Traveller's Literar___
to
Africa

Oona Strathern

TRAVELLER'S
LITERARY COMPANIONS

Read your
way around
the world

In Print
1994

Titles in the Traveller's Literary Companion series:
South and Central America (1993)
Africa (1994)
Eastern and Central Europe (1994)
The Indian Subcontinent (1994)
Japan (1994)
South-East Asia (1994)

British Library Cataloguing in Publication Data: A catalogue record for this book is available from the British Library.

Paperback ISBN 1 873047 55 X
Hardback ISBN 1 873047 50 9

Cover design by Russell Townsend
Front cover and spine photograph taken in Rora Habab, north-east Eritrea by Bill Robinson
Back cover photograph of Rimbaud House in Harar by Oona Strathern
Maps drawn by Andy Prigmore
Additional artwork by Zana Juppenlatz
Typeset by MC Typeset Ltd
Printed by Utopia Press

First published in 1994 by
In Print Publishing Ltd, 9 Beaufort Terrace, Brighton BN2 2SU, UK. Tel: (0273) 682836. Fax: (0273) 620958.

SERIES FOREWORD

This series of *Traveller's Literary Companions* is the series I have been looking for all my travelling life. Discovering new writers and new countries is one of the greatest pleasures we know, and these books will greatly increase the enjoyment of all who consult them. Each volume is packed with scholarly and entertaining historical, geographical, political and above all literary information. A country lives through its literature, and we have here an illustrated survey not only of a country's own writers, but also of the views of foreigners, explorers, tourists and exiles. The only problem I foresee is that each volume will bring about a compulsive desire to book a ticket on the next flight out.

The writers take us back in the past to each country's cultural origins, and bring us right up to the present with extracts from novels, poems and travel writings published in the 1980s and 1990s. The chapter introductions and the biographical information about the writers are invaluable, and will give any traveller an easy and immediate access to the past and present state of each nation. Conversation with hosts, colleagues or strangers on trains will be greatly assisted. An enormous amount of work has gone into the compiling and annotating of each volume, and the balance of fact and comment seems to me to be expertly judged.

Margaret Drabble

CONTENTS

List of Maps

Using the Companion

Each country has its own chapter and each chapter is divided into four distinct sections: (1) an introduction to the geography and cultural and political background; (2) a Booklist giving full publishing details of all the books mentioned in the introduction and extracted; (3) a selection of extracts; (4) biographical details and summaries of major works.

Extracts are ordered alphabetically by place and each is assigned a number to make it easy to locate from elsewhere in the chapter.

The **symbol** ◊ after an author's name indicates that there is a biographical entry in the chapter. If there is a biographical entry in another chapter, the author's name is followed by the symbol and the relevant chapter in parentheses – eg 'Wole Soyinka (◊ Nigeria)'.

In each chapter there is a **Fact Box** showing area, population, capital city, a selection of the most common languages, former colonial powers, and date of independence.

Also in each chapter, a list of **Literary Landmarks** is given. This is followed by a short list of **Libraries and Bookshops** – while every effort has been made to keep these up to date, there will inevitably be address changes and closures.

Bold type is used to highlight references to places.

There is an **index of authors** at the end of the book.

INTRODUCTION

It is said that there are as many Africans as there are books about Africa – and as many books about Africa as you could read in a leisurely lifetime. With more emphasis on the leisurely than the lifetime, this companion is a survey of the literature from 51 African countries. It embraces work by natives, exiles, explorers and foreign visitors alike. Alongside the acknowledged 'great and good' lie works by lesser-known poets, prose writers and playwrights.

As a continent with over 2000 languages and dialects, almost every form of religious worship, climatic zone and political persuasion, there is neither a homogeneous body of literature, one dominant means of expression, nor one piece that could be said to unlock the soul of Africa alone. Poetry, prose, oral tales and war songs all make up the diversity of the literature, and to say that African literature is in its infancy is a common misconception. Most underestimated is the role and influence of the traditional oral historians and story-tellers, for today it is still said that when an elder of a tribe or village dies it is as if a whole library has burned down.

While oral literature has long been an important part of the social and private fabric of African life, the written and published word arrived relatively late – Somalia, the so-called 'land of poets', did not have a formal Somali script until 1972. The absence of a written language is argued to have made Africa vulnerable to the white invaders. Indeed Ethiopia, which early on had a widely used written language, escaped the exigencies of prolonged colonial occupation. As elsewhere on the continent, it did not however protect the country from subsequent rule by eccentric emperors and ramshackle dictatorships.

Many of the first big printing presses were brought to the continent by the missionaries for their own evangelical aims. The scurrilous European scramble for Africa brought a foreign culture and literacy and spawned the long struggle for identity and independence. The approach of independence saw the dawn of a new literary era in many countries. The role of the native writers and intellectuals in liberating their countries was to liberate thought. It is noticeable that in countries such as Angola and Mozambique, which have suffered periods of protracted (pre and post) independence struggle, the dominant literary medium is poetry, and a list of the leading writers is comparable with that of the key freedom fighters. As short-story writer Luís Bernardo Honwana of Mozambique remarked, there simply were neither the time nor the resources to write prose.

One of the first clearly definable Africa-wide literary movements was *Négritude*. Emerging in Paris in the 1930s from a group of African and Caribbean students, it sought to define and assert African culture in the face of (French) colonial assimilation policies. Led in Africa by Senegal's Léopold Sédar Senghor, *Négritude* drew protagonists and praise from across the continent for decades to come. 'A black poet naturally partakes of *Négritude*' claimed the Mauritian poet Edouard Maunick. 'Suddenly, men became aware of belonging naturally in the world, as themselves . . . In doing so they do not exile themselves from others; they do not go into a museum filled only with mirrors; they do not scratch their navel to touch the centre of the earth; they do not turn to the past; they simply *recognize* themselves.'

As happens to many pioneering movements, *Négritude*, which was described by Jean-Paul Sartre as an 'antiracist racism', has long since been decried by a new generation of post-independence writers. They claim that the proponents of *Négritude* simplified the image of Africa. Not unlike the criticism levelled against the early explorers and colonizers, it is said that they heralded Africa as a veritable Garden of Eden, either to further dubious political propaganda, or worse still simply out of romantic naivety and idealism.

Meanwhile, so-called 'Euro-assimilationist' or 'Euromodernist' literature containing traces of colonial cultural influence has been lambasted by purists, who argue that work originating in any foreign tongue does not merit the title 'African' literature. Kenya's foremost contemporary writer Ngugi believes if you write in the language of the colonizers, your mind is colonized. However there are some, such as Nigeria's Chinua Achebe and Amos Tutuola, who have, in very different ways, turned this so-called handicap to their advantage. This cultural transvestism and its accompanying bilingualism can mean that writers' work is available not only to a greater Africa-wide audience, but to a worldwide audience. Replies South Africa's Lewis Nkosi to Ngugi's radicalism: 'If we don't publish in a world language, do you not think there will be problems of communication – between Africans?' Achebe answers the charge of Eurocentricity more directly, 'If Africa is illiterate, it makes no difference what language my books are in.'

Three Nobel Prize winners (Nigerian Wole Soyinka 1986, Egyptian Naguib Mahfouz 1987, and South African Nadine Gordimer 1991), are witness to the status, scope and worldwide standing of African literature. But while schools in Africa today include many more

African writers in their curriculum, distribution and resources remain a recurrent problem on the continent. Author Syl Cheney-Coker recently bought up 100 copies of one of his books that was published in England, took them back to Sierra Leone and sold them at an affordable price. Paradoxically the range and accessibility of books by African writers in Europe is steadily improving, thanks to a few persistent publishers, such as Heinemann which recently celebrated 30 years and over 200 titles of its African Writers Series.

The one regrettable gap in the African literary repertoire is work by native female writers. The exigencies of different religions, work traditions and childbearing have resulted in fewer educational opportunities and generally lower literacy rates among women in Africa. Those who have successfully made it to the shelves have frequently done so at remarkable personal cost or risk – such as Egypt's Nawal El Saadawi and Senegal's Mariama Bâ, and Botswana's Bessie Head.

Writing by non-natives – including Paul Bowles, Graham Greene, David Livingstone, Isak Dinesen (Karen Blixen) and C.J. Jung – is included in this companion as a literary, political and cultural counterpoint. This category has its own, often very different and sometimes controversial merits. Without wishing to be 'politically incorrect' or worse still fall foul of the reflex tendency, 'political correctness anxiety', this book is not governed by particular politics or prejudice and is compiled out of a sense of pleasure rather than duty. Simply it is a literary journey through the work and thoughts of people who like myself have lived, breathed and been inspired by Africa.

ACKNOWLEDGMENTS

From a cast of many without whom this book would not have been possible, and certainly not so enjoyable to write, I nominate the following for the 'Out of Literary Africa Awards':

Best female supporting roles: The West London Ladies Literary Group (Ailish Heneberry, Sabine Pusch and Charlotte Sankey); Toni Swindells; and Kathleen Strathern.

Best male supporting roles: Paul Strathern and Colin Dowarris for research; publishers Alastair Dingwall and John Edmondson; consultant, Dr Alastair Niven (Director of Literature, Arts Council of Great Britain); Matthias Horx who arrived when I began the book; and Tristan Oliver who appeared in the middle and arrived at the end.

Oona Strathern
Hamburg, Germany

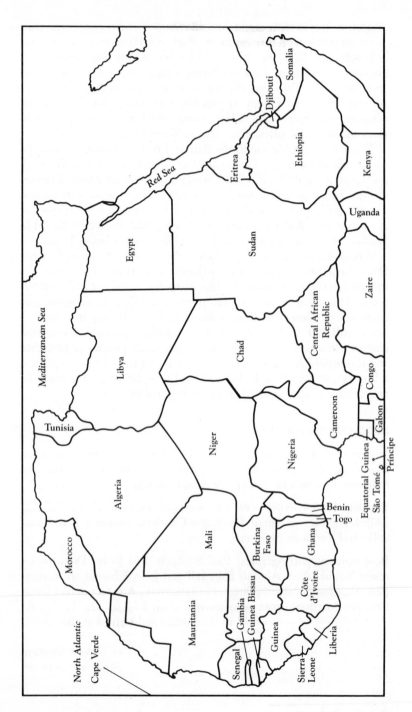

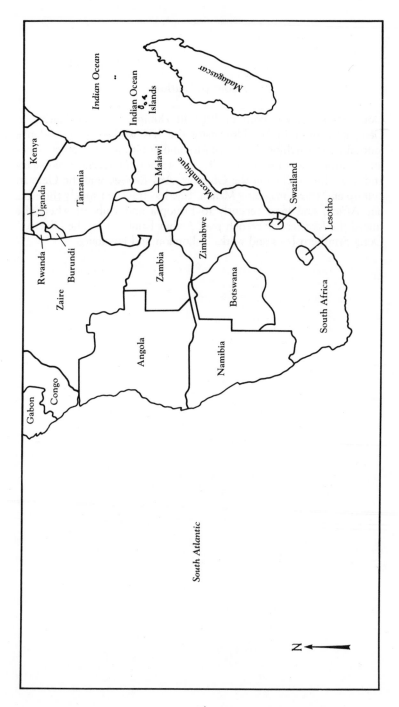

About the author

Oona Strathern was born in 1963 in Dublin. Since graduating in Geography from Bristol University she has worked as a freelance journalist, researching documentaries and environmental programmes for Central Television in the UK and writing for several newspapers and magazines including the *Observer*, *Arts Review*, and the German culture and travel magazine *Merian*. She has travelled widely throughout Africa, and most recently to Ethiopia and Djibouti where she traced the footsteps of French poet Arthur Rimbaud for the *Observer*. Oona Strathern lives and works in London and Hamburg.

BENIN

'Beware and take care
Of the Bight of Benin
Of the one that comes out
There are forty go in'
*Slavers' proverb, from The
Viceroy of Ouidah*

The tiny country of Benin, previously known as Dahomey, lies on a stretch of the West African coast that was the scene of a flourishing slave trade between the sixteenth and nineteenth centuries. It was here in the south of this tiny country that the Fon people established their powerful kingdom of Dan-Homey in 1625. Until 1885, when the last Portuguese slave ship officially sailed out of **Ouidah**, the kingdom reigned supreme over this corner of the African slave market.

The lure of an indomitable kingdom ruled by a series of mad mercurial kings, and with a lucrative slave trade, attracted the greedy, the curious and the nefarious – the most colourful and infamous of whom was Francisco Felix de Souza, a Brazilian who sailed to Africa in the early 1800s to make his fortune in the slave trade. According to Bruce Chatwin's ◊ brilliant and captivating account in *The Viceroy of Ouidah* (Extract 2), de Souza 'took to the Trade as if he had known no other occupation . . . he believed it was his heaven sent vocation to fuel with black muscle the mines and plantations of his country . . .'.

In exchange for rum and tobacco and in recognition of a like spirit, de Souza was awarded the title of Viceroy of Ouidah, by King Adandozan. This granted him a monopoly over the sale of slaves and an inexhaustible supply of women – he is said to have fathered over 100 children. Chatwin's book is a masterly evocation of the macabre dealings of the maverick Brazilian with King Adandozan (who eventually dyed de Souza black by dipping him in a tub of indigo) and King Gezo (who rescued him and then ruined him).

'The King lay lounging on a bolster of carmine velvet, thronged by naked women, who fanned him with ostrich feathers and wiped the perspiration from his forehead. He was a tall sinewy man with dry red

1

FACT BOX

AREA: 112 600 sq km
POPULATION: 4 900 000
CAPITAL: Porto-Novo
LANGUAGES: French, Bariba, Fon-Ewe, Yoruba
FORMER COLONIAL POWER: France
INDEPENDENCE: 1960

---

eyes, automatic gestures and the bonhomie of the seasoned slaughterer. The rising sun shone on his chest. His fingernails curled like cock's feathers. His loincloth was purple and his sandals were of twisted gold wire. At his feet were the heads of a boy and a girl, sent half an hour earlier to tell the Dead Kings that their descendant had woken up. He glared at the Brazilian and spat.' (*The Viceroy of Ouidah*)

Although his disposition lay more with East and North Africa, Sir Richard Burton's (◊ Ethiopia) writings on West Africa also make fascinating reading. His book A *Mission to Gelele, King of Dahome* (Extract 6), is an absorbing account of an assignment he undertook as British Consul to West Africa (1861–64) to investigate and 'woo' the opprobrious King Gelele. In a textual footnote to his 1873 translation of *Lacerda's Journey to Cazembe*, Burton gives us an idea of the character of the King: 'King Gelele, wishing to send a message to his (dead) father, summons a captive, carefully primes him with the subject of his errand, generally some vaunt, adhibits a bottle of rum, and strikes off his head. If an important word be casually omitted he repeats the operation, a process which I venture to call a postscript.'

Needless to say, accounts of infidelity among Burton's Amazonian aides, aphrodisiacs, abortion and decapitation ceremonies pleased neither his long-suffering wife Isabel (whose task it was to edit the report) nor his Victorian audience. Although he was undoubtedly a better explorer and writer than he was a statesman, it is perhaps some measure of Burton's acceptance there that he was presented by the King with a necklace of human bones, and not made into one.

After the collapse of the Empire in 1892, the country was known under the French as Dahomey. Then, following a series of coups in the early 1970s, it became the République du Benin (after an ancient West African Kingdom in Nigeria) under Marxist–Leninist General Mathieu Kerekou, who strictly controlled all news media. A particularly dramatic attempt to overthrow him in 1977 is said to have inspired scenes in *The Dogs of War* by Frederick Forsyth.

An intriguing history of rule by despots, mercurial kings, colonists and the heavy hand of revolutionary rhetoric has left a relatively reclusive country and culture. Despite the European and Arab influences, the Beninois are still principally governed by ancient African religious beliefs. The literary reputation of the country has, however, been strongly formed by the influence of the French Catholic mission schools: Benin soon became known as the Latin Quarter of West Africa. It is not surprising to find that the few twentieth century Beninois writers who have been published and gained some international standing have spent time in France, and in particular have been strongly influenced by the Paris-born *Négritude* movement.

In this spirit of reviving interest in traditional cultures, Maximilien Quenum's writing was designed to introduce to the European reader legends and myths as told by the elders of his village and recounted from his childhood. In *Légendes Africaines*, 1946, he tells how Dahomey got its name. According to legend, when Aho-Dako-Dogbaglin conquered the northern Kingdom of King Dan in the seventeenth century he founded his capital on the belly of Dan by dropping the King's body into the foundations. The kingdom was henceforth named Dan-hô-me, literally 'on the belly of Dan'. Sadly Quenum's work has not yet been translated from the French.

Another product of the French colonial system is Paul Hazoumé ◊ whose lengthy historical novel *Doguicimi*, 1938 (Extract 1) is a romantic fictionalized account of the rise and fall of the Dan-Homey kingdom through the adventures of a Dahomean princess. Despite a prose style heavily influenced by nineteenth century French fiction, this epic book – said to be the first Dahomean novel – is a rich source of information on the pre-colonial kingdom. Hazoumé's views on colonialism, in the appendix to his book, are rather more controversial: 'the French flag was to succeed magnificently . . . bringing in a reign of peace, liberty, and humanity to Dahomey'.

Characteristic of literature in the post-war years are the writings of novelist and short story writer Olympe Bhêly-Quénum ◊ who has lived in France for many years. His best known book, *Snares Without End* (Extract 3), is the only piece of his work to have been translated into English and is an unrelenting tale of misfortune and tragedy: 'Trapped as I was in the heart of the absurd, there was nothing left for me but to hurl myself into the void, to crash against the sheer face of Mount Kinibaya, like a pebble ricocheting across the surface of the lake, to fall dead, down below among the animals in the middle of the pasture . . .'.

Like his novels, only a sprinkling of Benin's poetry has been translated from the French. Emile Ologoudou ◊ and Richard Dogbeh, are both products of the *Négritude* movement and draw on the themes of despair and hopelessless amid the chaos of revolution (by 1972 there had been some five insurrections in Benin) – see Extract 4. Dogbeh's best known work *Cap Liberté*, 1969, displays a familiar rhetoric: urging the slum-bound populace to rise up and claim their rights. In *Salut Lagos* Dogbeh describes the appalling conditions of the economic and political refugees who have crossed the border into neighbouring Nigeria: 'Lagos/Where do they sleep, these teeming crowds of men women and children ragged feverous swarming your streets endless as ant-processions/why do these two mothers loiter by the roadside clutching their shaven-headed infants/why so many waifs polluting the great avenues?' (from Robert Fraser's *West African Poetry*).

Since independence in 1960 literature has been slowly moving away from familiar themes of traditional life, kingdoms and colonials. Prize-winning writer Jean Pliya's satirical play *La Secrétaire Particulière*, 1973 (not translated) deals with the problems of a new élite – corruption and inefficiency among a new generation of African civil-servants. There have also been increasing signs since 1975 of a revival in writing in the indigenous Yoruba, Bariba and Fon-Ewe languages.

The decades of deconstructive government in Benin have, one hopes, come to an end. In 1991, a national conference modelled on the French 'Tennis Court Oath' (which contributed to the overthrow of the French monarch in 1792) ousted General Kerekou. The country voted overwhelmingly for civilian and reformist Nicephore Sogolo, a former employee of the World Bank and a Paris-trained economist. Benin's population of five million appears to be in a better position than ever to see some order brought to the country's chaotic finances, and to bear the fruits of freedom of expression.

LITERARY LANDMARKS

Abomey. Centre of the Kingdom of Dahomey, where an unpredictable welcome awaited traders, slaves and visitors. Today the remains of the **Palace** are one of Benin's greatest attractions.

    Cotonou. A modern, European-built city and the *de facto* capital of Benin (**Porto-Novo** is the official capital). Described by *West Africa, The Rough Guide* as one of West Africa's least enticing cities. Birthplace of Olympe Bhêly-Quénum.

    Ouidah. Named Ajuda, which means 'help', by the Portuguese, the port became one of the largest slave trading posts on the Bight. As the British consul, Sir Richard Burton was welcomed in Ouidah by 'the usual decapitation' (*Mission to Gelele*) and at the **English Fort** by 'sherry, gin, rum and other chief-like delicacies' (*ibid*). Chatwin came here in 1971 to trace the descendants and steps of the Brazilian slaver de Souza who 'landed at Ouidah between two and three of a murky May afternoon smelling of mangrove and dead fish' (*The Viceroy of Ouidah*).

The Portuguese fort of Sao João Batista that was coveted by de Souza is now the **Ouidah Museum of History.**

Libraries and Bookshops

Cotonou. Bibliothèque de L'Université Nationale du Benin; Marché San Michel – bookstalls with English and French books.
Porto-novo. Bibliothèque Nationale.

BOOKLIST

The following selection includes the extracted titles in this chapter as well as those mentioned in the introduction which are available in English and other titles for further reading. In general, paperback editions are given when possible. The editions cited are not necessarily the only ones available. For most of the extracted works, the original publisher in English can be found in 'Acknowledgments and Citations' at the end of the volume, as can the exact location of the extracts and the editions from which they are taken. Extract numbers are highlighted in bold for ease of reference.

Bhêly-Quénum, Olympe, *Snares Without End*, Longman, Harlow, 1981. **Extract 3.**

Blair, Dorothy S., *African Literature in French*, Cambridge University Press, Cambridge, 1976.

Burton, Sir Richard, *A Mission to Gelele, King of Dahome*, Routledge and Kegan Paul, London, 1966. **Extract 6.**

Chatwin, Bruce, *The Viceroy of Ouidah*, Pan, London, 1982. **Extract 2.**

Chatwin, Bruce, 'A Coup', in *The Best of Granta Travel*, Granta Books, London, 1991. **Extract 5.**

Forsyth, Frederick, *The Dogs of War*, Corgi, London, 1975.

Fraser, Robert, *West African Poetry: A Critical Introduction*, Cambridge University Press, Cambridge, 1986.

Hazoumé, Paul, *Doguicimi*, Richard Bjornson, trans, Three Continents Press, Washington, DC, 1990. **Extract 1.**

Ologoudou, Emile, 'Liberty', Gerald Moore, trans, in *The Penguin Book of Modern African Poetry*, Gerald Moore and Ulli Beier, eds, Penguin, London, 1984. **Extract 4.**

Extracts

(1) ABOMEY

Paul Hazoumé, *Doguicimi*

Princess Doguicimi witnesses King Ghezo calling for traditional celebrations in his Kingdom.

Ajahi, the principal market at Agbomê, was at its liveliest. Because the sun had still not turned his face toward home on the other side of Coufo, buyers and sellers who had come from distant villages had not yet thought about starting back toward their compounds.

Suddenly a twin bell launched its 'Kioun-go! Kioun-go!' to the four winds. Initially drowned out by the sounds of the market, its ringing finally reached the ears of the people, and everyone quickly fell silent.

The women fell to their knees. The men flattened themselves in the dust and covered their heads with it.

The tall figures of Migan and Panligan dominated the scene. One of their attendants clasped a small raphia basket to his chest; the others surrounded a Mahinou whose arms were tied behind his back.

The group halted in front of Ayizan – the protective fetish of the market. Having remained standing beside the first minister, the public crier recited the epithets of King Guézo at great length, punctuating them with the ringing of his double bell; at the end he added: 'The Predestined King has ordered that it be announced to all Danhomê that the traditional celebrations will begin tomorrow evening.

'Starting tomorrow, the Father of Wealth will distribute glass beads, cloths, and silver to his people. At this very place, feasts and libations will follow the forwarding of messages to King Agonglo.'

'The King of the Universe invites his people to the feast. The festivities will last for seven days.'

'Danhomênous who have heard the good news directly from the mouth of Panligan, go and pass it on to the ears of friends and allies who are not present.'

With a forceful rap on the bell, he marked the end of his message and stepped aside. Migan made an offering of water and rum to the fetish. Standing in front of the Mahinou, who was on his knees and facing Ayizan, the sacrificial priest seized the victim by the hair and said: 'You, go and carry this news to the land of the dead!' The scimitar ·swung rapidly to the left. The neatly severed head of the Mahinou spattered blood upon the fetish above which Migan was holding it.

Two servants subdued the body, bundled it up, and carried it toward the Ditch.

The sacrificial priest handed his weapon and the head to his assistants.

The twin bell of Panligan resumed its 'Kioun-go! Kioun-go!' as the people in the crowd covered themselves with dirt to express their gratitude for the festivities that had just been promised to them.

(2) Benin: Amazons

Bruce Chatwin, *The Viceroy of Ouidah*

Slaver Dom Francisco (Francisco Felix de Souza), the ruthless wars, and the 'Amazon' tribeswomen of the Dahomey kingdom were legendary.

Each year, with the dry season, he would slough off the habits of civilization and go to war.

His first task had been to reform the Dahomean army. He and the King got rid of the paunchy, the panicky and the proven drunks. And since Dahomean women were far fiercer fighters than the men – and could recharge a muzzle-loader in half the time – they sent recruiting officers round the villages to enlist the most muscular virgins.

The recruits were known as the 'King's Leopard Wives'.

They ate raw meat, shaved their heads and filed their teeth to sharp points. They learned to fire from the shoulder not the hip, and never to fire at rustling leaves. On exercises they were made to scale palisades of prickly pear, and they would come back clamouring, 'Hou! Hou! We are men!' – and since they were obliged to be celibate, were allowed to slake their lusts on a troop of female prostitutes.

Dom Francisco insisted on sharing all the hardships of the march.

He crossed burning savannahs and swam rivers infested with crocodiles. Before an attack on a village, he would lash leaves to his hat and lie motionless till cockcrow. Then, as the dawn silhouetted the roofs like teeth on a sawblade, a whistle would blow, the air fill with raucous cries and, by the end of the morning, the Amazons would be parading before the King, swinging severed heads like dumb-bells.

Dom Francisco greeted each fresh atrocity with a glassy smile. He felt no trace of pity for the mother who pleaded for her child, or for the old man staring in disbelief at the purple veil spread out over the smouldering ruins.

For years he continued in this self-directed nightmare. But one day, before the sack of Sokologbo, he was hiding behind a rock when some small boys came skipping down the path, waving bird-scarers to shoo the doves off the millet fields. He would never forget their gasps as the Amazons pounced from the bushes and garrotted them one by one.

All that morning, as the Dahomeans did their work, he buried his face in his hands, muttering, 'No. Not the children!' and never went to war again.

(3) BENIN: PLAGUE

Olympe Bhêly-Quénum, *Snares Without End*

Ahouna and his family are dogged by misfortune throughout their lives. Here, their farm is destroyed by disease.

One morning, early in the harvest season, when my father went to open the cowshed he found two cows lying dead, with black, protruding tongues, bared teeth and glazed eyes that still bore the expression of acute suffering. Overcome with surprise and distress he called me – I had never seen him in such a state – and asked me where I had taken the cattle to graze the previous day.

'Why, in our pasture, father!' I replied, surprised at the question, and added, 'What's the matter, father? You look very upset.'

'Look, son!' he said, opening the cowshed once more.

I burst into tears at the horrible sight which still seems to be before my eyes. Still weeping, I drove out the rest of the herd. As soon as they were outside thirteen of them set up a continuous, loud lowing; their eyes took on a rabid stare and they leapt into the air to fall heavily to the ground. My parents and I watched trembling, weeping and praying to Allah to save our beasts, for we know from their jerking limbs that these thirteen cows too were dying. Their tongues protruded, already turning black, and saliva streamed from between their clenched teeth. Some of them were biting off their own tongues. They were lying on the ground, jerking convulsively like fetishists in a trance, when suddenly two of our three bulls made straight for us. We just managed to avoid them, but they were not attacking us. They continued their mad rush to be brought up short by our *naseberry* trees. These they nearly uprooted, then they circled round several times, leapt into the air and fell down, bellowing furiously, to lie stiff and foaming at the mouth.

At the sheepfold the same fearful sight met our eyes. Faya was dead, with two thirds of the flock. I don't know if I have mentioned our farmyard – well, it was almost completely wiped out. Except for three hens and two cocks wandering miserably around, there was not a creature left alive there. Oh! I can scarcely bear to think of that period of our existence.

Our whole household was plunged in grief. My father ran round in circles, like a man demented; then he pulled up short and, to our astonishment, he, who did not believe in witch-doctors, ran off to call Adanfô, a man from Agonli who lived in our area and had the reputation of being a great sorcerer.

Adanfô arrived, undid a raffia bundle from which he set out bones, minute calabashes, an 'agoumagan' – his instrument for looking into the future – and all the rest of his paraphernalia. Then he consulted the gods.

Adanfô, the soothsayer, was a man of slender build, and of graceful, unruffled demeanour; he would have been most handsome, had he not had a head like that of a wild boar. About a quarter of an hour after the beginning of his operations, he informed us – without having any previous knowledge of what had occurred – that the 'coal sickness' had come upon us.

(4) BENIN: REVOLUTION

Emile Ologoudou, *Liberty*

Benin-born poet Ologoudou conveys the sadness of his revolution-torn country. 'Liberty' is included in The Penguin Book of Modern African Poetry – see Booklist.

The White carcases
of
ships
sought desperately
the visible island with its golden mist,
the native isle of insurrection,
stage at evening of the most tragic adventures,
we were tossed
on the waves of the same sorrow,
and discord
had not yet blown us towards the sands
of
its evidence,
exuberance still reigned over the happy bay,
that day when we made long funeral
for all the things
we had to bury . . .

(5) COTONOU

Bruce Chatwin, *A Coup*

*When Chatwin visited Benin in 1971 to gather material for The
Viceroy of Ouidah, he found himself unwittingly caught up in a
coup and mistaken for a mercenary.*

The coup began at seven on Sunday morning. It was a grey and
windless dawn and the grey Atlantic rollers broke in long even lines
along the beach. The palms above the tide-mark shivered in a current
of cooler air that blew in off the breakers. Out at sea – beyond the surf –
there were several black fishing canoes. Buzzards were spiralling above
the market, swooping now and then to snatch up scraps of offal. The
butchers were slaughtering, even on a Sunday.

We were in a taxi when the coup began, on our way to another
country. We had passed the Hôtel de la Plage, passed the Sûreté
Nationale, and then we drove under a limply-flapping banner which
said, in red letters, that Marxist–Leninism was the one and only guide.
In front of the Presidential Palace was a road-block. A soldier waved us
to a halt, and then waved us on.

'Pourriture!' said my friend, Domingo, and grinned.

Domingo was a young, honey-coloured mulatto with a flat and
friendly face, a curly moustache and a set of dazzling teeth. He was the
direct descendant of Francisco-Félix de Souza, the Chacha of Ouidah, a
Brazilian slaver who lived and died in Dahomey, and about whom I was
writing a book.

Domingo had two wives. The first wife was old and the skin hung in
loose folds off her back. The second wife was hardly more than a child.
We were on our way to Togo, to watch a football game, and visit his
great-uncle who knew a lot of old stories about the Chacha.

The taxi was jammed with football-fans. On my right sat a very black
old man wrapped in green and orange cotton. His teeth were also
orange from chewing cola nuts, and from time to time he spat.

Outside the Presidential Palace hung an overblown poster of the
Head of State, and two much smaller posters of Lenin and Kim Il-Sung.
Beyond the road-block, we took a right fork, on through the old
European section where there were bungalows and balks of bougainvil-
laea by the gates. Along the sides of the tarmac, market-women walked
in single file with basins and baskets balanced on their head.

'What's that?' I asked. I could see some kind of commotion, up
ahead, towards the airport.

'Accident!' Domingo shrugged, and grinned again.

Then all the women were screaming, and scattering their yams and
pineapples, and rushing for the shelter of the gardens. A white Peugeot

shot down the middle of the road, swerving right and left to miss the women. The driver waved for us to turn back, and just then, we heard the crack of gunfire.

'C'est la guerre!' our driver shouted, and spun the taxi round.

'I knew it.' Domingo grabbed my arm. 'I knew it.'

The sun was up by the time we got to downtown Cotonou. In the taxi-park the crowd had panicked and overturned a brazier, and a stack of crates had caught fire. A policeman blew his whistle and bawled for water. Above the rooftops, there was a column of black smoke, rising.

'They're burning the Palace,' said Domingo. 'Quick! Run!'

We ran, bumped into other running figures, and ran on. A man shouted 'Mercenary!' and lunged for my shoulder. I ducked and we dodged down a sidestreet. A boy in a red shirt beckoned me into a bar. It was dark inside. People were clustered round a radio. Then the bartender screamed, wildly, in African, at me, and at the boy. And then I was out again on the dusty red street, shielding my head with my arms, pushed and pummelled against the corrugated building by four hard, acridly-sweating men until the gendarmes came to fetch me in a jeep.

'For your own proper protection,' their officer said, as the handcuffs snapped around my wrists.

The last I ever saw of Domingo he was standing in the street, crying, as the jeep drove off, and he vanished in a clash of coloured cottons.

(6) KANA

Sir Richard Burton,
A Mission to Gelele, King of Dahome

As Consul to West Africa, Burton was despatched to seek an audience with the notorious King Gelele. Kana (today spelt Cana) was the village where the Dan-Homey kings were traditionally buried.

The king was detained at Kana, as we were afterwards informed, by sundry cases affecting human life. Not less than 150 'Amazons' were found to be pregnant – so difficult is chastity in the Tropics. They confessed, and they were brought to trial with their paramours. The King has abolished the 'Brehon judges' established by his father: the malversation of these 'justices in eyre' rendered reference to them like 'going', as the old traveller has it, 'to the Devil for redress'. He now investigates each case personally, often sitting in judgement till midnight, and rising before dawn on the next day; moreover, every criminal has a right of personal appeal to him. The crime was *lèse-majesté* rather than simple advowtry; all the soldieresses being, I have said, royal wives. Eight men were condemned to death, and will probably be executed at the Customs. The majority were punished either by imprisonment or by a banishment to distant villages, under pain of death if they revisit the capital, and some were pardoned. The partners of their guilt were similarly treated. Female criminals are executed by officers of their own sex, within the palace walls, not in the presence of men. Dahome is therefore in one point more civilized than Great Britain, where they still, wondrous to relate, 'hang away' even women, and in public.

In the afternoon of Sunday, December 20th, we effected a departure from the English house. Sundry boxes were left behind, owing to the desertion of the carriers, who are fast learning bad habits: yesterday they stole an enamelled iron cup. The Court being at Kana, bell-women were a nuisance on the road; at every five minutes the hammock-men huddled us into the bush. Arrived at the Akoreha, or eastern market-place, we sat down near the Buko-no's house, awaiting his escort. Here fetish women crowded upon us, clapping palms for a present. They were easily dispersed by their likenesses being sketched.

Already the sun began to cool, though the sky was still all ablaze with golden glory. After half an hour's delay the old Buko-no came up, leaning on the Bo-kpo, or crutch staff, which wards off the evils of the way. Presently we remounted hammocks, and he, by means of a chair, climbed upon the back of his little *bidet* – a mare followed by a foal. The animals here are not larger than Shetland ponies, but they are generally, as is the Maharatta-land 'tattoo', shaped like stunted horses, showing the remains of good blood. They have fine noses, well-opened eyes, and sharp ears. As in Yoruba generally, the tits are excessively vicious, and if approached by a stranger, they will fly at him with a scream. This is doubtless owing to the brutality of their Negro grooms. They are, when mounted, invariably led, like donkeys, by a halter – the bridle, like the stirrup, being unknown. The little jades are almost hid in the local saddle, enormous housings of blue cloth, padded, quilted, and worked outside with white thread, while huge curtain tassels depend to their knees. As a rule, the rider is lifted on and off by his slaves. Whilst on horseback he passes his arm round the neck of a man walking by his side, and his waist is supported by the same attendant's near arm.

Bruce Chatwin

Biographies and important works

BHÊLY-QUÉNUM, Olympe (1928–). Born on the coast at **Cotonou**, Bhêly-Quénum has lived most of his life abroad working for UNESCO in France. He has written several short stories and novels, and is the only Beninois writer readily available in translation. *Snares Without End* (Extract 3) is the compassionate and tragic tale of Ahouna, a man for whom life is a catalogue of misfortune and despair. Thwarted in his search for relief in the form of hope or death, like a sleepwalker he travels helplessly through a life of snares without end.

BURTON, Sir Richard (see under Ethiopia).

CHATWIN, Bruce (1940–1989). English-born journalist, travel writer and novelist, Chatwin visited Benin in 1971 when it was still 'a belly of laughs and French brasseries'. Here he researched *The Viceroy of Ouidah* (Extract 2), a fictionalized account of the maverick Brazilian slave trader Francisco Felix de Souza's dealings with the mad mercurial kings of Dahomey, his struggle for identity, power, favour and eventually survival. A true literary and historical compliment was paid by Werner Herzog with his inter-pretation of the book in his 1988 film *Cobra Verde*, starring a suitably manic Klaus Kinski as de Souza. Chatwin died of Aids on 18 January 1989.

HAZOUMÉ, Paul (1890–1980). Born in **Porto-Novo**, Hazoumé was descended from the Dahomean nobility. He was a teacher, anthropologist, author and politician. During the first world war, Hazoumé worked in Paris in the African Department of the Musée de L'Homme. His political career began with the launch of an anti-government newspaper in 1915, and ended when he stood unsuccessfully for election in Benin in 1968. His literary career was more notable. In 1938, he published *Doguicimi* (Extract 1), an historical blockbuster which is credited as the first Dahomean novel. In the 1940s Hazoumé helped launch the famous French literary and cultural magazine *Présence Africaine*.

OLOGOUDOU, Emile (1935–). The poet Ologoudou was born in **Ouidah**. After studying law and sociology in Senegal, he went to the University of Cologne in the 1960s. His poems have appeared in *Présence Africaine* (see under Hazoumé).

Burkina Faso

'Upper Volta wore its badge of poverty without shame, and suffered neither from the illusion of grandeur nor the expectation of false hopes.'
David Lamb, quoting journalist Stanley Meisler in The Africans

Burkina Faso, previously known as Upper Volta, suffers from what might be called an 'image problem'. Landlocked, and geographically indistinct, the country is frequently remembered for its poverty and isolation. Since independence from France in 1960, it has blundered from coup to coup, and the life-expectancy here of 33 years is cited as one of the lowest in the world. This dismal picture is not improved by the fact that the country's major export is people. Along with a constant brain drain of the educated élite, over half a million people travel every year to neighbouring countries for seasonal work.

With so many people on the move, it is not surprising to find first that there is but a small body of written literature available, and second that what there is deals frequently with the question of migration. Several authors, such as Kollin Noaga (writing in French and as yet untranslated), explore the economic necessity of migration and the disruptive emotional and social impacts on traditional life in the villages and towns.

Another prevalent theme in the body of Burkinabe literature is the demise of the empires. The first acknowledged Burkina novel, written by Nazi Boni, a former deputy in the French parliament, traces the rise and fall of the old Bwamu empire. The empire was eventually overthrown in 1916 by French colonial troops who were present until independence in 1960. During this period of severe economic hardship, the colonists employed forced labour, a popular theme among the country's dramatists. Pierre Dabire took up this topic in his prize-winning play *Sansoa*. Today his, and similar works are regularly performed in the country's schools and in numerous theatres by travelling troupes.

FACT BOX

AREA: 275 000 sq km
POPULATION: 9 300 000
CAPITAL: Ouagadougou
LANGUAGES: French, Mossi, Dyula
FORMER COLONIAL POWER: France
INDEPENDENCE: 1960

Burkina Faso's lively local cultural scene is also expressed on the radio. Transmitting in over 15 indigenous languages, radio has taken off as a great source of literary entertainment in the years following independence. Look out for the stories by local chief Tiendrebeogo Yamba.

News and translations of Burkinabe literature may not have reached the shores of Europe, but another important popular form of expression has – the film. In a country with a high literacy rate (it was until recently one of the most poorly educated countries in the world), the medium of film has played an important part in education and the dissemination of information. Idrissa Ouédreago, producer of the prize-winning film *Yaaba* and one of Burkina's top talents, has won several awards on the international film circuit, and his films are screened throughout the world. For a full feast of 'visual' literature, the best time to visit is during the biennial Pan-African Film Festival when the country turns into the 'Cannes of West Africa'.

LITERARY LANDMARKS

Ouagadougou. Capital and centre of one of the ancient **Mossi** kingdoms. Hosts Burkina's only university and the Pan-African film festival. The main library is at the **University of Ouagadougou.**

BOOKLIST

Baxter, Joan, and Somerville, Keith, *Benin, Congo and Burkina Faso,* Pinter, London, 1989.

Lamb, David, *The Africans,* Vintage Books, New York, 1987.

Nnaji, B.O., *Blaise Compaoré, The Architect of the Burkina Faso Revolution,* Spectrum, Ibadan, 1989.

Sankara, Thomas, *Thomas Sankara Speaks,* Pathfinder Press, London, 1988.

CAPE VERDE ISLANDS

'Islands lost
in the midst of the sea
forgotten
in an angle of the World
– where the waves
cradle
abuse
embrace . . .'
Jorge Barbosa

According to local lore, when God was satisfied that he had finished creating the world and brushed his hands together, the crumbs that fell unnoticed from his fingers into the sea formed Cape Verde. Far flung, and oft forgotten, the sprinkling of ten islands and five islets that make up this archipelago located 620 km off the coast of Africa are an extraordinary mix of the beautiful and the barren, from desert and salt wastelands to rich volcanic landscapes. According to their relative geographical desirability for settlement, agriculture, goats (a long-standing pillar of the Cape Verdean economy), penal colony, salt excavation or slave labour, the islands were variously settled between the fifteenth and nineteenth centuries. The first settlers arrived in **Santiago** from Portugal in 1462, but it was not until the beginning of the nineteenth century that **São Vincente**, one of the most barren islands, had a population to boast of.

The history and culture of the archipelago are born out of a strategic seafaring position. In much of the local literature and lore, the sea and the subsequent development of the slave trade are dominant themes. Also, some of the most readable foreign books about the islands are written from a position of navigational expertise. In his book *Atlantic Islands*, T.B. Duncan writes, 'The archipelago enjoyed a superb geographical position, at the very crossroads of the Atlantic, where wind and current brought together the ships of Europe, Africa, the West Indies, and North and South America.' The captains found it 'desirable, even essential, to put in at a Cape Verdean Port to procure beverages, victuals, or nautical supplies, or to undertake indispensable repairs.'

The position of the islands also made them vulnerable to pillage, plunder, and piracy, and many of the isolated hillside communities are

FACT BOX

AREA: 4032 sq km
POPULATION: 379 000
CAPITAL: Praia (on Santiago)
LANGUAGES: Portuguese, Creole (Crioulo)
FORMER COLONIAL POWER: Portugal
INDEPENDENCE: 1975

witness to the time when the inhabitants fled from invaders. In 1585, Drake landed at today's capital **Praia**, with 25 ships and some 2300 men. During the march overland one of his men was killed – Drake burned almost every house in **Ribera Grande**, and the inhabitants took to the hills.

Though dominated by the Portuguese, as an increasing variety of nations (and lonely sailors) visited the islands so the genetic jumble increased. The rough seas that separate them meant that each island developed its own characteristics, and today there are marked linguistic, literary and cultural differences (and rivalry) between them. In **São Vincente**, the Portuguese/African derived Creole language (locally known as Crioulo) includes some English and French words, while in **Santiago** it has a stronger African influence. After independence from Portugal in 1975, there was an attempt to make Creole the official language. However standardization was virtually impossible, and the government soon reverted to Portuguese, which is today the dominant literary tongue.

Cape Verdean literature reflected very early the first rumblings of dissent over Portuguese rule. In 1936 a small clique of mixed race Cape Verdean intellectuals – Baltasar Lopes, Jorge Barbosa and Manuel Lopes – founded the literary journal *Claridade*. Its title meaning 'clarity', the journal expressed a growing Cape Verdean identity and was published intermittently until 1960. Baltasar Lopes's work *Chiquinho* was one of Portuguese Africa's first novels, and Lopes deliberately used the Creole language in an attempt to elevate the perception of this so-called 'pidgin' language to one with literary potential and merit.

Jorge Barbosa, born in **Praia** in 1902, was meanwhile establishing a reputation as the country's first major poet, with his collection entitled *Arquipélago*. Laden with melancholic reflections on the sea and longings for liberation, his poetry spoke for generations that were bound by a contradictory desire to leave a country with a declining economy and to establish a national identity: 'The demand at every hour/to go away is brought to us by the sea./The despairing hope for the long journey/and yet always be forced to stay.' (from *Poema do mar*).

The general mood of *weltschmerz* that characterized the work of these writers also pervades the work of a later generation of the nation's poets. Onésima Silveira ◊ was identified as one of the first distinctly militant poets and his works, like those of the above-mentioned writers, are not readily available in translation (Extract 1). Kaoberdiano Dambara ◊, who was, like Silveira, also a member of the influential PAIGC (The Independence Party of Guinea and Cape Verde), wrote some of the first Cape Verdean poems in the *Négritude* tradition (Extract 2).

While the 1970s and 1980s saw something of a hiatus in the Cape Verdean literary scene, more recently under comparatively democratic rule there has seen a revival in both Portuguese and Creole writing, including a new literary journal *Raizes*, in the tradition of the inspirational *Claridade*. As well as an increasingly lively local scene, Cape Verdean literature and theatre is said to be flourishing in Massachusetts, USA, where curiously enough there live more Cape Verdeans than in Cape Verde itself.

Libraries and Bookshops

Praia. French Cultural Centre; Instituto Caboverdiano do Livro; National Library.

BOOKLIST

The following selection includes extracted titles in this chapter as well as those mentioned in the introduction which are available in English and other titles for further reading. In general, paperback editions are given when possible. The editions cited are not necessarily the only ones available. For most of the extracted works, the original publisher in English can be found in 'Acknowledgments and Citations' at the end of the volume, as can the exact location of the extracts and the editions from which they are taken. Extract numbers are highlighted in bold for ease of reference.

Barbosa, Jorge, *Two Languages, Two Friends – A Memory*, Rendall Leite, trans, Instituto Caboverdeano do Livro, Cape Verde, 1986.

Dambara, Kaoberdiano, 'Judgement

of the Black Man', Margaret Dickinson, trans, in *Poems of Black Africa*, Wole Soyinka, ed, Heinemann, Oxford, 1987. **Extract 2**.

Davidson, Basil, *The Fortunate Isles*, Century Hutchinson, London, 1989.

Duncan, T.B. *Atlantic Islands*, University of Chicago Press, London, 1972.

Foy, Colm, *Cape Verde; Politics, Economics and Society*, Pinter, London, 1988.

Lyall, Archibald, *Black and White Make Brown*, Heinemann, London, 1938.

Silveira, Onésima, 'A Different Poem', Margaret Dickinson, trans, in *The Penguin Book of Modern African Poetry*, Gerald Moore and Ulli Beier, eds, Penguin, London, 1984. **Extract 1**.

Extracts

(1) Cape Verde: Identity

Onésima Silveira, *A Different Poem*

Prior to independence, a small group of poets like Silveira were outspoken about the desire to feel an own national identity and the need for dramatic political, economic and social change. The poem from which this extract is taken is included in The Penguin Book of Modern African Poetry – see Booklist.

The people of the islands want a different poem
For the people of the islands;
A poem without exiles complaining
In the calm of their existence;
A poem without children nourished
On the black milk of aborted time
A poem without mothers gazing
At the vision of their sons, motherless.

. . .

A poem with shaking hips and laughing ivory.
The people of the islands want a different poem
For the people of the islands:
A poem without men who lose the seas' grace
and the fantasy of the main compass points.

(2) Cape Verde: Origins

Kaoberdiano Dambara, *Judgement of the Black Man*

While 70% of today's Cape Verde population are creole, a result of a long history of the mixing of the white Portuguese and black slaves, Dambara reminds us that the union was not born out of an equal relationship. 'Judgement of the Black Man' is included in Poems of Black Africa – see Booklist.

The white man looked him in the face
my black brother did not stir

The white man shouted, roared, beat and kicked him
my black brother did not tremble

In his eyes there kindled flames
of rage, of dried tears, of force
My black brother did not stir, did not answer, did not tremble

In his steady eyes there kindled the flame
of a force which only the black man knows.

Biographies and important works

DAMBARA, Kaoberdiano (1939–). Dambara was born in Cape Verde. He is a member of the PAIGC (African Party for the Independence of Guinea and Cape Verde). He writes mainly in Guinea Creole, and his collection of poetry *Noti* (meaning 'Night') was considered one of the first Cape Verdean expressions of *Négritude*.

SILVEIRA, Onésima (1936–). Born in Cape Verde, Silveira lived for several years in São Tomé and Angola. He is a member of the PAIGC (see under Dambara), and was the Party's European Representative while he was studying in Sweden. His first published collection of poems was entitled *Hora Grande*.

CÔTE D'IVOIRE

'Our people . . . is a people who has, more than any other right, the right to an intelligible literature . . . Literature . . . is a resource, a weapon, I mean to say that it is foremost, an alarm or war drum . . .'
Bernard Binlin Dadié

The literary father figure of the Côte d'Ivoire is Bernard Binlin Dadié ◊. Not only a prominent poet, dramatist and short story writer, he has championed the collection, preservation and dramatization of ancient myths and tales. Born in 1916, he was one of the voices in the first wave of writers across Africa who challenged the rationale of the colonialist system, who wrote and spoke openly about his beliefs, and who was imprisoned for them. While many of his literary compatriots were in full swing with the *Négritude* movement in Paris, Dadié was more often to be found in Africa engaged in his own, though equally resonant writing – 'I thank you God for creating me black./White is the colour for special occasions/Black is the colour for every day/And I have carried the World since the dawn of time./And my laugh over the World, through the night, creates the Day.' (from 'I Thank You God', in *Voices from Twentieth Century Africa*).

An immensely prolific writer, Dadié is also one of the most widely translated writers of Francophone Africa. *Climbié* (Extract 2), which means 'some other day', is an autobiographical account of his childhood. At first it appears very similar to Camara Laye's *African Child* (see under Guinea), to which it is often married as part of a pre-independence genre in West Africa. However, Dadié develops more deeply and directly his dissatisfactions while maintaining a warmth and simplicity which are absent from the works of many of his contemporaries. Writing about his journey to France, he explained, 'Paris has not digested me because I resisted. The Gods from home, obstinate and patient, pulled me in another direction.'

Other writers following similar autobiographical patterns at the time

22

FACT BOX

AREA: 322 463 sq km
POPULATION: 12 400 000
CAPITAL: Abidjan (*de facto*) Yamoussoukro (official)
LANGUAGES: French, Akan, Krou, Malinké, Bambara
FORMER COLONIAL POWER: France
INDEPENDENCE: 1960

---

were not so resistant, or perhaps not so lucky. Aké Loba's first and autobiographical novel *Kocoumbo* tells of an African suffering the effects of being uprooted and poverty-stricken in Paris, who is drawn towards militant communism and into the dark underworld of the Pigalle. When he is rescued and educated as a magistrate, he falls foul of politicians back in his homeland who see him as a threat.

The biggest hit of the post-independence genre overseas was Ahmadou Kourouma's ◊ *The Suns of Independence* (Extract 1). Tackling the well worn literary topic of post-independence dissatisfaction, Kourouma nevertheless maintains an original wry humour and a dignified style. Fama, the hero, is a deposed and disgruntled chief who has lost his subjects and his power and has to readjust to an altogether different way of life – 'He, Fama, born to gold, food in plenty, honour and women! Bred to prefer one gold to another, to choose between many dishes, to bed his favourite of a hundred wives! What was he now? A scavenger . . . A hyena in a hurry.'

Less popular, though significant as one of the few Côte d'Ivoire novels translated into English, is Jean-Marie Adiaffi's *The Identity Card*. In a classic case of lost and mistaken identity, a displaced Ashanti prince is arrested by the French on spurious charges, tortured, blinded and then given seven short days to find his missing identity card. The novel is fraught with simplistic symbolism, though it contains some interesting dialogues on the dilemma of Africans adopting a colonial language. Says one teacher controversially, 'It is the language of the future . . . since it has become our mother tongue, we must speak it fluently.' His countryman replies, 'If we bury all our languages in the same coffin, we are parting forever with our cultural values . . . because our oral languages are our only archives.'

The writers who have had the most widespread literary success in Francophone Africa are undoubtedly those who have mastered two languages. Instead of fighting against another language, they have turned it to their advantage and used it as another tool of their trade. This is particularly noticeable in poetry, which is sometimes, for example, found to be directly influenced by the teaching of the French surrealist literature, though it is often combined with and complemented by the virtuosity and imagery of the indigenous language. Poets such as Joseph Bognini and Charles Nokan ◊ writing in the 1960s bring some interesting imagery into their country's repertoire (Extract 3).

Another interesting perspective on this country is provided by the Trinidad-born writer V.S. Naipaul ◊ who came to the Côte d'Ivoire in 1982 to write part of *Finding the Centre: Two Narratives*, his so-called 'prologue to an autobiography'. The people here, he remarked, were like himself, looking to find their 'centre'. He was also attracted to the country for sentimental reasons: 'France in Africa was a private fantasy . . . I imagined the language in the mouths of elegant Africans; I thought of wine and tropical boulevards'. Naipaul was drawn north to **Yamoussoukro**, the birthplace of the President and home to his crocodile-guarded palace. Here, he found, 'You get a glimpse of an African Africa, an Africa which – whatever the accidents of history, whatever the current manifestations of earthly glory – has always been in its own eyes complete, achieved, bursting with its own powers.' Mesmerized by the city's megalomaniacal proportions and its emblematic inhabitants (which with great ritual are fed live chickens in a daily ceremony), he named the narrative 'The Crocodiles of Yamoussoukro' (Extract 4).

An equally fascinating subject, and one which has long-since surrounded many deep-seated prejudices and popular myths about Africa, is the controversial question of cannibalism. One of the most bizarre stories I have come across is that told by John Gunther in his renowned book *Inside Africa*: 'Some years ago [the Côte d'Ivoire] elected a distinguished Negro lawyer, Victor Biaka-Boda, as a senator to Paris. Mr Biaka-Boda returned to his constituency in 1950 to do some electioneering and disappeared out in the bush. All efforts to trace him failed. On March 30, 1953, he was officially declared dead by a court sitting at Bouafle which on inspecting the evidence decided that he had been eaten by cannibals. "*Debris humain*" was the proof. There are cases innumerable in the world of senators feasting with the constituents, but this must surely be the only instance on record of constituents feasting on a senator.'

LITERARY LANDMARKS

Grand Bassam. 'Grand Bassam . . . is for connoisseurs of decay.' So said Richard West in his *White Tribes of Africa*. Bernard Dadié spent much of his childhood and education here.

Yamoussoukro. Birthplace of President Houphouët-Boigney. V.S.

Naipaul, staying at the opulent 12-storey French **Sofitel Hotel**, described the city as 'one of the wonders of black Africa'.

Libraries and Bookshops

Abidjan. American Cultural Centre Library; Central Public Library; Centre d'Édition et de Diffusions Africaines, BP 541; French Cultural Centre Library; Maison des Livres, 23 Boulevard de la République, BP 4645; National Library.

BOOKLIST

The following selection includes the extracted titles in this chapter as well as those mentioned in the introduction which are available in English and other titles for further reading. In general, paperback editions are given when possible. The editions cited are not necessarily the only ones available. For most of the extracted works, the original publisher in English can be found in 'Acknowledgments and Citations' at the end of the volume, as can the exact location of the extracts and the editions from which they are taken. Extract numbers are highlighted in bold for ease of reference.

Adiaffi, Jean-Marie, *The Identity Card*, Zimbabwe Publishing House, Harare, 1993.

Dadié, Bernard, *Climbié*, Heinemann, London, 1971. **Extract 2**.

Dadié, Bernard, *The Black Cloth*, K.C. March, trans, University of Massachusetts Press, Amherst, MA, 1987.

Dadié, Bernard, *The City Where No One Dies*, Three Continents Press, Washington, DC, 1986.

Gunther, John, *Inside Africa*, Hamish Hamilton, London, 1955.

Horn, Aloysious, *The Ivory Coast in the Earlies*, Jonathan Cape, London, 1927.

Kourouma, Ahmadou, *The Suns of Independence*, A. Adams, trans, Heinemann, Oxford, 1981. **Extract 1**.

Loba, Aké, *Kocoumbo*, extracted in *African Writing Today*, Ezekiel Mphahlele, ed, Penguin, London, 1967.

Matthiessen, Peter, *African Silences*, Random House, New York, 1991.

Naipaul, V.S., *Finding the Centre: Two Narratives*, Penguin, London, 1985. **Extract 4**.

Nokan, Charles, 'My Head is Immense', Gerald Moore, trans, in Gerald Moore and Ulli Beier, eds, *The Penguin Book of Modern African Poetry*, Penguin, London, 1984. **Extract 3**.

Voices from Twentieth-Century Africa, Chinweizu, ed, Faber and Faber, London, 1988.

West, Richard, *White Tribes of Africa*, Cape, London, 1965.

Extracts

(1) ABIDJAN

Ahmadou Kourouma, *The Suns of Independence*

Fama, a deposed chief who has been forced by circumstance to live beneath his class, hurries through the capital to the funeral of a fellow Malinké.

Fama grumbled: 'Hell and damnation! *Nyamokode!*'

Everything conspired to exasperate him. The sun! the sun! the cursed sun of Independence filled half the sky, scorching the universe so as to justify the unhealthy late-afternoon storms. And the people in the street! the bastards lounging about in the middle of the pavement as if it were their old man's backyard. You had to shove, threaten and curse your way past. All this in the midst of an ear-splitting din: horns hooting, motors racing, tyres flapping, passers-by and drivers shouting. Beyond the left-hand railing of the bridge, the lagoon glittered with the blinding flash of many mirrors, shattering and coalescing as far as the distant bank, the ash-grey horizon set with small islands and fringed with forest. The bridge was crowded with many-coloured cars, coming and going; beyond the right-hand railing was the lagoon, still glittering in places, but elsewhere choked with laterite soil; the harbour with its ships and warehouses, the edge of the forest and at last a bit of blue: the sea, soon lost in the blue of the horizon. God be praised! Luckily Fama hadn't much further to walk now; he could see the end of the harbour, over there where the road disappeared in a hollow, where other warehouses, their tin roofs gleaming or dull grey, clustered about palm-trees and clumps of foliage from which emerged a few two-storey houses with shuttered windows. It was an immense disgrace and shame, as great as that of the old panther caught fighting with hyenas over carrion, for Fama to be chasing after funerals in this way.

(2) GRAND BASSAM

Bernard Dadié, *Climbié*

As a child Dadié was sent to the local Catholic school in Grand Bassam. In Climbié he recounts some of the schoolboy tricks they used to play on the non-native teachers. He was later to be employed by the Ministry of Education.

The Headmaster, because of his rotund body and his long moustache, had been nicknamed *Cabou* by the students. The word made no sense in any of the dialects. But it sounded nice. Every time the Headmaster appeared, the students whispered '*Cabou, Cabou*', without raising their heads, their noses deep in a book or notebook.

One day the Headmaster wanted to get to the bottom of this. He prepared a lecture on the magnifying glass. His paunch was heaving, and his moustache, which he kept pulling and twisting all the time, looked like the tails of a scorpion. The students looked at each other, smiling. Someone breathed the word *Cabou*, which was passed to a third, until it swarmed through the classroom.

'Who are you calling *Cabou*?' asked the Headmaster. A chill passed over the class, and the students lost their smiles. How could anyone explain this word to the Headmaster, who, because he hit so hard, was greatly feared?

But Assè, the most mischievous of the students, without losing his wits, stood up and said:

'In our language, that's what we call a magnifying glass.'

'Ah! You call the magnifying glass *Cabou*!

'Yes, sir,' replied the students, smiling. '*Cabou*!'

'Well, why are you snickering like that?'

'The name is rather funny,' replied Assè. '*Magnifying glass* sounds better than *Cabou*.'

'*Cabou*, that sounds nice, too. I like it . . . *Cabou*?'

'Yes, sir, *Cabou*!'

The Headmaster marked the word down in his notebook.

How many scholars must have been misled in the same way as the Headmaster! Then one day, somewhere, he would defend to his death the proposition that the Negroes in the Ivory Coast call the magnifying glass *Cabou*.

(3) CÔTE D'IVOIRE: IDENTITY

Charles Nokan, *My Head is Immense*

Nokan's writing in French, dominated by concerns for true liberation and independence, often uses strange and powerful imagery that is a combination of his traditional and his 'adopted' culture. His poem 'My Head is Immense' is included in The Penguin Book of Modern African Poetry – see Booklist.

My head is immense
I have a toad's eyes
A horn stands on the nape of my neck
But a magical music surges
from me.

. . .

You who look on, you think
that the voice of my instrument
buys my freedom, that I am fluidity, thought
which flies.
No, there is nothing in me
but a pool of sadness.

(4) YAMOUSSOUKRO

V.S. Naipaul, *The Crocodiles of Yamoussoukro*

*When V.S. Naipul visited the birthplace of President
Houphouët-Boigney he found the ancient ancestral village swept
aside and the wilderness stripped back to make way for all the
manifestations of the President's ego. 'The Crocodiles of
Yamoussoukro' forms part of Naipaul's Finding the Center.*

The two ideas go together. The ultra-modern dream also serves old
Africa. It is pharaonic: it has a touch of the antique world. Away from
the stupendous modern frivolities of the golf course and the golf club
and the swimming pool of the Hotel President there is the presidential
palace with its artificial lake. Outside the blank walls that hide the
president's ancestral village and the palaver tree from the common
view, the president's totemic crocodiles are fed with fresh meat every
day. People can go and watch. But distances in Yamoussoukro are so
great, and the scarred, empty spaces so forbidding, that only people
with cars can easily go; and they tend to be visitors, tourists.

The feeding ritual takes place in the afternoon, in bright light. There
are the cars, the tourists in bright clothes, the cameras. But the
crocodiles are sacred. A live offering – a chicken – has to be made to
them; it is part of the ritual. This element of sacrifice, this protracted
display of power and cruelty, is as unsettling as it is meant to be, and it
seems to bring night and the forest close again to the dream of
Yamoussoukro.

Biographies and important works

DADIÉ, Bernard Binlin (1916–). Born in **Assinie**, Dadié is a short story writer, dramatist and poet. Like many of the most prominent writers in Africa, he has combined an active political life with a large literary output. He first became known for his collection of African folk tales, told to him by his uncle with whom he lived as a child (to protect her son from what she believed was a curse which had resulted in the deaths of her first three children, the author's one-eyed mother sent him to live with his uncle and aunt in **Bingerville**). The stories in *The Black Cloth* concern Ananzè the spider, who represents the eternal trickster, appearing in many guises and through whose devious dealings Dadié explores simple, ageless truths and morals. He came to political prominence when he worked as a journalist for the newspaper of the Parti Démocratique de Côte d'Ivoire in the late 1940s. It was as a result of this affiliation that he was to spend over a year in prison. Never far from politics, Dadié has since worked for UNESCO and in several government ministries of the Côte d'Ivoire. His most recent post was Minister of Culture.

KOUROUMA, Ahmadou (1927–). Born in **Boundiali**, in the Malinké area, Kourouma studied in Guinea, Mali and France. A one-book wonder, he was discovered in 1967 when he submitted the manuscript of *The Suns of Independence* to a literary competition. Originally written in French, it was later translated into English. It is the archetypal novel of post-independence disillusionment, though

distinguished by its originality of style and powers of observation of ordinary life. The title refers to the hopes of the Malinké that when the suns of independence dawn the wrongs suffered under colonialism will be righted.

NAIPAUL, V.S. (1932–). Born in Trinidad to an Indian family, Naipaul was educated in England and has travelled widely. Of his passion for travelling, he has said that it 'took me out of my own colonial shell'. *Finding the Centre* took the author to the Côte d'Ivoire, and is the result of his search for a balance in his life, and a point from which to look back at his own biography. Here he met many interesting characters, including a pro-

V.S. Naipaul

Bernard Dadié

fessor of Drummologie, the controversial so-called 'science' of talking drums, and a poet who had given up journalism because 'like smoking it could damage your health'. The author's experience, encounters and *raison d'être* are not so different from those of most travellers to this part of the world. However, he manages to travel through the narrative without boring the reader with dreary shock-of-the-new tensions that occupy so much travel writing. It is interesting to remember that Naipaul is a Hindu, travelling in a country where Hindus have a great reputation as magicians. Also inspired by Africa is *In a Free State*. Part fact and part fiction, it explores the illusion of freedom in South Africa in particular and of Africans in general. In *A Bend in the River*, set in a central African state, he paints a disturbing and violent picture of the emergence of the 'new Africa'. The novel owes much to Conrad's *Heart of Darkness*. In 1993, Naipaul was the first recipient of the British Literature Prize, awarded for a lifetime's achievement.

NOKAN, Charles (1936–). As well as an accomplished poet, Nokan, who writes under several names, is also a novelist and playwright (his real name is Zégoua Konan). Written in French, little of his work has been translated outside of anthologies. His writing, like much of the literature from the Côte d'Ivoire, reveals a preoccupation with colonialism, and is concerned with poetic and passionate pleas for a real and liberating post-independence.

THE GAMBIA

'Can any good thing come
out of Gambia? Wait.
nay; go and see.'
Lenrie Peters, Katchikali

When Mungo Park (◊ Mali) arrived on the banks of the **Gambia River** in May 1795, he described the view as the 'most enchanting prospect'. Some 70 years later Sir Richard Burton (◊ Ethiopia) was decrying the area as a 'whiteman's grave'. It did not, however, prevent Africa's smallest mainland country from becoming a major slave trading post (the name 'Gambia' is said to come from the word *cambio*, meaning 'change' in Spanish). Nor did it prevent the country from becoming a long-standing British colony, and today probably West Africa's most popular traveller's destination.

As the last British colony in Africa to win independence in 1965, the Gambia's literature has undoubtedly been heavily influenced by the English language. During the colonial period it was the language of the élite, though the oral tradition has throughout the centuries remained a strong and important part of literary expression – be it in music, dance or poetry. As Gambian poet Lenrie Peters ◊ pointed out in an interview, 'It is only recently that a new generation of people from the provinces have become involved with the international language of English, and while a few of them may write in it, the language isn't *in* the country to any depth.' Shallow maybe, but strong. Strong enough for the main momentum of today's growing body of well known and well received Gambian literature to be written in English.

Ironically, if there is an English-language book that has put Gambia on the international map, it is one that was only possible thanks to the extraordinary tenacity of the local oral story-telling traditions. For it was through listening to the local *griots* (oral historians), who traditionally carry family and national history down through the generations, that enabled the American author Alex Haley ◊ to write *Roots*. A worldwide best-selling book, *Roots* follows four generations of an American family, for which Haley traced his own family back some 200

FACT BOX

AREA: 11 295 sq km
POPULATION: 901 000
CAPITAL: Banjul
LANGUAGES: English, Fulani, Mandingo, Wolof
FORMER COLONIAL POWER: Great Britain
INDEPENDENCE: 1965

---

years not just to the Gambia, but to the very village where his forefathers lived. It was in **Juffure** that Haley's great-great-great-great-great-grandfather, Kunta Kinte, grew up and where he was captured, sold into slavery, and taken to Maryland, USA. From a peaceful and traditional existence, village life was changed forever, and the families uprooted for life (Extract 4).

Although Haley is an American rather than a Gambian writer, the story was important and symbolic for many people. In particular, it entered into the black American consciousness and many who felt dispossessed and without real roots were able to identify with Haley and Kunta Kinte's story, and were inspired to search for their own roots.

Juffure, today a major tourist attraction, has also inspired local writers. Poet Lenrie Peters wrote, 'Juffure, your years of violence/return, your years of grief/after three centuries of sleep./In your old age,/lost children return to you/from a different world.' (from *Selected Poetry*). Peters's first major literary achievement was in fact a novel, *The Second Round*, which follows the consequences and difficulties of return to native culture after a period of absence abroad. The look is semi-autobiographical – the life of the main protagonist who practises as a surgeon in England and then returns to his homeland is almost a mirror of the author's own. The theme of alienation, lost idealism and confrontation with uncompromising materialistic change characterizes much of the poetry of Lenrie Peters (Extract 3).

The Gambia's second major writer, William Conton ◊, made his name with *The African*, published in 1960. The sometimes bizarre and often strangely humorous story of an African student in England, it traces a doomed love affair with a white South African in the Lake District (Conton was a student at nearby Durham) and his return home. The embittered returnee throws himself into fighting for his country's independence, and rises to power as its first nationalist leader. Although ostensibly a mythical place, the country he returns to is drawn from his allegiances to Sierra Leone. While, as John Povey wrote, 'the novel cannot be critically admired for its technical qualities . . . its influence has been considerable'. It has been translated into several languages and inspired several writers to tackle this increasingly commonplace theme.

The new generation of successful Gambian writers is represented by Ebou Dibba ◊ and Tijan Sallah ◊. Dibba's first novel *Chaff on the Wind* (Extract 1) secured his reputation as a contributor to the body of national literature. Set in the Gambia in the 1930s, it follows the fortunes of two boys from different villages who meet on a boat heading for the capital. Dinding is a conventional Muslim, and the archetypal good-boy intends to establish himself in a respectable career. His raffish companion Pateh, the antithesis of Dinding, is looking for little more than a good time and advises his friend 'try to find yourself a girlfriend. She might help you change your village ways.' As we follow the boys to manhood, Dibba makes examples of them both. In spite of all the hard work and diligence on the one hand, and guile and cunning on the other, they are unable to change their destinies. Dibba shows them both as victims of fate, or mere *Chaff on the Wind* (Extract 1).

Sallah is a more radical writer. Poet and novelist, he takes a questioning view of the politics and pretences of present-day Gambia and Africa. Delicacy and subtlety are not his trademarks (Extract 2). His first collection of poetry, *When Africa Was a Young Woman*, was marked by directness and includes the memorable lines 'Let us not live in/Phantasmagoria: Tarzan never lived in my Africa'. 'Tarzan Never Lived in my Africa', and 'If You Ask Me Why My Teeth Are White' are titles designed to make the reader sit up and take notice. It is this sort of reaction which is a welcome and encouraging response to the new-found confidence of the Gambia's small collection of writers. Tiny but not lost, the country is an increasingly strong literary lighthouse shining on the West African coast.

Literary Landmarks

Banjul. Capital and birthplace of William Conton and Lenrie Peters. The only really large town in the Gambia. Banjul is a magnet for people seeking work or the wild life as characterized by Ebou Dibba in *Chaff on the Wind*.

Karantaba Tenda. Site of explorer Mungo Park's **memorial obelisk**. The stone marks the spot where he disembarked in 1804 on his second expedition to find the source of the River Niger.

Juffure. The **Trading Post** was the euphemistic name given to the slaving post. The one reconstructed here is allegedly the one from which Alex Haley's forefather was sold into slavery. The village and Trading Post are now major tourist attractions.

Libraries and Bookshops

Banjul. British Council Library; Chaaka's Bookshop, Clarkson Street; Methodist Bookshop, Buckle Street; National Library.

BOOKLIST

The following selection includes the extracted titles in this chapter as well as those mentioned in the introduction which are available in English and other titles for further reading. In general, paperback editions are given when possible. The editions cited are not necessarily the only ones available. For most of the extracted works, the original publisher in English can be found in 'Acknowledgments and Citations' at the end of the volume, as can the exact location of the extracts and the editions from which they are taken. Extract numbers are highlighted in bold for ease of reference.

Conton, William, *The African*, Heinemann, London, 1960.

Dibba, Ebou, *Chaff on the Wind*, Macmillan, London, 1986. **Extract 1.**

Dibba, Ebou, *Fafa*, Macmillan, London, 1989.

Dibba, Ebou, *Alhaji*, Macmillan, London, 1992.

Haley, Alex, *Roots*, Doubleday, New York, 1976. **Extract 4.**

Park, Mungo, *Travels in Africa*, Everyman, New York, 1969.

Peters, Lenrie, *Katchikali*, Heinemann, London, 1971.

Peters, Lenrie, *Satellites*, Heinemann, London, 1967. **Extract 3.**

Peters, Lenrie, *The Second Round*, Heinemann, London, 1969.

Peters, Lenrie, *Selected Poetry*, Heinemann, London, 1981.

Sallah, Tijan, *Before the New Earth: African Short Stories*, Writers Workshop, Calcutta, 1988.

Sallah, Tijan, *Kora Land: Poems*, Three Continents Press, Washington, DC, 1989.

Sallah, Tijan, 'Shadows of Banjul', in Samuel Baity Garren, 'Exile and Return: The Poetry and Fiction of Tijan Sallah', *Wasafiri*, Spring 1992. **Extract 2.**

Sallah, Tijan, *When Africa was a Young Woman*, Writers Workshop, Calcutta, 1980.

Extracts

(1) BANJUL

Ebou Dibba, *Chaff on the Wind*

Dinding and Pateh, just arrived in Banjul, have been sitting by the wharf watching the labourers at work. The restless Pateh sets off alone leaving Dinding to contemplate his fate as a new boy in the capital.

The extraordinary capacity of the human mind to adapt to assimilate quickly the differences between these new surroundings and one's original habitat makes the process of familiarisation barely noticeable to the unsuspecting onlooker, to the extent that such an onlooker is often heard to say, 'You are settling down well.' Those, however, of a poetic disposition are forever, so to speak, strangers even in their own indigenous surroundings. For those with such poetic sensibilities are forever aware of the differences between environments and of the constant changes that each environment is forever undergoing. This sensibility does not have to be expressed to become poetic; it suffices that it be directed at the objects around and that these objects be given the full attention that they deserve for them to display their uniqueness, not only from other objects but from other previous states such objects might have been in. For sensibility, the essential is to have a capacity at once to be surprised and not to be surprised.

Dinding was usually disposed to giving his environment almost childlike attention unless practical considerations dictated otherwise, and even then such practical considerations were never totally dominant. Thus it was that even when he talked to Pateh on the wharf he could not help but marvel at the way in which the cranes and their pulleys swung and lifted; at the up and down movement of the boat anchored against the wharf opposite, and all this against the background of an expanse of water, larger than any he had ever seen.

Now, as he walked the streets, he wondered what it was that gave this part of the town its naked, light aspect. It was not till he came to the point where he had left the letter writer, who now sat camouflaged under the big tree, his mouth drooling as he snoozed, his face held in his cupped hands, and his elbows resting on the makeshift writing desk, that Dinding knew the answer. There was, compared to his village, a relative absence of big trees, not even many baobabs or mango trees, most of the mango trees being confined to compounds. The ubiquitous giants of the woods around his village, with their thorny bark, were here nowhere to be seen. Equally, all those white buildings that seemed carved out of the still glare of the burning sun with their imposing presence, the white relieved only by the green, blue or brown of shutters and doors, contrasted sharply with the sun-baked brown, rounded and pointed, straw huts that had until recently given him shelter.

(2) BANJUL

Tijan Sallah, *Shadows of Banjul*

This impassioned, angry and despairing view of what has befallen the capital is characteristic of Sallah's rough and radical poetic style. The Wabenzi are the wealthy – literally 'people of the (Mercedes) Benz'. These lines from 'Shadows of Banjul' are taken from the journal Wasafiri – see Booklist.

There was a time when there was
Hygiene in the city. But now . . .
Gutters of assorted refuse assault
Your breath. Mosquitoes siphon life
With their tiny needle jackhammers-of-a-mouth.

. . .

Long shadows of Banjul haunt me.
The streets are arthritic with
Leper's dust. Scrawny ribs rattle
Their pots before the obese Wabenzi.

Everyone asks for a passport to exit.
No one faces up to the challenge
Of hope, except the hyenas,
Who dream of scavenging more coffers.

(3) THE GAMBIA: HOMELAND

Lenrie Peters, *Home Coming*

Returning to the Gambia from England after several years, Peters is apprehensive about what greets him, and how his country has changed. 'Home Coming' is included in Satellites – see Booklist.

Too strange the sudden change
   Of the times we buried when we left
The times before we had properly arranged
   The memories that we kept

. . .

There at the edge of town
   Just by the burial ground
Stands the house without a shadow
   Lived in by new skeletons

That is all that is left
   To greet us on the home coming
After we have paced the world.
   And longed for returning.

(4) JUFFURE

Alex Haley, *Roots*

It is the spring of 1750 and a boy has just been born to Omoro and Binta Kinte in the village of Juffure. As they name the child, the sense of ceremony and tradition is timeless.

As Binta proudly held her new infant, a small patch of his first hair was shaved off, as was always done on this day, and all of the women exclaimed at how well formed the baby was. Then they quieted as the jaliba began to beat his drums. The alimamo said a prayer over the calabashes of sour milk and munko cakes, and as he prayed, each guest touched a calabash brim with his or her right hand, as a gesture of respect for the food. Then the alimamo turned to pray over the infant, entreating Allah to grant him long life, success in bringing credit and pride and many children to his family, to his village, to his tribe – and, finally, the strength and the spirit to deserve and to bring honor to the name he was about to receive.

Omoro then walked out before all of the assembled people of the village. Moving to his wife's side, he lifted up the infant and, as all watched, whispered three times into his son's ear the name he had chosen for him. It was the first time the name had ever been spoken as this child's name, for Omoro's people felt that each human being should be the first to know who he was.

The tan-tang drum resounded again; and now Omoro whispered the name into the ear of Binta, and Binta smiled with pride and pleasure. Then Omoro whispered the name to the arafang, who stood before the villagers.

'The first child of Omoro and Binta Kinte is named *Kunta!*' cried Brima Cesay.

As everyone knew, it was the middle name of the child's late grandfather, Kairaba Kunta, Kinte, who had come from his native Mauretania into The Gambia, where he had saved the people of Juffure from a famine, married Grandma Yaisa, and then served Juffure honorably till his death as the village's holy man.

One by one, the arafang recited the names of the Mauretanian forefathers of whom the baby's grandfather, old Kairaba Kinte, had often told. The names, which were great and many, went back more than two hundred rains. Then the jaliba pounded on his tan-tang and all of the people exclaimed their admiration and respect at such a distinguished lineage.

Out under the moon and the stars, alone with his son that eighth night, Omoro completed the naming ritual. Carrying little Kunta in his strong arms, he walked to the edge of the village, lifted his baby up with his face to the heavens, and said softly, '*Fend kiling dorong leh warrata ka iteh tee.*' (Behold – the only thing greater than yourself.)

Biographies and important works

BURTON, Sir Richard (see under Ethiopia).

CONTON, William (1925–). Conton is a historian and teacher. Although born in **Banjul**, *The African*, his most famous work, now also translated into Hungarian, Russian and Arabic, recalls his childood and early education in Sierra Leone. Conton went on to study in England, and taught in Ghana and Freetown, Sierra Leone, where he joined the Ministry of Education. He now lives in Paris.

DIBBA, Ebou (1943–). Dibba grew up in the Gambia but came to England after winning a scholarship at

Cambridge. Fellow writer Lenrie Peters, in a special Gambian issue of *Wasafiri*, has described him as 'a novelist of real stature'. Following up *Chaff on the Wind* (Extract 1), the novel *Fafa: An Idyll on the Banks of a River*, moves on a generation with two of the minor female characters, and celebrates the river that dominates the country as a character in itself.

HALEY, Alex (1921–1992). Author of the 1977 Pulitzer Prize winning *Roots* (Extract 4), Haley was born in New York but was brought up in Tennessee by his grandmother, whose stories first inspired him to search for his roots. Haley first worked for the US Coast Guard as a cook and then become a journalist, eventually writing for *Readers' Digest* and *Playboy*. His nine years of research for the 700-page *Roots* took him to the Gambia and Lloyds of London where he discovered the records listing Kunta Kinte as one of the slaves to survive the crossing in 1767. For Haley, the moment the connection was completed was when the *griot* said, 'About the time the King's soldiers came . . . the oldest of the four sons, Kunta, went away . . . and he was never seen again . . .'. In 1971, Haley set up the Kinte Foundation for black genealogical research.

PARK, Mungo (see under Mali).

PETERS, Lenrie (1932–). Peters is a surgeon as well as a writer. Born in Banjul, he was educated in Sierra Leone and at the Universities of Cambridge and London. While he lived much of his early life in Sierra Leone, where he is something of a literary adoptee (his novel *The Second Round* was set mainly there), in some of his writing his roots are clearly in the Gambia. The collection of poems *Satellites* (Extract 3), his best collection, described as almost surgical in its execution, was written while Peters was studying in England, and expresses his fears about returning to his homeland (upon his return he worked as a government surgeon specialist and later privately). The title poem of his collection *Katchikali* celebrates the Gambian **Crocodile Pool**, a traditional shrine that symbolizes ancient gods and history, and that has been desecrated by developers. Lenrie Peters now lives in the Gambia.

SALLAH, Tijan (1958–). Born in **Serekunda**, Sallah has spent several years abroad in the USA. The title of his best received collection of poetry, *Kora Land*, refers to the 21-stringed instrument used by West African *griots*. As well as several collections of poetry, Sallah has published *Before the New Earth*, a collection of 16 short morality tales which appeared in 1988. They comment bluntly on stories such as how Africans were allegedly sold contaminated milk from Chernobyl. He is noted in much of his work not only for his observation of the corruption of the motherland itself, but more unusually for his sensitivity to women's suffering. Sallah currently works for the World Bank.

GHANA

The capital of Ghana, **Accra**, is one of Africa's biggest but liveliest cities. Beset by overcrowding and poverty, it is a far cry from the Accra that awaited the Portuguese when they arrived here in the fifteenth century. Writing to his neighbours Ferdinand and Isabella of Aragon–Castille, King Manuel of Portugal boasted how seamen from his country 'found land in which there are mines of gold'. Hence Ghana became known as the Mina d'Ouro and later under the British colonists, the Gold Coast.

Rich in natural resources, Ghana was also a magnet for those in search of spices, palm oil, cocoa and slaves. Within a century of arriving here the Portuguese were all but a spent force. They were soon to be supplanted by the Dutch, Danish and English, all of whom began to establish trading posts along the coast. Despite this, when Ghana became the first African country to retrieve its independence from Britain in 1957, it was also one of the richest. Since then the population has nearly doubled and Ghana is today one of West Africa's most densely populated countries – some 15 million people live in an area roughly the size of Great Britain.

Of the 50 ethnic groups, the largest are the Fante and Asante who each speak an own dialect of the Twi language. This rich ethnic and linguistic mosaic has to a remarkable extent resisted centuries of colonists and Christians for whom it was a priority to create a unified mode of oral and written communication. Traditional proverbs, legends and folktales, including the famous Anansi spider stories, maintain a tenacious hold in the indigenous culture.

Both in spite of, and partly as a result of this history of linguistic

---

FACT BOX

AREA: 238 533 sq km
POPULATION: 15 300 000
CAPITAL: Accra
LANGUAGES: Fanti, Twi, Ewe
FORMER COLONIAL POWER: Great Britain
INDEPENDENCE: 1957

---

imperialism, there have been many publications in the main indigenous languages – Fante, Twi and Ewe. Ironically, many of these works were sponsored by the eighteenth century missionaries who introduced a formal literary education into West Africa. Consequently Ghana is said to have one of the longest written literary histories in Africa, although, not surprisingly, most of the early works are either religious or emulate colonial literature.

It was this clash of traditional African beliefs and European Christianity that inspired one of West Africa's very first novels. *Ethiopia Unbound* (Extract 5) was published in 1911 and describes the journey of a young man who returns to his native Gold Coast after a period in England. It tells of the reactions and anger of a man finding himself a stranger in his own country surrounded by men 'with the gin bottle in one hand, and the bible in the other.' The hero Kwamankra is 'resolved to devote the rest of his life in bringing back his people to their primitive simplicity and faith . . . "If my people are to be saved from national and racial death, they must be proved as if by fire – by the practice of a virile religion, not by following emasculated sentimentalities which men shamelessly and slanderously identify with the holy One of God, His son, Jesus Christ."'

The title *Ethiopia Unbound* came from the fact that at the time, apart from Liberia, Ethiopia was the only independent country in Africa. The author, J.E. Casely Hayford ◊, spoke clearly for the need for African unity, and for a political, religious and educational realignment on the continent. His beliefs were essentially an early expression of *Négritude*, inspired by the Pan African Movement at the turn of the century and the writings of their prime spokesman W.E.B. Du Bois (1868–1963). Du Bois, an American who died in Ghana, was critical of the status of Afro–Americans in America and pioneered a campaign to raise the consciousness of and promote the culture of black people across the world.

African nationalism rose in quick response to British imperialism, and was marked by books such as the curiously titled *Eighteen Pence*, published in 1941. Written by R.E. Obeng, it was one of the first West African novels to appear in English. Set in the rural and isolated **northern** part of the country, it is a classic moral rags-to-riches story, and begins when the hero Obeng-Akrofi buys a cutlass for 18 pence but has to work on a farm to pay for it. Accused of rape by his employer's wife, the book deals with the conflict between native Akan laws and the British judiciary system: 'I will be answerable to the British Court', swears the rebellious Konaduwa when herself charged with several offences at the ancient rural Akan court, 'I am a lamb who has fallen amongst wolves! . . . There is nobody in this court who will listen to my defence, for all of you are interested in the case. Therefore I will reserve my defence until the case is tried by others who have no interest in it.'

Kwame Nkrumah became Ghana's first post-independence Prime Minister in 1957. Poor economic policies, hard military repression and widespread civil unrest led to a coup in 1966. So restrictive was Nkrumah's socialist regime that it was only after the coup that any significant literature could develop. One of the first novels to criticize the regime openly came from writer Ayi Kwei Armah ◊. *The Beautyful Ones Are Not Yet Born* (Extract 1) is a sharp, sardonic observation of post-independence politics. The title comes from a misspelled inscription on an Accra bus, and alludes to the ugliness of a corrupted population. Armah is Ghana's 'angry young man', and in all of his work he expresses undisguised disgust both at the violation of Africa by the West, and the complicity of Africa's new élite. *Fragments*, Armah's second novel, is a semi-autobiographical tale of a young intellectual returning to his home from several years in America only to find his country spiritually in fragments, with his countrymen eager to adopt the values he is escaping from. Armah has written several other novels, including *The Healers* which relates the demise of the Ashanti Empire to that of Africa in general.

Another of the anguished young writers of this period is Kofi Awoonor ◊ who spent nearly a year in a jail for allegedly harbouring a criminal. He established his literary career as a poet who, as he remarks, 'soils his hands in the despair of the people'. His first novel, *This Earth, My Brother . . .* (Extract 2), tells of a young lawyer who searches for his identity. Awoonor uses a bold combination of poetic prose and narrative to explore the relationship between the contemporary and the traditional. Following his imprisonment, Awoonor returned to pure poetry and published *The House by The Sea*, a reference to an old slaving post and symbolic of the prison he was detained in.

The Gab Boys by Cameron Duodo, a contemporary of Awoonor's, is so-called after the gaberdine trousers sported by delinquents who drop out of school. Mistrusted by their village elders, the boys symbolize the tensions and dangers in a country of burgeoning Westernization and urbanization.

Of all the 'political' books set in post-revolutionary Ghana, one of the most powerful and engaging is Amu Djoleto's ◊ *Hurricane of Dust* (Extract 3). Small-time crook Doe Hevi is an ardent supporter of the revolution, but falls foul of the regime and ends up at the mercy of the military.

The movement towards realism has also been reflected in Ghana's poetry, short stories and plays. Ama Ata Aidoo uses all three forms, but is celebrated primarily for her short stories which are, following the country's strong oral tradition, written to be heard. Another voice that cries out to be heard is that of poet Kwesi Brew ◊. *The Shadows of Laughter* (Extract 6) is a collection of melancholic love poetry set in the beautiful **central** and **northern Ghana** and by the **River Volta**. These poems provide something of a romantic respite from the hard political leanings of Ghana's leading literary figures.

Clearly however, throughout the 1970s and 1980s, Ghana became a by-word for political instability and corruption. In 1979, Flight Lieutenant Jerry Rawlings sought to inject some stability and led Ghana from military to civilian rule. Shortly after leading the coup, he relinquished power to an elected president, only to reclaim his presidency via another coup in 1981. His Provisional National Defence Council (PNDC) became known for the war he waged on corruption, but there was no attempt to return to civilian rule. His degree of success is best measured by the national referendum in April 1992, which voted overwhelmingly to end 11 years of his socialist military rule.

Meanwhile, in spite of the instability, Ghana's contemporary writers enjoy rather better success that those of its neighbours, and figures such as novelist and poet B. Kojo Laing ◊ are gaining Africa-wide attention with their lively contemporary portraits of a society in flux (Extract 4).

Despite severe restrictions on the media, there is an erratically published literary magazine *Okyeame*, and a growing hunger for both popular and more traditional literature.

Literary Landmarks

Accra. The **W.E.B. Du Bois Memorial Centre for Pan African Culture**, at 22 1st Circular Road, was the home of the American campaigner for pan-Africanism who died there in 1963. Today it is a cultural centre with a library, photographs, documents and memorabilia. **Achimota School** was responsible for the education of several of Ghana's leading writers, including Ayi Kwei Armah, and Kofi Awoonor. Established primarily as a technical school, it was believed that a literary education was superfluous to ordinary Africans' require-

B. Kojo Laing

ments. **Independence Square** was built under President Nkrumah to celebrate African liberation, and hosts the Eternal Flame of African Liberation that he lit.

Sekondi. The second most important port of Ghana, described at the turn of the century by pan-Africanist J.E. Casely Hayford in *Ethiopia Unbound* (Extract 4).

Takoradi. Birthplace of writer Ayi Kwei Armah.

Libraries and Bookshops

Accra. Accra Central Library; Alliance Française; American Library. The Atlas Bookshop, Ambassador Hotel Gardens; British Council Library.
Legon. University Bookshop, University of Ghana, PO Box 1.

BOOKLIST

The following selection includes the extracted titles in this chapter as well as those mentioned in the introduction which are available in English and other titles for further reading. In general, paperback editions are given when possible. The editions cited are not necessarily the only ones available. For most of the extracted works, the original publisher in English can be found in 'Acknowledgments and Citations' at the end of the volume, as can the exact location of the extracts and the editions from which they are taken. Extract numbers are highlighted in bold for ease of reference.

Aidoo, Ama Ata, *No Sweetness Here: A Collection of Short Stories*, Longman, Harlow, 1979.

Armah, Ayi Kwei, *The Beautiful Ones Are Not Yet Born*, Heinemann, London, 1988. **Extract 1.**

Armah, Ayi Kwei, *Fragments*, Heinemann, London, 1970.

Armah, Ayi Kwei, *The Healers*, Heinemann, London, 1979.

Armah, Ayi Kwei, *Two Thousand Seasons*, Heinemann, London, 1979.

Awoonor, Kofi, *This Earth, My Brother . . .*, Heinemann, London, 1972. **Extract 2.**

Awoonor, Kofi, *The House by the Sea*, Greenfield Review Press, New York, 1978.

Awoonor, Kofi, *Rediscovery and Other Poems*, Mbari, Lagos, 1964.

Awoonor, Kofi, *Night of My Blood*, Doubleday, New York, 1971.

Brew, Kwesi, *The Shadows of Laughter*, Longman, London, 1968. **Extract 6.**

Casely Hayford, J.E., *Ethiopia Unbound: Studies in Race Emancipation*, Frank Cass, London, 1969. **Extract 5.**

Djoleto, Amu, *Hurricane of Dust*, Longman, Harlow, 1987. **Extract 3.**

Djoleto, Amu, *The Strange Man*, Heinemann, London, 1967.

Djoleto, Amu, *Money Galore*, Heinemann, London, 1975.

Du Bois, W.E.B., *The Suppression of the African Slave Trade to the USA 1638–1870*, Louisiana State University Press, 1970.

Du Bois, W.E.B., *The Conservation of the Race*, American Negro Academy, 1897.

Du Bois, W.E.B., *The Negro*, Oxford University Press, Oxford, 1970.

Duodo, Cameron, *The Gab Boys*, Fontana, London, 1969.

Gunther, John, *Inside Africa*, Hamish Hamilton, London, 1955.

Laing, B. Kojo, *God-Horse*, Heinemann, Oxford, 1989.

Laing, B. Kojo, *Major Gentl and the Achimota Wars*, Heinemann, Oxford, 1992.

Laing, B. Kojo, *Search Sweet Country*, Picador, London, 1987. **Extract 4.**

Laing, B. Kojo, *Woman of the Aeroplanes*, Heinemann, London, 1988.

Obeng, R.E., *Eighteen Pence*, Ghana Publishing Corporation, Accra, 1941.

Extracts

(1) ACCRA

Ayi Kwei Armah,
The Beautyful Ones Are Not Yet Born

The hero, called simply 'The man', takes a bus through Accra. He watches the conductor counting out the piles of grubby small change. It was a rare day in this poor country that he was ever handed a note on the bus.

The cedi lay there on the seat. Among the coins it looked strange, and for a moment the conductor thought it was ridiculous that the paper should be more important than the shiny metal. In the weak light inside the bus he peered closely at the markings on the note. Then a vague but persistent odor forced itself on him and he rolled the cedi up and deliberately, deeply smelled it. He had to smell it again, this time standing up and away from the public leather of the bus seat. But the smell was not his mistake. Fascinated, he breathed it slowly into his lungs. It was a most unexpected smell for something so new to have: it was a very old smell, very strong, and so very rotten that the stench itself of it came with a curious, satisfying pleasure. Strange that a man could have so many cedis pass through his hands and yet not really know their smell.

After the note the conductor began smelling the coins, but they were a disappointment. Not so satisfying, the smell of metal coins. The conductor started stuffing them into his bag, first checking everything against the tickets to make sure how much he had gained. He felt reasonably contented. It would, he hoped, be a good day for him. Passion Week or no Passion Week. Again his nostrils lost the smell of the cedi's marvelous rottenness, and they itched to refresh themselves with its ancient stale smell. He took the note, unrolled it this time, and pressed it flat against his nostrils. But now his satisfaction was mixed with a kind of shame. In his embarrassment he turned round, wishing to reassure himself that the bus was empty and he was alone in it.

(2) ACCRA

Kofi Awoonor, *This Earth, My Brother* . . .

*Amamu, a brilliant young African lawyer in Accra, works
within the confines of a judicial system inherited from the British.
The courts have just adjourned their morning session.*

A long line of lawyers, sweating freely in their black coats and their
pin-stripe trousers, some struggling with their wigs and their black legal
bags, are chatting animatedly as they descend the stairs through the
Palladian pillars of the colonial edifice which now houses the Supreme
Court of Accra. Following them, a host of clients, petitioners, litigants,
pocket lawyers – case farmers, old men tired in their combat with the
law, young men who have won a brief reprieve and have had their cases
postponed. All listening intently to the lawyers. These brilliant
children of our soil who have wrenched from the white man the magic
of his wisdom. Their clients spoke in every tongue of the land. The
lawyers inclined their heads gently to one side and listened to these
men and women on whom their livelihoods depended as they strode
towards their cars parked between the plots of zinnias, milkbushes and
bougainvillea and the main road beyond which lay the sea . . .

Traffic was heavy. Especially traffic coming from the northern side of
the city, from the centre near the banks and the shopping centres. He
pulled up at the junction in patient anticipation of a lull that would
enable him to turn left. He was patient. After a few minutes, he saw
the lull he was waiting for. But he had misjudged the speed of the taxi
from the centre of town. As he turned into the road, swinging left,
tyres screeched, the taxi driver jammed on his brakes, eased opposite
him, and said without venom or bitterness, Your mother's arse, don't
you know how to drive? He drove on. He had heard what was said. It is
part of the day's driving in the capital. He smiled a little smile and
continued. The taxi sped on, horns hooting, and swung to the left near
Parliament House.

(3) ACCRA

Amu Djoleto, *Hurricane of Dust*

*Doe Hevi, a petty thief and supporter of the revolution, has been
'collected' by the military. His ordeal by torture and prison
begins in an army carrier on a main Accra road.*

As we drove along the Survey School–Achimota Broadway and we got
to Accra Girls School, I gave a loud cry with all my strength, with all
the acute pain and with all the big worries welling up in my heart. The

imperturbable handsome man was patiently and carefully applying a giant pair of pliers to my right big toe. He pressed and pressed until it burst and the blood flowed out from under the nail. He then loosened the pliers and asked the private soldier sitting next to me on the right to ease a drop of iodine tincture on the wound and all I heard was, 'Yes, Corporal Dakubu,' and the iodine was dropped. Then Corporal Jovan Dakubu, as I later learnt his full name to be, sitting on the seat along the side of the vehicle right opposite me, asked in a slow, gentle voice: 'Where are the others?'

'Which others, sir?' I asked feebly.

Suddenly, I saw bright stars and fell sideways on the other private soldier sitting on my left; then another bunch of brilliant stars and I straightened up. Corporal Dakubu spoke again but I could not hear him well because of the practised, shattering earslaps I had received from the soldiers between whom I sat. I knew Ghanaian soldiers and policemen are the best, happiest, earslappers in the world. By training and animal pleasure going way back to the period of British occupation, once they've been asked to take a person into custody, no matter whether the person would be proved innocent or guilty later, the mere fact that they have him at all constitutes sufficient ground for brutality, to render him half-blind, half-deaf or permanently injured for the rest of life.

I decided, therefore, to cooperate as much as I could to save at least my hearing and sight. I looked intently at the Corporal's lips to catch what he was saying. He must out of practice have noticed my inability to hear properly now, so he poked his shapely nose right into my face and shouted: 'Where are the other Peugeot 504 windscreen removers?'

'I don't presently know, honestly.'

'Iodine!' he said, and a drop was let on the bleeding toe once again. I was in hell.

(4) ACCRA

B. Kojo Laing, *Search Sweet Country*

> *In his innovative, freewheeling prose-poem of a novel, Laing connects and inter-relates people, places, and ideas. Here one of his many characters, Kofi Loww, walks through bustling Accra. Laing employs Ghanaian words, and words he has coined himself. Here, 'Bebree' means 'a lot', 'fufu' is a food made from pounded roots, and 'pito' is a kind of beer.*

Passing Ussher Fort by Sraha Market where the Pentecostal church clapped its wall, Loww saw how clearly everything – from fresh water and churches to governments and castles – could fit so easily in reflection in the gutters. This city could not satisfy the hunger of gutters, for there was nothing yet which had not been reflected in them. The Bukom building gaped through its small windows at the ancient coconut tree . . . which danced with the odd rhythm of his own heartbeats. The old fisherman mending his net had hair the same colour as the passing clouds; and this same colour was thrown down in different shades onto so many buildings, buildings sharing among themselves the poverty and richness of different decades, different centuries. One hundred feet from Kofi Loww to the shore, the tides threw up good and evil as plentiful as Keta-schoolboys: he found no answer there, not even with the one shell that defined the entire dirt of the Jamestown sea. Each piece of doubt had the status of a grain of sand. Bebreee. And the sun rose from the prison yard after thirty minutes of custody. Everyone took the sunshine, the earth, and the streets freeee! The sun was the brightest sister! The sun was a baker: heads, laws, fish, backs, beauty, chiefs, and history all browned under it; and the deepest assessment of the two-sided coin of life, the life of fufu, the life of pito, ended up with the same brown. And it was exactly this brown that Kofi Loww saw in the faces that laughed, frowned, mocked, and loved.

(5) Sekondi

J.E. Casely Hayford, *Ethiopia Unbound*

Kwamankra, who has returned home to the Gold Coast from England, describes the port of Sekondi.

Now, if you want to see Sekondi at its best and the water question at its worst, you must approach the town in the month of March on one of Messrs Elder Dempster's boats, at the season of the year, that is to say, when other parts of the country are already being bathed in refreshing showers. As you round off Tacradi Bay, you see the mother of Gold Coast civilisation enveloped in a sheet of overhanging clouds charged with electricity. The side view that is presented shows a city of great promise. Already there are signs of the heavens giving way, and raindrops patter on the ship's deck. But even while you are wondering what a wet landing you are going to have, a blaze of light breaks out on the north-east, and the Titan of the upper sphere leaps forth triumphantly over thunder and storm. As you divest yourself of your mackintosh, a cynical old coaster says to you: 'That's Sekondi all over; I shouldn't be surprised if the tanks are all dry.' . . .

If you had known Sekondi in the days of its pristine innocence, you will find that an iron bridge now spans the ancient natural boundary between the English and the Dutch towns. From the echoes beneath proceeds forth the monotonous dirge of an asthmatic engine which appears to be trying to do the work of two engines in a climate which, according to some, is bad for man, beast, and locomotive.

(6) TAMALE

Kwesi Brew, *The Woods Decay*

Lost time, love and hope are symbolized by the coming and going of the harmattan, a dry dusty wind which blows off the Sahara into northern Ghana. 'The Woods Decay' is included in The Shadows of Laughter.

O there are flowers in Tamale
That smell like fire.
The harmattan winds twiddle and toss them
But they never blink a colour.
I see the cross on the hill
And your hair scattered on the grass;

. . .

But I no longer understand
The love-taught tongue
Of trees and winds,
The language I learned
In the childhood of our love.
I now speak the tittle-tattle of men,
Bewildered men meditatively kicking
White pebbles along unfrequented paths;
I speak their tittle-tattle
And the earth presses firmly against my feet.
Oh, I am tired of the winds,
And the long unheeded calls of a heart
Shrouded with pain.

Biographies and important works

AWOONOR, Kofi (1935–). Formerly known as George Awoonor-Williams, Awoonor is a poet, folklorist and novelist. Born in Wheta, he was educated at **Achimota School** and the **University of Ghana** in **Accra**, to which he later returned as a lecturer in English and African literature. He has travelled widely in the USA, China and the former Soviet Union. Apart from writing several novels and anthologies of poetry, Awoonor has been Director of the Ghana Film Corporation, a TV scriptwriter, and an editor for *Okyeame*, an erratically published literary magazine. His literary career was established early with the publication of *Rediscovery and Other Poems* in 1964 and *Night of My Blood* in 1971. Since his imprisonment in 1975, he has become more involved with politics, reflected in his collection of poetry *The House by the Sea*. His best known novel, *This Earth, My Brother* . . . (Extract 2) is a sharp observation of a nation's conflict and despair through the eyes of a young African lawyer who has trained abroad.

ARMAH, Ayi Kwei (1939–). Armah, the so-called 'angry young man' of Ghana, was born in **Takoradi**. He is one of West Africa's most outspoken writers. He was educated at the **Achimota School** in **Accra**, and later at Harvard in the USA. He has worked variously as a teacher in Tanzania, a translator in Algiers, a television scriptwriter in Ghana, and as an editor–translator for the Paris-based news magazine *Jeune Afrique*. His first and most famous work is the

memorably titled *The Beautyful Ones Are Not Yet Born* (Extract 1). A substantial career in fiction followed, including *Fragments*, *Why are We So Blessed?*, *Two Thousand Seasons*, and *The Healers*. Armah currently lives quietly in Dakar, Senegal, and does not give interviews.

BREW, Kwesi (1928–). A poet and diplomat, Brew was educated at the **University of the Gold Coast**. He has held several government posts, including Ambassador to Mexico, Senegal and Lebanon. In 1969, he published *The Shadows of Laughter* (Extract 6), a collection of 46 poems. This is his only published volume, but it has been well received and widely anthologized.

CASELY HAYFORD, J.E. (1860–1930). Casely Hayford was a writer, lawyer, publisher and founder of the National Congress of British West Africa, the leading movement for African nationalism. He became a leading player in the nationalist movement that led to Ghana becoming the first colony to achieve independence. He was educated in Sierra Leone. In 1911, Casely Hayford published *Ethiopia Unbound* (Extract 5), which deals with Africa's need for a good self-consciousness in the light of centuries of colonialism. It is generally regarded as the first West African novel.

DJOLETO, Amu (1929–). Born and educated in Ghana, Djoleto went on to study in England. In his role as

Ayi Kwei Armah

an educationalist, he worked for the **Ministry of Education** in Ghana, edited the *Ghana Teachers' Journal*, and has written several handbooks on education. Djoleto's first novel, *The Strange Man*, is a rags-to-riches tale which spans the life of Mensah from his boyhood in a village to becoming a successful businessman. The parallel theme is the transition of his country from the Gold Coast to Ghana.

Money Galore is an irreverent tale of corruption and is full of unscrupulous and colourful characters. His best-known novel is *Hurricane of Dust* (Extract 3).

LAING, B. Kojo (1946–). Laing was born in **Kumasi** and was educated in Ghana and Scotland. He graduated from Glasgow University in 1968 and returned to Ghana the same year. He has worked in central and local government, and was Secretary for the Institute of African Studies at the **University of Ghana**. Since 1985, he has managed a private school in **Accra**, which was established by his mother in 1962. Laing is both a novelist and a poet. His first novel, *Search Sweet Country* (Extract 4), was published in 1986. This experimental and poetic novel is an exuberant explosion of imagery and language which fuses people, places, things and thought in an attempt to convey a society and country in the process of change. He subsequently published *Woman of the Aeroplanes* in 1988 and *Major Gentl and the Achimota Wars* in 1992. For his poetry, see his collection *God-Horse*, published in 1989, or the anthology *The Heinemann Book of African Poetry in English*.

GUINEA

When Sékou Touré sent his prophetic message to de Gaulle (see box), rejecting the offer of a Franco–African community, it was said to be with the backing of 95% of the population. While he never underestimated the desire of his people to rid themselves of the rigours of colonial rule, Touré did underestimate the effect on French–Guinean relations and the subsequent impact on the economy. For when Guinea became independent on 28 September 1958, France immediately stopped all financial and technical aid, removed all government records and civil servants, and the latter half of his bold declaration to de Gaulle became an unfortunate reality.

The charismatic and provocative Touré first rose to power as a union leader, and was a founding member of the RDA (Democratic Party of Guinea). Following a humiliating defeat in an apparently rigged election in 1954, Touré became Vice-President of the Council of Government and *de facto* Prime Minister in 1957. When he declared independence in 1958, the country had a mere handful of graduates, few government records (which went with the departing civil servants), and no foreign credit.

After a brief honeymoon period, the hard edge of his socialist policies started to bite. A market crackdown led to the banning of all private trade in 1975, and his campaign against 'degenerate intellectuals' was likened to the Chinese cultural revolution.

'If we regard artistic and cultural activities as a means of education, and if we intend to use them as the media of our revolutionary thinking', wrote Touré in *Africa on the Move*, 'we must ruthlessly reject from our artistic and cultural expression everything that does not contribute to the diffusion of revolutionary thinking or foster the reinforcement of revolutionary action. The control over our artistic

FACT BOX

AREA: 245 855 sq km (approx same area as the UK)
POPULATION: 5 900 000
CAPITAL: Conakry
LANGUAGES: French, Fulani, Malinké, Sousou, Poular, Kissi,
   Guerzé, Conaigui, Toma
FORMER COLONIAL POWER: France
INDEPENDENCE: 1958

and cultural production will be effected by a censorship committee, which will authorize the publication and distribution of works found to be in keeping with the orientation and aims of our revolution.'

The irony of the title of his book of dogma, *Africa on the Move*, was not lost on the intellectual and artistic community, many of whom were either imprisoned or exiled during his rule. In a particularly nasty twist of fate, poet, songwriter and soldier Fodeba Keita mysteriously 'disappeared' and was thought to have died in the prison he had helped to build. Another victim of the regime was the writer Camara Laye ◊ who, following independence, had become the country's first ambassador to Ghana. Laye is undisputedly the country's most celebrated writer. His novels *The African Child* (Extract 4) and *Radiance of the King* were born out of the pre-independence period and rank among West Africa's first significant works. *The African Child* is a poetic autobiographical tale of growing up in Africa, written while homesick in Paris, and features the countryside around **Kouroussa** where Laye was born. *Radiance of the King* is a more surrealistic and symbolic novel about a white man who, shortly after arriving in Africa, loses all his money gambling, and then seeks work in the service of the king. Clarence tries to assimilate Africa and Africans: 'If anyone who had known him in those days could have seen him now . . . crouching in the manner of black men under the arcade, and dressed in a *boubou* like a black man, he would have appeared quite unrecognizable.' However, after fathering several coloured children his European sensibilities catch up with him and he is overcome with guilt and shame for his lustful pursuits: 'Buttocks and breasts – that's all one saw'.

Laye's post-independence novel *A Dream of Africa*, 1966, deals with disillusionment with the new political systems which were forming throughout West Africa at the time. It was his expression of these views which led to his exile in 1965, and to his wife's imprisonment (she spent seven years in prison). In exile from Guinea, Laye researched the life of Almamy Samory Touré, Guinea's national hero whose guerilla army unsuccessfully put up opposition to the French colonists in the

1880s. Before his death in 1980 Laye recorded many of the traditional songs and tales of the *griots* (oral historians) of his Malinké tribe, the dominant ethnic group in Upper Guinea, who formed the empire of Mali under Sundiata in the thirteenth century. Another *griot* version of the forming of the empire is retold by D.T. Niane in *Sundiata: An Epic of Old Mali* (see Mali, Extract 3).

Aside from Laye, there are barely a handful of Guinean writers whose work has been translated into English from the French. Tierno Monénembo ◊ was, like Laye, forced into exile. His sharp and poetic novel *The Bush Toads* (Extract 1) is dedicated to 'Guinea, the little patch of earth where I first saw the light . . . and the darkness.' Through the eyes of a civil servant (or 'bush toad') working in a **Conakry**-like city he describes the frustations of the educated élite forced into incongruous and often ineffective positions.

Such was the oppressive nature of Sékou's regime that many of those that dared to speak out against the government were forced to write under pseudonyms. As Alioum Fantouré ◊ says in the introduction to the original version of *Tropical Circle* (Extract 2), 'you don't know anything about me, nothing, I beg you, listen to my story that I'm going to tell you . . .'. The story is the tragic tale of a 'ficticious' country and of a strikingly familiar repressive and ruthless ruler who rises to power in the events leading up to independence – 'We were no longer citizens, but his subjects, forced to submit to him . . .'.

One of the few British writers to visit Guinea was the ubiquitous Graham Greene (◊ Sierra Leone) who came here long before independence. Greene briefly entered south eastern Guinea during his journey across Liberia in 1935 and devoted a chapter to his experiences in *Journey Without Maps*, which he entitled 'Black Montparnasse' (Extract 3). He was particularly taken by what he interpreted as the 'Frenchness' of the people: 'The men in the village had their hair curiously cut into patterns and tufts: I had seen nothing of the kind in Liberia. Their heads were often completely shaved except for two tufts, at the crown and the nape; they looked like poodles, and a poodle of course is a French dog. The women in French Guinea too, lived up to the standard of a country which provides the handsomest whores and the most elegant brothels; their hair was gummed up into complicated ringlets like watch-springs round the ears, they were sometimes painted on the face with blue and ochre, as well as the usual white stripes, and this gave them the thick rather unfinished look of a modern portrait.'

Guinea is still said to be the most authentic Francophone country in West Africa, despite the fact that President Touré did his best to eradicate all cultural and intellectual influences of the colonists – he eliminated the teaching of French in schools and today barely 20% of the population understand French. However, in 1962 he initiated an ambitious and laudable programme to encourage the Guineans to learn their national tongues. Reading and writing in the eight national languages was made possible with the use of a modified Latin alphabet. Some, like the Muslim Peul people of Middle Guinea, translated the Koran into Poular and the subsequent growth in Poular literature was largely confined to religious prose and poetry.

Since Touré's death in 1984, French has been reintroduced into schools and is again both the administrative and official language of the country. In an attempt to nurture and rebuild artistic confidence, the capital hosts an annual arts fortnight and a cultural season from October to June. However, under the new government, the Military Committee for National Recovery (CMRN), there are at present no legal political parties. Consequently, widespread scepticism and mistrust both within and outside the country continue to inhibit literary and artistic activity.

LITERARY LANDMARKS

Conakry. Once celebrated as the 'Paris of Africa', today Conakry is unanimously described in guidebooks as 'remorseless' and 'morbidly dirty'. Looking back at the capital from the sea in *A Dream of Africa*, Camara Laye describes it as an 'African Florida'. In the book, Fatoman and his sweetheart take a boat ride out to the **Isles de Los** two miles off the coast. Tales of treasure buried here at the time of the slave traders were said to have inspired Robert Louis Stevenson's *Treasure Island*.

Galaye. 'A populous little town with the remains of old mud walls at the back like pieces of abandoned scenery', remarked Graham Greene as he passed through on his way back into Liberia.

Faranah. Native village of President Sékou Touré. The family villa is now the **Hôtel de Ville** and furnished with characteristically over-the-top furniture and presidential presents.

Koinya/koyama. The first village Greene's entourage stayed in when they crossed the border at Zorzor. Greene never knew the exact name of the village but it 'sounded like Koinya' and is thought to be modern-day Koyama (Extract 3).

Kouroussa. Camara Laye's place of birth, described in his autobiographical *The African Child*. From here he often used to travel to **Tindican**, a small village a few miles to the west where his mother was born. The long-suffering French explorer René Caillé stumbled upon Kouroussa in 1827 (see under Mali).

Niani. Capital of the ancient Mali Empire founded by Sundiata Keita in the thirteenth century.

Siguiri. Nineteenth-century guerilla leader Samory Touré fought against the **French Post** here.

Libraries and Bookshops

Conakry. National Library (includes special collection on slavery); National Museum.

BOOKLIST

The following selection includes the extracted titles in this chapter as well as those mentioned in the introduction which are available in English and other titles for further reading. In general, paperback editions are given when possible. The editions cited are not necessarily the only ones available. For most of the extracted works, the original publisher in English can be found in 'Acknowledgments and Citations' at the end of the volume, as can the exact location of the extracts and the editions from which they are taken. Extract numbers are highlighted in bold.

Fantouré, Alioum, *Tropical Circle*, Longman, Harlow, 1981. **Extract 2.**

Greene, Graham, *Journey Without Maps*, Penguin, London, 1976. **Extract 3.**

King, Adele, *The Writings of Camara Laye*, Heinemann, London, 1980.

Laye, Camara, *The African Child*, Fontana, London, 1977. **Extract 4.**

Laye, Camara, *A Dream of Africa*, Fontana, London, 1970.

Laye, Camara, *Radiance of the King*, Fontana, London, 1965.

Monénembo, Tierno, *The Bush Toads*, Longman, Harlow, 1983. **Extract 1.**

Touré, Ahmed Sékou, *Africa on the Move*, Panaf Books, London, 1979.

Extracts

(1) CONAKRY

Tierno Monénembo, *The Bush Toads*

Diouldé is an electrician and has just landed himself the incongruous position of Director of the Eastern European Service in the new government ministry. The novelty of being in the capital soon wears off . . .

Most of the time he sits biting his nails, or goes trotting from office to office like a lost dog. Gradually he even got tired of taking a walk into town – a habit he had acquired in order to escape from that stifling enclosure of idleness and boredom that is the Ministry.

The town, it's true, is nauseatingly dull. And a sort of restrictive bottleneck of land, formed by the sea's repeated erosions and endlessly-beating waves, cuts the place in two: into two assymetrical sections, so that one looks in vain for its true centre . . . A sort of long arm of earth, almost worn to nothing, with an almost non-existent wrist.

A few official buildings lift their lugubrious storeys towards the heavens. Luxury villas hide away in desperation, behind flowering hedges. They are ranged all along the corniche and encircle the city. The rest is a jumble of dilapidated shacks. Dry straw, branches of trees, rough bricks, rusty corrugated iron mingle in a crazy jigsaw puzzle of crooked walls and collapsing roofs. Hovels, huts, shacks all crumbling away together, crowding in on one another, clinging to one another as if holding one another up, grouping together in dismal bidonville clusters; an unending repetitive mess . . .

(2) GUINEA: INDEPENDENCE

Alioum Fantouré, *Tropical Circle*

The new Head of State has just declared the fictitious Republic of the Tropical Circle independent.

We were independent, happy, optimistic, but for my part, I felt something lacking. I was disappointed. I would have liked to see, as if by some miracle, a sudden change in the atmosphere around me: the sun going black and then gradually becoming light again, turning red, yellow, green and then an unblemished white to shed beams of clemency upon us. I would have liked, the moment we were declared 'independent', for the clouds to take on different colours, to drift more rapidly across the sky, for a wind to arise, for the sun to disappear suddenly, for thunder to be heard, for lightning to flash, for rain to fall, watering the fields and making plants grow, then everything to return to normal, only more beautiful than before. There should have been some miracle, like in the different religions, to celebrate the independence of South Majiland, but miracles only proliferate in our imagination. This dream made me lose touch with reality for several minutes. I was happy; I had to be happy!

Then the flag of the Republic of South Majiland was presented to the people. The people applauded, then, squatting on their heels, they bowed their foreheads to the ground, doing homage with dignity.

The people are independent.

The new Republican Guard plays our national anthem. The people stand to attention, bareheaded, silent, lost in thought. When the last bars fade, the people applaud with pride.

The people are independent.

(3) 'KOINYA'

Graham Greene, *Journey Without Maps*

On his travels through Liberia in 1935, Greene briefly entered French Guinea, or 'France', as it was referred to by his Liberian carriers. Greene was not sure of the name of the village he first stayed in when he visited Guinea, but he approximated it as 'Koinya'. It is thought to be modern-day Koyama.

The country was stamped as French from the first village we stayed in, which was neither Bamakama nor Jbaiay as I had intended: French in its commercial sense, in its baits which I should have believed to be intended for tourists, if there had been any hope of tourists. It was astonishing what a difference the invisible boundary made. You could not have mistaken this land for Liberia. Tourists would have been quite at home here among the round huts and the scarlet fezzes of the Mandingo traders. For these traders were indistinguishable, except that their dignity was less tarnished, from the men who sell carpets in the Dôme and the Rotonde. The only difference was we had followed them home. It was as if we had shadowed them all the way from the Boule Miche, sitting in third-class carriages, travelling steerage, riding up the long way from Konakry on horseback.

(4) Kouroussa

Camara Laye, *The African Child*

*Laye recalls the exhausting and terrifying circumcision ceremony
that all Malinké boys must endure in order to become 'men'.
The 'coba' is a special dance performed only on the eve of
circumcision.*

Three times that day we appeared in the main square to dance the
'coba'; and three times again during the night, by torchlight; and each
time the men enclosed us in a living hedge. We did not get any sleep;
no one went to bed: the whole town stayed awake and danced all
through the night. As we left our hut for the sixth time, dawn was
breaking.

'*Coba! Aye coba, lama!*'

Our bonnets still moved in time to the rhythm, our boubous were
still stretched over our straddling legs; but we were beginning to flag,
our eyes were burning feverishly and our anxiety was mounting. If we
had not been urged on, carried away by the tom-tom beat . . . But it
urged us on, carried us away! And we danced on obediently, our heads
curiously light from lack of sleep, curiously heavy, too, with thoughts of
the fate that was to be ours.

'*Coba! Aye coba, lama!*'

As we came to the end of the dance, dawn began to lighten the main
square. This time, we did not go back to our hut; we went immediately
into the bush; we went a long way, to where there was no risk of our
being disturbed. In the main square the dancing had stopped: the
people had all gone home. Nevertheless, a few men followed us out.
The rest awaited, in their huts, the ceremonial shots that would
announce to all that one more man, one more Malinke, had been born.

Biographies and important works

FANTOURÉ, Alioum (1938–).
Born in **Forécariah**, near **Conakry**,
Fantouré was educated in Paris and
Belgium, where he studied science
and economics. He worked as an
economist for several international
organizations and is a specialist in
industrial development. As an exile,
he writes under the pseudonym Fantouré, and claims that 'Bohi Di'
(which means 'son of the earth') is his
real name. His first novel *Tropical
Circle* (Extract 2) won him the Grand
Prix Littéraire d'Afrique Noir in
1973.

GREENE, Graham (see under Sierra
Leone).

LAYE, Camara (1928–1980). Laye was born in **Kouroussa**, Upper Guinea, into a Malinké family. Although his family name is Camara and Laye his first name, he always used Camara Laye for his work. Eldest of twelve children, he was educated first at a Koranic and then a local government school where his talents for writing were noted (his teacher apparently urged his father to 'push him to study, don't beat him'.) At 14 he went to **Conakry** to study in one of the few secondary schools in the country, and was then awarded a scholarship to study mechanics in France. In Paris he worked variously as a market porter and a mechanic while discovering French culture, Parisian nightlife, and the *Négritude* movement. One of few Africans in Paris at the time, he suffered much loneliness, and out of his memories of his childhood in Kouroussa came his first novel *L'Enfant Noir* (*The African Child* – Extract 4). He returned briefly to Guinea in 1954, where he was honoured by *griots* who had composed numerous songs to him. Following the success of his first two novels he had several pieces published in *Présence Africaine*. He returned to Africa again in 1956, and lived in Dahomey and Ghana. Censorship, disillusionment and the impending publication of *A Dream of Africa* forced him to leave Guinea again in 1965. Laye died in 1980 aged 52 in Dakar, Senegal, where he was engaged in recording traditional culture and oral literature, as well as writing a collection of African children's stories.

MONÉNEMBO, Tierno (1947–). Like many of his compatriots, Monénembo was forced into exile because of his outspoken opposition to the Guinean government. He moved first to Senegal and then to the Côte d'Ivoire, and eventually to Algeria where he taught biochemistry at a university in Algiers. His relaxed and conversational style of writing draws on the customs, culture and idioms of his native Guinea. His first novel *The Bush Toads* (Extract 1) was highly critical of the new style of African politics and was originally written in French.

GUINEA-BISSAU

'Guinea Bissau is a microcosm of a continent where events have conspired against progress, where the future remains a hostage of the past . . .'
David Lamb, The Africans

Guinea-Bissau is a small but significant country. Barely half the size of Scotland, it was the last Portuguese colony to gain independence (in 1974). It was first visited by Europeans in the 1450s, and by the turn of the century there was a notable presence of Portuguese immigrants. The country officially became a colony in 1885, but in the years that followed the Portuguese took little responsibility for their charge. Guinea-Bissau was merely a far-flung trading post, the people were classified as second-class citizens, hut taxes were imposed, and little money was put into social infrastructure or education.

Somehow during this pre-independence period emerged Guinea-Bissau's first novels. The author Fausto Duarte was born in Cape Verde in 1903, but, as he spent most of his working life in Guinea-Bissau, he was quickly 'adopted' as the country's first writer of note. Other writing during this period was limited to pseudo-ethnographic Portuguese-language works, though there remained a lively indigenous oral literature.

Against a background of economic repression there developed a small but strong cry for political reform. Several nationalist groups emerged in the 1950s, including Amilcar Cabral's Partido Africano da Indepenência da Guiné e Cabo Verde (PAIGC). He was joined by the likes of Carlos Miranda (Extract 1). Cabral first rose to prominence following the 1959 Pidjiguiti massacre, when over 50 striking dockers in the capital **Bissau** were killed by police. Cabral was born in Guinea in 1925 and first became politically active in Lisbon in 1945, where as a student he was involved with the Portuguese anti-facist movement. It was here too that he turned his hand to poetry, submitting it unsuccessfully to the Seara Nova review: 'Leave poetry: take my arms to bind the world/give me your arms to bind life/My poetry is me.'

FACT BOX

AREA: 36 000 sq km
POPULATION: 1 000 000
CAPITAL: Bissau
LANGUAGES: Portuguese, Creole, Balante, Fula, Malinké
FORMER COLONIAL POWER: Portugal
INDEPENDENCE: 1974

Cabral led the country through a protracted and bitter fight towards independence, and paid with his life. When he was assassinated in 1973, his brother Luis Cabral succeeded him as the leader of the PAIGC, and, following independence in 1974, became the new head of state.

The 'state', as the Portuguese had left it, consisted of one beer factory (built for the Portuguese soldiers), a handful of university graduates, a literacy rate of 2%, and not one indigenous doctor, lawyer or accountant. Even starting from this sorry base, the first few years of independence did not live up to the people's expectations. Under the Marxist–Leninist economy of Luis Cabral the country lived quite literally on peanuts, and quickly earned the title of 'The Albania of West Africa'.

On the literary front, things looked a little more promising. The war of independence had brought forth a (relative) flurry of literary and cultural activity in Guinea-Bissau. There was a revival of Creole as the *lingua franca* in schools, several projects were launched to record the riddles and tales of the oral tradition and Mário de Andrade, a leading intellectual and writer, became Guinea-Bissau's Minister of Culture. Andrade also collected indigenous poetry, and published several important anthologies in both Portuguese and Creole.

Andrade was unfortunately one of the casualties of the 1980 coup that brought yet another president to power. Commander Joao Vieira, as one journalist put it, 'did not go overboard on democracy', and exile has since become a popular option for many of Guinea-Bissau's promising writers.

LITERARY LANDMARKS

Bissau. The **Pidjiguiti** pier was the scene of the historical dockers' strike which became a turning point in the struggle for independence.

Cacheu. Headquarters of the slave trade in the sixteenth century and today resting place for the odd ex-guerrilla fighter (see Extract 1).

Libraries and Bookshops

Bissau. French Cultural Centre, Avenida Domingos Ramos, CP 129; National Library, 28 Rua Dr Severino G.de Pina, CP 294. The one and only bookshop in the country, called Casa de Cultura, is in Bissau and is reputed to sell very good Creole comics.

BOOKLIST

The following selection includes the extracted title in this chapter as well as those mentioned in the introduction which are available in English and other titles for further reading. In general, paperback editions are given when possible. The editions cited are not necessarily the only ones available.

Cabral, Amilcar *Unity and Struggle*, Heinemann, London, 1980.
Davidson, Basil, *No Fist is Big*

Enough to Hide the Sky: The Liberation of Guiné and Cape Verde, Zed Books, London, 1981.
Lamb, David, *The Africans*, Vintage Books, New York, 1987. **Extract 1.**
Lopes, Carlos, *Guinea-Bissau: From Liberation Struggle to Independence*, Zed Books, London, 1987.
McCulloch, Jock, *In the Twilight of Revolution: The Political Theory of Amilcar Cabral*, Routledge and Kegan Paul, London, 1983.

Extract

(1) CACHEU

David Lamb, *The Africans*

During the war of independence, Carlos Miranda was a soldier and then a prisoner of the Portuguese. Today he sits in the sleepy town of Cacheu, happy to impart his story to the rare passing visitor or journalist.

Carlos Miranda, former guerrilla fighter and one-time prisoner of war, sat with his friends in the barren little café, idling away the Saturday afternoon over a bottle of Portuguese wine and a few memories. There really wasn't much else to do, anyway. Cacheu, in Guinea-Bissau, is a small quiet town and the day was hot. So the men sat at their rickety wooden table, just talking quietly or doing nothing at all, expending little energy except that needed to brush away the flies. The walls of the bar were bare save for a faded photograph of the president, Luis de Almeida Cabral, and the stock of refreshments had dwindled to a dust-covered jug of rum, a case of Coca-Cola and an odd assortment of white wines, served lukewarm because the refrigerator, like the electricity in Cacheu, had long since broken down. The near-sighted bartender was propped like a broom against the refrigerator, squinting and sweating, and when a bottle slipped from his hands and shattered at his feet, he kicked the glass under the counter without a word and wiped his damp hands across his T-shirt. His family – a wife and seven young children – was sprawled out on the concrete floor nearby, fast asleep.

'Francisco broke another bottle,' Miranda said. 'No wonder there's nothing left to drink.' Francisco had indeed been dropping too many precious bottles of Coke lately, and his carelessness had become a source of much annoyance.

Biography and important works

LAMB, David. A journalist for the *Los Angeles Times*, Lamb has travelled extensively throughout Africa and spent eight years roaming the continent for his newspaper. His account of his impressions and experiences in Africa has been written up as *The Africans* (Extract 1). He has also written *The Arabs: Journeys Beyond the Mirage*. David Lamb has been nominated for the prestigious Pulitzer Prize six times.

LIBERIA

The so-called 'land of liberty', Liberia had a venerable start. In 1822 it was hailed as the 'promised' land, bought by American philanthropists from native chiefs to establish a homeland for freed American slaves. As a self-governing, Christian state with a constitution similar to that of the USA it was to be an example to the rest of Africa. As early as 1847, Liberia had proclaimed independence and was ruled by a non-white governor. But Africa's oldest republic has long since failed to live up to its name or fulfilled the heady sentiments of its national anthem.

For well over a century the ruling class were the returnees or 'Americos', who were notoriously indifferent to the needs and rights of the indigenous population. The President in 1934 was exposed as privately exporting slaves to Fernando Po. From the 1940s to the 1980s, Liberia was dominated by two charismatic characters – Presidents William Tubman and William Tolbert. Tubman was famous for amending the constitution to allow indigenous people to be represented in government, meanwhile pursuing an 'open-door policy' to encourage foreign investment (this spawned an assortment of books with titles such as *Investing in Liberia*). Tolbert carried on in his predecessor's tradition, though he abandoned the state limo in favour of a VW Beetle, and took great pleasure in composing slogans such as 'lifting the people from mats to mattresses'.

A bloody coup in 1980 marked the end of political domination by these 'Americos', but did little to relieve the country from years of economic decline (Liberia has one of the lowest GNPs in the world). As a result, literary activity has until very recently been dominated by blatantly patriotic and religious propoganda, intended to keep up the flagging morale of the settlers over the centuries. A number of simple stories by indigenous writers were collected and published privately by writer Henry S. Corder around 1950. Dominated by religious and moral themes they have occasional touches of humour: 'You're always at a party and somebody is always rubbing up against you', complains one disgruntled wife as her husband rolls back from yet another night on the town.

One of the earliest Liberian writers to gain recognition was Roland Tombekai Dempster ◊. It was his greatest ambition to become one of Africa's most outstanding poets, writers and philosophers: 'Ah, make Liberia like Augustin Virgil's Rome/And lend me fire and wit to sing my nation's name' ('A Song out of Midnight'). He achieved fame as Tubman's court poet, composing odes dedicated to the President, with titles such as 'Anniversary Ode' and 'To Monrovia Old and New' (Extract 2).

This was praise poetry indeed, but it reached mainly the ears of the élite Americos, as it bore little relation to the traditional praise songs of the indigenous people. Covering every subject from the cradle to the grave, the oral tradition is very strong in Liberia, and there are songs for every occasion, from secret society gatherings to work and courtship. Liberian writer Bai T. Moore ◊ recorded many of these during his travels, and incorporated sayings such as 'A woman is like a vine, which creeps up on any tree' and secret symbols such as 'each member's buttock is marked X' into his poetry.

Described by his friend Roland Dempster as 'one of West Africa's outstanding jungle poets', Moore is best known for his novel *Murder in*

Notes to map (facing page): [a]*The dotted line shows the route through Liberia taken by Graham and Barbara Greene and described in Graham's Journey Without Maps (which includes a map showing this route with the names of many of the places they visited) and Barbara's Too Late to Turn Back;* [b]*Compared and contrasted in Journey Without Maps (see Liberia, Extract 3);* [c]*After crossing the border near Zorzor into Guinea, the first village Greene encountered 'sounded like Koinya' and is thought to have been Koyama (see Guinea, Extract 3);* [d]*Described in Journey Without Maps as 'A populous little town with the remains of old mud walls at the back like pieces of scenery';* [e]*Greene almost died here, according to his cousin Barbara in Too Late to Turn Back (see Liberia, Extract 4);* [f]*Barbara and Graham Greene stayed here for nine days at the end of their journey;* [g]*The Greene's arrived here en route for their journey through Liberia and Graham gives his impressions in Journey Without Maps (see Sierra Leone, Extract 3). He was later based in the city during the second world war. While here he wrote The Ministry of Fear and gathered material for The Heart of the Matter, which features among other things the City Hotel (the model for the 'Bedford') and the old cotton tree on Kroo Bay (see Sierra Leone, Extract 2).*

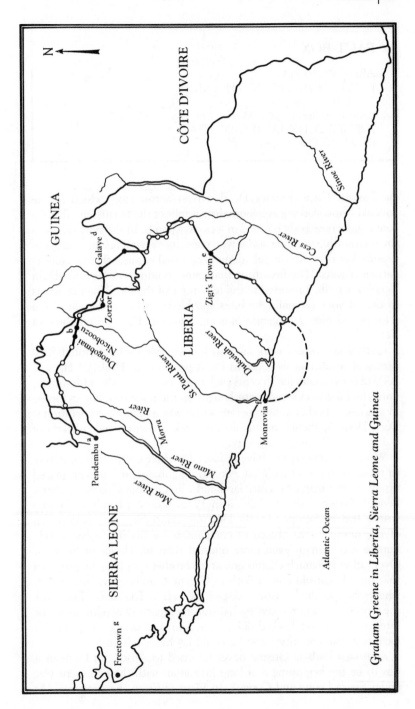

Graham Greene in Liberia, Sierra Leone and Guinea

FACT BOX

AREA: 99 067 sq km
POPULATION: 2 639 000 (44% urban)
CAPITAL: Monrovia
LANGUAGES: English, Mande, Kru, Bassa, Vai, Kpelle
FORMER COLONIAL POWER: USA
INDEPENDENCE: 1847

---

the Cassava Patch (Extract 1). Based on a true story which Moore covered while working as a journalist, it tells of the horrific murder of a young girl whose body is found in a cassava patch. In the story he traces the relationship with her suitor who consults a crystal reader in order to capture her heart for himself alone. The ritual requires that he collects various objects: 'The first thing that came to mind was, how to obtain Tene's toe nails. I resorted to the technique of the rat. When he wants to eat off your toe nails, he bites and blows. So with the aid of the scissors and plenty of gentle blowing I managed to clip off three of Tene's toe nails.'

Outlets for writers' work are still limited. Moore first printed 5000 copies of *Murder in the Cassava Patch* privately in Holland. He sold 2000 of these copies for 75 cents each from a street corner in Monrovia, until the Liberian Government bought up the remaining copies for use in schools. Another contemporary writer who is gaining recognition is Doris Henries, though mainly for her work as a critic and collector of indigenous folk tales and poetry.

While Liberia may not have produced a writer comparable in stature to those born out of its West African neighbours, it has been placed firmly on the map of literary landmarks by Graham Greene (◊ Sierra Leone). Greene came to Liberia in 1935, one of a handful of young writers leaving Europe to make long uncomfortable journeys in search of the unusual. His choice of companion for his first foray outside Europe was perhaps even more unusual than his choice of location. Over rather too much champagne at his brother's wedding he proposed that his 23-year-old cousin Barbara Greene ◊ accompany him. Later, when sober, he did his best to discourage her: in *Too Late to Turn Back* she writes: 'He sent me endless hair-raising reports of conditions in the interior, lists of unchecked diseases, accounts of savage campaigns by local tribes and anything else he could lay his hands on.'

Although Barbara Greene never returned to Africa, for Graham it was to be the beginning of a long love affair with the continent (see under Sierra Leone and Congo). In *Ways of Escape* he confesses, 'At thirty one in Liberia I had lost my heart to West Africa.' But initial impressions suggested otherwise. After four weeks of walking some 350 miles through dense jungle, and suffering a near-fatal illness, Greene sent his publisher 'You Can Keep Africa' as the draft title of his journal. This later became *Journey Without Maps* (Extract 3), part reference to the fact that the only map he had was from the American military – on which large expanses of the country were marked simply 'cannibals'.

Journey Without Maps is a detailed diary of his travels, and written very much in the style in which he travelled, with 'an instinctive simplicity, a thoughtless idealism'. As such it is more of anthropological interest than literary merit, and a great guide if one were to try to follow in his footsteps as did one intrepid biographer, Norman Sherry.

Unbeknown to Graham, his young cousin was busily keeping her own account of their tortuous journey, and he was mildly surprised when she published *A Land Benighted*, later more sympathetically entitled *Too Late to Turn Back* (Extract 4). For Barbara, Liberia was 'a dream of pure beauty and peace, a vision of moonlit villages in the jungle, friendly people dancing to the beat of a drum, simplicity where material values were of no account and where understanding could be reached without words.' A somewhat naive but thoroughly readable account, it is of great biographical and pictorial interest and hence the perfect companion volume to *Journey Without Maps*. The compliment was not, however, returned by Graham and the reader is barely made aware of his cousin's presence in all 250 pages of his account.

Theoretically, it is still possible to travel through Liberia and trace the Greenes' original journey, as did Norman Sherry while researching *The Life of Graham Greene*. Sherry visited Liberia shortly before the 1980 coup, and noted, much as Greene had experienced, that it was the 'most corrupt of countries'. The leader of the coup, Samuel K. Doe, took office in 1986 and Liberia remained under military rule until 1989, when notorious rebel leader Charles Taylor invaded from the Côte d'Ivoire and assassinated the President in 1990. Taylor's rebels led a reign of terror, with widespread looting, indiscriminate burning of villages and killings. An estimated 13 000 citizens have been killed in this civil war and nearly one million Liberians forced to seek refuge in neighbouring countries. Since then several ceasefires, conferences, interim governments, peacekeeping forces and the promise of elections have done little to reassure the war-weary population or to foster literary spirit.

LITERARY LANDMARKS

Monrovia. Barbara and Graham Greene spent nine days here at the end of their journey, and noted just 30 white residents, and tennis at the British Legation. The whole of their epic journey is charted town by town, and village by village, in *Journey Without Maps* (Extract 3) and *Too Late to Turn Back* (Extract 4). 'To Monrovia Old and New' by Roland Dempster described the capital as 'once worst of cities e'er known,/Here today men of State have flown.' Bai T. Moore composed several of his poems at Dempster's parties, while standing on the balcony, admiring the sunset over Monrovia.

Tosoh. Birthplace of poet Roland T. Dempster.

Zigi's Town. Here, according to his cousin Barbara, Graham Greene almost died (Extract 4).

Libraries and Bookshops

Monrovia. Government Public Library; University of Liberia Library.

BOOKLIST

The following selection includes the extracted titles in this chapter as well as those mentioned in the introduction which are available in English and other titles for further reading. In general, paperback editions are given when possible. The editions cited are not necessarily the only ones available. For most of the extracted works, the original publisher in English can be found in 'Acknowledgments and Citations' at the end of the volume, as can the exact location of the extracts and the editions from which they are taken. Extract numbers are highlighted in bold for ease of reference.

Corder, Henry S., ed, *New Voices from Liberia*, Liberian Studies, University of Delaware, Newark, DE, 1979.

Dempster, Roland Tombekai, *To Monrovia Old and New*, privately published, 1959. **Extract 2**.

Dempster, Roland Tombekai, *A Song Out of Midnight*, privately published, 1959.

Greene, Barbara, *Too Late to Turn Back*, Penguin, London, 1990. **Extract 4**.

Greene, Graham, 'A Chance for Mr Lever', in *Twenty One Stories*, Penguin, London, 1973.

Greene, Graham, *Journey Without Maps*, Penguin, London, 1973. **Extract 3**.

Greene, Graham, *Ways of Escape*, The Bodley Head, London, 1980.

Liberian Writing, Horst Erdmann Verlag, Tubingen, 1970.

Moore, Bai T., 'Murder in the Cassava Patch', in *Liberian Writing*, Horst Erdmann Verlag, Tübingen, 1970. **Extract 1**.

Sherry, Norman, *The Life of Graham Greene, Volume 1, 1904–1939*, Jonathan Cape, London, 1989. (Chapters 34–35 follow Greene's footsteps through Liberia.)

Extracts

(1) BENDABLI

Bai T. Moore, *Murder in the Cassava Patch*

The body of Tene, the daughter of a well known family in Bendabli, is found mutilated in a cassava patch. Based on a true story.

Like dry time thunder, Tene's murder shocked every one in the area. The news spread throughout the countryside like wildfire. A few hours following the discovery, hundreds of horrified persons had arrived on the scene to get a glimpse of the corpse. Mothers made it a point to bring along adolescent daughters cautioning them in these terms, »you see eh, when we old people tell you children to listen to your parents, you say this is a new age.« »The person, who killed this child is a madman . . . . A blood thirsty fiend seeking her vital organs to make sacrificial medicine, perhaps,« stricken onlookers remarked, as hundreds of them passed by the body of Tene lying under a palm tree in the center of the cassava patch.

The twelve man jury appointed by the local clan chief to examine the body reported that Tene was murdered with a sharp instrument, a razor or a cutlass. Her throat had been slashed, both wrists cut to the bone, and there was a gash above the eyes. From the appearance of the spot, Tene and her murderer must have fought for a good while before she was finally overpowered.

After much palavering on the scene, the elders all agreed that because of the advanced state of decomposition of the body, it should be immediately interred. »According to tradition,« remarked one elder, »Tene cannot be buried in the town.« The chief ordered a grave hastily dug and Tene was thrown into it.

(2) MONROVIA

Roland T. Dempster, *To Monrovia Old and New*

The country's so-called poet-laureate, Roland Dempster, wrote several highly optimistic odes in praise of the 'wonderful transformation' of the country in the late 1950s and early 1960s.

Where the drums beat, the Sangba echoed long,
And shouts of merriment trailed the cloud,

And, now, now has changed and formed anew –
The streets paved, the houses with newer view;
The shooting water has replaced the dangered well
And now the high or low where'er they dwell
Today have access to the shooting thing;
Ah, what joy the light and telephone bring!

(3) NICOBOOZU

Graham Greene, *Journey Without Maps*

Not far into Liberia, Greene was surprised to find how villages not more than a day's walk apart could be so different.

If we seldom sank as low as Duogobmai we seldom rose as high as Nicoboozu, which we reached next day after an easy cheerful trek of only three hours. Alfred had gone home; he had decided that the journey was not going to be a holiday; and in his place Vande had taken a friend of Babu's, a Buzie man called Guawa. Guawa was an asset; he had the carriers singing before Duogobmai had slipped behind the trees. He sang and he danced, danced even when he carried a hammock or a load; I could hear his voice down the trail, proposing the line of an impromptu song which the carriers took up, repeated, carried on. These songs referred to their employers; their moods and their manners were held up to ridicule; a village when the carriers pressed through in full song would learn the whole story of their journey. Sometimes a villager would join in the chant, asking a question, and I could hear the question tossed along the line until it became part of the unending song and was answered. . . .

Nicoboozu was a clean little town, the huts wide apart, and the chief was old, hospitable and incurious. He dashed us a chicken and a hamper of rice, saw that the hut we were to sleep in was swept, and then retired to his hammock and shade from the midday sun while we had a bath in a tin basin and the jiggers were cut out of our toes.

Nicoboozu was as favourable an example as we could find of a village touched by the Buzie culture. Here the women wore little silver arrows in their hair and twisted silver bracelets, beaten by the blacksmith out of old Napoleon coins brought from French Guinea, and heavy silver anklets; the men wore rings, primitive signet rings with a flattened side, and decorative beaded rings and rings twisted to match the bracelets. The weavers were busy, and every piece of craftsmanship we saw was light and unselfconscious. There was an air of happiness about the place which next day we did not find in Zigita. Zigita is the principal town of the Buzie tribe, it is a town where even the commonest bush cutlass is beautiful, but it isn't happy. It is Buzie in another fashion, the fashion of witchcraft and fear.

(4) ZIGI'S TOWN

Barbara Greene, *Too Late to Turn Back*

In the heart of Liberia, more than halfway through a 350-mile, four-week treck through uncharted country, Barbara Greene's cousin, Graham, fell ill with malaria.

Although he was feeling so ill, Graham ate an enormous lunch. His eternal hunger seemed to be one of the symptoms of his strange illness. After lunch he raced on ahead again, refusing to walk more slowly, and looking every moment as if he were going to faint. We were still walking downhill. The air was as damp as the hottest of the greenhouses at Kew Gardens. There was thunder in the air again. We could hear it rumbling in the distance. We had no idea how far we were from the coast. Some said ten days, others said a week, but no one seemed to know.

'Only two days,' lied Mark brightly, thinking it would cheer me up.

'Two more weeks,' lied Laminah, knowing that I liked the villages and thinking that that was what I would like to hear.

I gave it up.

We had nine hours steady walking to Zigi's town. The forest now seemed more luxuriant; it was greener and looked less dead. I thought I might find some orchids, but it seemed to be the wrong season for them, and I saw only little pink star-like flowers.

'De cook plenty tired,' said Laminah to me. There was nothing I could do for the old man. We were all plenty tired. Our carriers no longer joked or sang. We walked silently and no one spoke. The atmosphere grew heavier and the thunder got louder.

Graham was tottering as we got to Zigi's town; he was staggering as though he was a little drunk. He could get no rest from the carriers while he was up, for they came to him as usual with all their troubles, but I managed to persuade him to go to bed. I took his temperature and it was very high. I gave him plenty of whisky and Epsom salts, and covered him with blankets, hoping that I was doing the right thing.

I had supper by myself while the thunder roared; and the boys served me with grave faces. The same thought was in all our minds. Graham would die. I never doubted it for a minute. He looked like a dead man already.

Biographies and important works

DEMPSTER, Roland Tombekai (1910–1965). Born at **Tosoh**, which literally means 'keep quiet', Dempster ironically became one of the loudest protagonists of patriotic literature and was dubbed the poet-laureate of Liberia. Educated at a missionary school, he later became a government employee. In 1948–54 he was Editor-in-Chief of *Liberian Age*, a bi-weekly newspaper. He became Professor of English, History and Creative Writing at the **University of Liberia** from 1948 to 1960, but took time out to study journalism in the USA. Dempster died in **Monrovia**.

GREENE, Barbara (1907–1991). Born in Sao Paulo, Barbara Greene lived in Berkhamsted, Berlin, Liechtenstein, Argentina and Gozo. At the age of 23, she abandoned a leisurely and safe society life in Berkhamsted to walk across Liberia with her cousin Graham Greene. Undeterred by reports of elephantitis, leprosy and illegal slavery, nor by her father (he was reputedly glad she was showing some initiative), she survived this tortuous journey with her apparently uncommunicative cousin. Her first book, *Too Late to Turn Back* (Extract 4), is a vivid and direct account of their travels, best read as an accompaniment to Graham Greene's *Journey Without Maps* (Extract 3). Her photographs of the journey illustrate both books.

GREENE, Graham (see under Sierra Leone).

MOORE, Bai T. (1916–). A poet and folklorist, Moore was born in the **Vai** area to the northwest of Monrovia. Educated mainly in Richmond, Virginia, he returned to Liberia in 1941 as an agricultural expert. Moore held several positions as a civil servant, including Under-Secretary for Cultural Affairs. In 1958 he survived a plane crash in Guinea, and while in hospital composed several poems. *Golah Boy in America* came out of his experiences in the USA and contrasts life there with the customs and beliefs of his Golah people. His *Murder in the Cassava Patch* (Extract 1), published in 1968, is the best known novel to have come out of Liberia and has since been translated into several languages including German, Hebrew and Russian.

MALI

'Salt comes from the north, gold from the south, but the word of God and the treasures of wisdom are only to be found in Timbuctoo.'

Fifteenth-century Mali proverb (quoted in The White Monk of Timbuctoo)

Sandwiched between the black African nations to the south and the Arab world to the north, the land-locked country of Mali has over the centuries found itself at both a cultural and economic crossroads. From as early as 300 AD, trade routes were established across the Sahara, linking the bend in the **River Niger** to northern Africa and thence to Europe. Along these caravan routes flourished a trade in gold, salt, slaves and ostrich feathers, and upon this wealth was founded an illustrious history dominated by empires and emperors and, most famously, the legendary city of **Timbuktu** (or Timbuctoo).

In its heyday, Timbuktu was one of the main thoroughfares for West African gold, and one of the world's most important centres of learning. Founded by nomadic Tuaregs in the eleventh century, it was named after 'the old women with a big belly button', who looked after the oasis while they were out in the pastures. The city flourished in the fifteenth and sixteenth centuries, when under the rule of the Muslim Songhai empire it boasted (long before Oxford and Cambridge) a university with a reputed 25 000 students and one of the world's greatest collections of classic Arabic manuscripts. Several hundred of the most learned men of the black Islamic world came to live here, each with their own libraries and manuscripts, and it was noted at the time that 'books sell very well there'.

Following the Moroccan invasion in 1591, the Songhai empire was crushed and Timbuktu thenceforth saw a rapid decline in fortune. However, the legend lived on, and a motley assortment of European travellers, explorers and mavericks set out in search of riches and/or enlightenment. Of the forty or so who set out before the 1850s, only a

---

FACT BOX

AREA: 1 240 101 sq km
POPULATION: 8 700 000
CAPITAL: Bamako
LANGUAGES: French, Arabic, Bambara, Fulani, Malinké
FORMER COLONIAL POWER: France
INDEPENDENCE: 1960

---

handful actually arrived (hence no doubt the immortal euphemism 'to go to Timbuktu'). The first white man to set eyes on Timbuktu was said to be a French sailor named Paul Imbert who in 1591 was taken captive, sold as a slave and died there.

In 1795 the English dispatched Mungo Park ◊ to explore the region and map the course of the River Niger, but he failed to reach Timbuktu. Not long into the trip, Park was captured by a local Arab chief and, though he managed to escape after four months, he had only a horse and a compass to accompany him. Eventually he reached the River Niger at **Ségou** and managed to set off just 80 miles downstream before being forced to turn back (there were still 1500 miles to go to the sea). After surviving astonishing hardships and adventures, including a seven-month bout of fever, Park made it to the coast and returned to Britain. In 1805 he was sent off once more to explore the course of the River Niger, this time with a party of 40 Europeans. By the time Park reached the shores of the Niger, the party was down to eleven. They then set off downstream. Astonishingly, they managed to travel over 1000 miles of the Niger, to Bussa (in modern Nigeria), when they were attacked by natives and Park drowned (Extract 5).

A few years later, a compatriot of Park was to reach Timbuktu successfully. The hardy Gordon Laing arrived after untold difficulties in 1826, and was killed shortly after leaving the city. The innumerable difficulties of undertaking a journey in Mali at the time were summed up by Lord Byron in *Don Juan*, 1819–24; 'To that impracticable place Timbuctoo/Where geography finds no one to oblige her/With such a chart as may be safely stuck to.'

The achievement of being the first European to return from Timbuktu is credited to a Frenchman, René Caillé, who was distinctly unimpressed and stayed there a mere fourteen days in 1828: 'I looked around and found that the sight before me did not answer my expectations. I had formed a totally different idea of the grandeur and wealth of Timbuktu.' One image that has not changed over centuries of descriptions and 'discoveries' of Timbuktu are the long slow processions of camel caravans which to this day carry salt across the Sahara. Writer Leland Hall, arriving in the 1920s, observed like many before him that 'Timbuctoo was nothing, and I was nothing that went into it.' But he too was mesmerized by the timeless trail of camels and eloquently captured the scene in his book *Timbuctoo* (Extract 4).

While many people came and went, few stayed. The first foreign resident was Père Dupuis Yakouba (the so-called 'White Monk of Timbuctoo'), who was born in France in 1865. Described as a combination of Benvenuto Cellini, St Francis of Assisi and Marco Polo, he came to live here in 1895, promptly took up residence with a local woman and fathered some thirty children. Rumours of this renegade (and by now defrocked) monk filtered back to Europe, and intrigued journalist, foreign correspondent and sometime explorer William Seabrook ◊. In a vain attempt to 'coax, bribe, buy, bully' Yakouba into writing his autobiography, Seabrook visited Timbuktu several times. On his first visit in 1928 he 'arrived one dark Christmas night on a donkey' and his first impressions of Yakouba were of 'a benevolent patriarchal bull disguised as Santa Claus.' The author spent most of the week drinking absinthe with Yakouba, and trying to drag the 'true' story of his life out of him. Eventually Seabrook was to write Yakouba's extraordinary and amusing life story himself, entitling it *The White Monk of Timbuctoo* (Extract 6).

While Seabrook took much of Yakouba's tale with a long caravan of salt, the local history has for centuries been 'safeguarded' by professional oral story tellers who are said to speak 'free from all untruth'. These *griots* are the minstrels of West Africa and play an important part in the education of a people where loyalties are tribal as opposed to national, and where oral literature is more accessible and traditional than written literature. In recognition of this, there is currently talk of developing 'sound libraries', important in a country with an illiteracy rate of around 91%.

Many of the contemporary Malian writers recount tales and legends that are oral in origin in their work. Writer D.T. Niane ◊, born of *griot* ancestors, has collected and transcribed stories and folk tales from all over Mali. *Sundiata: An Epic of Old Mali* recalls the legend of the rise to power of the Sundiata, one of the emperors of the Mali empire in the thirteenth century (Extract 2). The story was originally recited in Malinké to Niane. He transcribed it and it was later translated into French and English. Niane highlights the historical importance of the role of the *griots*: 'Kings have prescribed destinies just like man . . . They have knowledge of the future, whereas we griots are depositories of the knowledge of the past. But whoever knows the history of a country can read its future. Other people use writing to record the past, but this invention has killed the faculty of memory among them. They do not feel the past any more, for writing lacks the warmth of the human voice . . . What paltry learning is that which is congealed in dumb books.'

Another popular legend is that of Kaidara. Taken from the traditional literature of Macina, Kaidara was transcribed by the gifted linguist and historian Amadou Hampâte Bâ ◊. Described as a 'Fulani Cosmological Epic from Mali', *Kaidara* is an allegorical poem about the quest for power and knowledge (Extract 1). Bâ has collected innumerable epics, initiation texts, tales and chronicles, though very few have been translated into English.

Drawing upon the country's history in a completely different way is Yambo Ouologuem ◊, who is without doubt one of the country's sharpest, wittiest and most original writers. 'When Negro Teeth Speak' is a brilliant, one-off poem that challenges perceptions about Africans from a surprising angle (Extract 3). Ouologuem is himself a fairly controversial character. His novel *Bound to Violence* caused a stir not only for its explicitly violent and sexual passages (in a country where 90% of the population is Muslim), but also because it was claimed several passages were cribbed from an early work by Graham Greene. *Bound to Violence* traces the three stages in the turbulent history of a ficticious Mali-like country and is, like Ouologuem's poetry, direct, honest, and highly entertaining: 'The Empire was crumbling . . . The Saif dynasty went from bad to worse with the grandsons of Saif Rabban Johanan the eldest of whom, Jacob, so the griots relate, "spent his nights expounding all manner of abstruse theological problems to his cat." The animal's discretion was such that, to spare Jacob any excessive fear of the horrors that awaited him here below, it crept away at daybreak.'

Following publication of this prize-winning first novel in 1968, Ouologuem produced a satirical pamphlet, *Open Letter to Black France*, addressed to General de Gaulle. This set out his controversial theories on the three periods of colonialism and the consequent 'slave' mentality. Domination by African emperors (of whom Ouologuem is himself a descendant), the Arabs and then the French in 1890 resulted, he argues, in a 'slave' mentality: 'The white slave traders only proposed – it was the African notables who disposed.'

Mali eventually became independent in 1960, but it was not until 1992, following years of repressive and economically disastrous socialist and military rule, that the country saw its first democratically elected President. The poll, which was attended by a mere 16% of the population, speaks for the fact that here, as in much of West Africa, the people's loyalties, as well as their educational and literary priorities, are primarily tribal rather than national.

With little prominence given to the written word, Mali has

developed, with government support, world-renowned film and music industries. Film-maker Souleymane Cissé achieved international acclaim with *Finye* and *Yeleen*, and musicians such as Salif Keita and Kasse Mady Diabaté have cultivated a unique modern popular music which is still faithful to their roots.

LITERARY LANDMARKS

Bamako. Explorers and adventurers René Caillé and Mungo Park both reached here. When Mali gained independence from France in 1960, Bamako became the capital of the country. Mali's first internationally recognized 'star', musician Salif Keita launched his career at the **Buffet Hôtel de la Gare**.

Sansanding. Explorer Mungo Park wrote his last letter to his wife from here on 19 November 1805 – 'Impressed with a woman's fears . . . you may be led to consider my situation as a great deal worse than it really is.' It was.

Ségou. Here Mungo Park first encountered the object of his travels – the mighty **River Niger**. Ségou was capital of numerous kingdoms after the fall of the Songhai empire.

Timbuktu. The **Sankore** mosque housed a world-renowned university during the city's heyday. Plaques mark the crumbling **houses of René Caillé, Gordon Laing**, and a German explorer **Heinrich Barth** who were among the first Europeans to reach the city alive. Rock singer and famine fund-raiser Bob Geldof visited Timbuktu, looked round, and said 'Is that it?'

Libraries and Bookshops

French Documentation Centre, Bamako; National Library of Mali, Bamako.

BOOKLIST

The following selection includes the extracted titles in this chapter as well as those mentioned in the introduction which are available in English and other titles for further reading. In general, paperback editions are given when possible. The editions cited are not necessarily the only ones available. For most of the extracted works, the original publisher in English can be found in 'Acknowledgments and Citations' at the end of the volume, as can the exact location of the extracts and the editions from which they are taken. Extract numbers are highlighted in bold for ease of reference.

Bâ, Amadou Hampâté, *Kaidara*, Three Continents Press, Washington, DC, 1988. **Extract 1.**

Bowles, Paul, *Too Far from Home*, Peter Owen, London, 1994.

Caillé, René, *Travels Through Central Africa to Timbuktu*, Frank Cass, London, 1968.

Hall, Leland, *Timbuctoo*, Harper and Brothers, London, 1927. **Extract 4.**

Hudson, Peter, *Two Rivers: Travels in West Africa on the Trail of Mungo Park*, Chapmans, London, 1991.

Niane, D.T., *Sundiata: An Epic of Old Mali*, Longman, London, 1971. **Extract 2.**

Ouologuem, Yambo, *Bound to Violence*, Heinemann, London, 1977.

Ouologuem, Yambo, 'When Negro Teeth Speak', Gerald Moore, trans, in *The Penguin Book of Modern African Poetry*, Gerald Moore and Ulli Beier, eds, Penguin, London, 1984. **Extract 3.**

Park, Mungo, *Travels in the Interior of Africa*, Eland, London, 1983. **Extract 5.**

Seabrook, William, *The White Monk of Timbuctoo*, Harrap, London, 1934. **Extract 6.**

Extracts

(1) MALI: FULANI EPIC
Amadou Hampâté Bâ, *Kaidara*

In his quest for eternal knowledge and enlightenment (not to mention political power), King Hammadi spent large amounts of money bringing scholars from all over the world to explain the mystery of the land of Kaidara. It was to elude him until . . .

One day a beggar appeared
at Hammadi's door after being driven away everywhere else.

He was more dead than alive.
He walked by habit more than by strength.
This little man, covered with wretched rags,
soaked in sweat, said 'At last, I'm here!'
'And where do you suppose you are?' said the guard.
'At Hammadi's, father of Hammadi, the great,
the generous, the benefactor of his people, there I am!'
'What do you want?' the guard asked.
'To see Hammadi' answered the old man.
The chief guard found that this went too far,
and to intimidate the old man and change his mind,
asked him, 'Want me to kick you out of here?
What you need is rice, not a royal audience.'
The little man beat the air, hammered the ground
and said:
'I want no charity! I want to see
and meet the King, and sup with him!
My hand and his in the same muck,
so I can spread my fleas and lice to him.'

(2) MALI: GRIOTS

D.T. Niane, *Sundiata*

These are the words of Djeli Mamoudou Kouyaté, one of a long line of griots, who from time immemorial have taught the kings of Mali the history of their ancestors. Here he begins the epic of the empire of Sundiata, passed down 'free from all untruth'.

Listen now to the story of Sundiata, the Na'Kamma, the man who had a mission to accomplish.

At the time when Sundiata was preparing to assert his claim over the kingdom of his fathers, Soumaoro was the king of kings, the most powerful king in all the lands of the setting sun. The fortified town of Sosso was the bulwark of fetishism against the word of Allah. For a long time Soumaoro defied the whole world. Since his accession to the throne of Sosso he had defeated nine kings whose heads served him as fetishes in his macabre chamber. Their skins served as seats and he cut his footwear from human skin. Soumaoro was not like other men, for the jinn had revealed themselves to him and his power was beyond measure. So his countless sofas were very brave since they believed their king to be invincible. But Soumaoro was an evil demon and his reign had produced nothing but bloodshed. Nothing was taboo for him. His greatest pleasure was publicly to flog venerable old men. He had defiled every family and everywhere in his vast empire there were villages populated by girls whom he had forcibly abducted from their families without marrying them.

(3) MALI: PERCEPTIONS

Yambo Ouologuem, *When Negro Teeth Speak*

Ouologuem tries both to shock and amuse his readers into examining perceptions of Africans. These opening lines are taken from the translation of the poem included in The Penguin Book of Modern African Poetry – see Booklist.

Everyone thinks me a cannibal
But you know how people talk

Everyone sees my red gums but who
Has white ones
Up with tomatoes

Everyone says fewer tourists will come
Now
But you know
We aren't in America and anyway everyone
Is broke

Everyone says it's my fault and is afraid
But look
My teeth are white not red
I haven't eaten anyone

People are wicked and say I gobble
the tourists roasted
Or perhaps grilled
Roasted or grilled I asked them
They fell silent and looked fearfully at my gums
Up with tomatoes

(4) MALI: SALT CARAVANS

Leland Hall, *Timbuctoo*

For centuries caravans of camels have plodded their way, two by two, 700 km across the desert from the Taoudenni salt mines to Timbuktu.

The fall of their soft padded feet was muffled in the sand, not a thud, not a scuff; and save for the singularly unpleasant grunts which are their own discourse – and they were too weary to do much grunting – the only sound was the tinkle of the slabs of salt slung in pairs over their humps. So that, did a man turn his back on that caravan, he lost it altogether, while it streamed on not fifty feet behind him. Thus, finding it so vague and so silent, I came to believe what I had so often heard – that if you are journeying with a caravan across the desert and lie asleep through the departure from the night's camp, small are the chances that you will ever overtake it. . . .

On the line moved, with no hastening but so steadily that one lost count altogether. There seemed no end to what trailed itself into sight from behind the dunes, passed us, went up the light rise between us and the city, and out of sight again, without ever a break in the so slender and so unimpressive double line. And the markers stood on the roof of the house with the tower which was by the edge of the city and kept tally; and we knew later that more than three thousand camels came in with salt that day to Timbuctoo.

In the narrow streets you were dodging camels the rest of the day; and there, between the walls, they seemed anything but small. You could not wander far without having to squeeze yourself against some door to let camels with scornful heads, no matter how flabby the hump, go by.

(5) SÉGOU

Mungo Park,
Travels in the Interior Districts of Africa

After a 700-mile trek eastwards from the coast, British explorer Mungo Park rests for the night in a small village before seeing, for the first time, the banks of the River Niger at Sego (modern-day Ségou).

The thoughts of seeing the Niger in the morning, and the troublesome buzzing of mosquitoes prevented me from shutting my eyes during the night; and I had saddled my horse in readiness before daylight; but on account of the wild beasts, we were obliged to wait until the people were stirring, and the gates opened. This happened to be a market day at Sego, and the roads were everywhere filled with people carrying different articles to sell. We passed four large villages, and at eight o'clock saw the smoke over Sego.

As we approached the town, I was fortunate enough to overtake the fugitive Kaartans, to whose kindness I had been so much indebted in my journey through Bambarra. They readily agreed to introduce me to the king; and we rode together through some marshy ground, where, as I was anxiously looking around for the river, one of them called out, *goe affili* (see the water), and looking forwards I saw with infinite pleasure the great object of my mission – the long sought for majestic Niger, glittering to the morning sun, as broad as the Thames at Westminster, and flowing slowly *to the eastward.* I hastened to the brink, and, having drank of the water, lifted up my fervent thanks in prayer to the Great Ruler of all things, for having thus far crowned my endeavours with success.

(6) Timbuktu

William Seabrook, *The White Monk of Timbuctoo*

Since his arrival in May 1895 Yakouba, The White Monk of Timbuctoo, has caused something of a stir in the town. An unofficial and somewhat embarrassed delegation of Frenchmen from the nearby fort have come to have words with his Superior.

Not that they were prudes, you understand. On the contrary! In fact, that was just it. There was Lita, for instance, the Peuhl girl, you know, whose father makes those doughnuts dipped in honey. Well, she had agreed to come and keep house for Lieutenant Aubade, and now she wouldn't, and you know why. What did he do to them anyway? Put a sign of the Cross on them, or something? There was Moussa too – the one nicknamed Elizabeth, you know – and, while he might have done it inadvertently, he had also practically stolen one of Captain Doussol's mistresses. Please understand – a priest was a man, *bien entendu*, as much so as a soldier. They didn't mean to be unreasonable, but would the Superior please ask this young Père Yakouba to be a little reasonable himself.

Yakouba was duly scolded, confessed, penanced, absolved, and repentant, but it wasn't very easy for a young priest of his peculiar temperament and vitality to be reasonable in Timbuctoo. Its women are as free and warm and expert as ever were the women of ancient Alexandria or Montmartre in Mimi's time. It is a great port, a camel port, as Alexandria was a seaport, sacred to Aphrodite, but with this difference that the priestesses here are of no special class. Though predominantly Moslem, veils and harems are practically unknown, and its women generally are just as free as among the great Moslem desert tribes of Arabia the Blessed. They sleep for pleasure with whom they please – and apparently this young white marabout had pleased them inordinately.

Biographies and important works

BÂ, Amadu Hampaté (1920–   ). Bâ was born into a Fulani family of religious Muslim leaders, and known as the 'sage' of **Bamako**. A historian, Bâ is renowned for developing an Arabic script for the Fulani language and has devoted his life's work to the preservation of oral traditions. He was for a while Mali's ambassador to the Côte d'Ivoire and delegate to UNESCO. He has also been Director of Radio Bamako's cultural programmes. Bâ has published many works in the field of Islamic theology and African religions.

NIANE, Djibril Tamsir (c1930–   ). A historian, a story teller and a collector of legends, Niane was born of *griot* ancestory in Conakry, Guinea, and was educated in Senegal and France. His best known work, *Sundiata* (Extract 2), is based on the legends of ancient Mali and tells the story of a crippled boy who rose to become one of the emperors of the Mali empire in the thirteenth century. Niane has taught history at several schools and universities in Senegal. He also works in theatre and radio production.

OUOLOGUEM, Yambo (1940–   ). Ouologuem was born in the **Dogon** country of Mali. He was the only son of a school inspector, and was educated in **Bamako** and Paris, where he studied philosophy, literature and sociology. His first novel, *Le Devoir de Violence* (*Bound to Violence*), is an account of the history of a fictitious African empire, and the Preface states, 'any resemblance to real persons would be fortuitous'. Liberally sprinkled with sorcery, cannibalism and eroticism, it attracted widespread attention and won a major literary prize – the Prix Renaudot – in 1968. He followed this with a vigorous attack on colonialism, *Lettre Ouverte à la France–Nègre*, addressed to the then President, General de Gaulle. Ouologuem also writes poetry (Extract 3).

PARK, Mungo (1771–1806). Park was born in Scotland and studied medicine at the University of Edinburgh. He then became a ship's medical officer and embarked on a study of the flora and fauna of Sumatra. This brought him to the notice of the African Association, which had been formed in 1788 for the purpose of exploring the Niger region. In 1795 Park was dispatched to map the course of the River Niger. After an unsuccessful first attempt he returned to Europe, wrote about his travels, married and settled down to become a doctor in Perthshire. On his second foray into Africa, Mungo Park drowned during a skirmish with natives. It took over seven years before full details reached the British Government.

SEABROOK, William (1886–1945). Born in Maryland, USA, Seabrook was a journalist and adventurer. He wrote several books about his travels in Arabia, Kurdistan, Haiti and Africa. His best known book, *The White Monk of Timbuctoo*, about Père Dupuis Yakouba, the first European resident in **Timbuktu**, is illustrated with Yakouba's drawings of local tools, fashions and hairstyles. Their love–hate relationship and the numerous arguments that developed over absinthe and several visits are amusingly recounted by Seabrook: 'But damn it, you're not Moses, even if you did marry a big black negress the same as he did.' Seabrook's hobby was collecting African masks.

MAURITANIA

'For a while we sat listening to them and watching their deft fingers as they played. Finally, Barka stopped and, drawing once more her veil across her face, went off to her tent. Then all was silence, but for the thousand different rumours that make up the desert night.'
Odette du Puigaudeau, *Barefoot Through Mauritania*

Barren and isolated, the published literature about the Islamic Republic of Mauritania can all too often be likened to the country itself. First to blow off the shelves are dunes of travelogues by heroic adventurers and explorers who have over countless centuries ventured across the desert and written at length about their 'unique' and often woeful experiences.

Secondly, to quench your cultural thirst you could investigate the indigenous Arabic literature which is almost wholly untranslated and unappreciated by an audience outside of Moorish Mauritania itself. A harsh climate and nomadic lifestyle have not led to a flourishing and varied literary tradition, and mighty manuscripts of a judicial or religious nature far outweigh secular prose and poetry on the library shelves. Poet and collector of Peul prose, Oumar Ba, born in 1900, is one of the rare writers whose work has been translated into French (though barely anything has been translated into English). Also translated into French, and paradoxically illustrating the point, was his controversial pamphlet entitled *Should We Keep the French Language?*

The real oasis in this literary desert can be found in the oral stories and poetry passed down and recalled by the *ighyuwn*, the Moorish bards. The Saharan equivalent of the West African *griots*, they traditionally play a lute, drum or flute with the recital. The stories take the form of moral fables, and are typically short and unsophisticated. Poetry telling is an important pastime, unparalleled in ritual by anything in Western culture. A well versed *griot* is an asset to any encampment, and will sing everything from satirical verse to the praises of his hosts and sometimes even himself.

FACT BOX

AREA: 1 030 700 sq km
POPULATION: 2 024 000
CAPITAL: Nouakchott
LANGUAGES: French, Hassaniya Arabic, Poular, Soninke, Wolof
FORMER COLONIAL POWER: France
INDEPENDENCE: 1960

Less innocently, the poetry also plays an exciting and key part of the wooing and flirtation rites between young couples. 'A woman's charm includes her ability to excite with provocative remarks,' noted A.G. Gerteiny in his chapter on Moorish language and literature in his book *Mauritania* (Extract 1). Reporting in the 1960s, a shocked Gerteiny was surprised to find, 'In the course of a polite evening with Moorish friends, one hears seemingly harmless *double-entendre* verses which actually are erotic and contain propositions and obscene comments. A gentleman is expected to flatter, flirt, and even propose to a girl; if he does not do so, she will lead him in that direction.'

Apart from being quoted in those books with purely academic interest, recordings of traditional poems and recitals can be found scattered throughout travelogues of the nineteenth and twentieth centuries. The flamboyant Frenchwoman Odette du Puigaudeau ◊ travelled across the country by camel with a female companion in 1933–34. In her book *Barefoot Through Mauritania* (Extract 3) she records many meetings with nomadic poets, and many days spent in the company of the *griots*: 'These minstrels are the joy and poetry of the desert . . . How indeed could gifts be refused to those who, according to their whim or interest, could humiliate you with their mockery or sing your praises across the plains.' The ambience of the book suggests the two clearly enjoyed their celebrity status as female travellers – which afforded them numerous poems in their honour, invitations and hospitality from Emirs en route. In **Boutilimit** the local religious leader showed du Puigaudeau his private library, kept in a rather dusty and dilapidated hut. Locked away in wooden chests was 'all the wisdom of Islam', hundreds of rare books in sumptuous bindings, including a thirteenth-century copy of the Koran.

Europeans had taken an interest in Mauritania long before the arrival of the lone French ladies. The first explorer to boast of his arrival here was a Roman General, Suetonius Paulinus, who was stationed in the country around AD42. Mercantile European contact began with Portuguese Alvise de Cadamosto, the so-called 'Navigator' who sailed here in 1455, though it was eventually the French in 1920 who were officially to claim colonial control. But it was not only territorial or trading possibilities that brought people here over the years. Surprising numbers of travellers were drawn to this barren and inhospitable landscape, embarking on spiritual quests to test the limits of their endurance, in the face of loneliness and extreme physical hardships.

When writer Bruce Chatwin (◊ Benin) felt the need for broad new geographical, literary and metaphysical horizons, he embarked on a journey that was to take him from Afghanistan to Mauritania. The aim was to study the nomads of the world, for a book on man's nomadic instinct. In Mauritania he found the Nemadi, a 'hunting caste' living near **Walata**. Although Chatwin gave up on the original book and destroyed the manuscript, he kept his notebooks, several select morsels of which are included in his excellent though eclectic book, *The Songlines* (Extract 4).

During his travels in 1972, writer Geoffrey Moorhouse ◊ questioned several times, not without undue cause, the sanity of his decision to undertake such a journey. His physical and mental preparations were admirably thorough. He sought advice from well seasoned Saharan travellers, such as Wilfred Thesiger, who pointed out 'it was not the most intelligent route to be taken by a man intent on making the first camel crossing of the Sahara from Atlantic to Nile.' He also took Arabic lessons and made frequent visits to the camel keepers at London Zoo to study camels' characters and peculiarities. The highly ambitious original route was to take him from the capital **Nouakchott**, through to Mali, Algeria, Libya and thence to the Nile at Luxor in Egypt. Beset by troubles and tiredness, Moorhouse ended his pilgrimage at Tamanrasset in Algeria, where he had quite literally been driven to the end of his and his camel's tether – 'There was nothing but pain in this desert, for human beings and animals alike. Life was pain. Only in death was there relief.' He entitled the book of his journey *The Fearful Void* (Extract 2).

Literary Landmarks

Boutilimit. Religious capital and site of a renowned Arab library. Birthplace of Mokhtar Daddah, who in 1960 became the country's first President.

Nouakchott. The name means 'place of the winds'. In *Fantastic Invasion*, 1980, Patrick Marnham writes 'The sand blows across the streets and piles up between the shacks of the metropolis; sweeping it into heaps is about the only source of steady employment that the city can offer.' Many travellers, including Geoffrey Moorhouse and Odette du Puigaudeau, passed through here, the latter enjoying 'hospitality, champagne, gramophones, and a good clean up'.

Libraries and Bookshops

Nouakchott. Central Public Library; French Cultural Centre ('The usual pleasant, chauvinistic retreat' according to *Rough Guide to West Africa*); National Library; University of Nouakchott Library.
 Boutilimit and Chinguetti. Arab Library.

BOOKLIST

The following selection includes the extracted titles in this chapter as well as those mentioned in the introduction which are available in English and other titles for further reading. In general, paperback editions are given when possible. The editions cited are not necessarily the only ones available. For most of the extracted works, the original publisher in English can be found in 'Acknowledgments and Citations' at the end of the volume, as can the exact location of the extracts and the editions from which they are taken. Extract numbers are highlighted in bold.

Ba, Oumar, in *The Penguin Book of Modern African Poetry*, Penguin, London, 1984.

Chatwin, Bruce, *The Songlines*, Jonathan Cape, London, 1987. **Extract 4.**

Du Puigaudeau, Odette, *Barefoot in Mauritania*, Routledge, London, 1937. **Extract 3.**

Gerteiny, A.G., *Mauritania*, Pall Mall Press, London, 1968. **Extract 1.**

Hudson, Peter, *Travels in Mauritania*, Virgin Publishing Ltd, London, 1990.

Marnham, Patrick, *Fantastic Invasion: Dispatches from Contemporary Africa*, Penguin, London, 1987.

Moorhouse, Geoffrey, *The Fearful Void*, Penguin, London, 1986. **Extract 2.**

Extracts

(1) MAURITANIA: LOVE POETRY
A.G. Gerteiny, *Mauritania*

The oral poetry of Mauritania is, noted Gerteiny, an intriguing vehicle for flirtation, and the sexual innuendos are far from covert. Unashamedly leading the proceedings, a young woman might well tease a young and timid man thus:

> The jewel-case of a woman
> Has a lock and a key.
> A girl still not a woman
> Owns the lock but not the key.

Wishing to impress her (and the audience), the man's reply should be quick and witty, and might be along these lines:

> *Iblīss* (Satan) kept me awake all night,
> My heart beating through my vein
> As a deer tracked all night
> By the hunter in the plain.

(2) TIDJIKA
Geoffrey Moorhouse, *The Fearful Void*

November 1972, and a few days into the long camel journey across the Mauritanian desert with his native guides, the author is beginning to wonder if he can make it to the next settlement, let alone all the way to Egypt.

Mohamed was at his best now. When our pace showed signs of slackening, he took the headrope of the leading camel, with the second one hitched behind, and all but hauled the beast along. When it was his turn to march at the back of our small column, he would clap his hands and make yipping noises to encourage both beasts to longer strides. When I lay feebly in a heap at a midday camp, he stoned my share of the dates and handed them to me one by one; then he fell back exhausted himself. Since the day before Chig we had marched in almost total silence, for neither of my companions now had the energy to continue their early chatter. Each day Mohamed had asked me to ride, and each day I had refused. I finally gave way in the middle of a blazing afternoon, when we had already been on the move for twelve hours . . .

I climbed up gratefully and experienced the marvellous relief of just sitting as the camels plodded on. Quietly we went along, our bodies swinging in the saddles, heavy with fatigue. There was a new perspective up there. The world was no longer simply an excruciating obstacle, to be attacked and overcome step by step. It was a thing of vistas, which one could absorb thoughtfully again. The camels seemed to move with little effort here, their legs going down with metronomic regularity: left rear, left fore, right rear, right fore, left rear, left fore, right rear, right fore . . . As I watched the beast in front carefully pacing the gravel, I could feel myself beginning to doze off.

(3) Tin-Deïla

Odette du Puigaudeau,
Barefoot Through Mauritania

The 'barefoot' Christian French ladies have been invited to stay in the tents of the grandson of an Emir, Mohammed-Fall, and his illustrious family. After a traditional meal and tea they are entertained by travelling minstrels Baraka and her husband Souidate.

Slaves wearing amber and silver ornaments were grouped behind the musicians, and they clapped their hands in unison with the plucking of strings and the beating of calabashes. A barbaric odour emanated from these people, the smell of the Moors, composed of sweat, leather, tea and spices. And the perfume of the yellow flowers of the *tahla* floated in with the lowing of the cattle on the night air . . .

This evening Souidate and Barka had no other thought than to 'do beautiful things for the Christians.' They sang *El Bial*, which is a love song, and *Z'rac* meaning 'Resignation,' by the poetess El Khansa, who lived in the second century of the Hegira, and *Zeïni* by Omar-ben-Khalssum, who was born before Mahomet.

> *Before we separate,*
> *I pray you stay awhile.*

For a long while we sat listening to them and watching their deft fingers as they played. Finally Barka stopped and, drawing once more her veil across her face, went off to her tent. Then all was silence but for the thousand distant rumours that make up the desert night.

(4) WALATA
Bruce Chatwin, *The Songlines*

At Walata, the ancient capital of the Almoravid Empire, Chatwin is at the mercy of a bored Governor as he waits patiently for permission to visit the nomadic Nemadi tribe.

The Governor, a morose hypochondriac, had been longing for someone to share the memory of his student days in Paris, or to argue doctrinal points of *la pensée maotsetungienne*. His favourite words were *tactique* and *technique*, but whenever I raised the question of the Nemadi, he'd let fly a brittle laugh and murmur, 'It is forbidden.'

At mealtimes, a pink-fingered lutanist would serenade us through the couscous while the Governor reconstructed, with my prompting, a street map of the Quartier Latin. From his palace – if four mud-brick rooms were a palace – I could see a tiny white tent of the Nemadi beckoning me across the hillside.

'But why do you wish to see these people?' the Governor shouted at me. 'Walata, yes! Walata is a historical place. But this Nemadi is nothing. It is a dirty people.'

Not only were they dirty, they were a national disgrace. They were infidels, idiots, thieves, parasites, liars. They ate forbidden food.

'And their women', he added, 'are prostitutes!'

'But beautiful?' I suggested, if only to annoy him.

His hand shot out from the folds of his blue robes.

'Ha!' he wagged a finger at me. 'Now I know! Now I see it! But let me tell you, young Englishman, those women have terrible diseases. Incurable diseases!'

Biographies and important works

CHATWIN, Bruce (see under Benin).

DU PUIGAUDEAU, Odette. In 1933 the French adventurer and her friend Marion Sénones left for Mauritania on a Breton fishing boat. They landed at Port Étienne (**Nouadhibou** today) with 'four letters of introduction, two small revolvers, a Junior Kodak, and our heads filled with good advice.' Travelling principally by camel, and occasionally by car, they travelled east via **Nouakchott** and **Boutilimit** to **Kiffa**. The lively pair took to the 'poetic' people, and their experiences, as recalled in *Barefoot Through Mauritania* (Extract 3), maintain a remarkable humour and patience, and display neither deep prejudice nor mistrust.

Geoffrey Moorhouse

MOORHOUSE, Geoffrey (1931–). Moorhouse was born in Bolton, UK, and spent many years as a journalist working for various newspapers, including *The Guardian*. His published books cover such diverse subjects as essays on cricket, a study of an American fishing community, and monastic life in India. *The Fearful Void* (Extract 2) was the result of a long and difficult journey from Mauritania to Algeria, undertaken when the author was 40 years old. Moorhouse set out in the manner of many an adventurer, to explore the limits of his fears and endurance – 'There were extremities that I hadn't touched, which I hadn't been able to examine, where my belief in the necessity of forward movement had not been tested.'

NIGER

'The (floating) log never becomes a crocodile'
Songhai proverb

Compared to the bite of neighbouring Nigeria's literary teeth, land-locked Niger is something of a literary log. Most of the literature is written in the mother tongue of the colonialists, and a mere trickle from this small spring of creativity has been translated from the French.

A prominent figure is Boubou Hama, who was born in 1909. Like many writers he was of a strong political persuasion – an early member of the Rassemblement Démocratique (RDA) and later President of the Partie Progressiste Nigérien (PPN). Among his works is *Kotia–Nima*, his three-volume autobiography which won the 1970 Grand Prix Littéraire de l'Afrique Noire for its depiction of his perceptions of and struggles against colonialist culture. He has also written several historical works which interweave history with local legends, and spirit stories of dwarfs and witchcraft.

The other key figure is dramatist André Salifou. Born in 1924 he was educated in the Côte d'Ivoire and has founded several theatre groups in West Africa, which he believes are an important instrument of education. His play *Tanimoune* is based on historical events in Sudan in the nineteenth century, and has been performed in Algeria.

Following various nineteenth-century travellers, such as German Heinrich Barth (the first European to explore what is present-day Niger) and Mungo Park (the first European to discover the River Niger flowed eastwards), we find equally strange obsessions luring twentieth-century 'explorers' here. Legends of Songhai sorcery and magic were among the things that drew Paul Stoller to the country in 1976. A professor of anthropology, Stoller came here to study the Songhai, who have inhabited the region since the eighth century. *In Sorcery's Shadow* is the story of his apprenticeship under Djibo the *sorko*. *Sorko* is the name given to a Songhai sorcerer, or, to demystify it a little, a praise singer to the spirits.

FACT BOX

AREA: 1 186 410 sq km
POPULATION: 7 900 000
CAPITAL: Niamey
LANGUAGES: French, Fulani, Hausa, Songhai, Tuareg
FORMER COLONIAL POWER: France
INDEPENDENCE: 1960

Once the would-be sorcerer has gained the trust of the Songhai and found a *sorko* willing to initiate him into the secret rituals, becoming a sorcerer is very time-consuming for a Westerner – even for a fluent Songhai-speaking one like Stoller. There are over 150 spirits, with a poem each which has to be memorized, and texts, songs and various rituals to be endured. Having coped with that, there are various job hazards – Stoller suffered temporary paralysis, a priestess sent spirits to attack him, and he suffered much stomach ache on account of the strange potions he had to swallow as part of the initiation process (Extract 1).

Returning from the USA in 1981 to complete his apprenticeship, Stoller stepped even further across the boundaries of professional ethics and objectivity: 'I could no longer be a dispassionate observer of Songhay society . . . I was inexorably drawn to the power, the people, and the mystery of the world of Songhay sorcery.'

The requirements and research methods of anthropologists are often something of an amusement and mystery to the subjects (see also Nigel Barley, Cameroon). One of Stoller's first self-appointed tasks was a study of the relationship between the use of language and local politics, and a language attitude survey. The dialogue between his first two respondents reveals more about local politics than language. Here the frustrated Stoller stomps between the two rival shopkeepers:

'Abdou, Mahamane has just told me that you speak only two languages. Is it true?'
'Yes it is true. I speak only two languages.'
'Why did you tell me you speak four languages?'
Abdou shrugged his shoulders and smiled. 'What difference does it make?' He looked skyward for a moment. 'Tell me, Monsieur Paul, how many languages did Mahamane tell you that he spoke?'
'Mahamane told me that he speaks three languages.'
'Hah! I know for a fact that Mahamane speaks only one language . . .'

Less sorcery and more success was had by Carol Beckwith and Marion van Offelen, whose book *Nomads of Niger* is the result of time spent with the Wodaabe, a nomadic people who inhabit large areas of southern Niger. A large and luxurious book, it has striking photographs, text printed on paper as sandy and grainy as the desert, and definite anthropological as opposed to literary ambition. Particularly impressive are the photographs of the Geerewol, an annual traditional celebration or beauty pageant which signifies the end of the season of migration. The homecoming single men make up their faces, concoct elaborate hairstyles and line up to be inspected by the women. For seven full days the men dance, sing, roll their eyes and flash their teeth in the hope of attracting a partner. As Richard Burton remarked in *Wanderings in West Africa*, 'The Niger, as has been well observed, is not a lottery in which men may win fortunes, but a field of labour in which they may earn them.'

LITERARY LANDMARKS

Agadez. An important trading point at the time of the Songhai empire of the sixteenth century. The German explorer Heinrich Barth found the town in decline when he reached it in 1850. Here you can witness the remarkable traditional Geerewol or 'bachelors' party' at the end of the rainy season.

Libraries and Bookshops

Niamey. American Cultural Centre; Franco–Nigerian Cultural Centre; University of Niamey Library.

BOOKLIST

The following selection includes the extracted title in this chapter as well as those mentioned in the introduction which are available in English and other titles for further reading. In general, paperback editions are given when possible. The editions cited are not necessarily the only ones available.

Beckwith, C., and van Offelen, Marion, *Nomads of Niger*, Harry N. Abrams, New York, 1983.

Burton, Sir Richard, *Wanderings in West Africa*, Dover, New York, 1992.

Norris, H.T., *Sufi Mystics of the Niger Desert*, Clarendon, Oxford, 1990.

Sanche de Gramont, *The Strong Brown God: The Story of the Niger River*, Granada, 1975.

Stoller, Paul and Olkes, Cheryl, *In Sorcery's Shadow*, University of Chicago Press, Chicago, IL, and London, 1987. **Extract 1.**

Extract

(1) MEHANNA

Paul Stoller and Cheryl Olkes, *In Sorcery's Shadow*

In the Songhai village of Mehanna, anthropologist Paul Stoller is under the apprenticeship of Djibo the sorko. As part of the initiation process he has eaten specially prepared food, and now he tests his powers.

Djibo tapped my arm. He pointed to a woman who was walking toward us. Balanced on her head was a mountain of brightly decorated enameled metal pots. 'Paul, you have the sorko food in your belly, do you not?'

'Yes, I do', I responded, though for the life of me I could not understand how something that I had eaten three days before could remain in my belly for the rest of my life.

'And,' he continued as he watched the woman with the pots, 'you are now wearing on the third finger of your left hand a ring which has drunk, are you not?'

'Yes, I am.'

'Well . . .?'

'Does it mean that I have strength?'

'Yes, of course it does.'

'But how am I to know it? I do not feel any different, just a bit more constipated.'

'I am sorry about your dried-out intestines, but this usually happens when one has eaten the food of strength.' He waved his hand in the direction of the woman with the pots on her head. She had stopped to talk with another woman going toward the river. 'Go up to that woman with the pots on her head. Look at her eyes even if she attempts to avoid your gaze. When your eyes meet, a tear will roll out of her left eye.'

'Sure it will,' I said sarcastically. Hoping to prove Djibo wrong, I approached the woman with the pots on her head; she was slowly walking away from the market. When she realized that I intended to intercept her, she quickened her pace. She lost her balance and some of her pots thumped into the sand. Like a conqueror, I stood over this woman as she picked up two of her pots. For a second our eyes locked. A large tear dropped from the corner of her left eye and ran down her cheek. She stood up stiffly and ran away, somehow holding on to her pots. I returned to Djibo, stupefied.

'I don't believe it, Djibo. The woman would not look at me, and when she did, a tear dropped onto her cheek from her left eye.'

'Did you smell her?'

'No, I didn't.'

Djibo shook his head. 'One day you will be able to smell them, but that lies ahead of you on your path.'

'Smell what?' I asked.

'Witches, you fool.'

NIGERIA

'In our country a long American car driven by a white-uniformed chauffeur and flying a ministerial flag could pass through the eye of a needle.'
Chinua Achebe,
A Man of the People

Chinua Achebe Ɖ, Nigeria's leading novelist–philosopher, has not been sparing in his criticism of the country. In *The Trouble with Nigeria*, 1983, he wrote 'It is one of the most corrupt, insensitive, inefficient places under the sun . . . It is dirty, noisy, ostentatious, dishonest and vulgar. In short it is one of the most unpleasant places on earth! . . . Only a masochist with an exuberant taste for self-violence will pick Nigeria for a holiday.' If these words seem surprising, it is even more surprising that Achebe still lives there. But Nigeria, the undisputed giant of West Africa, has, he claims, an energy and inspirational quality that are at once extremely frustrating and incredibly exciting. In the world of literature, like the country itself, Nigeria is the land of beautifully blurred borders, where reality and fiction and tradition and modernism are often indistinguishable. In the words of Achebe, 'Soon we won't be able to write novels because anything you can concoct has already been surpassed yesterday. Our society itself is catching up with fiction.'

The story of Nigeria's disproportionate literary success (compared to its neighbours) must start with acknowledgment of the multitude of indigenous languages and peoples. It is said to be the most linguistically complicated country in the world, with 250 peoples, as many languages, some 400 dialects and a multitude of own mythology and traditions. Administratively, the country is today divided into 30 states, but the simplest common denominators are the three basic cultural conglomerations – **Yorubaland** focusing around **Lagos** in the southwest, **Igboland** in the southeast, and **Hausaland** to the north.

Literature in the indigenous languages took off early. The Muslim north was renowned for Arabic poetry in the fifteenth century and later

FACT BOX

AREA: 923 850 sq km
POPULATION: 99 000 000
CAPITAL: Abuja (official), Lagos (de facto)
LANGUAGES: English, Edo, Efik, Fulani, Hausa, Igbo, Ijaw, Yoruba
FORMER COLONIAL POWER: Great Britain
INDEPENDENCE: 1960

flourished when Hausa was transliterated into Arabic script. The arrival of the missionaries then brought the Roman script to Hausa, and in the 1930s there was a flourish of prose writers and poets, including the future first Prime Minister of independent Nigeria, Tafawa Balewa.

Yoruba was also adapted to further the Christian cause when a freed slave, Samuel Crowther (born in 1809), transcribed the language to translate the bible. The rich fabric of oral literature and folklore began to be recorded and was quickly woven into short stories and novels: '. . . To plant yam is costly – but it amply repays its own debt./You put the yam to bed in the ground/it will bring you money/that will plant you on top of a beautiful woman.' (Yoruba saying from *Voices from Twentieth-Century Africa*). After independence and the emergence of an increasingly urbanized population, and a university-educated class of teachers and intellectuals, the narrations were ever more clearly a sign of the times: 'Here peace is lying exhausted on the ground/and belligerence dances on his back./Ibadan, the town where the owner of the land/does not prosper like the stranger . . .' (*Voices from Twentieth-Century Africa*).

One of the great contemporary spokesmen and campaigners for the preservation of traditional 'non-academic' literature is Nigeria's Chinweizu. An engaging defender of popular literature, he is a radical, making clear distinctions between 'Euro-assimilationist junk . . . upheld as the flower of African literature' and that which is genuinely traditional and of relevance to his people. In his excellent outspoken book *Voices from Twentieth-Century Africa* are collections and comparisons of both types, and a call for a redrawing of the map of African literature. In his own compositions, Chinweizu makes his message loud and clear, and speaks bluntly of '. . . this land/This black whore . . ./tied to a post and raped by every passing white dog . . .'. He sees his task as correcting the distortions perpetrated by the arrival of a foreign body, with its incumbent tongue, heavy hand and selfish soul. In his couplet 'Colonizer's Logic', he takes a characteristically ironic look at the problem of language: 'The natives are unintelligent – /We can't understand their language'.

The language an African writer chooses to use brings up the delicate issues of pride, prejudice and practicality. There is a strong and passionate lobby in Nigeria in particular to abandon European languages completely and revive the indigenous ones. For Nigerian writers such as Ben Okri ◊ who choose to live in England, there is little obvious practical choice. For writers who remain in their homeland the decision is harder. Edo-speaking poet Odia Ofeimun ◊, author of the controversial *The Poet Lied* (Extract 8), chooses to write in English because, as he explains, 'it is the shortest course to reach the 250 different ethnic groups. The Nigerian language I speak is spoken by less than a million people in a country of 120 million. I had to make a choice. I chose English.' Chinua Achebe takes a more philosophical and political view on the matter and maintains that abandoning the European languages would not solve the country's problems. Speaking from a country made up of permanently increasing numbers of states he says, 'As an African and a nationalist looking at the situation now, there is a real value in keeping our countries together using a language that has been imposed upon us. It may not last for all time, but writers are not only there for all time, they're here for now as well.' (*Wasafiri*, Autumn 1991).

The first English-language best-seller by a Nigerian was *The Interesting Narrative of the Life of Olaudah Equiano, or Gustavus the African, Written by Himself*. His autobiography, which was into its ninth edition by the time of his death in 1797, follows Equiano ◊ from boyhood when he had 'never heard of white men or Europeans, or of the sea' to his capture and sale to white slave traders. As a slave and later as a free man, Equiano travelled all over the world. He eventually settled in England where he and his book were important activators in the movement to abolish slavery (Extract 2).

It was not until over 150 years later, with the appearance of Amos Tutuola ◊, that another Nigerian author enjoyed such international celebrity. Tutuola's idiosyncratic style was as distinct from Equiano's stiff Victorian English as any work could hope to be. *The Palm-Wine Drinkard* (Extract 12), his first piece of prose fiction, was published in 1952 and was anarchic in its originality, causing a stir among the conservative British press of the time. 'I was a palm-wine drinkard since I was a boy of ten years of age. I had no other work more than to drink palm wine in my life . . . But when my father noticed that I could not do any more work than to drink, he engaged an expert palm-wine tapster for me; he had no other work than to tap palm-wine every day . . .'. Thus begins a tale that, influenced by Tutuola's native Yoruba folklore (and no doubt a little native palm-wine), leads the imagination into a never-never underworld of spirits, ghosts, mythology and morality. His fiercest critics were, surprisingly, his fellow-educated

Nigerians who disapproved of his borrowing from tradition and were embarrassed by his unconventional, 'incorrect' and eccentric use of the English language. Despite harsh criticism, Tutuola did not compromise his style and so was a pioneer in building literary bridges between two worlds, two cultures, and two languages.

Speaking in defence of this increasingly popular style, Chinua Achebe, the godfather of the African novel whose work is taught in schools throughout Africa, remarked, 'there is a way in which the vigour of one language, its imagery and metaphors, can be transferred across.' This was the trademark of poet Gabriel Okara ◊ who attempted to render the expressive idiom of his native Ijaw into English. As with Tutuola's work, the critics were initially uncomfortable with the outcome, though his first novel *The Voice* is today considered one of the classic Nigerian novels (Extract 3).

This dexterity is the key to the accessibility and success of Achebe's writing also. His first novel, *Things Fall Apart* (Extract 10), has sold some eight million copies in 30 different languages worldwide (and there is even a shorthand version). The novel forms part of a trilogy which examines the colonial encounter with traditional African values. It starts with an Igbo community when the missionaries were beginning to penetrate into the minds and geography of the country. *No Longer at Ease* takes up the story of a so-called 'been-to', a headstrong young idealist who returns from abroad to find himself and his morality 'ill at ease' with that of his homeland. Achebe's own favourite is *Arrow of God*, which completes the cycle of the trilogy as it returns to the early colonial era and the clash of two belief systems. The delightfully characterized Captain Winterbottom is the epitome of the stiff British District Officer, who drinks brandy and ginger ale and dresses for dinner, and sees himself as the saviour of the people and the local chief.

Two of Achebe's noted fellow Igbo writers at this time were carried in a different direction by the winds of change. *One Man, One Matchet* by Timothy Aluko revisits the impact of Christianity and colonialism. Set in the cocoa producing area of **western Nigeria**, the book is full of fascinating local lore: 'Here he paused to sneeze, which earned him a murmur of congratulation from his chiefs. To sneeze is believed to be an operation for expelling evil through the nose and the mouth. A royal person doing this is therefore congratulated on getting through a successful operation.'

The intriguingly titled *Toads for Supper* by Chukwuemeka Ike is set, like many of his books, in one of the country's flourishing universities and takes us through the corridors, novelties and temptations of campus life. The hero, who finds himself simultaneously engaged to three girls, pays no heed to the advice proffered: 'My friend . . . you are

Chinua Achebe

a freshman. Like a chicken transported to a strange environment you should stand on one leg till you are sure of your ground.'

The real successor to the legacy and epic style of Achebe and Tutuola is Ben Okri, whose novel *The Famished Road* (Extract 7) took a languid literary world by surprise when it won the Booker Prize in 1991. When people suggested that you had to know about Africa to read it, Okri retorted with the quip that he had to sit at school in Nigeria reading Dickens and Jane Austen. 'I have this desire to abolish boundaries' declares Okri, whose book follows the journey of an *abiku* or spirit child whose fate it is to float between human and spirit form. Azaro chooses to abandon his spirit companions and join the road travelled in the human realm of suffering, hunger and pain. 'I was born not just because I had conceived a notion to stay, but because in my coming and going the great cycles of time had finally tightened around my neck. I prayed for laughter, a life without hunger. I was answered with paradoxes. It remains an enigma how it came to be that I was born smiling.' *Songs of Enchantment*, 1993, continues Azaro's story and has him re-affirming his commitment to mortal life – 'for the living life is a story and a song, but for the dead life is a dream.'

The title and symbolism of *The Famished Road* recall the words of Nigeria's foremost dramatist, essayist and Nobel Prize winner, Wole Soyinka ◊. In his poem 'Death in the Dawn' he writes 'Traveller, you must set out/At dawn. And wipe your feet upon/The dog-nose wetness of the earth . . ./And the mother prayed, Child/May you never walk/When the road waits, famished.' Soyinka is one of the most energetic and prolific of contemporary Nigerian writers. His work, which shows the influence of both traditional and European drama, spans centuries and blends social criticism with both comedy and sharp philosophical satire (Extract 13). The secret of Soyinka's success is his kaleidoscopic versatility, and his dexterity with prose that recollects the pace and pathos of both Yoruba oral legends and Shakespeare. *The Swamp Dwellers*, one of his early plays written just before independence, uses the metaphor of the rituals of the sinister **swamplands** to mirror the evils lurking in the burgeoning city of **Lagos**. As in many of his works, Soyinka is concerned with man's adaptability in the face of factors both within and outside his control. *The Lion and the Jewel*, set in a Yoruba village, is by contrast his lightest work. It takes a sharp dig at the pomposity of Westernized schoolteachers and has been described as delightfully amoral. *Opera Wonyosi* is the curiously successful and engaging transformation of Brecht's *Threepenny Opera* into a Nigerian setting.

While Soyinka dominated drama in the early years of independence, there were other important writers slowly gaining ground. One of these was John Pepper Clark, or John Pepper Clark-Bekederemo ◊ as he is known today. Clark's battle, as for many writers of his generation, was how to make the English language inhabit the indigenous imagination. His epic poetic drama *The Ozidi Saga* (Extract 4), about the myths of the Ijo people of the **Niger River delta**, took fifteen years to record and needs seven days to perform. He has received equally high acclaim for his pure poetry. *Casualties*, regarded as his finest poetic accomplishment, makes heavy reading and is entirely about the Biafran civil war; 'The casualties are not only those who escaping/The shattered shell become prisoners in/A fortress of falling walls . . .'.

Wole Soyinka

Following independence in 1960, the Biafran war, which fought itself out between 1967 and 1970, was the most influential and destructive force on Nigerian society and literature. Ostensibly a result of long-standing tribal rivalries, this bitter and bloody war of attrition started when the eastern region declared the independent Republic of Biafra. Claiming the lives of 100 000 soldiers, it was a war which no writer could disregard even if he were – as one critic (and poet) was said to have claimed of Clark – physically safely outside of the war zone at the time. Clark's collection includes an ode to Christopher Okigbo ◊, a close friend and fellow poet who died on the battlefront at **Nsukka** in 1967. Okigbo is to Biafra what Wilfred Owen was to the first world war. At the time of his death, he was generally considered to be Nigeria's finest modern poet and his loss symbolized the senseless destruction unleashed by war (Extract 9).

The ire that was unleashed during the war proved a genuine inspiration for many writers in their formative years at the time. For others it was, as one critic put it, 'on its way to becoming a mere literary cliché.' Poets, novelists and essayists poured out their memories, and their anger in considerable quantities and qualities. Novelist Elechi Amadi ◊, who was detained twice during the war and eventually joined the Federal Army, has written in semi-autobiographical fashion around his wartime experiences. His novel *Estrangement* (Extract 14) is set in the broken landscape of the aftermath of war. Permeated with a sad sense of relief, the bars and the towns are alive with people greeting each other with exclamations of 'happy survival'.

Ken Saro-Wiwa's novel about the Biafran war, *Sozaboy*, has been described by William Boyd (◊ Congo) as 'one of the great achievements of African literature'. A novelist, journalist and publisher, Sara-Wiwa is also known as the writer and producer of the immensely popular Nigerian television programme *Basi and Co.* He was imprisoned in1993, presumably because of his fierce campaigning for the rights of the Ogoni people, of whom he is one.

The story of the war from a woman's point of view is told by Flora Nwapa in *Never Again*. Nwapa says 'to a certain extent the civil war liberated women . . . it was hard for us to find food and useful materials, so the women would dress as Yorubas and go into the enemy villages to trade. It was us who found food for the men and kept the family going. We were the backbone of the war. And for some women, this was the start of a highly successful career in trading.' Nwapa is best known as the author of *Efuru*, the first novel to be published by a woman writer in Nigeria. In a softly-softly feminist style, she portrays the permanent social pressures on women to procreate and to be judged according to their ability to do so: in her novel *Idu* she writes 'What we are all praying for is children. What else do we want if we have children?' Nwapa herself has forged a formidable career and reputation in government ministries and owns her own publishing company. She has also written several children's books and short stories which she says 'aim to teach moral lessons'. Of her reputation as a feminist, she has said 'If you say you are a feminist in Nigeria you are asking for trouble . . . I write about what is rather than what ought to be, not what women should do but what they are. I'm not radical, just honest.'

A more dynamic and radical writer on the same theme is Buchi Emecheta ◊. Her sardonically entitled book *The Joys of Motherhood* (Extract 6) tells the tragic tale of 'Nnu Ego, who gave all her energy, all her money and everything she had to raise kids . . . She was so busy doing all this that she had no time to cultivate any friends among her own sex.' Plagued by lack of male offspring and the subsequent failure of her first marriage, the heroine Nnu Ego takes a second chance, and leaves her village for the city where awaits a slob of a second husband. Emecheta's pioneering handling of the subjects of migration, urbanization, and subtle repression of women gives us a bleak and touching autobiographical look at her life both in Nigeria and abroad. *In the Ditch* is, despite the terrible circumstances, a remarkably humorous account of the life of a single Nigerian woman and her children on a council block in the East End of London. She survived winters, racism and eventually found friendship – 'One of the methods she had found to be very helpful in securing friendship in England was to pretend to be stupid. You see, if you were black and stupid, you were conforming to what society expected of you.' In her foreword Emecheta says simply, 'everything in this book really happened'.

In this realm of a struggling social realism, Cyprian Ekwensi ◊ has done for the modern urban novel what Nwapa did for the feminist novel. While Nwapa's success opened the way for women writers such as Emecheta, playwright Zulu Sofolam, and more recently Zaynab Alkali from Muslim-dominated northern Nigeria, Ekwensi led the way into the licentious literary domain of urban decay and decadence. Ekwensi is a popular writer, who emerged from the vast stable of **Onitsha** market literature writers (see below). His novel *Jagua Nana* (Extract 5) is the racy and compassionate story of an ageing prostitute who hangs out in the Tropicana, a seedy club in **Lagos**. Called Jagua after the British car, she makes her money while 'courted' by rich businessmen, oil workers, and diplomats. It is the bright and sharp portrait of a woman who, like the city, is chaotic, losing her charms, seeking both intensity and the means to escape her fate. *Jagua Nana* is a striking evocation of the seedy, seamier side of life in a post-oil and independence boom town.

Among the new wave of modern writers are Biyi Bandele-Thomas ◊ (Extract 11) and Festus Iyayi who have taken up familiar themes with new energies. Iyayi's *Heroes* is set in Benin City back in 1969 and tells the story of a journalist who has to face up to the moral realities of the war: 'There are times, he thought, when tragedies not only bind us hand and foot but tie our tongues as well.' Since independence and the civil war, there has been an unprecedented loosening of literary tongues. The courage and energy that emerged brought women, sex, money and politics out of the moral closet. Today, at the cutting edge of African literature, Nigeria's writers are some of the most powerful and inspirational on the continent. Writing in *How to Be a Nigerian* in 1966, Enahoro said, 'In the beginning God created the universe. Then he created the moon, the stars and the wild beasts of the forests. On the sixth day he created the Nigerian. But on the seventh day while God rested, the Nigerian invented noise.' Perhaps he should have added, on the eighth day he invented the Nigerian writer.

MY SEVEN DAUGHTERS
ARE AFTER
YOUNG BOYS
(A CLASSICAL DRAMA)
FOR SCHOOLS & COLLEGES

A STORY ABOUT A MAN WHO MARRIED SO MANY WIVES

The seven Daughters *(Good for Nothing)*

This is the picture of a man who married many bad wives. This man does not rest in his house. Everyday his wives will fight him. Look at the man running and the wives pursue him with sticks and knife.

One wife means one trouble and two wives mean two troubles. This man bought troubles with his money. He thinks that he is very wise and rich. I am very sorry for him.

ONITSHA MARKET LITERATURE

Drunkards Believe Bar is Heaven, Beware of Harlots and Many Friends, Miss Cordelia in the Romance of Destiny – these are just some of the wonderful titles of the so-called 'Onitsha market literature' which sprang up in eastern Nigeria in the 1940s–60s. Not so much books as thin pamphlets, they are the Mills and Boon of West Africa. The phenomenon germinated up in the busy market trading town of **Onitsha** on the banks of the Niger, which as Chinua Achebe explains, 'had always attracted the exceptional, the colourful and the bizarre'. Old missionary presses were put to new ownership and uses, there was a constant traffic of different people, tribes and ideas through the large covered market, and growing demand from a rapidly expanding literate urban lower middle class. The writers themselves were mostly part-time amateurs – teachers, students and even pharmacists like Cyprian Ekwensi (the most famous author to emerge from this style) – who had a gift for story telling and a head full of a library of lively native oral literature. *How to Write Love Letters, How to Become Rich and Avoid Poverty, My Seven Young Daughters are After Young Boys* – the pamphlets offered every kind of practical advice, ready-made principles and moral checklists. It was a kind of free-for-all democratic form of literature that replaced the role of the *griot*. The pamphlets were cheap to produce, cheap to purchase, and there was a steady stream of would-be writers. No-one ever gained real fame or fortune out of such literature, and often the titles became more legendary than their authors. Pamphlets such as *Our Modern Ladies Characters Towards Boys* typically sold around 3000 to 4000 apiece, though *The Nigerian Bachelors Guide* sold an outstanding 40 000. This popular style spread rapidly, came to a standstill during the Biafran war, and currently enjoys modest success in the markets throughout southern Nigeria.

For further reading, see *Market Literature from Nigeria* (British Library) and E.N. Obiechina's *Onitsha Market Literature*.

LITERARY LANDMARKS

Abeokuta. Birthplace of Nobel Prize winner Wole Soyinka, and the setting for his *Aké: The Years of Childhood*. First founded as a homeland for freed Yoruba slaves.

Ibadan. In the 1950s the **University** was an important hatching ground for new young writers. Students and graduates including Wole Soyinka, John Pepper Clark and Christopher Okigbo all published their work in their student magazine *The Horn*. Here too was founded *Black Orpheus*, the famous literary periodical founded by two Germans and later edited by Soyinka. Named after Jean-Paul Sartre's preface to an anthology of French black poetry published by Senegal's Senghor, it developed into the influential Mbari Club and publishing house. Adewale Maja-Pearce describes a visit to the University in his autobiographical *In My Father's Country* (Extract 1).

Lagos. The British first seized **Lagos Island** in 1861 and it took a century before the country became independent again. Today the city of nearly 8 million people is one of the recurring festering sores in the urban novel. Lagos boasts a great **National Theatre** and the best English-language bookshops in West Africa.

Onitsha. Home of popular author Cyprian Ekwensi and hub of Nigeria's market literature.

Libraries and Bookshops

Ibadan. University of Ibadan bookshop and library, Oyo Road.

Lagos. Best Seller Bookshop, Falamo Shopping Centre; British Council Library, 54 Okunola Martins Close, Ikoyi; Eko Meridian Hotel Bookshop, Kuramo Waters; Federal Palace Hotel Bookshop, Ahmadou Bello Road; National Library, 4 Wesley Street; New World Bookshop, Tafawa Balewa Square; S.S. Bookshop, Broad Street.

BOOKLIST

The following selection includes the extracted titles in this chapter as well as those mentioned in the introduction which are available in English and other titles for further reading. In general, paperback editions are given when possible. The editions cited are not necessarily the only ones available. For most of the extracted works, the original publisher in English can be found in 'Acknowledgments and Citations' at the end of the volume, as can the exact location of the extracts and the editions from which they are taken. Extract numbers are highlighted in bold for ease of reference.

Achebe, Chinua, *The African Trilogy – Things Fall Apart*, **Extract 10**, *No Longer at Ease*, and *Arrow of God*, Pan, London, 1988.

Achebe, Chinua, *Anthills of the Savanna*, Heinemann, London, 1987.

Achebe, Chinua, *Beware, Soul Brother and Other Poems*, Heinemann, London, 1972.

Achebe, Chinua, *A Man of the People*, Heinemann, London, 1966.

Achebe, Chinua, *The Sacrificial Egg and Other Stories*, Etudo, Onitsha, 1962.

Achebe, Chinua, *The Trouble with Nigeria*, Heinemann, London, 1983.

Alkali, Zaynab, *The Stillborn*, Longman, Harlow, 1988.

Aluko, Timothy, *His Honourable Majesty*, Heinemann, London, 1973.

Aluko, Timothy, *One Man, One Matchet*, Heinemann, London, 1964.

Aluko, Timothy, *One Man, One Wife*, Heinemann, London, 1967.

Amadi, Elechi, *The Concubine*, Longman, Harlow, 1989.

Amadi, Elechi, *Estrangement*, Heinemann, London, 1986. **Extract 14.**

Amadi, Elechi, *The Great Ponds*, Heinemann, London, 1969.

Amadi, Elechi, *Sunset in Biafra*, Heinemann, London, 1973.

Bandele-Thomas, Biyi, *The Man who Came in from the Back of Beyond*, Bellew, London, 1991. **Extract 11.**

Clark-Bekederemo, John Pepper, *Casualties*, Longman, Harlow, 1970.

Clark-Bekederemo, John Pepper, *Collected Plays 1958–1988*, Howard University Press, Washington, DC, 1991. **Extract 4.**

Clark-Bekederemo, John Pepper, *A Decade of Tongues*, Longman, Harlow, 1981.

Clark-Bekederemo, John Pepper, *A Reed in the Tide*, Longman, London, 1965.

Ekwensi, Cyprian, *Jagua Nana*, Heinemann, Oxford, 1988. **Extract 5.**

Ekwensi, Cyprian, *Lokotown and Other Stories*, Heinemann, London, 1966.

Ekwensi, Cyprian, *Survive the Peace*, Heinemann, London, 1976.

Emecheta, Buchi, *The Bride Price*, Fontana, London, 1978.

Emecheta, Buchi, *Double Yoke*, Fontana, London, 1989.

Emecheta, Buchi, *Head Above Water*, Fontana, London, 1986.

Emecheta, Buchi, *In the Ditch*, Fontana, London, 1988.

Emecheta, Buchi, *The Joys of Motherhood*, Fontana, London, 1988. **Extract 6.**

Enahoro, Anthony, *How to Be a Nigerian*, quoted in *The Travellers' Dictionary of Quotation*, Peter Yapp, ed, Routledge, London, 1988.

Equiano, Olaudah, in *The Life of Olaudah Equiano*, Paul Edwards, ed, Longman, Harlow, 1988. **Extract 2**.

The Heinemann Book of African Poetry in English, selected by Adewale Maja-Pearce, Heinemann, Oxford, 1990.

Ike, Chukwuemeka, *The Bottled Leopard*, University of Ibadan Press, Ibadan, 1985.

Ike, Chukwuemeka, *The Naked Gods*, Harvill, London, 1970.

Ike, Chukwuemeka, *Our Children are Coming*, Spectrum, Ibadan, 1990.

Ike, Chukwuemeka, *Toads for Supper*, Harvill, London, 1965.

Iyayi, Festus, *Heroes*, Longman, Harlow, 1986.

Maja-Pearce, Adewale, *In My Father's Country: A Nigerian Journey*, Heinemann, London, 1987. **Extract 1**.

Market Literature from Nigeria, British Library, London, 1990.

Nwapa, Flora, *Efuru*, Heinemann, London, 1966.

Nwapa, Flora, *Idu*, Heinemann, London, 1969.

Nwapa, Flora, *Never Again*, Nwamife Publishing, Enugu, Nigeria, 1976.

Obiechina, E.N., *Onitsha Market Literature*, Heinemann, London, 1972.

Ofeimun, Odia, *The Poet Lied*, Longman, London, 1981. **Extract 8**.

Ofeimun, Odia, *Handle for the Flutist*, Update Communications, Lagos, 1986.

Okara, Gabriel, *The Fisherman's Invocation*, Heinemann, London, 1978.

Okara, Gabriel, *The Voice*, Heinemann, London, 1970. **Extract 3**.

Okigbo, Christopher, *Labyrinths with Path of Thunder*, Heinemann, London, 1971. **Extract 9**.

Okri, Ben, *The Famished Road*, Vintage, London, 1992. **Extract 7**.

Okri, Ben, *Flowers and Shadows*, Longman, Harlow, 1980.

Okri, Ben, *The Landscape Within*, Longman, Harlow, 1981.

Okri, Ben, *Songs of Enchantment*, Cape, London, 1993.

Saro-Wiwa, Ken, *Sozaboy: A Novel in Rotten English*, Saros International, Port Harcourt, 1985.

Soyinka, Wole, *Aké: The Years of Childhood*, Rex Collings, London, 1981.

Soyinka, Wole, *The Interpreters*, Heinemann, London, 1970.

Soyinka, Wole, *The Lion and the Jewel*, Oxford University Press, Oxford, 1963.

Soyinka, Wole, *Mandela's Earth and Other Poems*, Methuen, London, 1990.

Soyinka, Wole, *The Man Died*, Penguin, London, 1975.

Soyinka, Wole, *Six Plays* (including *Opera Wonyosi* and *Death and the King's Horseman*), Methuen, London, 1984. **Extract 13**.

Soyinka, Wole, *Three Short Plays* (*The Swamp Dwellers*, *The Trials of Brother Jero*, and *The Strong Breed*), Oxford University Press, Oxford, 1989.

Tutuola, Amos, *My life in the Bush of Ghosts*, Faber and Faber, London, 1990.

Tutuola, Amos, *The Palm-Wine Drinkard*, Faber and Faber, London, 1977. **Extract 12**.

Tutuola, Amos, *The Witch Herbalist of the Remote Town*, Faber and Faber, London, 1990.

Voices from Twentieth-Century Africa, Chinweizu, ed, Faber and Faber, London, 1988.

Extracts

(1) IBADAN

Adewale Maja-Pearce, *In My Father's Country*

Maja-Pearce's journey to discover his African roots contains many acute observations on Nigerian life. Here he recounts his experience at the hands of petty library officials at Ibadan University (which includes Wole Soyinka and Chinua Achebe among its alumni).

My initial impression was disappointing. The place looked a wreck. There were broken windows in the lecture halls, dirty marks on the walls and puddles of stagnant water in many of the buildings. There was also the problem of toilets. This was not unique to the university. It was a problem which was to plague me throughout my journey and eventually resulted in a severe case of constipation. Even though we were still in the rainy season – in many ways the best time to travel since it is also the coolest, with an average temperature of 75°F – there was no running water. All the toilets were blocked with dried shit and soiled newspaper. I did the best I could and then went to the library. It was nine o'clock. I envisaged a full day's work ahead of me. I should have known better. Life is never simple or straightforward in Nigeria, particularly when one is obliged to deal with officials.

Six men stood around the check-in counter, only one of whom could be said to be working. I ignored them and headed towards the periodicals' section. Before I got very far one of them hissed at me. There is nothing unusual in hissing. It is the way people attract each other's attention. But I have always found it disconcerting. It has a way of sounding both rude and menacing.

'What do you want?' he asked. I began to explain but he quickly cut me short.

'Go and wait there,' he ordered, pointing to a corner near the entrance. Ten minutes passed; fifteen minutes. The men continued chatting and laughing. I knew it would be a mistake to give in to my anger. They were simply doing what all officials do in Nigeria, which is to exploit to the limit whatever powers they possess. It wasn't personal, unless I made it so.

(2) Igboland

The Life of Olaudah Equiano

Born in ·'a charming fruitful vale named Essaka' Equiano described his region as 'one of the most remote and fertile . . . called Eboe'. At the time it was written, in the eighteenth century, the book was an important counter to the myths and lies perpetuated by Europeans about the lives and customs of the African people that were used to justify the slave trade.

As to religion, the natives believe that there is one Creator of all things, and that he lives in the sun, and is girted round with a belt that he may never eat or drink; but, according to some, he smokes a pipe, which is our own favourite luxury. They believe he governs events, especially our deaths or captivity; but, as for the doctrine of eternity, I do not remember to have ever heard of it: some however believe in the transmigration of souls in a certain degree. Those spirits, which are not transmigrated, such as our dear friends or relations, they believe always attend them, and guard them from the bad spirits or their foes. For this reason they always before eating, as I have observed, put some small portion of the meat, and pour some of their drink, on the ground for them; and they often make oblations of the blood of beasts or fowls at their graves . . .

We practised circumcision like the Jews, and made offerings and feasts on that occasion in the same manner as they did. Like them also, our children were named from some event, some circumstance, or fancied foreboding at the time of their birth. I was named *Olaudah*, which, in our language, signifies vicissitude or fortune also; one favoured, and having a loud voice and well spoken. I remember we never polluted the name of the object of our adoration; on the contrary, it was always mentioned with the greatest reverence; and we were totally unacquainted with swearing, and all these terms of abuse and reproach which find their way so readily and copiously into the languages of more civilised people. The only expressions of that kind I remember were 'May you rot, or may you swell, or may a beast take you.'

(3) IJAW

Gabriel Okara, *The Voice*

Okolo (his name means 'the voice') returns to his village in Ijaw country searching for 'it' or the meaning of life. Here he comes into conflict with the elders of the village who are suspicious about his questions and feel their traditional position and powers threatened.

'Your head is not correct!' Chief Izongo shouted at Okolo.

'Me, my head not correct?' Okolo said laughing in disbelief.

'I know that you do not agree as one that palmwine has held does not agree that palmwine has held him; or as one who sleeps at a meeting does not agree that he sleeps. So whether you agree or do not agree means nothing to me because one whose head is not correct never agrees that his head is not correct,' said Chief Izongo closing his mouth as if nothing would come out of it again.

'My head is as clear and cool like rain water,' said Okolo. 'So if you want me for another thing, say so without fear.'

'You think I fear?' Chief Izongo spoke, his inside smelling with anger 'I have given you plenty of time to come. If you waste more time wrestling with me with words I will burn the hut down.' . . .

The people snapped at him like hungry dogs snapping at bones. They carried him in silence like the silence of ants carrying a crumb of yam or fish bone. Then they put him down and dragged him past thatch houses that in the dark looked like pigs with their snouts in the ground; pushed and dragged him past mud walls with pitying eyes; pushed and dragged him past concrete walls with concrete eyes; pushed and dragged him along the waterside like soldier ants with their prisoner. They pushed and dragged him in panting silence, shuffling silence, broken only by an owl hooting from the darkness of the orange tree in front of Chief Izongo's house. Okolo became tired. His mouth opened slackly and his breath came out without reaching his chest. His feet belonged to him no longer. But his head was clear and his inside was unruffled like water in a glass. He spoke with his inside:

'I am moving round and round caught in a whirlpool of hate and greed and I smell the smell of hate in their sweat glistening on their backs . . .'

(4) Ijo

J.P. Clark-Bekederemo, *Ozidi*

This play is adapted from the epic tale of the Ijo area of the Niger delta, the author's birthplace. Temugedege, the mad brother of Ozidi, has just been appointed King by the Council state of Orua which includes Ofe the Short, Azezabife the Skeleton Man, Agobogidi the Nude and Oguaran the Giant. Five days into 'office' and his brother pays a visit and finds him talking merrily to himself.

Temugedege: Now am I king,
    King Temugedege of Orua, terror of all our
    Territories beyond these creeks and
    Keeper of our common store of wealth.
    That doesn't sound bad at all, no not at all.
    I Temugedege a king! No longer shall I be
    Harried to sea; no longer into the forest.
    Stacks of fish shall be brought to me daily; bundles of
    Fire-wood to keep the fire warming our backside
    Now I am king.
Ozidi: [*coming upon him.*] Temugedege, what are you doing with a
    chewing-stick in your mouth at this time of day?
Temugedege: [*starts but recovers himself quickly.*] You forget yourself,
    young man. I am
    King now, you know. So learn not to talk to me
    As you have done in the past. I am King
    Of Orua now.
        . . .
Temugedege: You wait and see. The Council of State
    Shall be dissolved forthwith by royal command.
    In place of those conspiratorial characters, I shall myself
    Select a caretaker committee of seven virgin girls who will
        whisper
    Appropriate words into our ears. Do you
    Hear that? One shall fetch me my royal chewing-stick, another
        my goblet
    Of morning glory, three shall pick the grey hair
    And lice on our sacred head, and any climbing up
    Our arm-pits; all this as we recline
    Basking in the evening glow of our life,
    Two shall pare our finger and toe nails, and one
    Shall scratch our tender back although we both know
    The itch in the flesh is far down elsewhere.

(5) LAGOS

Cyprian Ekwensi, *Jagua Nana*

Jagua's boyfriend Freddie wants to be a 'been-to'. As part of his preparations for his trip to England, he frequents the British Council and has taken Jagua along to a lecture there on the passing of British imperialism. Feeling overdressed and out of place she walks out and they make their way to the Tropicana night club instead.

Jagua was not listening. Looking up for a moment she saw in the rear-view mirror the angry eyes of Freddie. She knew he must be angrier than ever because he had failed again to drag her up into the society of the snobs. Instead she had won. She was pulling him down to the *Tropicana*, trying to teach him to relax. You die, you're dead, Jagua thought. It's over. You've left nothing, not a mark. Freddie always resisted her own philosophy but she would go on trying.

When the taxi passed over the bridge she barely glimpsed the half-naked fishermen in the canoes on the flat lagoon. They had their sails out, so she guessed they must be fishing. Now, these fishermen did not worry about lectures, Jagua thought; and they were happy. She loved this hour when the lights were coming up in the causeway: white and blue and orange lights and the hotels and coloured adverts ablaze but not yet effective in the pale twilight.

The taxi rattled over a level-crossing and pulled into the side of a road. She heard the trumpet shrieks from the *Tropicana* and felt genuinely elated. Jagua got out on the side of the road near the woman selling cooked yams. She stopped for a moment to straighten her dress, and the woman stopped blowing the fire and started looking at Jagua's sheath dress, painted lips and glossy hair.

'Heh! . . .' the yam seller burst out. 'One day ah will ride motor car and wear fine fine cloth . . .'

She said it aloud to Jagua's hearing and Jagua felt her ego pumping up. She pulled Freddie across the road to the little hatch of a door and they went inside. The *Tropicana* to her was a daily drug, a potent, habit-forming brew. Like all the other women who came here, alone or with some man, Jagua was looking for the ray of hope. Something will happen tonight, this night, she always told herself.

(6) Lagos

Buchi Emecheta, *The Joys of Motherhood*

It is the 1930s, and Nnu Ego from Ibuza in the heart of Iboland is forced to leave her first husband because they had no children. She lives in Lagos with her second husband who has just fathered their second child. The first one died mysteriously.

Nnaife, fully saturated with drink, announced to his friends that although their first baby was thrown into 'the bush' – the term for a burying place – this one, he was sure, was going to live and be a man. Most of the Ibos present agreed with him that the name Oshiaju, meaning 'the bush has refused this', was appropriate.

Though Nnaife was not skilled at speaking Yoruba, the language commonly used in Lagos, he had made a lot of palm-wine friends among the Yoruba people, and on that evening one of these friends said, 'You Ibos think you are the only ones with such names. We have our own version, and I will give it to the boy.' Suiting his actions to his words, he marched up to the mother and child, gave them two shillings and said, 'Your name is "Igbo ko yi", which also means "the bush has refused this".'

So weeks later when Nnu Ego sang and rocked her new child Oshia on her knees, she was more confident. The voices of all the people who knew them had said she deserved this child. The voices of the gods had said so too, as her father had confirmed to her in his messages. She might not have any money to supplement her husband's income, but were they not in a white man's world where it was the duty of the father to provide for his family? In Ibuza, women made a contribution, but in urban Lagos, men had to be the sole providers; this new setting robbed the woman of her useful role. Nnu Ego told herself that the life she had indulged in with the baby Ngozi had been very risky: she had been trying to be traditional in a modern urban setting. It was because she wanted to be a woman of Ibuza in a town like Lagos that she lost her child. This time she was going to play it according to the new rules.

(7) NIGERIA: ABIKU

Ben Okri, *The Famished Road*

*Azaro is one of the abiku or spirit children whose many lives flow
into each other and who float in a world without boundaries.
They do not look forward to being born into the world of the
living.*

Being born was a shock from which I never recovered. Often, by night
or day, voices spoke to me. I came to realise that they were the voices
of my spirit companions.
'What are you doing here?' one of them would ask.
'Living,' I would reply.
'Living for what?'
'I don't know.'
'Why don't you know? Haven't you seen what lies ahead of you?'
'No.'
Then they showed me images which I couldn't understand. They
showed me a prison, a woman covered with golden boils, a long road,
pitiless sunlight, a flood, an earthquake, death.
'Come back to us,' they said. 'We miss you by the river. You have
deserted us. If you don't come back we will make your life unbearable.'
I would start shouting, daring them to do their worst. On one of
these occasions Mum came into the room and stood watching me.
When I noticed her I became silent. Her eyes were bright. She came
over, hit me on the head, and said:
'Who are you talking to?'
'No one,' I replied.
She gave me a long stare. I don't remember how old I was at the
time. Afterwards my spirit companions took great delight getting me
into trouble. I often found myself oscillating between both worlds. One
day I was playing on the sand when they called me from across the road
with the voice of my mother. As I went towards the voice a car almost
ran me over. Another day they enticed me with sweet songs towards a
gutter. I fell in and no one noticed and it was only by good fortune that
a bicyclist saw me thrashing about in the filthy water and saved me
from drowning.
I was ill afterwards and spent most of the time in the other world
trying to reason with my spirit companions, trying to get them to leave
me alone. What I didn't know was that the longer they kept me there,
the more certain they were making my death. It was only much later,
when I tried to get back into my body and couldn't, that I realised they
had managed to shut me out of my life. I cried for a long time into the
silver void till our great king interceded for me and reopened the gates
of my body.

(8) NIGERIA: BIAFRAN WAR

Odia Ofeimun, The Poet Lied

In an attempt to set some kind of moral standard for the poets of post-war Nigeria, Ofeimun touches ironically on the privilege and ethics of the poet who claims, by virtue of his vocation, to feel and see more of what is happening around him. These lines are taken from The Heinemann Book of African Poetry in English – see Booklist.

He asked this much:
to be left alone
with his blank sheets on his lap
in some dug-out damp corner
with a view of the streets and the battlefields
watching the throng of calloused lives,
the many many lives stung by living.
He would put them into his fables
sandwich them between his lions and eagles,
between his elephants and crocodiles

Sometimes if he felt like it
he would come away from his corner
to take a closer look at things
fishermen in their canoes, hounded by tides,
swimmers drowning, hounded by tides
And he would take snapshots –
no need to caption them –
he would not mind at all
if he was called the poet of snapshots,
a quack of visions, a quack of visions.

(9) NIGERIA: BIAFRAN WAR

Christopher Okigbo, Hurrah for Thunder

Part of a series entitled Path of Thunder written shortly before the outbreak of the war, this poem was, like so many of Okigbo's verses, prophetic of war and his own fate. These lines from 'Hurrah for Thunder' are taken from The Heinemann Book of African Poetry in English – see Booklist.

Alas! the elephant has fallen –
Hurrah for thunder –

But already the hunters are talking about pumpkins:
If they share the meat let them remember thunder.

The eye that looks down will surely see the nose;
The finger that fits should be used to pick the nose.

Today – for tomorrow, today becomes yesterday:
How many million promises can ever fill a basket . . .

If I don't learn to shut my mouth I'll soon go to hell,
I, Okigbo, town-crier, together with my iron bell.

(10) NIGERIA: MISSIONARIES

Chinua Achebe, *Things Fall Apart*

*The missionaries have arrived in Nigeria. As they start to spread
out to the remoter villages on their quest, things begin to 'fall
apart' within the tribes.*

The missionaries spent their first four or five nights in the marketplace,
and went into the village in the morning to preach the gospel. They
asked who the king of the village was, but the villagers told them there
was no king. 'We have men of high title and the chief priests and the
elders,' they said.

It was not very easy getting the men of high title and the elders
together after the excitement of the first day. But the missionaries
persevered, and in the end they were received by the rulers of Mbanta.
They asked for a plot of land to build their church.

Every clan and village had its 'evil forest'. In it were buried all those
who died of the really evil diseases, like leprosy and smallpox. It was
also the dumping ground for the potent fetishes of great medicine-men
when they died. An 'evil forest' was, therefore, alive with sinister forces
and powers of darkness. It was such a forest that the rulers of Mbanta
gave to the missionaries. They did not really want them in their clan,
and so they made them that offer which nobody in his right senses
would accept.

'They want a piece of land to build their shrine,' said Uchendu to his
peers when they consulted among themselves. 'We shall give them a
piece of land.' He paused, and there was a murmur of surprise and
disagreement. 'Let us give them a portion of the Evil Forest. They boast
about victory over death. Let us give them a real battlefield in which to
show their victory.' They laughed and agreed, and sent for the
missionaries, whom they had asked to leave them for a while so that

they might 'whisper together.' They offered them as much of the Evil Forest as they cared to take. And to their greatest amazement the missionaries thanked them and burst into song.

'They do not understand,' said some of the elders. 'But they will understand when they go to their plot of land tomorrow morning.' And they dispersed.

The next morning the crazy men actually began to clear a part of the forest and to build their house. The inhabitants of Mbanta expected them all to be dead within four days. The first day passed and the second and third and fourth, and none of them died. Everyone was puzzled. And then it became known that the white man's fetish had unbelievable power. It was said that he wore glasses on his eyes so that he could see and talk to evil spirits. Not long after, he won his first three converts.

(11) NIGERIA: THIEVES

Biyi Bandele-Thomas,
The Man who Came in from the Back of Beyond

Between teaching literature and tending to two small pet sharks he keeps in an aquarium, schoolteacher Maude spins out fantastic tales about his previous life to Lakemf, one of his pupils. While sitting in his master's study, the gullible young boy is quickly drawn deep into the web of lies about his former occupations.

My eyes bulged out wide. 'A thief?'

'Yes, a thief. Nothing serious though. A purse here, a wallet there. The picking of pockets is not just a crime, you know. It is an art of precision, a science of calculating to the nearest zero. Take the man under whose tutelage I was; he could remove the socks on your feet and still leave you with your shoes on and you wouldn't know a thing had happened, let alone that someone had touched you. He was a master of the art. He used to say to us, "Patience, my boys, patience is the name of the game. Softly, softly." And he was an epitome of patience, believe me. I once followed him, watched him stalk a man on a train from Lagos to Port Harcourt. The trains were tortoises in those days. Five to six days it took between Lagos and Port Harcourt. And my master followed this Okrika businessman five nights and four days before, on the fifth night, as the locomotive head of the monstrous snake of the soot-covered train sputtered into Port Harcourt, he struck while the man, who had not dared sleep a wink throughout the journey, was piling his luggage together preparing to detrain. The coach, as all coaches on our trains are, was packed with human cargo.

One could hardly move. In fact I remember one portly gentleman clad in double-breasted, who bowed, rightly too I must say, and without shame, to the call of nature, right in the middle of a coach. He had unsuccessfully tried to get to the toilet for three days. The air in that coach was immediately fouled up of course. But the difference was not that noticeable. And come to think of it, you can't beat a train for fetor. It appeared to me that the most vile-smelling classes of humanity were mostly to be found on our trains. I was one of them.

(12) NIGERIA: UNDERWORLD

Amos Tutuola, *The Palm-Wine Drinkard*

Five months after leaving town, the palm-wine drinkard finds a man who knows where his dead palm-wine tapster is. First he must help him find his daughter, who has followed a handsome and expensively dressed man from the market. Twelve miles out of the village they enter an endless forest where curious creatures live, and she discovers the 'complete gentleman' is not as complete as he seemed . . .

When he reached where he hired the left foot, he pulled it out, he gave it to the owner and paid him, and they kept going; when they reached the place where he hired the right foot, he pulled it out and gave it to the owner and paid for the rentage. Now both feet had returned to the owners, so he began to crawl along on the ground, by that time, that lady wanted to go back to her town or her father, but the terrible and curious creature or the complete gentleman did not allow her to return . . .

When they went furthermore, then they reached where he hired the belly, ribs, chest etc, then he pulled them out and gave them to the owner and paid for the rentage.

Now to this gentleman or terrible creature remained only the head and both arms with neck, by that time he could not crawl as before but only went jumping on as a bull-frog and now this lady was soon faint for this fearful creature whom she was following. But when the lady saw every part of this complete gentleman in the market was spared or hired and he was returning them to the owners, then she began to try all her efforts to return to her father's town, but she was not allowed by this fearful creature at all.

When they reached where he hired both arms, he pulled them out and gave them to the owner, he paid for them; and they were still going on in this endless forest, they reached the place where he hired the neck, he pulled it out and gave it to the owner and paid for it as well.

'A FULL-BODIED GENTLEMAN
REDUCED TO HEAD'

Now this complete gentleman was reduced to head and when they reached where he hired the skin and flesh which covered the head, he returned them, and paid to the owner, now the complete gentleman in the market reduced to a 'SKULL' and this lady remained with only 'Skull'.

(13) Oyo

Wole Soyinka, *Death and the King's Horseman*

The king of the Yoruba city of Oyo has died. Elesin's fate, as his horseman, is to accompany his master to 'the other side'. Here the praise-singer is calling to him as he slips into a trance. Based on real events of 1946, the District Officer prevents Elesin's suicide.

Does the deep voice of *gbedu* cover you then, like the passage of royal elephants? Those drums that brook no rivals, have they blocked the passage to your ears that my voice passes into wind, a mere leaf floating in the night? Is your flesh lightened Elesin, is that lump of earth I slid between your slippers to keep you longer slowly sifting from your feet? Are the drums on the other side now tuning skin to skin with ours in *osugbo*? Are there sounds there I cannot hear, do footsteps surround you which pound the earth like *gbedu*, roll like thunder round the dome of the world? Is the darkness gathering in your head Elesin? Is there now a streak of light at the end of the passage, a light I dare not look upon? Does it reveal whose voices we often heard, whose touches we often felt, whose wisdoms come suddenly into the mind when the wisest have shaken their heads and murmured; It cannot be done? Elesin Alafin, don't think I do not know why your lips are heavy, why your limbs are drowsy as palm oil in the cold of harmattan. I would call you back but when the elephant heads for the jungle, the tail is too small a handhold for the hunter that would pull him back. The sun that heads for the sea no longer heeds the prayers of the farmer. When the river begins to taste the salt of the ocean, we no longer know what deity to call on, the river-god or Olokun. No arrow flies back to the string, the child does not return through the same passage that gave it birth. Elesin Oba, can you hear me at all? Your eyelids are glazed like a courtesan's, is it that you see the dark groom and master of life? And will you see my father? Will you tell him that I stayed with you to the last? Will my voice ring in your ears awhile, will you remember Olohun-iyo even if the music on the other side surpasses his mortal craft? But will they know you over there? Have they eyes to gauge your worth, have they the heart to love you, will they know what thoroughbred prances towards them in caparisons of honour? If they do not Elesin, if any there cuts your yam with a small knife, or pours you wine in a small calabash, turn back and return to welcoming hands. If the world were not greater than the wishes of Olohin-iyo, I would not let you go . . .

(14) PORT HARCOURT
Elechi Amadi, *Estrangement*

Ibekwe is just back from the Biafran war and is shocked to find his wife happily ensconced with another soldier. Angry and hurt, he wanders off into the Hotel de Aburi and finds himself caught up in the hubbub of people swapping stories of the war.

Ibekwe ordered a plate of *garri* and sat down on the bench on one side of the rough long table covered with a dirty blue plastic table cloth. Flies hovered incessantly. Yet there was a cosiness about the place in spite of the squalor, and a comforting comradeship among the customers that defied their grim poverty. Suddenly there was a burst of laughter. Ibekwe looked up.

A tall bearded man in a dirty badly sown white gown with a red sash was holding forth. His listeners called him professor.

'In Biafra, I was called father, not professor,' he said, 'and I will tell you how it happened. Every other day Biafran soldiers came on recruitment drives. Each time I ran away or hid in the ceiling under the bed or even under a heap of cassava.' The audience laughed. 'So I was, in fact, a prisoner. Sometimes I said, why not join and end this hide-and-seek business? My wife said no, they would kill me. So one day a friend gave me an idea. I collected all the money I had and made this long gown you see here and borrowed my wife's rosary and bible. My wife nearly died of laughter when she saw me in my priest's dress.' The audience roared 'Father! Father!' The professor made the sign of the cross. There was more laughter. 'The next day the recruitment team came. I came out boldly – but brother, my heart was beating – I said: "*Pax vobiscum*" and made the sign of the cross. The Biafran soldiers greeted me as Father, and asked for a blessing. Wonders will never end!' Another roar of laughter. 'They knelt down and I prayed for them, for Ojukwu, for Nzeogwu, for anyone I could think of. After that I joined the welfare people, but my eyes were on the food distribution centres. In the end I was asked to work in one of them. I made sure I did not come within a mile of any real Catholic priest. Brothers, I did not lack food after that. That is how I survived.'

Biographies and important works

ACHEBE, Chinua (1930–). Generally regarded as the godfather of the modern African novel, Achebe is one of the first names to trip off European tongues when discussing African literature. He grew up in the village of **Ogidi** in **Igboland** where his grandfather and father were among the first men in Nigeria to convert to Christianity. After winning a scholarship, Achebe studied literature at the **University of Ibadan**, from which he was one of the first graduates. In 1961 he took up what he describes, in a characteristically modest way, as 'the rather important position of Director of External Broadcasting'. When the Biafran war broke out, Achebe was working in **Lagos** and was forced to leave as the result of his satirical *A Man of the People*, 1966, an exposé of a corrupt and all too recognizable government. He narrowly escaped when a call warned him that soldiers were looking to test 'which was stronger, my pen or their gun'. In 1972, he was appointed to the Literature Department at the University of Massachusetts and subsequently to the **University of Nsukka**, Nigeria. His three classic novels *Things Fall Apart*, 1958 (Extract 10), *No Longer at Ease*, 1960, and *Arrow of God*, 1964, form a trilogy that chronicles three generations of Nigerian history and culture – from the traditional environment of his early childhood, through colonialism, and into post-independence. Following the Biafran conflict – during which he took up the cause working for the Biafran government – Achebe's work, as ever, moved with the times, and progressed with the politics. *Anthills of the Savanna*, 1987, is set in an anonymous West African country two years after a military coup. The relationship between the dictator and his old friends from the Ministry of Information and a poet and editor of a national paper, are strained. Their days are good or bad depending on which side of the bed his Excellency got out of – 'On a bad day . . . keep your mouth shut, for nothing is safe, not even the flattery we have become such experts in disguising as debate.' Achebe has also published children's books, short stories, critical essays and poems. Following a recent car accident, he spends most of his time in his homeland.

AMADI, Elechi (1934–). Born in **Aluu** near **Port Harcourt**, Amadi graduated from **University College Ibadan** with a degree in mathematics and physics. He has been a land surveyor, a teacher, a fighter in the Nigerian Army, and more recently has worked in the Ministry of Education. *The Concubine*, his first novel, is rooted in the rural lives of the people in the **Niger delta** area. It was hailed by critics as 'a novel of classic simplicity'. Amadi's direct and unpretentious style continued to impress in *The Great Ponds* and *Sunset in Biafra*, which reveal his experiences during the Biafran civil war. *Estrangement* (Extract 14), published in 1986, deals with the aftermath of the war. During the 1970s Amadi also published several plays.

BANDELE-THOMAS, Biyi (1967–). Bandele-Thomas is a novelist, poet and playwright. His first novel, *The*

Man who Came in from the Back of Beyond (Extract 11) was published in 1991. Set in the northern town of **Kaduna**, it tells of the strange relationship between a maverick secondary school teacher and one of his boys to whom he tells one very long and tall tale (or what the boy terms an 'aprilphoolologism'). The teacher excuses his monstrous lies to the boy by claiming, 'You caused it with your insatiable appetite for sensationalism, your *Lagos Weekend* mentality. If I may call it that.' The poems of Biyi Bandele-Thomas have already been widely anthologized and published in several literary magazines.

CLARK-BEKEDEREMO, John Pepper (1935–). A poet and playwright, Clark-Bekederemo was born in **Kiagbodo** in the Ijo region of the Niger delta which features in *The Ozidi Saga*. As well as drawing on his native traditions, he was influenced by Greek tragedy and Elizabethan and Brechtian drama while a student of English literature at the **University of Ibadan**. He edited the student literary magazine *The Horn* here in 1957–58. While critics are divided about his work, it has undoubtedly had an impact on his contemporaries. *A Reed in the Tide* was his second volume of poetry, and said to be the first by a single African poet to be published internationally (rather than in an anthology). Clark-Bekederemo's essays focus on the use of language and the influence of the English education system in Nigeria. As well as teaching at the **University of Lagos**, he is involved with a theatre company there. His plays were first produced by Wole Soyinka ◊.

EKWENSI, Cyprian (1921–). Ekwensi is an Igbo, born in **Minna**, and educated in Nigeria, Ghana and

Cyprian Ekwensi

London. He worked as a forestry officer and teacher, and then discovered broadcasting, journalism and writing. Since 1957 he has been Head of Features at the Nigerian Broadcasting Corporation, a position which inspired his novel *Survive the Peace*, about a radio journalist for Biafra. Coming out of the tradition of Onitsha market literature, he unashamedly declares himself as a writer for the masses, a man of the people, and admits to no pretensions: 'I don't regard myself as one of the sacred writers writing for some audience locked up in the higher seats of learning.' After the war, during which he campaigned for the Biafran cause, he opened a pharmacy and declared he was 'happy to be a Nigerian again'. In 1981, Ekwensi, who has written for several newspapers, was appointed Managing Director for a new paper, *The Weekly Eagle*, in **Imo** state.

Throughout his extraordinarily varied career, he has continued to write – by popular demand – and is one of Nigeria's most prolific authors. His best tackled themes relate to urban life and his novels are written in a natural and popular style that has attracted more fans than critics. *Lokotown and Other Stories* is a sweep through the seductions and sleaze of **Lagos** life. An early edition of his most popular work, *Jagua Nana* (Extract 5), was subtitled *The Earthy Novel of a Calculating Seductress*. The most recent edition is more modestly subtitled *A Brilliant Evocation of Modern Lagos*.

EMECHETA, Buchi (1944–). Born into an Ibuza family in **Lagos**, Emecheta was married early and she had a child by the age of seventeen. In 1962 she came to London with her five children and her husband. After leaving her husband she read sociology at London University, struggled hard to bring up her children, and started to write at night. She worked as a teacher, a librarian and a community worker, until her unswaying determination to have her work read and published reaped results. Of her novels, *The Bride Price*, 1978, is perhaps her best known work, and concerns a fifteen-year-old girl who is set to be married-off by her greedy uncle for a high bride price, but she defies tradition by falling in love. Among her other works is *The Joys of Motherhood* (Extract 6), a tragic story of unhappy marriage and a woman who devotes all her personal and material resources to bringing up children. *Head Above Water*, her 'real' autobiography, was published in 1986. In 1980 Emecheta was appointed Senior Research Fellow in the Department of English and Literary Studies at the **University of Calabar**, Nigeria. However she left this post because of 'frustration with Nigerian society,

Buchi Emecheta

[and] the chauvinism of the men'. She has won several literary prizes, and, while her works tend to receive mixed reviews, she has most significantly helped to redress the balance of a male-dominated Nigerian literary scene, and given hope to many women writers and readers there.

EQUIANO, Olaudah (c1745–1797). Born in eastern Nigeria to a chief, Equiano was sold as a slave to an English naval officer while still a small boy. The officer, as was the custom of the time, gave him the name of a European hero, Gustavus Vassa. Equiano, who had hitherto never seen or even heard of the sea, became a skilled sailor, gained the respect of his employees, and eventually managed to buy his freedom. He travelled widely, from Britain to the Arctic, and worked variously as a gentleman's valet in the Mediterranean and an assistant doctor while among the Miskito Indians of Central America. The published story of his extraordinary life (Extract 2) was hailed in 1791 as 'a principal instrument in bringing about the motion for the repeal of the Slave-act'.

MAJA-PEARCE, Adewale (1953–). Maja-Pearce was born in London, the son of a Nigerian father and English mother. He grew up in **Lagos**, but returned to London to complete his education (he obtained a degree at the School of Oriental and African Studies). He has published a volume of short stories entitled *Loyalties*, 1987, and the travelogue *In My Father's Country*, 1987 (Extract 1), which recounts in perceptive and entertaining detail a personal odyssey back to Nigeria. More recent works include *How Many Miles to Babylon?*, 1990, and *Who's Afraid of Wole Soyinka?*, 1991. Maja-Pearce is active in the literary publishing world in the UK, specializing in African poetry and prose. His positions include Africa Editor of the journal *Index on Censorship*, and Series Editor of the path-breaking Heinemann African Writers Series. In the latter capacity he compiled the 1990 anthology *The Heinemann Book of African Poetry in English*.

Adewale Maja-Pearce

OFEIMUN, Odia (1950–). Born in mid-western Nigeria, Ofeimun studied at **Ibadan University**, and took up political service in 1979. His first collection, *The Poet Lied* (Extract 8), was published in 1980, and became famous when fellow poet J.P. Clark-Bekederemo threatened to sue him for libel. Clark believed the title poem, an ironic attack on the righteousness and morality of those who fought the civil war with pen in hand, to be about him. The book was eventually re-issued and Ofeimun's second collection, *Handle for the Flutist*, sold out immediately in Nigeria. He is on the Editorial Board of the *Lagos Guardian* and General Secretary of the Association of Nigerian Authors.

OKARA, Gabriel (1921–). Often described as a 'natural' poet, Okara was born in the **Ijaw** country of the Niger delta. The son of a chief, his creative talents were first expressed in painting. He later studied bookbinding, and it was from this profession that Okara moved into the publishing business and thence to the civil service. He studied journalism in the USA, and during the civil war was an active supporter of Biafra, touring America with Achebe in 1969 to promote the cause. Following the war he founded and edited *The Nigerian Tide*, a local government newspaper. Okara's poems were originally published in the magazine *Black Orpheus*. His collection *The Fisherman's Invocation* won him the Commonwealth Poetry Prize. He is best known for *The Voice* (Extract 3), with its unorthodox and poetic use of the colonial language combined with African philosophy, folklore and imagery.

OKIGBO, Christopher (1932–1967). Born in **Ojoto** in eastern Nigeria,

Okigbo studied at the **University of Ibadan**, where he was apparently more interested in jazz than Classics. While he was at university, his work was published in the magazines *The Horn* and *Black Orpheus*. He later became a librarian at the **University of Nsukka** and was a member of the famous Mbari literary club. Okigbo died at the age of 34 while serving as a major in the Biafran army during the civil war. He was killed in one of the first battles of the war. His work owes much to the oral tradition of his Igbo people and, among others, Keats and Eliot. Since his death he has been admired by many Nigerian poets. *Labyrinths with Path of Thunder* was published posthumously and brings together in one volume his collections of poetry.

OKRI, Ben (1959–). When Okri was still a baby his family moved from his birthplace, **Minna**, to London where his father studied law. He returned reluctantly to Nigeria at the age of seven – 'My mates told me that in Africa people lived in trees and lions walked about so I told my mum I was going to stay in south London with my comics.' Schooling in Nigeria was sporadic, while Okri's father worked as a poor man's lawyer. Okri wrote his first novel, *Flowers and Shadows*, about the corrupt business world of **Lagos**, while he was still a teenager. When it was published, all the elders of his village clubbed together to buy him a pen. His second novel, *The Landscapes Within*, about a suffering artist, was published shortly afterwards, while he was a literature student at the University of Essex. Despite his early success, Okri could not afford to complete his degree and he spent the early 1980s sleeping rough and writing. Since winning the Booker Prize in 1991 with *The Famished Road* (Extract 7) he has been

writer in residence at the University of Cambridge. In 1993, Okri published *Songs of Enchantment*, a sequel to *The Famished Road*.

SOYINKA, Wole (1934–). Soyinka was born in **Abeokuta** and educated at **University College Ibadan** and the University of Leeds. While writing, he has taught drama and literature at several universities, both in Nigeria and abroad. Returning from England, where he spent time as play reader at the Royal Court Theatre in London, and saw several of his plays staged there, Soyinka founded a national theatre group and has since been a driving force in the development and production of theatre in Nigeria. His plays have been performed in his native Yoruba and in English, and Soyinka has also acted in, directed and produced them. *The Interpreters*, 1965, was Soyinka's first novel. It is the story of a group of young **Lagos** intellectuals who meet regularly, get drunk and try to 'interpret' their experiences, disorderly lives and surroundings. Soyinka has written two autobiographical works, *Aké: The Years of Childhood* and *The Man Died: Prison Notes*. The latter is the story of his arrest at the beginning of the civil war, when he was accused of backing the Biafrans, and his detention from 1967 to 1969. When he received the Nobel Prize for Literature in 1986, he was the first African writer to have done so.

TUTUOLA, Amos (1922–). Tutuola is a Yoruba and a native of **Abeokuta**, a large town in western Nigeria. Son of a Christian cocoa farmer, educated in mission schools, he was eventually forced to abandon his highly successful studies because of lack of family funds. He took up farming, worked as a blacksmith, and joined the RAF.

Ben Okri

The idea for the story of *The Palm-Wine Drinkard* (Extract 12) came to him while working in the Department of Labour in **Lagos**. With his talent for story-telling, he wrote the book within a few days, submitted it to The United Society for Christian Literature, who passed the manuscript to Faber and Faber. In his later books, Tutuola continues the themes from oral tradition, of what happens when a mortal strays into the world of ghosts. In *My Life in the Bush of Ghosts*, the hero spends 24 years in a ghost land inhabited by 'smelling ghost', 'homeless ghost', and even the 'Television-handed ghostess'. The mythological tenants of *The Witch Herbalist of the Remote Town*, 1990, are equally weird and wonderful, and include the Abnormal Squatting Man of the Jungle.

SENEGAL

> 'Négritude is the awareness, defence and development of African Cultural Values . . . In works of art, . . . it is sense of image and rhythm, sense of symbol and beauty.'
> *Léopold Sédar Senghor*

Senegal is unique in Africa for the fact that its main literary figure was also the founding father of the nation. Léopold Sédar Senghor ◊ is known the world over for his poetry, his philosophies, and his statesmanship. Senghor had already established a high political and literary profile outside Senegal when in 1960 he became the country's first President. This was the year when Senegal finally gained independence from France – the French had established a presence here as early as 1658 and ratified their claim in 1885.

What first brought Senghor onto the stage of world politics and literature was his vocalization of the concept of *Négritude*, which emerged from a group of African and Caribbean students living in Paris in the early 1930s. *Négritude* was in essence a reaction against colonialism and the French policy of assimilation that prevailed at the time, and was summed up by Senghor as 'the sum total of the values of the civilization of the African world'. For a long time, the term *Négritude* inspired many writers and students, particularly those writing in French. It spoke for the growing movement towards independence in the 1950s, and became a buzzword with which to categorize the consequent emerging African literature. Today *Négritude* is often criticized by the younger generation of black intellectuals as romanticizing Africa. Like all neologisms, it was in itself something of a myth, though in Senghor's words, a 'true myth'.

The impetus and energy created by this movement was to give the greatest ever stimulus to Black African writing, the publishing house and literary magazine, *Présence Africaine*. Launched in Paris in 1947 by a compatriot of Senghor, Alioune Diop, it published the work of many promising young writers and poets, such as David Diop ◊ (Extract 5), and in doing so attracted the attention and support of many African

---

FACT BOX

AREA: 196 720 sq km
POPULATION: 7 600 000
CAPITAL: Dakar
LANGUAGES: French, Wolof, Peul, Serer, Tukulov, Malinké
FORMER COLONIAL POWER: France
INDEPENDENCE: 1960

---

and European writers and intellectuals, including Jean-Paul Sartre, André Gide and Albert Camus.

Naturally *Présence Africaine* published much of Senghor's work over the years, including his essays setting out his concept of *Négritude* and his poetry. His poems, like his philosophies, are born out of optimism, humanism, and a deep love for his motherland. They are a rich and rhapsodic expression of his feelings, and to read them is to understand both why *Négritude* was so influential, and why it is so often criticized today. His collection *Éthiopiques* (Extract 6) was written at the height of his powers as a poet and during the peak of his success as a politician. Politically, the country fared better under Senghor's moderate version of socialism than many of its neighbours. Senghor remained President until 1981, and when he handed over power to his Vice-President, Abdou Diouf, he was celebrated as the first African President to ever retire voluntarily!

Unlike Senghor, who was born into a Catholic family, Diouf is from the Wolof, the dominant tribe in Senegal. The majority of Wolof were converted to Islam in the eighteenth century, when Muslim marabouts overthrew the local dynasty, planted a number of zealous fundamentalist missionaries and sponsored *jihads*. Consequently Wolof, the largest language group, was first written in Arabic script and much of this early literature is religious. The Arabic script also served over the centuries to transcribe and record the ancient oral literature. These tales and 'virtual' histories, which were traditionally told by *griots*, today are enjoying something of a revival in the written form.

Birago Diop ◊ is one of a number of twentieth century Senegalese authors to draw on the rich well of oral literature. Primarily a poet and short story writer, Diop, who lived for a long time in Paris, collected oral literature from the Wolof tradition to bring it both to the French public and to Africans living abroad (Extract 1).

Unfortunately, neither the Francophone literature nor that of the many indigenous languages has been extensively translated into English. *Karim*, which was published in 1935, was one of the earliest Senegalese novels to appear in French. Written by Ousmane Socé ◊, it is an observant and evocative tale of a young man drawn by the bright lights to the city of **Dakar** (Extract 2).

The hero of poet Malick Fall's ◊ sardonic novel *The Wound* meets an even more unpleasant fate on his way to the metropolis. Injured in a lorry crash, his festering wounds result in his treatment as a madman (Extract 3).

Sembène Ousmane ◊ is Senegal's foremost author and film-maker. Renowned for his sharp character analysis and social commentary, Ousmane turned to his other talent – film-making – in his quest to disseminate his message to a wider (and non-literate) audience. Ousmane, whose work aims to provide both a mirror and motivator for change, has of necessity always been controversial. *Xala*, meaning 'temporary sexual impotence' in Wolof, was a film and novel produced in 1973, which exposed the privileged class of Senegal. The film was cut without his permission before it was shown in Senegal, and many of his subsequent films have been banned or heavily censored. His books, which reach a smaller audience, have therefore not been subjected to the same degree of censorship, though they are no less political, and have sold well throughout Francophone Africa. His third and best novel, *God's Bits of Wood*, relates the story of the 1947 Dakar–Niger railroad strike in which the author had participated (Extract 7). The title refers to a local superstition that if people are counted their lives are shortened – therefore when looking at the numbers of strike supporters, for example, pieces of wood are counted in place of people.

A tale of a very different strike is *The Beggar's Strike* (Extract 4) by Aminata Sow-Fall. Inspired by a group of beggars Sow-Fall witnessed on the streets of **Dakar** fighting over food they had been given, her prize-winning novel examines the morality and altruism behind 'giving'. In *The Beggar's Strike*, an official clears the streets of 'human flotsam' in order to gain promotion. Almsgiving is a local custom here, and when he suddenly finds himself in need of the beggars in order to carry out a sacrifice, he discovers much to his horror they have gone on strike in protest at their treatment.

Women novelists are something of a rarity in Muslim-dominated countries, but one of the most important writers to emerge from Senegal is Mariama Bâ ◊. When Bâ died tragically in 1981 following a long illness, she had written only two novels, both of which have been translated from the French. Her unforgettable first novel, *So Long a Letter (Une Si Longue Lettre)*, is a semi-autobiographical portrait, taking the form of a letter from Ramatoulaye, a Muslim woman, to her best friend. Ramatoulaye candidly reveals the hurt she feels when her husband takes one of her daughter's friends for a second wife (Extract 8). The picture she paints is of the painful struggle to come to terms with this 'legitimate' betrayal, and the struggle of women fighting for

Mariama Bâ

education and opportunity within the traditions and constraints of a Muslim community – 'Because, being the first pioneers of the promotion of African women, there were very few of us. Men could call us scatter-brained. Others labelled us devils. But many wanted to possess us.'

The power and influence of Bâ's writing lies in its accessible style and the careful politicization of women's issues which aims both to make women aware of their inferior status and give them fuel for change. At the same time she is aware of the resistance to change, the danger of alienation from a potential male audience, and of the 'privilege of our generation to be the link between two periods in history, one of domination, the other of independence.'

Bâ is undoubtedly one of the great inspirations in African women's literature. As a former schoolteacher she is emphatic about the role of education in a society in which tradition serves to discriminate against women attending school for longer than is absolutely necessary. As the heroine of *So Long a Letter* recalls, 'To lift us out of the bog of tradition, superstition and custom, to make us appreciate a multitude of civilisations without renouncing our own, to raise our vision of the world, cultivate our personalities, strengthen our qualities, to make up for our inadequacies, to develop universal moral values in us; these were the aims of our admirable headmistress.'

LITERARY LANDMARKS

Dakar. Leaving Dakar along the **corniches**, the dramatic cliff roads, provides a respite from the stifling city, with beautiful beaches and picturesque views. Mariama Bâ remembers the **Dakar Corniche** in *So Long a Letter* as 'a sheer work of art wrought by nature. Rounded or pointed rocks, black or ochre coloured, overlooking the ocean. Greenery sometimes a veritable hanging garden spread out under the clear sky.' The legend of the formation of **Les Mamelles**, the two distinctive hills at **Alamadies Point** is retold by Birago Diop (Extract 1). The World Black Arts Festival in Dakar in 1966 placed Senegal at the centre of the cultural African map.

Joal. On the scenic **Petite Côte**, and birthplace of Léopold Senghor.

Gorée. Occupied variously by the Portuguese and the French who built warehouses for goods, Gorée in fact became famous as a slave depot. The **Maison des Esclaves** (the Slave House) still houses the small cells, chains and shackles.

St Louis. Third largest city at the mouth of the Senegal River, founded on an island by French colonists. Used as a base by explorers such as René Caillé. The suburb of **N'Dar Tout** features in Malick Fall's *The Wound*. Birthplace of Aminata Sow-Fall and Ousmane Socé.

Thiès. Major railhead and one of Senegal's most ancient cities.

Libraries and Bookshops

Senegal apparently has the most active library scene in the whole of Francophone Africa.

Dakar. Alliance Française Library; American Cultural Centre, Place de l'Indépendence; British Senegalese Institute, 18 Rue de 18 Juin; Cultural University Library; Libraire Clairafrique, Place de l'Indépendence; Libraire Sankore, 25 Ave William Ponty.

St Louis. Centre Recherches et Documentation du Sénégal.

BOOKLIST

The following selection includes the extracted titles in this chapter as well as those mentioned in the introduction which are available in English and other titles for further reading. In general, paperback editions are given when possible. The editions cited are not necessarily the only ones available. For most of the extracted works, the original publisher in English can be found in 'Acknowledgments and Citations' at the end of the volume, as can the exact location of the extracts and the editions from which they are taken. Extract numbers are highlighted in bold.

Bâ, Mariama, *So Long a Letter*, Virago, London, 1982. **Extract 8.**

Diop, Birago, *Tales of Amadou Koumba*, D.S. Blair, trans, Oxford University Press, London, 1966.

Diop, David, *Hammer Blows*, Heinemann, London, 1975.

Diop, David, 'Sell-Out', John Reed and Clive Wake, trans, in *Poems of Black Africa*, Wole Soyinka, ed, Heinemann, Oxford, 1987. **Extract 5.**

Fall, Malick, *The Wound*, Heinemann, 1973. **Extract 3.**

The Gambia and Senegal, Insight Guides, APA Publications, London, 1990. **Extract 1.**

Ousmane, Sembène, *Black Docker*, Heinemann, Oxford, 1987.

Ousmane, Sembène, *God's Bits of Wood*, Francis Price, trans, Heinemann, Oxford, 1986. **Extract 7.**

Ousmane, Sembène, *Xala*, C. Wake, trans, Heinemann, London, 1976.

Senghor, Léopold Sédar, *Prose and Poetry*, John Reed and Clive Wake, trans, Heinemann, London, 1976. **Extract 6.**

Senghor, Léopold Sédar, *Selected Poems*, C. Williamson, trans, Rex Collings Publishers, London, 1976.

Socé, Ousmane, *Karim*, in *African Writing Today*, Ezekiel Mphahlele, ed, Penguin, London, 1967. **Extract 2.**

Sow-Fall, Aminata, *The Beggar's Strike*, D.S. Blair, trans, Longman, Harlow, 1986. **Extract 4.**

Extracts

(1) DAKAR

Birago Diop

*Recounting traditional oral tales, Diop explains how Les Mamel-
les, the two hills at Almadies Point on the Dakar peninsular,
originated. This passage is quoted in the Insight Guide to The
Gambia and Senegal – see Booklist.*

There once was a peasant named Momar who had two hunchbacked
wives. Khary, his first wife, had a very tiny hunchback, which made
her envious of all normal women. Koumba, his second wife, was badly
deformed, but her heart was warm and open to everyone. Unfortunately, Khary was not touched by Koumba's pleasant nature and never
forgave her for being reconciled to her deformity.

One day, Momar and Koumba were sleeping under a tamarind tree
which was frequented by genies. An old woman appeared to Koumba
and showed her a trick that would unburden her of her great hunchback
on to a genie. As soon as Khary saw what had happened to her rival,
she pestered Koumba to learn the secret, which she at once set to use.
Alas, the genie was delighted to find someone on whom to unload the
heavy burden she had acquired and she placed on Khary's back
Koumba's hump. Khary in desperation threw herself into the sea. But
the sea could not completely cover her and poor Khary's two humps
surfaced alongside Cap-Vert. These humps are what we call the
Mamelles.

(2) DAKAR

Ousmane Socé, *Karim*

*Karim is drawn to the bright lights of Dakar, and spends an
evening at a ball in pursuit of a young girl.*

Four o'clock in the morning.

The same feverish atmosphere still reigned in the room, the same
thirst for pleasure.

Excitement was growing like a river swollen by torrential rain. The
dancers were flinging themselves about more and more.

They were tired of Latin emotionalism, so the orchestra started
playing tunes of their own country, *goumbés*. The couples had broken
up and everyone was dancing by himself . . .

'Hi, Papa Charles,
The *goumbé* is the devil!
Old men, come and try it.
The *goumbé* is the devil!

The accordion led the music, accompanied by the banjo and the mandolin. A jazz tom-tom rhythm was beaten out on tambourines, the *assicots*, while keys were knocked against empty bottles and pebbles rattled in tin cans.

'Oh, what times we live in!
The men are bad today.
They have a wife and children
And a mistress tucked away . . .'

The women formed an inner circle, standing shoulder to shoulder. They moved in a nimble, jigging round, the men dancing on the outside and answering their satirical song with another:

'Oh, what times we live in!
The girls are bad today.
They have a man and children
And a lover tucked away . . .'

The more they jigged about, the more they needed to jig about, each man following his partner's twitching rump.

(3) Gaya

Malick Fall, *The Wound*

Like many of his generation, Magamou wants to migrate from his small village to the bright lights of N'Dar, a suburb of Saint-Louis. His mother warns him against the folly of such a decision.

'Don't go to N'Dar, my son. Don't ever go to the town.'
As she spoke, Yaye Aida knotted, for the third time, the shabby cloth that covered her to the waist.
'I must go to the town, Yaye,' the young man insisted.
'Think, what have the men who have gone to the town ever brought back for us from N'Dar, N'Dakaru or Thiès-Diankhene? Nothing but misery, terrible misery.'
Magamou was only half listening to her.
'But, mother, what about all those trunks full of clothes, all those baskets packed with strange things to eat, and those metal beds, those tables. No, mother, I will go to the town.'

'That magic harvest has made you take leave of your senses. It has put the clan at sixes and sevens, and made your imagination sick. It has ruined us, don't you see? Ruined us!'

Beside herself with desperation, Yaye Aida held her son's hands in hers as she tried to make him understand how the false wealth of the towns had undermined the life of the tribe and insidiously drawn its members away from the simplicity of their customs and moderation of their needs. Old Aida talked and talked, using every argument she could think of to try and convince her obstinate son of his folly. He pretended to be listening attentively, but in his imagination he was already watching the town traffic speeding by.

(4) Senegal: Beggars

Aminata Sow-Fall, *The Beggar's Strike*

After clearing his town's streets of 'human flotsam', the Director of Public Health and Hygiene suddenly finds he is in need of their services and instructs his assistant to bring them back.

'Yes . . . yes. But Keba, I must tell you . . . I need these beggars today. I need them . . . I've got to distribute a sacrifice among them. I need them to go back to their vantage points for one day, for one day only . . . It won't even be for one day, only for a few hours!

Keba, completely nonplussed, slightly loosened his tie to give himself time to think; he felt himself growing hot all over and his head began to swim. He had difficulty in getting his breath. In a timid, almost inaudible voice, he asked Mour, 'You want the beggars back in the City? . . . Is that what you're saying?'

'Yes, for a very personal reason . . . I'd like you to go to see them with a few members of the former clearance squads to give them confidence and to persuade them to come back on the streets for a few hours. Tell them they risk nothing, absolutely nothing!'

Keba did not reply immediately. He lowered his eyes to his note-book for a few minutes during which Mour watched the vein which stood out on the forehead of his faithful assistant, and said to himself that Keba was certainly trying to find a solution, a way of dealing with the beggars. Finally, Keba raised his head, and prompted by some violent emotion stared at his chief and cried passionately, 'No! Who do you take me for! It's madness what you're saying! I've hunted down these beggars, I've destroyed them physically and morally, and finally they leave us in peace, and now you want me to go and tell them to come back! What would I look like? Now that we can finally breathe freely, you want me to pollute the atmosphere again! You ask me to open a sore that has not yet healed. No! Not on your life! I won't do it!'

(5) SENEGAL: NÉGRITUDE
David Diop, *Sell-Out*

*As these lines from his poem 'Sell-Out' show, Diop's poetry was
a clear and loud product of the Négritude movement though it
was still in its infancy while he was writing. 'Sell-Out' is
included in the anthology Poems of Black Africa – see Booklist.*

Poor brother in your silk-lined tuxedo
Chatter and whisper and swagger through condescending
    drawing rooms
We pity you
The sun of your land is no more than a shadow
Across the calm brow of a civilised man
And your grandmother's hut
Reddens a face whited by the bowing and
Scraping of years
But when you are sick of the words as sounding empty
As the cash-box perched on your shoulders
You will tread the African earth bitter and red . . .

(6) SENEGAL: NÉGRITUDE
Léopold Sédar Senghor, *Congo*

*Senghor often uses the theme of women and love as a symbol for
Africa as the motherland. His poem 'Congo' is included in Prose
and Poetry – see Booklist. 'Ouzougou' is a type of very hard
wood.*

By my head by my tongue you are woman, you are woman by
    my belly
Mother of all things in whose nostrils is breath, mother
    of crocodiles and hippopotami
Manatees and iguanas, fishes and birds, mother of floods
    that suckle the harvests.
Great woman! Water wide open to the oar and the canoe's
    stem
My Sao my lover with maddened thighs, with long calm
    waterlily arms
Precious woman of ouzougou body of imputrescible oil,
    skin of diamantine night.

(7) SENEGAL: RAILWAY STRIKE

Sembène Ousmane, *God's Bits of Wood*

*The strength of the 1947 railway strike has been fortified by the
arrival of the workers' wives, or 100 of 'God's Bits of Wood'
(for according to local superstition counting people themselves
shortens their lives). On the long hot march from Thiès to Dakar
they stop for a rest under makeshift shelters.*

Penda could no longer control her anger. She strode rapidly over to the
embankment and began kicking down the branches and snatching
away the skirts and blouses. The women cried out in protest, and Awa
screamed, 'The whore won't dare to touch my cloth!' but Penda went
grimly on with her work until she had destroyed the last of the flimsy
shelters.

Then she looked around her and, seeing that some of the women
were still lying or kneeling on the ground, she began to count them
out, lifting her fingers one by one.

'One, two, three, four . . .'

'Witch!' Awa cried. 'You have no right to do that!'

'No, no! Don't count us, please!' Séni said, getting quickly to her
feet. 'We are God's bits of wood, and if you count us out you will bring
misfortune; you will make us die!'

'I want to know how many of you are against the strike,' Penda said.
'. . . five, six, seven, eight . . .'

'Stop!' Awa cried, scrambling to her feet. 'We will be eaten alive!
My dream was true! I dreamed that spirits carrying pointed knives came
and cut me in pieces to devour me!'

With fear and anger dividing their hearts, the women gathered
together their clothing, knotted the cloths around their heads, and
went back to the road.

(8) SENEGAL: WOMEN

Mariama Bâ, *So Long a Letter*

*Following the death of her husband, Ramatoulaye's friends and
family-in-law arrive to offer condolences and, as is the tradition,
she sacrifices her possessions as gifts to them. 'Lakh' is a
traditional food made from millet flour.*

On the third day, the same comings and goings of friends, relatives, the
poor, the unknown. The name of the deceased, who was popular, has
mobilized a buzzing crowd, welcomed in my house that has been
stripped of all that could be stolen, all that could be spoilt. Mats of all

sorts are spread out everywhere there is space. Metal chairs hired for the occasion take on a blue hue in the sun.

Comforting words from the Koran fill the air; divine words, divine instructions, impressive promises of punishment or joy, exhortations to virtue, warnings against evil, exaltation of humility, of faith. Shivers run through me. My tears flow and my voice joins weakly in the fervent 'Amen' which inspires the crowd's ardour at the end of each verse.

The smell of the *lakh* cooling in the calabashes pervades the air, exciting.

Also passed around are large bowls of red or white rice, cooked here or in neighbouring houses. Iced fruit juices, water and curds are served in plastic cups. The men's group eats in silence. Perhaps they remember the stiff body, tied up and lowered by their hands into a gaping hole, quickly covered up again.

In the women's corner, nothing but noise, resonant laughter, loud talk, hand slaps, strident exclamations. Friends who have not seen each other for a long time hug each other noisily. Some discuss the latest material on the market. Others indicate where they got their woven wrappers from. The latest bits of gossip are exchanged. They laugh heartily and roll their eyes and admire the next person's *boubou*, her original way of using henna to blacken hands and feet by drawing geometrical figures on them.

Biographies and important works

BÂ, Mariama (1929–1981). Bâ was a novelist, a schoolteacher and a campaigner for women's rights in Senegal. Born in **Dakar** and raised by her grandparents following the early death of her mother, she was educated in French schools and studied the Koran at the main mosque in Dakar. She had nine children by her husband, a former Minister of Information whom she later divorced. Her writing began with newspaper articles at the time of her involvement in Senegalese women's associations, though her first novel, *So Long a Letter* (Extract 8), was not published until 1979. In 1980 she won the Noma Award for publishing in Africa, and she was at the forefront of the literary scene. Her second novel, *The Scarlet Song*, was published posthumously, and traces the marriage between a poor Senegalese man and a French woman.

DIOP, Birago (1906–). A poet and collector of traditional tales, Birago Diop was born in **Dakar**, and educated in **Saint Louis** and at the University of Toulouse, France, where he studied veterinary medicine. He travelled to Paris where he met and was influenced by many of the young

African and Caribbean students involved in the *Négritude* movement. When Senegal became independent, Diop was made Ambassador to Tunisia, but later returned to **Dakar** to open a veterinary clinic. He has devoted much of his time to collecting oral tales from the Wolof, and while working as a vet collected many stories about animals. *Tales of Amadou Koumba* is a collection of tales handed down to him from his household *griot*. It has also been translated into Russian and Lithuanian.

DIOP, David (1927–1960). Diop was born in Bordeaux, France, to a Cameroonian mother and Senegalese father. He spent most of his early life in France, but later taught in **Dakar** and considered Senegal his homeland. His one published book of poetry, *Coups de Pilon*, translated as *Hammer Blows*, is an attack on the French colonialists and appeared shortly after his tragic death in a plane crash off the coast of Senegal, in which his family also died and the rest of his manuscripts were lost.

FALL, Malick (1920–1978). Fall was a poet and diplomat, who worked for a time in the Senegalese Department of Information. Writing in French, he gained a wider audience and recognition with the publication and translation of his novel *The Wound* (Extract 3). Like many of his contemporaries, his work dealt with the search for spiritual and moral fulfilment in the post-independence period.

OUSMANE, Sembène (1923–). Son of a fisherman and largely self-taught, Ousmane was drafted into the French army at the outbreak of the second world war. He returned to Senegal and took part in the famous

Sembène Ousmane

1947 strike of the Dakar–Niger railroad workers, which was later to be incorporated into his book *God's Bits of Wood* (Extract 7). He then moved to France to further his literary ambitions, where he worked as a docker in Marseille for ten years and joined the French Communist Party. Out of this hard experience came his semi-autobiographical novel *Black Docker* which described the appalling exploitation of black workers there. In the 1950s in Paris, he met and was influenced by Aimé Césaire, Camara Laye (◊ Guinea), and Sartre. In the 1960s he was invited to study at the Moscow Film School. When he returned to **Dakar**, he combined his novels and short stories with film-making to 'show Africans some of the deplorable conditions under which they live.'

SENGHOR, Léopold Sédar (1906–). Senghor was born in **Joal**, a coastal village 120 km south of Dakar, into a prosperous Serer Catholic family in a predominantly Muslim community. In

1931, he won a scholarship to France, where he ended up studying at the Sorbonne in Paris and becoming the first African to pass the *agrégation*, enabling him to teach. In the 1930s he joined the French army and was captured in the second world war. In 1946, he was elected as a Senegalese member to the National Assembly in Paris. In 1960 he became President of Senegal, a post which he held until 1981, when he retired. Senghor is generally regarded as the first African statesman – a brilliant intellectual and an able politician, who managed to combine vision and awareness of pan-African culture with the difficult day-to-day business of running a country (and also found time to write several collections of poetry – Extract 6). A socialist who believes in democracy, he is also the major African poet in French, as well as a distinguished theorist.

SOCÉ, Ousmane (1911–). Born in **Saint Louis**, Socé began his education at a Muslim school and went on to study medicine in France. He founded and edited several journals, including *Bingo*, which published Senegalese short stories and poems. He joined Senghor's new political party in the 1950s as Editor of the party journal and Assistant Secretary. Socé wrote one of the first popular Senegalese novels in French: *Karim* (Extract 2), published in 1935, was

his first novel. Set in **Dakar** in the early 1930s, the novel observes the effect of French colonialism and the cultural differences between the Catholics and the Muslims. His second novel, *Mirages de Paris*, is a love story that centres on the problems of an educated African in Paris in the 1930s, when he falls in love with a French girl. In the 1960s, Socé was Senegal's Ambassador to the USA and the United Nations.

SOW-FALL, Aminata (1941–). Sow-Fall was born in **Saint Louis**. She was educated first in Senegal, and then went to the Sorbonne in Paris. When she published her first novel, *Le Revenant*, in 1976, she was hailed as the first woman novelist in Francophone Africa. The hero of the novel – a young and ambitious African man – faces a familiar fate. Caught up in the challenges and economies of a changing society he is forced to fake his own death to survive. Her second novel, *The Beggar's Strike* (Extract 4), also carries a strong moral message, but is delivered with a wry sense of humour. It won the prestigious Grand Prix Littéraire d'Afrique Noire in 1980 and has since been translated into Russian, Spanish and English. Sow-Fall has taught French in a number of schools and worked in Senegal's Ministry of Culture as Director of Letters and Intellectual Ownership.

SIERRA LEONE

'I never knew and never heard mention of so villainous a place as Sierra Leone. I do not know where the Devil's Poste Restante is, but the place surely must be Sierra Leone.'
Captain Chamier, Life of a Sailor, 1833

Sierra Leone was for many years the first port of call for European shipping to Africa, and **Free-town**, its capital, was known as the 'Liverpool of West Africa'. Thus for many European writers and travellers arriving in the nineteenth and early twentieth century, Sierra Leone provided their first impressions of Africa. In *Wanderings in West Africa*, 1863, Sir Richard Burton (◊ Ethiopia) claimed, 'nothing can be viler than the site selected for Freetown', while traveller Mary Kingsley (◊ Gabon), passing through in 1895, noted more kindly that there were 'things one wants the pen of a Rabelais to catalogue' (*Travels in West Africa*, 1897).

While first impressions are notoriously varied, Sierra Leone is more often distinguished from the rest of West Africa by its coastline of swamps and peninsulars, a flamboyant Creole population, and the fact that from 1808 to 1961 it was the quintessential African British colony.

A few years before the British Parliament made the slave trade illegal in 1807, British philanthropists founded a 'free' town (**Freetown**) here for runaway and freed slave refugees. Their descendants, the Creoles, who still dominate the Freetown peninsular, make up less than 2% of the country's population today but have played a key role in its development. Krio, their language, is a curious mixture of English and indigenous languages, and is written phonetically (eg 'Ivinin-o' is 'good evening'). Numerically dominant, however, are the Temne, who first sold the Freetown peninsular to the settlers, and the Mende, who are legendary for their secret societies (books on which disappear mysteriously from libraries).

In terms of both modern history and literature, Sierra Leone was an early starter. The first newspaper was founded in 1801, but it was not

FACT BOX

AREA: 72 323 sq km
POPULATION: 4 200 000
CAPITAL: Freetown
LANGUAGES: English, Temne, Mende, Limba, Krio
FORMER COLONIAL POWER: Great Britain
INDEPENDENCE: 1961

until 150 years later that the country produced its most notable writers, with most found in the Roman alphabet or Arabic (the dominant religions are Islam and Christianity). Of pre-twentieth century writing, the most accessible and entertaining is that of James 'Africanus' Horton, a local doctor who travelled along the West African coast forming elaborate theories on all known ills – from politics (particularly the capability of the African for self-government)' to education and science. Investigating the cause of malaria along Sierra Leone's lagoon and bog-ridden coast, Horton quotes from Caliban in Shakespeare's *The Tempest*: 'All the infections that the sun sucks up/From bogs, fens, flats, on Prosper fall, and/Make him by inch-meal a disease.'

Another unique character was the so-called 'African Victorian Feminist', Adelaide Smith Casely-Hayford who completed her autobiography at the age of 91. Born into the Creole élite in 1868, Casely-Hayford's life spanned the reign of Queen Victoria to Queen Elizabeth. The year she died, 1960, also marked the publication of one of Sierra Leone's first popular 'modern' novels, *Kossah Town Boy*. Written by Richard Cole, it is a simple autobiographical tale of growing up in **Kossah**, eastern Freetown. Cole, also remembered as the first African Fellow of the Royal College of Surgeons in England, warmly recollects life under the British colonial system, from Sunday school and picnics to singing 'Britons never, never, N-E-V-E-R shall be slaves!!'. Of his first year at school he wrote: 'We did not feel strange about these songs. We were British if not Britons. They were part of the treasures of the language in which we were educated. And slavery had meant a lot to our race.'

A few years later, another medical graduate of Sierra Leone, Dr Davidson 'Abioseh' Nicol ◊, published *The Truly Married Woman* (Extract 5), a collection of short stories about pre-independence Africa. Like Cole, Nicol concentrates on everyday life with a kind of jolly realism. Also like Cole, and typical of much of the literature of the 1960s, he was accused of unquestioning capitulation to the ruling colonial system and values.

Sarif Easmon ◊ is yet another Sierra Leonean from the medical profession who has turned his hand to writing (Extract 4). His first play, *Dear Parent and Ogre*, is a stiff domestic comedy that deals with the whole gamut of tensions between generations, tribes, cultures and class at the onset of a country's election. Set in a tastefully decorated sitting room, the key characters are frequently found drinking champagne and talking politics: 'I said you were talking bosh, Daddy. These are days of democracy in Africa, and handkerchief-sized kingdoms went out with the dodo . . .'

In many people's eyes, however, democracy fared little better than the dodo. Playwright Yulisa (Pat) Amadu Maddy ◊ was one of the first of the 'angry young men' – a generation of writers and intellectuals who, disillusioned by a period of post-independence characterized by dictatorships, coups and differing states of emergency, left the country to find freedom of expression. In doing so he did not abandon his roots: in Lee Nicol's *Conversations with African Writers*, he says 'I'm not interested in the still-born or archaic traditions of imported culture. I love original cultures as they are.' *Obasai and Other Plays* is a collection of four short plays that spring to life with traditional chants, songs and myths. Drawing on Maddy's own bitter experiences of imprisonment in Sierra Leone, *Yon Kon* describes the tensions between inmates in a prison. His first novel, *No Past, No Present, No Future* (Extract 1) describes how three friends save money to travel to England together and in so doing systematically corrupt their relationship with their home country, each other, and subsequently destroy any hopes for the future: 'It was the best season for the gem; the "puss-yie" – diamond – illicit mining and smuggling was up one hundred per cent. Every man, woman and child coming from the East Province was worth knowing and befriending.'

Another of this outspoken generation of intellectuals who, like Yulisa Amadu Maddy, fell out with the oligarchical government of President Siaka Stevens in the 1970s, is Syl Cheney-Coker ◊. One of the lively new generation of West African poets, Cheney-Coker wrote much of his work while living in Europe and America. In 'Letter to a Tormented Playwright', dedicated to Maddy, he writes 'remember Amadu how terrible I said it was/that you were in exile and working/in the Telephone office in touch with all/the languages of the world but with no world/to call your own . . .'. *The Graveyard Also has Teeth*, the collection in which that poem appears, is his second collection of poems and was written after the death of his brother. It encompasses a bold mixture of traditions and styles, with a range of influences from Shakespeare's sonnets to the stories of Argentinian Jorge Luis Borges. Homage is paid to poets and artists worldwide. His subsequent collection, *The Blood in the Desert's Eyes* (Extract 6), was published in

1990. Cheney-Coker's first novel, *The Last Harmattan of Alusine Dunbar* (Extract 7), is a magical odyssey following the fortunes of the freed black American slaves who returned to Africa, through the eyes of Sulaiman the Nubian (aka Alusine Dunbar).

Cutting through cultures and timescales in quite a different way is Mukhtarr Mustapha, a Muslim poet from **Freetown**. Obsessed by the ancient rituals and cults that enjoy sporadic revival in West Africa, he uses the imagery of their bizarre rituals as a chilling comment on the torture that is carried out on political prisoners of oppressive regimes: 'Lift my tongue and tie it/With a rope from a tethered goat/Lacerate my lips with deep sanguine/gutters splattering blood like a/Bellow in full blaze – blazing yellow . . .' ('Gbassy – Blades in Regiment').

These were the kinds of ancient tales and rituals that European travellers and writers arriving in West Africa were warned of and in some cases lured by. Following on the heels of several genteel Victorian 'ladies' who wrote distinctly unmemorable memoirs was a young journalist, Graham Greene ◊. He arrived in **Freetown** in 1935 en route for a 'journey without maps' through Liberia and did not expect to return to Sierra Leone. But when the second world war broke out, Greene volunteered for the Secret Service in Liberia. Not surprisingly, the publication of *Journey Without Maps* (Extract 3), about his travels there, was not looked upon favourably by the Liberian government and Greene was forced to take up duties in neighbouring Sierra Leone. After three months 'training' in Lagos, Nigeria, he found himself in Freetown for a year. His flat was below **Hill Station**, in the European Quarter, and perilously close to the outdoor lavatories of the nearby slums which were infested with flies and vultures and which turned into a swamp in the rainy season. His experiences in these dingy lodgings were said by Greene to have robbed *The Ministry of Fear* (written while in West Africa) of humour ('an entertainment' underwrites the title page). Nevertheless Greene's fondness for seediness and for Sierra Leone were illustrated in his best-selling novel *The Heart of the Matter* (Extract 2). In *Ways of Escape*, Greene notes, 'There are pages in *The Heart of the Matter* (and one character, Yusef) for which I care, descriptions which bring back many happy months and some unhappy ones. The Portuguese liners with their smuggled letters and smuggled diamonds were very much part of the odd life I lived there in 1942–3 . . . Those days – I am glad to have had them; my love of Africa deepened there in particular for what is called, the whole world over, the Coast, this world of tin roofs, of vultures clanging down, of laterite paths turning rose in the evening light.'

Graham Greene

LITERARY LANDMARKS

Bauya. The confluence of two main railway lines and a centre of diamond trading and smuggling. In Maddy's *No Past, No Present, No Future*, the three main characters come here in their quest to make money. Maddy himself once worked for Sierra Leone Railways.

Freetown. By the site of the birth of the American slave trade in the 1560s is **King Jimmy Market**, now trading in fruit and vegetables. The **City Hotel**, immortalized in Graham Greene's *The Heart of the Matter* as the cockroach-ridden Bedford, is still reported to be supremely seedy and frequented by colourful characters. The **City Bar** was favoured by ex-pats and Greene because people 'are rather more dashing, get a little drunk and tell indecent stories.' (*Journey Without Maps*, p 42). **Lumley Beach** was introduced to Greene as the healthiest place along the coast. The beaches are still noted as among the finest in Africa. When Greene disembarked in Sierra Leone, he was greeted by a Kru from **Krutown**, often described as one of the few parts of Freetown with any beauty. **Kroo Bay** is still inhabited by the Krus who are famed as the great sailors of the coast and claim never to have dealt in slaves nor to have been slaves, and to have escaped Anglicanization. Slaves were once sold, and then years later freed, under the **old cotton tree**, which appears in Greene's *The Heart of the Matter* and is celebrated by the famous Gambian poet Lenrie Peters (◊ The Gambia): 'But come what may/her very root and hope/lie in the cotton tree/which overlooks the bay.' **Fourah Bay** is West Africa's oldest surviving university. Many writers from Africanus Horton MD to Richard Cole studied here. The modern university has been relocated, but you can visit the original red brick building in the east end of the town.

Kailahun District. The **railway** which Greene took to **Pendembu** stopped functioning in 1971 and there is little sign of resurrection. The **Moa Falls** on the **Moa River** provides the dramatic backdrop for Sarif Easmon's short story 'Bindeh's Gift' (Extract 4).

Libraries and Bookshops

Freetown. American Cultural Centre Library; British Council Library; Fourah Bay College Library and Bookshop, University of Sierra Leone; Government Bookstore, Wallace Johnson Street; New Horizons, Howe Street; Sierra Leone Library, Rokel Street.

In *Journey Without Maps*, Greene notes, with a touch of amusement and disappointment, an advertisement for 'literature' available in the Freetown Ededroko Store which listed Corelli's *Sorrows of Satan* and Caine's *The Woman Thou Gavest Me*.

BOOKLIST

The following selection includes the extracted titles in this chapter as well as those mentioned in the introduction which are available in English and other titles for further reading. In general, paperback editions are given when possible. The editions cited are not necessarily the only ones available. For most of the extracted works, the original publisher in English can be found in 'Acknowledgments and Citations' at the end of the volume, as can the exact location of the extracts and the editions from which they are taken. Extract numbers are highlighted in bold for ease of reference.

Allain, Marie-Françoise, *The Other Man: Conversations with Graham Greene*, The Bodley Head, London, 1983.

Burton, Sir Richard, 'Three Days at Freetown', in *Wanderings in West Africa*, Dover Press, New York, 1992.

Chamier, Captain, *Life of a Sailor*, quoted in *The Travellers' Dictionary of Quotation*, Peter Yapp, ed, Routledge, London, 1988.

Cheney-Coker, Syl, *The Blood in the Desert's Eyes*, Heinemann, Oxford, 1990. **Extract 6.**

Cheney-Coker, Syl, *The Graveyard*

Also has Teeth, Heinemann, London, 1980.

Cheney-Coker, Syl, *The Last Harmattan of Alusine Dunbar*, Heinemann, Oxford, 1990. **Extract 7**.

Cole, Richard, *Kossah Town Boy*, Cambridge University Press, Cambridge, 1960.

Cromwell, Adelaide M., *An African Victorian Feminist, Adelaide Smith Casely-Hayford 1868–1960*, Frank Cass, London, 1986.

Easmon, Sarif, 'Bindeh's Gift', in *African Writing Today*, Ezekiel Mphahlele, ed, Penguin, London, 1967. **Extract 4**.

Easmon, Sarif, *Dear Parent and Ogre*, Oxford University Press, Oxford, 1964.

Greene Graham, 'Convoy to West Africa', diary of Greene's journey to Sierra Leone in 1941, in *In Search of a Character*, Penguin, London, 1969.

Greene, Graham, *The Heart of the Matter*, Penguin, London, 1971. **Extract 2**.

Greene, Graham, *Journey Without Maps*, Penguin, London, 1976. **Extract 3**.

Greene, Graham, *The Ministry of Fear*, Penguin, London, 1970.

Greene, Graham, *Ways of Escape*, The Bodley Head, London, 1980.

Horton, James 'Africanus', in *Africanus Horton, The Dawn of Nationalism in Modern Africa: Extracts from Political, Educational and Science Writings by J. A. B. Horton MD 1835–1883*, selected by Abioseh Nicol, Longman, London, 1969.

Kingsley, Mary, *Travels in West Africa*, Virago, London, 1986.

Maddy, Yulisa Amadu, *No Past, No Present, No Future*, Heinemann, London, 1973. **Extract 1**.

Maddy, Yulisa Amadu, *Obasai and Other Plays*, Heinemann, London, 1971.

Maddy, Yulisa Amadu, *Two African Tales*, Cambridge University Press, Cambridge, 1965.

Mustapha, Mukhtarr, 'Gbassy – Blades in Regiment', in *A Selection of African Poetry*, K.E. Senanu and T. Vincent, eds, Longman, London, 1976.

Nicol, Davidson (aka Abioseh), *The Truly Married Woman and Other Stories*, Oxford University Press, Oxford, 1965. **Extract 5**.

Nicol, Lee, *Conversations with African Writers*, Washington, DC, 1981.

Peters, Lenrie, *The Second Round*, Heinemann, London, 1969.

Sherry, Norman, *The Life of Graham Greene, Volume One, 1904–1939*, Jonathan Cape, London, 1989.

Extracts

(1) BAUYA

Yulisa Amadu Maddy,
No Past, No Present, No Future

Ade, the son of a civil servant, and Santigie, a chief's son, are contemplating what they will miss when they leave for England.

'Padre, the lot, Christianity, God, white men, they have stripped our parents of any self-respect. Our parents' parents were worse. Our parents talk now of Freedom because our generation has stimulated them with its courage, and they don't like to feel we are telling them what to do.'

Ade took another bottle of beer and opened it with his teeth. He continued his declamations.

'They are the last unproductive generation of our race. They have not left a single worth-while page of history.' Santigie spat, as if with hate. 'God! my dad wants to become a knight. To be called Sir Madras Toronto Bangwango Okiki John, shit.'

'Very original Bauyan,' Santigie yelled. 'They seem to remember all their tucked-away native names the moment they kneel before the Queen.'

'He will die broken-hearted if his ambition fails.'

'Ambition for long service, hating and persecuting his own people.'

'Do you know,' Ade was on his feet, 'some of our African knights don't know how to use knives and forks. They don't even understand the white man's table manners. I hear that some of our so-called great men eat their sweets before they have their hors d'oeuvres when they go to England. Some have the main course and ask for repeat after repeat. Others disgrace themselves with simple things like not knowing when to say thank you and no thank you.'

Santigie and Ade were enjoying themselves. The night air outside the town dance hall was warm and full of music and laughter, and the voices of the sober and drunk. The music issuing out of the dance hall upstairs was a conglomeration of West African, West Indian calypso, hi-life and indigenous African rhythms, interspersed with occasional jive, foxtrots and waltzes. From below, the dance floor reverberated and thundered. Ladies coming out for fresh air looked radiantly sweaty and tantalizing, some accompanied by their men friends and others single but not apparently neglected. The men were elegant in gabardine and sharkskin suits.

'Give me a big fat-chested momma with a big fleshy protruding bottom tonight, and I am saved for eternity!' Santigie shouted, looking at a plumpish lady in a green silk dress who had just emerged. The dress was nearly topless and showed her legs above the knees. She stood there alone, enjoying the fresh air.

(2) FREETOWN

Graham Greene, *The Heart of the Matter*

Scobie, the hero of the novel, is a second-rate police officer coming to terms with life in a fly-blown colony. According to Greene in Ways of Escape, 'Scobie was based on nothing but my own unconscious. He had nothing to do with my Commissioner of Police . . . Nor on any of the MI5 agents who trailed – in two cases disastrously – down the West African coast in those days.'

Scobie turned up James Street past the Secretariat. With its long balconies it had always reminded him of a hospital. For fifteen years he had watched the arrival of a succession of patients; periodically at the end of eighteen months certain patients were sent home, yellow and nervy, and others took their place – Colonial Secretaries, Secretaries of Agriculture, Treasurers and Directors of Public Works. He watched their temperature charts every one – the first outbreak of unreasonable temper, the drink too many, the sudden stand for principle after a year of acquiescence. The black clerks carried their bedside manner like doctors down the corridors; cheerful and respectful they put up with any insult. The patient was always right.

Round the corner, in front of the old cotton tree, where the earliest settlers had gathered their first day on the unfriendly shore, stood the law courts and police station, a great stone building like the grandiloquent boast of weak men. Inside that massive frame the human being rattled in the corridors like a dry kernel. No one could have been adequate to so rhetorical a conception. But the idea in any case was only one room deep. In the dark narrow passage behind, in the charge-room and the cells, Scobie could always detect the odour of human meanness and injustice – it was the smell of a zoo, of sawdust, excrement, ammonia, and lack of liberty. The place was scrubbed daily, but you could never eliminate the smell. Prisoners and policemen carried it in their clothing like cigarette smoke.

(3) FREETOWN

Graham Greene, *Journey Without Maps*

Graham Greene disembarked at Freetown en route for Liberia.
It was his first encounter with West Africa.

Freetown, the capital of Sierra Leone, at first was just an impression of heat and damp; the mist streamed along the lower streets and lay over the roofs like smoke. Nature, conventionally grand, rising in tree-covered hills above the sea and the town, a dull uninteresting green, was powerless to carry off the shabby town. One could see the Anglican cathedral, laterite bricks and tin with a square tower, a Norman church built in the nineteenth century, sticking up out of the early morning fog. There was no doubt at all that one was back in home waters. Among the swarm of Kru boats round the ship the *Princess Marina* with its freshly painted name was prominent. '*Princess Marina*,' the half-naked owner kept on calling. 'Sweetest boat on the coast.'

Tin roofs and peeling posters and broken windows in the public library and wooden stores, Freetown had a Bret Harte air without the excitement, the saloons the revolver shots or the horses. There was only one horse in the whole city, and it was pointed out to me by the proprietor of the Grand Hotel, a thin piebald beast pulled down the main street like a mule. There had been other horses from time to time, but they had all died. Where there wasn't a tin shed there were huge hoardings covered with last year's Poppy Day posters (the date was January the fifteenth). On the roofs the vultures sat nuzzling under their wings with horrible tiny undeveloped heads; they squatted in the gardens like turkeys; I could count seven out of my bedroom window. When they moved from one perch to another they gave no sensation of anything so aerial as flight; they seemed to hop across the street, borne up just high enough by the flap-flap of their dusty wings.

This was an English capital city; England had planted this town, the tin shacks and the Remembrance Day posters, and had then withdrawn up the hillside to smart bungalows, with wide windows and electric fans and perfect service. Every call one paid on a white man cost ten shillings in taxi fares, for the railway to Hill Station no longer ran. They had planted their seedy civilization and then escaped from it as far as they could. Everything ugly in Freetown was European: the stores, the churches, the Government offices, the two hotels; if there was anything beautiful in the place it was native: the little stalls of the fruit-sellers which went up after dark at the street corners, lit by candles; the native women rolling home magnificently from church on a Sunday morning, the cheap European cottons, the deep coral or green flounces, the wide straw hats, dignified by the native bearing, the lovely roll of the thighs, the swing of the great shoulders. They were dressed for a garden party and they carried off cheap bright grandeur in the small back-yards among the vultures as nature couldn't carry off Freetown.

(4) KAILAHUN

Sarif Easmon, *Bindeh's Gift*

Looking down on the Moa Falls in Kailahun, Kallon tells how in the 1860s tribal leader Kai Borie used to punish war boys whose nerves had failed them in battle. Easmon's story 'Bindeh's Gift' is included in the anthology African Writing Today – see Booklist.

Kai Borie stood on the great boulder by the Moa Falls, big, black, and magnificent, a human almost as charged with energy as thunder and lightning, bursting out of black, nimbus clouds.

'Bring Bensali here,' he roared above the thunder of the waterfalls. 'He is my sister's child and, therefore, by tribal custom and fact, more precious to me than my own would be. But if in the attack he did behave like a coward, he shall die as other cowards have died before him.'

A movement like a shock-wave passed through the concourse of men assembled on this side of the river. Overhead the stars, numberless and brilliant in a moonless heaven, looked down on a river scene as brilliant and certainly more colourful than themselves. For five hundred palm-oil flambeaux were blazing on the Moa's near bank, making the stretch of water look like a hungry, roaring river of blood. Black men held the torches up, and they lined the rocks right down to the water's edge; men as thick as palisades right up to the forest roots, perched on trees – all fearful, all expectant of the horror that might have been the individual lot of any one of them. Upstream, downstream ten thousand 'war boys' awaited this royal execution. The light picked out their bodies like statues carved in ebony, here in chiaroscuro, there as clear as day – while here and there spear points glinted like stars answering the stars overhead.

From the river bank to the forest behind, the King's command was passed from mouth to mouth. It made a murmur from the ranks of men, a sound indefinite and eerily moving – as if the earth on which they stood had grumbled in protest.

The prisoner, sitting under guard by a fire in the forest, trembled as the shaft of a spear touched him on the shoulder, and he was ordered to rise.

Two soldiers, their bodies mirrored in the firelight, helped Bensali to rise – for his hands were bound behind his back. He set his teeth with the pain as they pulled him up: there was a wound festering high up on his right arm, on the inner side.

'Courage, Bensali!' whispered the man on his left.

'I am not afraid to die,' Bensali answered back, briefly.

They marched him down through the forest, from the fireside down the shadow of death ablaze with torches, to the destiny awaiting him by the Moa Falls.

(5) KISSY HILLS

Abioseh Nicol, *The Devil at Yolahun Bridge*

Sanderson, a district officer for the British colonial administration, sets off on his daily rounds with one of his military policeman. 'The Devil at Yolahun Bridge' is in The Truly Married Woman and Other Stories – see Booklist.

He felt buoyant and in an inspecting mood again this morning, and the sun was not yet too hot. He tried to converse with his escort in the local language. He always seized an opportunity to do this in preparation for the language test which each officer of the Administrative Service had to take before confirmation of his appointment. The tall powerfully built African walked slightly in front of him pushing aside the twigs of branches overhanging the path. He smiled respectfully when Sanderson addressed him and answered with as good an accent as he could in English to show that he should be promoted a corporal and interpreter if the opportunity offered.

Sanderson gave up the struggle early and they trudged on silently. Sometimes a bird would be disturbed by the noise of a cracking twig and would veer off angrily chirping, its plumage an iridescent streak of red, green and blue, to settle on a higher branch. They soon came to a clearing where there was a long low shed and some huge cotton trees. This was the market and it was crowded with people from neighbouring villages, buying, selling, bartering and gossiping. The women sat with an easy grace on low stools with their wares on mats spread on the ground in front of them under the shade of the trees. The more successful ones were in the shed with their goods on rickety stalls. There were only women and children about except in one or two of the larger stalls where grave middle-aged men sat aloof from the gossiping women. The women had their hair done up in elaborate plaits half concealed under gay cotton scarves. They had on simple dyed cloth wrapped around their body from the knees up to just above the breast and some wore blouses. The children played about in the dust while the older ones organised themselves into bands and raided stalls or played complicated games, chanting and clapping as they did so. The mats on the ground and the stalls in the shed were crowded with goods and foodstuffs of all descriptions. Dried fish, salted fish and raw fish; okras, sorrel leaves, and red pepper; cassava, sweet potatoes, bananas, and plantains; rice, and ground-nut, and millet seed heaped up in separate piles in pyramid form, the apex crowned with a cylindrical cigarette tin as measure; palm oil, groundnut oil, and coconut oil placed in empty gin bottles and stopped with a bit of rag or crumpled paper; little oil lamps and dishes made from kerosene tins; some scrawny fowls and guinea-hens lying on the ground with their feet tied, squawking and flapping their wings adding to the general bustle of the whole scene.

(6) SIERRA LEONE: EXILE
Syl Cheney-Coker, The Philosopher

In these lines from his poem 'The Philosopher', Cheney-Coker displays his grief and feelings of exile and estrangement both as a poet within and outside his country. The poem forms part of the collection The Blood in the Desert's Eyes *– see Booklist.*

Who lived here when the stones were green
verdigris of age when the reptilians marched like men
into the night before that morning the sea
emptying its cup of wounds like a chasm of revolt.
like a castaway an old man kept his books in a cave
desolate his memory of life a portrait
like an abstraction of years, he lived
forgotten by others before the last tidal wave
I consecrate him seer his beard was a white book
where we read about kings and prophet
planners of the ruins astride our stormy conscience
to write what history the moon already dripping its sea of red blood

(7) SIERRA LEONE: 'MALAGUETA'

Syl Cheney-Coker,
The Last Harmattan of Alusine Dunbar

Travelling through time and space, Alusine Dunbar looks down from the plateau of the dead at the fortunes of the Malagueta settlers, black pioneers who sought freedom in a Sierra-Leone-like fictional country.

Now, he was returning to Malagueta because, as he told Garbage, 'I had seen the leopards going for the goats and I had to come before they ate all of them.'

He came through the idyllic gardens of the savannah and saw the pageant of the migratory birds going back to Europe with their impertinent looks and their fanciful plumages. Not having been in that part of the world for a while, he strayed into the sandy desolation of the desert, to see what changes the discovery of the compass had made since the days of the camel. His patience was rewarded: on the vast plateau in the awesome silence of the sand, Alusine Dunbar saw the majestic castles and caves of Tassili n' Ajir, the fantastic drawings of the nomadic painters; he rested on the stones in the rock garden of antiquity and read the epigram, 'Gold is the king of jewels but do not love it more than the sands of the desert', that a witty poet had scrawled on the tomb of the gold king over whom N'jai the gold merchant had forsaken the pleasures of enjoying the weasel-like body of Mariamu.

A herd of oryx brought him out of the desert and, keeping to the clouds of the locusts which have no respect for the borders between wet and dry regions, he arrived, invincible, in Malagueta, because Alusine Dunbar had conquered the last mystery of how to be alive in the same place where he had died over a hundred years before. Nothing in his occult weaponry had prepared him for the vandalism that greeted him. Gone were the enchanting bazaars that the sedentary Tuaregs had built when they had given up hawking the condiments of the Moors; he looked in vain for the chapman corner where the female beggars had peddled the imitation jewellery from Tangiers and read the palms of fortune seekers. The courtyard where he had brought back the armadillo from extinction was lost in the revolting expanse of shops, and, in the swamps where he had hoped to find the world unchanged, he was aghast to see that the pigmy hippos were being reduced to curiosity jokes, while the peaceful siestas of the crocodiles had been disturbed by the cunning skinhunters.

'The destruction has started,' the old man lamented.

Biographies and important works

CHENEY-COKER, Syl (1945–). Cheney-Coker was born in **Freetown**. He studied both in Sierra Leone and in the USA, and lived for several years in Nigeria, teaching at the University of Maiduguri. His first collection of poems, *Concerto for an Exile*, published in 1973, gives the reader a dizzy sense of his homesickness for his Creole roots, and the feelings of disorientation and disillusionment associated with his imposed exile in America. *The Last Harmattan of Alusine Dunbar* (Extract 7), his first novel, is dedicated to his mother, whose Creole story-telling inspired the character of Sulaiman the Nubian, a spirit who transcends the divide between past, present and future. The novel won the African Commonwealth Writers Prize in 1991. *The Graveyard Also has Teeth*, written while in the USA, is his second collection of poems, and *The Blood in the Desert's Eyes* (Extract 6) his third. Cheney-Coker currently lives in **Freetown**, where he publishes *The Vanguard*, a fortnightly newspaper.

EASMON, Sarif (1913–). A writer and physician, Easmon was educated in England. He returned to Sierra Leone, where he wrote plays, short stories and novels while working in a private medical practice in **Freetown**. *Dear Parent and Ogre*, his first play, was produced by Wole Soyinka's (◊ Nigeria) troupe in Ibadan in the 1960s. *The Feud* is a collection of cosmopolitan short stories set variously in Africa and Europe that deal passionately with love, revenge and justice. His first novel, *The Burnt-Out Marriage*, is about a liberal village chief who has to resort to traditional magic to control his even more progressive and powerful wife.

GREENE, Graham (1904–1991). Greene was born in Berkhamsted, England. He travelled to West Africa for the first time in 1935 when he embarked on a journey across Liberia with his cousin Barbara Greene (◊ Liberia), described in *Journey Without Maps* (Extract 3). Greene returned in 1941 when he was dispatched to undertake work for the Foreign Office. While here he wrote *The Ministry of Fear* and gathered the material for *The Heart of the Matter* (Extract 2), the anguished and beguiling story of a police officer in a West African colony during the war. It is one of his more explicitly 'Catholic' novels (Greene converted to the Roman Catholic Church in 1926) and is considered by many to be his finest book. In *Ways of Escape*, his second volume of autobiography, Greene described it as 'a success in the vulgar sense of that term' and his apparent excuse for writing it was 'swamps, rain and a mad cook'. *A Burnt-Out Case* (see under Zaire) is set in a leper colony in central Africa.

MADDY, Yulisa Amadu (1936–). Born in **Freetown**, Maddy is a Creole writer, actor and director. He studied drama and literature in France and England and then, in the early 1960s, worked as a radio producer first for the BBC in London, and subsequently in Denmark. He returned to Sierra Leone in 1968 and became Head of Drama for Radio Sierra Leone. Since then, his plays, published as *Obasai and Other Plays* and *Big Berrin and Pulse*, have been staged everywhere from Edinburgh to Freetown. His first novel, entitled *No Past, No Present, No Future* (Extract 1), was published in 1973.

NICOL, Abioseh (1924–). Also known as Davidson Nicol. A poet, short story writer and biochemist, Nicol was educated in Nigeria and Sierra Leone. He was awarded the Margaret Wrong Prize and Medal for Literature in Africa in 1952, and in 1957 he was elected the first African Fellow at Cambridge. He is best known for his short stories – see *The Truly Married Woman and Other Stories* and *Two African Tales*. However, his poem 'The Meaning of Africa' became well known and oft quoted as a stark reminder of the mixed feelings of the country's élite towards indigenous culture at the time.

TOGO

'Things official didn't work very well in Togo. From the education of children to my toilet that never flushed, development seemed to fail at every turn – foreign, misunderstood, abused . . .'
George Packer,
The Village of Waiting

When Peace Corps worker George Packer came to Togo in the 1980s things were not quite as he had expected. First, and much to his disappointment, 'It turned out there were no French existentialists hanging out in Lomé.' Second, he was posted to **Lavié**, a small dusty village north of the capital, whose name means an unpromising 'wait a little more'. The reluctant Packer went on to write a frank, funny and moving exposition of life there. *The Village of Waiting* (Extract 1), is an important and intriguing book if only for the fact that there is little known or written about this tiny country outside of the region.

Tucked inconspicuously between Ghana and Benin, Togo was nevertheless colonized during the great 'scramble for Africa'. First came the Germans, and then, following the war, Togoland was divided between Britain and France. The western part that was administered by the British merged with Ghana in 1956 and the larger poorer portion became the Republic of Togo in 1960.

Subjected to artificial bureaucratic boundaries, the added burden of several colonial languages, the Togolese managed to defend and develop their own languages and culture to a remarkable extent. During German rule, there was extensive linguistic research into the indigenous languages and the Togolese were apparently encouraged to use their own languages. Indeed, the first-ever West African play to be published in an African language was in Togolese. *Toko atolia*, published in 1937 by Kwasi Fiawoo, heralded the beginning of a lively local publishing scene.

Things changed for a time with the arrival of the British and French. The latter were more insistent on imposing their own language than

FACT BOX

AREA: 56 000 sq km
POPULATION: 3 800 000
CAPITAL: Lomé
LANGUAGES: French, English, Mina (verbal only), Ewe, Kabyé
FORMER COLONIAL POWER: Germany, France and Great Britain
INDEPENDENCE: 1960

their European counterpart, and there emerged a French–Togolese literature. Initially the works were mainly religious in sentiment and noticeably not anti-colonial. Meanwhile the voices of protest – the nationalists – were heard by a lively local publishing scene that was patronised by the United Nations, and therefore to some degree protected from censorship.

The numbers of French-speaking intelligentsia in Togo grew, and following independence in 1960, more diverse themes emerged in the literature. One of the writers to dominate the post-independence period was Felix Couchoro, who was born in 1900. A prolific writer, Couchoro published four novels in book form, and eighteen others were printed in serial form in the country's daily newspaper, *Togo-Presse*. His novels deal principally with tribal and village conflicts, and centre around tricksters and the tricked. The work for which he is best known, *Les Secrets d'Éléonore*, published by Togo's national publishing house Éditogo in 1963, is about rights, ownership and paternity in a Togolese family. David Anaou addresses similar themes in *Le Fils du Fetiche*, which was first published in 1955.

Following the success of Couchoro's serializations, novellas became a popular literary form in Togo. Several writers turned to the short punchy paperback, including Victor Aladji (1941–   ), whose works rarely numbered more than 55 pages. *L'Équilibriste*, which means 'the tightrope walker', is the improbable tale of a Togolese Dick Turpin, who steals only from the rich, and successfully evades the law until he falls in love with a policeman's daughter. Boasting 64 pages, it is one of Aladji's longer works.

Yves-Emmanuel Dogbé, born two years earlier than Aladji, is one of Togo's noted poets who has also collected and published work by his contemporaries. Although playwrights, like poets, have gained less notice than novelists in Togo, the work of Senuovo Nestor has been a great success among the French-speaking ex-colonies. Sadly, while there are clearly several popular writers of note to have emerged from Togo, practically nothing has been translated into English. One of the few books accessible to English-language readers is Tété-Michel Kpomassie's ◊ extraordinary autobiography, *An African in Greenland* (Extract 2). Nothing short of an oddity, it tells the story of his decision at the age of sixteen to run away from his tiny forest village to the Arctic, evading his certain fate as an acolyte of the local python cult. Twelve years later, and facing a temperature differential of 75°C, Kpomassie found 'I had started on a voyage of discovery, only to find that it was I who was being discovered.'

The apparent lack of hard political discourse in the indigenous literature is largely due to the 'popularity' of President Eyadéma's single-party state. The coup he staged in 1963 and which brought him to power was memorable as the first-ever coup in independent Africa. The Rassemblement du Peuple Togolais has been in power ever since. As the only candidate in the country's 1972 'election', Eyadéma secured a resounding 99.95% of the vote. The President has since survived several coup attempts and a plane crash, after which he celebrated his 'miraculous' survival with a 'Triumphal Return'. This resulted in a new national holiday, several hotels and statues commissioned in his honour, and most recently a comic book in which he plays a dynamic Superman-like character.

LITERARY LANDMARKS

Kara. Home of the President, and the 'capital' of the north. Here you can buy wristwatches with the illuminated face of you-know-who.

Lavié. George Packer's 'village of waiting', where he was reluctantly stationed as a Peace Corps instructor (Extract 2).

Lomé. Capital, described by the *Rough Guide* as 'one of West Africa's best capitals – laid back but not chaotic, stylish.' The **Grand Marché** is a good place to look for books.

Togoville. Where the Germans first arrived in 1884 and carved out their deal with the local chief that made the country a protectorate. Visitors are apparently expected to visit the chief and sign the so-called 'golden book'.

Libraries and Bookshops

Lomé. American Cultural Centre, rue Caventou; Centre Culturel Francais, rue 24 Janvier; Éditions Akpagnon, BP 3531; Éditions Éditogo, BP 891; Librare Bon Pasteur, rue du Commerce; Maladise Books, rue du Commerce.

BOOKLIST

Kpomassie, Tété-Michel, *An African in Greenland*, James Kirkup, trans, Secker and Warburg, London, 1983. **Extract 2**.

Packer, George, *The Village of Wait-*ing, Vintage, New York, 1988. **Extract 1**.

Voices from Twentieth-Century Africa, Chinweizu, ed, Faber and Faber, London, 1988.

Extracts

(1) LAVIÉ

George Packer, *The Village of Waiting*

By late February in Lavié, there had been no rain for nearly four months. The villagers and the author are beginning to feel the effects of the heat and dust . . .

During the evil hours, ten to three, movement out in the village was at a minimum. Figures hurried through the white light from shade to shade. Girls spent hours indoors plaiting each other's hair. The old men on the rocks and logs outside the bistro drank palm wine and waved at the flies that had materialized out of the heat, and quarreled or slept through the worst hours. Their greetings to me shriveled to hoarse grunts. Their fields were hard and cracked, like their old skin, and vegetation on the plateau had thinned to the point where I could see its rocky contours for the first time. Nobody ventured out there, except Faustus and his pals to tap palm trunks and bring back the cure-all; nothing was out there now, just the dead earth and the withered stalks of last year's corn. The farmers had nothing to do but wait.

Their wives worked. The chores didn't stop for lack of rain, but the women moved more slowly, talked less, and kept to their houses.

The one who sold beans next to Ama's rice every morning in the public place was pregnant, her belly swollen under layers of *pagne*. It was about the only thing growing in the village. One morning I asked her when the baby was due. Normally cheerful, she dropped her ladle and stared. 'Why? Are you the father?' It wasn't a question to ask a married woman – not in this heat, with the rains delayed. By mid-March they were two weeks late and no sign of them on the horizon.

(2) LOMÉ

Tété-Michel Kpomassie, *An African in Greenland*

At sixteen years old Kpomassie chances on an extraordinary inspiration for a means to escape becoming an acolyte of the local python cult.

The Evangelical Bookshop, in the commercial quarter at the other end of town, was one of Lomé's modest bookstores, run by missionaries. As the missionaries concentrated on the conversion and instruction of an illiterate people who were mostly pagans and idol-worshipers (there are very few Muslims in the country), the shelves of their shop were laden with school textbooks and religious primers. However, from time to time, as if in error, the occasional travel book or a novel would find its way onto the shelves, and, every week before my accident, I had fallen into the habit of spending the money I made by selling my mats, on books which were never on our school syllabus.

So one morning when my brothers had left early for the coconut plantation, and there was no one left at home to take me for a walk along the seashore, I went out alone and visited the Evangelical Bookshop. Inside there were two shelves against the walls on either side of the counter. I went up to one of these, attracted by a book laid flat on a half-empty shelf, with a cover showing a picture of a hunter dressed in clothes made of animal skins and leaning on a spear. I was struck at once by the title: *The Eskimos from Greenland to Alaska* by Dr Robert Gessain. The book was illustrated with photographs and engravings: I liked the look of it, bought it, then went on my way to the beach. By noon I had finished my new book, the first I had read about the life of the little men of the North.

Was it the author's praise of their hospitality that triggered my longing for adventure, or was it fear of returning to the sacred forest? I hardly remember. But when I had finished reading, one word began to resonate inside me until it filled my whole being. That sound, that word, was *Greenland*. In that land of ice, at least, there would be no snakes!

Biography and important works

KPOMASSIE, Tété-Michel (1941–). Kpomassie was born into a traditional Togolese family in the village of **Atoéta**. His father had eight wives, and Kpomassie had 26 brothers and sisters. His autobiographical *An African in Greenland* (Extract 2) recounts how, after a strange encounter with a sacred python in the forest, he is taken to a local priestess who 'cures' him and then tries to enrol him. A week before his father sends him off for initiation, Kpomassie discovers a book about Greenland in a **Lomé** bookstore, and concludes that the Arctic is a better option. Finally arriving in Greenland – via Dakar, Marseille and Copenhagen – his initial observations of the Inuit are not promising; 'dancing and drinking were all they had in life. This was not the Greenland of my dreams.' But as he travels further north, he discovers another world. *An African in Greenland* contains Kpomassie's fascinating and unique perspective on Arctic life. Self-taught from the age of six, he now works in Paris for a Japanese electronics firm, and is married to a Frenchwoman. In 1981 he was awarded the Prix Littéraire Francophone International.

ALGERIA

'Men and societies have succeeded one another in this place; conquerors have marked this country with their non-commissioned officers' civilization. They entertained a vulgar and ridiculous idea of greatness, and measured that of their empire by the surface which it covered.'
Albert Camus,
The Wind at Djemila

Over the centuries, conquerors and colonists from the Vandals to the French have all played their part in the transformation of Algeria and its people. The earliest inhabitants, according to legend, were the Berbers, who gave their name to the notorious Barbary Coast. The Phoenicians began to set up colonies along this coastline around 500 BC, ruling from their stronghold at Carthage (in modern Tunisia), but during the second and third centuries BC, the Romans defeated the Carthaginians and colonized the coast for themselves.

Following the collapse of Roman rule in the fifth century, there was a succession of conquests. First came the fearsome Vandals, the Teutonic tribe which sacked Rome and gave its name to vandalism. The Vandals were followed by the Byzantines, the Arabs, and finally the Turks.

The Barbary Coast became notorious between the sixteenth and eighteenth centuries as a haunt of pirates who preyed on Mediterranean trading ships which plied too close to the African shore. In 1575 the 28-year-old Cervantes was captured by pirates off Marseille, taken to **Algiers** and held as a slave. Despite several daring and almost successful attempts at escape (after which he was kept in a dungeon in manacles), Cervantes was to remain in captivity in Algiers until 1589, when a ransom was paid by the Spanish authorities. One of the rare descriptions of Algeria during this period comes from a French soldier, Nicholas Nicholay ◊ who lived in the sixteenth century and travelled throughout North Africa in his capacity as a diplomat (Extract 4), managing somehow to evade the pirates. Less fortunate was the cousin

---

FACT BOX

AREA: 2 381 745 sq km (second largest country in Africa)
POPULATION: 25 363 000
CAPITAL: Algiers
LANGUAGES: Arabic, French, Berber
FORMER COLONIAL POWER: France
INDEPENDENCE: 1962

---

of Josephine Bonaparte, Aimée Dubucq de Rivery, who was captured by Corsair pirates on her way to Europe from the West Indies in 1784. She was given by the Dey of Algiers to the Sultan of Turkey who promptly made her part of his harem and she became known as the 'French Sultana'.

On the pretext of putting an end to the kidnapping, pillage and plunder, the French invaded Algeria in 1830. They seized control of the country proper in 1847 and during the century of French rule which followed, Algeria changed almost beyond recognition. The population was transformed with the arrival of some 800 000 European settlers, and with the mushrooming of the indigenous Muslim population from three to nine million. During this period romantic European curiosity about Algeria was at its peak. The mysteries and lure of the Arab world were to fulfil the dreams of a few intrepid travellers, including the extraordinary Isabelle Eberhardt ◊. In her diary (Extract 5), she tells how, disguised as a man, she travelled on horseback at the turn of the century through 'infinite stretches of sand' seeking out 'utter peace and silence all around'. Stories about her fraternizing with 'natives' and her tragic death still linger on in the villages through which she journeyed.

By the second world war, a strong independence movement had begun to form among the Muslims. Within ten years of the end of the war, open rebellion broke out. A bitter civil war ensued between the *colons* (the Europeans) and the FLN (the National Liberation Front), with acts of terror, brutal oppression and repeated atrocities on both sides. This period is the subject of Gillo Pontecorvo's 1965 film, *The Battle of Algiers*. Finally an agreement was signed and Algeria became an independent state in 1962. Following a brief internal power struggle, Boumedienne came to power in 1965 with the task of reviving an economy sapped by the long civil war and finally sabotaged by the abrupt colonial withdrawal.

After Boumedienne's death in 1978, Algeria continued as an authoritarian socialist republic, attempting to reform the deeply conservative habits of the people. The economy was modernized, education programmes instituted, and there was a drive to bring about a measure of equality for women, who hitherto had been treated as little more than chattels. Yet the majority of the population still remain poor, with many forced to emigrate to France in search of work. Nowadays many families throughout the country rely on money sent back from France by these economic exiles.

The souring of the socialist ideals in the light of continued economic hardship turned many people against the authoritarian government, in favour of Muslim fundamentalism. With increasing support, especially from the urban poor, the Islamic Salvationist Front (FIS) is today a force to be reckoned with. Elections planned for 1992 were hastily 'postponed' when it was realized that the FIS might succeed. Today the army and the now officially banned FIS (which threatens to bring an end to what democracy there is in Algeria) are in permanent conflict and there is widespread civil unrest and rioting. Victims too are liberalism and literature. The Algerian Novelists' Union was recently forced to cancel an Albert Camus Day because of Islamic fundamentalist rioting, and the writings of Albert Camus ◊ are purposely left off the school syllabus.

Long-since considered a controversial figure for his humanitarian line on the war of independence, Camus has arguably produced the finest literature to come out of Algeria (Extract 3). Despite the fact that he was born here and wrote much of his finest work with an Algerian setting, many Algerians are not so generous in their literary appraisal. For them, he represents the voice of the colonial oppressors, and is considered as one of a spurious category of European *colon* authors. Yet some, like the Algerian Novelists' Union, claim that far from being an 'outsider', Camus still speaks for the young people caught up in the absurdities of life in Algeria today.

When Algerian writing in Arabic got off the ground in 1925 with the

---

Notes to map (facing page): [a]*Birthplace of* **Camus**, *who included many descriptions of the city in his work – see especially* The Outsider *and his essay 'Summer in Algiers' (Extract 3). In 1575,* **Cervantes** *was held as a slave here. A picture of the city as it was in the sixteenth century is provided by* **Nicholas Nicholay** *(Extract 4).* **Fettouma Touati's** Desperate Spring *(Extract 2) tells the stories of women working in Algiers. The city was the setting for* **Pontecorvo's** *1965 film,* The Battle of Algiers; [b]*This ancient Roman city near Constantine is described by* **Camus** *in 'The Wind at Djemila';* [c]*Roman ruins described by* **Camus** *in 'Ruins at Tipasa';* [d]**Camus** *set his novel* The Plague *here;* [e]**Isabelle Eberhardt** *stayed at the Moorish Baths;* [f]*This desert village was where* **Isabelle Eberhardt** *died in a flood at the age of 27 – she is buried in the Muslim cemetery;* [g]**Isabelle Eberhardt** *lived here (see Extract 5);* [h]*This remote and mountainous region is the birthplace of several Algerian novelists, including* **Fadhma Amrouche, Fettouma Touati,** *and* **Mouloud Feraoun.**

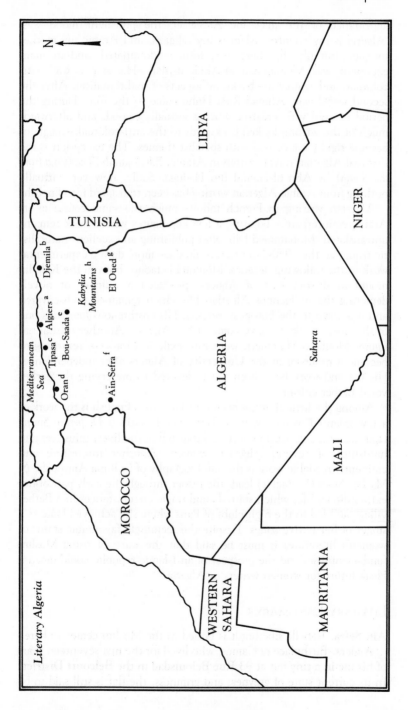

appearance of the magazine *Al-Shihab*, the prevalent mood was: 'Algeria is my country, Islam is my religion, and Arabic my mother tongue.' Initially the short story form predominated, and its main exponent was Muhammad al-Abid al-Jilali. His stance was anti-colonial, and against the backward aspects of traditionalism. After the second world war, Ahmad Rida Huhu came to the fore. During the period of civil war, creative writing virtually ceased, and afterwards much of the writing looked backwards to the anti-colonial struggle or became rigidly concerned with socialist themes. The exception is the first real Algerian novel written in Arabic, *Rih al-janub* (*The Wind from the South*) by Abn al-Hamid Ibn Haduga. Sadly, however, virtually nothing from Arabic Algerian writing has been translated into English.

Algerian writing in French follows much the same course as its Arabic counterpart – boasting a few key figures whose work remains untranslated. Mohammed Dib, after publishing an excellent naturalistic trilogy in the 1950s, went on to produce more daring experimental work in the following decades. Mouloud Feraoun, born in the **Kabylia** mountain district east of Algiers, produced a number of novels depicting the indigenous Algerian life which remained undiscovered and unknown to the European settlers. His posthumous *Journal* is one of the finest works to have come out of Algeria. Another substantial figure, Mouloud Mammeri, went into exile in Morocco, returning to become a professor at the **University of Algiers** after independence. His life and work have been much devoted to preserving the earlier vocal Berber culture.

Among the little that has been translated into English is the work of a few talented women writers. Fettouma Touati's ◊ *Desperate Spring* (Extract 2) is a collection of stories that tell of the lives, injustices and hardships of several Algerian women. Another interesting and eminently readable work is the autobiography of Fadhma Amrouche ◊. *My Life Story* (Extract 1) leads the reader through the early part of her extraordinary life, which started amid tragic circumstances in a Berber village and led to the nightclubs of Paris where she achieved fame as a singer of her native songs. Despite the seemingly favourable status of women's literature, it must be said that the wave of rising Muslim fundamentalism and the prospect of an Islamic republic could mean a bleak future for women writers in Algeria.

LITERARY LANDMARKS

Aïn Sefra. Isabelle Eberhardt is buried in the Muslim cemetery here.

Algiers. Birthplace of Camus, who lived for the first seventeen years of his life in a tiny flat at **93 Rue Belouisdad** in the **Belcourt District**. In its current state of greyness and grimness, the flat is still said to be recognizable as the setting for the home of Mersault, protagonist of *L'Étranger* (*The Outsider*) who sat on the minute balcony 'half way between misery and the sun'. According to a journalist who recently visited the flat, its present occupants were not only ignorant of their home's 'celebrity' status, but confessed that they had not read one word of Camus. Formerly notorious as a heavily working class, *pied-noir* area, today the neighbourhood of his old home is a hotbed of Islamic fundamentalism. In 1924, Camus was enrolled at the nearby **Lycée Abd-el-Kadr** (then named 'Bugeaud' after the French colonialist) on a scholarship, though none of his works are on the curriculum there today. Camus describes many parts of the city in his works, especially in *The Outsider* and his essays *Les Noces*. **Government Square** and **the Kasbah** are just two of the many recognizable places captured in his work. Pontecorvo's film *The Battle of Algiers* portrays life in Algiers at the time of the civil war and is a powerful evocation of a city in conflict, with many scenes in **the Kasbah**.

Bou-Saâda. Isabelle Eberhardt rented a small room at the **Moorish Baths** during her last years in Algeria.

Djemila. Ancient Roman city of Cuicul, near **Constantine**, described by Camus in his essay 'The Wind at Djemila': 'Wherever you walk, along the paths through the ruined houses, along wide paved roads under shining colonnades, along the vast forum between the triumphal arch and the temple set upon a hill, you always end up at the ravines which surround Djemila on every side, like a pack of cards opened out under a limitless sky.'

Kabylia. The remote mountain region east of Algiers and birthplace of several prominent Algerian writers. Fadhma Amrouche was born here, and achieved fame in France singing the haunting traditional songs of the region. Novelists Fettouma Touati and Mouloud Feraoun were also born here. Isabelle Eberhardt travelled through this region and settled at **El Oued**.

Oran. The city which provided Albert Camus with the backdrop for his novel *The Plague*.

Tipasa. Roman ruins 64 km west of Algiers, described by Albert Camus in his essay 'Ruins at Tipasa'.

Libraries and Bookshops

Algiers. Bibliothèque Universitaire and Librarie Papeterie, 2 Rue du 19 May 1956; Libraire Algerienne, 11 Rue Bab Azoun; Libraire Hachette, Rue Ben Mehidi Larbi 49 bis; SNED (Société Nationale d'Édition et de Diffusion), 3 Boulevard Znout Youcef.

Constantine. Libraire Chapelle, Place d'Orléans 1.

BOOKLIST

The following selection includes the extracted titles in this chapter as well as those mentioned in the introduction which are available in English and other titles for further reading. In general, paperback editions are given when possible. The editions cited are not necessarily the only ones available. For most of the extracted works, the original publisher in English can be found in 'Acknowledgments and Citations' at the end of the volume, as can the exact location of the extracts and the editions from which they are taken. Extract numbers are highlighted in bold for ease of reference.

African Women's Writing, Charlotte Bruner, ed, Heinemann, London, 1993.

Amrouche, Fadhma, *My Life Story*, Dorothy S. Blair, trans, The Women's Press, London, 1988. **Extract 1**.

Blanch, Lesley, *The Wilder Shores of Love*, Sphere, London, 1984 (includes chapters on Isabelle Eberhardt and Aimée Dubucq de Rivery).

Camus, Albert, *The Outsider*, Stuart Gilbert, trans, Penguin, London, 1961.

Camus, Albert, *The Plague*, Stuart Gilbert, trans, Penguin, London, 1963.

Camus, Albert, *Selected Essays and Notebooks* (includes 'The Wind at Djemila', 'Summer in Algiers' and 'Ruins at Tipasa'), Philip Thody, trans, Penguin, London, 1979. **Extract 3**.

Eberhardt, Isabelle, *In the Shadow of Islam*, Sharon Bangert, trans, Peter Owen, London, 1993.

Eberhardt, Isabelle, *The Oblivion Seekers*, Paul Bowles, trans, Peter Owen, London, 1988.

Eberhardt, Isabelle, *The Passionate Nomad: The Diary of Isabelle Eberhardt*, Beacon/Virago, London, 1988. **Extract 5**.

Fanon, Frantz, *Studies in a Dying Colonialism*, Earthscan Publications, London, 1989.

Horne, Alistair, *A Savage War of Peace*, Macmillan, London, 1977.

Mackworth, Cecily, *The Destiny of Isabelle Eberhardt*, Quartet, London, 1977.

Nicholay, Nicholas, 'Navigations at Peregrinations Orientales', in *Purchas his Pilgrimes*, 1625. **Extract 4**.

Purchas, Samuel, *Hakluytus Posthumus, or Purchas his Pilgrimes, Contayning a History of the World in Sea Voyages and Land Travell by Englishmen and Others*, 1625. Published in 20 volumes by AMS Press, New York (reprint of 1907 edition).

Touati, Fettouma, *Desperate Spring*, Ros Schwartz, trans, The Women's Press, London, 1987. **Extract 2**.

Wilkins, Anthony, *Among the Berbers of Algeria*, Fisher Unwin, London.

Albert Camus

Extracts

(1) ALGERIA: MARRIAGE

Fadhma Amrouche, *My Life Story*

In her autobiography Fadhma Amrouche describes how at the
age of sixteen she was married and presented to the Amrouche
family. As is the tradition, she spends the first night at the home
of her in-laws where live a myriad of relations and her husband's
second wife-to-be.

When night fell my mother-in-law took us to the upper storey above
the small storeroom, where she had prepared our bed: rugs laid out on a
rush mat, with a printed cotton sheet to cover us. The room was
enormous, over thirty foot long by twenty or twenty-five feet wide. Jars
of oil were lined up along the floor at the bottom of every wall, and
there were as many in the four other rooms, downstairs as well as
upstairs. The windows had heavy shutters that were closed with a sort
of wooden bolt: you turned a latch to the vertical position and the bolt
shot into the wall into which the window frame was fixed; to open it,
you turned the wooden latch back to the horizontal and the bolt fell
back; to get in from the outside you'd have to burn the doors down.

There was no ceiling, so we could see the roof-tiles. There was no
comfort, nothing was kept clean and tidy; the floor was paved with
bricks, the same as downstairs. Next to us, over the vestibule,
Taïdhelt, the grandfather's wife, had her bedroom.

I slept like a log that night. I was so tired! Next morning, it was
already late when I woke up. Everybody was busy: Taïdhelt had drunk
her coffee and was winding wool on to her distaff; my mother-in-law,
Reskia and Hemama, Douda's daughter, as well as my husband's
fiancée, had all been out to pick prickly pears, and were setting out the
fruit in rows in a shady corner of the courtyard. They had filled up a big
wooden dish which anyone could help themselves to at any time; but
first you had to pour water over them to blunt the prickles and then cut
off the heads and tails with a sharp knife and finally peel off the thick
skin.

I watched this procedure with amusement and curiosity. Meanwhile
my mother-in-law had taken off the clothes she had worn to pick the
fruit and was rubbing herself down hard with a sort of brush made of
alfalfa grass, to remove any remaining thorns.

Douda beckoned me over to the hearth, where she stood surrounded
by egg-shells. In a large earthenware dish on the fire, a huge *galette*
made of very white semolina beaten up with a number of eggs, was

frying in oil. This is the traditional breakfast in Aïth-Abbas, reserved for mothers of newborn babies. But that morning Douda had made a much bigger *galette* and she gave me and my husband a good quarter of it. She had poured some honey into a bowl and that was our breakfast.

(2) ALGERIA: WOMEN

Fettouma Touati, *Desperate Spring*

In her novel, Touati describes the lives of a number of Algerian women, interlinking the tales of the different characters and different dilemmas.

Djohra was widowed in the first year after the war. She had just turned twenty-four. Her younger daughter Fatma was three, Salah seven, and Yasmina five. She continued living in her husband's house. Her father-in-law, her brother-in-law and her mother-in-law looked after her. There was no question of a widow of twenty-four being alone, even if she was a mother. They kept a close watch on her chastity. As time went by and the children grew older, they relaxed their guard. A boy of fifteen is supposed to keep an eye on his mother, for she is merely a woman.

Salah was her only son. She spoiled him outrageously. When she and her daughters ate couscous with a soup made from a handful of chick-peas and a courgette, he ate chips or eggs. When Fatma protested, her mother retorted: 'But he's a man!'

From the age of thirteen, Salah proved to be a hooligan. His thefts became increasingly serious. Djohra had to reimburse an ever-growing number of plaintiffs. He would sell the proceeds of his thefts for the price of a cinema ticket, or he would go drinking and wander around Algiers. When he needed a large sum of money, he wheedled it out of his mother. As he grew older, he became more demanding, sometimes asking for the equivalent of a third of his mother's pension. He didn't care that it left them without enough to eat.

'You'll always manage!' he would say to his mother.

'I shouldn't have to manage! You are eighteen! It's your turn to go out to work. You wear a moustache, and I keep you in idleness!'

(3) ALGIERS

Albert Camus, *Summer in Algiers*

*Albert Camus describes summer in the city in which he grew up
and which he longs for when away from the country. Algiers is
often described in his novels and his essays. 'Summer in Algiers'
is included in his Selected Essays and Notebooks – see Booklist.*

You spend the whole morning diving in the sea, with garlands of
laughter among spouts of water, in long paddling trips around red and
black cargo vessels (the ones from Norway smell of all kinds of wood,
the ones from Germany reek of oil, the ones going from port to port
along the coast smell of wine and old casks). When the sun is brimming
over from every corner of the sky, the orange-coloured canoe laden
with sunburnt bodies brings us back in a mad race. And when, in a
sudden pause in the rhythmic stroke of the fruit-coloured blades of the
double paddle, we glide smoothly into the harbour, how can I help but
know that I am carrying across the smooth waters a tawny cargo of gods
in whom I recognize my brothers?

But, at the other end of the town, the summer already offers us the
contrast of its other wealth: I mean its silences and boredom. These
silences do not always have the same quality, according to whether
they are born of shadow or of sun. There is the silence of noon on
Government Square. In the shade of the trees that grow each side
Arabs sell penny glasses of iced lemonade, perfumed with orange
blossom. Their cry of 'cool, cool' echoes across the empty square.
When it fades away, silence falls again under the sun: in the merchant's
pitcher, the ice moves and I can hear it tinkling. There reigns the
silence of the siesta. In the streets round the docks, in front of the
squalid barbers' shops, you can measure the silence by the melodious
buzzing of the flies behind the hollow reed curtains. Elsewhere, in the
Moorish cafés in the Kasbah, it is men's bodies which are silent, which
cannot drag themselves away, leave the glass of tea, and rediscover
time through the pounding of their own pulse.

(4) ALGIERS

Nicholas Nicholay,
Navigations at Peregrinations Orientales

*The French diplomat provides one of the few available descrip-
tions of Algiers in the sixteenth century.*

Shee is scituated upon the Mediterranean Sea, upon the hanging of a
Mountaine environed with strong Walls, Ramperds, Ditches, Plat-

formes, and Bulwarks, in forme almost three-square; the largenesse which goeth towards the Sea side stretcheth narrowly almost unto the highest part, whereas there is a great building made in forme of a Citadell, to command the Towne and entrie of the Haven. As for the buildings being beyond the Pallace Royall, are very faire Houses belonging to particular men, with a great number of Bathes and Cookes houses. The places and streetes are so well ordained, that every one in his Occupation apart: there are about three thousand Hearthsteeds. At the bottome of the Citie which is towards the North joyning to the Walles, which are beaten with the Surges of the Sea in a great place, is by great Artifice and subtill Architecture builded their principall and head Mosquee; and a little below that is the Arcenall, which is the place into which are hailed up, and trimmed the Gallies and other vessels. This Citie is very Merchant-like, for that she is situated upon the Sea, and for this cause marveilously peopled, for her bignesse: she is inhabited of Turkes, Moores, and Jewes in great number, which with marveilous gaine exercise the Trade of Merchandise, and lend out money at Usury.

(5) EL OUED

Isabelle Eberhardt, *The Diary of Isabelle Eberhardt*

Disguised as a man Isabelle Eberhardt journeyed on her horse Souf (named after the region) through remote desert regions of Algeria, few of which had been visited by Europeans. Slimène is the Algerian whom she eventually married.

Shortly after the maghreb last night, rode Souf by the back of the café through the white sandy streets along houses that are half in ruin.

A few moments earlier, just as the sun had been about to set and El Oued had been ablaze in gold, I had spotted the silhouettes of two Arabs garbed in white standing on top of the little dune where the lime kiln is; they looked as if set against a heavenly light. The impression was a biblical one, and I suddenly felt as if transported back to the ancient days of primitive humanity, when the great light-giving bodies in the sky had been the object of veneration . . .

At that frontier between town and desert, I was reminded of those autumn and winter sunsets in the land of exile, when the great snow-capped Jura mountains seemed to come closer in an expanse of pale bluish hues.

It is chilly in the morning now. The light has changed colour. We no longer have the flat glare of stifling summer days. The sky is now a violent shade of blue, pure and invigorating.

Everything has come to life again, and so has my soul. Yet, as always, I feel a boundless sadness, an inarticulate longing for something I cannot describe, a nostalgia for a *place* for which I have no name.

For several days now, intellectual endeavour has seemed less repellent to me than it did this summer, and I think I shall go on writing. The wellspring does not seem to have run dry.

For the moment I do not feel up to taking off and parting from Slimène for ever, even if I could afford to do so. And why should I?

I feel a tranquil heart is mine at last; the same cannot be said for any peace of mind, alas!

Biographies and important works

AMROUCHE, Fadhma (1882–1967). The poet and singer Amrouche was born in a mountain village in the remote **Kabylia** region of eastern Algeria, the illegitimate daughter of a young local widow. A strict 'code of honour' in her Berber village meant that to avoid persecution and possible death for Fadhma, her mother walked six days through the mountains to place her child in a Catholic mission. Amrouche was married at sixteen to a local Berber schoolteacher, and later moved to Tunis and Paris. Here she achieved fame as a singer of the haunting songs of her native Kabylia. In her 70s she wrote her autobiography *My Life Story* (Extract 1) which has come to be regarded as a classic.

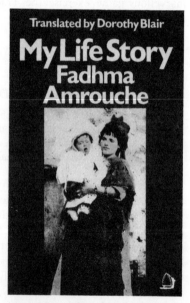

Translated by Dorothy Blair
My Life Story
Fadhma
Amrouche

The cover portrait is of Fadhma Amrouche and her son

CAMUS, Albert (1913–1960). Camus was born in Algeria when this region of North Africa was in French possession. His parents were of Spanish descent and he grew up in a working class, *pied-noir* district of **Algiers**. While studying at **Algiers University** in the mid 1930s, he engaged in left-wing political activities, campaigning against facism. He was also a keen athlete and played in goal for Racing Algiers, the local football team. During the second world war he became a resistance leader in France and was associated for a time with Jean-Paul Sartre and the existentialists. He is best known for his novels *L'Étranger* (*The Outsider*) and *La Peste* (*The Plague*), both of which have Algerian settings. He also wrote several plays and books of essays (Extract 3). Camus was awarded the Nobel Prize for Literature in 1957. He was killed in a road accident in January 1960.

Fettouma Touati
Desperate Spring
Translated by Ros Schwartz

EBERHARDT, Isabelle (1877–1904). Eberhardt is a legend in Algeria, despite her short life. She was born in Geneva of Russian parents. Her father was a Muslim, and after his death her guardian brought her up as a boy. Initially she studied medicine, but when her guardian died she took her inheritance and went to live in North Africa. With the intention of becoming a writer, she travelled on horseback dressed as a man through remote regions of Algeria. She married a native Algerian, which resulted in her persecution, and a mysterious assassination attempt by the French colonial authorities who eventually expelled her. She later returned with her husband, continuing her work as a journalist and writer (Extract 5). She was killed at the age of 27 in a flash flood in Aïn Sefra, a wadi-village in the desert.

NICHOLAY, Nicholas (1517–1583). Nicholay served as a soldier in the army, campaigning all over Europe. He was posted as a diplomat to Constantinople in 1551, and in the course of this work travelled widely through

the Levant and visited North Africa. His is one of the few descriptions of Algeria during this period (Extract 4).

TOUATI, Fettouma. Born in the remote southern region of **Kabylia**, Touati later moved to **Algiers** to work at the **University of Tzi-Ouzou**, where she encountered the difficulties endured by so many working women in modern Algerian society. This experience inspired her to write her first novel, *Desperate Spring* (Extract 2), which relates the stories of a number of women working in Algiers.

EGYPT

'The entire country is transformed into a sea and you can see nothing but the cities, which look like islands in the Aegean Sea. During this season the boats no longer follow the course of the river, they sail straight over the plain. On the voyage from Naucratis [near the site of modern Alexandria] to Memphis you sail right past the pyramids.'
Herodotus, Book II

When the great traveller and historian Herodotus ◊ arrived in Egypt in the fourth century BC he was surprised to find it 'transformed into a sea' (Extracts 11 and 12). With the advent of flood control, first impressions are rather different for the travellers of today. However the **Nile** remains now, as then, the life blood of Egypt.

From the earliest stirrings of civilization around 5000 BC, the river has provided Egypt with its food and drink, its building materials, its power and its climate. Without the Nile there would simply be no Egypt. The rest of the country is largely desert, and the population of some 50 million (increasing by over one million each year) live crammed into the Nile valley region, the delta and the coastal strip. **Cairo**, the capital and the third largest city in the world, is now so overcrowded that it even has a district known as the **City of the Dead**, where the inhabitants live in the mausoleums of the graveyards.

The picture of poverty, overpopulation and of a Third World state belies Egypt's rich and celebrated history. As early as 3500 BC, papyrus was in use and in 3200 BC the unification of Upper and Lower Egypt led to the age of the great dynasties which produced the **Pyramids** and the **Valley of the Kings**. The earliest papyrus writing was in hieroglyphics and was primarily used for official, commercial and funerary records. Two fragments from this period record what is thought to be the earliest purely personal writing. The first is a note from a creditor to one of his debtors, loosely translated: 'Do not think you will get away

---

FACT BOX

AREA: 1 002 000 sq km
POPULATION: 54 059 000
CAPITAL: Cairo
LANGUAGES: Arabic
FORMER COLONIAL POWER: Ottoman Empire (Turkey), French
    and British Administration, British Protectorate

---

with this debt which you owe me.' The second contains the observations of a disgruntled official: 'Things are going to the dogs; the end of the world is at hand.' Even 5000 years ago it seems these elements that play such a role in modern civilization were already flourishing in Ancient Egypt. Even the earliest dice yet discovered, which dates from this period, was found to be loaded!

During the later dynasties, writing on magic and religion began to proliferate. Among these was the so-called *Book of the Dead*. Copies of this book were buried with the dead in order to give them instructions on what to do when they woke up and found that they were no longer living. Sections included 'The Book of Knowing What is in the Underworld', 'The Book of the Gates', and the seemingly superfluous 'Book of Breathing'. Examples of folklore also began to appear, such as the *Tale of the Eloquent Peasant*, the story of a cunning peasant who always managed to get the better of his enemies and rivals, often by means of wily tricks. This form of folklore, handed down orally, has taken on a new lease of life today in the streets and cafés of the poorer districts of Cairo and other large cities, many of whose inhabitants fondly remember their upbringing in the countryside.

It was during the rule of the Pharaohs that the Israelites set out on their journey to the Holy Land, as recorded in the Book of Exodus in the Bible (Extract 8). In 332 BC Alexander the Great invaded Egypt, **Alexandria** was founded and the period of Ptolemaic rule began (Ptolemy was the name of the Macedonian kings of Egypt). Alexandria became one of the leading cities of the Ancient World, with the Pharos lighthouse hailed as one of the Seven Wonders of the World (the Pyramids are the only 'wonder' to have survived). Now Egypt began to look north towards Hellenic culture. Ptolemy I (Soter, a favourite general of Alexander the Great) established the greatest library of the Ancient World in Alexandria. It contained over 400 000 priceless volumes and manuscripts, including many ancient Greek and Roman texts – all of which were lost to history when the library burned down in 277 AD. Another Ptolemy, Claudius Ptolemaeus, the celebrated astronomer, mathematician and geographer was to have a profound influence for many centuries. Unfortunately, his calculation of the length of the Equator was out by some 30% and led Columbus over a thousand years later to believe he had sailed as far as China when in fact he had only reached America.

The last of the Ptolemaic rulers was Cleopatra, whose celebrated affair with Mark Anthony was to inspire Shakespeare's play *Antony and Cleopatra* (Extract 6). In the seventh century AD, Egypt was overrun by Arabs and became a largely Muslim country. Cairo soon established itself as one of the great centres of Islamic learning, attracting scholars from all over the Muslim world, including West and Central Africa. Apart from religious writing, the main literature of this period was story-telling and folklore. Out of this tradition in fourteenth century **Cairo** grew many of the stories of *The Thousand and One Nights*. Similar stories continue to circulate in the villages of Egypt today, retailing anecdotes from the court and bazaars of the Caliphate era over 500 years ago.

Meanwhile Egypt continued to attract a stream of writers, travellers and explorers. Bruce (◊ Ethiopia), Burton (◊ Ethiopia), Burckhardt, Flaubert ◊, de Lesseps ◊ were to be followed in this century by everyone from crime writer Agatha Christie (who wrote *Death on the Nile* here) to the lyric poet Rainer Maria Rilke (◊ Tunisia) who wrote of his visit in a letter to his wife Clara of 18 January 1911, 'I gazed and gazed – my God how one summons up one's strength, willing one's eyes to believe all they can see.'

Despite many rapturous and colourful descriptions (see for example, Extracts 13 and 14), for the most part these travellers understood little of the country they saw. The real Egypt often remained a closed book to them. When the French poet Gerard de Nerval rented a house in **Cairo** for six months, he was surprised when his landlord asked him to leave after a week because he had offended the neighbours by not buying any women to live with him!

Only in **Alexandria** did the Europeans seem to get a little closer to the locals. E.M. Forster came to work in the **International Red Cross Hospital** here in 1915 and was later to publish several books based on his experiences, including *Alexandria: A History and a Guide*. During his stay he befriended the Greek–Alexandrian poet Cavafy ◊, whom he remembered, in *Pharos and Pharillon*, as a 'Greek gentleman in a straw hat' standing on a street corner 'absolutely motionless at a slight angle to the universe'. The fact that Forster got to know a Greek–Egyptian was not so unusual in the circumstances. Alexandria had always been a city with unusual and cosmopolitan 'leanings' due its polyglot population and variety of religious affiliations (including Coptic Christian, Muslim and Judaic). Like Dublin and Prague, the two other cities on the fringes of European cultural life at this time, Alexandria was to produce more than its fair share of leading European cultural figures. The futurist Marinetti, the Italian hermetic poet Ungaretti, and Cavafy, the greatest poet in the Greek language this century (Extract 1), all hailed from the cultural and racial melting pot of Alexandria. Later, drawing on experiences gained in the city during the second world war, Lawrence Durrell ◊ was to describe the last colourful era of the city's cosmopolitan history in his celebrated *Alexandria Quartet* (Extract 2): 'The grim mandate which the city exercised over its familiars, crippling sentiment, steeping everything in the vats of its own exhausted passions.'

But in 1956 all this came to an end when Nasser seized the Suez Canal and the British, French and Israelis invaded. As a result of this fiasco the foreign communities were forced to leave Egypt, their influence vanished overnight, and the modern state of Egypt was born.

Indigenous Egyptian writing now came into its own. Before this century it had faced great difficulties, while the great art of story-telling (largely in the vernacular) flourished. Literary Arabic was simply not suited to the novel form. Realistic dialogue was impossible (people did not speak in literary Arabic) and narrative was stilted owing to the formality of the written language. The first really modern novelist in Egypt was Muhammad Husayn Haykal (1888–1956), who later became a member of the Cabinet. His novel *Zaynab*, 1917, the story of a girl from the countryside of the **Nile Delta**, pioneered colloquial dialogue. Meanwhile Tewfik Al-Hakim ◊, an Alexandrian by birth who studied law in Paris, was developing the traditions of poetic drama. He was to become Egypt's greatest playwright, and is best known abroad for his novel *The Maze of Justice*, an intriguing and amusing murder story which is also set in a village on the **Nile Delta**.

Not until the advent of Naguib Mahfouz ◊ did the Egyptian urban novel take off. Mahfouz drew on his early experiences in the old **Gamiliyya quarter** of Cairo, and later used his Dickensian eye for detail in his celebrated *Cairo Trilogy* (Extract 5), set in three different suburbs of Cairo. This saga depicts the fortunes of a middle-class family during the 1920s and 1930s up to the beginning of the second world war. Mahfouz won the Nobel Prize for Literature in 1988 and is now the best known of all Egyptian writers, with many of his works available in translation.

The best account of the influential Suez Crisis from the Egyptian point of view is in *Don't Shut off the Sun* by Ehsan Abdel Kuddous, who started his career as a journalist with progressive views. After 1956 and the resultant foreign exodus, life in Egypt changed dramatically. The life of the 'lost' generation, the people who were immediately affected by the evacuation, is carefully observed by Waguib Ghali ◊ in his novel *Beer at the Snooker Club* (Extract 3): 'There he was then. Selling cucumbers. Cucumbers of all things . . . a degree in his pocket and selling cucumbers.'

Since then, Egypt has undergone great changes and several traumatic events, most notably the wars with Israel and the final reconciliation, and the assassination of Sadat. This has left contemporary Egypt, under Mubarak, in a volatile situation, exacerbated by population explosion and rapid but uneven modernization. Progress and liberalization on the one hand now have to compete with the rising Muslim fundamentalism.

A writer whose career has been central to this struggle is Nawal El Saadawi ◊, who trained as a doctor and became the Director of Public Health. Her novels and campaigning for women's rights led to her eventual dismissal from this post. Under Sadat she was imprisoned, and to avoid censorship many of her novels have been published in Beirut and more recently several have been translated into English. Perhaps the best introduction to her writing is in the collection of stories *She has No Place in Paradise* (Extract 7), whose title is indicative of her struggle for women in Egyptian society.

Of the same calibre is Yusuf Idris ◊ whose celebrated short stories (Extract 9) confront the sensitive themes of politics, sex and poverty (equally controversial is his combined use of colloquial and classical Arabic styles). *The Cheapest Nights* is his collection of short punchy stories with titles such as 'The Freak', 'Did You Have to Turn on the Light Li-Li?', and 'The Dregs of the City', set in **Cairo**: 'The deeper inside, the narrower the streets. The houses shrink and shed their numbers. Windows have no shutters . . . Faces are paler and darker. Clothes are old and faded. Language degenerates into abuse, and the air carries the smell of spices and leather and glue and sawdust.'

His contemporary and fellow short story writer, Gamal Al-Ghitani ◊, has had most success with *Zayni Barakat* (Extract 4), an historical novel set in sixteenth century **Cairo**. It charts the rise to power of the puritannical Zayni Barakat – 'He made his way with difficulty atop a high mule with a modest saddle and plain saddle-cloth (this pleased the people; they said, 'Look, that is how justice and just rulers should be!) . . . As for Zayni he kept nodding his head slowly, with a pious and righteous look on his face.' His novel boldly echoes the threat of rising Muslim fundamentalism, which recently precipitated the imprisonment of one writer who published a cartoon version of the Koran, and which threatens to censor many more writers in Egypt today.

LITERARY LANDMARKS

Alexandria. Cavafy used to frequent the Greek bookshop on what was then Rue Debanne. He lived the last years of his life, at his flat at **10**

Rue Lepsius in the disreputable old Greek quarter called **Massalia**, which was near the harbour. His flat was above a brothel, across the street from the **Greek hospital** and around the corner from **St Sabas Church**. As he said, according to E.M. Forster in *Pharos and Pharillon*, 'Where could I live better? Below the brothel caters for the flesh. And there is the church which forgives sins. And there is the hospital where we die.' Though he never visited the brothel – it didn't cater for homosexuals – he was to die in the hospital and his funeral was held at St Sabas. The **Metropole Hotel**, a modernized Art Nouveau hotel, was formerly the offices of the Third Circle of Irrigation where Cavafy worked – on the first floor above what is now the **Trianon Patisserie**. Durrell, Churchill, Noel Coward and Somerset Maugham are among the many guests who have passed through the **Hotel Cecil** and admired the views of the Eastern Harbour. Ask to see the Visitor's Book for the full roll call. Alexandria is Durrell's vivid backdrop for his *Alexandria Quartet* (Extract 2). In *Clea*, the final part, he magically describes a German air raid on the city: 'The Alexandria I saw now, the first vision of it from the sea was something I could not have imagined.'

Aswan. Agatha Christie wrote her best-selling novel *Death on the Nile* while staying at the **Hotel Pullman**. The hotel, which also featured in the 1978 film of the novel, is still referred to by the *cognoscenti* under its former name, the Old Cataract. The style is an eclectic mix of Edwardian and Moorish, though it is said to have been largely spoiled by modernization.

Cairo. Naguib Mahfouz was born in the **old Gamiliyya quarter**. The suburbs of **Bayn al Qasran**, **Qasr ash-Shawq** and **as Sukkanyya** are the backdrops to his *Cairo Trilogy*. His favoured pastime is a long walk to the famous **Aly Baba Coffee Shop** in **Tahrir Square**. The **Pyramids** were visited by almost all the great European writers and travellers who came to Egypt. Incurable romantics like Flaubert wrote about them before actually setting foot near them; 'When the traveller has reached the top of the pyramid his hands are torn and bleeding . . . Look and you will see cities with domes of gold and minarets of porcelain . . . marble rimmed pools where sultanas come to bathe their bodies . . .' (*Flaubert in Egypt*). The **Shepheard's Hotel** on **Opera Square** was a favourite stopping place for the passing literati on their way to the 'marvels' and Alexandria. The **Opera House** itself was the venue for Verdi's *Aida*, performed for the extravagant opening celebrations of the **Suez Canal**. Pierre Loti, the flamboyant French nineteenth century writer, secured the rare and perverse privilege of being allowed to wander alone at night amid the mummies of Cairo's **Museum of Egyptology**. He is said to have found his former self in the form of Rameses II.

Valley of the Kings. Howard Carter discovered **Tutankhamen's**

Tomb (Extract 15) in the Valley of the Kings in November 1922: 'Hardly had I arrived on the work next morning than the unusual silence made me realise something out of the ordinary had happened.'

Libraries and Bookshops

Alexandria. Al-Ahram, 10 Sharia Horriya; Book Centre, 51 Sharia Sa'ad Zghloul.

Cairo. American University in Cairo – the bookshop is at the back of the campus on Mohammed Mahóud Street; Anglo–Egyptian Bookshop, 196 Sharia Khaliq Sarwat.

BOOKLIST

The following selection includes the extracted titles in this chapter as well as those mentioned in the introduction which are available in English and other titles for further reading. In general, paperback editions are given when possible. The editions cited are not necessarily the only ones available. For most of the extracted works, the original publisher in English can be found in 'Acknowledgments and Citations' at the end of the volume, as can the exact location of the extracts and the editions from which they are taken. Extract numbers are highlighted in bold for ease of reference.

African Women's Writing, Charlotte Bruner, ed, Heinemann, London, 1993.

Al-Ghitani, Gamal, Zayni Barakat, Farouk Abdel Wahab, trans, Penguin, London, 1990. **Extract 4**.

Al-Hakim, Tewfik, The Maze of Justice: Diary of a Country Prosecutor, A. Eban, trans, Saqi, London, 1989. (Note: Al-Hakim's forename is spelt 'Tawfiq' in this edition.)

Al-Hakim, Tewfik, 'Miracles for Sale', in Modern Arabic Short Stories, Denys Johnson-Davies, trans, Oxford University Press, Oxford, 1967. **Extract 10**.

Carter, Howard, The Tomb of Tutankhamen, Cooper Square, Savage, MD, 1963. **Extract 15**.

Cavafy, C.P., The Complete Poems, Rae Dalven, trans, Chatto and Windus, London, 1961. (**Extract 1** translated by Paul Strathern.)

Christie, Agatha, Death on the Nile, Fontana, London, 1987.

Durrell, Lawrence, Alexandria Quartet, Faber and Faber, London, 1965. **Extract 2**.

Folk Tales of Egypt, Hasan M. El Shamy, trans, University of Chicago Press, Chicago, IL, 1980.

Flaubert, Gustave, Flaubert in Egypt, Francis Steegmuller, ed and trans, The Bodley Head, London, 1972. **Extract 13**.

Forster, E.M., Alexandria: A History and a Guide, M. Haag, London, 1983.

Forster, E.M., Pharos and Pharillon, M. Haag, London, 1986.

Ghali, Waguib, Beer at the Snooker Club, Serpent's Tail, London, 1987. **Extract 3**.

Haywood, John, *Modern Arabic Literature 1800–1970*, Lund Humphries, London, 1971.

Herodotus, *Histories, Book II*, H.H. Huxley, ed, Bradda, Oxford, 1979. (**Extracts 11 and 12** translated by Paul Strathern.)

Idris, Yusuf, *The Cheapest Nights*, Heinemann, London, 1978.

Idris, Yusuf, 'Faharat's Republic', in *Modern Arabic Short Stories*, Denys Johnson-Davies, trans, Oxford University Press, Oxford, 1967. **Extract 9.**

Lesseps, Ferdinand de, *The History of the Suez Canal: A Personal Narrative*, Blackwood, London, 1876. **Extract 14.**

Lively, Penelope, *Cleopatra's Sister*, Viking Penguin, London, 1993.

Lively, Penelope, *Moon Tiger*, Penguin, London, 1988.

Mahfouz, Naguib, *Palace of Desire*, Part Two of the *Cairo Trilogy*, Doubleday, New York, 1991.

Mahfouz, Naguib, *Palace Walk*, Part One of the *Cairo Trilogy*, Doubleday, New York, 1990. **Extract 5.**

Mahfouz, Naguib, *Sugar Street*, Part Three of the *Cairo Trilogy*, Doubleday, New York, 1992.

Nerval, Gerard de, *Travels to the East*, Peter Owen, London, 1972.

Ptolemy (Claudius Ptolemaeus), *The Geography*, Dover, New York, 1992.

Saadawi, Nawal El, *The Fall of the Imam*, Minerva, London, 1987.

Saadawi, Nawal El, *She has No Place in Paradise*, Shirley Eber, trans, Minerva, London, 1989. **Extract 7.**

Shakespeare, William, *Antony and Cleopatra*, in *Complete Works of Shakespeare*, Collins, London, 1951. **Extract 6.**

Tales from The Thousand and One Nights, N.J. Dawood, ed, Penguin, London, 1973.

Extracts

(1) ALEXANDRIA

C.P. Cavafy, *The City*

The 'city' referred to in the poem is Alexandria, where Cavafy lived for the rest of his life after his return from abroad.

You said; 'I'll go to another land, go to some other sea.
I'll find another city to live in that's better than this one.
All I've ever done has been damned, thwarted by fate;
and my heart, like a cadaver, is buried in this tomb.
How long must my mind remain in this wilderness?
Wherever I look about me, wherever I turn my eyes

all I see are the dark ruins of my life here
where I've spent so many years, wasting and destroying them utterly.'

You will find no other lands, you will find no other sea.
The city will follow you. You will roam
the same streets, grow old in the same quarters.
and turn grey amongst these same houses.
Always you will arrive in this city. Don't hope for any other.
There is no ship to take you away, no road out of town.
As you have destroyed your life here
In this small corner, you have ruined it throughout the world.

(2) ALEXANDRIA

Lawrence Durrell, *Alexandria Quartet*

In this passage from 'Clea', the final part of his Alexandria Quartet, Durrell describes the hero's arrival off Alexandria harbour at night, and his witnessing of a German air raid on the city.

It was still dark when we lay up outside the invisible harbour with its remembered outworks of forts and anti-submarine nets. I tried to paint the outlines on the darkness with my mind. The boom was raised only at dawn each day. An all-obliterating darkness reigned. Somewhere ahead of us lay the invisible coast of Africa, with its 'kiss of thorns' as the Arabs say. It was intolerable to be so aware of them, the towers and minarets of the city and yet to be unable to will them to appear. I could not see my own fingers before my face. The sea had become a vast empty ante-room, a hollow bubble of blackness.

Then suddenly there passed a sudden breath, a whiff like a wind passing across a bed of embers, and the nearer distance glowed pink as a sea-shell, deepening gradually into the rose-richness of a flower. A faint and terrible moaning came out across the water towards us, pulsing like the wing-beats of some fearful prehistoric bird – sirens which howled as the damned must howl in limbo. One's nerves were shaken like the branches of a tree. And as if in response to this sound lights began to prick out everywhere, sporadically at first, then in ribbons, bands, squares of crystal. The harbour suddenly outlined itself with complete clarity upon the dark panels of heaven, while long white fingers of powder-white light began to stalk about the sky in ungainly fashion, as if they were the legs of some awkward insect struggling to gain a purchase on the slippery black. A dense stream of coloured rockets now began to mount from the haze among the battleships, emptying on the sky their brilliant clusters of stars and diamonds and smashed pearl snuff-boxes with a marvellous prodigality. The air shook in strokes. Clouds of pink and yellow dust arose with the maroons to shine upon the greasy buttocks of the barrage balloons which were flying everywhere. The very sea seemed to tremble. I had no idea that we were so near, or that the city could be so beautiful in the mere saturnalia of a war. It had begun to swell up, to expand like some mystical rose of the darkness, and the bombardment kept it company, overflowing the mind. To our surprise we found ourselves shouting at each other. We were staring at the burning embers of Augustine's Carthage, I thought to myself, we are observing the fall of city man.

(3) Cairo

Waguib Ghali, *Beer at the Snooker Club*

The engaging hero of Beer at the Snooker Club describes the start of another hard day's idling in Cairo.

I left and went to Groppi's. I drank whisky and ate peanuts, watching the sophisticated crowd and feeling happy that my aunt had refused to give me the money. I had asked simply because my conscience was nagging. It was something I vaguely had to do but had kept putting off. Soon Omar and Jameel came in, then Yehia, Fawzi and Ismail. Groppi's is perhaps one of the most beautiful places to drink whisky in. The bar is under a large tree in the garden and there is a handsome black barman who speaks seven languages. We drank a bottle of whisky between us and I watched them fight to pay for it. Yehia paid, then we all left together. They each possess a car.

I am always a bit bored in the mornings because they are all either at the university or working. Sometimes I go and play snooker with Jameel at the billiards' club. You can find him there anytime – in fact he owns it. I would go there more often if it weren't for Font. Whenever I reproach myself for drinking too much, I tell myself it's Font who is driving me to drink. 'Font,' I told him once, 'just tell me what you want me to do?'

'Run away, you scum,' he answered. So I went to Groppi's and drank more whisky.

(4) Cairo

Gamal Al-Ghitani, Zayni Barakat

This is a report of the Head Spy of Cairo on the activities of the puritanical Zayni Barakat, who is trying to assert his power in the city in the sixteenth century.

On the old pulpit of al-Azhar he stood. The mosque was overflowing with people of all colours and walks of life. They shouted and the pillars shook and the minarets almost leaned. It appeared that nothing on earth could quiet them, but Zayni raised his right hand, fingers outstretched (it was a normal, five-finger hand), and it was as if a magical force flowed from him and silence shut the people's mouths. It was said later on that he had the ability to make people fall silent and that if he wanted people to shed tears, he would make them do that. His voice flowed quietly among the people. This, in effect, is what he said.

Firstly, he would never have accepted the Inspectorship had he not informed the emirs of the conditions that his soul had laid down for the comfort of the people. Besides, had it not been for the Shaykh, learned in the foundations and the various branches of knowledge, the ascetic hermit, the friend of God, Shaykh Abu al-Su'ud, he would never have accepted. (At this point the clamour of the people rose, saying, 'We want nobody but you!', 'No one would do but you!', and such slogans that expressed the same idea in different words and phrases. Once again, his hand gestured calmly. The people's clamour subsided and they listened.)

Secondly, he fears nobody but God . . . Hence, should an act of injustice be committed against anyone, poor or rich, near or far, he should immediately go to his deputy and he would surely right the wrong and punish the transgressor, after the case was heard and the truth established.

Thirdly, he is not going to stay in Cairo all the time . . . There shall be nothing to stand between him and the people, great and humble, and should any wrong befall anyone, let that be righted publicly, in front of everyone.

Fourthly (and this is very serious), in every alley, street, village, town and fief, he will have agents monitoring, policing and staking out inequities wherever they occur; and these agents will inform him.

(5) Cairo

Naguib Mahfouz, *Palace Walk*

*Young Kamal returns home from school at the end of the day,
making his way through the streets of Cairo. Palace Walk is the
first part of the Cairo Trilogy.*

Kamal left the Khalil Agha School in the afternoon, bobbing along in the
swelling current of pupils who blocked off the road with their flow. They
began to scatter, some along al-Darrasa, some on New Street, others on
al-Husayn. Meanwhile bands of them encircled the roving vendors
stationed to catch them at the ends of the streets that branched out from
the school. Their baskets contained melon seeds, peanuts, doum palm
fruit, and sweets. At this hour, the street also witnessed fights, which
broke out here and there between pupils forced to keep their disagreements
quiet during the day to avoid school punishment . . .

He reached the pastry shop and stretched out his hand with the small
change he had hung on to since morning. He took a piece of pastry
with the total delight he experienced only on such a sweet occasion. It
made him frequently dream of owning a candy store one day, not to sell
the candy but to eat it. He continued on his way down al-Husayn
Street, munching on the pastry with pleasure . . .

On his way, he passed by the tobacco store of Matoussian. He
stopped under its sign, as he did every day at this hour, and raised his
small eyes to the colored poster of a woman reclining on a divan with a
cigarette between her crimson lips, from which rose a curling plume of
smoke. She was leaning her arm on the windowsill. The curtain was
drawn back to reveal a scene combining a grove of date palms and a
branch of the Nile. He privately called the woman Aisha after his
sister, since they both had golden hair and blue eyes. Although he was
just going on ten, his admiration for the mistress of the poster was
limitless. How often he thought of her enjoying life in its most splendid
manifestations. How often he imagined himself sharing her carefree
days in that luxurious room with its pristine view that offered her, in
fact both of them, its earth, palms, water, and sky. He would swim in
the green river valley or cross the water in the skiff that appeared
ghostlike far off in the picture. He would shake the palm trees till the
dates fell around him or sit near the beautiful woman with his eyes
gazing at her dreamy ones.

(6) EGYPT: CLEOPATRA

William Shakespeare, *Antony and Cleopatra*

Antony has just been betrayed by Cleopatra in his battle against
Caesar's fleet at the Battle of Actium.

All is lost:
This foul Egyptian hath betrayed me:
My fleet hath yielded to the foe, and yonder
They cast their caps up, and carouse together
Like friends long lost. Triple-turn'd whore, 'tis thou
Hast sold me to this novice, and my heart
Makes only wars on thee. Bid them all fly:
For when I am reveng'd upon my charm,
I have done all. Bid them all fly, be gone,
O sun, thy uprise shall I see no more,
Fortune and Antony part here, even here
Do we shake hands. All come to this? The hearts
That spaniel'd me at heels, to whom I gave
Their wishes, do discandy, melt their sweets
On blossoming Cæsar: and this pine is bark'd,
That overtopp'd them all. Betray'd I am.
O this false soul of Egypt! this grave charm.
Whose eye beck'd forth my wars, and call'd them home . . .

(7) EGYPT: HEAT

Nawal El Saadawi, *Thirst*

In Saadawi's short story, the heroine sets out on a hot day for
market. 'Thirst' is included in She has No Place in Paradise –
see Booklist.

The tarmac of the street beneath her feet had softened from the intensity
of the sun's heat. It burned her like a piece of molten iron and made her
hop here and there, bumping and colliding, unconsciously, like a small
moth against the sides of a burning lamp. She could have made for the
shade at the side of the street and sat for a time on the damp earth, but her
shopping basket hung on her arm and her right hand clutched at a tattered
fifty piastre note. She recited to herself the things she had to buy from the
market so as to remember them . . . half a kilo of meat at thirty-five
piastres, a kilo of courgettes five piastres, a kilo of tomatoes seven piastres,
three piastres change . . . half a kilo of meat at thirty-five piastres, a kilo of
courgettes five piastres, a kilo of tomatoes seven piastres, three piastres
change . . . half a kilo of meat . . .

(8) EGYPT: THE PHARAOHS

The Bible, Book of Exodus

The Israelites are living in slavery in Egypt at the time of the Pharaohs.

Now there arose a new king over Egypt, which knew not Joseph.

And he said unto his people, Behold, the people of the children of Israel are more and mightier than we:

Come let us deal wisely with them; lest they multiply, and it will come to pass, that, when there falleth out any war, they also join themselves unto our enemies, and fight against us, and get them up out of the land.

Therefore they did set over them taskmasters to afflict them with their burdens. And they built for Pharaoh store cities, Pithom and Raamses.

But the more they afflicted them, the more they multiplied and the more they spread abroad. And they were grieved because of the children of Israel.

And the Egyptians made the children of Israel to serve with rigour:

And they made their lives bitter with hard service, in mortar and in brick, and in all manner of service in the field, all their service, wherein they made them serve with rigour.

(9) EGYPT: A POLICEMAN

Yusuf Idris, *Faharat's Republic*

In his short story, Idris describes an ageing local police sergeant. 'Faharat's Republic' is included in the anthology Modern Arabic Short Stories – see Booklist.

The duty officer made no reply till the man had addressed him by 'Sergeant-Major . . . Sir!'

I had drawn close and was leaning, as were several others, on the wooden railing. I was thus able to hear his accent which contained faint traces of the countryside of Upper Egypt; his high-pitched voice betrayed the wide open spaces in which he had grown up, betrayed too the bellowing and barking required by his job: it had added to it the sort of grating rattle that befalls the local café wireless from having its volume turned up too high too often. The image of the general went completely from my mind as his features took on an aura of awesome authority. I saw him then purely as Upper Egyptian: a nose as big as that of Rameses, a high angular brow like that of Mycerinus, and the imprint of his advancing years that indicated a crowded history in the service of the police, for he had inevitably spent whole decades in it to reach the rank of Sergeant-Major, having joined the force as a simple private. I saw his ageing body as it really was, straight in parts, twisted in others, forced into its uniform, heavy boots and leather belt, which had themselves imposed a shape upon his body in the same way as the iron gives shape and dimension to a tarboosh. It was quite apparent he enjoyed being duty officer and wanted people to treat him like a real honest-to-God officer, which no doubt he had been dreaming of becoming for three-quarters of his lifetime dreaming of the day when his shoulder would carry its one pip. It was clear, though, that this shoulder would be carrying nothing of the sort, for though he would sometimes undertake the role of duty officer, the time for his being pensioned off was imminent and for him the dawn star was more attainable than that of a second lieutenant . . .

(10) EGYPT: A PRIEST

Tewfik Al-Hakim, *Miracles for Sale*

At the beginning of his short story, Al-Hakim describes a priest at home early one morning. 'Miracles for Sale' is included in the anthology Modern Arabic Short Stories – see Booklist.

The priest woke early as was his wont, preceded only by the birds in their nests, and began his prayers, his devotions, and his work for his diocese in that Eastern land whose spiritual light he was and where he was held in such high esteem by men of religion and in such reverence by the people. Before his door there grew a small palm tree planted by his own hands; he always watered it before sunrise, contemplating the sun as its rim, red as a date, burst forth from the horizon to shed its rays on the dewy leaves, wrapping their falling drops of silver in skeins of gold.

As the priest finished watering the palm tree that morning and was about to return inside, he found himself faced by a crowd of sad and worried-looking people, one of whom plucked up the courage to address him in beseeching tones:

'Father! Save us! No one but you can save us! My wife is on her death-bed and she is asking for your blessing before she breathes her last.'

'Where is she?'

'In a village near by. The mounts are ready,' replied the man, pointing to two saddled donkeys standing there waiting for them.

'I am willing to go, my sons,' said the priest. 'Wait a while so that I may arrange my affairs and tell my brethren and then return to you.'

'There's no time!' they all said as one voice. 'The woman is dying. We may well reach her too late. Come with us right away if you would be a true benefactor to us and a merciful saviour to the dying woman. It is not far and we shall be there and back before the sun reaches its zenith at noon.'

'Well, then, let us go at once!' the priest agreed with enthusiastic fervour.

(11) THE NILE IN FLOOD

Herodotus, *Book II*

Writing in the fifth century BC, Herodotus describes his first arrival in Egypt. It is August, and the Nile is in flood.

The entire country is transformed into a sea and you can see nothing but the cities, which look like islands in the Aegean Sea. During this season the boats no longer follow the course of the river, they sail straight over the plain. On the voyage from Naucratis [near the site of modern Alexandria] to Memphis you sail right past the pyramids.

(12) THE PYRAMIDS

Herodotus, *Book II*

Herodotus' description of the Pyramids also shows that things were very different in his day.

The construction of the pyramid took 20 years. It is covered with smooth concrete slabs, each jointed together, all over 10 yards long. The pyramid was initially constructed in the form of a flight of steps. When the workmen had completed the pyramid in this form, they hauled up the smooth slabs with machines made of short beams, which raised the slabs up the steps. The top of the pyramid was thus finished off first with smooth casing, the slopes below it next, and finally the part nearest the ground.

(13) The Pyramids and the Sphinx

Gustave Flaubert, *Flaubert in Egypt*

The French novelist travelled to Egypt in the mid-nineteenth century. Here, he first sees the Pyramids and the Sphinx.

Departure. Friday [7 December 1849], set out at noon for the Pyramids.

Maxime is mounted on a white horse that keeps jerking its head, Sassetti on a small white horse, myself on a bay, Joseph on a donkey.

We pass Soliman Pasha's gardens. Island of Roda. We cross the Nile in a small boat: while our horses are being led aboard, a corpse in its coffin is borne past us. Energy of our oarsmen: they sing, shouting out the rhythm as they bend forward and back. The sail swells full and we skim along fast.

Gizeh. Mud houses as at Atfeh – palm grove. Two waterwheels, one turned by an ox and the other by a camel.

Now stretching out before us is an immense plain, very green, with squares of black soil which are the fields most recently plowed, the last from which the flood withdrew: they stand out like Indian ink on the solid green. I think of the invocation to Isis: 'Hail, hail, black soil of Egypt!' The soil of Egypt *is* black. Some buffaloes are grazing, now and again a waterless muddy creek, in which our horses sink to their knees; soon we are crossing great puddles or creeks.

About half-past three we are almost on the edge of the desert, the three Pyramids looming up ahead of us. I can contain myself no longer, and dig in my spurs; my horse bursts into a gallop, splashing through the swamp. Two minutes later Maxime follows suit. Furious race. I begin to shout in spite of myself; we climb rapidly up to the Sphinx, clouds of sand swirling about us. At first our Arabs followed us, crying 'Sphinx! Sphinx! Oh! Oh! Oh!' It grew larger and larger, and rose out of the ground like a dog lifting itself up.

View of the Sphinx. Abu-el-Houl (Father of Terror). The sand, the Pyramids, the Sphinx, all gray and bathed in a great rosy light; the sky perfectly blue, eagles slowly wheeling and gliding around the tips of the Pyramids. We stop before the Sphinx; it fixes us with a terrifying stare; Maxime is quite pale; I am afraid of becoming giddy, and try to control my emotion. We ride off madly at full speed among the stones. We walk around the Pyramids, right at their feet. Our baggage is late in arriving; night falls.

(14) THE SUEZ CANAL

Ferdinand de Lesseps,
The History of the Suez Canal

This passage describes the discovery the day before the official opening of the Suez Canal that an Egyptian frigate had run aground and was lying across the Canal. It is taken from a speech delivered by de Lesseps in Paris and includes the reactions of his audience.

Powerful assistance was placed at the disposal of the Prince, who took with him a thousand seamen of his squadron. We agreed that there were three methods to be employed: either to endeavour to bring back the vessel to the middle of the channel, or to fix it to the banks; and if these two means fail, there was a third. We look into each other's eyes. 'Blow it up!' cried the Prince. 'Yes, yes; that's it. It will be magnificent.' And I embraced him. (*Salvos of applause.*) 'But at least,' added the Khedive, smiling; 'you will wait till I have taken away my frigate, and that I have announced to you that the passage is free.' I would not even grant him this respite. (*Laughter.*) The next morning I went on board the Aigle, without mentioning the accident to any one, as you may well believe.

The fleet started, and it was only five minutes before arriving at the site of the accident that an Egyptian admiral, sailing on a little steamer, signalled to me that the Canal was free. (*Bravo!*) On arrriving at Kantara, which is thirty-four kilometres from Port Saïd, the Latif, dressed in flags, saluted us with her guns, and every one was charmed with the attention which had thus placed a large frigate on the passage of the fleet of inauguration. (*Cheers and laughter.*) On arriving at Ismaïlia, the empress told me that during the whole journey she had felt as though a circle of fire were round her head, because every moment she thought she saw the Aigle stop short, the honour of the French flag compromised, and the fruit of our labours lost. (*Sensation.*) Suffocated by emotion, she was obliged to leave the table, and we overheard her sobs – sobs which do her honour, for it was French patriotism overflowing from her heart. (*Applause.*)

We passed without difficulty the rock of Serapium; and what gave me great pleasure as we were skirting it, was that the workmen near it, after looking to see if we touched the bottom of the Canal, expressed their transports of joy by a gesture which no expression can render. (*Here M. de Lesseps, by imitating the action of the workmen, brings down the applause of all the hall.*)

(15) TUTANKHAMEN'S TOMB

Howard Carter, *The Tomb of Tutankhamen*

Carter describes how he discovered the Tomb.

It was clear by now beyond any question that we actually had before us the entrance to a tomb, but doubts, born of previous disappointments, persisted in creeping in . . . and it was with ill-suppressed excitement that I watched the descending steps of the staircase, as one by one they came to light. The cutting was excavated in the side of a small hillock, and, as the work progressed, its western edge receded under the slope of the rock until it was, first partially, and then completely, roofed in, and became a passage, 10 feet high by 6 feet wide. Work progressed more rapidly now; step succeeded step, and at the level of the twelfth, towards sunset, there was disclosed the upper part of a doorway, blocked, plastered, and sealed.

A sealed doorway – it was actually true, then! Our years of patient labour were to be rewarded after all, and I think my first feeling was one of congratulation that my faith in The Valley had not been unjustified. With excitement growing to fever-heat I searched the seal impressions on the door for evidence of the identity of the owner, but could find no name: the only decipherable ones were those of the well-known royal necropolis seal, the jackal and nine captives. Two facts, however, were clear: first, the employment of this royal seal was certain evidence that the tomb had been constructed for a person of very high standing; and second, that the sealed door was entirely screened from above by workmen's huts of the Twentieth Dynasty was sufficiently clear proof that at least from that date it had never been entered.

Biographies and important works

AL-GHITANI, Gamal (1945–). A novelist and short story writer, Al-Ghitani is widely regarded as the best of his generation. He grew up in **Cairo**, worked as a rug designer and then became a journalist, covering all the major recent conflicts in the Middle East. He has written six collections of short stories, but is best known internationally for his historical novel *Zayni Barakat* (Extract 4).

AL-HAKIM, Tewfik (1902–). Al-Hakim grew up in **Alexandria**, but went to Paris to study law. He later worked as a lawyer for the Public Prosecutors' Office in provincial Egypt, and it was these experiences that were to provide much of the material for his writing. He is best known as Egypt's leading playwright, but he has also written novels and short stories (Extract 10) that are equally distinguished for their sophistication and realism. His best known novel, *The Maze of Justice*, is a wittily observed detective story about a murder in the **Nile Delta** which gives a revealing picture of life in the Egyptian countryside. True to his training, Al-Hakim's collection of plays, *Fate of a Cockroach*, explores the complexities that face man in his search for freedom and justice.

CARTER, Howard (1873–1939). Carter will be forever remembered as the Englishman who discovered the **tomb of Tutankhamen**. He started in archaeology young: at 17 he was working on an archaeological survey in Egypt, and by 1902 was in charge of evacuations in the *Valley of the Kings* where he discovered the tombs of Hatshepsut and Thutmose IV. In 1922, while working in the Valley of the Kings he came across the first tell-tale evidence of what turned out to be the tomb of Tutankhamen who reigned from 1361–1352 BC. Carter spent the next ten years painstakingly removing and cataloguing the contents of the tomb which have contri-

Lawrence Durrell

buted significantly to our understanding of Ancient Egypt.

CAVAFY, C.P. (1863–1933). Born in **Alexandria** of Greek parents, Cavafy spent some of his early childhood in England. Returning to Alexandria, he spent the rest of his life writing poetry, indulging in brief homosexual liaisons, and supporting himself by working as a clerk for the Water Board. His poetry evokes the provincial seediness of life in Alexandria, drawing deeply on minor events from the classical history of the Middle East while using a daring mixture of purist and demotic Greek.

DURRELL, Lawrence (1912–1991). Durrell was born in India and educated at a minor English public school. After a spell as a jazz pianist in a nightclub he went into exile, living in Paris and Corfu. At the outbreak of the second world war he was shipped from Greece to Egypt, where he worked as a press officer for the British Information Office for the duration of the war. Durrell's experience of **Alexandria** was to provide him with the material for his greatest work, his *Alexandria Quartet*, comprising *Justine*, *Balthazar*, *Mountolive* and *Clea*. When this work appeared in England in the late 1950s, its exoticism struck a nerve among the travel-starved and sexually repressed English and became hugely popular despite being largely scorned by the critics. The *Quartet* remains essential reading for all travellers to Alexandria.

FLAUBERT, Gustave (1821–1880). The French novelist is best known as the pioneer of realism and the great stylist of French literature. After a sickly childhood and early manhood, Flaubert set off in 1849 on a two-year tour of the Near East with his friend the writer Maxime du Camp. He started his career as a typical French romantic and had in fact written, in the first draft of *L'Éducation Sentimentale*, an imaginary description of climbing to the top of the **Pyramids** four years before he actually saw them. Flaubert drew partly on his Eastern travels for background material for his novel *Salammbô*, which is set in ancient Carthage. His experiences and impressions during his trip to Egypt are recorded in *Flaubert in Egypt* (Extract 13).

GHALI, Waguib (1938–1969). Ghali was a member of the sadly lost 'post-Suez' generation, who had been educated to European ways but found themselves practically exiles in their own country after the Europeans left. *Beer at the Snooker Club* (Extract 3) is his only novel, and describes much of the sense of futility and alienation from the 'real' Egypt felt by him and his social contemporaries (as well as a description of life in London as seen by a young Egyptian). Ghali committed suicide in 1969, and his tragic life has been described in *After a Funeral* by Diana Anthill (Jonathan Cape, London, 1969).

HERODOTUS (484–424 BC). The Greek historian Herodotus has become known, thanks to Cicero, as the 'Father of History'. Herodotus was the first historian to travel widely and see the world for himself. He took great care to describe the customs and history of the countries he visited, though he sometimes misinterpreted these and some of his information has been questioned. He visited Egypt during the autumn of 450 BC, and described the Egyptians, their history and country in *Book II* of his history (Extracts 11 and 12).

IDRIS, Yusuf (1927–). Idris was born in a country village and studied to become a doctor. He eventually became a government health inspector. It is probably this background which gave him his preoccupation with the darker side of life. Many of his stories are concerned with death, though often treated in a characteristically humorous manner. Idris is a short story writer of very high quality. His essentially realist manner and his use of accurate colloquial speech – whose comic veuve often enforces his overt political beliefs – are employed to great effect in his early book of short stories *The Cheapest Nights*.

LESSEPS, Ferdinand de (1805–1894). A French diplomat de Lesseps achieved lasting fame as the man who built the **Suez Canal** (although his was actually only the last of a number of schemes). He raised money by public subscription and work on the Canal began in 1859. Ten years later, despite the fierce desert heat, primitive equipment (picks and baskets), labour troubles and a cholera epidemic, the Canal was completed. The great opening ceremony on 17 November 1869 was attended by the Khedive of Egypt Ismail Pasha and the Empress Eugenie of France.

MAHFOUZ, Naguib (1911–). Winner of the 1988 Nobel Prize for Literature, Mahfouz was born and spent his earliest years in the old **Gamiliyya quarter** of **Cairo** which he has used as the setting for several of his novels. Throughout his long and distinguished career, Mahfouz has written prolifically. One of his earliest works, *Midaq Alley*, is a colourful insight into the lives of the people of Cairo in the 1940s, and has long been a bestseller in Egypt. His best work, however, is the celebrated *Cairo Tril-*

ogy: Bayn al Qasran (Extract 5), *Qasr ash-Shawq* and *as-Sukkahyya*, each volume named after a suburb of Cairo. The books depict the fate of three generations of a Cairo family during the 1920s and 1930s. These were the first truly urban Egyptian novels, and with them Mahfouz transformed Egyptian writing in to a sophisticated art form worthy of comparison with its European counterparts.

SAADAWI, Nawal El (1931–). After training to be a doctor, Saadawi began writing her stories and novels over thirty years ago. She eventually became Director of Public Health but her involvement in women's move-ments and the increasingly controversial nature of her writing caused her to be dismissed, and later imprisoned by Sadat. Her experiences in prison were captured in the highly acclaimed *Memoirs from the Women's Prison*. Her novels and short stories (especially *She has No Place in Paradise* – Extract 7) have a refreshingly direct quality and often deal with sexual problems that are still considered controversial in Egypt. Her opinion on women's liberation is also considered highly subversive in a country where women are still very much second-class citizens. Yet Saadawi is far from being a mere polemicist, and her stories have an artist's eye for the subtlety of human behaviour.

LIBYA

'I remembered what I knew about this Libyan desert. When, in the Sahara, humidity is still at forty per cent of saturation, it is only eighteen here in Libya. Life here evaporates like a vapour. Bedouins, explorers, and colonial officers all tell us that a man may go nineteen hours without water. Thereafter his eyes fill with light, and that marks the beginning of the end.'
Antoine de Saint-Exupéry,
Wind, Sand and Stars

In *Purchas his Pilgrimes*, published in 1625, John Leo gives his impressions of Libya: '. . . the Inhabitants of Libya live a brutish kind of life; who neglecting all kinds of goods Arts and Sciences, doe wholy apply their minds unto theft and violence. Never as yet had they any Religion, and Lawes, or any good forme of living . . . They spend all their dayes either in most lewd practices, or in hunting or else in warfare . . .'. At that time, Libya was still part of the Ottoman Empire and the Turks' last foothold along the North African coast. The Turks were eventually ousted by the Italians in 1911, who then enjoyed a brief period as colonists. The country became independent in 1951. In 1969, an earnestly religious man in his twenties staged a successful military coup against the ageing King Idris. That young man was none other than Colonel Moammar Gadhafi.

Gadhafi and his vision of pan-Arabism are synonymous with modern-day Libya. Under his close guard (opposition parties are banned), Arabic is the official tongue. The use of any other language has been successfully and actively discouraged, resulting in a largely impenetrable and untranslated body of literature for those familiar with only the Roman alphabet. One of the few Libyan books that has been widely translated is Gadhafi's own *The Green Book*. Described by one guidebook as chiefly 'pure eccentric eyewash', it propounds the theory that the Western parliamentary system is actually undemocratic as it takes the power *from* the people – 'The most tyrannical dictatorships

```
FACT BOX

AREA: 1 759 537 sq km
POPULATION: 4 544 000
CAPITAL: Tripoli
LANGUAGES: Arabic, Italian
FORMER COLONIAL POWER: Italy
INDEPENDENCE: 1951
```

the world has known have existed under the shadow of parliaments.'

Numerous journalists and writers have attempted to get round Gadhafi's polished evasiveness. The editor of *Zagreb*, a newspaper in former Yugoslavia, was no more or less successful than most. To his question, 'You are known as an unpredictable person: others consider you to be vague. I would like to hear your views on these opinions.', Gadhafi replied, 'The question of the expected and the unexpected, the vague or the non-vague is something usually noticed by observers, not by the person concerned.' (see *The Battle of Destiny*).

Non-religious literature has only really developed in Libya since the 1960s, though this has had many Egyptian influences and is predominantly nationalistic in its disposition. National literature is actively supported by a group of professionals and intellectuals who belong to the al-Fikr society, and, in the apparent absence of a Ministry of Culture, by the Ministry of Information and Education. Nevertheless, the government's support of the arts in the literary field is admirably aimed at encouraging awareness of traditional Islamic folklore.

Despite Libya's proximity to Europe and the popularity of its neighbours, the country has never been a mecca for Europe's travellers and writers (Libya's entries in African guidebooks are among the shortest, and one book warns unmarried women under 35 that they have no hope of obtaining a visa, despite Gadhafi's alleged preference for female bodyguards). The English poet Philip Ward spent several years as a librarian here, and produced his two collections of poetry. In the poem 'Letter from Tripoli' in *At the Best of Times*, he answers to perplexed friends the common enquiry 'What am I doing?'; 'I married here the girl I love . . ./I create words, books, libraries./I write at night,/my mind going lighthouse-blank,/like our celibate sky./Poems come oftener than clouds.'

One of the most celebrated literary figures to visit Libya (albeit unexpectedly) was Antoine de Saint-Exupéry ◊. An avid flyer, while working for the African mail service Saint-Exupéry flew 'on a wing and a prayer' across the Sahara: 'My world was the world of flight. Already I could feel the oncoming night within which I should be enclosed as in the precincts of a temple – enclosed in the temple of night for the accomplishment of secret rites and absorption in inviolable contemplation. Already this profane world was beginning to fade out . . . I know nothing, nothing in the world, equal to the wonder of nightfall in the air. (*Wind, Sand and Stars*). One night, on a journey to Saigon, his plane passed over **Banghazi** on Libya's coast, flew off course and crashed in the desert. Leaving Paris, Saint-Exupéry said, 'I had no idea that the sands were preparing me for their ultimate and culminating ordeal.' His book *Wind, Sand and Stars* (Extract 1) tells the extraordinary tale of his survival and eventual rescue by a Bedouin. As Gadhafi says in *The Green Book*, 'the strong always rule'. And survive.

Libraries and Bookshops

Tripoli. Egyptian Cultural Centre; Government Library.

BOOKLIST

The following selection includes the extracted title in this chapter as well as those mentioned in the introduction which are available in English and other titles for further reading. In general, paperback editions are given when possible. The editions cited are not necessarily the only ones available. For most of the extracted works, the original publisher in English can be found in 'Acknowledgments and Citations' at the end of the volume, as can the exact location of the extracts and the editions from which they are taken. Extract numbers are highlighted in bold for ease of reference.

Gadhafi, Colonel Moammar, *The Battle of Destiny: Speeches and Interviews*, Kalahari Publications, London, 1976.

Gadhafi, Colonel Moammar, *The Green Book: Part 1, The Solution to the Problem of Democracy*, Martin Brian and O'Keeffe, London, 1976.

Leo, John, in *Purchas his Pilgrimes*, 1625.

Purchas, Samuel, *Hakluytus Posthumus, or Purchas his Pilgrimes, contayning a History of the World in Sea Voyages and Land Travell by Englishmen and others*, 1625. Published in 20 volumes by AMS Press, New York (reprint of 1907 edition).

Saint-Exupéry, Antoine de, *Southern Mail & Night Flight*, Curtis Cate, trans, Penguin, London, 1971.

Saint-Exupéry, Antoine de, *Wind Sand and Stars & Flight to Arras*, Lewis Galantière, trans, Picador, London, 1987. **Extract 1.**

Ward, Peter, *At the Best of Times*, The Oleander Press, North Harrow, Middlesex, and Stoughton, Wisconsin, 1968.

Ward, Peter, *Maps on the Ceiling*, The Oleander Press, North Harrow, Middlesex, and Stoughton, Wisconsin, 1970.

Extract

(1) THE DESERT

Antoine de Saint-Exupéry, *Wind, Sand and Stars*

In 1935 Saint-Exupéry set out to break the record for flying from Paris to Saigon. The plane came down in the Libyan desert and he and his mechanic Prévot miraculously survived the crash. One day Saint-Exupéry wanders off alone to look for signs of life, chatting all the while to himself. After several days without food or water things are beginning to get unreal.

Over the hilltop. Look there, at the horizon! The most beautiful city in the world!

'You know perfectly well that is a mirage.'

Of course I know it is a mirage! Am I the sort of man who can be fooled? But what if I *want* to go after that mirage? Suppose I enjoy indulging my hope? Suppose it suits me to love that crenellated town all beflagged with sunlight? What if I choose to walk straight ahead on light feet? – for you must know that I have dropped my weariness behind me, I am happy now . . . Prévot and his gun! Don't make me laugh! I prefer my drunkenness. I am drunk. I am dying of thirst.

It took the twilight to sober me. Suddenly I stopped, appalled to think how far I was from our base. In the twilight the mirage was dying. The horizon had stripped itself of its pomp, its palaces, its priestly vestments. It was the old desert horizon again. . . .

I had been walking two hours when I saw the flames of the bonfire that Prévot, frightened by my long absence, had sent up. They mattered very little to me now.

Another hour of trudging. Five hundred yards away. A hundred yards. Fifty yards.

'Good Lord!'

Amazement stopped me in my tracks. Joy surged up and filled my heart with its violence. In the firelight stood Prévot, talking to two Arabs who were leaning against the motor. He had not noticed me, for he was too full of his own joy. If only I had sat still and waited with him! I should have been saved already. Exultantly I called out:

'Hi! Hi!'

The two Bedouins gave a start and stared at me. Prévot left them standing and came forward to meet me. I opened my arms to him. He caught me by the elbow. Did he think I was keeling over? I said:

'At last, eh?'

'What do you mean?'

'The Arabs!'
'What Arabs?'
'Those Arabs there, with you.'
Prévot looked at me queerly, and when he spoke I felt as if he was very reluctantly confiding a great secret to me:
'There are no Arabs here.'
This time I know I am going to cry.

Biography and important works

SAINT-EXUPÉRY, Antoine de (1900–1944). Born and educated in Le Mans, France, Saint-Exupéry joined the French Air Force in 1921 and flew in Morocco and France until he was demobilized in 1923. Not giving up his love of flying, he joined the Air Mail Service in North Africa and wrote *Courrier Sud* (*Southern Mail*). In *Wind, Sand and Stars* (Extract 1), he wrote of this time, 'We, pilots of the Sahara line were like prisoners of the sands, navigating from one stockade to the next with never an excursion outside the zone of silence.' In 1931 Saint-Exupéry returned to Paris and established his literary reputation with *Vol de Nuit* (*Night Flight*). He served as a pilot in the second world war until France fell. He escaped to America, where he wrote several books including that for which he is best known, *Le Petit Prince*. Saint-Exupéry returned to North Africa as a reconnaissance pilot in 1943, and in 1944 disappeared for the last time into the North African desert.

MOROCCO

'Morocco is like a tree
nourished by roots deep in
the soil of Africa which
breathes through foliage
rustling to the winds
of Europe.'
*King Hassan II of Morocco,
The Challenge*

Culturally, economically and
politically Morocco has for many
years been stirred by the 'winds' of
Europe. The colonial legacy was
such that following the end of
French rule in 1956, French was
the favoured language of expression for many writers here. Literary
activity in Arabic was, for most of
the twentieth century, confined
to classical poetry, history and the
defence of Islam. This work,
however, was an important part of
the journey towards establishing a
national identity and awareness in the face of colonialism. As such it
was the precursor to the nationalist literature that was to emerge in
Arabic in the decades preceding independence.

Ironically, some of the most popular nationalistic literature to
emerge in the 1930s–50s was that written in the foreign tongue. The
most provocative figure of the 1950s was Driss Chraïbi ◊ who, while
living and writing in Paris, attacked both the French intellectual
liberals *and* the traditional Moroccan Islamic establishment. In an
oblique apology to his countrymen, *Heirs to the Past* (Extract 2) follows
a man returning home after 16 years abroad and learning to reconcile
himself with his family who mockingly call him 'Mister Postman'.
Chraïbi emphasizes his protagonist's feelings of alienation on his return:
'It was as if I were returning from school, wearing shorts and clutching a
heavy satchel of books that told of civilisation.'

The original rebellious tone of Chraïbi's writing inspired a number of
young Moroccan writers in the 1960s. Tahar Ben Jelloun's ◊ thoughts
were similarly not compromised by writing in the language of the
colonists. He sought instead to decolonize the French tongue. In his
bold and remarkable book *The Sacred Night* (Extract 4) Jelloun tells of
the torments and tragedies suffered by a woman who has been brought

FACT BOX

AREA: 458 730 sq km (excluding Western Sahara)
POPULATION: 25 138 000
CAPITAL: Rabat
LANGUAGES: Arabic, Berber, French, Spanish
FORMER COLONIAL POWER: France
INDEPENDENCE: 1956

up as a boy because of her father's shame about his lack of male heirs. Leaving the humilities of her past behind her, she leaves home to start a new independent life: 'I was fighting against guilt, religion, morality, and all the things that threatened to rise again to compromise me, sully me, betray me, destroy what little I sought to preserve deep within myself.' The heroine finds herself in **Marrakesh** among the traditional story-tellers, with whom she searches for a way to release the burdens of her past. The strengths and surprises of the book lie in the candid exploration of female sexuality and the clear denouncement of female circumcision and repression in an Islamic, male-dominated society.

This comparatively closed and secretive society so close to the shores of Europe was an endless source of fascination for outsiders, and it had a curious and powerful effect on visitors. From the turn of the century, Morocco became a magnet for those in search of unusual, even 'specialist' pastimes, pleasures and sights that could not be found easily or openly on their own shores.

When the American novelist Edith Wharton arrived in 1917 and discovered there was no guidebook, she promptly set about writing one herself. Drawn breathlessly into the dense network of the **Marrakesh souk** she was at once both fascinated and horrified by what she saw. In her book *In Morocco*, she writes 'Fanatics in sheepskins glowering from the guarded thresholds of the mosques, fierce tribesmen with inlaid arms in their belts and the fighters' tufts of wiry hair escaping from camel's-hair turbans, mad Negroes standing stark naked . . . consumptive Jews . . . lusty slave girls . . . almond-eyed boys leading fat merchants by the hand, and bare-legged Berber women, tattooed and insolently gay . . .'.

Wharton was followed almost a decade later by the French novelist Colette ◊, a reluctant traveller who preferred to stay in her native France. Once in Morocco, however, she fell in love with the senses, smells and lifestyle of North Africa, as revealed in her book *Places* (Extract 6): 'They have vagabond, disinterested souls who commit themselves to a motionless siesta on divans stuffed with fine wool and contemplate the Mediterranean through half-closed eyes.'

Close on Colette's heels arrived Richard Hughes, author of *A High Wind in Jamaica*, who, in the winter of 1926–27, lived in the **Kasbah** of **Tangier**. He later published *In the Lap of Atlas*, a collection of stories creatively re-worked from traditional oral tales recounted to him over dinner by his Moorish friends.

Writer Percy Wyndham Lewis ◊ arrived in spring 1931, escaping from the great depression that had enveloped Europe. He threw himself into what he called the 'Islamic sensations', visiting sheiks, brothels and remote mountain ranges in an attempt to absorb himself in the country's history and to explore the characteristics and lives of the inhabitants. This he did with an obsessional, almost missionary zeal, and the descriptions in the resulting *Journey into Barbary* (Extract 3) are dense, often surprising – 'The French Protectorate in Morocco . . . is a great European enterprise . . .' – and frequently amusing, especially those pertaining to the French who had taken over in 1912: 'It shows the French at their best – as the humane, civilising, most genially-acquisitive, of all powers . . .'

One of the strongest (though apparently indifferent) literary magnets in the 1950s was the American writer and bohemian Paul Bowles ◊ who lives in **Tangier** and is the most famous of the 'tangerinos' (permanent European residents). Bowles is best known outside Morocco for his first novel *The Sheltering Sky* (Extract 1), which was filmed by Bertolucci in 1990 (Bowles himself makes a cameo appearance). It is a strangely fascinating tragic tale of three bored rich Americans, a couple (Port and Kit) and a male friend, who come to Morocco to forget about the war and who drift aimlessly through the country. 'Because neither she nor Port had ever lived a life of any kind of regularity, they both had made the fatal error of coming to regard time as non-existent. One year was like another year. Eventually everything would happen.' They are curiously dispassionate about each other, about **Tangier** ('this colourless mess here that calls itself a town'), and about their journey as it rolls towards its climax.

The real contribution made by Bowles to the Moroccan literary scene lies not in attracting a sycophantic wave of writers, would-be-writers and their attendant groupies, but in the time he spent transcribing and translating the works of the indigenous writers with whom he had become friends. *Love with a Few Hairs* (Extract 7) was recounted to Bowles by a young Arab, Mohammed Mrabet ◊. Set in **Tangier**, it candidly tells the story of a seventeen-year-old Moroccan boy who has a homosexual relationship with a wealthy and adoring European hotel owner, but who also wants to marry the girl next door. More of Mrabet's work is found in Bowles' *Five Eyes*, an anthology of stories recounted by five Moroccan writers. It often happened that one of his (Moroccan) writer friends would start to tell a story, Bowles would grab a notebook and write down his translation there and then. It was in such a manner that he transcribed extraordinary tales like *The Man Who Dreamed of Fish Eating Fish* from Yacoubi, a painter. The story comes from the rich repertory of Moroccan folk humour, which Yacoubi's artistic licence has enriched with his wilful imagination.

By far the most important and extraordinary work that Bowles has in part been responsible for bringing to the English-speaking world is that of Mohamed Choukri ◊. After a desolate upbringing in **Tangier**, during which he survived as a minor criminal selling hashish, his body, and anything else of value he could lay his hands on, Choukri finally learnt to read and write at the age of 21. His first novel, *For Bread Alone* (Extract 8), is a raw and disturbingly honest autobiography. Choukri recalls the famine in the **Rif Mountains** which forced his family to leave their home when he was a young boy: 'One afternoon I could not stop crying. I was hungry. I had sucked my fingers so much that the idea of doing it again made me sick to the stomach. My mother kept telling me; be quiet. Tomorrow we're leaving for Tangier. There's all the bread you want there. You won't be crying for bread any more, once we get to Tangier.' Sparing no space for pleasantries, he describes graphically how they walked to the city along roads littered with dead rotting animals, and how in desperation in Tangier his father killed one of his babies which was permanently howling with hunger.

In the summer of 1973, shortly after Choukri had written *For Bread Alone*, he heard that the American playwright Tennessee Williams had been seen in Tangier and decided to track him down. Pondering over how to approach the great writer, as he records in *Tennessee Williams in Tangier*, he thought logically, 'He's a writer and I'm a writer. He's famous and I'm not famous. That's the difference. The apprentice thief usually learns from a master thief.' Despite their differences of temperament and language, the two writers nevertheless appeared to find a mutually beneficial affection and understanding. *Tennessee Williams in Tangier* recounts their meetings and conversations over the two-week acquaintanceship. As well as expressing constant surprise over Williams' frequent outbursts of laughter Choukri includes a memorably bizarre conversation about the French writer Jean Genet, whom Choukri had spotted and interviewed in Tangier a few years previously. Williams, himself fond of pretty young boys, asked, 'What happened here between Genet and the blacks? Did they let them into the hotel with him?' Choukri: 'How do you know he likes blacks?' Williams: 'I know he does. He likes them to look like Idi Amin.'

The Tangier trail to decadence and discovery attracted writers of the calibre of William Burroughs, Christopher Isherwood and later Joe Orton, but for the most part the pleasure-seeking principle obscured any literary longings. While their literary legacy was meagre to say the least, their exploits recently resulted in two fascinating books: *Tangier: City of the Dream* and *The Dream at the End of the World: Paul Bowles and the Literary Renegades in Tangier* by Iain Finlayson and Michelle Green respectively. The full excesses and legendary scandals of the behaviour of these 'renegades' is candidly and amusingly revealed. As visiting journalist Robert Ruark said of the place, 'Sodom by comparison was a church picnic, and Gomorrah a convention of Girl Scouts'.

One of the few visiting writers to Morocco who did not appear to be distracted by the availability of drugs or young boys, and who stayed somewhat longer than the average visitor, was the English writer Peter Mayne ◊. Arriving in **Marrakesh** for what turned out to be a productive year-long stay, he acquired himself the best form of companion and guide – a bicycle. In *A Year in Marrakesh* (Extract 5), he writes 'My object in bicycling in such discomfort round and round the city is to din into myself the shape and sound and smell of it. It will take months and months and then suddenly I shall possess the place. It will be mine – or in any case I shall have become part of it, which amounts to the same thing.'

LITERARY LANDMARKS

Casablanca. Morocco's largest city, or as Wyndham Lewis put it, 'an enormous whitewashed fungus-town'. Internationally associated with the 1942 film starring Humphrey Bogart and Ingrid Bergman that took its name.

Marrakesh. A mecca for travellers since the 1960s, and in former times one of the most important cultural centres of the Muslim world. The Bulgarian/English novelist and Nobel Laureate Elias Canetti spent time here and wrote *The Voices of Marrakesh*, which opens with the intriguing line 'I came into contact with camels on three occasions, and each occasion ended tragically'. Ogden Nash's limerick about the city in *Everything but Thee and Me* was also inspired by the camel population ('The agricultural economy/Suggests the Book of Deuteronomy./The machine has not replaced the camel.').

Rio de Oro. An ethereal description of the Rio de Oro or Spanish Sahara occupied by Morocco is given by French pilot and author Antoine de Saint-Exupéry (◊ Libya), who landed here during a minor accident: 'I was thrilled by the virginity of a soil which no step of man or beast had sullied. I lingered there, startled by this silence that never had been broken. The first star began to shine, and I said to myself that this pure surface had lain here thousands of years in sight only of the stars.'

Tangier. In the heydey of the 1930s and 1940s Tangier was known for its refined decadence. In his Journal for 1987, Paul Bowles said

'Three and a half decades ago Said Kouch, Jane's Arabic Professor said to her; "*Tous les agréments de Tanger ont disparu.*" It was true then, and meaningless now. Whatever charms the town once had have long since been forgotten.' Today find a copy of the local *Rogue's Guide to Tangier*, to help steer you round the streets and past the hungry hustlers that hang out there.

Libraries and Bookshops

Fès. English Bookshop, 68 Ave Hassan II.

Rabat. Bookshop, 7 Zenkat Alyamama; British Council Library, 3 Zankat Descartes; City Library.

Casablanca. City Library; French Cultural Centre.

Tangier. City Library.

BOOKLIST

The following selection includes the extracted titles in this chapter as well as those mentioned in the introduction which are available in English and other titles for further reading. In general, paperback editions are given when possible. The editions cited are not necessarily the only ones available. For most of the extracted works, the original publisher in English can be found in 'Acknowledgments and Citations' at the end of the volume, as can the exact location of the extracts and the editions from which they are taken. Extract numbers are highlighted in bold for ease of reference.

Bowles, Paul, *The Sheltering Sky*, Paladin, London, 1990. **Extract 1.**

Bowles, Paul, *Let It Come Down*, Peter Owen, London, 1980.

Bowles, Paul, *Pages from Cold Point*, Abacus, London, 1991.

Bowles, Paul, *Points in Time*, Peter Owen, London, 1990.

Bowles, Paul, *The Spider's House*, Abacus, London, 1991.

Bowles, Paul, *Their Heads are Green*, Abacus, London, 1990.

Bowles, Paul, *The Thicket of Spring*, Black Sparrow Press, Santa Barbara, CA, 1972.

Bowles, Paul, *Two Years Beside the Strait: Tangier Journal 1987–1989*, Peter Owen, London, 1990.

Canetti, Elias, *The Voices of Marrakesh*, Marion Boyars, London, 1978.

Choukri, Mohamed, *For Bread Alone*, Paul Bowles, trans, Grafton, London, 1987. **Extract 8.**

Choukri, Mohamed, Paul Bowles, trans, *Tennessee Williams in Tangier*, Cadmus Editions, Santa Barbara, CA, 1979.

Chraïbi, Driss, *Heirs to the Past*, Len Ortzen, trans, Heinemann, London, 1971. **Extract 2.**

Chraïbi, Driss, *Flutes of Death*, Three Continents Press, Washington, DC, 1985.

Colette, *Places*, David Le Vay, trans, Peter Owen, London, 1970. **Extract 6.**

Finlayson, Iain, *Tangier: City of the Dream*, HarperCollins, London, 1992.

Five Eyes: Stories, Paul Bowles, ed and trans, Black Sparrow Press, Santa Barbara, CA, 1979.

Green, Michelle, *The Dream at the End of the World: Paul Bowles and the Literary Renegades in Tangier*, Bloomsbury Publishing, London, 1992.

Hassan II, King, *The Challenge*, Anthony Rhodes, trans, Macmillan, London, 1978.

Hughes, Richard, *In the Lap of Atlas*, Chatto and Windus, London, 1979.

Jelloun, Tahar Ben, *The Sacred Night*, Alan Sheridan, trans, Quartet, London, 1989. **Extract 4.**

Jelloun, Tahar Ben, *Silent Day in Tangier*, D. Lobdell, trans, Quartet, London, 1991.

Jelloun, Tahar Ben, *Solitaire*, G. Stanton and N. Hindley, trans, Quartet, London, 1989.

Lewis, Wyndham, *Journey into Barbary*, C.J. Fox, ed, Penguin, London, 1987. **Extract 3.**

Mayne, Peter, *A Year in Marrakesh*, Eland, London, 1984. **Extract 5.**

Mrabet, Mohammed, *The Big Mirror*, Peter Owen, London, 1989.

Mrabet, Mohammed, *Love with a Few Hairs*, Paul Bowles, trans, Arena, London, 1986. **Extract 7.**

Mrabet, Mohammed, *The Lemon*, Paul Bowles, trans, Peter Owen, London, 1986.

Mrabet, Mohammed, *Look and Move On*, Paul Bowles, trans, Peter Owen, London, 1989.

Nash, Ogden, *Everything but Thee and Me*, J.M. Dent and Sons, London, 1963.

Saint-Exupéry, Antoine de, *Southern Mail & Night Flight*, Curtis Cate, trans, Penguin, London, 1971.

Saint-Exupéry, Antoine de, *Wind, Sand and Stars & Flight to Arras*, Lewis Galantière, trans, Picador, London, 1987.

Wharton, Edith, *In Morocco*, Hippocrene Books, New York, 1984.

Extracts

(1) BOU NOURA

Paul Bowles, *The Sheltering Sky*

Alone together in the desert town of Bou Noura, the uneasy relationship between Kit and Port is showing signs of strain. In this chapter, 'The Earth's Sharp Edge', one senses impending doom. Here Kit asks Port why he bothers to drink if, as he has just cried, it makes him 'disgusted and miserable'.

'I told you,' he said. 'I wanted to be with you. And besides, I always imagine that somehow I'll be able to penetrate to the interior of somewhere. Usually I get just about to the suburbs and get lost. I don't think there *is* any interior to get to any more. I think all you drinkers are victims of a huge mass hallucination.'

'I refuse to discuss it,' said Kit haughtily, climbing down from the bed and struggling her way through the folds of netting that hung to the floor.

He rolled over and sat up.

'I know why I'm disgusted,' he called after her. 'It's something I ate. Ten years ago.'

'I don't know what you're talking about. Lie down again and sleep,' she said, and went out of the room.

'I do,' he muttered. He crawled out of the bed and went to stand in the window. The dry desert air was taking on its evening chill, and the drums still sounded. The canyon walls were black now, the scattered clumps of palms had become invisible. There were no lights; the room faced away from the town. And this was what he meant. He gripped the windowsill and leaned out, thinking: 'She doesn't know what I'm talking about. It's something I ate ten years ago. Twenty years ago.' The landscape was there, and more than ever he felt he could not reach it. The rocks and the sky were everywhere, ready to absolve him, but as always he carried the obstacle within him. He would have said that as he looked at them, the rocks and the sky ceased being themselves, that in the act of passing into his consciousness, they became impure. It was slight consolation to be able to say to himself: 'I am stronger than they.' As he turned back into the room, something bright drew his eye to the mirror on the open door of the wardrobe. It was the new moon shining in through the other window. He sat down on the bed and began to laugh.

(2) CASABLANCA

Driss Chraïbi, *Heirs to the Past*

Driss Ferdi, the protagonist of Chraïbi's novel, has returned home to Casablanca after 16 years of living in France, for the funeral of his father. It is the end of the ceremony and everybody is going home.

The crowd had gone, even the countless beggars had resigned themselves to going, weighed down with food and alms, dates and figs. And there remained only the two of us, sitting near the fresh grave and watching the sun sink into the sea. The earth had long ago drunk up the rain, and looked as though there had never been any at all. From the cemetery rose a smell of slaked lime.

When the sun had been swallowed up, when all that remained on the horizon was a streak of emeralds, rubies and opals, Madini sighed and said:

'The dead are dead, Driss, and nobody thinks of asking them questions. They're dead, you understand?'

He looked at me with the eyes of a beaten dog.

'But there are those who remain,' he went on, 'those who are still alive and can be questioned. Explain it all to me, Driss. I want to know why all these people who were here a little while ago and who know what human suffering is – I just want to know why they become animals. If you could explain that, I swear that I'd lie down here and remain here until I became a skeleton.'

He seized my arm with both hands and began to pump it up and down.

'I want to understand, understand, to know why these people, not so long ago, caught an old Jew in the street, a poor old fellow who just happened to be passing, poured petrol over him and burned him alive. Do you understand, Driss? It's not the advice given by my father that keeps going through my head, but the awful screams of that Jew. Tell me, brother. You're educated, you've read a lot of books. Can you explain it?'

I've never known what to say. I just looked at his pleading eyes.

No, I had not returned to my native land to be present at my father's funeral – the dead are well and truly dead – not even to collect my share of the inheritance; but to see what was happening after such a long absence. Night fell suddenly. I got to my feet and said to him, 'Come on, let's go home.'

That is all I found to say. It had perhaps all happened by chance, but I could not help thinking that something had been staged, and well staged. By putting his question to me at that particular moment, he had abruptly destroyed my peace and plunged me once again into the world of men.

(3) Casablanca

Wyndham Lewis, *Journey into Barbary*

After a curious comparison with New York (both are 'modern as modern' and have the same 'unmistakable sensations of violent impermanence'), Lewis launches into a vitriolic description of the city of Casablanca in 1931.

Its shell, the dazzling balanced plaster walls, what are they, the suspicious traveller asks, but a gigantic architectural confectionery? Tap them, they must be hollow, or filled with *marsh mallow* – certainly of a mushroom flimsiness, porous rag-pulp or paper-mulberry-hearted.

In fact no one has been there long enough to saturate any cubic foot of it with his presence. There is no personality in its hasty palaces: this densely-peopled city might still be empty, for all the human aura with which it is charged. Organically it is a hoax: here is not an organism, but a preposterous assemblage of discrete and self-sufficing cells, which would collapse at a touch, administered with force enough, almost anywhere.

All its inhabitants, too, are a huge scratch-population, blown together by a big newspaper puff from the four ends of the earth, gold-diggers in posh city-quarters, ten-a-penny filibusters in plaster palaces: the 'big noises' in this mushroom metropolis are adventurers of a decade's standing at the longest – not like the old and crusted harpies of Tangier and Tunis: the biggest 'men of substance' here, you feel, would, anywhere else, be straw-magnates, with big question-marks against their names.

(4) MARRAKESH

Tahar Ben Jelloun, *The Sacred Night*

In the marketplace of Marrakesh the heroine is looking for the story-teller her tale 'had ruined'. A young beautiful woman from the south of the country appears and begins to tell a story.

'We're here to listen to music and to see you dance. This is not a mosque, you know.'

'I'm happy to listen to you, Madame,' a good-looking young man broke in. 'Pay no attention to what they say; they're cousins of bedouins themselves.'

'A story is a story, not a sermon,' another young man said. 'And since when do women not yet old dare to flaunt themselves like this? Have you no father, brother, or husband to guard you from harm?'

She must have expected comments of that kind, for she was ready with a gentle, ironic answer:

'Are you perhaps the brother I never had, or the husband so overcome with passion that his body trembles between fat, hairy legs? Are you perhaps the man who collects forbidden pictures and takes them out in icy solitude, crumpling them under his loveless body? Or perhaps you are my long-lost father, carried off by fever and shame, by the feeling of damnation that has driven you to exile in the southern sands?'

She leaned forward, laughed, took a corner of her haïk and tied it to her waist; then she asked the young man to hold the other end. She turned slowly, barely moving her feet, until she was entirely wrapped in it.

'Thank you,' she said. 'May God guide you on the right path! You have beautiful eyes. Get rid of that moustache. Virility lies not in the body, but in the soul. Farewell. I have other books to open.'

She looked at me, suddenly motionless, and said:

'Where are you from, you who never speak?'

She left without waiting for an answer.

I would have liked to tell her of my life. She would have made it a book to carry from village to village. I can see her opening the chapters of my story one by one, keeping the final secret to herself.

(5) MARRAKESH

Peter Mayne, *A Year in Marrakesh*

> *One evening, as Mayne made his way across the Djema'a el-Fna for his evening aperitif, he was stopped by a Moor whom he had often seen at the café, but had never previously spoken to.*

He is obviously a respected person, and I have remarked that he gets served promptly by all the *garçons*. I have also remarked that he arrives at the café on a bicycle which has two little 'driving-mirrors'. These are fastened on the handlebars and I believe he uses them more for looking at himself in, than to warn him of traffic coming up behind, because they are both tipped up into his face. He is rather a handsome fellow, as well as respected. Anyway, this time he greeted me as if we met regularly. I begin to manage the standard greetings fairly fluently now, unreeling my 'no-harms' and 'peace-on-you's' with quite an air. He suggested that we share the expenses of a lady wrapped in a *hāik* who was hurrying not very fast across the *place* in the opposite direction.

'Do you think . . . ?' I began, as best I could in Arabic.

He said: 'You want or you don't want?'

I started to say that I must look at my watch and consider my engagements for the evening, but by now the lady was hurrying back again at about the same speed and the man said urgently:

'You will pay her two parts and I will pay one part. Yes? I shall ask her?'

'Do you know her?' I inquired, still anxious to gain time. The lady was quite near now.

'No,' he said. 'But I will ask her.'

I said: 'I would like to see her properly first.' She was completely covered by her *hāik* and I am not one who can judge from a pair of thick ankles. She looked like any other woman would look wrapped up in a cloth bundle. There was nothing to indicate her business at this hour and place that I could see.

'Why?' he demanded.

'Well, because . . .' But by this time the lady was several yards beyond us again.

'You are as nothing!' the man cried angrily and hurried after her.

(6) MOROCCO: FOOD

Colette, *Places*

Invited to Morocco in 1926, the French novelist describes with characteristic sensuality and delectable slowness the pleasures of a long, large and languid Moroccan luncheon.

'Azil!'

A silken scarf, modelled like a Parisian hat, revealed nothing of her hair. Azil was young and zealous and did not allow herself to smile. Her soft cheeks and bare round arms captured the blue from without whenever she passed the bay-window opening on to the sea. Azil mirrored the blue of the sky, the green of foliage; from each ear a glass pendant swung to its own bluish reflection on her strong neck. Azil was beautiful like a polished jar, beautiful like a young seal, beautiful like any well-treated, well-fed, sixteen-year-old slave.

She had already placed before us pale girdle-cakes soaked in sugared butter and sprinkled with almonds; pigeons bathed in succulent juice with green olives, chick-peas melting in flour, sweet onions; chickens buried under fresh beans with wrinkled skins and lemon cooked and re-cooked and reduced to a savoury purée. We had also had mutton, and mutton again, and once more; mutton stuffed with fennel, mutton with cumin and courgettes, mutton with twenty spices; and an exquisite diversion – girdle-cake flaky to the limit of flakiness, rendered transparent, concealing a soft nugget of minced fowl, sugared and flavoured with nutmeg . . .

Ceaselessly Azil fetched and carried the red bowls. The spring vegetables took pride of place – broad beans, asparagus, new peas in a pot decorated with orange-trees, artichokes round as roses; small turnips, marrows and carrots appeared under swelling yellow enamel, with whole eggs broken over the dish a quarter of an hour before serving. Finally came couscous, at once soft and granular – conscous, discreet harbinger of desert and fruit – couscous with a surrounding rampart, a small fortress, of sweet onions and muscat grapes swollen to the sweating-point, couscous and bowls of barely soured buttermilk. We lifted our heads, we began to look at the sea, beyond an abyss of greenery tumbling to the shore.

(7) MOROCCO: RELATIONSHIPS

Mohammed Mrabet, *Love with a Few Hairs*

*In order to get Mina, his childhood sweetheart, to fall in love
with him, Mohammed visits a local witch who has created a spell
with the help of a few of his loved one's hairs. Unfortunately for
him, as he is later to find out, the spell works rather too well.*

Mohammed was standing in a bar on the beach in the city having a
beer. Mustafa came in.

So here you are! You've forgotten all about us. What news of the
girl-friend?

Beautiful, said Mohammed. He laughed.

Have you been back to pay the witch?

No, but I will.

And the powder really worked?

Worked! I just this minute left her. What are you having?

Beer, said Mustafa. Soon he looked at Mohammed and said: You're
not really going to marry her, are you?

Is that what you think? Don't you know what love is? When I was
this big I used to take care of her. I've always loved her.

Mohammed went on drinking. After a while he was saying, again
and again: She could die or I could die. But there's nobody alive who
could pull us apart.

That's the way to talk! said Mustafa. Marry her, get yourself a good
house, and fill it with young ones. This is a hard world. You might as
well try to be happy.

Mustafa did not really believe this, but they were drinking in a bar.

Incha' Allah, said Mohammed, already feeling happy. He was
thinking: There's nothing wrong with a world where you can get love
with a few hairs. It's wonderful!

(8) TANGIER

Mohamed Choukri, *For Bread Alone*

*To escape his violent father, Choukri leaves home and sleeps rough
in places such as the city graveyard, 'the only place you can go into
at any time of the day or night without having to ask permission'.
One morning he goes to the market to pick some pockets and spots
a European woman buying something at a stall . . .*

She paid and put her change purse back into her handbag. Then she
caught sight of me, staring fixedly at the handbag. Her eyes seemed to
be saying: Aren't you ashamed? And so I felt ashamed, and went out of
the market. I spent the whole day letting the alleys swallow me up and

spew me out. In the evening I discovered that you could sleep in the Fondaq ech Chijra. You paid only one peseta at the gate in order to get in, and you could sleep where you liked. There are two levels. The animals sleep below and the people above. It was nine o'clock when I went in. A café, a restaurant, small rooms they rented out, shops, fruit and vegetable stands. The Fondaq is like a city. On the stairway I ran into a drunk. He reached out to touch my face, saying: Aha, gazelle! Where are you off to, beautiful? I pushed his hand away violently, ran up two steps and glared at him. He guffawed.

What are you so nervous about? Afraid of me?

In his hand he held an empty bottle. I'm going to fill us this bottle, he said. I'll be back.

He went on downstairs, laughing, and I continued up, feeling more frightened each minute. He called back to me: Wait for me, handsome. I'll be right up. I'm not going to let you get away.

There were scores of men on the balcony, some of them already asleep, but most of them sitting up, drinking, smoking kif, chatting and singing. I caught sight of a drunk hugging a boy. Then he kissed him on the cheeks. One of the others cried: Leave him alone! Not now! Later, later.

No. I'm not going to sleep here, I told myself. I'd rather sleep in the graveyard.

Biographies and important works

BOWLES, Paul (1910–). Born in New York, Bowles first went to Europe to study music with Aaron Copland. By a bizarre arrangement in 1938 Bowles, a homosexual, married lesbian writer Jane Auer, and they settled in **Tangier** where he still lives. As well as the cult success of *The Sheltering Sky* (Extract 1), Bowles has written other acclaimed novels, a collection of poems, *The Thicket of Spring*, and short stories. He is still recognized as a composer and has written a number of musical and ballet scores. His transcriptions and translations of stories by Choukri ◊ and Mrabet ◊ and many other Moroc-

can writers have been invaluable in bringing their hitherto unknown works to an English-speaking audience. His 1994 novel, *Too Far from Home*, is set in Mali and is illustrated with drawings by the American artist Marguerite McBey, a long-time resident of Tangier. See Christopher Sawyer-Laucanno, *An Invisible Spectator: A Biography of Paul Bowles*, Bloomsbury, London, 1989; and *Paul Bowles, By His Friends*, Gary Pulsifer, ed, Peter Owen, London, 1992.

CHOUKRI, Mohamed (1935–). The key figure in contemporary

Moroccan literary life, Choukri was born at **Beni Chiker** in the **Rif**. His family fled the area when famine hit, and in **Tangier** they led a life of extreme poverty and deprivation during which eight of his siblings died of malnutrition. During the riots for independence Choukri was jailed with a poet who inspired him, at the age of 21, to learn how to read and write. Soon after he had learnt classical Arabic, he started writing poetry and fiction. He still lives in Tangier, where over the years he had made contact with many visiting writers, including Jean Genet and Tennessee Williams. His most creative contact has been with Paul Bowles ◊ who has translated much of his work and thus brought it to international attention. *For Bread Alone* (Extract 8), his first autobiographical novel, was described by Tennessee Williams as 'a true document of human desperation, shattering in its impact'. The book is now available in thirteen languages, though is censored in most Arab countries. Today Choukri is a professor of Arabic and teaches at **College Ibn Batuta** in Tangier.

Paul Bowles

CHRAÏBI, Driss (1926–). Born in **El Jadida**, Chraïbi left for Paris at the age of nineteen where he studied chemical engineering. Eventually he turned away from a promising career in order to devote himself to literature. His first novel, *Le Passé Simple*, was published in 1945 and caused a stir with its fresh, modern style denouncing Moroccan society. At home it was slated by the nationalist press but it brought him to the attention of the French. He has since published over a dozen novels, most of which have each been translated into four or more languages. *Heirs to the Past* (Extract 2) tells of a man's return to **Casablanca** after sixteen years in France.

COLETTE, Sidonie Gabrielle (1873–1954). The French novelist, essayist and short story writer was born in Burgundy. She moved to Paris at the age of 20 with her first husband, the notorious Henri Gauthiers-Villars. Willy, as he was known, forced her to ghost-write the *Claudine* books by locking her in a room. Colette left her husband in 1906, and married twice more. Meanwhile, she had become recognized in her own right as one of France's most sensual and sensuous writers. Her experiences in Morocco are recounted in *Places* (Extract 6).

JELLOUN, Tahar Ben (1944–). A poet and novelist, Jelloun is one of the new generation of Moroccan writers. He expresses himself in French and has found himself well received abroad. In 1987 he won the coveted Prix Goncourt with *The Sacred Night* (Extract 4). Among his other works available in English translation is *Silent Day in Tangier*, the moving story of a young man who leaves **Fès** to find work in the **Rif**, and becomes a man 'led astray by the wind, forgotten by

Tahar Ben Jelloun

time, and scorned by death'. *Solitaire* recounts the experiences of his fellow North Africans in France. Jelloun currently lives in Paris.

LEWIS, Percy Wyndham (1882–1957). Lewis was born in a boat off the North American coast and educated in England. Later as a bohemian in Paris he moved in both literary and artistic circles. Principally an artist, he also spent much time writing satirical works directed at movements such as the Bloomsbury Group. That habit, coupled with his right-wing ideology (he was associated with the British Fascist Party), left him rather isolated from the literary and intellectual world of the 1930s. In 1931, Lewis spent several months writing and sketching and travelling throughout Morocco, during which time he developed a great admiration for the native Berbers, whom he named 'the Norsemen of the African steppes', and wrote *Journey into Barbary* (Extract 3).

MAYNE, Peter (1908–1976). Mayne was an English writer and traveller who spent *A Year in Marrakesh* (Extract 5). His reason for coming to live here, as he explained to two visiting acquaintances, was that 'I suddenly realised that I was an illiterate intellectual . . . *and* over-civilised'. Mayne rented a small house here and while writing his book attempted to learn Arabic.

MRABET, Mohammed (1940–). Born into the Temsamani tribe in the **Rif**, Mrabet lived in **Tangier** as a child and spent much of his subsequent life there. His early education was purely Koranic, but he has since taught himself to read Spanish and a little English. His works have since been translated into several languages. As he has done for many of his protégés, Paul Bowles ◊ has transcribed and translated Mrabet's tale *Love with a Few Hairs* (Extract 7). A short but intriguing tale of promiscuity and naivety, it deals with the difficult blend of the traditional and modern morality in Arab city life.

TUNISIA

> 'Walk five hundred steps in
> my city, and you change
> civilizations: here is an Arab
> town . . . Then the busy
> Jewish alleys . . . Further on,
> little Sicily . . . and then the
> *fondouks*, the collective
> tenements of the Maltese,
> those strange Europeans with
> an Arab tongue and a British
> nationality.'
> Albert Memmi,
> *The Pillar of Salt*

The novel, like independence, is relatively new to Tunisia. During the seventy-five years of French rule, a brief attempt to encourage Tunisian writers to develop lengthy works in French failed to ignite the collective imagination. It was evident that the Tunisians were still deeply attached to and inspired by traditional tea-house tales, short stories and poetry in the Arabic language.

It was also apparent when colonial rule ended in 1956 that, in the search for a sense of national identity and a way to protect against continuing French influence, there was a need to develop more themes and new forms of literary expression in the non-colonial tongue. Two of the key writers in Arabic – Muhammad Al'Arusi Al-Matwi and Al-Bashir Khuray-Yif – came from small towns in southern Tunisia and produced very successful novels about changing village life and the migrations to and from the city.

However Tunisia's most distinguished contemporary novelist and virtually the only one translated into English is Albert Memmi ◊ who writes in French. His intriguing background as an intellectual Jewish Tunisian brought up in **Tunis**, and currently living in France, has enabled Memmi to experience both the advantages and prejudices of many societies. His experiences identify him variously with colonizers, the colonized, traditional Arab culture, and Western intellectualism. His first autobiographical novel, *The Pillar of Salt* (Extract 3), was published in 1953. He describes it as 'a trial balloon to help me find the direction of my own life. However it became clear to me that a real life for a cultured man was impossible in North Africa at that time.' The

---

FACT BOX

AREA: 164 149 sq km
POPULATION: 8 168 000
CAPITAL: Tunis
LANGUAGES: Arabic, French
FORMER COLONIAL POWER: France
INDEPENDENCE: 1956

---

obstacles to his education were great – income (or lack of it), family background (semi-illiterate parents), as well as religion and race. 'The number of obstacles that ill luck made me contend with was really very considerable. But fate's first gift to me was to open the doors of high school.' Under a scholarship and sponsorship, Memmi enrolled at the French lycée where he learnt French. 'The language I spoke was a dreadful mixture of literary or even precious expressions and of idioms translated word for word from our dialect, of schoolboy slang and of my own more or less successful inventions . . . My language was thus as wild and turbulent as I was.'

Albert Camus (◊ Algeria), whose experiences of estrangement in Algeria were not dissimilar to those of Memmi in Tunisia, says in the introduction to *The Pillar of Salt*, 'He has been able to describe with so much detail the split personality of a young Jew who rises, thanks to his will power and his intelligence, to a full awareness of what he is or is not . . . Whether French or North African native, we remain what we are, contending with contradictions that steep our cities in blood and which we cannot solve by evasion, but only by experiencing them to the bitter end. It is in this light alone that one can understand how much I prize Albert Memmi's book.'

Rather more rare in the published and translated Arab literary world is a successful female writer. Also Jewish and living in France, Gisèle Halimi ◊, a civil rights lawyer, is the author of *Milk for the Orange Tree* (Extract 4), a fascinating autobiographical account of growing up in **Tunis** and her subsequent work on cases of political and racial and sexual discrimination – themes that were close to her heart. The title of her story comes from the time when, as a young girl, she used to water her orange tree in the family garden with milk so she did not have to drink it herself. She later realized 'The milk for the orange tree produced no miracle. Because orange trees do not like milk. They like tender soil, pure water and sun. And, above all, they only put down strong roots and bear fruit when nurtured with their own truth. People are like orange trees. They must choose what helps them to live, what makes them thrive. As a little girl, I did not yet know that. I disliked milk and I detested restraint. But I thought it was fair to impose it on the tree which was so dear to me.'

While many Tunisians found a life in France, some Jewish Tunisians settled in Israel after the second world war. Irene Awret's *Days of Honey* is the result of the meeting of Rafael Uzan, a shoemaker from a small town on the north coast of Tunisia, and Awret, who as a teenager fled from Hitler's Germany. Both their families settled in Safed, where Uzan recounted his Tunisian boyhood to Awret. 'Rabbi Hai synagogue', begins Uzan, 'has been closed up for over twenty years now. It closed the day that the last Jew left Bab Salah Street to settle in Israel . . . Never again have I set eyes on Nabeul, but deep in my memory my town lies glowing in the sun as on the day I left it . . .'.

Although nearby Egypt and Morocco were stronger cultural magnets for many foreign literary adventurers, the great ruins of Carthage and the religious centre of **Kairouan** lured the likes of Rilke ◊ (see Extract 2), and inspired Shakespeare, Belloc, Flaubert (◊ Egypt), and Alexandre Dumas. Flaubert's *Salammbô* describes in luxuriant and decadent detail, the period after the first Punic war when Carthage was besieged by unpaid mercenaries. Their leader, the Libyan giant Matho, falls in love with Salammbô, the daughter of the Carthaginian leader Hamilcar. When the book was first published in 1862 it was called 'bloody, dirty and sadistic'. Full of sultry breezes, orgies of eating and drinking, and 'barbaric opulence' it is a shamelessly romantic, voluptuous and kitsch evocation of the period.

Even Augustine of Hippo, one of the more august visitors to the place, who came here to complete his education from Algeria at the age of 17 in the fourth century, claimed: 'I came to Carthage where the cauldron of illicit loves leapt and boiled around me.' As biographer Peter Brown said, in *Augustine of Hippo*, 'The cauldron was very much of Augustine's own boiling.'

Like many who were to follow, Augustine of Hippo was seduced by the warm Mediterranean colours, senses and aromas in Tunisia. He described the African sunlight here as the 'Queen of all Colours pouring down over everything.' Many centuries later Swiss painter Paul Klee came here to paint, sketch and travel, and allowed himself and his work to be infused with the warmth of the place. One day in **Kairouan** in 1914, Klee wrote in his diary 'I now abandon work. It penetrates so deeply and so gently into me, I feel it and it gives me confidence in myself without effort. Color possesses me. I don't have to pursue it. It will possess me always, I know it. That is the meaning of this happy hour: Color and I are one. I am a painter.'

Today's writers in Tunisia have been encouraged and stimulated by a number of initiatives. Lively debates on radio and television have fuelled interest, as have an association of writers set up in the early 1970s and several literary magazines of which the best known is *al-Fikr*, meaning 'thought'. Modern literature is also supported by several government schemes, including so-called Maisons de la Culture. These 'Houses of Culture' are gradually being established in the larger towns throughout Tunisia, bringing a variety of books and films to otherwise culturally remote religions. However, while there are still few Tunisian works of great international standing, today's younger generation of readers is turning back to French literature for inspiration.

LITERARY LANDMARKS

Carthage. 'She was of *Carthage*, not of *Tunis./*This *Tunis* Sir was *Carthage.*' (William Shakespeare, *The Tempest.*) Shakespeare's ship-wrecked courtiers are, of course, discussing Dido, Queen of Carthage, immortalized in Virgil's *Aeneid* (Extract 1). The grandeur of the Phoenician trading post and Roman Christian centre, where marble was said to be 'so abundant that if all the inhabitants of Africa were to assemble to carry away the blocks they could not accomplish the task', has lived on in literature long since it fell to ruins. Noted disappointed Graham and Ashbee in the 1880s, 'For any indication of monumental grandeur one may look in vain.' Or, as Hilaire Belloc wrote in *Esto Perpetua*, 'Carthage had not desired to create, but only to enjoy: therefore she left us nothing.' It was here too that St Augustine, a Berber from Libya, was educated.

Hammamet. The Swiss painter Paul Klee wrote fondly of Tunisia in his diaries, and described the many scenes, sensations and colours that his work from this time captures: 'What a day! Birds sang in every hedge. We looked into a garden where a dromedary was working at the cistern. Downright biblical. The setup certainly hasn't changed.'

Kairouan. In historical terms, Kairouan is the most important town in Tunisia. On the Islamic scale of religious importance it is said that seven visits here are said to be the equivalent to one visit to Mecca. When the poet Rainer Maria Rilke visited here in 1910 he was moved by the 'simplicity and intensity of Islam . . .'.

Sidi Bou Said. 'As chic as they come' boasts one guidebook about this cliff-top town. Indeed almost every artist and writer who visited Tunisia, including Paul Klee, Cervantes, Simone de Beauvoir and André Gide, spent some time hanging out here.

Tunis. 'Nothing can give you any idea of the streets of Tunis', wrote Alexandre Dumas in *Tangier to Tunis*, 1846, 'Almost every day some house or other, burnt to powder by the fierce sun, collapses in a heap of dusty rubble . . .'.

Libraries and Bookshops

Rabat. The Royal Library.

Tunis. British Council Library, 141–143 ave de la Liberté; Claire Fontaine Bookshop, 4 rue d'Alger; Éditions Alif Bookshop, 5 rue d'Hollande; Maison de la Culture Ibn Khaldoun, 16 rue Ibn Khaldoun; National Library, rue Jemaa Zitouna.

BOOKLIST

The following selection includes the extracted titles in this chapter as well as those mentioned in the introduction which are available in English and other titles for further reading. In general, paperback editions are given when possible. The editions cited are not necessarily the only ones available. For most of the extracted works, the original publisher in English can be found in 'Acknowledgments and Citations' at the end of the volume, as can the exact location of the extracts and the editions from which they are taken. Extract numbers are highlighted in bold for ease of reference.

Awret, Irene, *Days of Honey*, Schocken, New York, 1984.

Belloc, Hilaire, *Esto Perpetua: Algerian Studies and Impressions*, Duckworth, London, 1906.

Brown, Peter, *Augustine of Hippo: A Biography*, Faber and Faber, London, 1969.

Dumas, Alexandre, *Tangier to Tunis*, A.E. Murch, trans, Peter Owen, London, 1959.

Flaubert, Gustave, *Salammbô*, A.J. Krailsheimer, trans, Penguin, London, 1977.

Graham and Ashbee, *Travels in Tunisia*, Dulan, London, 1887.

Halimi, Gisèle, *Milk for the Orange Tree*, Dorothy S. Blair, trans, Quartet, London, 1990. **Extract 4.**

Klee, Paul, *The Diaries of Paul Klee 1898–1918*, Felix Klee, ed, Peter Owen, London, 1965.

Marlowe, Christopher, *Dido, Queen of Carthage*, in *Complete Plays and Poems*, E.D. Pendry, ed, Dent, London, 1990.

Memmi, Albert, *The Pillar of Salt*, Elek Books, London, 1956. **Extract 3.**

Memmi, Albert, *The Colonizer and the Colonized*, H. Greenfield, trans, Earthscan Publishing, London, 1990.

Memmi, Albert, *Portrait of a Jew*, Eyre and Spottiswoode, London, 1963.

Rilke, Rainer Maria, *Letters of Rainer Maria Rilke*, 2 vols, W.W. Norton, New York, 1947. (**Extract 2** translated by Paul Strathern from *Rilke: Briefe 1907–1914*, Insel Verlag, Leipzig, 1933.)

Roumani, Judith, *Albert Memmi*, Celfan, Philadelphia, PA, 1987.

Virgil, *Aeneid*, in John Dryden, trans, *Works of Virgil*, Oxford University Press, Oxford, 1961. **Extract 1.**

Extracts

(1) Carthage

Virgil, The Aeneid

Aeneas is dallying in Carthage with his lover, Dido, the Queen of Carthage. The Gods send Mercury to remind him of his destiny – to found Rome. Seeing his ships sailing away, Dido seizes the sword Aeneas left behind, flings herself on her funeral pyre, and dies cursing her faithless lover. These lines are from the seventeenth century translation by the poet John Dryden.

But furious Dido, with dark thoughts involved,
Shook at the mighty mischief she resolved.
With livid spots distinguished was her face;
Red were her rolling eyes, and discomposed her pace:
Ghastly she gazed; with pain she drew her breath;
And nature shivered at approaching death.
   Then swiftly to the fatal place she passed,
And mounts the funeral pile with furious haste;
Unsheaths the sword the Trojan left behind
(Not for so dire an enterprise designed).
But when she viewed the garments loosely spread,
Which once he wore, and saw the conscious bed,
She paused, and with a sigh, the robes embraced;
Then on the couch her trembling body cast,
Repressed her ready tears, and spoke her last:
'Dear pledges of my love, while heaven so pleased,
Receive a soul, of mortal anguish eased.
My fatal course is finished; and I go,
A glorious name, among the ghosts below.
A lofty city by my hands is raised;
Pygmalion punished, and my lord appeased.
What could my fortune have afforded more,
Had the false Trojan never touched my shore?'
Then kissed the couch; and 'Must I die (she said),
And unrevenged? 'tis doubly to be dead!
Yet e'en this death with pleasure I receive:
On any terms, 'tis better than to live.
These flames, from far, may the false Trojan view;
These boding omens his base flight pursue!'
She said, and struck: deep entered in her side
The piercing steel, with reeking purple dyed.

Clogged in the wound the cruel weapon stands;
The spouting blood came streaming on her hands.
    Her sad attendants saw the deadly stroke,
And with loud cries the sounding palace shook.
Distracted, from the fatal sight they fled,
And through the town the dismal rumour spread.
First from the frighted court the yell began;
Redoubled, thence from house to house it ran:
The groans of men, with shrieks, laments and cries
Of mixing women, mount the vaulted skies.
Not less the clamour, than if – ancient Tyre,
Or the new Carthage, set by foes on fire –
The rolling ruin, with their loved abodes,
Involved the blazing temple of their gods.

(2) Kairouan

Rainer Maria Rilke

*In 1910–11, the Austrian poet Rilke travelled in North Africa,
visiting Algeria, Egypt and Tunisia. Here, in a letter to his wife
Clara written on 21 December 1910, he describes his visit to
Kairouan.*

I have come for the day to the holy city of Kairouan, which after Mecca
is the great pilgrimage centre of Islam. The city was founded by Sidi
Okba, a comrade of the Prophet, in the great plains; and it has risen
again and again out of its own ruins around the enormous mosque in
which hundreds of pillars from Carthage and all the ancient Roman
coastal colonies have come together again to support the dark cedar
ceilings and white cupolas, so luminescent today against the broken
grey skies, out of which the longed-for rain has now been falling for
three days. The flat white city lies like a vision amidst the rounded
pinnacles of its ramparts, surrounded by nothing but plains and tombs,
as though besieged by the never-stirring ever-increasing army of its
dead. Here one feels the simplicity and intensity of Islam as though the
Prophet lived only yesterday, and the city remains his kingdom.

(3) TUNIS

Albert Memmi, *The Pillar of Salt*

Here Memmi captures the feeling of estrangement and bewilder-
ment of growing up as a Jew in Tunis.

My native city is after my own image. Through Tarfoune Street, our
alley led to the Alliance School; and between home and the
schoolyard, the atmosphere remained familiar, all of a piece. We were
among Jews of the same class, and we had no painful awareness of our
situation, no pretenses. At school, we persisted in speaking our own
dialect despite the director's posters which demanded French. Sometimes I crossed a Moslem quarter as if I were fording a river. It was not
until I began attending the lycée that I really became acquainted with
the city. Until then, I had believed that, by some special privilege, the
doors of the world were being opened to me and that I need only walk
through them to be greeted with joy. But I discovered I was doomed
forever to be an outsider in my own native city. And one's home town
can no more be replaced than one's mother . . .

Walk five hundred steps in my city, and you change civilizations:
here is an Arab town, its houses like expressionless faces, its long,
silent, shadowed passages leading suddenly to packed crowds. Then,
the busy Jewish alleys, so sordid and familiar, lined with deep stalls,
shops and eating houses, all shapeless houses piled as best they can fit
together. Further on, little Sicily, where abject poverty waits on the
doorstep, and then the *fondouks*, the collective tenements of the
Maltese, those strange Europeans with an Arab tongue and a British
nationality . . .

And within this great variety, where everyone feels at home but no
one at ease, each man is shut up in his own neighbourhood, in fear,
hate, and contempt of his neighbor. Like the filth and untidiness of this
stinking city, we've known fear and scorn since the first awakening of
our consciousness. To defend or avenge ourselves, we scorned and
sneered among ourselves and hoped we would be feared as much as we
ourselves experienced fear. This was the atmosphere in which we lived
at mealtimes, in school and in the streets. If any youthful ingenuous-
ness or skepticism allowed us still to hope, we were promised nothing
but treachery and blood-red dawns. Slowly, as if a poison administered
drop by drop had at last had its effect, my sensibility, my sentiments,
my entire soul was permeated with it and reshaped; I learned to check
the odious inventory of it all. Beyond a ceremonious politeness,
everyone remained secretly hostile and was finally horrified by the
image of himself that he discovered in the minds of others.

One can make a mess of one's childhood or of one's whole life.

Slowly, painfully, I understood that I had made a mess of my own birth by choosing the wrong city.

(4) TUNISIA: FRENCH PROTECTORATE

Gisèle Halimi, *Milk for the Orange Tree*

Halimi illustrates the racial discrimination and exclusion that was fostered by the 'closed circles of the French Protectorate' with stories she remembers from her childhood.

As if in a habitat designed by a Machiavellian architect for needs of policy, the European masters at the top commanded Jews and Arabs, themselves separated from each other in parallel circles. The Arab, at the lowest level, being held in the most perfect contempt by the Jew, whether French or Tunisian.

According to the teachings of the European settler, the Arab (dirty, a thief and a liar) had no claim to the status of an equal. Whether he be a ragged *yaouled*,[1] a *beldi* intellectual, city-dweller, or land-owner. This same settler insinuated to this Arab that the Jew, from time immemorial, aimed at dominating the world by money and intrigue. The proof: although he was a Tunisian like the Arab, he had the advantage of certain privileges. Had he not become a French citizen in Algeria, while Muslims had remained 'French subjects'?[2] There must have been some justification for the pogroms. These concentric hatreds divided and the occupying power ruled.

Two stories circulate in corroboration of this enmity.

The first belongs to colonialist folklore. It goes as follows: 'If you meet a viper on the right of your path and an Arab on your left, kill the Arab and continue on your way.'

My grandfather had told me the second story, a glint of amusement in his eyes, while his voice indicated the serious lesson to be learned: A Jew, seeing an Arab funeral procession passing in the street, bursts into noisy sobs which arouse the curiosity of his neighbour, also a Jew, who inquires, 'Why are you weeping? It's only an Arab after all!' The first Jew's tears flow all the faster. 'That's just it,' he gasps through his sobs. 'One dead Arab. *Only one!* How many years or centuries will it need for them all to disappear if they only depart *one by one?* . . .'

[1]Street-urchin, beggar or shoe-shine boy.
[2]Crémieux Decree, 24 October 1870.

Biographies and important works

HALIMI, Gisèle (1927–). Halimi was the second child of impoverished, highly orthodox Jewish parents. Her father, a lawyer's clerk, was bitterly disappointed not to have another son. Books were banned from the family house – distrusted especially for women's eyes – and Halimi fought hard for her education. She secretly borrowed books from every library in **Tunis**, took a scholarship for the **French lycée** whereupon she decided to become a lawyer, and eventually got to Paris to study law. *Milk for the Orange Tree* (Extract 4) is about her experiences as a child and an adolescent in a French protectorate, and under German occupation. She talks freely about the pains of being beaten by her schoolteacher at the age of eight (for being 'a filthy Jew'), joining the Tunisian communist party, and in 1971, founding *Choisir*, a non-political movement for women's rights, with Simone de Beauvoir in Paris. Halimi is now a celebrated barrister in France.

Gisèle Halimi

MEMMI, Albert (1920–). A novelist, a sociologist and a poet, Memmi was born in **Tunis** to a Jewish family and spent most of his youth there. During the second world war he was arrested, interned in a labour camp, and managed to escape. After the war he studied at the University of Algiers and the Sorbonne in Paris, where he graduated in philosophy. *The Colonizer and the Colonized*, with an introduction by Jean-Paul Sartre, is an essayistic book on the personal and worldwide legacies of colonialism. His first novel, *The Pillar of Salt* (Extract 3), addresses the same themes in novel form: the feelings of 'a native in a colonial country, a Jew in an anti-Semitic universe, an African in a world dominated by Europe.' Memmi's work has been influenced by his native tradition of story-telling, and is an overlap of autobiography and fiction. He has taught in Tunis and Paris and now lives in Paris.

RILKE, Rainer Maria (1875–1926). Rilke was born in Prague, studied philosophy, literature and art history in his home town and Munich, and travelled to Russia. In Paris he was influenced by Rodin and Cézanne and his early *fin-de-siècle* sentimentality turned into melancholy. His wanderings to North Africa in 1910–11 took him to Algeria, Tunisia and Egypt. After 1919, he lived in Switzerland.

VIRGIL (70–19 BC). Virgil, or Publius Vergilius Maro, was born near Mantua. Generally held to be the greatest of the Roman poets, his works have influenced poets through the centuries. He is best known for his epic poem in 12 books, the *Aeneid*. This tells the story of the wanderings of the Trojan prince Aeneas after the destruction of Troy, and connects its hero with the foundation of Rome. On his deathbed, Virgil expressed the wish that the work should be burned, and he left instructions to that effect in his will.

However, the uncompleted manuscript was edited by two of his friends and survived to become one of the major titles in literary history. The *Aeneid* has attracted various translators. The version by the seventeenth century poet John Dryden (Extract 1) is perhaps the most famous. The 1952 translation by the poet C. Day Lewis is also recommended.

DJIBOUTI

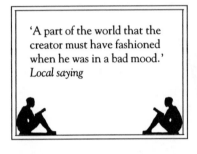

'A part of the world that the creator must have fashioned when he was in a bad mood.'
Local saying

Djibouti is commonly associated with two things: the heat and the French. Before independence in 1977, Djibouti was for almost a century a French colony, and to-day is inhabited by some 20 000 French people. It was probably a Frenchman who coined the phrase 'the hell of Africa' for Djibouti. Even in mid-winter the temperature on the coast frequently rises to over 30°C, rain is infrequent, and there are no cool mountain retreats to boast of.

The entire territory is less than half the size of Denmark and consists mostly of barren, inhospitable desert – parts of which are volcanic outcrops and black lava fields where nothing lives or grows. French writer and eccentric Pierre Loti observed, 'Nothing moves at all: everything has died of the heat. One doesn't even hear the singing of insects, which in other countries of the world, are the persistent noise of life.' The hinterland forms a strip around the **Gulf of Tadjoura**, which lies on the Gulf of Aden at the entrance to the Red Sea. The inland mountains rise to 2000 m, and the inland depression of about 150 m below sea level contains the Horn of Africa's own Dead Sea, the beautiful and eerie **Lake Assal**.

Despite its overwhelmingly bad press, this part of Africa is men-tioned in ancient Roman records dating from as early as the first century AD, and Arab traders record encounters with local tribesmen at the port of **Tadjoura** in the seventh century. In the latter half of the nineteenth century, this hot but strategic strip of coast became notorious for illegal gun-running expeditions and for the persistence of the internationally outlawed slave trade (running slaves from the interior across to Arabia and the Persian Gulf). The French poet Arthur Rimbaud (◊ Ethiopia), who came to Africa after abandoning poetry at the age of 21, was involved in the former if not also the latter of these illegal trades (Extract 4). Yet, despite this unashamed absence

---

FACT BOX

AREA: 21 755 sq km
POPULATION: 441 000
CAPITAL: Djibouti
LANGUAGES: French, Arabic, Somali, Afar
FORMER COLONIAL POWER: France
INDEPENDENCE: 1977

---

of literary pursuit, Rimbaud's stay here is variously honoured throughout the capital (see below, under 'Literary Landmarks').

It was around this time that the French began to take over the coast, seeing it as a strategically important counterbalance to the British post of Aden across the Gulf. With the opening of the Suez Canal, this area had now become an important trading crossroads between Africa, the Middle East and Asia. This importance was further enhanced when the French started to build a railway at the capital, **Djibouti**, in 1897. It was not until twenty years later that the railway reached the Ethiopian capital Addis Ababa, and to this day it remains its only rail link with the coast. A highly unreliable service, the journey has been the bane of many a traveller's life. Evelyn Waugh (◊ Ethiopia) was one such customer. He spent several days sulking in Djibouti town in 1930 (Extract 3), claiming 'no one voluntarily spends long in Djibouti'. Indeed, aside from the most esoteric of literary sports (such as attempting to follow Rimbaud's footsteps across Africa), there is little of popular interest to recommend to the literary traveller.

Modern-day Djibouti is populated predominantly by two distinct peoples – the Afars and the Issas, who inhabit the north and south of the country respectively. The Afars are a nomadic people, formerly known as the Danakils, and inhabit the area north of the Gulf of Tadjoura, their tribal lands spreading throughout the **Danakil Desert** region into Ethiopia. In the nineteenth century the Danakil earned themselves a reputation among anthropologists as the most fearsome tribe in Africa and their custom of cutting off the penises of unwelcome male visitors ensured that they were left largely undisturbed. Anthropologists and explorers such as Wilfred Thesiger ◊ discovered that this apparently primitive people had a highly developed hierarchy of customs, and it was only through strict adherence to this exact (if vicious) system that they were able to survive in such an inhospitable region (Extract 1).

The Issas are a Somali people – culturally and linguistically attached to their fellow Somalis living in Somalia and south-east Ethiopia, but divided by purely artificial boundaries. This exclusively colonial concept remains largely ignored by the nomadic tribesmen to this day. Census-taking is thus a highly unreliable indicator of the country's population, which is estimated at anywhere between 300 000–500 000. Over half the population live in the capital **Djibouti** which provides the main economic hub of the country. The town relies heavily on service industries, the major French naval base and a large international port (when the Suez Canal was closed in 1967 the economy came to a virtual standstill).

Despite colonial interference, the Afars and Issas have managed to preserve a large portion of their indigenous culture. The Somali people are known as the 'people of poets' and their traditional poetry and story-telling remains as alive and imaginative today as ever (Extract 2). However, this is an oral tradition and it was not until 1972 that a written form of the Somali language was established. Only now are many of the centuries-old Somali tales being recorded against the day when 'progressive' culture takes over, and these time-honoured cultural customs succumb to more ephemeral international popular culture.

LITERARY LANDMARKS

Djibouti. The Djibouti–Addis Ababa **railway** was started in 1897 at Djibouti and eventually reached Addis Ababa in 1917. Evelyn Waugh stayed somewhat reluctantly at the **Hotel des Arcades** while he waited for the reliably unreliable train (Extract 3). There is a **Centre Arthur Rimbaud** (French Cultural Centre and Library), on the **Boulevard Bonhoure**. However, when the author of this book visited the Centre, there was not one work on Rimbaud to be found. The main bus terminus, **Place Mahamoud Harbi**, used to be called 'Place Arthur Rimbaud'.

Danakil Territory. Wilfred Thesiger led an expedition into this desert region occupied by the much-feared, fine-featured Danakil Tribe (today known as the Afars). The Danakils were renowned for procuring somewhat unusual trophies from their victims. 23-year-old Thesiger was one of the earliest explorers who survived to tell the legendary tale of their rituals (Extract 1).

Tadjoura. Small sleepy coastal port where Arthur Rimbaud was forced to spend a year waiting to embark on his gun-running expedition to Ethiopia's King Menelik in 1886 (Extract 4). En route he passed **Lake Assal**, Djibouti's Dead Sea.

Libraries and Bookshops

Djibouti. Centre Arthur Rimbaud, Boulevard Bonhoure.

BOOKLIST

The following selection includes the extracted titles in this chapter as well as those mentioned in the introduction which are available in English and other titles for further reading. In general, paperback editions are given when possible. The editions cited are not necessarily the only ones available. For most of the extracted works, the original publisher in English can be found in 'Acknowledgments and Citations' at the end of the volume, as can the exact location of the extracts and the editions from which they are taken. Extract numbers are highlighted in bold for ease of reference.

Blise, Loren F., 'Afar Songs', *Northeast African Studies*, Vol 4, No 3, 1982–1983.

Contes de Djibouti (in French and Somali), Conseil International de la Langue Française, Paris, 1980. (**Extract 2** freely adapted from the French by Paul Strathern.)

Rimbaud, Arthur, *Collected Poems* (in French with prose translations – includes selected letters), Oliver Bernard, ed, Penguin, London, 1962.

Rimbaud, Arthur, *Complete Works and Letters*, Wallace Fowlie, trans, University of Chicago Press, Chicago, IL, 1967. (**Extract 4** translated by John Edmondson from *Illuminations, Suivi de Correspondance 1873–1891*, Flammarion, Paris, 1989.)

Sayed, William F., *Cantiques* (Somali poems in English and French), Les Nouvelles Éditions Africaines, Dakar.

Thesiger, Wilfred, *The Life of My Choice*, Fontana, London, 1987. **Extract 1**.

Thompson, Virginia, and Adloff, Richard, *Djibouti and the Horn of Africa*, Stanford University Press, Stanford, CA, 1968.

Waugh, Evelyn, 'When the Going was Good', in *A Book of Traveller's Tales*, Eric Newby, ed, Picador, London, 1986. **Extract 3**.

Extracts

(1) Djibouti: Danakil

Wilfred Thesiger, *The Life of My Choice*

The Danakil, inhabiting one of the most inhospitable deserts on earth, were considered by many as the most fearsome in Africa.

Every man wore, strapped across his stomach, a formidable curved dagger known as a *jile*, with a sixteen-inch blade sharp on each side.

Nearly all these daggers had one or more brass-bound leather thongs dangling from the scabbard, each thong denoting a man killed.

I thought the Danakil an attractive-looking people, and despite their murderous reputation they appeared to manifest a genuine friendliness. I was prepared to accept the fact that they would kill a man or boy with as little compunction as I would shoot a buck. Their motive would be much the same as that of an English sportsman who visited Africa to shoot a lion and, like him, they preferred to take their quarry unawares.

The Danakil invariably castrated any man or boy whom they killed or wounded, removing both the penis and the scrotum. An obvious trophy, it afforded irrefutable proof that the victim was male, and obtaining it gave the additional satisfaction of dishonouring the corpse. Nesbitt stated in *Desert and Forest* that 'the Danakil wore the testicles of their victims round their wrists . . .' I never came across an instance of this, though I encountered a number of individuals who had just killed someone, including a complacent fourteen-year-old near Bilen. The boy's hair was plastered with ghee, or clarified butter, as evidence of his achievement.

All that mattered to these people was to kill; how they did so had little significance. Nesbitt described how one of his servants, accompanied by the Danakil guide, went to bathe in the river. He put his rifle down and entered the water. The guide picked up the rifle, shot and castrated him, and made off. It is impossible to exaggerate the importance that the Danakil attached to this practice, rating as they did a man's prowess by the number of his kills; many raids were undertaken principally for this purpose. On returning from a raid, any who had never killed were often ragged by their more competent companions, their clothes dirtied and cow dung, instead of ghee, rubbed in their hair.

(2) Djibouti: Traditional Tales

The Jackal and the Cockerel

Traditional Djibouti tales have been handed down orally from generation to generation. They usually contain a simple and direct moral and many are centuries old. This extract is adapted from Contes de Djibouti – see Booklist.

Once upon a time the Jackal went to see the Cockerel. 'Since you've got such a wonderful voice,' said the Jackal to the Cockerel, 'why don't you sing me one of your pretty songs.' Overcome by this unexpected compliment, the Cockerel puffed out his chest, closed his eyes, and sang: 'Cock-a-doodle-do!' While the Cockerel had his eyes closed, the Jackal leapt forward and seized the Cockerel.

As the Jackal was carrying off the Cockerel between his teeth, he came to some sheep-dogs who began to attack him. The Cockerel immediately advised the Jackal: 'Say to them, "What are you doing? I haven't stolen any of your flock. Leave me alone!" '

As soon as the Jackal opened his mouth and began to speak, the Cockerel ran off and flew to the top of a nearby tree. 'A curse on my mouth which spoke when it should have remained silent,' said the Jackal regretfully. 'A curse on my eyes which should have remained open!' said the Cockerel.

(3) Djibouti Town

Evelyn Waugh, *When the Going was Good*

In 1930 Evelyn Waugh travelled to Ethiopia to cover the coronation of Haile Selassie for an English newspaper. On his way he docked at Djibouti where he was forced to wait for several days before catching the train for Addis Ababa.

After luncheon, the rain having stopped, we drove for a tour of the town. We bumped and rocked along in a one-horse cab through pools of steaming mud. The streets, described by the official guidebook as 'elegant and smiling,' were mere stretches of waste-land between blocks of houses. These, in the European quarter, were mostly built on the same plan as the hotel, arcaded and decaying.

'They look as though they might fall down any minute,' remarked my companion as we drove past one more than usually dissolute block of offices, and while we looked they actually did begin to fall. Great flakes of stucco crumbled from the front; a brick or two, toppling from the coping, splashed into the mud below. Some scared Indian clerks scampered into the open, a Greek in shirt-sleeves appeared from the house opposite, a group of half-naked natives rose from their haunches and, still scouring their teeth with sticks of wood, gazed apprehensively about them. Our driver pointed excitedly with his whip and admonished us in Somali. It had been an earthquake which, in the more sensible motion of the cab, had escaped our notice.

(4) TADJOURA
Arthur Rimbaud

Arthur Rimbaud, French poet turned illegal gun-runner writes to his family from the small port of Tadjoura. At the time he was trying to break an embargo by running a shipment of guns from here across the Danakil desert to King Menelik in Ethiopia.

Tadjourah, 3 December 1885

My dear friends,

I am here getting together my caravan for Choa. As usual, it is a slow process; but anyway I am intending to set out from here towards the end of January 1886 . . .

This place Tadjourah has been annexed for a year to the French colony of Obock. It is a small Dankali village with a few mosques and palm trees. There is a fort, originally built by the Egyptians, where six French soldiers now sleep under the orders of a sergeant in command of the post. The country has been allowed to keep its little sultan and its native government. It is a protectorate. The main business of the place is the slave trade.

The caravans of Europeans leave here for Choa, which is no great distance; and yet they get there only with much difficulty because the natives all around the coast have become hostile to Europeans since the English Admiral Hewett made Emperor Jean du Tigré sign a treaty abolishing the slave trade, the only business here which shows any signs of flourishing. However, under the French protectorate, nobody is trying to stop the traffic in slaves, and that is so much the better.

Don't go thinking I have become a slave trader. The goods we import are rifles (old piston rifles, 40 years out of date), which you can get for 7 or 8 francs apiece from the dealers in old weapons, in Liège or France. To the King of Choa, Menelik II, they sell for about 40 francs. But the expenses are enormous, not to mention the dangers of the journey there and back. The people along the road are Dankalis, Bedouin shepherds, fanatical Muslims: they are to be feared. It is true that we travel with firearms and the Bedouins have only spears: but all the caravans are attacked . . .

I wish you health and prosperity in 1886.

Sincerely

A. *Rimbaud*

Biographies and important works

RIMBAUD, Arthur (see under Ethiopia).

THESIGER, Wilfred (1910–). Born in Addis Ababa, where his father was British Minister at the Legation, Thesiger grew up in Ethiopia, was educated in England, and eventually returned to Africa. At the age of 23 he led an expedition into the **Danakil territory**, which was at the time largely unexplored. During the second world war he served with the British forces in the liberation of Ethiopia from the Italians. He consequently travelled to many remote parts of East Africa and the Middle East, and has a home in northern Kenya where he lives among the pastoral Samburu tribe. Wilfred Thesiger has made a name for himself as a fearless if somewhat eccentric explorer, and has written a number of books about his travels, including *The Life of My Choice* (Extract 1).

WAUGH, Evelyn (see under Ethiopia).

ETHIOPIA AND ERITREA

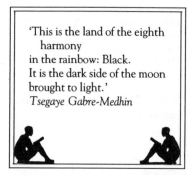

'This is the land of the eighth
   harmony
in the rainbow: Black.
It is the dark side of the moon
brought to light.'
   Tsegaye Gabre-Medhin

Geographically, politically, and historically Ethiopia has no parallel throughout Africa. Commonly associated with famine and desert, the country is in fact centred on the climatically beneficent **Ethiopian Highlands**. Neither too hot in summer nor too cold in winter, the gently rolling landscape around the capital **Addis Ababa** resembles the fertile hills of Tuscany and the south western highland region known as **Kefu** gives its name to the drink we call coffee.

Ethiopia is also unique in Africa in having virtually no colonial past. It was the last country on the continent to be overrun by European colonists when the Italians invaded in 1935. Consequent Italian rule lasted a mere six years and features as little more than a brief interruption in the country's long history.

Ethiopian culture, one of the most ancient in the sub-Sahara, came into being when Europe was still tribal. The country's remote mountain fastness enabled this culture to survive outside influences and develop independently during its long periods of isolation. The earliest mention of Ethiopia and its people comes in hieroglyphic records of Ancient Egypt, and tells of trade with people from the Highlands which began in 2000 BC. The Egyptians called these people Habashat, which later became corrupted to give the name Abyssinia.

In the last centuries of the first millenium BC, Abysinnia fell under the influence of the Sabaeans, who occupied Saba (today the Yemen). It was during this period that the Hebrew King Solomon visited the legendary Queen of Saba (known to us as Sheba). Unlike modern state visits, this one included more than the usual public displays of affection, and the Queen later gave birth to a son. This son was to become King Menelik I, who was the founder of the Ethiopian dynasty of kings.

FACT BOX

AREA: Ethiopia – 898 050 sq km; Eritrea – 125 000 sq km
POPULATION: Ethiopia – 52 800 000; Eritrea – 3 500 000
CAPITAL: Ethiopia – Addis Ababa; Eritrea – Asmara
LANGUAGES: Amharic, Arabic, English, Gallinya, Tigrinya
FORMER COLONIAL POWER: Italy

The golden era of the Aksumite kingdom which centred on the city of Aksum in the north, emerged in the second century AD. Its rulers claimed descent from King Solomon and the kingdom remained under Jewish influence until the reign of Ezana in the fourth century when it converted to Christianity. When the Muslims invaded Egypt in the seventh century, Ethiopia was cut off from the rest of Christendom. During the ensuing centuries it was to develop its own unique form of Christianity, unaware of the doctrinal schisms and theological developments which affected its European counterpart.

When the Crusaders invaded the Holy Land they heard talk of a powerful Christian king called Prester John who ruled a great kingdom beyond the lands conquered by the Muslim Arabs. Unsuccessful attempts were made to contact Prester John and many came to believe that the kingdom of Prester John was just a myth. Not until the fifteenth century, when some Ethiopian monks attended an ecumenical council in Florence, was the rumour confirmed.

The earliest Ethiopian literature was written in Ge'ez, the archaic literary language of the country. Today this survives only in the liturgy of the Ethiopian Orthodox Church, and is incomprehensible to most Ethiopians – though it continues to be spoken by members of the Falasha, Ethiopia's Jewish community, which was recently shipped to Israel in a secret exodus. Ge'ez literature flourished in the thirteenth century and consisted mainly of translations of religious tracts. The classic of this period is *Kebra Negast* (*Glory of the Kings*), which describes the romantic meeting of Solomon and Sheba.

Throughout this time, the spoken language of the people was Amharic and in the sixteenth century this began to develop as a written language for royal chronicles. Still employed today it is a unique and beautiful syllabic script, appearing to the Western eye as a blend of Hindu, Hebrew and Arabic.

For literature about secular life and descriptions of the countryside, we have to rely mainly on the descriptions of the few early European travellers who visited the country. Most came in search of the source of the Nile, speculated on by Europeans since Ancient Greek times. One such quest was undertaken in 1613 by the Portuguese missionary Father

Message from H.I.M. Emperor Haile Selassie I to
2nd International Conference of Ethiopian Studies, Manchester, 1963.

ኢየብልዩ ፡ በ.ት ፡ መንግሥት ፡
አዲስ ፡ አበባ ።

JUBILEE PALACE
ADDIS ABABA

ጦሳ ፡ እንበሳ ፡ ዘእምነገደ ፡ ይሁዳ ፡
ቀዳማዊ ፡ ኃይለ ፡ ሥላሴ ፡
ሥዩመ ፡ እግዚአብሔር ፡ ንጉሠ ፡ ነገሥት ፡ ዘኢትዮጵያ ፡

በማንኛስተር ፡ ለምትሰበሰቡ ፡ የኢትዮጵያ ፡ ጥናት ፡ ሊቃውንት ፡

ሰላምታችን ፡ ይድረሳችሁ ።
ኢትዮጵያ ፡ ከጥንት ፡ ጀምሮ ፡ ቋንቋዋን ፡ ታሪኳንና ፡ ባህሏን ፡ ለዓይጠኑ ፡
የውጭ ፡ አገር ፡ ሊቃውንት ፡ እርዳታዋንና ፡ በጎ ፡ ፈቃድዋን ፡ እንደሰጠቻና ፡
አሁንም ፡ እንደማታቋርጥ ፡ አደዘነጋም ። እናንተም ፡ ተሰብስባችሁ ፡ ስለ ፡
ኢትዮጵያ ፡ ጥናት ፡ በምትነጋገሩበት ፡ ጊዜ ፡ ጥናታችሁ ፡ መልካም ፡ ውጤት ፡
እንዲኖረው ። ተስፋችን ፡ ነው ። ዝርዝሩ ፡ የምትነጋገሩበትን ፡ እስክንረዳ ፡
ፍሬውን ፡ እናብ ፡ ለናንተ ፡ ትተናል ።
በዩኒቨርስቲያችን ፡ የኢትዮጵያ ፡ ጥናት ፡ እንስቲትዩት ፡ ስለተከፈተ ፡
የሚቀጥሉ ፡ ከብሶባቸሁ ፡ በዩኒቨርስቲው ፡ አማካይነት ፡ አዲስ ፡ አበባ ፡ ላይ ፡
በጻረነ ፡ ደስ ፡ ይሉናል ። ደኸንንም ፡ ግብጎ ፡ የምናደርግላቸ ፡ ስለቀዳማዊ ፡
ኃይለ ፡ ሥላሴ ፡ ሽልማት ፡ የወጣውን ፡ ማስታወቂያ ፡ ተመልክታችሁታል ፡
ብለን ፡ ነው ። ~ ስኔ ፡ ፳፯ ፡ ቀን ፡ ፲፱፻፶፭ ፡ ዓ.ም ፡

Amharic script

Paez who discovered what he believed to be the source of the river:
'Near a little mountain, that did not seem of any particular height . . .
I discovered two round springs one of which might be about two feet
diameter: the sight filled me with a pleasure which I knew not how to

express, when I considered that it was what Cyrus, Cambyses, Alexander and Julius Caesar had so ardently and so much in vain desired to behold.' (quoted in *A Short Relation of the River Nile* by Father Lobo).

Just over a century and a half later, the Scottish explorer James Bruce ◊ arrived at the same spot, believing himself to be the first European to set eyes on it. In *Travels to Discover the Source of the Nile* (Extract 8), he writes 'Kings had attempted this discovery at the head of armies . . . Though a mere private Briton, I triumphed here.' Unfortunately for both Father Paez and James Bruce, this was merely the source of the **Blue Nile**, a tributary of the main White Nile.

European interest in Ethiopia grew in the eighteenth century with Dr Samuel Johnson's translation from the French of an account (originally in Portuguese) of a *Voyage to Abysinnia* by Portuguese Jesuit, Father Lobo. This detailed if sometimes fanciful picture of life there inspired the scholarly Johnson to write several morality tales set in seventeenth-century Ethiopia. In *Rasselas* (later translated into Amharic) the hero grows tired of his life surrounded by 'soft vicissitudes of pleasure and repose' and in disgust sets off to Egypt with a philosopher. His work later seduced the English Romantics – Coleridge's *Kubla Khan* has visions of an 'Abysinnian maid' and Wordsworth eulogizes about 'Abyssinian privacy'.

That same century, the indefatigable Victorian explorer Sir Richard Burton ◊ set out to discover the source of the Nile, but beforehand, in 1855, he became the first European to enter the forbidden Muslim city of **Harar** without being executed (Extract 6). Twenty-six years later the maverick French poet Arthur Rimbaud ◊ became the first permanent European resident of the city when he set up here as a coffee and ivory trader (Extracts 4 and 7).

It was during this century that the semi-autonomous provinces which today form Ethiopia began to be merged under Tewodros II, who ruled from 1855 to 1868. The country eventually came together under the great King Menelik II who ruled from 1889–1913 and who successfully resisted the first Italian attempts at colonization. His successor, Haile Selassie, who later became a figurehead for Rastafarians worldwide, was not so successful (see Extract 2 by Evelyn Waugh ◊). It was under the diminutive Selassie that modernization of Ethiopia began – accompanied by widespread corruption, economic stagnation and civil war. After 40 years of rule he was deposed in favour of a Marxist government which was later taken over by the equally notorious Mengistu. This ramshackle dictatorship lasted throughout the terrible famines of the 1980s and the continuing civil wars in **Eritrea** and the **Ogaden**, until 1991 when Mengistu fled, leaving the country in shambles. On 24 May 1993, Eritrea declared itself an independent nation, with Isayas

Aferwerki, leader of the Eritrea People's Liberation Front, elected President. (On Eritrea, see Jeremy Harding's *Small Wars, Small Mercies*.)

A unique religious legacy had a strong influence on the genesis of twentieth century Ethiopian literature. Following the translation into Amharic of John Bunyan's *Pilgrim's Progress* in 1892 came the first Amharic novel. Written in 1908, *Libb wallad tarik* by Afawarq Gabre Yesus is a religious–allegorical work. Few outside Ethiopia can read the enchanting script, and it was not until after the second world war that a few Amharic novels began to be translated and Ethiopian literature gained a wider currency. Among these were the works of Tsegaye Gabre-Medhin ◊ whose best known book is *The Oda-Oak Oracle*. This is a powerful work, in the tradition of Greek tragedy, but derived purely from Ethiopian culture. In it, the hero Ukutee is under a curse, and his future bride Shanka consults the tree oracle of the Oda Oak, who warns her that her first-born son must be sacrificed to appease the curse. More recently, Gabre-Medhin has written a number of plays, including *Collision of the Altars*, set 1500 years ago in the Aksumite Kingdom, but dealing with a situation of national disintegration not so far removed from the present day.

His contemporary, Sahle Sellassie ◊, writes mainly of life in the Ethiopian villages. *Shinga's Village*, his first novel, was written in

Rimbaud House in Harar is shown to tourists as the house where Rimbaud lived . . .

. . . but local research suggests he actually lived here

Chaha, an Amharic dialect. It describes in the form of fictional memoirs the conflicts which arise in a 1950s village when traditional ways come up against the first effects of modernization. Later Sellassie wrote a novel directly in English, *The Afersata*. In this a village hut is burnt down, and the local court (or Afersata) carries out an investigation using both rational and more traditional superstitious methods to try to discover the culprit. His novel *Warrior King* (Extract 5) is based on the life of Emperor Tewodros II.

By coincidence the third noteworthy writer of modern Ethiopia, Daniachew Worku ◊, was, like Sellassie and Gabre-Medhin, born in 1936. Worku has written poetry and plays in Amharic, but remains best known for his novels, some of which have been written in English. The most successful of these is *The Thirteenth Sun* (Extract 3), whose title derives from the unique Ethiopian calendar which has thirteen months (modern tourist posters boast of 'thirteen months of sunshine'). The book describes a pilgrimage up **Mount Zewkala** to visit the Abbo Shrine by the hero Goytom, accompanied by his half-sister Woynitu and his father, who is dying. Worku uses this setting to attack the superstition and social exploitation of the poor villagers, as well as the iniquities of the medievalist church. This is a directly anti-traditionalist novel, and is indicative of a move by today's authors (see also Extract 1 by Tolossa ◊) to deal with contemporary issues and morals in the harsh light of what must feel like an extremely uncertain future.

LITERARY LANDMARKS

Addis Ababa. The **Cherkos district** is the home of the poor coffin-dealer and the grave digger in the play by Fikré Tolossa (Extract 1). The **road south to Bishoftu** is described by Daniachew Worku in *The Thirteenth Sun* (Extract 3).

Aksum. Ancient centre of the great Aksumite Empire which flourished in the second to fourth centuries.

Blue Nile. The legendary **Coy Springs** south of **Lake Tana**, the source of the Blue Nile, was visited by the Portuguese missionary Father Paez (1613) and the Scottish explorer James Bruce (1770), who both mistakenly thought they had discovered the source of the main White Nile (Extract 8).

Entoto. On the northern outskirts of Addis Ababa, the capital founded by King Menelik II who completed the unification of modern Ethiopia. The **Longhouse** in which he held court, and in which Rimbaud bartered his guns, can still be seen.

Harar. Much of the original **wall** and **gates** of the ancient Islamic stronghold and 'Forbidden City' remain. The city was first penetrated by Sir Richard Burton in 1854 and was home for ten years (1880–90) to French poet Arthur Rimbaud. The splendid **Rimbaud House**, in which he is rumoured to have lived, still stands.

Libraries and Bookshops

Addis Ababa. Birham Bookshop and Stationery, PO Box 302; City Library – author Ryszard Kapuściński (◊ Angola) visited the library in 1991 after Mengistu fled the capital, and was surprised to find it 'well stocked as it had been 30 years ago'; ECA Bookshop Co-op Society, PO Box 1236; G.P. Giannopoulos, PO Box 120; Menno Bookshop, PO Box 1236.

BOOKLIST

The following selection includes the extracted titles in this chapter as well as those mentioned in the introduction which are available in English and other titles for further reading. In general, paperback editions are given when possible. The editions cited are not necessarily the only ones available. For most of the extracted works, the original publisher in English can be found in 'Acknowledgments and Citations' at the end of the volume, as can the exact location of the extracts and the editions from which they are taken. Extract numbers are highlighted in bold for ease of reference.

Bruce, James, *Travels to Discover the Source of the Nile*, Gregg, Godstone, Surrey, 1971. **Extract 8.**

Buchan, John, *Prester John*, Penguin, London, 1956.

Burton, Sir Richard, *First Footsteps in East Africa*, Dover, New York, 1988. **Extract 6.**

Casely Hayford, J.E., *Ethiopia Unbound: Studies in Race Emancipation*, Frank Cass, London, 1969 (see under Ghana).

Gabre-Medhin, Tsegaye, *The Oda-Oak Oracle*, Oxford University Press, Oxford, 1965.

Gabre-Medhin, Tsegaye, *Collision of the Altars*, Longman, London, 1977.

Harding, Jeremy, *Small Wars, Small Mercies: Journeys in Africa's Disputed Nations*, Viking, London, 1993.

Johnson, Samuel, *History of Rasselas, Prince of Abyssinia*, Penguin, London, 1985.

Kapuściński, Ryszard, *The Emperor*, Picador, London, 1984.

Lobo, Father, *Itinerario of Jeronimo Lobo*, D.M. Lockhart, trans, Hakluyt Society, London, 1984.

Lobo, Father, *A Short Relation of the River Nile*, London, 1673.

Lobo, Father, *A Voyage to Abyssinia*, Samuel Johnson, trans, Yale University Press, Yale, CT, 1985.

Marsden-Smedley, Philip, *A Far Country*, Arrow, London, 1990.

Menghista, Lemma, *The Marriage of Unequals*, Macmillan, London, 1970.

Moorehead, Alan, *The Blue Nile*, Penguin, London, 1984.

Murphy, Dervla, *In Ethiopia with a Mule*, Century, London, 1984.

Rimbaud, Arthur, *Collected Poems* (in French with prose translations – includes selected letters), Oliver Bernard, ed, Penguin, London, 1962.

Rimbaud, Arthur, *Complete Works and Letters*, Wallace Fowlie, trans, University of Chicago Press, Chicago, IL, 1967. (**Extract 7** translated by John Edmondson from *Illuminations, Suivi de Correspondance 1873–1891*, Flammarion, Paris, 1989.)

Sellassie, Sahle, *The Afersata*, Heinemann, London, 1968.

Sellassie, Sahle, *Warrior King*, Heinemann, London, 1974. **Extract 5.**

Strathern, Paul, *A Season in Abyssinia: An Impersonation of Arthur Rimbaud*, Macmillan, London, 1972. **Extract 4.**

Tolossa, Fikré, *The Coffin-Dealer and the Grave-Digger*, Ubersee-Museum, Bremen, 1982. **Extract 1.**

Waugh, Evelyn, *Waugh in Abyssinia*, Longman, London, 1936. **Extract 2.**

Worku, Daniachew, *The Thirteenth Sun*, Heinemann, London, 1973. **Extract 3.**

Extracts

(1) ADDIS ABABA

Fikré Tolossa,
The Coffin-Dealer and the Grave-Digger

Tolossa's play is set in Cherkos, one of the poorest areas of Addis Ababa. A coffin-dealer and a grave-digger are talking together in the coffin-dealer's workshop, surrounded by all sorts and sizes of coffins.

Coffin-dealer: Oh you can't imagine how hungry I am! I think we'd better close the workshop and go and get ourselves some food.

Grave-digger: Wait a second. somebody might drop in to buy one more coffin. (*With his right hand raised to his brow, he stares into the distance dramatically.*) I see someone far away, dying in a big, big, bed! The man dying is fat, and his villa is as grand as a princely palace! Rejoice, Kassa, soon your purse will be filled!

Coffin-dealer: I think it's me myself, and nobody else who is dying. I wish you knew how hungry I am!

One of the coffins starts moving

Grave-digger: (*sees this first and shivers, terror-stricken. Then he cries out in a choked voice*) a-a-a-a!

Coffin-dealer: (*also noticing the coffin*) What is that?

Grave-digger: I d-o-n'-t k-n-o-w! aa! a-a-a-a!

Coffin-dealer: Is this a nightmare?

(*They retreat from the coffin. The coffin opens slowly and out comes a corpse covered with a shroud. It takes a few steps towards the two. They run towards the exit. The corpse runs faster and blocks their way . . . They run all over the room with cries and the corpse follows them everywhere. At last they fall down . . . After a reasonable moment of suspense, the corpse uncovers itself and it proves to be Ashebir, the rich man.*)

(2) ADDIS ABABA

Evelyn Waugh, *Waugh in Abyssinia*

Waugh returned to Ethiopia in 1935 as a journalist for the Daily Mail to cover the Italian invasion.

Addis Ababa on the eve of war seemed little changed in character and appearance from the city I had known five years before. The triumphal arches that had been erected for the coronation had grown shabbier but they were still standing. The ambitious buildings in the European style with which Haile Selassie had intended to embellish his capital were still in the same rudimentary stage of construction; tufted now with vegetation like ruins in a drawing by Piranesi, they stood at every corner, reminders of an abortive modernism, a happy subject for the press photographers who hoped later to present them as the ravages of Italian bombardment. The usual succession of public holidays paralysed the life of the country; we arrived on the eve of one of them and for two days were unable to cash cheques or collect our luggage from the customs. There was a new Palace and some new shops. The lepers, driven into the villages for the coronation, had returned; that was the most noticeable change.

The newspapermen in their more picturesque moods used often to write about the cavalcades of fighting men who swept through 'the narrow streets of the mountain capital', evoking for their readers the compact cities of North Africa. In fact the streets were very broad and very long. Everything lay at a great distance from everything else. The town was scattered over the hillside like the litter of a bank holiday picnic party.

(3) BISHOFTU

Daniachew Worku, *The Thirteenth Sun*

Worku describes the route from the capital Addis Ababa to the township of Bishoftu.

Along the main street leading to the hills of the little township, Bishoftu, thirty miles south of Addis Ababa, billboards are planted at every conspicuous curve, advertising various commodities, most of them products of the tobacco monopoly. They carry names of beautiful animals, some of them rare and on the verge of becoming extinct, names of queens and famous places from the grandness of Ethiopia's past, heralding them, it seems, to the new era of civilization. 'Smoke Gureza', 'Smoke Nyala', 'Smoke Walya', 'Smoke Elleni', 'Smoke Axum

– Filter American blend', 'Smoke Marathon – little cigars', and 'Fly Ethiopian Airlines – Thirteen Months of Sunshine', they announce.

To the right and to the left, electric and telephone poles criss-cross the sheltering trees and hedges studding the sides of the hills: 'the devil's business' the villagers are pleased to call them. And haven't they succeeded? With the help of nature, of course. More often than not, thunder storms and lightning shatters these poles to pieces. White ants eat them from beneath the ground. Monkeys swinging on the wires loosen the ties at the top. And gales of wind from the side give a helping hand to down them on every storm-swept slope. And the natives? Sure enough, they are always ready to give a finishing touch to the 'God-sent' mishap. They tear up the ties to clear up the way, cautiously pull out the steel rails and pull down the telegraph wires. No – not for mischief's sake, as some people say, but from goodwill and fine co-operative zeal. The rails to beat into plough-shares, sickles, spears and knives. And the wire for bracelets and anklets with which to adorn their females.

(4) DANAKIL DESERT

Paul Strathern, *A Season in Abyssinia*

In Strathern's novel, based on the life of Rimbaud during his years in Africa, the 26-year-old poet ventures into the Danakil desert on his way towards Harar.

From Zeyla, Rimbaud set off inland on the first caravan leaving for Harar. At the edge of the narrow coastal plain, the mountains rose sharply to the inland plateau: a vast barren wilderness. Each night the caravan camped in a small water hollow, and fires were lit. As Rimbaud ate the spicy rice hash that the tribesmen shared around a large heaped bronze platter, the drifting smoke of the fire would blend with the white mist which rose from the water hole, and soon all that was visible under the light star-peppered sky was a smooth-surfaced sea of mist with twists of orange flickering smoke rising from the fires. Amidst the murmurs of the tribesmen, the bells of the cropping camels would tinkle through the silence of the surrounding night.

In the morning at first light the tribesmen would be already up stamping out the grey dusty embers of the fires and loading up the camels. All through the day you simply endured, willing your mind to focus on some distant peak as your horse's hooves clinked against the stones. You could make out no trail and merely followed Youssif, the surly dark-eyed Somali leader, as he picked his way between the boulders, up over the ridges, down along the curving shadowless valleys, while the string of camels carrying the barter and other goods for Harar plodded silently behind.

Each night when the air froze around you and your thoughts became solid once more as your body woke from its heat-induced stupor, you became increasingly possessed by this feeling of inconsolable aching loneliness. What kind of a place lay at the end of a track like this? What the hell ever possessed men to travel day after unending day through such a completely dead world? But you knew, all right. And while you endured, blindly following the nodding robed figure of Youssif as he rode on ahead, you let the heat purge all other thoughts from your mind.

Each morning, before the heat of the day had melted all but the tightening knot of my will, I feasted on the traces of dreams, slaking my thirst with memories of the life I'd left behind me. If I'd have had any tears I'd have shed them, but my eyes were dry and only threads of woollen foam grew at the edges of my lips, glueing them together. And as the desert levelled out into flat dusty rock, Rimbaud's disgust at all he was, all that he had done and been, hardened until it became as unrelenting as the sun that pressed down on the rocky, sunburnt floor of that upper world.

(5) GONDER

Sahle Sellassie, *Warrior King*

Sellassie bases his novel on the life of Emperor Tewodros II who started to unite Ethiopia in the mid-nineteenth century.

The royal drums started to rattle at dawn when the sky was grey, grey like ash. They rattled until the sky turned scarlet red; they continued to rattle until long after sunrise, until the last man in Gonder arrived at the place of calling. This was the day the emperor was to make a speech . . .

The emperor – attended by the empress, the bishop, Ingida, Gebreye, Gelmo and other dignitaries, including John Bell and Walter Chichile Plowden, the British envoy who had lately arrived from Massawa – stood on the balcony of the famous castle and looked down upon the crowd. [The crowd] pushed and pulled and jostled and nudged each other's sides and stepped on each other's toes in an effort to be a little closer to the castle, to see the face of the emperor and hear his new proclamation.

'Everyone must return to his father's profession,' the emperor pronounced. 'The farmer to his plough, the trader to his trade. I shall have no mercy on idlers and disturbers of the peace. Those who have no land may come and see me about it, and they shall get land. And those who have no oxen may come and see me too, and they shall get oxen. But woe to robbers and highway cut-throats, woe to idlers and disturbers of the peace, for I shall have no mercy on them.'

(6) HARAR

Sir Richard Burton, *First Footsteps in East Africa*

Burton makes his final approach to the forbidden city of Harar in 1854. He originally planned to enter disguised as an Arab (as he had entered Mecca) but changed his mind as he neared the city.

About noon we crossed the Erar River. The bed is about one hundred yards broad, and a thin sheet of clear, cool, and sweet water, covered with crystal the greater part of the sand. According to my guides, its course, like that of the hills, is southerly towards the Webbe of Ogadayn: none, however, could satisfy my curiosity concerning the course of the only perennial stream which exists between Harar and the coast.

In the lower valley, a mass of waving holcus, we met a multitude of Galla peasants coming from the city market with new potlids and the empty gourds which had contained their butter, ghee, and milk. . . As we commenced another ascent appeared a Harar Grandee mounted upon a handsomely caparisoned mule and attended by seven servants who carried gourds and skins of grain. He was a pale-faced senior with a white beard, dressed in a fine Tobe and a snowy turban with scarlet edges: he carried no shield, but an Abyssinian broadsword was slung over his left shoulder. We exchanged courteous salutations, and as I was thirsty he ordered a footman to fill a cup with water . . . Upon the summit was pointed out to me the village of Elaoda: in former times it was a wealthy place belonging to the Gerad Adan.

At 2 pm we fell into a narrow fenced lane and halted for a few minutes near a spreading tree, under which sat women selling ghee and unspun cotton. About two miles distant on the crest of a hill, stood the city – the end of my present travel – a long sombre line, strikingly contrasting with the white-washed towns of the East. The spectacle, materially speaking, was a disappointment: nothing conspicuous appeared but two grey minarets of rude shape: many would have grudged exposing three lives to win so paltry a prize. But of all that have attempted, none ever succeeded in entering that pile of stones: the thorough-bred traveller . . . will understand my exultation.

(7) HARAR

Arthur Rimbaud

Shortly after his arrival in Harar, the restless French poet turned traveller and trader, wrote to his family. In between requests for books such as Construction in Metal and Jokes, Puns in Arabic, he describes his life there a little. This letter is headed 'Harar, 15 February 1881'.

I don't intend to stay here for long; I will soon know when I can leave. I have not found what I thought I would find; and I am leading a very tedious and unprofitable life here. As soon as I have 1500 or 2000 francs, I will leave, and will be very glad to go. I am counting on finding something better a little farther on. Write and give me news on the Panama project: as soon as it is open I will go there. I will even be glad to leave here, now. I have contracted an illness, not dangerous in itself; but this climate is treacherous for any kind of sickness. A wound never heals. A one-millimetre cut on a finger festers for months and becomes gangrenous very easily. At the same time, the Egyptian administration has a shortage of doctors and medicines. The climate is very damp in summer; I dislike it intensely, it is much too cold for me. . .

You mustn't think that this country is completely uncivilized. We have the Egyptian army, artillery and calvary, and their administration. All this is just the same as in Europe; except here they are a pack of dogs and bandits. The natives are Gallas, all farmers and shepherds: peaceful people, as long as they are not attacked. The country is excellent, although relatively cold and humid; but agriculture has not modernized. Trade is in the main restricted to the hides of animals, which are milked when they are alive and then skinned; and then there are coffee, ivory, gold; perfumes, incense, musk, etc. The trouble is that we are 60 leagues from the sea and transport is expensive. . .

I will say now: see you soon! in the hope of better weather and less stupid work; because, if you imagine I am living like a prince, I for my part am sure that I am leading a very foolish and tiresome life.

This is leaving with a caravan, and won't reach you before the end of March. That is one of the pleasures of this situation. It is even the worst thing of all.

Yours

Rimbaud

(8) THE NILE

James Bruce,
Travels to Discover the Source of the Nile

*The hardy Scottish explorer arrives at the object of his travels –
the source of the Nile. Unfortunately, unbeknown to Bruce, this
was in fact only the source of the Blue Nile, a tributary of the
White Nile.*

'Come, said I, . . . no more words; it is late now, lose no more time,
but carry me to the head of the Nile directly . . .'. He then carried me
round to the south side of the church, out of the grove of trees that
surrounded it. 'This is the hill, says he . . . that when you was on the
other side of it, was between you and the fountains of the Nile; there is
no other, look at that hillock of green sod in the middle of that watery
spot, it is in that the two fountains of the Nile are to be found . . . if
you go the length of the fountains pull off your shoes as you did the
other day, for these people are all Pagans, worse than those that were at
the ford, and they believe in nothing that you believe, but only in the
river, to which they pray every day as if it were God; but this perhaps
you may do likewise.' Half undressed as I was by the loss of my sash, and
throwing my shoes off, I ran down the hill towards the little island of
green sods, which was about two hundred yards distant; the whole side
of the hill was thick grown over with flowers, the large bulbous roots of
which appearing above the surface of the ground, and their skins
coming off on treading upon them, occasioned two very severe falls
before I reached the brink of the marsh; I after this came to the island of
green turf, which was in form of an altar, apparently the work of art,
and I stood in rapture over the principal fountain which rises in the
middle of it.

It is easier to guess than to describe the situation of my mind at that
moment – standing in the spot which had baffled the genius, industry
and enquiry of both ancient and moderns, for the course of near three
thousand years.

Biographies and important works

BRUCE, James (1730–1794). The
Laird of Kinnaird was an early African
explorer. A rugged individualist with
a flaming red beard, Bruce set out in
1761 to see if he could discover the
source of the Nile – thought in those
days to be at the **Coy Springs**. After
travelling, with many hair-raising

adventures, through Egypt and down the Red Sea, he eventually arrived in Ethiopia. Here he travelled to **Lake Tana**, and finally on 14 November 1770 reached the celebrated fountains (which were the source of the Blue Nile only). He returned to his estate in Scotland and wrote up his adventures into the five-volume *Travels to the Source of the Nile* (Extract 8) which was published in 1790.

BURTON, Sir Richard (1821–1890). After being sent down from Oxford, Burton went to India where he learnt several native languages (he eventually mastered some 40 languages and dialects from four continents). He travelled in disguise to Mecca, becoming the first non-Muslim to penetrate the Holy City. He then travelled to Ethiopia, where in 1854 he became the first European to enter the forbidden Muslim stronghold of **Harar**. Later he travelled with Speke in search of the source of the Nile. He then entered the diplomatic service, a career for which he was temperamentally unsuited. One of his postings was to 'the white man's graveyard' Fernando Po, from which he travelled up the Congo and visited Dahomey (now Benin). Burton wrote many books describing his travels, the best known of which are *First Footsteps in East Africa* (Extract 6) and *A Mission to Gelele, King of Dahomey* (see under Benin).

GABRE-MEDHIN, Tsegaye (1936–). Gabre-Medhin was educated in Ethiopia. He then travelled to Chicago where he studied law, graduating in 1960. From there he went to London, where for a while he was attached to the Royal Court Theatre. When he returned to Ethiopia he began by writing plays and eventually became director of the Haile Selassie I Theatre in **Addis Ababa**. His first English-language play *Tewodros* was produced here in 1963. His novel *The Oda Oak Oracle* is considered by many to be the finest English-language work his country has produced. He has also written some fine poetry.

RIMBAUD, Arthur (1854–1891). Rimbaud was a French visionary poet and the *enfant terrible* of French poetry. In order to become a 'visionary', he embarked on his notorious 'derangement of the senses', which consisted of a life of vagabondage, drug taking and drunkenness. During this period he wrote some of the finest poetry in the French language. At the age of 21, he abandoned poetry to wander around the globe, finally settling in Ethiopia, where he set up as a trader in the remote city of **Harar**, and became its first European resident. He lived in Ethiopia for ten years, trading in coffee, ivory and hides, and also involving himself in illegal gun-running (and possibly slave trading). In 1891 he returned to France where he died in Marseille.

SELLASSIE, Sahle (1936–). Sellassie went abroad to complete his education, studying at Aix-en-Provence in France and the University of California at Los Angeles (UCLA). He was the first to write literature in the Amharic dialect of Chaha, though he also produced works in English. He first achieved widespread recognition with his English novel *The Afersata*. To support himself he worked for a while as a government employee, training staff for the civil service.

STRATHERN, Paul (1940–). Born in the UK, after completing his education at Trinity College Dublin

Strathern joined the merchant navy. During the following years he published five novels, including A Season in Abysinnia (Extract 4), based on the life of the French poet Arthur Rimbaud ◊ during his 'lost' years in Africa. Besides his novels he has also written a number of travel books. He has travelled extensively around Africa, and most recently visited Ethiopia and Djibouti.

TOLOSSA, Fikré (1955–). Tolossa is a playwright and short story writer. He was educated at the **University of Addis Ababa**. He later studied at the Gorki Institute of Literature in Moscow, and then moved to Germany where he taught Russian and creative writing at Bremen. Tolossa's plays contain much broad comedy, but also face up to themes of death, justice and the need for human beings to fulfil themselves.

WAUGH, Evelyn (1903–1966). Waugh first travelled to Ethiopia as a journalist to cover the coronation of Haile Selassie in 1930, and returned five years later to cover the Italian–Abyssinian war for the *Daily Mail*. He

drew on these experiences to write several of his books. *Scoop* is a humorous novel describing the adventures of an inept British reporter sent to Africa to cover a crisis in the fictitious country of Ishmaelia. *Black Mischief* describes how a dissolute British adventurer arrives in the fictitious country of Anzania and assists the Emperor to reform his country, often with farcical results. *Waugh in Abyssinia* (Extract 2) is a factual account of Waugh's visit to Ethiopia in 1935.

WORKU, Daniachew (1936–). A playwright and novelist, Daniachew (aka Daniel) Worku was educated in Ethiopia. His first novel *The Thirteenth Sun* was initially suppressed but eventually came out just before the fall of Haile Selassie at the end of 1974. This sophisticated novel fights against backwardness in the country, and especially against the exploitative power of the Church. His finest play, *The House with the Big Worku*, is about a village mother who comes to the city in search of her son who is a teacher. Worku is generally considered one of the finest writers in English to have emerged from Ethiopia.

KENYA

> 'When the missionaries arrived, the Africans had the land and the missionaries had the Bible. They taught us to pray with our eyes closed. When we opened them, they had the land and we had the Bible.'
> Jomo Kenyatta

First president of independent Kenya, Jomo Kenyatta was also the author of one of the earliest Kenyan literary works in English. *Facing Mount Kenya* was an anthropological tribute to the Kikuyu – his people and the dominant tribe of Kenya. Like many of his generation, Kenyatta learned to read and write at a local missionary school and it was here that he first encountered the colonial attitudes with their system of *de facto* apartheid. The charismatic Kenyatta soon became involved in fighting for the rights of the Kikuyu to claim back their land from the white settlers who had been arriving since the turn of the century. The independence movement, called Mau Mau, became renowned for its fearful oaths, its fearless fighters and its patriotic songs adapted from traditional Kikuyu oral literature (Extract 4). In the ensuing struggle, which lasted from 1952 to 1956, thousands of Africans died, and although they were defeated by the British, they won an important psychological battle which ensured independence a few years later.

Although he was just 14 at the start of the Mau Mau emergency, it was to play an important part in the work of another Kikuyu, Kenya's foremost writer, thinker and critic, Ngugi wa Thiong'o ◊. Ngugi, as he is simply known, is to East African literature what Chinua Achebe (◊ Nigeria) is to West. His work closely mirrors the changes that have taken place in Kenya since he was a child. His first novel, *Weep Not Child*, about the devastating effect of the emergency on a Kenyan family, was the first English-language novel to be published by an East African writer. Ngugi's distinctly direct and restless style – speaking out against the inequalities and injustices of both pre- and post-independence governments – earned him a formidable reputation as

263

FACT BOX

AREA: 582 644 sq km
POPULATION: 25 000 000
CAPITAL: Nairobi
LANGUAGES: Swahili, English, Gikuyu
FORMER COLONIAL POWER: Great Britain
INDEPENDENCE: 1963

---

well as a year in **Kamiti Maximum Security Prison**, during which time he wrote *Devil on the Cross* (Extract 2). As well as being a vigorous defender of the Mau Mau struggle and workers' rights, Ngugi has campaigned vigorously for the revival of indigenous languages. In *Teaching of African Literature in Schools*, Ngugi recalls a time when no African books were taught in schools and how his son struggled to relate to the poems of Wordsworth. He asked his son, what are the 'host of golden daffodils?'. His son replied, 'just little fishes in the lake'. Since then, Ngugi has written only in his native Gikuyu.

The disorientating and demoralizing experience of being educated into an unnatural tongue and culture is the main essence of David Mulwa's ◊ novel *Master and Servant* (Extract 3). The suffering endured under a rule-by-fear education system is slowly and systematically described in this authentic pupil's-eye account. Regularly caned and permanently browbeaten by the school's mottoes 'you must speak English' and 'avoid vernacular, it makes you stupid', the pupil questions the benefit of such an education: 'Once my father had told me that I was far more superior to these cows because God had given me a mind. What use was that mind if it forbade the experience of joy and happiness.'

The resonance and stamina of Ngugi's work has been a hard act for many East African authors to follow. There are a few, however, who stand out with distinctive styles and followings of their own. Grace Ogot ◊ is conspicuous as one of the few female writers to have achieved notice (Extract 6). When she first approached the East African Literature Bureau with her fiction she was shocked to find 'They really couldn't understand how a Christian woman could write such stories, involved with sacrifices, traditional medicines and all, instead of writing about Salvation and Christianity.'

One writer who has successfully stepped out of Ngugi's shadow is Meja Mwangi ◊. *Going Down River Road* (Extract 8), featuring the 'hungry, horny toed barefoot son of the rusty concrete mixer', and *The Cockroach Dance* are his best works and are compelling narratives of post-independence urban life. He portrays a limbo world of the young and disorientated, found in the seedy bars and brothels of the infamous **River Road in Nairobi**. Mwangi's earlier works focus on the mechanics of the Mau Mau struggle. Although he was just a boy at the time of the emergency, it affected him deeply and he believes every Kenyan author has to write about this period at some point in his life.

Charles Mangua's ◊ catharsis of his war-time experiences resulted in rat-a-tat-tat style popular fiction. Candid, crude and racy, he started a trend towards lighter literature that has made him one of the country's bestselling authors. His irreverent style spares no subject nor sentimentality. The anti-hero of *A Tail in the Mouth* (Extract 11) has tried everything in life, from an aborted career as a priest and a holiday in the steamy brothels of **Mombassa** to fighting on both sides during the civil war. Mangua influenced writers of his generation such as David Maillu who went one step further and who has produced a number of controversial mini-novels under his own imprint, Comb Books. Works such as *Unfit for Human Consumption* and *The Flesh* tend to speak for themselves. Classified by many as soft-porn for the masses, his bestselling books are banned in neighbouring Tanzania. In defence of his motives and methods he says simply, 'Life does not hesitate to say anything so why should I hesitate?'

One of the most important literary catalysts and outlets was the literary magazine *Busara*, born out of the energies of students at the **University of Nairobi**. During its short life from 1968 to 1976, it stimulated a writers' workshop, poetry, and critical analysis. Amin Kassam, once Assistant Editor of *Busara*, went on to become a fairly successful poet and short story writer. His recurrent theme is the feeling of helplessness – in 'Trapped in a Puddle' he writes 'how long will you fight/little ant/before you are crushed . . . not even the printed page/floating so invitingly/can save you from the wrath.' Given the traditional importance of Swahili poetry on the coast (Extract 5), it is strange to find that there are few strong modern poets. One of the few is the flexible Jared Angira ◊ who uses both modern and traditional techniques in his work. Angira's poetry is a sad plea for he who, he says in the introduction to his collection *Cascades* (Extract 1), 'yearns to be understood before he is lumped on to the conveyor belt' – for the silent majority, 'the group on whose behalf philosophies are propounded'.

One group of writers who were notorious for their amateur philosophizing about Kenyan society were the white settlers and their groupies. For many Europeans, the enduring image of Kenya is still rooted in the impressions created by a small set of rich, titled misfits and mavericks who ventured here after the turn of the century. Drawn here by the climate, the lifestyle and (some) by the apparent decadence, the scandals and legends of some of their lives make shamefully fascinating reading.

Of the least salacious were the lives and works of Karen Blixen ◊ and Elspeth Huxley ◊, who come out of what Ngugi describes frankly as the racist tradition. Karen Blixen came here with her husband in 1914 to manage a 6000 acre coffee plantation. Her autobiography *Out of Africa* (Extract 10), made into a film in 1985 starring Meryl Streep and Robert Redford and remembered for its romantic connotations, is also a very naive and covertly racist book: 'Part of the farm was native forest, and about one thousand acres were squatters' land . . . The squatters are Natives, who with their families hold a few acres on a white man's farm, and in return have to work for him a certain number of days in the year. My squatters, I think, saw the relationship in a different light for many of them were born on the farm, and their fathers before them, and they very likely regarded me as a sort of superior squatter on their estates.'

Judging by her book, Blixen was equally detached and naive when it came to the carnal activities of her European compatriots. She dwells instead on her guests (including the Prince of Wales who was memorable for having complemented her on her Cumberland sauce), the failure of their ambitious plantation scheme, her divorce in 1921 and her affair with the dashing Denys Finch-Hatton. Blixen's descriptions of the landscape were fuelled by the bird's-eye view of the land she experienced flying with Finch-Hatton in his old Moth machine. The locals were much less impressed by his aviation skills than Blixen. When they landed after one trip an old Kikuyu approached them and asked Denys, 'Will you get up high enough in your aeroplane to see God?' When he replied that he didn't know, the old gentleman replied 'Then, I do not know at all why you two go on flying.' Finch-Hatton died when his plane crashed near **Voi**.

Apart from Blixen, another lady to mourn his death was fellow aviator, Beryl Markham, who had been a rival for his love. Markham came to East Africa with her father when she was just five years old,

---

Notes to map: [a]**Elspeth Huxley**'s *family set off from this famous settlers' meeting place at the start of* The Flame Trees of Thika; [b]*The influential literary magazine* Busara *(1968–76) was launched by students here.* **Jared Angira** *was one of its editors.* **Ngugi wa Thiong'o** *was head of the Literature Department until his imprisonment in 1978;* [c]**Evelyn Waugh** *drank champagne at the exclusive Muthaiga Club, recalled in his A* Tourist in Africa. **Elspeth Huxley**'s *parents were members, as was* **Karen Blixen** *– and the Club is featured in the film of Out of Africa;* [d]*Setting for* **Meja Mwangi**'s Down River Road *(Extract 8);* [e]*Described by* **V.S. Naipaul** *in* North of South *(Extract 9), who visited the famous Thorn Tree cafe here;* [f]*Suburb named after* **Karen Blixen** *whose farm was about 20 km out of Nairobi. The farmland was converted to residential plots in the 1930s and her house is now the Karen Blixen Museum.*

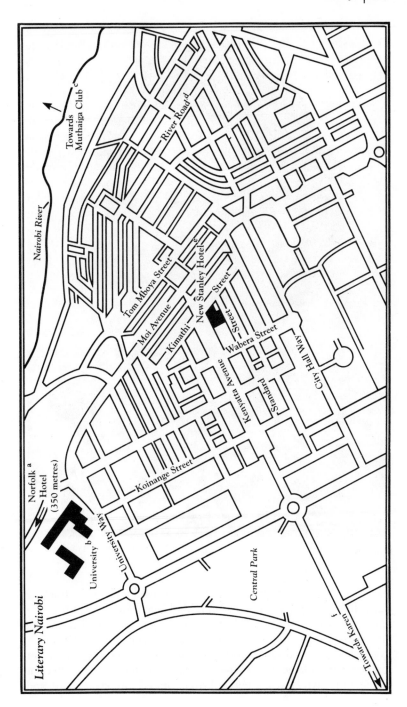

Literary Nairobi

Norfolk [a]
Hotel
(350 metres)

University [b]
Way

University Way

Koinange Street

Central Park

Towards Karen [f]

Tom Mboya Street

Moi Avenue

Kimathi Street

New Stanley Hotel [e]

Street

Kenyatta Avenue

Wabera Street

Standard

City Hall Way

Nairobi River

Towards
Muthaiga Club [c]

River Road [d]

Elspeth Huxley

learned to hunt warthogs with a spear, and used a plane for tracking game. In her book *West with the Night* Markham wrote, 'All of it makes sense – the smoke, the hunt, the fun, the danger.' She later became the first woman to attempt a solo east-to-west crossing of the Atlantic.

The legendary salacious stories of the so-called 'Happy Valley' set can be found in James Fox's *White Mischief*, the story of the mysterious murder of Josslyn Hay, the Earl of Erroll. Graced with great charm and good looks, Hay was the playboy of the colonial community – taking particular and indiscreet pleasure in the arms of married ladies. In 1925 he was installed in 'Clouds' in the **Wanjohi Valley** with the much sought-after Lady Idina Gordon. Fox writes of her, 'Idina was only happy, according to survivors of her house parties . . . if *all* her guests had swapped partners, wives or husbands by nightfall . . . She would organise, from time to time, after dinner games of 'blowing the feather' across a sheet held out by the guests around a table. It was a frantic game that was designed to create near hysteria; when the feather landed all eyes would be on Idina, who, like a high priestess presiding over a sacred ritual, would divine and then announce who was to sleep with who.' *White Mischief* was made into a film in 1987.

An altogether more sober book is Elspeth Huxley's bestseller, *The Flame Trees of Thika* (Extract 12), which opens in 1913 as the family set off by ox and cart from the **Norfolk Hotel** in **Nairobi** to **Thika**. Thika was then a popular area for big-game hunters and where the family had purchased some land 'on the bar of the Norfolk Hotel, from a man wearing an Old Etonian tie'. One of Huxley's best contributions to the literature about Kenya is an anthology called *Nine Faces of Kenya*, which includes writings on war, exploration, local legend, poetry and wildlife. She includes the exploits of big-game hunters the Prince of Wales (in 1928), ex-President Theodore Roosevelt, and Winston Churchill, who poached himself a Rhino here in 1907. Along with the resident gun-happy and gin-happy set, the trophy hunters wrote extensive diaries of their exploits, and contributed to the demise of the once-abundant game. In 1977 the government banned the hunting of all wild animals.

Some imperialist traditions die hard. With barely concealed colonial manner, many writers were lured to Kenya. When Ernest Hemingway (◊ Tanzania) talked about going back to Africa he wanted to 'live – really live. Not just watch life gliding by . . . I want to go somewhere else [other than America] just as we've always had the right to go somewhere else.' Looking for an alternative tourist retreat in 1958, writer Evelyn Waugh (◊ Ethiopia) looked to East Africa. *A Tourist in Africa* is an idiosyncratic diary of his travels in Kenya, Zimbabwe and Tanzania. In it, he recalls the spirit of his first trip here in the 1930s when he fell in love with the country and indulged in 'traditional' decadences. He drank champagne at the **Muthaiga Club**, enjoyed the hospitality of the up-country farmers, and recorded the 'enchanting contradictions of Kenyan life; a baronial hall straight from Queen Victoria's Scottish Highlands . . . sherry is brought in, but instead of a waistcoated British footman a bare-footed Kikuyu boy in a white gown and red jacket.'

Literary Landmarks

Mombassa. Portuguese explorer Vasco da Gama dropped anchor here in 1498. Swahili culture and poetry flourished under the influence of the Arab raiders and traders. Karen Blixen described the town as having 'all the look of a picture of Paradise, painted by a small child.'

Mount Elgon. Home of the Elgonyi people, whom C.G. Jung ◊ studied and wrote about in *Memories, Dreams, Reflections* (Extract 7) when he came here in 1925.

Mount Kenya. Jomo Kenyatta's autobiography, *Facing Mount Kenya*, recalls the Kikuyu tradition of building the doors of their houses to face the mighty mountain because they believe that this is where Ngai (God) rested.

Nairobi. In 1899, at Mile 327 of the **East African Railway**, the Europeans created Nairobi, which means 'Stream of Cold Water' in Swahili. Noted as the 'quintessential white suburb', **Karen** is named after Karen Blixen whose farm in 1914 was 20 km from Nairobi. When she first came here they travelled to town by mule-pulled cart. Today there is a constant stream of minibus tours to **Karen House** where she lived and **St Austin's Church** where she prayed. About town life she said, 'Our Quasi Smart Set of the Colony from time to time enlivened the town with rows of quick melodrama. Nairobi said to you: "Make the most of me and of time. *Wir kommen nie wieder so jung* – so undisciplined and rapacious – *zusammen*".' This was the spirit of the **Norfolk Hotel**, the so-called solar plexus of settlers' Nairobi. As well as a notorious flirting ground, it was a starting point for the hunts. Most of the settlers were a bloodthirsty lot – including the women – and sported Savile Row red coats, white breeches and imported foxhounds. In *The Flame Trees of Thika*, Elspeth Huxley remarked that her parents had been sold their farm 'across the bar of the Norfolk Hotel by a man wearing an old Etonian tie'. The **New Stanley Hotel**, Nairobi's other traditional traveller's meeting place, is described by V.S. Naipaul ◊ in *North of South* (Extract 9). At **Dageretti Corner**, Josslyn Hay, Earl of Erroll, was found with a bullet through his head on 24 January 1941. The unsolved murder became colonial Kenya's *cause célèbre*, and is the subject of the book (and later film) *White Mischief*. The notorious lively and poor **River Road**, which runs through the inner city, is the setting for much of Meja Mwangi's bestselling book *Going Down River Road* (Extract 8). One of the early members of the **Muthaiga Club** was Karen Blixen (Isak Dinesen), and the Club is featured in the film *Out of Africa*. Elspeth Huxley's parents (whose early lives were immortalized in *The Flame Trees of Thika*) were also members.

Ngong Hills. Traditionally the land of the Maasai. Local legend recalls that the strange form of the hills was created when a clumsy

giant tripped over Kilimanjaro and squashed the earth with his hand –
hence the knuckle-like form. Described somewhat differently by Karen
Blixen in *Out of Africa* (Extract 10).

Thika. Elspeth Huxley's first memories of Kenya were of the journey
to the flame tree covered land that her father had bought here.

Wanjohi Valley. The so-called 'Happy Valley', where in the 1920s
and 1930s many of the gin-soaked settlers lived, like Lady Idina who
got through six husbands.

Libraries and Bookshops

Mombassa. Bahari Book Centre, Moi Avenue; British Council Library.

Nairobi. Book Corner, Mama Ngina Street; British Council, ICEA
Building, Kenyatta Avenue; East African Publishing House, POB
30571; Kenyatta University College Library; McMillan Memorial
Library, Banda Street; Nation Bookshop, corner of Kenyatta Avenue
and Kimathi Street; National Central Library; Prestige, Mama Ngina
Street; Select, Kimathi Street; University of Nairobi Library.

BOOKLIST

*The following selection includes the ex-
tracted titles in this chapter as well as
those mentioned in the introduction
which are available in English and other
titles for further reading. In general,
paperback editions are given when possible. The editions cited are not necessarily the only ones available. For most of
the extracted works, the original publisher in English can be found in 'Acknowledgments and Citations' at the end
of the volume, as can the exact location
of the extracts and the editions from
which they are taken. Extract numbers
are highlighted in bold for ease of reference.*

Adamson, Joy, *Born Free*, Fontana,
London, 1960.

Allen, James de Vere, *Swahili Origins*, James Currey, London,
1993.

Angira, Jared, *Cascades*, Longman,
London, 1979.

Angira, Jared, 'No Coffin, No
Grave', in *Poems of Black Africa*,
Wole Soyinka, ed, Heinemann,
London, 1987. **Extract 1.**

Angira, Jared, *Silent Voices*, Heinemann, London, 1972.

Blixen, Karen (Isak Dinesen), *Letters
from Africa 1914–1931*, Weidenfeld and Nicolson, London,
1981.

Blixen, Karen (Isak Dinesen), *Out of
Africa*, Penguin, London, 1984.
Extract 10.

Blixen, Karen (Isak Dinesen), *Shadows on the Grass*, Penguin, London, 1985.

Churchill, Winston, *My African
Journey*, The Holland Press,
Neville Spearman, London,
1962.

Four Centuries of Swahili Verse, Jan Knappert, ed, Darf, London, 1988.

Fox, James, White Mischief, Jonathan Cape, London, 1983.

Hemingway, Ernest, Green Hills of Africa, Cape, London, 1992.

Huxley, Elspeth, The Flame Trees of Thika, Penguin, London, 1977. **Extract 12.**

Huxley, Elspeth, The Mottled Lizard, Penguin, London, 1981.

Huxley, Elspeth, Nine Faces of Kenya, Collins Harvill, London, 1990.

Huxley, Elspeth, Out in the Midday Sun, Chatto and Windus, London, 1985.

C.G. Jung, Memories, Dreams, Reflections, Rand C. Winston, trans, Flamingo, London, 1983. **Extract 7.**

Kassam, Amin, Pulsations, East African Literature Bureau, Nairobi, 1977.

Kenyatta, Jomo, Facing Mount Kenya, Secker and Warburg, London, 1937.

Maillu, David, Kisalu and His Fruit Garden and Other Stories, Heinemann, Nairobi, 1989.

Maina wa Kinyatti, ed, Thunder from the Mountains, Zed Books, London. **Extract 4.**

Markham, Beryl, West with the Night, Houghton Mifflin, Boston, MA, 1942.

Mangua, Charles, Son of Woman, East African Publishing House, Nairobi, 1971.

Mangua, Charles, A Tail in the Mouth, East African Publishing House, Nairobi, 1972. **Extract 11.**

Mulwa, David, Master and Servant, Longman, Harlow, 1979. **Extract 3.**

Mwangi, Meja, Carcase for Hounds, Heinemann, London, 1974.

Mwangi, Meja, The Cockroach Dance, Longman, Harlow, 1989.

Mwangi, Meja, Going Down River Road, Heinemann, London, 1984. **Extract 9.**

Mwangi, Meja, Kill Me Quick, Heinemann, London, 1973.

Mwangi, Meja, Taste of Death, East African Publishing House, Nairobi, 1975.

Myths and Legends of the Swahili, collected and translated by Jan Knappert, Heinemann, Nairobi.

Naipaul, V.S., North of South, André Deutsch, London, 1978. **Extract 8.**

Ngugi wa Thiong'o, Devil on the Cross, Heinemann, London, 1987. **Extract 2.**

Ngugi wa Thiong'o, A Grain of Wheat, Heinemann, Oxford, 1988.

Ngugi wa Thiong'o, I Will Marry When I Want, Heinemann, London, 1982.

Ngugi wa Thiong'o, Matigari, Wangui wa Goro, trans, Heinemann, Oxford, 1989.

Ngugi wa Thiong'o, Petals of Blood, Heinemann, Oxford, 1988.

Ngugi wa Thiong'o, The River Between, Heinemann, London, 1965.

Ngugi wa Thiong'o, Weep Not Child, Heinemann, London, 1987.

Ogot, Grace, Land without Thunder, East African Publishing House, Nairobi, 1968.

Ogot, Grace, The Promised Land, East African Publishing House, Nairobi, 1968. **Extract 6.**

Poems of Black Africa, Wole Soyinka, ed, Heinemann, London, 1987. **Extracts 1 and 5.**

Ruark, Robert, Something of Value, Doubleday, New York, 1955.

Ruark, Robert, Uhuru, McGraw-Hill, New York, 1962.

Teaching of African Literature in Schools, Kenyan Literature Bureau, Nairobi, 1978.

Theroux, Paul, Girls at Play, Penguin, London, 1983.

Thurman, Judith, *Isak Dinesen: The Life of Karen Blixen*, Penguin, London, 1986.

Trzebinski, Errol, *The Kenya Pioneers: The Frontiersmen of an Adopted Land*, Mandarin, London, 1991.

Waugh, Evelyn, *A Tourist in Africa*, Methuen, London, 1985.

Voices from Twentieth-Century Africa, Chinweizu, ed, Faber and Faber, London, 1988. **Extract 4,** the Mau Mau.

Extracts

(1) KENYA: COMPATRIOTS

Jared Angira, *No Coffin, No Grave*

Here Angira expresses feelings of loss, confusion and change for Kenya's compatriots during the 1960s and early 1970s. This poem forms part of his collection Silent Voices, which he says 'consists of crude voices gasping in the dark . . . trapped between despair and existence . . . caught up in a maze but always trying to get through.' 'No Coffin, No Grave' is also included in the anthology Poems of Black Africa – see Booklist.

who could signal yellow
when we had to leave politics to the experts
and brood on books
brood on hunger
and schoolgirls
grumble under the black pot
sleep under torn mosquito net
and let lice lick our intestines
the lord of the bar, money speaks madam
woman magnet, money speaks madam
we only cover the stinking darkness
of the cave of our mouths
and ask our father who is in hell to judge him
the quick and the good.

(2) Kenya: Culture

Ngugi wa Thiong'o, *Devil on the Cross*

Two men travelling in a matatu or small bus strike up a conversation about cultural imperialism. Written while the author was detained without trial, this novel is hailed as one of the most powerful critiques of modern Kenya ever written. Today Ngugi lives in exile, writing only in his native Kikuyu.

Gatuĩria cleared his throat again. He looked at Mũturi. 'You talk as if you knew I came from the university, and it is true. I am from there. I'm a kind of research student in culture. I'm *a junior research fellow in African culture. Our culture* . . . *sorry, I mean,* our culture has been dominated by the Western imperialist cultures. That is what we call in English *cultural imperialism.* Cultural imperialism is mother to the slavery of the mind and the body. It is cultural imperialism that gives birth to the mental blindness and deafness that persuades people to allow foreigners to tell them what to do in their own country, to make foreigners the ears and mouths of their national affairs, forgetting the saying: Only he who lives in the wilderness knows what it is like. Hence a foreigner can never become the true guide of another people. It is about our generation that the singer sang:

> The deaf man, the deaf man,
> The deaf man is he who can't hear for the nation!
> The blind man, the blind man,
> The blind man is he who can't see for the nation!

'Let us now look about us. Where are our national languages now? Where are the books written in the alphabets of our national languages? Where is our own literature now? Where is the wisdom and knowledge of our fathers now? Where is the philosophy of our fathers now? The centres of wisdom that used to guard the entrance to our national homestead have been demolished; the fire of wisdom has been allowed to die; the seats around the fireside have been thrown on to a rubbish heap; the guard posts have been destroyed; and the youth of the nation has hung up its shields and spears. It is a tragedy that there is nowhere we can go to learn the history of our country. A child without parents to counsel him – what is to prevent him from mistaking foreign shit for a delicious national dish?

(3) KENYA: EDUCATION

David Mulwa, *Master and Servant*

*It is towards the end of the colonial period and Kituku has come
to complete his education in Kyambe Primary School, which is
run along the lines of an English public school. The pupils learn
everything in English, and live in constant fear of the headmaster
and his cane.*

English lesson! English lesson and blanks and interminable pronuncia-
tions of guttural sounds, of lisping sounds, of nasal sounds and *ba-ba*
sounds and *baa* sounds and *um*-sounds, in which the forty-five of us
make blabbering idiots of ourselves, and the whole classroom is a
perfect bedlam. English lessons and vocabulary; the same procedure day
in day out: 'Take our your dictionaries' and *whup*! Flash comes green
Dic (as we christened that Authority), who says on his front cover that
he is a very concise dictionary and gives a formidable impression of
guarding most jealously, what lies thereafter: 'Take out your dictionaries – and study the words on page . . .' I *am* studying the words on page
. . . but they don't mean anything to me. There's a word called
'gargoyle' – which sounds rather funny. We make no attempt to *learn
the words nor even define* them. They come from the dictionary into our
heads and evaporate with the evening air at the end of the lesson. We
are told to write a composition about any of the words we have been
studying. I like this word 'gargoyle'. I couldn't make head or tail of the
definition. But it *must* be a good word, or the teacher would not have
chosen the page that bore it. I seek to uplift the word and define it in
terms of the invincible mortals of this school that I dread most, in order
to please them, using *gargoyle* as an adjective of praise. Thus my
composition reads, 'Our English teacher is very gargoyle, the headmaster is very gargoyle, and we have a school motto that says English
should be spoken even in our dreams instead of our vernacular and,
God's truth! that's very gargoyle! – the Chapel is gargoyle, Reverend
Wranglem is gargoyle, punishment and school rules are very gargoyle
because they make us grow to be good boys when we leave Kyambe
School, which I think is altogether very gargoyle indeed . . .'

(4) KENYA: MAU MAU

The Mau Mau, *The Call*

During the Mau Mau struggle for independence the oaths and rituals to recruit supporters (and to get rid of adversaries) were legendary. Many of the traditional chants and poems of the Kikuyu were used and adapted to woo recruits and to keep up morale. Extracted from the anthology Voices from Twentieth-Century Africa – see Booklist.

Have you not yet joined,
What are you waiting for?
Join our Mau Mau army,
What are you waiting for?

. . .

What sort of man are you,
What are you waiting for?
Or are you one of the whites,
What are you waiting for?

And you, man of religion,
What are you waiting for?
Remember land is the source of national strength,
What are you waiting for?

. . .

Mau Mau is the people's movement,
What are you waiting for?

(5) KENYA: SWAHILI

Swahili traditional verse

Kenya's first literature has its origins in oral Swahili poetry which was written in the Arabic script and spread throughout the East African Coast. These praise songs and poems often use a simple rhyming form to relay a great variety of morality tales and advice. A warning: they are not renowned for their egalitarian portrayal of women. Extracted from the anthology Poems of Black Africa – see Booklist.

Give me the minstrel's seat that I may sit and ask you a word
my friends.

Let me ask for what reason or rhyme women refuse to marry?
Woman cannot exist except by man, what is there in that to
   vex some of them so?

. . .

When man goes on his road he goes with a friend, for he who
   walks alone has no good fortune
As man goes through life soon he is pierced by the thorn of
   misfortune
Or the sand-mote enters his eye and he needs a friend to
   remove it.
Even so do I advise you, the rich man and the poor man join
   hands across the shroud.
Better a loin-cloth without disgrace than a fine-flowered shawl
   of shame.

(6) KISUMU

Grace Ogot, *The Promised Land*

*Ochola and his wife have left the Luo village of Nyanza and are
on their way to start a new life in neighbouring Tanzania. Here
they arrive at Lake Victoria from where they will take the boat
with other pioneers who are moving away from their homeland.
The book is subtitled A True Fantasy.*

The ground seemed to slope, yet the water did not spill; the sunlight
made it sparkle and the beauty of it was overwhelming. At the little
pier small boats tossed about lazily in the morning wind. Beyond the
boats, stood the great SS 'Rusinga', the giant of Lake Victoria which
was to carry Ochola and his wife away to the unknown land. From time
to time, thick black smoke puffed up from the steamer and, from a
distance, it looked like a burning island.
    Ochola turned to his wife excitedly. 'Can you see that big ship at the
pier head?'
    Nyapol nodded, her mouth full of sour saliva.
    'Can you imagine that within a short time we shall be aboard that
giant and sailing away on the Lake? I'm sure you'll enjoy the journey.'
    'Let's hope the lake will be calm,' Nyapol said slowly, with a sinking
feeling in her stomach.
    Ochola could not help feeling important. He had looked forward to
this time ever since he was a boy. The day he would take his wife to
town, as he had seen many of his clansmen do. It was a matter of great

prestige in those days to go to town and be in contact with the new ideas and acquire the new ways of life. People living in towns obviously ate better food than those who lived in the country. They ate at regular hours too. Nyapol listened to her husband patiently; she wished she could be as excited as he was about the journey. There was so much she was going to lose by leaving Nyanza. Now and again she glanced at the hills of Nyahera and thought of her birthplace beyond.

She thought of her mother and sisters who were, perhaps, even now enjoying the tales of old times in the village they had lived for so many years. She wished she had not married. Marriage was a form of imprisonment in which the master could lead you where he wished.

(7) MOUNT ELGON

C.G. Jung, *Memories, Dreams, Reflections*

> *Dr Carl Jung visited Mount Elgon in 1925 to learn from the elders of the Elgonyi people about their rituals, symbolism and spirits.*

At the end of that palaver an old man had suddenly exclaimed, 'In the morning, when the sun comes, we go out of the huts, spit into our hands, and hold them up to the sun.' I had him show me the ceremony and describe it exactly. They held their hands in front of their mouths, spat or blew vigorously, then turned the palms upwards towards the sun. I asked what this meant, why they blew or spat into their hands. My questioning was in vain. 'We've always done it,' they said. It was impossible to obtain any explanation, and I realized that they actually knew only that they did it, not what they were doing. They themselves saw no meaning in this action. But we, too, perform ceremonies without realizing what we are doing – such as lighting Christmas tree candles, hiding Easter eggs, etc.

The old man said that this was the true religion of all peoples, that all Kevirondos, all Buganda, all tribes for as far as the eye could see from the mountain and endlessly farther, worshipped *adhísta* – that is, the sun at the moment of rising. Only then was the sun *mungu*, God. The first delicate golden crescent of the new moon in the purple of the western sky was also God. But only at that time; otherwise not.

Evidently, the meaning of the Elgonyi ceremony was that an offering was being made to the sun divinity at the moment of its rising. If the gift was spittle, it was the substance which in the view of primitives contains the personal mana, the power of healing, magic, and life. If it was breath, then it was *roho* – Arabic, *ruch*, Hebrew, *ruach*, Greek, *pneuma* – wind and spirit. The act was therefore saying: I offer to God my living soul. It was a wordless, acted-out prayer which might equally well be rendered: 'Lord, into thy hands I commend my spirit.'

Besides *adhísta* the Elgonyi – we were further informed – also venerate *ayík*, the spirit who dwells in the earth and is a *sheitan* (devil). He is the creator of fear, a cold wind who lies in wait for the nocturnal traveller. The old man whistled a kind of Loki motif to convey vividly how the *ayík* creeps through the tall, mysterious grass of the bush.

(8) NAIROBI: KENYA

Meja Mwangi, *Going Down River Road*

Ben, who has just been sacked from his job, goes to his favourite club on River Road, the New Garden Hotel, to spend his last month's pay. He picks up a young 'student', one of the regular girls who hang out looking for free drinks and 'friends' for the night.

'Would you like to see my place?' he tested.

She looked up, her large eyes glassy with indecision.

'Is it far?'

'No, but we could take a taxi.'

'I would prefer to walk.' He took her books, put them under his arm. They turned down the street to Government Road. He slipped his hand into hers.

'It is cold,' she uttered. He got his arm round her waist. She felt warm, so good. He trimmed his strides to match hers. Her hip rubbed against his leg, soft and hard at the same time. His mind raced ahead of him and tried to figure out how it would be at home.

A late bus jammed with late-drinkers ground gears and shuddered up the road towards Kebete. Along River Road, watchmen stirred awake by their fires to watch them pass. Somewhere in the bowels of the twisted dark lanes between Grogan and River Roads someone screamed for help. No-one was likely to answer the call. Robbers were earning their bread today too.

The Karara Centre was still open. The barman could not close at the usual time. Never. The patrons would murder him, wreck the joint and set it on fire. The police did not harass him about keeping to the regulations. They got a tip to keep away and more than that they did not care. Even then as now, the whole town knew that the Centre and its crowd were lost to the Devil. A kind of emergency filling-station half-way between here and Hell.

The Hell crowd was gathered outside the Bar watching a man fight a woman. Nobody helped the woman. She had drunk his beer and would not go to bed with him. He was just paying himself for the trouble. She protested that she had not had anything from him. All he wanted was a free lay, which he definitely would not get. No one cared for the truth. This was fun just to watch.

(9) Nairobi

V.S. Naipaul, *North of South*

Visiting in 1978, writer Naipaul found himself at the famous Thorn Tree Café in the New Stanley Hotel. A well-known meeting place for travellers it is also the haunt of the new colonists – an unscrupulous breed of hustlers who home in on newcomers.

It was mid-morning and the open-air pavement terrace attached to the New Stanley Hotel was crowded with tourists dressed for Africa. Bush-shirts and sun hats banded with leopard skin of synthetic garishness were everywhere in evidence. Cameras and binoculars dangled from sun-tanned necks. German, French and American voices rang in the air. Out on the street was parked a convoy of zebra-striped Volkswagen vans. The smell of safari – of tented bush, of elephant, of hippopotamus, of lion – suffused the bright morning. Noisy traffic choked the broad expanse of Kenyatta Avenue. Fashionably dressed blacks streamed along the pavements, the men carrying briefcases, the women swinging handbags. Nairobi vibrated with cosmopolitan splendour. A crippled beggar, his knees padded with foam rubber, his hands encased in sandals, crawled nimbly on the periphery of the terrace. 'Jambo . . . jambo . . .' The waiters, smartly dressed in white and green tunics, kept him at bay. A thorn tree, rising centrally from the terrace, threw a dappled green shade across the metal tables.

Without asking if they could, two Americans came over and sat down at my table. . .

'From distant parts?'

I nodded.

'What kind of currency are you carrying?'

I told him.

He clucked his tongue. 'Sterling . . . that's not so good. Still, I could give you eighteen shillings to the pound.'

I said I preferred to change my money legally.

He laughed. 'Hear that, Andy? The guy says he prefers to change his money *legally*.'

'The guy's a sucker,' Andy said.

Stan leaned towards me. 'How about a woman?'

'Not now, thanks.'

'A boy?'

'You deal in those too?'

'I deal in most things – currency, dope, women, boys. I'll fix you up with anything you want. You could say I'm one of the pillars of the tourist trade in these parts.' . . .

'Business must be good.'

'Booming,' Stan said. 'The only comparison is Jo'burg. Nairobi is the finest city north of South.'

(10) NGONG HILLS

Karen Blixen, *Out of Africa*

Karen Blixen's coffee farm lay at the foot of the Ngong Hills which run in a ridge from north to south. For the young Dane, it was unlike anything she had ever seen or experienced before.

The geographical position and the height of the land combined to create a landscape that had not its like in all the world. There was no fat on it and no luxuriance anywhere; it was Africa distilled up through six thousand feet, like the strong and refined essence of a continent. The colours were dry and burnt, like the colours in pottery. The trees had a light delicate foliage, the structure of which was different from that of the trees in Europe; it did not grow in bows or cupolas, but in horizontal layers, and the formation gave to the tall solitary trees a likeness to the palms, or a heroic and romantic air like full-rigged ships with their sails furled, and to the edge of a wood a strange appearance as if the whole wood were faintly vibrating. Upon the grass of the great plains the crooked bare old thorn-trees were scattered, and the grass was spiced like thyme and bog-myrtles; in some places the scent was so strong that it smarted in the nostrils. All the flowers that you found on the plains, or upon the creepers and liana in the native forest, were diminutive like flowers of the downs – only just in the beginning of the long rains a number of big, massive heavy-scented lilies sprang out on the plains. The views were immensely wide. Everything that you saw made for greatness and freedom, and unequalled nobility.

The chief feature of the landscape, and of your life in it, was the air. Looking back on a sojourn in the African highlands, you are struck by your feeling of having lived for a time up in the air. The sky was rarely more than pale blue or violet, with a profusion of mighty, weightless, ever-changing clouds towering up and sailing on it, but it has a blue vigour in it, and at a short distance it painted the ranges of hills and the woods a fresh deep blue. In the middle of the day the air was alive over the land, like a flame burning; it scintillated, waved and shone like running water, mirrored and doubled all objects, and created great Fata Morgana. Up in this high air you breathed easily, drawing in a vital assurance and lightness of heart. In the highlands you woke up in the morning and thought: Here I am, where I ought to be.

(11) Tana River

Charles Mangua, *A Tail in the Mouth*

It is the time of the Mau Mau revolution and somewhere along the steep banks of the Tana River the homeguards are launching an attack on the gangsters they believe are hiding in the forest. For Samson Moira it is just another job in a long line of disasters.

Ta-ta-ta-ta. God's teeth! This is no goddam joke. I only joined the homeguards to earn an honest living but – jeez. This don't look like no goddam way of earning a living. I'll resign tomorrow for Chrissake. Tomorrow. To hell with a goddam living – ta-ta-ta. Hey, not again. Our folks are shooting too. Whenever they give us a tata-ta-ta from the other side we give them a pe-pepe-pe-toah-toah. Trouble is I can give nothing. Not with a goddam spear. I don't even know what I am following the others for. Those with spears should remain behind. They should go home. I make up my mind. I creep fast and catch up with Kariuki.

'Do I have to come? This blunt spear is no good.'

'You heard my order. Keep behind the others, idiot. Hey – you there, keep shooting! Damn!' A bullet just whizzed above his head.

'Aaaah! – oh-oh.' Nderitu leaps in the air and comes down with a thud. He is holding his stomach. They've got him. Right in the middle of the belly. He is on his knees clutching his belly. Blood is oozing out through his fingers. He collapses to the ground again. He's got his mouth shut tight and his face contorted with agony. Jesus. He is dead. Just like that. Dead. His eyes are glassy and vacant. Kariuki curses.

(12) THIKA

Elspeth Huxley, *The Flame Trees of Thika*

One morning the Huxley family and a group of settlers set off on mules and ponies from Thika for a picnic and some hunting in the bush.

The guinea-fowl could not be shot until the sun was more than half-way down the sky and so we found a shady tree some way from Kupanya's village for the picnic. In our circle of cool shade, as if under a rustling green parasol, we inhabited a different world from the sun-soaked Kikuyu ridges that stretched to meet a far, enormous sky, blue as a wild delphinium and decorated with vigorous clouds that threw shadows as large as islands on to the hillsides and valleys. It was as if we sat in a small, darkened auditorium gazing out at a stage which took in most of the world.

'If one followed those little rivers to their birthplace,' Lettice inquired, 'where would one be?'

'On top of the Aberdare mountains, where it's bleak and cold and marshy, and the lions are said to have spots,' Ian replied.

'And down there?' Lettice gestured with a sandwich towards the far distance where a brown smudge on the horizon showed us the beginning of the great plains.

'The valley of the Tana, where there's perhaps the finest concentration of game in all the world.'

'I must go there one day,' Lettice said.

'You would find it unhealthy and hot.'

'That is part of its attraction.'

Alec Wilson, with an air of plucking up his courage, observed: 'That's not the sort of thing you're cut out for, Mrs Palmer. That's to say, marching and camping and that sort of thing isn't the life for a lady of your – for someone who – well, I mean . . .' He grew not pink, but positively red, in his confusion.

'For someone as incompetent as I?'

'No, no, of course, I didn't mean to imply . . .'

'I'm sorry: I know you didn't.' She smiled at Alec with unusual warmth to make up for her remark.

'You mean that Mrs Palmer is too good for Africa,' Ian suggested. 'You are probably right.'

'That is rather a large claim,' Lettice said.

'Surely it isn't a question of which is superior, Lettice or the continent of Africa,' Tilly suggested. 'It's a question of adapting ourselves to the conditions.'

Biographies and important works

ANGIRA, Jared (1936–). Founder and treasurer of the Writers' Association of Kenya, the poet Angira was born and educated in Kenya. He studied commerce at **Nairobi University** where he was editor of *Busara*, a well known outlet for writers that was published under the auspices of the literature department there. He has published several collections of poetry – his best known are *Silent Voices* and *Cascades* – which, in his characteristic simple and sad way, run through the gamut of human and psychological suffering that is born out of political turmoil. As one critic said of his early work, 'for a poet so young, he speaks with a strikingly old voice'.

BLIXEN, Karen (1885–1962). Known also under her pen-name, Isak Dinesen.

Karen Blixen

Blixen arrived in Kenya newly married from Denmark in 1914, with her husband. Her life here was not happy – her marriage failed, and the farm was a disaster. She did however discover writing. Her autobiography, *Out of Africa* (Extract 10), was a 'sublime repair job' says biographer Judith Thurman. In contrast to her letters home, *Out of Africa*, says Thurman, 'rearranges the events of Karen Blixen's life on the farm so that there is no psychological or narrative ambivalence to them'. There was indeed a great sense of loss and sadness about her life in her writings. As another critic of her book said, she was able to 'recover in the imagination what she has lost in the external world'. She returned to Denmark in 1931. Her short stories *Shadows on the Grass* also take up a Kenyan theme.

HUXLEY, Elspeth (1907–). Daughter of Major Grant of Njoro, Huxley spent most of her childhood in Kenya. She was educated at a European school in **Nairobi**, then at Reading University, and later at Cornell, USA. After she married in 1931 she travelled widely. In the 1950s she joined the Monckton Advisory Commission on Central Africa. She has written several books about Africa, including *The Mottled Lizard*, the sequel to *The Flame Trees of Thika* (Extract 12), which takes up the story when the family return to Kenya after the second world war.

JUNG, Carl Gustav (1875–1961). The famous and influential Swiss psychologist, psychiatrist and philo-

Ngugi wa Thiong'o

sopher founded his own school of 'Analytical Psychology' following his collaboration with Freud from 1907 to 1913. His research into religious and spiritual processes and their symbolism took him, in 1925, to **Mount Elgon** in Kenya, where he learned about the rituals in the lives of the Elgonyi people.

MANGUA, Charles (1939–). Mangua's two novels, *A Tail in the Mouth* (Extract 11) and *Son of Woman*, inspired a new confidence and popular style in Kenyan fiction writing. Described as 'refreshingly flippant', the raw style of his first novel, *Son of Woman*, earned him near overnight success. The novel broke sales records when it sold out of its first printing of 10 000 within six months. *Son of Woman* is about the appropriately named Dodge, son of a prostitute who ends up in a mission and later at university. *A Tail in the Mouth*, Mangua's second novel, is about an equally irreverent character who lives (only just) through the Mau Mau rebellion. It won him the 1973 Kenyatta Prize for Literature.

MULWA, David. First published outside his native Kenya in 1987, Mulwa's debut novel, *Master and Servant* (Extract 3) has many sensitively observed layers. Primarily it tells of the sensitive relationship between a boy and his house servant, when the boy is sent away from his despotic father to attend school in another village. Set at the end of the colonial era, we follow the boy as he grows into the world of adult emotions and political realities.

MWANGI, Meja (1948–). Born in **Nanyuki** and confined during his childhood to a camp (to prevent contact with the Mau Mau), Mwangi studied science at **Kenyatta College**. While writing his books he has been employed by the British Council and French Television in **Nairobi**. His personal catharsis of childhood experiences resulted in books about the Mau Mau – his first novel, *Taste of Death*, and *Carcase for Hounds*. He is best known today for his sensitive but unsentimental preoccupation with the hardships of urban life. *Going Down River Road* (Extract 9) is a compelling and fascinating journey through the sleaze and cockroach-ridden life of a young man in the capital.

NAIPAUL, V.S. (see under Côte d'Ivoire).

NGUGI wa Thiong'o (1938–). Ngugi is a Kikuyu, born in **Kamir-iithu** village near **Limuru**, 12 miles north-east of Nairobi. His father, who had four wives and 28 children, was dispossessed by a greedy landowner and the large family found themselves squatting on their own land. Ngugi was educated at Makerere University in Uganda and later at Leeds, England. Back in Kenya, he became head of the Literature Department at **Nairobi University** until he was imprisoned in 1978 following the performance of his play *I Will Marry When I Want*. The play, written in Gikuyu, was designed to be performed

by peasants and workers, and on its first production was claimed to be subversive and provocative. The licence was revoked and Ngugi was detained for a year. *Devil on the Cross* (Extract 2) – originally written in Gikuyu (see below) – was sketched out on toilet paper while he was in detention. It is the story of a woman seduced by the 'satan of capitalism', and is dedicated 'To all Kenyans struggling against the neo-colonial stage of imperialism.' *Weep Not Child*, his first published novel, published under the name James Ngugi, was written while he was still a student in Uganda and won him an award from the 1966 Dakar Arts Festival in Senegal. *The River Between* was the novel he wrote first, and is very much born out of Kikuyu land and legend. His novels are, at heart, concerned with the colonial experience and legacy – including the Mau Mau incident and the problems of the new nation state. With each new book his reputation seems to increase and his resolve strengthen. His style is often not easy. It can be didactic and heady, but it is never boring or ambiguous. Ngugi has always been conscious of his role as a writer and his responsibility to address himself to the needs of the people. He says in relation to *Petals of Blood*, 'I am not . . . ashamed of speaking and writing about the peasants and workers who have built Kenya . . .'. This led Ngugi to abandon the English language, and today he writes only in Gikuyu, the language of the Kikuyu. Much to the chagrin of his supporters, he has still not been reinstated to his former position at Nairobi University. Extracts from some of his books banned in Kenya have been published in the journal *Index on Censorship*. Since his release from detention in 1979, Ngugi has been unable to live in Kenya and has mainly divided his time between the UK, Sweden and the USA.

OGOT, Grace (1930–). A Luo, born in **Central Nyanza** district, Ogot was educated at local schools and went on to train as a nurse in Uganda and England. She has since been employed as a scriptwriter and broadcaster for the BBC Overseas Service; a public relations officer; and as a delegate to the United Nations and UNESCO. One of the founding members of the Writers' Association of Kenya, she is primarily a short story writer concerned with everyday life and everyday problems. Her established themes are of village life in general, and women in particular. *Land Without Thunder*, her first collection of short stories, follows traditional life in her native Kenyan villages. *The Promised Land* (Extract 6) was her first novel. Ogot's work has appeared in several literary magazines, and she is also well known locally for her popular weekly radio show which is broadcast in the Luo language.

SOMALIA

'The country teems with poets – the fine ear of the people causing them to take the greatest pleasure in harmonious sounds and poetic expressions . . . Every chief in the country must have a panegyric to be sung by his clan, and the great patronize light literature by keeping a poet.'
Sir Richard Burton,
First Footsteps in East Africa

Somalia, the so-called 'land of poets', was known to the Ancient Egyptians as the Land of Punt. Trade with Egypt continued well into the first millenium AD, until this desert-dominated land fell under Arab control. A flourishing trade in slaves (destined for the markets of Baghdad and Damascus) and spices (for Europe) centred on the southern ports of **Mogadishu** and **Brava**, until the sixteenth century when the Portuguese discovered a route round the Cape of Good Hope into the Indian Ocean. The calls of Arab traders became less frequent, and the Somalis continued their timeless tribal way of life far from the prying eyes of the world.

Limited trading power, a largely inhospitable landscape, and a predominantly Muslim population, however, did nothing to deter expansionists, colonialists and explorers from as far afield as China. In 1854 the explorer Sir Richard Burton (◊ Ethiopia) arrived at Zeyla, today known as **Seylac** (Extract 2). Burton was distinguished from many of his contemporary travellers by the fact he could speak fluent Arabic and knew Muslim ways. Nevertheless, he was an intruder and his arrival is somewhat differently remembered from a local point of view. As recounted by the popular Somali novelist Faarax Cawl ◊ in his bestselling book *Ignorance is the Enemy of Love* (Extract 5), Burton had been sent on a 'reconnoitring mission' by the British Government: 'He told the Somali people that he was Sheikh Cabdalla, and disguised himself so that they would not know that he was a swindler whose intentions towards the Somali people and their land were robbery and oppression. This British infidel was in truth well acquainted with the

FACT BOX

AREA: 630 000 sq km
POPULATION: 8 041 000
CAPITAL: Mogadishu
LANGUAGES: Somali, Arabic, English, French
FORMER COLONIAL POWER: Great Britain, Italy
INDEPENDENCE: 1960

Muslim faith and the Arabic language, and sometimes led the prayers in the mosques of the town of Seylac. It seems that most of the time he wore a long robe such as clerics wear, and he never moved very far from the places frequented by learned clerics and students, so that no one else could find him out or even notice him.'

According to local lore, Burton's true identity was discovered when 'Sheikh Araye came upon this Briton when he had gone to relieve himself on open ground, and the Sheikh, hiding behind a tree, saw clearly that the man . . . had not been circumcised and that on his body there was that visible mark of being an infidel'. The 'hypocrite' was driven from Seylac and set out for Harar, considered then to be part of Somali territory.

Harar today is in Ethiopia, but these lands have long been contested and have often changed hands. In the latter half of the nineteenth century, King Menelik II of Ethiopia annexed a large part of the traditionally Somali Ogaden region, which today remains part of Ethiopia. In 1888 the British took over the north-eastern half of the country as a 'protectorate', and in 1893 the Italians annexed the southern half. During the second world war, the British occupied the Italian sector, which was returned to the Italians as UN trustees in 1950.

It was not until independence in 1960 that the halves of Somalia united. Nine years later, Mohammed Siyad Barre came to power and introduced a radical form of socialism, forming a close alliance with the Soviet Union. This alliance was ruptured in the 1970s, when Somalia invaded the Ogaden in an unsuccessful attempt to retrieve this predominantly Somali-occupied region from Ethiopian control.

However, to a largely nomadic people borders are an unnatural phenomenon – the Somali culture and language spread freely into neighbouring Djibouti, northern Kenya, and much of south-east Ethiopia. But ignoring international borders is not always so easy, as one pastoral poet discovered while trying to reach his family in Ethiopia shortly after the Somali–Ethiopian war of 1977–78. Denied permission to cross, he penned a poignant protest (Extract 6).

Nuruddin Farah

Migratory problems were also highlighted during the droughts and famines of the 1980s when Somalia, whose economy can barely support those officially within its borders, had to host vast numbers of Somali refugees who fled across the border from Ethiopia. The resulting catastrophe was only partly alleviated by massive overseas aid. Since then President Barre has been overthrown, the country has disintegrated into anarchy, and the great chiefs who once patronised poets today champion armed gangs in the struggle for ascendancy among the clans. As Burton aptly observed over a century ago, 'a false quantity or prosaic phrase excites their violent indignation'.

But what really identifies Somalia as the 'land of poets' is that the Somali tongue developed into a highly colourful and inventive language, unrestrained by the formality of written structures. Not until 1972 was a written script devised so that Somali could be set down. Before that, all formal writing and education had been conducted in Arabic, English or Italian.

Though the tradition of Somali oral poetry stretches back for centuries, it quickly learned to adapt to the changes of the twentieth century. The poetic genre known as 'Heelo' which developed after the second world war quickly began to be used for radio broadcasts, and was adapted to include such disparate topics as traditional love stories, drama, politics and popular songs. Meanwhile, traditional moralistic tales were starting to be recorded in various languages (see under Djibouti, Extract 2).

As far as written works are concerned, the most important figure to emerge is undoubtedly Nuruddin Farah ◊. His first book, *From a Crooked Rib* (Extract 1), appeared in 1970 when he was just 25 years old. Since at this time there was no formalized Somali script, Farah wrote in English. With considerable daring he chose to write this novel from the standpoint of a tribal girl who escapes from her family (which has arranged her marriage) and ends up in the capital **Mogadishu**. Farah pulls no punches, showing the bitter realities of Somali life (especially for women). Four more of Farah's novels have since appeared in English, each better than the last (see Booklist).

The popular poet, William F.J. Syad, born in 1930, writes mainly in French to overcome the language problem, but includes a number of poems in English in his published collections. Much of his work is simple love poetry, and a large amount of this consists of free translations of traditional oral verse.

Writing in Somali is dramatist Hassan Sheikh Mumin ◊. His play *Leopard Among the Women* (Extract 4) has been translated into English, and depicts life in a merchant's family. Mumin and his contemporaries seek to show how the modern influences and uncertain living are undermining traditional values, and threaten the disintegration of family life. The dilemma of life in Somalia today is summed up by the hero in Omar Eby's ◊ short story 'A Long Ride' (Extract 3). Ruminating on his truck journey out of **Mogadishu** he admits to 'romantic notions about living in the bush', and discovers that 'the land had begun to possess him, but with a few moments of reflection he knew it was better this way – to be possessed, than to possess. Again he looked about him as he shifted positions on the seat, smiling on the land that possessed him, feeling its fingers probing to fondle his heart.'

Literary Landmarks

Belet Wene. Somalia's foremost writer, Nuruddin Farah, describes a tribal girl's curiosity upon her arrival here in *From a Crooked Rib* (Extract 1). It is her first taste of a town.

Berbera. The landing point of Chinese traveller Yu-Yang-Tsa-Tsu some 500 years ago. He recorded that the people 'stick a needle into the veins of cattle and draw blood, which they drink raw, mixed with milk'.

Mogadishu. From Belet Wene, Farah's heroine Ebla eventually arrives here. The countryside along the road south of the capital is captured in 'A Long Ride', the short story by Omar Eby (Extract 3).

Seylac. Formerly named 'Zeyla', Seylac was Sir Richard Burton's first landing point in sub-Saharan Africa and is described in *First Footsteps in East Africa* (Extract 2). The sometimes dangerous sea journey across from Aden to this port is described in Faarax Cawl's popular novel *Ignorance is the Enemy of Love* (Extract 5).

Libraries and Bookshops

With the country in a seemingly permanent state of anarchy and the capital Mogadishu in ruins, any postal addresses will be highly unreliable. However: The New African Booksellers, PO Box 897, Mogadishu.

BOOKLIST

The following selection includes the extracted titles in this chapter as well as those mentioned in the introduction which are available in English and other titles for further reading. In general, paperback editions are given when possible. The editions cited are not necessarily the only ones available. For most of the extracted works, the original publisher in English can be found in 'Acknowledgments and Citations' at the end of the volume, as can the exact location of the extracts and the editions from which they are taken. Extract numbers are highlighted in bold for ease of reference.

Burton, Sir Richard, *First Footsteps in East Africa*, Dover, New York, 1988. **Extract 2**.

Cawl, Faarax, *Ignorance is the Enemy of Love*, Zed Press, London, 1982. **Extract 5**.

Cawl, Faarax M.J., *The Shackles of Colonialism*, UNESCO, Paris, 1978.

Eby, Omar, *A Long Dry Season*, Good Books, Intercourse, PA, 1988.

Eby, Omar, 'A Long Ride', in *The Sons of Adam*, Herald Press, Scottdale, PA, 1970. **Extract 3**.

Farah, Nuruddin, *From a Crooked Rib*, Heinemann, London, 1970. **Extract 1**.

Farah, Nuruddin, *Gifts*, Serif, London, 1993.

Farah, Nuruddin, *Sardines*, Heinemann, London, 1982.

Farah, Nuruddin, *Sweet and Sour Milk*, Heinemann, London, 1979.

Laitin, David D., and Samatar, Said S., *Somalia: Nation in Search of a State*, Gower, London, 1987. **Extract 6**.

Mumin, Hassan Sheikh, *Leopard Among the Women*, B.W. Andrzejewski, trans, Oxford University Press, London, 1974. **Extract 4**.

Syad, William, *Cantiques*, Nouvelles Éditions Africaines, Dakar and Abidjan, 1976.

Extracts

(1) Belet Wene

Nuruddin Farah, *A Crooked Rib*

Ebla, a tribal girl, arrives at this small town to the north of Mogadishu. It is the first time she has ever been in a town.

At the outskirts of the town, she could hear the hideous noise so common in Belet Wene, the smoke which could have smothered anybody, the peasants coming out of town after they had bought and sold what they wanted, and the young boys playing football, with a ball which was made out of pieces of worn-out clothes stitched together. Before she knew what was happening or where she was, she was somewhere near the bazaar.

Ebla stopped for a while to look closely at the townspeople. Inwardly she was annoyed, perhaps because nobody had noticed her aloofness or perhaps because she could not see anybody whom she knew. (But she had not known more than a hundred persons in her life; and perhaps, she never wanted to know more.) Her colleagues from the caravan had gone ahead. It was only when somebody called to her that she came back to her senses and woke up. Then she found nobody but herself, dressed in the long wide robe, which stretched out in all directions, down to the ground, to the sides, ruffling in the wind. She looked at her robe as she walked, lifting between her thumb and forefinger the corners which touched the ground. The wind blew on to her belly. Her right side was naked and one voluptuous breast could be seen, nodding, saying 'hello' to the robe which caressed it. Ebla thought that the clothes worn by the townspeople were indecent. 'But maybe I am wrong – let me get closer,' she told herself, 'and see how they dress exactly. Tomorrow; I will be able to pass judgement tomorrow, perhaps.'

(2) SEYLAC

Sir Richard Burton, *First Footsteps in East Africa*

*Victorian explorer Burton describes his first arrival in Africa in
1854 at the Port of Zeyla in what is now Somalia (Zeyla is now
Seylac). The indigenous population were not so enthusiastic (see
chapter introduction).*

On the morning of 31st October we entered the Zayla Creek, which
gives so much trouble to native craft. We passed, on the right, the low
island of Masha, belonging to the 'City of the Slave Merchant,' –
Tajurrah – and on the left two similar patches of seagirt sand, called
Aybat and Sa'ad al-Din. These places supply Zayla, in the Kharif or hot
season, with thousands of gulls' eggs – a great luxury. At noon we
sighted our destination. Zayla is the normal African port – a strip of
sulphur–yellow sand, with a deep blue dome above, and a foreground of
the darkest indigo. The buildings, raised by refraction, rose high, and
apparently from the bosom of the deep. After hearing the worst
accounts of it, I was pleasantly disappointed by the spectacle of
white-washed houses and minarets, peering above a long low line of
brown wall, flanked with round towers.

As we slowly threaded the intricate coral reefs of the port, a bark
came scudding up to us; it tacked, and the crew proceeded to give news
in roaring tones. Friendship between the Amir of Harar and the
governor of Zayla had been broken; the road through the Isa Somal had
been closed by the murder of Mas'ud, a favourite slave and adopted son
of Sharmarkay; all strangers had been expelled the city for some
misconduct by the Harar chief; moreover, small-pox was raging there
with such violence that the Galla peasantry would allow neither ingress
nor egress. I had the pleasure of reflecting for some time, dear L, upon
the amount of responsibility incurred by using the phrase 'I will'; and
the only consolation that suggested itself was the stale assurance that

'Things at the worst most surely mend.'

(3) SOMALIA: COUNTRYSIDE

Omar Eby, *A Long Ride*

*This is the start of Eby's short story, which takes the reader on a
journey through the harsh Somali countryside.*

In Somalia, all roads lead to Mogadishu, but the green truck riding high
on large, firm tires sped him in a cloud of white dust along a road
running away from the city sometimes south, sometimes southwest. A

thin eddy of silky dust whispering behind each tire gathered thickly, climbed white and orange-flecked in a tall column and hung motionlessly on the morning after the passing of the truck.

Under the brittle light of a midmorning sun, the road faded into a liquid mirage thrown up quivering against the horizon. Dancing and winking, the horizon mocked him, but it was surprising and pleasing him that it fled before the thunderous clamor of his charging 'tank,' as he had personally dubbed the old truck. On either side of the vehicle the silver thornbushes with small leaves of hammered steel gray scratched at the scene and snatched at his attention as they momentarily whipped into view.

Over the thornbushes a few baobabs lifted heavy arms in fright, a gauze of dust enshrouding their trunks. Above the dust and the truck, above the scrubs and trees, the sky soared and curved in an upward sweep of blue, stretching out joyfully its endless acres.

Through the open truck windows the day coughed on him hot bursts of its breath, smelling of strawy grasses and animal dung. Not unlike a zoo, he thought again, making the association for a hundredth time, but rather enjoying the dried and sharp odor and thinking it clean and satisfying.

He eased up unconsciously on the accelerator and smiled on the land God had given him for a home. Not a site of some few hundred feet by hundred feet, nor a plot of a couple acres, but the whole sweeping desolate country from the urgent Indian ocean on his left to the desperate backland desert, from the gulf to the river. Yet over the years he was learning that he could not possess it – that the land defied his anxious mental grasp.

(4) Somalia: Relationships

Hassan Sheikh Mumin, *Leopard Among the Women*

Shabeel, a young townsman, and Shallaayo, a merchant's daughter, meet in the street. Their conversation highlights traditional values, and the complicated relationship between men and women in a predominantly Muslim society.

Shabeel: Shallaayo!
Shallaayo: How are you?
Shabeel: I'm well.
Shallaayo: You seem to be angry!
Shabeel: No, no – I'm all right.
Shallaayo: In that case, Shabeel – greetings!
Shabeel: Greetings!

Shallaayo: I have good news.

Shabeel: That's good.

Shallaayo: A blessing came from the meeting we had together.

Shabeel: What blessing? Tell me!

Shallaayo: You seem to be angry again.

Shabeel: No, no – go on, go on. Jabber away!

Shallaayo: When God creates a person out of two human beings who lawfully belong to each other, is that not a blessing?

Shabeel: There is a great blessing in a person created by God out of two human beings who lawfully belong to each other – but in this case it's not so good, since we've done it by fraud.

Shallaayo: What?

Shabeel: We've done it by fraud!

Shallaayo: Done it by fraud?

Shabeel: Yes.

Shallaayo: By the name of God and by the Sura of Yaa Siin! [*Aside*] Oh, my belly! [*To* Shabeel] What did you say?

Shabeel: By the Zodiac and its signs! [*Aside*] Oh, my head! [*To* Shallaayo] What did you say, woman?

Shallaayo: [*addresses the audience*]: Oh noble ladies, listen how he dishonours me shamelessly!

Shabeel: [*addresses the audience*]: Oh men, listen how this girl pesters me in the street, she whom I've never seen before! [*To* Shallaayo] Get out of my sight!

(5) Somalia: Storm

Faarax M.J. Cawl, *Ignorance is the Enemy of Love*

During a crossing from Aden to Somalia, a ship full of Somali passengers is overtaken by a sudden violent storm.

Then, at about half-past eleven, the ship's mast broke in two in the middle, and the upper part crashed down on to the deck. Before this happened the captain had still had some hope, but with the breaking of the mast and the shouts which came from all sides of 'Help! Help! Crew! I'm lost!' he resigned himself to what was to come and put his trust in the words of the Profession of Faith.

It was obvious to anyone in his right mind, unless he were a child, that the ship would founder and that there was no chance of remaining on it. Calimaax took Nuur Ciise aside and asked him, 'What do you think of our position? What do you expect to happen, you who cannot swim?'

'Oh, don't leave me behind – the situation is terrible!'

'Nuur, you must just resign yourself to whatever fate God has written for you, since I myself am going to help one of these women.'

'What, Calimaax, do you give preference to a woman, whose bloodwealth is only fifty camels, over me who am worth a hundred? Still, God is all-powerful, and it's quite likely that I shall reach the coast even before you and the woman you're going to take with you.'

'If you're a saint, then obviously you'll get there before us. But I'd have you keep in mind, Nuur, that you shouldn't harbour resentment against me, for if God confronts one with men and women in distress, like these here tonight, it is one's right and duty to help those who should come first. But wait for me and I'll come back for you.'

(6) SOMALIA: WAR

Anon

The poet laments the fact that as a result of the war with Ethiopia (1977–78) he cannot cross the border to join his family in Ethiopia. This poem, taken from Laitin and Samatar's book Somalia: Nation in Search of a State *(see Booklist), was originally quoted by John Darnton in 'A Barren Ethiopian Desert is Promised Land to Somalis',* New York Times, *14 September 1978.*

My brother is there
I can hear the bells of his camels
When they graze down in the valley,
And the leaves of the bushes they browse at
Have the same sweetness as the bushes near my place
Because the rain which
Makes them grow comes from the same sky.
When I pray, he prays,
And my Allah is his Allah.
My brother is there
And he cannot come to me.

Biographies and important works

BURTON, Sir Richard (see under Ethiopia).

CAWL, Faarax M.J. (1937–). Cawl was born in **Sanag**, Somalia, and educated at Chelsea College, London. On his return to Somalia he worked as an engineer and later became a colonel in the police force. *Ignorance is the Enemy of Love* (Extract 5) was his first novel, and was written in the newly formalized Somali script. It was a huge success – its first print run of 10 000 copies sold out within six months. The novel is a simple love story, about a real and ill-fated romance between a Dervish leader and an educated young woman. Eventually the woman is forced by her father to marry a camel dealer. Cawl has since written several other books, including novels and political texts.

EBY, Omar (1935–). Eby was born in Hagerstown, Maryland, in the USA. He graduated from Syracuse University and the University of Virginia. He spent six years teaching in Africa – in Somalia, Tanzania and Zambia. *The Sons of Adam* is a collection of short stories that includes 'A Long Ride' (Extract 3), a poetic and evocative account of a lorry-driver's journey through the countryside, in which he muses on the dilemmas and sense of dislocation of his life in modern-day Somalia. Other published works include *A House in Hue*, *A Whisper in Dryland*, *Sense and Incense*, and *A Long Dry Season*. Omar Eby currently teaches writing and literature at Eastern Mennonite College, Harrisonburg, Virginia.

FARAH, Nuruddin (1945–). Farah was born in **Baidoa**, the fourth in a family of ten, in what was then the Somaliland Protectorate. After being educated in Somalia, and a brief spell as a civil servant, he went to India to study philosophy at the University of Chandigarh. Here he wrote his first novel, *From a Crooked Rib* (Extract 1). He married an Indian woman and studied for several years in England at the Universities of Essex and London. Other novels published in English include *Sweet and Sour Milk*, *Sardines* and *A Naked Needle*, about a teacher in **Mogadishu** who has been to England. On his visit he promises to marry an English girl, and then one day she turns up in Mogadishu. *Gifts*, published in 1993, is set in **Mogadishu** in the 1980s, before the destruction of the clan wars. Reviewing the book in the *Financial Times*, Jeremy Harding described it as 'an exemplary hybrid, in which the Somali habit of metaphor, grounded

Omar Eby

in oral tradition, gives depth and structure to a finely woven, rather English prose.' Nuruddin Farah is generally regarded as Somalia's leading writer.

MUMIN, Hassan Sheikh (1930–). Born the son of a local religious leader in the **Borama District** in northwestern Somalia, Mumin received a traditional Muslim education. He then worked variously as a businessman, teacher and a haberdashery instructor. In the 1960s he worked for **Mogadishu** radio and was later employed in the Cultural Department in the Ministry of Education. He has written several successful plays, including *Leopard Among the Women* (Extract 4) and *The World Depends on Brains for its Protection*, about a man who gets married fifty times (untranslated).

SUDAN

> 'The map of the Sudan looked like a face, the face of a man gazing down; the face of a man in mourning. The wars were carried on; tyrants come in all shapes and colours of the skin. So much hatred all together – not even this country was big enough to hide them all.'
> *Jamal Mahjoub,*
> *Navigation of a Rainmaker*

The giant of the African continent, Sudan straddles the divide between the rich Arabized north and the poor Black Christian and animist south. Within the country, whose name comes from Bilad al-Sudan, meaning 'Land of the Blacks', stark religious, linguistic and economic differences have embedded themselves into a permanent state of civil war between the people, which even the common enemy of British colonialism could not unite.

While Egypt and Britain juggled for power in the nineteenth century, the Mahdists, nationalistic Arab desert warriors, gained increasing support. In 1885 the famous British governor General Gordon (or Charles 'Chinese' Gordon as he was fondly known) was murdered when the followers of the Mahdi stormed the palace in **Khartoum** and took control. Then, in 1898, the Mahdist state was overthrown by Kitchener and the British made Sudan a British colony. To make his mark and exact revenge, Kitchener purportedly rebuilt the capital with the pattern of a Union Jack.

The rise of the Mahdist state and the infamous Mahdi warriors provided new themes for the country's writers. Poets were particularly prolific, glorifying them in the accepted traditional style with unashamed and abundant use of cliché. The legendary tenacity and bravery of the Mahdists even procured a poem from the British writer Rudyard Kipling. The 'tribute', 'Fuzzy Wuzzy', is not exactly what one would term today 'politically correct', and should be considered more as a reflection of Kipling's dubious political beliefs than a celebration of the nobility and bravery of the warriors: 'So 'ere's to you, Fuzzy-Wuzzy,

FACT BOX

AREA: 2 505 810 sq km
POPULATION: 25 800 000
CAPITAL: Khartoum
LANGUAGES: Arabic, English
FORMER COLONIAL POWER: Egypt and Great Britain
INDEPENDENCE: 1956

at your 'ome in the Soudan;/You're a pore benighted 'eathen but a first class fighting man; An 'ere's to you Fuzzy-Wuzzy, with your 'ayrick 'ead of 'air-/You big black bounding beggar – for you broke a British square!'

By the time Sudan gained its independence the literature had undergone several changes and influences. The movements in romanticism, realism and neo-classicism were closely linked to the undercurrents in the country's development, and the literary developments of the colonial power. Following the influence of Egyptian classicism on poetry there came, in the 1930s, a river of romanticism, influenced by the likes of the classic English romantics, Wordsworth, Shelley, and Keats – the remnants of this style are noted in an amusing story from Bruce Chatwin's (◊ Benin) visit (Extract 2). A backlash of realism later resulted in socialist poetry, short stories and essays. However, it was not until long after independence that literature began to move away from traditional and colonial influences, and that translations of Sudanese literature trickled through to a wider audience.

Tayeb Salih ◊ is the major writer to emerge in translation from Sudan. Unlike most of his predecessors, Salih is not easy to categorize, as he uses a rich mixture of metaphor, traditional story-telling methods, and contemporary themes. *Season of Migration to the North* (Extract 1), described as an *Arabian Nights* in reverse, explores the sufferings and schizophrenia of a man who by all appearances is African, though in terms of his beliefs he is Arab. Indulging in what he sees as the moral decadence of the West while a student in London, Mustafa enjoys and kills the women who are seduced by his tales of the Occident. Rejecting this abhorrent life, he returns to his village by the Nile and faces his dilemmas and his guilt for the murders. Also translated is *The Wedding of Zein*, a collection of traditional short stories illustrated with rather surreal but beautifully stark sketches by Ibrahim Salahi, one of Sudan's most famous artists.

The reported current vogue for short story writing may be attributable to the limited possibilities for journalists here in a climate of rising Islamic fundamentalism. All journalists and employees in the media are required to be members of the ruling National Islamic Front, and any overtly subversive writing is not, shall we say, encouraged.

One such victim was journalist and poet, Anai Kelueljang ◊. His finest collection, entitled *The Myth of Freedom* (Extract 3), was written between 1968 and 1985, roughly the period of the militarist Nimeiri regime. Kelueljang, who once ran a state-owned newspaper here, wrote an open farewell elegy to journalism in his poem 'My Chequered Career' – 'I must sink beneath time's flood,/And happily hibernate with elevated mind!' The poet spent a period in Juba jail, and includes in his book several poems that were written on toilet paper while he was held in detention.

The major literary 'export' of Sudan is Jamal Mahjoub ◊. His first book, *Navigation of a Rainmaker* (Extract 4), is set in modern-day Sudan and leads us through an unforgiving landscape during a relentless civil war. We follow the journey of Tanner, a young geologist who has left England to discover the land of his father and goes to work for an oil company. Escaping the boredom and bureaucracy of **Khartoum** he goes off into the desert of his dreams and nightmares – 'A broken place where the wind and the sand and the stars live'. Mahjoub guides us expertly along the dusty paths of the migrating masses and the rainmaker, through the realities of famine and war, and into the mind of a man coming to terms with his own disaffected and desecrated life.

Reading between the lines of the indigenous literature, it is all too apparent why Sudan has not proved a great temptation for foreign – especially British – writers. American Edward Hoagland ◊ visited Sudan in 1977 for that very reason. He had visited Africa before, but was drawn back to Sudan because of what he describes as its 'almost unequalled variety'. He noted it as one of the most hospitable countries on earth and, in *African Calliope* (Extract 5), explores with the manner of a grasshopper everything from politics to geography and history. As the author suggests, 'Plunge straight in, as befits the age of sudden air travel.'

English writer Charlie Pye-Smith ◊ took a different and more popular route overland into Sudan. Travelling down the Nile from Egypt, his first point of entry into the country was at **Wadi Halfa** on **Lake Aswan** (Extract 6). When he eventually arrived in **Khartoum**, not ten years after his first visit, he was shocked to find how much it had decayed and at the number of refugees and beggars who had arrived from war-torn neighbouring countries. Pye-Smith takes us around his favourite streets and hang-outs, including the camelburger café and the ice-cream parlour where you can buy a banana split distinguished by its lack of banana. Rising early one morning he takes a stroll along **Nile Avenue**, 'the finest street in Khartoum'. 'By the time I had reached the bridge which crossed the White Nile to Omdurman I was sweating profusely.

It was eight o'clock and over 100 degrees. Every guidebook tells you that from here you can see the different-coloured waters of the two rivers, the White and the Blue running side by side. I couldn't.'

LITERARY LANDMARKS

Khartoum. Taking the reader through the ex-pat clubs, the **Sudan Club** and the **Hilton**, Jamal Mahjoub, in *Navigation of a Rainmaker*, describes the city as 'a savage burlesque in which the war and the starvation were nothing more than sideshow stands'. A foreign eye here, Edward Hoagland, explained, in *African Calliope*, 'Khartoum is a ship in a sea, the expatriates will tell you. By which they sometimes mean they are going out of their minds.'

The White and Blue Nile. Khartoum was founded at the confluence of the two rivers, called by the country's poets, 'the longest kiss in history'. A less romantic vision is provided by Edward Hoagland in *African Calliope*: 'Three thousand miles from Alexandria, The White Nile is more gray than white, more brown than green.'

Libraries and Bookshops

Khartoum. American Cultural Centre; British Council; French Cultural Centre; The Khartoum Bookshop, PO Box 968; The Nile Bookshop, 41 New Extension Street, PO Box 8036; Soviet Cultural Centre; University of Khartoum Library.

BOOKLIST

The following selection includes the extracted titles in this chapter as well as those mentioned in the introduction which are available in English and other titles for further reading. In general, paperback editions are given when possible. The editions cited are not necessarily the only ones available. For most of the extracted works, the original publisher in English can be found in 'Acknowledgments and Citations' at the end of the volume, as can the exact location of the extracts and the editions from which they are taken. Extract numbers are highlighted in bold for ease of reference.

Chatwin, Bruce, *The Songlines*, Picador Books, London, 1988. **Extract 2.**

Fadl, El Sir Hassan, *Their Finest Days*, Three Continents Press, Washington, DC, 1969.

Hall, Marjorie and Ismail, Bakhita Amin, *Sisters Under the Sun: The Story of Sudanese Women*, Longman, Harlow, 1981.

Hoagland, Edward, *African Calliope:*

A *Journey to the Sudan*, Penguin, London, 1981. **Extract 5.**

Kelueljang, Anai, *The Myth of Freedom*, New Beacon Books, London, 1975. **Extract 3.**

Kipling, Rudyard, *A Choice of Kipling's Verse*, Faber and Faber, London, 1983.

Mahjoub, Jamal, *Navigation of a Rainmaker*, Heinemann, Oxford, 1989. **Extract 4.**

Pye-Smith, Charlie, *The Other Nile*, Penguin, London, 1987. **Extract 6.**

Salih, Tayeb, *Season of Migration to the North*, Denys Johnson-Davies, trans, Heinemann, London, 1976. **Extract 1.**

Salih, Tayeb, *The Wedding of Zein and Other Stories*, Heinemann, London, 1969.

Voices from Twentieth-Century Africa, Chinweizu, ed, Faber and Faber, London, 1988. **Extract 3.**

Extracts

(1) The Nile

Tayeb Salih, *Season of Migration to the North*

Back home at his village on the Nile, Mustafa tells the story of how he met and seduced one of his 'prey'. Unsure of his origins from his appearance, she asks where he is from. Appealing to her desire for all things Occidental, he woos her with stories about his home country.

'I'm like Othello – Arab-African,' I said to her.

'Yes,' she said, looking into my face, 'Your nose is like the noses of Arabs in pictures, but your hair isn't soft and jet black like that of Arabs.'

'Yes, that's me. My face is like the desert of the Empty Quarter, while my head is African and teems with a mischievous childishness.'

'You put things in such a funny way,' she said laughing.

'The conversation led us to my family, and I told her – without lying this time – that I had grown up without a father. Then returning to my lies, I gave her such terrifying descriptions of how I had lost my parents that I saw the tears well up in her eyes. I told her I was six years old at the time when my parents were drowned with thirty people in a boat taking them from one bank of the Nile to the other. Here something occurred which was better than expressions of pity; pity in such instances is an emotion with uncertain consequences. Her eyes brightened and she cried out ecstatically;

'The Nile.'

'Yes the Nile.'

'Then you live on the banks of the Nile?'

'Yes. Our house is right on the bank of the Nile, so that when I'm lying on my bed at night I put my hand out of the window and idly play with the Nile waters till sleep overtakes me.'

Mr Mustafa, the bird has fallen into the snare. The Nile, that snake god, has gained a new victim . . .

(2) OMDURMAN

Bruce Chatwin, *The Songlines*

Chatwin has come to Sudan to seek 'broader horizons'. On his travels he meets a man who tries to convert him to Islam with the help of a spirit or djinn.

Sheikh S lives in a small house overlooking the tomb of his grandfather, the Mahdi. On sheets of paper joined with Scotch tape to make a scroll, he has written a poem of five hundred stanzas, in the style and metre of Grey's *Elegy*, entitled 'Lament for the Destruction of the Sudanese Republic'. He has been giving me lessons in Arabic. He says I have the 'light of faith' on my forehead, and hopes to convert me to Islam.

I say I will convert to Islam if only he will conjure up a djinn.

'Djinns', he says, 'are difficult. But we can try.'

After an afternoon of combing the Omdurman souk for the right kinds of myrrh, frankincense and perfume, we are now all prepared for the djinn. The Faithful have prayed. The sun has gone down, and we are sitting in the garden, under a papaya, in a mood of reverent expectation, in front of a charcoal brazier.

The sheikh first tries a little myrrh. A wisp of smoke curls upward.

No djinn.

He tries the frankincense.

No djinn.

He tries everything we have bought, in turn.

Still no djinn!

He then says, 'Let's try the Elizabeth Arden.'

(3) Sudan: Islam

Anai Kelueljang, *My Cousin Mohamed*

*This symbolic and epic poem traces the background of a man
whose Arab father took an African woman for a mistress. It
explores Orouba, the cultural Arabization of non-Arab people,
and portrays the problems of perception, definition and religion
within the country.*

> My Cousin Mohamed
> Thinks he's very clever . . .
> With pride,
> He says he's an African who speaks
> Arabic language,
> Because he's no mother tongue!
>
> . . .
>
> Among the Arabs,
> My cousin becomes a militant Arab –
> A black Arab,
> Who rejects the definition of race
> By pigment of one's skin.
>
> He says,
> If an African speaks Arabic language
> He's an Arab!
> If an African is culturally Arabised
> He's an Arab!

(4) Sudan: Rains

Jamal Mahjoub, *Navigation of a Rainmaker*

*The arrival of rain here, after one of the many long and
desperate periods of drought, is a highly emotional time. It brings
joy, chaos, and above all relief.*

The torrent of rain falls upon the blistered land. Like a huge carpet, the
band of cloud unfurls itself across the length of the country. The drops
lick the surface of the parched soil as though it were the cracked lips of
a man driven by thirst to desperation. The pummelling waves fall in
time to the pleading wind . . .

On the heels of the rainbow the people in the west know the rain is
too late and too brief to be of any real significance; it is too late. They

run in delirious circles nevertheless, to collect what they can in buckets, in old milk tins, anything that will hold water. The wells will run again, they will survive this year. They say a prayer perhaps for those who did not last long enough to be able to say this.

In the South the fields of war are silenced by the rain. The drops clatter down like the rattle of bones in a grey mist of moving ghosts, like the echo of laughter, like the shadow of weeping.

In the offices of the government the clerks and the *murrasalas* are thankful because once more the hand of God has intervened and saved them the trouble of doing anything. They sit down and order more tea.

(5) Tokar

Edward Hoagland, *African Calliope*

Hoagland makes his way to Tokar at the delta of the Baraka River, an area of many Hadendowa people. His companion Izz Abdel, who is not completely au-fait with the Bedawiye language spoken there, takes his chances in the second language, Arabic. Not an uncommon problem in a country with an estimated 100 different languages.

Meeting an Arab peddler leading a donkey in the desert that afternoon, Izz Abdel, in his practised style, had stepped out of the Land Rover, patting his heart repeatedly, exclaiming, 'There is no god but God!'

The peddler, who was a butcher – his animal festooned with goat rib cages and legs – jerked the donkey's halter to bring it to a stop, and placed his right hand on his heart.

'Mohammed is the Apostle of God!' he said.

'Bless the Prophet!' said Izz Abdel.

'Peace be upon him,' the peddler answered.

The whole four-part formula had been gone through again, in leisurely, bountifully zestful fashion. Then again, the words for the first time starting to sound a bit slurred, both men dropping their eyes from what I took to be the beginnings of boredom. And then yet *again* – before Izz Abdel inquired about directions to Tokar – by which juncture the fate of the peddler's soul might seem to have been staked upon what he said. But these Hadendowa notables in their white robes did not respond to Izz Abdel's invocations except perfunctorily.

(6) WADI HALFA

Charlie Pye-Smith, *The Other Nile*

After travelling by boat down the Nile through Egypt, Pye-Smith disembarks onto Sudanese sand, en-route for Khartoum.

Wadi Halfa lay some way back from the dam: cadaverous, desolate and unwelcoming. Her ribs, stripped bare and bleached by the desert sun, poked through the drifting sands. It was midday when the Toyotas dropped us outside the station.

Wadi Halfa may not have courted fame but Flaubert and the weather have endowed the town with a certain mystique. Du Camp alleged that Flaubert, much preoccupied with a future novel, declared from the summit of Gebel Abusir, a hill near Halfa, 'I have found it! Eureka! Eureka! I will call her Emma Bovary!', thus settling on the title for his next novel and the name of the principal character. It is a nice story, and most probably nonsense.

I don't suppose people give much thought to Flaubert in Halfa. It is the heat that preoccupies the visitor. The old town, now below the Aswan Dam, holds the world record: 125.2°F. Once it gets above 100 degrees it seems to make little difference whether it is 105, 115 or 125 degrees. It is simply hell on a sliding scale.

Biographies and important works

CHATWIN, Bruce (see under Benin).

HOAGLAND, Edward (1932–). Hoagland was born in New York City, and educated at Harvard. He is a novelist, essayist, and short story writer. His first published journal of his travels was *Notes from the Century Before*, set in British Columbia. *African Calliope* (Extract 5) is his second book of travels and 'plunges' the reader into a 'bewildering' world of discovery. Hoagland currently lives in New York, teaches, and still travels.

KELUELJANG, Anai. His collection of poems, *The Myth of Freedom* (Extract 3) was written over seventeen years. Some of the poems were composed while he was held in a jail in **southern Sudan** in 1976. Publication of his poetry was refused by the government there, though this refusal added to his determination to get the outspoken collection published. Its title refers to the post-independence wave of politics that was sweeping through Africa at the time, and Kelueljang dedicates the book to '. . . the Sudanese youth/Who toil to build a Socialist Sudan/Where there is no exploitation of man by man . . .'. His recurrent themes relate to Sudan's struggle, though tucked away in the back is a little poem called 'Falklands', with a stark reminder of an ongoing British imperialism!

MAHJOUB, Jamal (1960–). Born of a Sudanese father and an English mother, Mahjoub spent part of his childhood in Liverpool until the family moved to Sudan. There he was educated by Italian Catholic priests at **Comboni College, Khartoum**, returning to England to study geology at the University of Sheffield. He abandoned geology as a potential profession and pursued a variety of careers, from cooking to dispatch riding and telephone sales. He rediscovered his Sudanese roots and geological training in his first novel, *Navigation of a Rainmaker* (Extract 4). Mahjoub currently lives in Denmark.

PYE-SMITH, Charlie (1951–). Pye-Smith was born in Huddersfield, England. He studied ecology at university and has written several books on the subject. Pye-Smith first travelled to the countries of the Nile in 1975, and his first travel book, *The Other Nile* (Extract 6), was inspired by his return some ten years later. It is a sensitively observed account of the changes he found, the multifarious lives of the people he met and the problems he encountered. Recalling novelist and traveller Evelyn Waugh's phrase, 'there is no room for tourists in a world of displaced persons', Pye-Smith writes 'Waugh was right: it is no place for tourists. Nevertheless I'm glad that for a little while I ventured between the barbed wire.'

SALIH, Tayeb (1929–). Salih was born in **northern Sudan** into a family of farmers and religious teachers. Educated at **Khartoum** and London universities, he spent time as Head of Drama in the BBC's Arabic Service. Salih took up writing late in life, mainly, he declares, for his own entertainment. *The Wedding of Zein* is his first collection of stories which thread together the life of Zein, from his general buffoonery (his trademark) to his wedding with the most sought-after girl of the village. *Season of Migration to the North* (Extract 1) is his second and widely acclaimed published work.

TANZANIA

> 'And thou, Swahili, my
> mother-tongue, art still the
> dearest to me . . ./The
> speech of my childhood, now
> I am fully grown/I realise thy
> beauty and have made it all
> on my own . . .'
> *Shabaan Roberts, Swahili*

If any East African country can lay claim to a truly national poet, then it is Tanzania. Shabaan Roberts ◊, the so-called Shakespeare or Dickens of Tanzania, became a national hero in a country which, before his emergence in the 1930s, had been undistinguished in literary terms. At the turn of the century there was a general mood of apathy and a predominance of pseudo-religious writing which was punctuated only briefly during the resistance against German colonialism. The Maji Maji rebellion, as it was known, momentarily inspired a surge in nationalistic Swahili *tenzis*, or epics. It was also to return in later years as a theme for poets such as Yusuf O. Kassam ◊.

Roberts, like many of his fellow writers, started with safe conservative themes, but his writing quickly began to embrace nationalistic themes unfettered by deference to particular religious tomes or the colonialists. Nevertheless, to read his poems is still like listening to a sermon – albeit an undogmatic and a gentle one. He is really a preacher-poet – encouraging education (of which he experienced little that was formal), good behaviour, and even laughing as a way of life (Extract 7). It has often been remarked that Roberts carried the weight of Tanzanian literature on his shoulders for some two decades. In terms of volume and dedication this is certainly true. Alongside producing some 14 fat volumes of Swahili verse, Roberts helped keep this indigenous language buoyant in the face of educational imperialism. He was one of the first campaigners for Swahili to become the national language, and likened it to milk from an African woman's breast while English was the dried powdered variety. There was some poetic justice in the fact that Roberts lived to see independence, though tragically he died a few years before Swahili was designated the national language in

---

FACT BOX

AREA: 945 087 sq km
POPULATION: 25 200 000
CAPITAL: Dar es Salaam
LANGUAGES: Swahili, English
FORMER COLONIAL POWER: Great Britain, Germany
(1891–1919)
INDEPENDENCE: 1961

1966. Following his death the main impetus to Swahili literature came from the country's first President. Nyerere, a socialist with a distinct leaning towards the Chinese model of Communism, translated Shakespeare into Swahili in his spare time.

Following independence, English-language literature was more or less limited to the **University of Dar es Salaam** and its literary magazine *Darlite*, which enjoyed a brief success in 1966–70. This was still a time when it was fashionable to mimic the English Romantics shamelessly, though many writers later turned their pen to Swahili as a tool for their trade. There are some, however, who have enjoyed a measure of success writing in English. One of the first was Peter Palangyo ◊ whose *Dying in the Sun* (Extract 2) is a bitter tale of love, suffering and survival in the arid interior of a man's heart and his native countryside. Peter Ruhumbika also took up the rural theme with *Village in Uhuru*, and describes what *uhuru* (freedom/independence) meant to one remote community.

The first popular post-independence urban novel was published in 1977. W.E. Mkufya's *The Wicked Walk* is a taste of the ever-emergent corruption, prostitution and temptations in **Dar es Salaam**. The title is from the psalm by David which the main character recalls upon finding the hanged body of a woman: 'The *wicked walk* on every side, when the vilest men are exalted.'

More recently, Kenyan-born Moyez Vassanji ◊ has provided a rare insight into the unique urban experiences of Asians in East Africa. His novel *The Gunny Sack* (Extract 1) opens many windows onto the corners of life in the capital of Tanzania: 'There were three dreams in this town that aspired to Baghdad once and New York afterwards . . .'. *Uhuru Street*, his collection of short stories, also set in **Dar es Salaam**, aims, he says, to 'turn off and turn on lights, in a manner of speaking, one by one so each short story would be a flicker of light and then you would have a whole street emerging or a whole city . . .' (interview in *Wasafiri*, Spring 1991).

The small and largely inaccessible body of European language work by Tanzanians is testimony in part to the pioneering work and legacy of poet Shabaan Roberts. When Swedish writer Per Wästberg ◊ visited the **University of Dar es Salaam** in 1971 he found the students weary of European literature and eager to study Swahili works.

Wästberg was accompanied to Tanzania by German novelist Günter Grass – the pair were working on developing a curious German–Swedish–Jugoslavian project, which, had it worked, would have meant several months here each year. As it was, the visit resulted in a few words from Grass in *From the Diary of a Snail* and some interesting and often amusing encounters in Wästberg's *Assignments in Africa* (Extract 5). One such incident occurred when Grass was challenged by two German electricians working in **Tanga**: 'Are you by any chance the fraudulent Herr Grass?' The hitherto happily incognito Grass was forced to admit that he was.

The preferred privilege of anonymity was not guaranteed for Evelyn Waugh (◊ Ethiopia) either. In his self-ironically entitled *A Tourist in Africa* (Extract 8), Waugh recounts how following his arrival at the **Chagga Council Offices** near **Kilimanjaro**, he was taken to a school at a coffee cooperative. There, he was expected to impart the benefit of his wisdom as a writer to the eager pupils. This amusing and uncomfortable experience – which all foreign writers must at once dread and feel duty-bound to comply with – is a lesson to all who write about a country and then hope to slip away unnoticed. Next in line may be William Boyd (◊ Congo) who set *An Ice Cream War* here (Extract 3) and Georgette Heyer, dubbed 'the most easily read author in the tropics', who lived in Tanzania for a few years. This is perhaps the least repayment to a country for providing such good pages of novel material.

Literary Landmarks

Bagamoyo. The **Old Prison** is where the Arab traders held their slaves en route for Zanzibar or Arabia. Sir Henry Morton Stanley ◊ set out from here with a blank map (relying only on his compass and his bearers) to search for the 'lost' Dr Livingstone (◊ Zambia). He took with him 8000 yards of calico, a bearskin, a bath tub, a bottle of Champagne and a bottle of Worcester Sauce. You can visit the **Chapel** where Livingstone's body was laid briefly before transfer to Westminster Abbey. When Evelyn Waugh visited here in the 1950s he noted, 'A very faint, inexpungible tinge of luxury lingers', on account of the time when the Oman Arabs occupied it in the 18th Century.

Dar es Salaam. The town, whose name means 'haven of peace', became the capital in 1891 when the German colonists moved their seat of government from **Bagamoyo**. **Uhuru Street** is the inspiration for

Moyez Vassanji

Moyez Vassanji's book of that name. The national poet–hero Shabaan Roberts has one of the main streets named after him. Richard West, in *The White Tribes of Africa*, described the city thus: 'The heat and damp gives Dar es Salaam an air of sweet decay which strikes African after the brisk highlands of Kenya. The plaster rots, the tin rusts and damp spreads like a stain over the side of the new flats . . . The mood is of working-class Athens or middle-class Bombay.' When Evelyn Waugh was here he frequented the **Dar es Salaam Club**, where he used the library and read the English papers.

Kilimanjaro. 'Far away in the distance the august mountain Kilimanjaro shone in the upper air like a vast celestial mould of Christmas pudding streaked with frozen rivers of brandy butter.' (Edward Marsh, *A Number of People*). Immortalized, in more senses than one, by Hemingway ◊ in 'The Snows of Kilimanjaro' (Extract 4).

Moshi. When Evelyn Waugh stayed in the **Livingstone Hotel** here, which looked 'like a liner unaccountably stranded', he noted sadly that Livingstone never came within 200 miles of it, and added 'Let me here give you a word of advice to fellow-tourists in East Africa: keep away from hotels run by the British. We have no calling to this profession.'

Olduvai Gorge. Site of the Leakey family archaeological excavations, and several historical finds.

Serengeti Plains. 'It is a microcosm of what most of East and Central Africa was like little more than half a century ago, a surviving pocket, a remembrance of one of the greatest sights the world has ever known. This is all we have left.' (Elspeth Huxley, *Forks and Hope*, 1964.)

Tabora. Bavarian-style half-timbering is the crumbling remains of German colonial presence. Stanley's travelling companion John Shaw died here in 1871 after a night of playing *Home Sweet Home* on his mouth organ.

Ujiji. On the eastern shore of **Lake Tanganyika**, site of the oft-quoted meeting between Livingstone and Stanley (Extract 9).

Zanzibar. This clove-covered island with the **Livingstone House** has attracted a number of comments: 'It is not worth while to go round the world to count the cats in Zanzibar' wrote Henry David Thoreau in *Walden* in 1854. 'It might be called Stinkibar rather than Zanzibar' said David Livingstone in 1866.

Libraries and Bookshops

Dar es Salaam. British Council Library; International Bookshop, corner of Samora Avenue and Pamba Road; National Central Library; University Library and Bookshop, PO Box 35091.

Zanzibar. Centre for Research on Oral Traditions and African Languages; Zanzibar Government Archives.

BOOKLIST

The following selection includes the ex-tracted titles in this chapter as well as those mentioned in the introduction which are available in English and other titles for further reading. In general, paperback editions are given when possible. The editions cited are not necessarily the only ones available. For most of the extracted works, the original publisher in English can be found in 'Acknowledgments and Citations' at the end of the volume, as can the exact location of the extracts and the editions from which they are taken. Extract numbers are highlighted in bold for ease of reference.

Boyd, William, *An Ice-Cream War*, Penguin, London, 1973. **Extract 3.**

Grass, Günter, *From the Diary of a Snail*, Pan, London, 1989.

Hemingway, Ernest, *The Snows of Kilimanjaro and Other Stories*, TriadGrafton, London, 1977. **Extract 4.**

Kassam, Yusuf, in *Poems of Black Africa*, Wole Soyinka, ed, Heinemann, London, 1987. **Extract 6.**

La Mana, Chaguo, *A Choice of Flowers, Swahili Songs of Love and Passion*, Heinemann, London, 1972.

Leakey, Mary, *Discovering the Past*, Weidenfeld and Nicolson, London, 1984.

Marsh, Edward, *A Number of People*, quoted in *The Travellers' Diction-ary of Quotation*, Peter Yapp, ed, Routledge, London, 1988.

Mkufya, W.E., *The Wicked Walk*, Tanzania Publishing House, Dar es Salaam, 1977.

Palangyo, Peter, *Dying in the Sun*, Heinemann, London, 1969. **Extract 2.**

Poems from East Africa, D. Cook and D. Rubadiri, eds, Heinemann, London, 1971.

Roberts, Shabaan, in *Anthology of Swahili Poetry*, Ali Jahadhmay, ed, Heinemann, London, 1977. **Extract 7.**

Ruhumbika, Gabriel, *Village in Uhuru*, Longman, London, 1969.

Stanley, H.M., *Life and Finding of Dr Livingstone*, Dean and Sons, London, 1874. **Extract 9.**

Vassanji, Moyez, *The Gunny Sack*, Heinemann, Oxford, 1989. **Extract 1.**

Vassanji, Moyez, *Uhuru Street*, Heinemann, London, 1991.

Wästberg, Per, *Assignments in Africa*, Olive Press, London, 1986. **Extract 5.**

Waugh, Evelyn, *A Tourist in Africa*, Methuen, London, 1985. **Extract 8.**

West, Richard, *The White Tribes of Africa*, Jonathan Cape, London, 1965.

Extracts

(1) DAR ES SALAAM

M.G. Vassanji, *The Gunny Sack*

Vassanji takes us into the maze of the Kariakoo Quarter, where streets from the Indian Quarter wiggle their way into the African Quarter. Once home to the German Carrier Corps, it is full of mud and wattle huts, strange sounds and even stranger people.

The nights were warm. Dim lights inside the house threw long shadows against the walls, leaving parts of it in permanent darkness. Outside was a thick darkness, a black, menacing universe, with faces occasionally illuminated by moving kerosene lamps, and eerie, momentary shadows, gigantic, cast by passing cars against building walls: a darkness that rang with shouts and cackles and squeals of laughter. A little after sunset a drum would start rolling at the nearby Pombe Shop and the sounds of singing would add to the other sounds of the night. We would sit in the shop with two or three panels removed from the door to let in the night air; the adults would talk in low murmurs, while we children watched the teeming darkness outside and waited for what it would next summon at our doorstep.

There was Timbi Ayah the fat mama, Boy Manda Kodi the notorious loafer, Tembo Mbili Potea and mad Goan, Chapati Banyani the mad African. This latter would stand outside and sing:

> Chapati Banyani, nani kula?
> Shamsi, Shinashiri, Khoja, nai?
> Akili potea kama ngombeeee!

> Who eats the chapatis of the Banyanis?
> Shamsis, Ithnashris, Khojas, no?
> They lose their senses like cows!

He would peep inside at the cowering kids all huddled together, making widely suggestive eyes, before stepping back into the darkness, into which his cackle then lost itself.

This was Dar es Salaam, frightening until you knew it, mysterious until you grew with it.

(2) KACHAWANGA

Peter Palangyo, *Dying in the Sun*

It is lunchtime in the carpentry shop at the southern end of the village and the carpenter and his assistants are eating ugali with curry-laden white ant sauce. Teresa, on an errand for her fiancé's family, is drawn into the proceedings and banter.

The carpenter was a middle-aged man with hair straying haphazardly on to his unshaven face. He had big fleshy lips which curled up like the snout of a pig. He wore a loin-cloth and an unbuttoned shirt exposed his well-rounded muscles of the chest and arms, which were a mark of his profession.

'Peace be to you, our sweetheart.'

'Peace be to you, my fiancee.'

'I can say the man whose bride is looking for a wedding box is not unlucky.' The assistants laughed. This was always the second sentence the carpenter addressed to his women customers. Teresa did not reply to the irony. 'A workman's place is his home, and as our people believed from long ago, if one enters a man's house without sharing the meal on the table, the house won't eat again,' he said, motioning towards the family table. The assistants grudgingly made way for Teresa. She sat down on the ground and with her dirty fingers started rolling a ball of ugali until it was a perfect sphere, then with her thumb she bored a hole in it and dipped it into the small amount of sauce in the bowl. She started to nibble at it unwillingly. She had not eaten at all that day but she was not hungry. 'I understand our sweetheart. When one is excited especially just before marriage one's stomach moves up and down so much it can't take anything.' The carpenter was laughing. 'He is handsome and rich, this young man of yours, isn't he?' . . .

'Tell me about this man of yours, our sweetheart.'

Teresa, who had not said a word so far, replied coldly, 'I'm looking for timber to make a box to bury his father in.'

(3) KILIMANJARO

William Boyd, *An Ice Cream War*

German born Liesl and Erich von Bishop, accompanied by British Temple Smith, are returning by train to their respective farms near Moshi. It is 1914 and the War has not yet been announced. 'British East' refers to Kenya.

Eventually they boarded the train and it pulled out of Buiko on the final leg to Moshi. The Usambara hills gave way to the gentler Pare range as they rattled steadily northwards through lush green parklands, the hills on their right, the Pangani river on their left.

'There is talk,' she heard her husband say, 'of banning native shambas and villages from a five mile-wide strip the entire length of the line. It's such good farmland and so close to the railway.'

'Sounds reasonable to me,' Temple observed, looking out of the window. 'They do it in British East. I only wish my farm was as good as this.' He looked to his left at the line of trees that marked the Pangani.

'Ha!' he exclaimed, making Liesl jump. 'There she is!'

The train was rounding a gentle curve to the right. They all crowded to the window. There, dominating the view ahead, was Kilimanjaro, bluey-purple in the distance, its snowy peaks unobscured by clouds.

'Magnificent,' Erich said. 'Now I know I'm home.'

The sun flashed on the window of the compartment, blinding Liesl momentarily. She reached into her bag and rummaged around inside it for a pair of coloured spectacles. Kilimanjaro dimmed slightly, subdued by the thick dark green lenses, but lost none of its grim majesty. Contrary to the elation the others felt, Liesl's heart felt weighted with the recognition. She had lived so long with the splendid mountain facing her house that she did not see it as a glorious monument, but rather as a hostile and permanent jailer, or some strict guardian.

(4) KILIMANJARO

Ernest Hemingway, *The Snows of Kilimanjaro*

In Hemingway's moving short story about a dying man, skilfully told in a narrative interwoven with flashbacks to his past life, the flight of the soul is equated with a plane flight to the heights of Kilimanjaro.

He waved to Helen and to the boys and, as the clatter moved into the old familiar roar, they wung around with Compie watching for wart-hog holes and roared, bumping, along the stretch between the fires and with the last bump rose and he saw them all standing below, waving, and the camp beside the hill, flattening now, and the plain spreading, clumps of trees, and the bush flattening, while the game trails ran now smoothly to the dry waterholes, and there was a new water that he had never known of. The zebra, small rounded backs now, and the wildebeeste, big-headed dots seeming to climb as they moved in long fingers across the plain, now scattering as the shadow came toward them, they were tiny now, and the movement had no gallop, and the plain as far you could see, grey-yellow now, and ahead old Compie's tweed back and the brown felt hat. Then they were over the first hills and the wildebeeste were trailing up them, and then they were over mountains with sudden depths of green-rising forest and the solid bamboo slopes, and then the heavy forest again, sculptured into peaks and hollows until they crossed, and hills sloped down and then another plain, hot now, and purple brown, bumpy with heat and Compie looking back to see how he was riding. Then there were other mountains dark ahead.

And then instead of going on to Arusha they turned left, he evidently figured that they had the gas, and looking down he saw a pink sifting cloud, moving over the ground, and in the air, like the first snow in a blizzard, that comes from nowhere, and he knew the locusts were coming up from the South. Then they began to climb and they were going to the East it seemed, and then it darkened and they were in a storm, the rain so thick it seemed like flying through a waterfall, and then they were out and Compie turned his head and grinned and pointed and there, ahead, all he could see, as wide as all the world, great, high, and unbelievably white in the sun, was the square top of Kilimanjaro. And then he knew that that was where he was going.

(5) Tanga

Per Wästberg, *Assignments in Africa*

In what they call 'in the documentary spirit of the day', and following the discovery of the identity of Günter Grass by two German electricians working nearby, Grass and Wästberg interview two girls at the bar of the Splendid View Hotel where they are staying. Later on in their shared room, Grass nearly loses part of his precious manuscript.

One was twenty-two, unmarried, with two children. She very badly wanted to go to Nairobi, just as others want to go to Paris. She worked from seven until midnight for about eight pounds a month. After that she worked at a night-club for four hours and was at the disposal of customers for one to three pounds according to appearance, status and period of time. The other woman was thirty-eight, had fifteen children and had no wish for any more. She came from an island in Lake Victoria and was thinking of returning, but the children had a better chance of schooling in Tanga. People on the island were proud of those who lived in town and earned money, no matter how. She was very open-hearted about this, and also aware of one thing – it was dangerous to feel anything for a customer, because then you gave him the power she herself had to have over him, and then she lost her protection, her integrity.

At night the temperature in the room rose to 35° Celsius. Every bulge in the lino concealed unknown creatures. Small lizards swirled round the bed's legs. Günter pulled his bed out under the ceiling fan, and I switched it on. It began with a weird groan, and something large and black fell off it on to Günter's eyelids.

The first light gradually crept like a snake across the crack under the door. What to do if it was a cobra? Advice I had been given was to set fire to some paper – one of Günter Grass' manuscript pages – to dazzle the death-dealing reptile.

(6) Tanzania: Maji Maji

Yusuf O. Kassam, *Maji Maji*

The so-called Maji Maji uprising was a war of resistance against the German colonialists. It took place between 1905 and 1907, and ended with brutal suppression and a sinister silence. Sitting outside his mud hut an old man recalls the fight. The poem is included in the anthology Poems of Black Africa – see Booklist.

'For many days,
They resounded with drum-beats and frenzied cries;
Then with the spirits of alien ancestors
They thundered with strange unearthly sounds.'
Placing both hands on his head,
He looked down on the earth and pronounced,
'They fired bullets, not water, no, not water,'
He looked up, with a face crumpled with agony,
And with an unsteady swing of his arm, he said,
'Dead, we all lay dead.'

. . .

'The Germans came and went,
And for many long years
No drums beat again.'

(7) TANZANIA: MORALITY

Shabaan Roberts, *Laugh with Happiness*

Here in one of his more 'modern' poems, Roberts, the so-called Shakespeare of Tanzania, implores people to laugh and be happy. Despite the apparent flippancy, Roberts was a great moralist and treats 'happiness as a gift bestowed upon the mortal'. 'Laugh with Happiness' is included in anthology of Swahili Poetry – see Booklist.

Laugh in order to rise should you fall
Rise and rise again, roll not on the ground,
Rise and laugh, laugh and continue to play.
Continue to laugh and in a big way you should celebrate.
Let yourself laugh to your heart's content, let your face light up as you
    laugh.
God, the creator of this world, happiness was His own thing,
Sorrow will perish, laughter is its sure cure.
Make it a habit to laugh every day.

(8) TANZANIA: A TOURIST

Evelyn Waugh, *A Tourist in Africa*

Evelyn Waugh's hoped-for anonymity as he travelled through East Africa as a 'tourist' was not to be. His reputation as a 'great' writer finally caught up with him on his travels.

I should have known better than to put my head into that classroom. I have been caught before in this way by nuns. I smirked and attempted to get away when I heard the fateful words '. . . would so much appreciate it if you gave them a little address'.

'I am awfully sorry I haven't anything prepared. There's nothing I could possibly talk about except to say how much I admire everything.'

'Mr Waugh, these boys are all wishing to write good English. Tell them how you learned to write so well.'

Like a P.G. Wodehouse hero I gazed desperately at the rows of dark, curious faces.

'Mr Waugh is a great writer from England. He will tell you how to be great writers.'

'Well,' I said, 'well. I have spent fifty-four years trying to learn English and I still find I have recourse to the dictionary almost every day. English,' I said, warming a little to my subject, 'is incomparably the richest language in the world. There are two or three quite distinct words to express every concept and each has a subtle difference of nuance.'

This was clearly not quite what was required. Consternation was plainly written on all the faces of the aspiring clerks who had greeted me with so broad a welcome.

'What Mr Waugh means,' said the teacher, 'is that English is very simple really. You will not learn all the words. You can make your meaning clear if you know a few of them.'

(9) Uꜱᴊɪᴊɪ

H.M. Stanley, *Life and Finding of Dr Livingstone*

As was customary, to announce one's arrival, Stanley arrived at Ujiji shouting and shooting guns. It was here on the shores of Lake Tanganyika where he finally found Livingstone and uttered those immortal words . . .

So we were firing away, shouting, blowing horns, beating drums. All the people came out, and the great Arabs from Muscat came out. Hearing we were from Zanzibar, and were friendly, and brought news of their relatives, they welcomed us. And while we were travelling down that steep hill – down to this little town, I heard a voice saying, 'Good morning, sar.' I turned and said sharply.

'Who the mischief are you?'

'I am the servant of Dr Livingstone, sar.'

I said, 'What! is Dr Livingstone here?'

'Yes, he is here. I saw him just now.'

'Do you mean to say Dr Livingstone is here?'

'Sure.'

'Go and tell him I am coming.'

Do you think it possible for me to describe my emotions as I walked down those few hundred yards? This man, David Livingstone, that I believed to be a myth, was in front of me a few yards. I confess to you that were it not for certain feelings of pride, I should have turned a somersault. But I was ineffably happy. I had found Livingstone; my work is ended. It is only a march home quick; carry the news to the first telegraph station, and so give the word to the world. A great many people gathered around us. My attention was directed to where a group of Arabs was standing, and in the centre of this group a pale, care-worn, grey-bearded old man, dressed in a red shirt, with a crimson joho, with a gold band round his cap, an old tweed pair of pants, his shoes looking the worse for wear. Who is this old man? I ask myself. Is it Livingstone? Yes, it is. No, it is not. Yes, it is.

'Dr Livingstone, I presume?'

'Yes.'

Biographies and important works

BOYD, William (see under Congo).

HEMINGWAY, Ernest Miller (1899–1961). Hemingway was born in Illinois in a suburb of Chicago. He worked in the USA as a journalist before moving to Paris where he became part of the expatriate literary scene, meeting, among others, Ezra Pound and Gertrude Stein. He wrote both novels and short stories, and is respected especially for the latter. His main collections are *Men without Women* and *Winner Take Nothing*. Somewhat out of time with contemporary culture, Hemingway was passionate about bullfighting, big-game hunting, and deep-sea fishing. He visited Spain during the Civil War and supported the Republicans. His experiences formed the basis for what is perhaps his most famous novel, *For Whom the Bell Tolls*. In the second world war,

he was a war correspondent in Europe (he had been wounded and decorated for his service as an ambulance driver in the first). Towards the end of his life, he lived mainly in Cuba. He committed suicide in July 1961, in the grips of a serious illness. 'The Snows of Kilimanjaro' (Extract 4) is one of Hemingway's finest short stories. It tells the story of a dying man, remembering his past life as he wanders in and out of delirium. The descriptions of the African environment are evocative and atmospheric, especially his dramatic description of Kilimanjaro which in the story becomes the destination of the soul. In *The White Album* the American writer Joan Didion remarks, 'Certain places seem to exist mainly because someone has written about them. Kilimanjaro belongs to Ernest Hemingway.' 'The Snows of Kilimanjaro' was made into a film in 1952, with Gregory Peck and Ava Gardner in the lead roles. Hemingway also wrote *The Green Hills of Africa*, about big-game hunting. He received the Nobel Prize for Literature in 1954.

Ernest Hemingway

KASSAM, Yusuf, O. (1943–). Kassam was born in Tanzania, but was educated at Makerere University in Uganda where he obtained a degree in English and History. He went on to teach in Uganda and Tanzania, where he is a member of the **Institute of Adult Education** in **Dar es Salaam**. He took up writing poetry in 1964, following an interest in the works of Wordsworth. His prize-winning work has been widely anthologized, and has been broadcast on the BBC African Service.

LIVINGSTONE, David (see under Zambia).

PALANGYO, Peter (1939–1993). Palangyo was born in **Arusha** and educated locally and later in Uganda and the USA. A biologist by training, he discovered a penchant for literature while studying in Minnesota. When he returned to Tanzania in 1972, he taught at the **University of Dar es Salaam** and several schools. *Dying in the Sun* (Extract 2) was his first novel and the first by a Tanzanian to be published in the Heinemann African Writers Series. Peter Palangyo died in a road accident on 18 January 1993.

Peter Palangyo

ROBERTS, Shabaan (1909–1962). Hailed as the Tanzanian Dickens *and* Shakespeare, and the first Tanzanian author to write literature in Swahili, Roberts was largely self-educated. According to the prevailing colonial laws at the time, a Muslim child was unable to enter higher classes unless he converted to Christianity. His main influences, which were combined in his work with traditional Swahili verse, were the English classics by Bunyan, Swift, Stevenson, and Lewis Carroll and more noticeably Shakespeare and Dickens. Roberts began writing in 1934 and started his own publishing house to get around the prejudices and problems he encountered as an outspoken nationalist. The project failed and most of his works were not published until after his death from tuberculosis. Some of his work, including poems written for his children's moral education, has since been translated and included in several anthologies.

STANLEY, Sir Henry Morton (1841–1904). Stanley was born in North Wales and emigrated to Africa. For several years he lived a wandering life, travelling through America and Asia, until in 1867 he joined the *New York Herald* as a special correspondent. When news began to filter out of Africa that the great explorer Livingstone (◊ Zambia) was lost somewhere in the interior, the *Herald* dispatched Stanley on an expedition to find him. This resulted in their historic meeting at **Ujiji** on the eastern shore of **Lake Tanganyika** (Extract 9). On a later expedition, Stanley mapped the course of the Congo River.

VASSANJI, Moyez (1950–). Born in Nairobi, Kenya, Vassanji was educated at the **Aga Khan School** in **Dar es Salaam** and later in the USA at the Massachusetts Institute of Technology and the University of Pennsylvannia. His books deal particularly with the experience of Asians in East Africa. *The Gunny Sack* (Extract 1), entitled symbolically after a particular type of packing trunk, was his first novel and won him the Commonwealth Novel Prize for Africa. *Uhuru Street*, a collection of short stories, is named after a main street in **Dar es Salaam**. Today Vassanji lives, writes and teaches in Toronto, Canada.

WÄSTBERG, Per (1933–). A Swedish novelist, journalist and sometime poet, Wästberg was Chief Editor of Sweden's major morning paper *Dagens Nhyeter* from 1976 to 1982, and the co-founder of Swedish Amnesty International. His interest in humanitarian issues has driven much of his work and his travels. He has written both fiction and documentary political analysis which has been translated into several languages. *Assignments in Africa* (Extract 5) about his travels in Eastern Africa is at once a poetic, sensitively observed and journalistic work. Subtitled modestly *Reflections, Descriptions and Guesses*, it is both personal and political, and above all a very readable introduction to changes in the area in the late 1960s and early 1970s.

WAUGH, Evelyn (see under Ethiopia).

UGANDA

> 'Almost for the first time in Africa I got the impression that this was a country where Africans were happy.'
> *John Gunther, Inside Africa*
>
> 'Uganda's history is like a crime to which there have been no witnesses.'
> *Sir John Grey*

Happiness is not a word normally associated with twentieth-century Uganda. Reputed to be a naturally happy people, the Ugandans have found themselves both witnesses to and victims of, a national tragedy.

The first tribal kingdoms began to appear in the region now called Uganda during the fourteenth century. In time the Bagandans, from whom Uganda takes its name, emerged as the predominant tribe, and Ganda, their language, was formulated into a written script in the 1880s. In the decades that followed there appeared a number of histories of the Bagandan kings and the customs of the country, written mostly by the king in question, and his advisers.

Surprisingly it was not until the nineteenth century that this landlocked country made contact with the coast. During this period Muslim traders began arriving from the Indian Ocean settlements. They were soon to be followed by the early European explorers, including John Hanning Speke ♭, the first European to set eyes on **Lake Victoria** and locate the **source of the Nile** (Extract 3). In the footsteps of the Victorian explorers came the inevitable flood of Christian missionaries, and by the turn of the century the Bible had appeared in Ganda. Importunate proselytizing and missionary zeal soon provoked the locals, and a series of bloody massacres ensued.

As was often the case in these Eurocentric centuries, Uganda's fate was decided at a treaty in faraway Berlin, and in 1894 the territory was declared a British protectorate. The British allowed Uganda a fair amount of authority, but tended to favour the Bagandans for posts in the administration. Seeing their way to administrative advancement blocked, other tribes turned to different professions – and thus the

---

FACT BOX

AREA: 236 040 sq km
POPULATION: 16 900 000
CAPITAL: Kampala
LANGUAGES: English, Swahili, Bante, Nilotic, Nilo-Hamitic
FORMER COLONIAL POWER: Great Britain
INDEPENDENCE: 1962

---

professions (army, law, civil, etc) became polarized. This sowed the seeds of trouble to come, in a country where artificially imposed unity was always precarious.

Uganda achieved independence in 1962, with Milton Obote as Prime Minister. Obote soon set about establishing himself as a dictator. He struck out at his tribal enemies (especially the Bagandans), rewrote the constitution giving himself virtually absolute power, set about a programme of rationalizing foreign assets, and of course arrested those who opposed him. Meanwhile, watching all this, and learning from Obote's Machiavellian example of how to rule a country, was his military Chief of Staff, Idi Amin.

In 1971 Amin seized power and thenceforth began Uganda's years of bloodiest suffering. During this period 300 000 Ugandans were brutally killed by the so-called 'Public Safety Unit' and the 'Bureau of State Research', professional and university classes were wiped out, 70 000 Asians were given 90 days to leave the country, and £500 million of assets were seized. The country fell apart – with services such as health care and transportation simply ceasing to function. Drunken soldiers roamed the country looting and killing at will; the foreign-currency-earning crop of coffee rotted in the fields; wildlife was killed for food; and inflation ran at over 1000%. When the exchequer's coffers were empty, Amin launched a diversionary war against his impoverished neighbour, Tanzania. By now the country (though not the people) had become an international leper, supported only by Colonel Gadhafi of Libya.

It was during this period that the British journalist Patrick Marnham ◊ sought an interview with Idi Amin. Commissioned by *Oui*, an American magazine, Marnham tells, in 'In Search of Amin', how he unsuccessfully approached numerous minor civil servants in the capital, **Kampala**. Finally reaching the Permanent Secretary, 'a threatened species', Marnham proffered information about the nature of his visit: 'He had never heard of *Oui* magazine, so I told him that it was owned by *Playboy*. He looked appalled. He himself was a Christian and unphased by the First World's obsession with saucy photographs, but the President was a Moslem. The possible juxtapositions worried him.'

Somewhere out of the bloodshed and terror, there emerged a strong opposition movement in the shape of Yoweri Museveni and his National Resistance Army. A long-term opponent of both Obote and Amin, Museveni, who took power in 1986, was determined that a new Uganda free from inter-tribal rivalry and corruption should emerge. Recruits to his army were trained in civil respectability, discipline, and national (rather than tribal) loyalty. Despite Museveni's neo-Marxist, although relatively pragmatic policies, the legacy of Amin's regime has left a strong mark on Uganda. It remains largely broke, ancient tribal rivalries are seldom far below the surface, and the country is under increasing threat from the AIDS epidemic.

Meanwhile, surviving all this was a distinctive body of literature. The first significant imaginative literature in Gandan began to appear after the second world war. This was largely through the encouragement of the East African Literature Bureau. However, at first the Bureau was largely concerned with encouraging literacy among schoolchildren. The rather patronizing quality of this juvenile literature can be surmised from such titles as 'The Obedient Servant'. However, the Bureau's horizons soon widened and it extended its interests to other Ugandan languages.

In 1953 it was responsible for the publication in Acholi (a dialect of Lwo) of poet Okot p'Bitek's ◊ first work *Lak tar miyo kinyero wi lobo*, which means 'Are Your Teeth White? Then Laugh'! Indicatively his next work, the epic *Song of Lawino: A Lament*, was published in English translation before it appeared in Lwo. This brought p'Bitek to wide attention in Britain and the United States, and he soon emerged as the major writer in Uganda. His third published work, *Two Songs* (Extract 7), won the Kenyatta Prize for Literature in 1972. His early death leaves an unfillable gap in the East African literary scene. Although he is remembered as a difficult character, given to prodigious alcoholic consumption, Alastair Niven, writing in *Africa Now* in 1982, characterized him as 'alive to the tips of his fingers and in every utterance he made'.

Imaginative literature in other Ugandan languages began to proliferate under Obote, who, for admittedly political reasons, wished to see an end to Gandan cultural supremacy (today they account for 20% of the population). But the main boost to Ugandan literature was provided by David Cook, who ran the English Department at Makere College (later to become the **University**) in **Kampala**. Under Cook, the founding of the magazine *Penpoint* in 1958 gave many young Ugandan writers a platform. When the Kampala Conference of African Anglophone writers was held in 1962, the new Ugandan writers received further encouragement by contact with their longer-established South and West African contemporaries.

Besides p'Bitek, one of the most notable writers to emerge during this period was Barbara Kimenye ◊, with her simple and amusing stories of tribal life in the Gandan villages (Extract 1). By contrast, her contemporary Enriko Seruma ◊ chose the more complex form of the novel, taking on board much of its Westernized sophistication. He describes his first novel, *The Experience*, as 'an expressionistic painting of contemporary Africa'. His collection of short stories *The Heart Seller* (Extract 6) includes the bizarre tale of a poor African who sells his heart to an aging American senator, who needs it in order to pursue his energetic love affair with his young secretary. In light of recent scandals of organ sales in the Third World, this satirical tale has proved unsettlingly prophetic.

The diversity of the Ugandan literary scene was further enhanced by the writings of the Asian (Goanese) writer Peter Nazareth ◊. His novel *In a Brown Mantle* (Extract 5), which deals among other things with the problems of mixed-race relationships, is representative of the type of literature that appeared in the 1960s. Racism, political intrigue and violence, the perils of both modernization and traditionalism, social division, sexual relations between races, and many other topics began appearing in novels, plays, radio drama and poems. Then Amin seized power and the years of terror, intimidation and silence began.

From this time onward, Ugandan literature was produced almost entirely in exile. In keeping with the resilience of the Ugandan character, Ugandan literature continued during this catastrophic period – despite the prospect of marginalization and an almost vanished reading public. The wildly sexy novel *The Sobbing Sounds* (Extract 4) was produced in 1975 by Omunjakko Nakibimbiri (a pseudonym) to widespread interest (by no means all of it literary!).

But most important of all was the emergence of Taban lo Liyong ◊, one of the great originals of African literature, and a worthy successor to the mantle of his fellow writer Okot p'Bitek who died in 1982. Liyong's family were from Sudan, but his writings are truly Ugandan in their jest, eccentricity and astonishing inventiveness (Extract 8). His perceptive observations in *The Last Word* on the meaning of African literature and its development are second only to his creative work. Not for nothing has he been called the Beckett of Africa. Although Liyong does not share Samuel Beckett's pessimism, his stylistic endeavours seem to spring from the same profound and anarchic source: 'I am going to tell you the story of my father's death. By and by. But I am a dictator; I hold the gavel. While it is in my hand, I shall wield a heavy dictatorial power. No need turning over the pages to see how much longer you have to submit. For I might never tell you about my father at all. On the other hand, I might. No knowing. My advice is: enjoy each moment of the time. If you *must* rush away for an appointment, or a wedding feast, go.' (From 'My Father, His Life and Death, My Wife, My Art and All That', in *The Last Word*).

LITERARY LANDMARKS

Acholi Province. Birthplace of the two leading figures of Ugandan literature, Okot p'Bitek and Taban lo Liyong.

Buganda. Setting for Barbara Kimenye's short stories of village life among the Ganda people.

Kampala. The capital, where journalist Patrick Marnham fought his way through a bureaucratic maze in an attempt to interview dictator Idi Amin.

Ripon Falls. John Hanning Speke became the first European to discover the **source of the Nile** in 1862.

Libraries and Bookshops

Kampala. Makerere University Bookshop, University College, Makerere; Uganda Bookshop, Coleville Street, PO Box 7145.

BOOKLIST

The following selection includes the extracted titles in this chapter as well as those mentioned in the introduction which are available in English and other titles for further reading. In general, paperback editions are given when possible. The editions cited are not necessarily the only ones available. For most of the extracted works, the original publisher in English can be found in 'Acknowledgments and Citations' at the end of the volume, as can the exact location of the extracts and the editions from which they are taken. Extract numbers are highlighted in bold.

Grey, Sir John, quoted by Alan Moorehead in *The White Nile*, Penguin, London, 1973.

Gunther, John, *Inside Africa*, Hamish Hamilton, London, 1955.

Kimenye, Barbara, *Kalasanda*, Oxford University Press, Oxford, 1965. **Extract 1**.

Liyong, Taban lo, *Fixions and Other Stories*, Heinemann, London, 1969. **Extract 8**.

Liyong, Taban lo, *The Last Word*, East African Publishing House, Nairobi, 1969.

Marnham, Patrick, 'You Still Exist', in *Fantastic Invasion: Dispatches from Contemporary Africa*, Penguin Books, London, 1987. **Extract 2**.

Marnham, Patrick, 'In Search of Amin', in *The Best of Granta Travel*, Granta, London, 1991.

Nakibimbiri, Omunjakko, *The Sobbing Sounds*, Longman, London, 1975. **Extract 4**.

Nazareth, Peter, *In a Brown Mantle*, East African Literature Bureau, Kampala, Uganda, 1972. **Extract 5**.

p'Bitek, Okot, *Song of Lawino: A Lament*, East African Publishing House, Nairobi, 1966.

p'Bitek, Okot, *Two Songs*, East African Publishing House, Nairobi, 1971. **Extract 7**.

Seruma, Enriko, *The Heart Seller*, East African Publishing House, Kampala, 1971. **Extract 6**.

Speke, John Hanning, *Journal of the Discovery of the Source of the Nile*, W.M. Blackwood, London, 1863. **Extract 3**.

Extracts

(1) KALASANDA

Barbara Kimenye, *The Village*

Life goes on in Kalasanda, a typical village of Buganda. The inhabitants are Bagandans, the predominant tribe in Uganda. 'The Village' is included in Kimenye's collection of short stories Kalasanda – see Booklist.

If it were possible to look down on Kalasanda from above, I imagine it reveals itself as a straggling collection of small, mud homesteads set in shambas of varying size, roughly covering two square miles of country, and showing a marked tendency to overflow into the neighbouring Ggombolola, with the same murram track which branches off the main highway snaking unsteadily through it like a narrow brown river. Rough though this track may be, it should never be underestimated, for it constitutes the main link between Kalasanda and the rest of the world, and all the obscure little paths which spring from it on either side, in differing degrees, lead to some segment of Kalasanda life . . .

Another path, which conveniently twists as if in conformity with the often unsteady feet that stumble along it, brings you to the Happy Bar, the tin-roofed dwelling where Maria Ssentamu's sumptuous curves shake in perpetual merriment as she serves warm beer in thick, greasy glasses to the thirsty locals. Maria must surely weigh over fourteen stones. Nevertheless, she is by far the most seductive woman in the village, and she has a number of children to prove it. It seems that a simple shake of her magnificent hips is enough to bowl a man over. Few can withstand the onslaught. Members of the Mothers' Union spitefully whisper that this unfailing charm is all something to do with what Maria puts in the drinks.

(2) Kampala
Patrick Marnham, *Fantastic Invasion*

British journalist Patrick Marnham picked up some extraordinary stories of life under Amin's reign while in Uganda. The title of the chapter from which this extract is taken, 'You Still Exist', refers to the exclamation commonly heard between people meeting again on the streets of Kampala after the dictator's demise.

The silence of the royal palace was largely accounted for by the collapse of the Ugandan tourist industry. The original Amin, the cheerful, no-nonsense army officer, was a British invention. But as the years passed and the business of running a modern state in Africa became steadily more difficult for Amin and his colleagues, there was no visible sign of British or any other Northern influence. Little that the government did had the intended effect. In 1974 an attempt was made to revive tourism as a useful source of foreign currency. A large party of East African travel agents were flown to Kampala from Nairobi. As they were ushered into the airport's VIP lounge for an official welcome, they met the head of the Ugandan Tourist Office being marched under armed escort to the plane which they had just left. He had come to the airport to greet them but had found, instead, that he was being deported. Amin had just discovered that an Englishman was running the tourist office. Uganda's tourist revival ended abruptly.

(3) Ripon Falls
John Hanning Speke,
Journal of the Discovery of the Source of the Nile

The Victorian explorer arrived after a tortuous journey at the exact spot where the Nile flows out of Lake Victoria.

We were well rewarded; for the 'stones,' as the Waganda call the falls, was by far the most interesting sight I had seen in Africa. Everybody ran to see them at once, though the march had been long and fatiguing, and even my sketch-block was called into play. Though beautiful, the scene was not exactly what I expected; for the broad surface of the lake was shut out from view by a spur of hill, and the falls, about 12 feet deep, and 400 to 500 feet broad, were broken by rocks. Still it was a sight that attracted one to it for hours – the roar of the waters, the thousands of passenger-fish, leaping at the falls with all their might, the Wasoga and Waganda fishermen coming out in boats and taking post on all the rocks with rod and hook, hippopotami and crocodiles lying sleepily on the water, the ferry at work above the falls, and cattle driven down to drink at the margin of the lake, – made, in all, with the pretty nature of the country – small hills, grassy-topped, with trees in the folds, and gardens on the lower slopes – as interesting a picture as one could wish to see.

The expedition had now performed its functions. I saw that old father Nile without any doubt rises in the Victoria N'yanza, and, as I had foretold, that lake is the great source of the holy river which cradled the first expounder of our religious belief.

(4) UGANDA: LOVE

Omunjakko Nakibimbiri, *The Sobbing Sounds*

This notorious and comical book was written by an author who wishes to remain anonymous. Here the narrator is still a young boy, curious about what creates the so-called 'sobbing sounds'.

Lusambya tiptoed to my room. But it was dark and obviously he could not see a thing. Even if he was capable of seeing anything, I was ready for him. The way they were whispering was exciting, and I was determined to share the fun, so I pretended to be asleep. I closed my eyes and emitted some sounds just short of snoring. I even half opened my mouth. The stage was set. When Lusambya came into my room he was convinced by his six senses that I was enjoying a delicious slumber. Satisfied, he went back to his room to report the good news to his sweetheart.

'He is fast asleep.'

'Good. He must be pretty tired, poor fellow.'

I did not like the 'poor fellow', but there was nothing I could do about it. From my childhood, I never liked people unnecessarily sympathising with me.

She asked Lusambya to light the *tadooba* so that she could see where to put her clothes. A match was struck and the room was lit. She began undressing. He began undressing. I had never seen grown-ups undressing, and I always wanted to. Now was my chance. . .

'Darling! I can't wait!', he said.

And I realised what he meant. The bed began squeaking and the sobbing sounds commenced. The performance was on the air – I wished they had not blown off that light!

It was the first time I had ever heard the real sobbing and hissing sounds of love. For the first time I became aware that one day, one day, 'if the beast does not eat the chicken; the chicken will lay eggs', and I too would cause those real sobbing sounds. In this expectant mood, I dozed off. The pair were now having their interval.

(5) UGANDA: LOVE

Peter Nazareth, *In a Brown Mantle*

The hero of the novel, P.D. Joseph D'Souza, a Goanese Ugandan, makes the acquaintance of Grace Umbowa, an African girl, whom he meets in the university library where they are both studying.

As I was in the library one day preparing for my first annual exam, I sat opposite a girl who looked like a Mark Eden 'After' photograph: she was generously endowed in the upper department. While I was reading, I looked up – to find her left-hand inside her blouse, apparently holding her right breast. It was an absent-minded gesture, just as one rubs one's nose or scratches one's head; she was deeply involved in the book she was reading.

I forced myself to keep reading my book. After some time, I was distracted by the sound of high heels descending the library staircase. I looked up. It was one of the English secretaries descending. Although it was the pre-miniskirt era, she was wearing a rather short skirt, and I had a generous eyeful of thigh. I watched. Then I realised that the girl opposite me was looking at me and grinning.

'You *are* studying hard, aren't you' she whispered. 'Biology, of course!'

I hastily looked down. Back to concentrating. Until I eventually looked up to find the left hand absently at work again. This time it was my turn.

'Let me hold it for you,' I whispered.

'What?' she said looking up.

I looked at her left hand. She followed my gaze. Although she was dark, I swear she blushed! Finally, she said,

'*Touché!*'

'I've been too distracted,' I said, 'Why don't we go to the canteen?'

She hesitated but finally agreed. That was the beginning of a relationship that lasted over a year.

(6) UGANDA: POVERTY
Enriko Seruma, *The Heart Seller*

In desperation, an impoverished young African tries to sell his heart for money to spend on the good life.

He picked up the ball-point pen, switched on the light and started writing: 'Editor, Newsweek . . .,' but the empty beer bottles beside the airletter he was writing on distracted him, so he picked them up, walked across the room and opened the door. The room-service man abruptly stood up, saying 'Yes, sir!' with such enthusiasm it was almost impossible to believe he was feigning it. Mwavu gave him the empty bottles and quickly turned around before he could see the man's disappointed frown. Mwavu knew the man expected him to order some more beer and subsequently give him a tip, but Mwavu had drunk his last shilling yesterday. He went back into Room 200 of the Hotel Africa and sat down at the desk again.

'Dear Sir,' he continued writing. 'I am a young African man who is so poor I feel like committing suicide – in fact I'm going to jump from the roof of this hotel I am staying in if this appeal to the world, made through your international newsmagazine, does not produce a favourable response. But before I commit suicide I'd like to give the world a golden chance. I would like to sell my heart for a transplant. Anyone who feels he or she may need a new heart shortly can buy my young, vigorous heart for only one million dollars. The money must be sent to me immediately by a Bank Transfer. The buyer will collect his heart in ten years' time. This delay is necessary so that I can spend the money. Upon termination of ten years, delivery will be punctual. Yours faithfully, Jackson Mwavu . . .'

(7) UGANDA: PRISON
Okot p'Bitek, *The Song of the Prisoner*

The prisoner describes his despair amid the intrigue and corruption that have blighted his country under Obote's regime. 'The Song of the Prisoner' is included in Two Songs – see Booklist.

The heavy smell
Of Death
Fills the room
Like darkness,
The alcohol
Of the black silence
Intoxicates me.

There is a carpenter
Inside my head,
He knocks nails
Into my skull.

My feet are a pair
Of pregnant women
Heavy like grinding stones
And full of the fangs
Of the cobra . . .

(8) Uganda: Story-Telling

Taban lo Liyong, *He and Him*

The innovative opening of this short story demonstrates Liyong's ever-imaginative approach to the ancient art of story-telling. 'He and Him' appears in Fixions – see Booklist.

A story doesn't have to have many characters in it. In this one, for example, we have two people, and we feel they are enough. One is he, the visitor from the country, and the other is him, the object of the visit. The subject, I may add, is the visit of he to town.

As we feel that what he ate for breakfast that morning has no relevance whatsoever on the visit, nor the colour of the sky while he passed through the countryside, nor how sharp his nose is, nor how blue his eyes – in fact, since we feel that these extraneous things other writers use for fleshing up scanty stories are not constitutional ingredients of the story, we shall cut them out – for the readers' benefit. We understand our readers are busy people, rushing from one phase of life to another.

One thing we must say, though: he coughed. That is important. Another: his friend smoked. Yet another: they both loved reading; this is something they picked up in their youth when they were in school together.

He had been in the country for some years now. Exactly how many does not affect the substance of the story very much. What absolutely matters is that whereas things stood still in the country, except the growth of weeds more than that of crops, and the multiplication of pigs in excess of cows, in the city changes had already become so topical that he had decided to come and see for himself.

Biographies and important works

KIMENYE, Barbara (1939–). Kimenye was born in Uganda and first achieved renown as a short story writer. Her three volumes, *Kalasanda* (Extract 1), *Kalasanda Revisited* and *The Smuggler*, all written in the mid-1960s, describe in orthodox style the comings and goings of Gandan village life. The last of the three, which describes how three Ugandan boys wander across the border into neighbouring Congo, is intended for children. Kimenye subsequently became well known as a newspaper columnist for a Kenyan newspaper, while living in exile in Nairobi.

LIYONG, Taban lo (1939–). Lo Liyong was born in **Kajokaji** near the Uganda/Sudan border. Although Sudanese by nationality, he grew up in Uganda and was educated first in **Acholiland** and later in **Kampala**. He went on to study in the USA, where

Taban lo Liyong

he received his BA at Howard University and Master of Fine Arts (Creative Writing) at Iowa University. At Iowa, he became a Fellow of the International Writers Workshop. Lo Liyong is a highly intelligent, utterly individual writer with a maverick style all his own, as revealed in his collection of short stories *Fixions* (Extract 8). His book of criticism *The Last Word* was the first to be published in East Africa and contains many superb if controversial insights into African culture. Unfortunately he is appreciated more abroad than at home – but his permanent place in African literature is assured. Lo Liyong has taught in various countries, including Kenya and Papua New Guinea. He is currently based at the University of Juba in Sudan.

MARNHAM, Patrick (1943–). Born in Jerusalem, Marnham studied law at Oxford. Since then he has abandoned practising law in favour of journalism and travel writing. He has written about several countries in Africa apart from Uganda. He worked among the nomads of the Sahel in West Africa for the Minority Rights Group, and has described this in his book *Fantastic Invasion: Dispatches from Contemporary Africa* (Extract 2).

NAZARETH, Peter (1940–). Nazareth is a Ugandan of Goanese Indian extraction. He writes novels and plays and is known for his collection of critical essays *Literature and Society in Modern Africa: Essays on Literature*. Though uneven in quality, the essays contain many perceptive insights. His best known novel, *In a*

Brown Mantle (Extract 5), analyses the problems which have faced many African countries in the decades following their independence. Though his literary style suffers from occasional lapses, the book remains lively and entertaining, not least in its descriptions of relations between the sexes.

P'BITEK, Okot (1931–1982). Born in **Gulu** in northern Uganda, p'Bitek wrote novels in his native Lwo, but he also wrote poetry and essays in English. His first novel, *Are Your Teeth White? Then Laugh*, was written in 1953 while he was a professional footballer. He subsequently went to Britain where he studied at Bristol, Aberystwyth, and Oxford. He is best known for his powerful 'poetic novel' *Song of Lawino* which was rendered into English from Lwo. This achieved wide recognition in Britain and America. It depicts the bitter effects of modernization on traditional African life.

SERUMA, Enriko (1940–). 'Enriko Seruma' is the pseudonym of Henry Seruma Kimbugwe. He is best known for his novel *The Experience* and his collection of short stories *The Heart Seller* (Extract 6), with stories set in both Africa and America. The book contains two award-winning stories – 'Love Bewitched' and 'The Calabash'.

SPEKE, John Hanning (1827–1864). Speke started his career as a subaltern in the British Indian Army, and by temperament remained a typical Victorian army officer throughout his life. His great stroke of fortune came in 1855 when he teamed up with Sir Richard Burton (◊ Ethiopia). Together they explored large regions of East Africa, enduring considerable hardships and danger. Withdrawn by nature, Speke fell out with the mercurial Burton during their second expedition in 1860. He then struck out on his own and discovered, almost by accident, **Lake Victoria**. This he rightly claimed was the **source of the Nile** (a claim which Burton jealously disputed). On a subsequent expedition in 1862, Speke proved his claim by finding the **Ripon Falls**, where the headwaters of the Nile disgorge from the Lake (Extract 3).

CAMEROON

Cameroon was and remains a totally artificial country. It was originally 'created' by the European powers in the nineteenth century and covers a region occupied by a wide variety of disparate tribes, linguistic groups and peoples. The first contact with Europe was with the early Portuguese explorers of the fifteenth century. During this period the coastal territory around the mouth of the **Wouri River** became known as Rio des Cameroes after the succulent prawns found there. Therein lies the origin of the name Cameroon.

Later this coastal region was, like much of Africa, to suffer from the blight of the slave trade. (At its height well over 100 000 slaves a year were being shipped to America.) The first inroads of colonialism were made when the British signed a commercial treaty with a Donala Chieftan in 1856. This eventually proved unsatisfactory, and in 1884 the Germans took over the territory as a protectorate. They instituted a 'pacification' programme, bringing all the far-flung tribes under their central control, as well as building railways and starting an education programme. After the German defeat in the first world war, the territory was divided in two – the north western strip of the country becoming British Cameroon, and the rest administered by the French.

As well as its linguistic and tribal diversity, the country also has a wonderfully varied geography. To the south there are coastal plains and dense forest inland. In the north the savannah extends to the shores of **Lake Chad,** and the central region rises 760–1370 m at the **Adamawa Plateau.** To the west lies Mount Cameroon, which, at 4070 m, is the highest mountain in West Africa. It is an awesome spot in the midst of the tropical thunderstorm season, as Victorian traveller Mary Kingsley (◊ Gabon) discovered. In *Travels in West Africa* she writes, 'One feels as if one were constantly dropping, unasked, and unregarded, among painful and violent discussions between the elemental powers of the universe.'

Yet despite the violent seasonal storms, the climate is largely beneficent – a pleasant 70–80°F throughout the year. Indeed in colonial times, **Yaoundé** was considered one of the best postings in the French African Empire. As Negley Farson wrote in 1940 in *Behind God's Back*, 'The 250 white people in this capital . . . seem always conscious of their good fortune in being stationed where a man can breathe.'

Early in the 1920s André Gide (◊ Congo) passed through the territory and was rather less complimentary about the French colonial administration (Extract 5). Ending his journey at the port of **Douala** he exclaimed, 'What a hotel! The most repellent of rest-houses is better than this. And what white people! Ugly . . . stupid . . . vulgar . . .' (*Travels in the Congo*).

The French colonial era, which remained heavily repressive towards the native population throughout its four and a half decades of existence, finally came to an end amid bloodshed in 1960. A year later the British Territory was given independence, and the two halves of the country were reunited after a referendum. According to a local saying: 'It is a long time before the pot where the goat is cooked loses its smell' – and heavy-handed government was to continue into independence under President Ahidzo. Unlike the situation in its neighbouring countries, stability in Cameroon was maintained – but at a cost. Ahidzo finally fled to France in 1983. Yet what had appeared to be stability to the outside world looked very different from the inside. In the words of the poet Mbella Sonne Dipoko ◊ in his poem 'Pain', 'All was quiet in this park/Until the wind, like a gasping messenger announced/The tyrant's coming./Then did the branches talk in agony.'

Written literature has an ambivalent place in Cameroonian culture. Partly because of their education, and partly to find an audience outside the narrow confines of their native land, most Cameroonian literary

---

Notes to map: [a]**Nigel Barley**, *The Innocent Anthropologist, lived with the Dowayo tribe in this remote region;* [b]*Where* **André Gide** *had an audience with the Sultan (Extract 5);* [c]**Mary Kingsley** *experienced Mt Cameroon in the nineteenth century in the midst of the tropical thunderstorm season;* [d]**Gide**'*s journey is recounted in Travels in the Congo;* [e]*Birthplace of* **Mbella Sonne Dipoko** *and* **Francis Bebey.** **Gide** *stayed here at the end of his journey through what is now Cameroon – and was not impressed with his hotel or the 'white people' he encountered;* [f]*Mbenda's passion for Agatha Moudi rages in a fishing village at the mouth of the Wouri River (Extract 6);* [g]**Negley Farson** *wrote about the desirability of being stationed here in Behind God's Back.* **Mongo Beti** *was born just outside Yaoundé.*

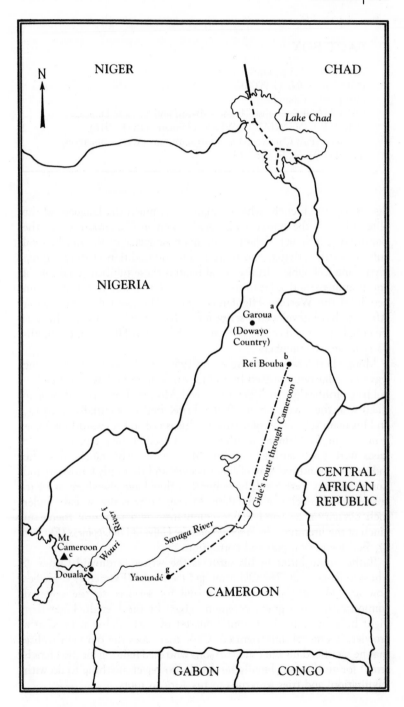

FACT BOX

AREA: 475 425 sq km
POPULATION: 11 900 000
CAPITAL: Yaoundé
LANGUAGES: English, French, Bantu and Sudanic languages
FORMER COLONIAL POWERS: Germany (1884–1916),
    France (East Cameroon) and Great Britain (West Cameroon)
INDEPENDENCE: 1960–61

---

figures write in French, which remains very much the language of the élite. Most of the native languages spoken in Cameroon are of the Bantu type, although Fulani is the main language of the north. Oral culture is still thriving, and there is a living tradition of story-telling, myths and folk fables. In the tribal regions these fulfil the dual role of entertainment and education. A unique exception is the Abmoun people of the **Western Highlands**, one of the few tribes throughout Africa to have developed a script for its own tribal language. This was invented at the end of the last century by Sultan Njoya, and contains 83 signs and 10 numbers.

Mongo Beti ◊ began writing in the 1950s and headed the first strong wave of indigenous written literature. Since then he has continued to publish prolifically. In 1957 his novel *Mission Terminée* (*Mission to Kala*) won the coveted Saint-Beuve Prize. Beti is essentially a satirist, and his main subject is colonialism. This is not so backward-looking as it may seem, for Cameroon still has to rid itself of the prejudices whose seeds were sown during that era. Missionaries who taught that the indigenous 'primitive' way of life was evil, and that only Christian and European ways were good, have here, as they have elsewhere, a lot to answer for. To achieve a modern African unity is not so easy under such circumstances, and hence colonialism is a recurring theme in much of the literature. In *Perpetua and the Habit of Unhappiness* (Extract 2), Beti focuses on political corruption.

Rather more bitter in his satire is the writer Ferdinand Oyono ◊ whose tragi-comedy *The Old Man and the Medal* (Extract 1) describes how an old man is awarded a medal for services to the colonial administration at a grand ceremony given by the French. Later that night he strays into the colonial quarter of town and is arrested as a prowler, his medal unrecognized. Only then does the old man realize that he sacrificed his life (and two sons who died fighting for the French army) for an illusion. Finally he decides to reject anything to do with 'civilization' and tries to return to his African roots.

A contemporary of Oyono is the novelist and short story writer Francis Bebey ◊. One of his novels, *Agatha Moudio's Son* (Extract 6), won the Black African Grand Prize for Literature. In the novel Bébey gives a humorous account of a young man's rebellion against the wishes of his family who have chosen a wife for him. He makes his own choice and falls in love with a rather less 'suitable' girl.

Perhaps the most talented writer of the modern generation is Mbella Sonne Dipoko, who has written a number of novels but will be best remembered for his lyric poetry. Unfortunately Cameroon was too small for Dipoko, its society too confused for such a poetic spirit, and he soon took up residence in Europe. His poems of love, experiences and sorrow as he wanders about Europe are shot through with moments of great feeling and beauty – yet it is when he writes about the suffering in his homeland that he is at his best (Extract 3).

An author who writes equally fondly of Cameroon, but from a completely different stance, is anthropologist Nigel Barley ◊. Coming from Britain, he stayed for two years among the Dowayo tribe in remote **northern Cameroon** and later wrote *The Innocent Anthropologist* (Extract 4), a bestselling account of this field trip: 'So off I went every day, armed with my tobacco and notebooks and paced out the fields, calculated the yields, counted the goats in a flurry of irrelevant activity.' This hilarious (often at the cost of the author) and frequently moving account is an excellent introduction for a visitor to the country.

LITERARY LANDMARKS

Douala. Birthplace of one of Cameroon's finest poets, Mbella Sonne Dipoko. André Gide ended his journey through Cameroon here.

Dowayoland. Scene of Nigel Barley's fieldwork and subject of his humorous book, *The Innocent Anthropologist*.

Mount Cameroon. Tallest peak in West Africa, visited by Victorian traveller Mary Kingsley.

Reï Bouba. French writer André Gide had an audience with the Sultan here during his travels through the country.

Libraries and Bookshops

Baffoussam. Libraire Populaire, BP 322.

Douala. American Cultural Centre; British Council Library; French Institute of Black Africa.

Yaoundé. American Cultural Centre Library; The Bilingual Bookshop, BP 727 Mvog-Ada; Centre du Diffusion du Livre Camerounais, BP 338; University of Yaoundé Library.

BOOKLIST

The following selection includes the extracted titles in this chapter as well as those mentioned in the introduction which are available in English and other titles for further reading. In general, paperback editions are given when possible. The editions cited are not necessarily the only ones available. For most of the extracted works, the original publisher in English can be found in 'Acknowledgments and Citations' at the end of the volume, as can the exact location of the extracts and the editions from which they are taken. Extract numbers are highlighted in bold for ease of reference.

An Anthology of Cameroon Literature in English, Genviève de la Taille, ed, Longman, Harlow, 1986.

Barley, Nigel, The Innocent Anthropologist, British Museum Publications, London, 1983. **Extract 4.**

Barley, Nigel, A Plague of Caterpillars, Viking, London, 1986.

Bebey, Francis, Agatha Moudio's Son, Heinemann, London, 1971. **Extract 6.**

Beti, Mongo, Mission to Kala, Peter Green, trans, Heinemann, London, 1964.

Beti, Mongo, The Poor Christ of Bomba, G. Moore, trans, Heinemann, London, 1971.

Beti, Mongo, Perpetua and the Habit of Unhappiness, J. Reed and C. Wake, trans, Heinemann, London, 1978. **Extract 2.**

Dipoko, Mbella Sonne, 'Autobiography', in African Writing Today, Ezekiel Mphahlele, ed, Penguin, London, 1967. **Extract 3.**

Dipoko, Mbella Sonne, A Few Nights and Days, Heinemann, London, 1966.

Farson, Negley, Behind God's Back, Victor Gollancz Ltd, London, 1940.

Gide, André, Travels in the Congo, Viking Penguin, New York, 1986. **Extract 5.**

Kingsley, Mary, Travels in West Africa, Virago, London, 1982.

Mokoso, Ndelely, Man Pass Man and Other Stories, Longman, Harlow, 1987.

Oyono, Ferdinand, The Old Man and the Medal, J. Reed, trans, Heinemann, London, 1967. **Extract 1.**

Philombé, René, Tales from the Cameroon, Three Continents Press, Washington, DC, 1984.

Extracts

(1) CAMEROON: COLONIALISM

Ferdinand Oyono, *The Old Man and the Medal*

Fouconi, a French colonial administrator, has just returned home after supervising the preparations for the decoration ceremony.

M Fouconi was one of those Europeans Africans find it difficult to tell the age of. He was taken to be a young administrator until the day when his first boy ran off with his false teeth. His nose stuck out sturdily from the middle of his bloated face which the sun had turned as red as the bottom of a chimpanzee. He had a terrible temper on an empty stomach but it fell off sharply after a glass of whisky. He lived with an African woman whom he used to hide in the storeroom on the ground floor when he had white visitors. The day before the Governor's arrival he sent her back to the location.

When M Fouconi got back to the Residence, the laundry-man had just brought his white suit. He snatched it out of his houseboy's hands. He turned it over and over and then he sniffed it.

'I told him he wasn't to starch this linen jacket with cassava . . . stupid bugger!' he shouted.

His eyes passed over the head of his houseboy and through the open-work matting of the door. A bottle of whisky was waiting for him on the table. His anger subsided. He lost interest in his white suit.

(2) CAMEROON: POLITICS

Mongo Beti, *Perpetua and the Habit of Unhappiness*

In an imaginary African country (taken to be Cameroon), local people learn of the downfall of the Commissioner of Oyolo and the dark and sinister circumstances of the fate of a man who falls foul of the ruling party.

Then, one evening in the middle of the eight o'clock news the national radio announced that M'Barg'Onana, *former* Chief Commissioner for the city of Oyolo 'guilty of misappropriation of funds and repeated extortions, had been removed from the opportunity to do further harm'. It was not a piece of news but a kind of coded message directed at those who knew the code, and at the same time a ritual incantation that a threatening and insatiable Moloch now trumpeted each time it devoured an important member of the regime. It took less than a month before the unpaid cryptographers of the secrets of Baba Tura's gloomy rule were whispering the truth into one another's ears. Their discovery was in some ways commonplace. The man who had protected Edward had been drawn into an unsuccessful conspiracy through his loyalty to an old schoolfriend, now Minister of the Interior. He had joined him, soon after his arrest, not in the famous prison at Fort-Nègre where so many nationalists and revolutionaries had been callously slaughtered but in a new temple of torture recently built inside the boundary of the football stadium where from this time onward, by a trick of fate, it was as often servants of the regime as its real or supposed enemies who found themselves . . . Then, in accordance with the custom of the regime, they were tried in a few minutes behind closed doors by a military tribunal which had been quietly waiting until the torturers had finished their task before sentencing the accused, just as quietly, to detention in a fortified enclosure – in other words, a northern concentration camp.

(3) DOUALA

Mbella Sonne Dipoko, *Autobiography*

Dipoko was born in the port of Douala and this extract from his 'Autobiography' speaks of the difficulties of growing up in Cameroon. The poem is included in the anthology African Writing Today – see Booklist.

We crawled and cried and laughed
Without hope
Without despair
We grew up
Fenced in by the forest.
But this world of uncles and fathers and mothers and others –
Our fine world of greenness and grins was blown away
By the terrible storm of growth
And the mind soon flung pebbles at the cranes of the offshore island.

(4) DOWAYO

Nigel Barley, *The Innocent Anthropologist*

Nigel Barley, 'innocent anthropologist', describes some of the extraordinary situations and pitfalls in which he found himself during his two-year field trip in remote Dowayoland.

My rather wobbly control of the language was also a grave danger. Obscenity is never very far away in Dowayo. A shift of tone changes the interrogative particle attached to a sentence to convert it into a question, into the lewdest word in the language, something like 'cunt'. I would, therefore, baffle and amuse Dowayos by greeting them, 'Is the sky clear for you, cunt?' But my problems were not exclusively with interrogative vaginas; similar problems haunted eating and copulation. One day I was summoned to the Chief's hut to be introduced to a rainmaker. This was a most valuable contact that I had nagged the Chief about for weeks. We chatted politely, very much sounding each other out. I was not supposed to know he was the rainmaker; I was the one being interviewed. I think he was much impressed by my respectful demeanour. We agreed that I would visit him. I was anxious to leave since I had acquired some meat for the first time in a month and left it in my assistant's care. I rose and shook hands politely. 'Excuse me,' I said, 'I am cooking some meat.' At least that was what I had intended to say; owing to tonal error I declared to an astonished audience, 'Excuse me. I am copulating with the blacksmith.'

(5) REÏ BOUBA

André Gide, *Travels in the Congo*

In 1925 André Gide set out on an expedition along the Congo River, turning off north, and then returning to the coast by way of the territory which now forms Cameroon. At Reï Bouba, 640 km from the coast, he has a meeting with the local Sultan.

More floods of people then succeeded each other more and more rapidly, pushed forward by a thick wall of foot-soldiers – archers in serried ranks and perfect order. Behind these could be seen something which seemed at first incomprehensible – this was a quantity of bucklers in hippopotamus hide; they were nearly black and held at arm's length by the performers in the rear. I myself was caught up into this extraordinary ballet, and everything seemed to melt into a glorious symphony; I lost count of details, and behind this last curtain of men as it parted, I beheld nothing but the sultan himself – surrounded by his body-guard and standing before the town walls, a bowshot from the door through which we were to enter, at the foot of a little slope and in the shade of a clump of enormous trees. At our approach, he descended from a kind of palankeen drawn by stooping, naked men. There were two parasols over him – one, of crimson, shaded him directly; the other, much larger one was black, flecked with silver, and was held over the first. We dismounted from our horses and, extremely desirous of representing as best we could France, civilization, the white race, we advanced with dignity, slowly and majestically, towards the sultan's outstretched hand . . .

(6) WOURI RIVER

Francis Bebey, *Agatha Moudio's Son*

Much to the horror of his parents, who have chosen a wife for him, Mbenda, a young man from a coastal fishing village at the mouth of the Wouri River, has fallen in love with the notorious and beautiful Agatha.

Agatha Moudio had taken some precautions before coming to visit me: she had thrown a whole handful of salt into the kitchen fire. At Douala, everybody knows how to make it rain; you merely burn a little salt, and immediately the heavens open as in the days of Noah's Ark. And not just a little shower, against which any old raincoat will protect you. No, real, rainy-season rain, water falling from the sky in thick, fat drops, when no one dares venture out.

Agatha came in and made me think furiously: what would Maa Médi say if she found this girl with me, alone with me? If only she had come on a weekday, it wouldn't have mattered much: my mother went to work in the fields every day, and the few gossips who might have made it their business to report to her that Agatha had been to see me would certainly not have succeeded in convincing her. But today, a Sunday afternoon when everybody was in the village, was not the day to choose to visit me, even though the visit did overwhelm me with joy.

'You mustn't stay here long,' I said to Agatha, 'you mustn't . . .'

I had hardly finished saying this when the clapping began on the roof of my house, so suddenly and so loud that I had to stop, taken aback. The burnt-salt trick had obviously been a great success.

'All the same you can't turn me out in such a downpour,' replied Agatha, assuming an expression of sublime innocence.

Biographies and important works

BARLEY, Nigel (1948–). Barley was educated at the University of London and became an assistant keeper at the Museum of Mankind, specializing in North and West Africa. In 1978 he did two years' field work among the remote Dowayo tribe. *The Innocent Anthropologist* (Extract 4), the story of this stay in Cameroon, became a bestseller. Unlike many such books, it is honest and its humour is not purely at the expense of his hosts. After much exasperation and disaster, Barley grew to love the Dowayo people. He later returned and wrote an equally entertaining sequel, A *Plague of Caterpillars*.

BEBEY, Francis (1929–). Born at Douala, Bebey went to study literature and musicology at the Sorbonne in Paris. He learnt to play several instruments before he could read, and today, as well as a novelist, he is also well known as a musician. His first novel, *Agatha Moudio's Son* (Extract 6), a tale of passion in the face of tradition, won the Grand Prix Littéraire de L'Afrique Noire. This and *Ashanti Doll*, set in Ghana, have been translated into English. Bebey has worked for Radio Ghana, and also for UNESCO in Paris.

BETI, Mongo (1932–). Beti was born just outside Yaoundé and completed his education at the University of Aix-en-Provence and the Sorbonne in France. He wrote his first novel under a pseudonym, but switched to his real name for his second novel, translated into English as *The Poor Christ of Bomba*. This caused a sensation with its frank sexual descriptions and sarcastic attacks on the church. Three other novels of Beti have been translated into English – *Mission to Kala*, *King Lazarus*, and *Perpetua and the Habit of Unhappiness* (Extract 2), a searching investigation into political corruption in his country.

DIPOKO, Mbella Sonne (1936–). Born in Douala, Dipoko spent part of his youth in Nigeria. In 1958 he became a news reporter for the Nigerian Broadcasting Corporation. After 1960 he left to live in Europe, basing himself in Paris. He has published several novels, of which A *Few Nights and Days* and *Because of Women* have been translated into English. But he is best known for his wild poems of love, anger and despair. The poems in *Black and White in Love* describe his amatory experiences against a wideranging European and North African background (including a spell in the north of England.)

GIDE, André (see under Congo).

OYONO, Ferdinand (1929-). After completing his education in France, Oyono served in the diplomatic corps. During this period he began writing novels and appeared on stage and television. He was later the Cameroon delegate to the UN. He has published many novels in French. *The Old Man and the Medal* (Extract 1) and *Houseboy* have been translated. His main aim is to portray, with fierce and often very humorous satire, the colonial situation and its effects on his people.

Mongo Beti

CENTRAL AFRICAN REPUBLIC

> 'Who is that jerk we have in Bangui?
>
> Charles de Gaulle on President Jean-Bédel Bokassa (from Squandering Eden)
>
> 'I've lost my papa.'
>
> President Jean-Bédel Bokassa on hearing of Charles de Gaulle's death (from Squandering Eden)

Once known more grandly as the Central African Empire under Emperor Bokassa I, the Central African Republic does not lack a source of literary inspiration. The rise to power of Bokassa reads like pure fiction. For the unfortunate inhabitants of this poor landlocked country, it was, for many years a terrible fact.

Jean-Bédel Bokassa, an ex-sergeant in the French army, was endorsed by France as the country's President a few years after independence. It was a decision the French were soon to regret. Living out his hedonistic fantasy to be like Napoleon I, the little Bokassa set about organizing a coronation to crown himself emperor (he was previously a mere 'life-long president'). In *The Africans*, David Lamb writes, 'On December 4, 1977, Bangui a dusty river town of 250 000 souls, was packed with several thousand guests – but not a single head of state. The temperature climbed past 100 degrees and the dignitaries sat sweating in their morning coats and Parisian gowns, waiting for Bokassa to fulfil his lifelong quest for Napoleonic glory. Finally a voice boomed over the loudspeaker, "Sa majesté impériale, l'empereur Bokassa Sa premier," and everyone struggled to attention.'

France footed most of the bill, estimated at anything between $20 and $90 million, which included a $2 million crown, a $150 000 coronation robe adorned with two million pearl and crystal beads, and imported white horses to pull the royal carriage. Meanwhile, back in the ex-colony rumblings of disapproval were silenced by a senior government minister who said it was racist to recognize England's extravagant celebrations for Queen Elizabeth's reign and not give the same credence to Bokassa's coronation.

FACT BOX

AREA: 622 999 sq km
POPULATION: 3 100 000
CAPITAL: Bangui
LANGUAGES: French, Sango
FORMER COLONIAL POWER: France
INDEPENDENCE: 1960

But Bokassa's credibility soon wore thin. To quote David Lamb again, 'For his fifty-fifth birthday he ordered each of his countrymen to give him a present of 500 local francs (about $2.50), and when he told his people they would have to help pay for his coronation, he offered a simple explanation: "One cannot create a great history without sacrifices, and this sacrifice is accepted by the population." '

The sacrifices were not just financial. In 1979 Bokassa was implicated in the massacre of nearly 100 schoolchildren who had refused to wear uniforms with his portrait on them, manufactured by a factory he owned. Not long afterwards, while Bokassa was on a trip abroad, France, as Rosenblum and Williamson put it in *Squandering Eden*, 'changed the locks on the country . . . Bokassa was sentenced to death in absentia for murder, cannibalism and massive embezzlement. But no one tried to bring him back.'

In fact, Bokassa voluntarily returned to Bangui in 1986. The original death sentence was commuted to life imprisonment and then reduced again. In 1993, he was released from prison. According to reports, Bokassa was in ebullient mood on his release, claiming to be the '13th apostle of Christ' and offering to return as emperor.

Perhaps not surprisingly, the literature that emerged in the Central African Republic during Bokassa's rule kept away from the obvious taboo (though no doubt very tempting) subject. Safer topics (and more believable ones) were found in the tales of the missionaries' contact with the tribes, and the effect of colonialism on traditional life. While these have not yet found their way into translation from the French, names to look out for in future include poet, novelist and prize-winning short story writer Pierre Makombo Bamboté and novelist Cyriaque Robert Yavoucko, both of whom have, unlike their ex-emperor, been well received in France. Watch out also for the as yet untranslated Faustin-Albert Ipeko-Etomane, Pierre Sammy, and Benoit Basile Siango, the Central African Republic's first playwright (his first work was published in Bangui in 1967).

LITERARY LANDMARKS

Bangui. Site of Bokassa's Napoleonic coronation in 1977. Negley Farson's impression in the 1930s, while the country was ruled by the French colonists, was: 'It was the only place in the world where I have seen almost the entire French community drunk at 10 o'clock in the morning.' (*Behind God's Back.*)

Bouali. French writer André Gide (◊ Congo) came to the **M'Bali Falls** here during his travels up the Congo in the 1920s (Extract 1).

BOOKLIST

The following selection includes the extracted title in this chapter as well as those mentioned in the introduction which are available in English and other titles for further reading. In general, paperback editions are given when possible. The editions cited are not necessarily the only ones available.

Gide, André, *Travels in the Congo*, University of California Press, Los Angeles, 1962. **Extract 1.**

Farson, Negley, *Behind God's Back*, Gollancz, London, 1940.

Lamb, David, *The Africans*, Vintage Books, New York, 1987.

O'Toole, Thomas, *Central African Republic: The Continent's Hidden Heart*, Westview Press, Boulder, CO, and Gower Press, London, 1986.

Rosenblum, Mort, and Williamson, Doug, *Squandering Eden*, Paladin, London, 1990.

Extract

(1) BOUALI

André Gide, *Travels in the Congo*

In 1925 French writer André Gide travelled up the Congo River and at Bangui the expedition turned north along the Ubangui tributary. To reach the M'Bali Falls at Bouali, he continued his journey across country by car.

The falls of the M'Bali, if they were in Switzerland, would be surrounded by enormous hotels. Here all is solitude; a hut, two huts with straw roofs, in which we are to sleep, do not spoil the wild grandeur of the scene. Fifty yards from the table where I am writing this, the cascade falls in a great misty curtain, silvered by the light of the moon between the branches of the great trees.

Bouali, 29 September

My first night in a camp-bed, where one sleeps better than in any other. At sunrise the waterfall, looking golden in the slanting rays, was an exceedingly beautiful sight. An immense island of greenery divides the current, and the water falls into two cascades, disposed in such a way that it is impossible to see them both at once. And one learns with astonishment that the first fall that strikes one owes its majesty and fullness to only half the waters of the river. When one draws near the bank, one discovers the second, hidden in the shade by some jutting rocks, and half buried, as it were, under the abundance of vegetation. The shrubs and plants are not, it must be admitted, the least exotic in appearance, and if it were not for a strange little island of pandanus with its aerial roots, nothing would remind one that this is almost the heart of Africa.

CHAD

Looking for literature in Chad is rather like looking for a time of peace and democracy in the country's history. Since the traditional balance of power was broken up by the French colonists in 1916, Chad has been plagued by bloody, unrelenting conflicts. Almost everyone has at one time been fighting against everyone else – Muslims against Christians; Northerners against Southerners; and every possible political group against each other.

Independence, which in 1960 brought 'Tombalbaye the terrible' to power, did little to relieve the situation. Once he had got rid of all French place and street names (reasonable enough), the dictator then banned all Christian names (not so reasonable for the indigenous Christian community) and made all his civil servants, officials and officers undergo the initiation rites of his tribe. He declared a one-party state and arrested the leaders of the main opposition party. Tombalbaye was assassinated during a successful coup in 1975 by General Malloum. Malloum's rule was equally inefficient, and a power struggle resulted in some five different fighting factions and the deaths of thousands of civilians. Next in this hall of horrors came Hissene Habré, who during his eight-year rule was responsible for the genocide of some 40 000 Chadians. Since Habré was deposed in 1990, his supporters have waged a war in the south of the country resulting in the deaths of more innocent civilians.

Over the years various fighting factions and governments have received 'generous' military, financial and development support from France, Libya and Russia. David Lamb in *The Africans* recalls Moscow's generous 'developmental' aid to the French-speaking country: 'twelve Soviet university professors, who knew only one language – Russian'.

FACT BOX

AREA: 1 270 998 sq km
POPULATION: 5 800 000
CAPITAL: N'Djamena
LANGUAGES: French, Arabic
FORMER COLONIAL POWER: France
INDEPENDENCE: 1960

Marginally more useful than the snowploughs that were given to Guinea. Libya, whose motives are not entirely altruistic, has also shown keen interest in Chad. The latest ruler, Colonel Deby, has it appears struck up a cosy relationship with his neighbour, though quite how long he will remain in power is an open question.

A lighter measure of just how complicated the power struggle became was illustrated by the arrival of two delegations at the Organization of African Unity summit in Tripoli in 1982. No one could decide which was the legal party, the meeting was cancelled, and the nickname the Organization of African Disunity was born.

If it has been difficult for the outside world to learn about and understand the events in landlocked, tumultuous Chad, it has been even more difficult for the country's writers to know what it is safe to write and when. Antoine Bangui, an ex-minister of Tombalbaye, tells how he survived three years in prison in *Prisonnier de Tombalbaye*. The country's other main published writers, Baba Moustapha and Kari Djimet, also write in French and are as yet unavailable in translation, and likely to remain so until the day democracy comes to Chad.

LITERARY LANDMARKS

N'Djamena. In *The White Tribes of Africa*, 1965, Richard West wrote, 'the capital of the Republic of Chad lies at the desolate centre of the immense continent; and feels like it. It was the rainy season when I arrived, with a climate like hot Irish stew.'

BOOKLIST

Bangui, Antoine, *Prisonnier de Tombalbaye*, Hatier, Paris, 1980 (in French).

Lamb, David, *The Africans*, Vintage, New York, 1987.

Rosenblum, Mort and Williamson, Doug, *Squandering Eden*, Paladin, London, 1990.

West, Richard, *The White Tribes of Africa*, Cape, London, 1965.

CONGO

> '. . . we need . . . no more than some priests and a few people to teach in schools, and no other goods except wine and flour for the holy sacrament. That is why we beg of Your Highness to help and assist us in this matter, commanding of your factors that they should not send here either merchants or wares, because it is our will that in these kingdoms there should not be any trade of slaves nor outlet for them.'
> *King Dom Affonso of Kongo to the King of Portugal, 1526 (The African Past)*

The rulers of the kingdom of Kongo were the first sub-Saharan Africans to write in any European language. In the sixteenth century, King Affonso of Congo sent 24 letters in Portuguese to the rulers of Portugal. These letters were for the most part a model of nobility and tact and show the initial friendliness of the indigenous people towards the early Portuguese explorers and traders (Extract 6). Affonso's hopes for mutually advantageous trade between the two countries were gradually eroded away with the increasing European avarice and brutality.

There then followed the terrible years of the slave trade. During the following centuries, over 13½ million slaves (the equivalent of the combined population of present-day London and Manchester) were exported from this part of the coast, which included Zaire and Angola.

In the 1880s the Italian–French explorer de Brazza (after whom **Brazzaville** is named) set up a number of commercial schemes for the further exploitation of this region – to the benefit of the French and to the utter detriment of the local people. This exploitation had reached such an appalling state that in the period 1914–24 the local population was reduced by two-thirds. It was in 1925, in the aftermath of this, that the French writer André Gide ◊ arrived (Extract 7), and revealed to the French people (and the world) the atrocities that were being committed in the name of France.

FACT BOX

AREA: 342 000 sq km
POPULATION: 2 351 000
CAPITAL: Brazzaville
LANGUAGES: French, Kongo, Tété and Lingala
FORMER COLONIAL POWER: France
INDEPENDENCE: 1960

After such colonial treatment, it is not surprising that, soon after independence in 1960, the Congo became the first avowedly Communist state in Africa. Through the ensuing years there followed a number of military takeovers and failed coups, accompanied by increasing corruption. Only gradually was corruption weeded out, and now the country is ruled by a more middle-of-the-road non-aligned government.

French remains the official language, but it is only spoken by a small élite. The wide local range of tribal languages remain the means of everyday communication. These have to some extent been standardized into the two main 'trade' languages: Lingala, spoken mainly in the north, and Kongo, which is used in the west. Most Congolese literature remains oral – with its wide range of fables, myths and stories passed from mouth to mouth in a living tradition (Extract 3).

Published Congolese literature is largely Francophone, with hardly any translated into English. Similarly, few English novelists have written about this region. The novel *Brazzaville Beach*, by British (but West African born) William Boyd ◊ is one of the most readable (Extract 5). The action of the novel is said to take place in an unnamed country. It is, of course, no coincidence that the events and political background bear a remarkably close resemblance to conflicts in this region of Africa, and that the title takes its name from the capital of the Congo.

One of the first Francophone poets was Martial Sinda. *Premier Chant de Départ* ('First Song of Leaving') was published in French in 1955 when the author was 35 years old. That same year there appeared the first book of poetry by Tchicaya U Tam'si ◊. This launched the career of one of the greatest Francophone poets to date. The poetry of the Paris-educated U Tam'si has frequently been concerned with his need to find his roots and the search for a true African identity: 'The flat horizon of this country splits my heart/If I recoil everything bristles suddenly!/I will stay at the gate with the wind in my side/but with tornadoes in my belly . . .' (from *Le Ventre*). Such concerns, and his profound treatment of them, have struck a chord with audiences well beyond the confines of Africa.

A similar sense of alienation can be found in the writings of Sylvain Bemba ◊. His short story 'The Dark Room' (Extract 1) won the Prix de la Nouvelle Africaine in 1964 organized by the French magazine *Preuves*. This established Bemba's reputation and he went on to become one of the country's leading dramatists. In 'The Dark Room', N'Toto simultaneously captivates and terrifies a French woman in Paris with his tongue-in-cheek philosophizing: ' "Yes," the Negro went on, "we are descended from india-rubber, and our great ancestor, if you like, was Michelin, or rather the fellow you see on the posters advertising that brand of tyres. That's why our forefathers and the slaves who were sent to America were able to adapt themselves to a situation that was new to them." '

Bemba, along with U Tam'si, could not be described as typical of Congolese writers. A major difference is that most of the Congolese writers remain within the traditions of their country and experience no such crisis of identity.

Another contemporary writer of note is Guy Mengawho. He was born in 1940, and won the Grand Prix of the Inter-African Theatre competition in Paris in 1968 for his play *L'Oracle*. Unfortunately his work has not been translated into English. One writer who has been lucky enough to cross this cultural divide is Henri Lopes ◊, whose novel *The Laughing Cry* (Extract 4) portrays with comic zest and insight the antics of a buffoonish African dictator known ironically as 'Daddy'. Before one of Daddy's rare visits to a province his minions are sent in: 'They . . . distributed handfuls of notes stamped with his effigy, made lists of the most appetizing virgins and drove off all evil spirits, in a thousand senses of the term.'

Surprisingly, Lopes managed to combine a career in literature and politics. After holding a string of ministerial appointments, he briefly became the country's Prime Minister in 1972–75. His miraculous survival in both spheres – considering the politicians he served with and the satirical force of his literature – must have required more than literary and political dexterity. We, and the standing of Congolese literature, can only be grateful for his good fortune.

LITERARY LANDMARKS

Brazzaville. Named after Italian–French explorer Pierre de Brazza (1852–1905) who 'founded' French Congo and Brazzaville in 1883.

Congo River. The river that forms part of the border between Congo and Zaire is today officially known as the **Zaire River** (the ancient local name for 'large river'), but was originally named after the Kongo tribe who inhabited its mouth. The kingdom of Kongo occupied this region from the fifteenth century and it was from here that the king sent his famous letters to the ruler of Portugal (Extract 6). Nineteenth-century explorer Sir Henry Morton Stanley (◊ Tanzania) came here to map the Congo River. **Pool Malebo** was once named 'Stanley Pool' after him. At the mouth of the river at Boma in present-day Zaire is where he is said to have carved his name on a baobab, in which the Portuguese traders hid illegal slaves. Joseph Conrad (◊ Zaire) captained a riverboat on the Congo upstream from Leopoldville (Kinshasa). Out of this experience he wrote *Heart of Darkness*. André Gide travelled up the Congo from **Brazzaville**, branching north along the **Oubangui River** on his way to what is now the Central African Republic. *Travels in the Congo* (Extract 7) is his journal of this experience. Graham Greene (◊ Sierre Leone) also travelled upstream from Kinshasa, a trip that is recorded in his *Congo Journal*.

Libraries and Bookshops

Brazzaville. Bibliothèque Publique de Brazzaville; French Cultural Centre; Marien Ngouabi University Libraries; People's National Library.

BOOKLIST

The following selection includes the extracted titles in this chapter as well as those mentioned in the introduction which are available in English and other titles for further reading. In general, paperback editions are given when possible. The editions cited are not necessarily the only ones available. For most of the extracted works, the original publisher in English can be found in 'Acknowledgments and Citations' at the end of the volume, as can the exact location of the extracts and the editions from which they are taken. Extract numbers are highlighted in bold for ease of reference.

Affonso, King Dom, in *The African Past*, Basil Davidson, ed, Penguin, London, 1966. **Extract 6**.
Bemba, Sylvain, 'The Dark Room',

in *African Writing Today*, Ezekiel Mphahlele, ed, Penguin, London, 1967. **Extract 1**.
Boyd, William, *Brazzaville Beach*, Penguin, London, 1990. **Extract 5**.
Carlson, Lois, *Monganga Paul*, Hodder and Stoughton, London, 1967.
Conrad, Joseph, *Heart of Darkness*, Penguin, London, 1982.
Gide, André, *Travels in the Congo*, University of California Press, Los Angeles, 1962. **Extract 7**.
Greene, Graham, *Congo Journal*, Penguin, London, 1987.
Lopes, Henri, *The Laughing Cry*, G. Moore, trans, Readers International, London, 1982. **Extract 4**.
Myths and Legends of the Congo, collected and translated by Jan

Knappert, Heinemann, London, 1971. **Extract 3.**

U Tam'si, Tchicaya, *Selected Poems*, Gerald Moore, trans, Heinemann, London, 1970. **Extract 2.**

U Tam'si, Tchicaya, in *The Penguin Book of Modern African Poetry*, Gerald Moore and Ulli Beier, eds, Penguin Books, London, 1967.

Extracts

(1) CONGO: EXILE

Sylvain Bemba, *The Dark Room*

So often we hear what it is like for a European to visit a distant unknown city, but here the tables are reversed. In his prize-winning short story, Bemba describes how it is for an African in Paris. 'The Dark Room' is included in the anthology African Writing Today – see Booklist.

N'Toko liked taking his hairy face, the face of a bearded, grimacing faun, round the streets of Paris. He was conscious of his ugliness and he derived a sort of secret pleasure from displaying his repulsive features with calm effrontery. He was visibly amused by the shuddering amazement which he caused in the street when he passed other people who turned round to watch the huge Negro walking away. Baggy clothes gave him an outline which was vague, unfinished, blurred, almost ghostly. And yet, when people came to know him better, they were surprised to find that they no longer felt the slightest malaise in his presence. Then they recognized that he had a certain charm, an irresistible magnetism . . .

N'Toko loved Paris. He still remembered his first days in the famous city. On his arrival he had been disappointed. He had expected to find a *de luxe* work in a handsome gilded binding. Instead, a dismal, dirty sky and sad-looking walls showed him Paris in the guise of an old book found in a box on the quays. The miracle occurred when he began leafing through the worn volume. On every page, at every line, he met the hypnotic gaze of the statues' vacant eyes. He lived again through those centuries of a history which he had learnt at school and whose tide still beat in foaming breakers against the cliffs of modern times.

The first joys N'Toko experienced in Paris were those of a conquista-
dor. He was discovering a new world.

(2) Congo: Homeland

Tchicaya U Tam'si, *The Scorner*

*The sterility of his land becomes a focus for the poet's sense of
rootlessness. 'The Scorner' is included in Selected Poems – see
Booklist.*

I drink to your glory my god
You who have made me so sad
You have given me a people who are not distillers of gin

What wine shall I drink to your *jubilate*
In this country which has no vines
In this desert all the bushes are of cactus
Shall I take their crop of flowers
for flames of the burning bush of your desire
Tell me in what Egypt my people's feet lie chained . . .

(3) Congo: Myths

Myths and Legends of the Congo

*The evil and greedy spirits that inhabit the oral literature of the
Congo often take the form of disfigured human forms. Here a
man is on his way to collect his wife and new-born from his
in-laws. This tale is typical of those told among the Bakongo
tribe.*

On the way he met a spirit in the form of a truncated body: no arms, no
legs, no head. The Trunk asked him politely where he was going and a
man answered him. The Trunk begged his permission to accompany
him, and offered to carry the wine-jar.

The man replied, surprised: 'But you have nothing to carry it with.'
The Trunk, however, insisted, and so the man put the jar on top of the
Trunk, who carried it all the way.

When they arrived at the in-laws' compound, a hut was assigned to
them and they were brought a lavish meal. The man ate until he was
satisfied; the Trunk ate the spoons and knives too.

The next day they had a goat for breakfast; the man ate his fill, but
the Trunk ate the bones, the horns, the skin, and the pots as well.

After this they went home, the man with his wife carrying her new baby, accompanied by the greedy Trunk.

When they reached the spot where the Trunk had crept out of the earth, it stopped and demanded:

> Now share with me your wife, be generous!
> Now share with me your child, be generous!

As soon as his fellows heard that the Trunk was singing for his prey they too crept out of the earth, one or two first, then a dozen, then a hundred, all writhing bodies. All demanded to eat live human flesh. The man despaired!

(4) CONGO: POLITICS

Henri Lopes, *The Laughing Cry*

'Daddy', the dictator of an unidentified African country, is described by 'his hapless valet and cuckolder'. Daddy loves to travel and is permanently on a state visit to one country or another.

My friend the young compatriot Cabinet Secretary, devoting himself to a mischievous calculation, was able to prove that the President passed an average of less than fifteen days a month in the country. According to radio grapevine, he was always careful on these journeys to carry with him all the cash in the Public Treasury, so as to paralyze anyone who might toy with the idea of playing the trick he had played on Polépolé. These were doubtless only stories, which were given a certain plausibility by Daddy's style, but which I am in no position to confirm. The spirit of objectivity, on the other hand, obliges me to record that Daddy took his journeys very seriously. How often have I not heard him complain:

'Nobody wants to understand me! We are in the age of Concorde and of personal diplomacy. Anyone would think I travel the world for the sake of tourism. Whereas, all this travelling exhausts me, it breaks my back . . . I'm no longer the right age for it . . . If it wasn't for the prestige of the country . . .'

And his gaze seemed to lose itself in rich, secret, Eden-like horizons of which he was deprived by public affairs and the spirit of sacrifice.

'Not to mention that I risk my life every time.'

'Your precious life.'

'Thank you, my boy, thank you, thank you, thank you. May God bless you.'

And he brandished his lion's tail above his obliging colleague's head.

'Whenever one embarks in those machines . . .'

And he plunged into long and knowing digressions.

The people of Moundié had their own vision of this politics of travel. When Daddy was in the capital, they loved to make fun of it.

'Eh! my brother, have you heard the latest? Daddy is on an official visit to our country!'

(5) CONGO: WAR

William Boyd, *Brazzaville Beach*

Hope Clearwater, an anthropologist, has been investigating the unusual territorial behaviour of 'gangs' of chimpanzees in the forest. On the way back from an expedition he and a colleague are captured by a renegade guerrilla group.

'I really don't think they want to hurt us,' I said. 'They're just kids.'

'The kids are the worst,' he said, fiercely. 'They don't care. Don't give a damn what they do.' He was shivering, his voice was a rasping whisper.

'Not this lot, surely,' I said.

'Look what they've got written on their fucking jackets! *Atomique Boum.* What the fuck does that signify? Some kind of commando? Some kind of death squad?' He was beginning to panic.

'For Christ's sake.' I stood up. The two boys were lounging at the fringe of the shade cast by the mango tree. They were talking quietly to each other, their weapons on the ground, their backs half turned away from us. I walked over to them.

'Where has he gone, Dr Amilcar?' I said. They spoke briefly to each other in a language I did not recognize. I suspected only one of them spoke English. One had understood me. Beneath each eye were three small vertical nicks – tribal scars.

'For gasoline,' he said. 'Please to sit down.'

I pointed at the other one's track-suit top.

'What does this mean?' I asked. '*Atomique Boum.*'

'Volley.' He smiled.

'Sorry?'

'It is our game. We play volley-ball. We are the team Atomique Boum.'

'Ah.'

I felt an odd subsidence in my gut, a hollow feeling that made me want to laugh and cry at the same time.

'It's a good game,' I said. Lost in Africa, prisoners of an armed volley-ball team.

'Very good,' he agreed.

Then the other one said something, more sternly. The boy with scarred eyes smiled apologetically, and motioned for me to return to my place. I rejoined Ian. Anxious Ian.

'Relax,' I said. 'We've been captured by a volley-ball team.'

(6) Kongo

King Dom Affonso of Kongo

This letter dated 6 July 1526 from King Dom Affonso of Kongo to the King of Portugal sheds an interesting light on the early contacts between the Europeans and the Congolese. Contrary to popular belief, in this case the local rulers wanted missionaries and priests and definitely did not want dealings with the slave traders. This letter is included in The African Past – see Booklist.

Sir, Your Highness [of Portugal] should know how our Kingdom is being lost in so many ways that it is convenient to provide for the necessary remedy, since this is caused by the excessive freedom given by your factors and officials to the men and merchants who are allowed to come to the Kingdom to set up shops with goods and many things which have been prohibited by us . . .

And we cannot reckon how great the damage is, since the mentioned merchants are taking every day our natives, sons of the land and the sons of our noblemen and vassals and our relatives, because the thieves and men of bad conscience grab them wishing to have the things and wares of this Kingdom which they are ambitious of; they grab them and get them to be sold; and so great, Sir, is the corruption and licentiousness that our country is being completely depopulated, and Your Highness should not agree with this nor accept it as in your service. And to avoid it we need from those [your] Kingdoms no more than some priests and a few people to teach in schools, and no other goods except wine and flour for the holy sacrament. This is why we beg of Your Highness to help and assist us in this matter, commanding your factors that they should not send here either merchants or wares, because it is our will that in these Kingdoms there should not be any trade of slaves nor outlet for them. Concerning what is referred above, again we beg of Your Highness to agree with it, since otherwise we cannot remedy such an obvious damage. Pray Our Lord in His mercy to have Your Highness under His guard and let you do for ever the things of His service. I kiss your hands many times.

(7) Oubangui River

André Gide, *Travels in the Congo*

After travelling along the Congo Gide turned off north up the Oubangui River. In the first of these passages, he is about 300 km up river.

18 September

The temperature is not very high (not more than 90° Fahrenheit), but the air is heavy with electricity and moisture, and thick with tsetses and mosquitoes. The latter particularly like attacking one's ankles, which are left unprotected by one's shoes; they even venture up one's trousers and attack one's calves; even through the stuff one's knees are bitten. Siestas are impossible; besides, it is the hour for butterflies. I am beginning now to know them almost all. When a new one appears, it is all the more delightful.

23 September

The forest is changing slightly in appearance; the trees are finer; their trunks, which are freed from creepers, are more distinct; their branches are hung with masses of light-green lichen, like the larches in the Engadine; some of these trees are gigantic, far bigger than any of our trees in France; but as soon as one is at some distance from them (owing also to the immense width of the river), it is impossible to judge of their size. The creeper-palm, which was so frequent a few days ago, has disappeared.

24 September

At ten o'clock we stopped opposite Bétou. The natives here, Mojembos by race, are healthier, more robust, handsomer: they seem freer and franker. While my two companions went along the river bank, I found my way to the Compagnie Forestière's station. A squad of very young girls were at work weeding the ground in front of the station. They were singing as they worked; they were dressed in a kind of ballet skirt made of plaited palm-fibre; many of them had on brass anklets. Their faces were ugly, but their busts admirable. I took a long, solitary walk across fields of manioc, chasing extraordinary butterflies.

Biographies and important works

BEMBA, Sylvain (1932–). Born in the Congo, Bemba also writes under the pseudonym 'Martial Malinda'. He first achieved fame with his prize-winning short story, 'The Dark Room' (Extract 1), which was joint winner of the Prix de la Nouvelle Africaine in 1964. He has since published several novels and plays (none of which is available in English). After returning from a spell in Paris he became Chief Editor of L'Agence Congolaise d'Information, **Brazzaville**.

BOYD, William (1952–). Boyd was born in Accra, Ghana, and brought up in West Africa and the UK. He studied at Oxford University, and later became a lecturer in English Literature. His first novel, A Good Man in Africa, is set in West Africa and has won two literary awards. Since then he has travelled widely in Africa. Brazzaville Beach (Extract 5), his bestselling novel, is set in an unnamed African country. It follows the career of the heroine Hope Clearwater, an anthropologist whose work at a chimpanzee station brings her into conflict with the station's famous director. Very much a 'postcolonial' work, it brilliantly evokes the situation in Africa as seen from an outsider's point of view – though its deeper implications go far beyond this.

GIDE, André (1896–1951). One of the most distinguished French writers of his era, Gide's novels were largely concerned with his own spiritual quest. The self revelations and honesty involved in this search caused him to recognize and confess to his own suppressed homosexuality – after which he set out for the Congo in 1925. He travelled through the territories now occupied by Congo, Zaire, Central African Republic, Cameroon and Gabon. When he returned to France he published Travels in the Congo (Extract 7), which was fre-

quently critical of the French administration in the region. His increasing concern with social matters led him to turn to Communism, though his sympathy evaporated after a visit to the Soviet Union. André Gide received the Nobel Prize for Literature in 1947.

LOPES, Henri (1937–). Lopes was born in Kinshasa (then the Belgian Congo) and educated in Paris. In 1968 he became Minister of National Education in the Congo, and after this held a series of ministerial posts until he became Prime Minister from 1973 to 1975. He was later Deputy Director General of UNESCO. He continued with his literary work during his political career and was awarded Le Prix Littéraire de L'Afrique Noire in 1972 for his novel Tribalques. He is also author of the Congolese National Anthem. His novel The Laughing Cry (Extract 4) is a superbly comic, penetrating and scathing picture of an African tyrant.

U TAM'SI TCHICAYA (1931–). Born in **Mpili**, Congo Republic, Tchicaya U Tam'si studied in France, where his father was a Deputy for Congo in Paris. Later when the neighbouring Belgian Congo (now Zaire) achieved independence, he crossed the river to Kinshasa and edited a newspaper there. Since then he has lived in France, but his work with UNESCO has meant that he has frequently returned to Africa. He has published many volumes of poetry, novels, and short stories. Several of these have been translated into English. He is considered by many critics to be the finest Francophone African poet of his generation.

EQUATORIAL GUINEA

'In every book I ever read
Of travels on the Equator
A plague, mysterious and
   dread,
Imperils the narrator.'
Hilaire Belloc,
The Modern Traveller

Noted principally by the early explorers for death and disease, Equatorial Guinea was possibly the least sought-after colony in the whole of Africa. 'Ever since 1827 [Fernando Po] has been accumulating for itself an evil reputation for unhealthiness,' noted Mary Kingsley (◊ Gabon) in the journal of her travels (Extract 1). The region is made up of three very disparate parts: **Río Muni** or **Mbini** on the mainland sits in the 'armpit' of Africa, while the rest of its territory is divided between the volcanic islands of **Fernando Po** (today named **Bioko**) and **Annobon** (or **Pagalu**) which lie 200 and 500 km respectively from the coast.

The charmingly named island of Fernando Po was chanced upon by Portuguese navigators in the fifteenth century, and variously claimed over the centuries by the Spanish, the British (who used it as a base from which to combat the slave trade), then Spain again in 1844. Visiting the island in 1884, Sir Henry Morton Stanley (◊ Tanzania) remarked that it was 'a jewel which Spain did not polish', while his even more disillusioned compatriot Sir Richard Burton (◊ Ethiopia), who had been given the obscure post as British Consul there in 1861, reported 'They sent me there hoping I'd die.'

The island was known during the colonial era as the 'Foreign Office grave'. Mary Kingsley gives an amusing account of a Spanish governor taking up his post there in 1893: 'As soon as his appointment as Governor was announced, all his friends and acquaintances carefully explained to him that this appointment was equivalent to execution, only more uncomfortable in the way it worked out . . . Still he kept up a good heart, but when he arrived at the island he found his predecessor had died of fever; and he himself, the day after landing, went down

---

FACT BOX

AREA: 28 051 sq km (Bioko 2017 sq km)
POPULATION: 426 000
CAPITAL: Malabo (on Bioko)
LANGUAGES: Spanish, Fang, Bubi
FORMER COLONIAL POWER: Spain
INDEPENDENCE: 1968

---

with a bad attack and he was placed in a bed – the same bed, he was mournfully informed, in which the last Governor had expired.'

Despite the dangers of disease Mary Kingsley grew very attached to this part of Equatorial Guinea, and spent a lot of time studying the fetishes, the fancies and the culture of the indigenous Bubis. Very different from the Fangs of the mainland, the Bubis suffered greatly when, following independence from Spain in 1968, they fell under the rule of Francisco Macias Nguema who renamed the island Bioko. Up to a third of the population fled the country during the time of his presidency, and estimates of the scale of genocide that was committed on the outlying islands between 1968 and 1979 reach tens of thousands. When the extent of Nguema's atrocities and corruption was finally realized, he was toppled from power and executed.

Contrary to expectations, the years following independence were not conducive to literary activity. The first printing press had actually been set up as early as 1875 by Methodist missionaries, and by the time of independence there were seven functioning throughout the country. But some five years of despotic rule later, very few were in operation and those that functioned were subject to heavy censorship. The media in all forms are still in a state of delayed shock, figures on literacy are mysteriously unavailable, and indigenous literary works are apparently as few and far between as the country's islands.

During the Nguema era all foreign literature, publications and journalists were banned from Equatorial Guinea. Indeed some of the first books to appear on the country followed visits by development experts such as American Robert Klitgaard ◊ who came here in the 1980s. His book *Tropical Gangsters* (Extract 2) contains many amusing, poignant and perceptive stories, including several abortive attempts at meeting ministers, and a wonderful scene where he composes a song about living in the capital with a motley assortment of musicians that include a Michael Jackson look-alike and two Equatorial Guinean rock stars: 'I came to Malabo by accident, on Air Iberia./Overslept my destination Lagos, Nigeria./I've been here ever since, and till I don't know when,/Oh lord I'm stuck in Malabo again!'

BOOKLIST

The following selection includes the extracted titles in this chapter as well as those mentioned in the introduction which are available in English and other titles for further reading. In general, paperback editions are given when possible. The editions cited are not necessarily the only ones available.

Fegley, Randall, *Equatorial Guinea:*

An African Tragedy, Peter Lang, New York, 1989.

Kingsley, Mary, *Travels in West Africa*, Virago, London, 1986. **Extract 1.**

Klitgaard, Robert, *Tropical Gangsters*, I.B. Tauris, London, 1990. **Extract 2.**

Liniger-Goumaz, Max, *Small is Not Always Beautiful*, Hurst and Co, London, 1988.

Extracts

(1) FERNANDO PO (BIOKO)
Mary Kingsley, *Travels in West Africa*

During her travels in West Africa in the 1890s, Kingsley, who had always been fascinated by this island, took a trip across from Calabar in Nigeria.

Fernando Po is the most important island as regards size on the West African coast, and at the same time one of the most beautiful in the world. It is a great volcanic mass with many craters, and culminates in the magnificent cone, Clarence Peak . . . Seen from the sea or from the continent it looks like an immense single mountain that has floated out to sea. It is visible during clear weather (and particularly sharply visible in the strange clearness you get after a tornado) from a hundred miles to seawards, and anything more perfect than Fernando Po when you sight it, as you occasionally do from far-away Bonny Bar, in the sunset, floating like a fairy island made of gold or amethyst, I cannot conceive . . . Its moods of beauty are infinite: for the most part gentle and gorgeous, but I have seen it silhouetted hard against tornado-clouds, and grandly grim from the upper regions of its great brother Mungo. And as for Fernando Po in full moonlight – well there! you had better go and see it for yourself.

(2) MALABO

Robert Klitgaard, *Tropical Gangsters*

As part of his brief as a representative from the World Bank, Klitgaard is eager to secure interviews with several of the country's top ministers. Despite his highly respected position the mission proves less than easy.

I kept trying to see Don Manuel, the Minister of Finance. No luck. Finally, I decided to work on Esmeralda, his surly secretary. How about lunch? Or a beer? Or a cup of coffee? One morning that week, I walked in and asked whether the minister was in, and Esmeralda said, 'No, but you can take me out now for coffee.'

Except for Harmon and me, the other team members had departed, and he was busy writing his report. So transportation was no longer a problem. I had a car and driver all day. I ushered Esmeralda into the back seat, and the driver drove us to a brand new spot that featured espresso coffee and Spanish sweets called *churros*. We went inside. The driver, emboldened by our buying his lunches most days, came along, sat at our table, and ordered a beer. I got a coffee. Esmeralda ordered a breakfast that would have surprised Mike Tyson.

Conversation came hard, if only because she kept eating and eating. Finally, she paused and touched my arm.

'What hotel are you staying at?'

Don't have one, staying at a house.

Esmeralda thought that one over. 'Well,' she said, leaning forward, 'let's go away together to Douala.' That's the commercial port of Cameroon.

Naw, don't have a visa. Um, let's get back to the ministry.

We drove there. Esmeralda got out and told the driver, 'Pick me up at three, that's when I get off work.' Then she instructed me. 'See you after work. Let's go do something.'

I muttered excuses. See you tomorrow, when I come back to see whether I can meet with the minister.

She disappeared, and I got back in the car. I looked at the driver, he looked at me, and we both laughed.

Biographies and important works

KINGSLEY, Mary (see under Gabon).

KLITGAARD, Robert. Klitgaard taught economic development at Harvard and has worked as a consultant around the world. Arriving for the second time in 1986, Klitgaard spent two years in Equatorial Guinea. His book *Tropical Gangsters* (Extract 2) unveils the recent political events, the history of the country, and a World Bank project that 'hopes to transform a ruined economy'. The book offers a detailed and interesting look at Equatorial Guinea from the development perspective, sprinkled with honest and evocative descriptions of the places Klitgaard visited all over the country – and his quest for good surfing beaches.

GABON

What Gabon lacks in literary weight, it more than makes up for in tales of post-independence presidential excess and eccentricities. Not long after independence from France in 1960, the first president was ousted and succeeded by 'an ambitious postal worker'. President El Hadj Omar Bongo (better known as Albert-Bernard before an efficacious visit to Mecca), who has ruled since 1967, holds annual elections on his birthday. Running unopposed, his re-elections have been a rather generous birthday present to himself. He also holds most of the government's ministerial posts, including those of National Guidance and Women's Advancement. There are countless legendary anecdotes about his rule of Gabon which have been endlessly retold and rolled around the world. They are perhaps not quite so entertaining if you happen to live there.

The oil boom, while it lasted, brought great illusions of grandeur to Bongo. He splashed out $2 billion on a three-day Organization of African Unity conference in 1977, complete with circular freeway (going nowhere in particular) and huge hotel–village (not much use now). He flew marble in from Italy to complete his palace for the occasion (the local quarry is full of the stuff). According to David Lamb in *The Africans*, Bongo's $800 million *Star Trek* style palace has 'a night club, a banquet hall for 3000 persons (which represents 1 percent of Gabon's population) and a bathtub big enough to swim several strokes in. For good measure, there are two theatres, separated by a central viewing room which Bongo can rotate at the push of a button to make his choice of presentations.'

FACT BOX

AREA: 265 001 sq km
POPULATION: 1 170 000
CAPITAL: Libreville
LANGUAGES: French, Fang, Eshira, Mpongwe
FORMER COLONIAL POWER: France
INDEPENDENCE: 1960

It would be nice to think that the theatre is used to stage works by national artists and writers. Indeed, the country has produced several playwrights, novelists and prose writers, whose work has been printed locally. The little Gabonese literature that has been translated into English comprises the Fang and Pygmy traditional praise songs, some of which meditate on the beauty and majesty of nature and the elements, while others lament the arrival of the whites and negro landlords (Extract 3). The Pygmies have an enchanting 'Invocation to the Rainbow', which is a symbol of hope and renewal: 'Among the black clouds,/Dividing the dark sky,/As a knife cuts through an overripe fruit,/Rainbow, Rainbow!/And it fled,/The thunder killer of men,/Like the antelope from the panther . . .' (from *Voices from Twentieth-Century Africa*). In Fang expiation ceremonies, fire is summoned and in the traditional 'Song of the Will-o'-the-Wisp' it is a heavily charged symbol of strength (Extract 2).

It is believed that the Pygmies were the original inhabitants of Gabon, but they were displaced by the migrating Fang and there are few remaining today. Larger population displacement was caused by the slave traders. Overlooked by the Portuguese, it was the British, Dutch and French who took an early interest in the country and plundered its human, ivory and hardwood resources. Subsequently, a few European migrants and explorers ventured here. Among the most interesting of these were Mary Kingsley ◊ and a German doctor, Albert Schweitzer ◊. Arriving in 1894, Kingsley was the first European to venture into parts of Gabon. Following the **Ogooué River** she entered Fang territory – a tribe which, according to the rumours of the time, had a taste for cannibalism. Kingsley's reports, while they were never actually proven to have been witnessed, had a lasting impact on the perception of this part of Africa (Extract 1).

The legacy of Nobel Prize winning Albert Schweitzer's work here is altogether more healthy. Born in 1875 in Germany he was a theologian and an organist. He gave up his university post at the age of 30, studied medicine and set off for Africa. In Gabon he established a hospital on the **Ogooué River** which later included a leper colony he ran with his wife (Extract 4). Throughout his stay he continued to return to Europe to give lectures on his work, and to play concerts. His writings contain many details about his invaluable work here and about his philosophies: 'In everything you recognize yourself. The tiny beetle that lies dead in your path – it was a living creature, struggling for existence like yourself, rejoicing in the sun like you. And now it is no more than decaying matter – which is what you will be sooner or later too.' He died in 1965, but his hospital is still running and is considered to be one of the finest in the country. Locally he is remembered less fondly for the following remark about his patients – 'I feel for them like a brother, but like an older brother. The Negro is a child in a primitive culture, and nothing can be done with children without authority.'

LITERARY LANDMARKS

Franceville. President Bongo's home town, connected to the rest of the country by the great **Transgabonese Railway**. The railway, which took 13 years to build through over 640 km of hardwood forest, was one of the world's largest construction projects. After a diversion to Franceville, the route missed the iron ore mining area.

Lambaréné. About 13 km from the town, on the **Ogooué River** lies the still functioning **Schweitzer Hospital**. It is one of Gabon's best hospitals.

Libreville. In 1849 the town was established as a settlement for freed slaves. Graham Greene (◊ Sierra Leone) passed though the **airport** on his way back from the Congo and noted the busy scene in his diary, later recorded in *In Search of a Character*: 'Complete mixing, not only of black and white, but men and women . . . Too great a cordiality and shaking of hands and noisy affability. Colonialism in hurried and undignified retreat.'

Libraries and Bookshops

Libreville. American Cultural Centre, Avenue de Colonel Parant; French Cultural Centre, Place de l'Indépendance; Libraire Nouvelle, BP 612.

BOOKLIST

The following selection includes the extracted titles in this chapter as well as those mentioned in the introduction which are available in English and other titles for further reading. In general, paperback editions are given when possible. The editions cited are not necessarily the only ones available. For most of the extracted works, the original publisher in English can be found in 'Acknowledgments and Citations' at the end of the volume, as can the exact location of the extracts and the editions from which they are taken. Extract numbers are highlighted in bold for ease of reference.

Brabazon, James, *Albert Schweitzer: A Biography*, Gollancz, London, 1976.

Greene, Graham, *In Search of a Character*, Penguin, London, 1968.

Kingsley, Mary, *Travels in West Africa*, Virago Press, London, 1986. **Extract 1.**

Lamb, David, *The Africans*, Vintage, New York, 1987.

Schweitzer, Albert, *From My African Notebook*, George, Allen and Unwin, London, 1938. **Extract 4.**

Schweitzer, Albert, *My Life and Thought*, George, Allen and Unwin, London, 1933.

Schweitzer, Albert, *On the Edge of the Primeval Forest*, A&C Black, London, 1922.

Seaver, George, *Albert Schweitzer: The Man and His Mind*, A&C Black, London, 1948.

The Unwritten Song, Willard Trask, ed, Jonathan Cape, 1969. **Extract 3.**

Voices from Twentieth-Century Africa, Chinweizu, ed, Faber and Faber, London, 1988. **Extract 2.**

Extracts

(1) GABON: FANG

Mary Kingsley, *Travels in West Africa*

Kingsley's emotive and horrific description of the customs of the Fan (or Fang) tribesmen served to fuel the Victorian appetite for wild fantasies and prejudices about Africa.

The Fan is full of fire, temper, intelligence, and go; very teachable, rather difficult to manage, quick to take offence, and utterly indifferent

to human life. I ought to say that other people, who should know him
better than I, say he is a treacherous, thievish, murderous cannibal. I
never found him treacherous; but then I never trusted him . . . 'The
cannibalism of the Fans, although a prevalent habit, is no danger, I
think, to white people, except as regards the bother it gives one in
preventing one's black companions from getting eaten. The Fan is not
a cannibal from sacrificial motives like the negro. He does it in his
common sense way. Man's flesh, he says, is good to eat, very good, and
he wishes you would try it. Oh dear no, he never eats it himself, but the
next-door town does. He is always very much abused for eating his
relations, but he really does not do this. He will eat his next door
neighbour's relations and sell his own deceased to his next door
neighbour in return; but he does not buy slaves and fatten them up for
his table as some of the Middle-Congo Tribes I know of do. He has no
slaves, no prisoners of war, no cemeteries, so you must draw your own
conclusions. No, my friend, I will not tell you any cannibal stories.

(2) GABON: FANG TRADITIONAL
Song of the Will-o'-the-Wisp

*The spirit of fire is a powerful symbol in Fang tradition. It moves
and acts unpredictably, invoking fear, awe and sometimes a
challenge. This Song is included in the anthology* Voices from
Twentieth-Century Africa – *see Booklist.*

Fire that men see only at night, dark night,
Fire that burns without warming, that shines without burning,
Fire that flies without body and without support, that knows neither
   house nor hearth,

. . .

Fire of sorcerers, spirit of the waters underground, spirit of the upper
   airs,
Flash that shines, firefly that lights the swamp,
Bird without wings, thing without body, spirit of the strength of fire,
Hear my words, a man without fear calls you.

(3) GABON: PYGMY

Pygmy Song

This Pygmy satire was improvised before whites against the tribe's negro overlords. Once the dominant tribe, the Pygmies were soon overtaken by the migrating Fang. This extract is taken from Willard Trask's The Unwritten Song – see Booklist.

The forest is vast, the wind is right.
Forward, the tribe, bow on arm!
This way, that way, that way and this.
A pig! – Who kills the pig? –
The Pygmy – But who'll eat it? – Poor Pygmy!
Still, cut it up: you'll get the entrails to chew on . . .

. . .

Without a house, like the monkeys.
Who gathers honey? – The Pygmy –
And who guzzles it and gets fat? – Poor Pygmy –
Still, bring it down; they'll leave you the wax! . . .

(4) LAMBARÉNÉ

Albert Schweitzer, *From My African Notebook*

Schweitzer, as well as serving as a brilliant doctor and organizer, often had to play the diplomat at Lambaréné. Having learnt much about the different tribes' customs and laws, he then applied his humanist approach to difficult decision making.

Very early one morning the noise of an altercation at the Hospital was wafted up to our dwelling-house. In the night a patient had taken another man's canoe and gone out fishing by moonlight. The owner of the boat surprised him as he returned at dawn and demanded for the use of the canoe a large monetary compensation as well as all the fish he had caught. By the laws current among the natives, this was his actual right.

The case was brought before me and, as often before, I had to act as judge. First I made known that on my land not native law, but the law of reason of the white man is in force and is proclaimed by my lips. Then I proceeded to examine the legal position.

I established the fact that both men were at the same time right and wrong. 'You are right,' I said to the owner of the canoe, 'because the other man ought to have asked for permission to use your boat. But you are wrong because you are careless and lazy. You were careless because you merely twisted the chain of your canoe round a palm-tree instead of fastening it with a padlock as you ought to do here. By your carelessness you led this other man into temptation to make use of your canoe. Of laziness you are guilty because you were asleep in your hut on this moonlight night instead of making use of the good opportunity for fishing.'

'But you,' I said, turning to the other, 'were in the wrong when you took the boat without asking the owner's permission. You were in the right because you were not so lazy as he was and you did not want to let the moonlight night go by without making some use of it.'

In view of the established legal usage, I then gave sentence that the man who went fishing must give a third of the fish to the owner as compensation, and might keep one-third for himself because he had taken the trouble to catch the fish. The remaining third I claimed for the Hospital, because the affair took place here and I had to waste my time adjusting the palaver.

Biographies and important works

KINGSLEY, Mary Henrietta (1862–1900). London-born Kingsley led a distinctly sheltered life until her late twenties. Then, following the death of her father, and casting off the conventions of the time, she set off to Africa. Her original aim was to study African law and religion to complete a book her father had left unfinished. Her extensive travels took her through western and equatorial Africa. Arriving in 1893 at Cabinda, Angola, she collected beetles and fish for the British Museum from the Congo River. In 1894 she became the first European to venture into parts of Gabon. Following the **Ogooué River** she entered Fang territory – a tribe which, according to the rumours of the time, had a taste for cannibalism. Kingsley also visited **Corisco** island off the coast. Back in England, with more for natural history collections, she gave numerous lectures across the country in 1896–99. *Travels in West Africa* (Extract 1) is an entertaining and informative account of her travels and researches. She returned to Africa and died of fever while looking after casualties of the Boer War.

SCHWEITZER, Albert (1875–1965). The German theologian, physician, moralist and musician (renowned for his interpretations of Bach) was born in Alsace (then in Germany) and studied theology at Strasbourg University. In 1904, after reading an article about the diseases of the area that is now Gabon, Schweitzer decided to become a missionary doctor in Africa, gave up his university posts and commenced with medical studies (whose fees were paid with money from his concerts). He and his wife, who by then had trained as a nurse, arrived at **Lambaréné** in April 1913. Initially their hospital was run out of a converted chicken coop from where Schweitzer dealt with a myriad of diseases, including malaria, leprosy and hernias. In 1914 he and his wife were thrown out of the French territory when war was declared against the Germans. In 1924, after a long illness and depression, Schweitzer returned to continue his work in Gabon. The original hospital was in ruins and he built a new one a few miles away. As more funds were raised the hospital grew into 75 bungalows treating up to 1000 patients a day who travelled from miles around. Once described as 'the greatest man in the world' by *Time* magazine, he was awarded the Nobel Peace Prize in 1952 and he used the money to build a village for 300 lepers. He died in Lambaréné at the age of 90. As well as several early theological books, he published *My Life and Thought*, an autobiography. Albert Schweitzer's experiences in Africa are described and analysed in *On the Edge of the Primeval Forest* and *From My African Notebook* (Extract 4).

RWANDA AND BURUNDI

'The Punch and Judy of Africa.'
Anon

The names of these two tiny mountainous countries, tucked away in the heart of Africa, trip poetically off the tongue together. But it is there that the pleasantries between these twinned countries end, and a murderous mirroring begins. Among the smallest and most densely populated countries on the continent, they were originally inhabited by the Twa Pygmies, who today make up only 1% of the population. Migrating Hutu from West Africa displaced them first, followed by the Tutsi who came from the East in the sixteenth and seventeenth centuries. While the Hutu dominated numerically in both countries (around 85%), it was the Tutsi who secured power, subjugating the Hutu with a feudal system that revolved around complicated land and cattle contracts.

As the countries entered the twentieth century, it was clear that this lord–peasant relationship could and should not last (despite the apparent compliance of the colonists and the Christian missionaries). In Rwanda in 1959, when the peasants tried to protest, their leaders were murdered. The reprisal was a bloody battle in which over 100 000 Tutsi were murdered, and the Hutu gained control at independence in 1962. That same year independence was declared in Burundi, but the minority Tutsi still ruled the roost. It was not until 1965 that the long-repressed Hutu there rebelled, making several unsuccessful coup attempts. In 1972 the Tutsi found a simple solution to the challenges – the genocide of every Hutu with education, money or a good job. Nearly 250 000 Hutu were killed and some 100 000 fled to Rwanda, Zaire and Tanzania.

It is hard to believe that these horrific purges in Burundi happened barely 20 years ago, and those in Rwanda just over 30 years ago. Amid the silence which was cast mysteriously over Africa and the rest of the world at the time, a few voices spoke out against the atrocities. What happened in Rwanda was, said Bertrand Russell in 1964, 'the most

---

FACT BOX

Rwanda
AREA: 26 335 sq km
POPULATION: 7 100 000
CAPITAL: Kigali
LANGUAGES: French, Kinyarwanda, Swahili
FORMER COLONIAL POWER: Belgium
INDEPENDENCE: 1962

Burundi
AREA: 27 731 sq km
POPULATION: 5 700 000
CAPITAL: Bujumbura
LANGUAGES: French, Kirundi, Swahili
FORMER COLONIAL POWER: Germany, Belgium
INDEPENDENCE: 1962

---

horrible and systematic human massacre we have had occasion to witness since the extermination of the Jews by the Nazis'. A *Los Angeles Times* correspondent entering the capital of Burundi in 1972 reported, 'It is a little like entering Warsaw after World War II, and finding few Jews there.'

Not only is it difficult to imagine any literary life under these circumstances, but before the purges the 'god-given' missionaries had concentrated their efforts almost solely on educating the Tutsi (effectively ignoring the Hutu). The literature that survives and thrives is oral. Identity-confirming songs, folk tales and fables set to music, take preference over written works with the majority of the population. 'Song of the Bridesmaids' is traditionally sung to the bride to calm her nerves. In a more emancipated country it might well have the opposite effect – 'Resign yourself, do like all the others./A man is not a leopard,/A husband is not a thunderstroke,/. . . It will not kill you to grind the grain,/Nor will it kill you to wash the pots./Nobody dies from gathering firewood/Nor from washing clothes . . . (from *Voices from Twentieth-Century Africa*).

One of the rare Rwandan poets who has appeared in English translation as representative of his country, is Jean-Baptiste Mutabaruka ◊. A Tutsi, he tries to combine traditional rhythms with formally grounded poetry (Extract 3). In his epic poem 'Song of the Drum', he recalls, 'The years of brutalization/When the awakening of the pattering mornings/Sounded on the dusty roofs/Of our burned huts . . .'. The same, of course, can be claimed by the Huti in Burundi, where he has since taken up residence.

Another Rwandan writer is J.S. Naigiziki, who has written two books, neither of which appear to have made their way into English from the French. One is a narrative of life in Rwanda and the other is a collection of plays, first published in Rwanda in 1956. Since literature and even a holocaust could not put Rwanda on the international map, it was left to the country's mountain gorillas to do the job. Under threat of extinction from poachers and disappearing forest, several researchers appeared on the mountainside in what is now the **Parc National des Volcans**. While there were many more qualified, the one who gained lasting fame was an eccentric American called Dian Fossey ◊, whose mentor and early supporter was the world famous anthropologist Dr Leakey. A dedicated loner, Fossey lived and worked for the best part of 13 years in a damp camp on the slopes of **Mount Visoke** and **Mount Karisimbi**. She gave the gorillas names like Beethoven, Peanuts and Macho, and was called 'Nyramacibili' ('small woman') by the local Rwandans. In *Gorillas in the Mist* (Extract 2) she records her most rewarding experiences as an anthropologist: 'Peanuts, Group 8's youngest male, was feeding about fifteen feet away when he suddenly stopped and turned to stare directly at me. The expression in his eyes was unfathomable. Spellbound, I returned his gaze – a gaze that seemed to combine elements of inquiry and of acceptance. Peanuts ended this unforgettable moment by sighing deeply, and slowly resumed feeding. Jubilant I returned to camp and cabled Dr Leakey I'VE FINALLY BEEN ACCEPTED BY A GORILLA.'

Much of Fossey's work was taken up with protecting the gorillas from poachers. Her battle with them ended in 1985 when she was found murdered in her tent. Since her death she has become something of a cult figure and several books and a film have subsequently appeared about her life. Her philosophy was appropriately summed up by Harold Hayes in *The Dark Romance of Dian Fossey* with a Rwandan proverb: 'You can outdistance that which is running after you but not what is running inside you.'

Unless attracted by the exclusive and expensive sport of gorilla watching, few people find the inclination to drop in on Rwanda or Burundi. Flying out of one trouble spot and unexpectedly into Burundi, Polish writer Ryszyard Kapuściński (◊ Angola) enthused: 'This was Africa the arch-beautiful, the fairy-tale Africa of forests and lakes, of a cloudless peaceful sky.' The magic wore off when, upon landing visa-less at **Bujumbura** (then known as Usumbura under the Belgians), he and his two travelling companions were locked up, interrogated, and awaited a certain death (Extract 1).

Similar experiences were had by the hero in V.S. Naipaul's (◊ Côte

Dian Fossey

d'Ivoire) *A Bend in the River* who passed through these countries driving from the east coast to Zaire ('That isn't the kind of drive you can do nowadays in Africa . . . too many of the places have closed down or are full of blood.'). Apart from the treacherous narrow, winding mountain roads of these countries, he had to deal with 'all that business at the frontier posts, all that haggling in the forest outside wooden huts that flew strange flags'. As he, the Tutsi, the Hutu, and Kapuściński discovered, 'You can always get into those places. What is hard is to get out.'

LITERARY LANDMARKS

Rwanda. On the slopes of **Mount Visoke** and **Mount Karisimbi** in the **Parc National des Volcans**, researcher Dian Fossey spent over ten years living, studying and working to protect the gorillas against poachers. When she was murdered in 1985 there were around 250 left.

Libraries and Bookshops

Burundi. American Cultural Centre, Chaussée Prince Rwagasore, Bujumbura; Burundi Literature Centre, BP 18, Gitega; French Cultural Centre, Chaussée Prince Rwagasore, Bujumbura.

Rwanda. Bookshop, Avenue de la Paix, Kigali; French Cultural Centre Library, Gisenyi and Kigali; US Embassy Library, Kigali.

BOOKLIST

The following selection includes the extracted titles in this chapter as well as those mentioned in the introduction which are available in English and other titles for further reading. In general, paperback editions are given when possible. The editions cited are not necessarily the only ones available. For most of the extracted works, the original publisher in English can be found in 'Acknowledgments and Citations' at the end of the volume, as can the exact location of the extracts and the editions from which they are taken. Extract numbers are highlighted in bold for ease of reference.

African Writing Today, Ezekiel Mphahlele, ed, Penguin, London, 1967. **Extract 3.**

Fossey, Dian, *Gorillas in the Mist,* Penguin, London, 1985. **Extract 2.**

Hayes, Harold, *The Dark Romance of Dian Fossey,* Chatto and Windus, London, 1991.

Kapuściński, Ryszard, *The Soccer War,* Granta Books, London, 1990. **Extract 1.**

H. Lane and R. Pillard, *The Wild Boy of Burundi,* Random House, New York, 1978.

Naipaul, V.S., *A Bend in the River,* Penguin, London, 1980.

Voices from Twentieth-Century Africa, Chinweizu, ed, Faber and Faber, London, 1988.

Extracts

(1) BURUNDI: BUJUMBURA

Ryszard Kapuściński, *The Soccer War*

Flying haplessly into Bujumbura, Kapuściński and his two companions find themselves held prisoners at the airport. Through the window they make contact with a steward who says he will try to contact the United Nations to help them. As Kapuściński sweats out the wait his thoughts speak too for the scars inflicted upon the countrymen of Burundi.

The hours of torture began. The steward had tossed a crumb of hope into our cell and it jolted us out of our state of paralysis and overpowering depression, a kind of self-deafening that I now see was a defence against insanity. For those awaiting death as we were, passive and apathetic, on the verge of collapse, ready to hit bottom, it takes only one flash of light in the darkness, one lucky break, and suddenly you rise up again and return to the living. What you leave behind, however, is an empty territory that you cannot even describe: it has no points of reference or shape or signposts, and its existence – like the sound barrier – is something you feel only once you have approached it. One step out of that emptiness and it disappears. No one, however, who has entered this emptiness can ever be the same person he was before. Something remains – a psychological scar, hardened, gangrened flesh – a fact, finally, more apparent to others than to himself, that something has burned out, that something is missing. You pay for every meeting with death.

(2) RWANDA: PARC DES VOLCANS

Dian Fossey, *Gorillas in the Mist*

The most memorable contact of her life with the gorillas, said Dian Fossey, was when a gorilla first touched her. Remarkably it was Peanuts, the same gorilla that two years previously had 'exchanged glances' with her.

The day had started out as an ordinary one, if any day working from Karisoke might be considered ordinary . . . I had just settled down on a comfortable moss-cushioned *Hagenia* tree trunk when Peanuts, wearing his 'I want to be entertained' expression, left his feeding group to meander inquisitively toward us. Slowly I left the tree and pretended to munch on vegetation to reassure Peanuts that I meant him no harm.

Peanuts' bright eyes peered at me through a latticework of vegetation as he began his strutting, swaggering approach. Suddenly he was at my side and sat down to watch my 'feeding' techniques as if it were my turn to entertain him. When Peanuts seemed bored with the 'feeding' routine, I scratched my head, and almost immediately, he began scratching his own. Since he appeared totally relaxed, I lay back in the foliage, slowly extended my hand, palm upward, then rested it on the leaves. After looking intently at my hand, Peanuts stood up and extended his hand to touch his fingers against my own for a brief instant. Thrilled at his own daring, he gave vent to his excitement by a quick chestbeat before going off to rejoin his group. Since that day, the spot has been called *Fasi Ya Mkoni*, 'the Place of the Hands.'

(3) RWANDA: TRIBES

Jean-Baptiste Mutabaruka, *Song of the Drum*

Mutabaruka, a Rwandan Tutsi who lives in exile in Burundi, sings of exile, war and tribal rivalry. His sentiments mirror the experiences of both the Tutsi and the Hutu tribes. This extract is taken from the anthology African Writing Today – see Booklist.

Tell me, yes tell me
Your word of advice
The dull-witted pebble
Oh no, it's the uncertain step . . .
A swallow of creamy milk
A handful of narrow-leaved sprays
A little walk behind the house
A blow at the friendly fire
A quick touch of father's weapons . . .
Who will reawaken this long-smothered flame
To its burning?

Biographies and important works

FOSSEY, Dian (1932–1985). The American Dian Fossey started her research on gorillas in Zaire, where she won the support of prominent anthropologist Louis Leakey. When her first camp and enthusiasm were lost to rebels, she moved to Rwanda and started work 3000 m up in the northern mountains. Her work to dispel the myth of gorillas as violent, aggressive and stupid carnivores earned her a doctorate from Cambridge University and is recorded in the book *Gorillas in the Mist* (Extract 2). Of her companions for many lonely years, she once hinted to a visitor, 'the more that you learn about the dignity of the gorillas, the more you want to avoid people'. Dian Fossey was murdered in 1985. *Gorillas in the Mist* was made into a film in 1988, starring Sigourney Weaver as Fossey.

KAPUŚCIŃSKI, Ryszard (see under Angola).

MUTABARUKA, Jean-Baptiste (1927–). Mutabaruka was born in eastern Rwanda, the son of a Catholic cattle farmer. He was brought up and educated in the traditions of the Tutsi people, and later attended a Catholic school in Leopoldville (now Kinshasa, Zaire). His work blends those backgrounds. Mutabaruka is now an exile in Burundi.

NAIPAUL, V.S. (see under Côte d'Ivoire).

SÃO TOMÉ AND PRÍNCIPE

'These volcanic islands are all of extreme beauty and fertility . . . and they are all exceedingly unhealthy.'
Mary Kingsley,
Travels in West Africa

So little known is the Republic of São Tomé and Príncipe that when delegates to these tiny islands arrived at the 1977 Organization of African Unity (OAU) summit in Gabon, they were reported to have been asked by the organizers 'Are you sure that's in Africa?'. Yet despite their apparent isolation and perceived insignificance, these islands were occupied by the greedy early European navigators who discovered them uninhabited in the 1470s. By the sixteenth century the islands were occupied by the Portuguese who had hastily established sugar plantations and settled convicts, exiled Jews and slaves from the mainland to work in them.

São Tomé soon became a significant slave entrepôt and as interest in the islands grew they attracted the attention of the Dutch who took over for part of the seventeenth century: 'San Thomé is still called "The Dutchman's Church-yard"', reported traveller Mary Kingsley (◊ Gabon) in the 1890s, 'on account of the devastation its climate wrought among the Hollanders when they once occupied it: as they seem, at one time or another, to have occupied all Portuguese possessions out here, during the long war these two powers waged with each other for supremacy in the Bights, a supremacy that neither of them attained to.'

Out of this cultural melting pot emerged three distinctive Creole languages whose vocabulary is based 90% on Portuguese while the grammar and pronunciation can be traced to the languages of the ancient Benin and Kongo kingdoms (whence came the most slaves). The main literary expression of the Principenses and the Santomense is oral – with poetry, dance and drama playing an important part in the Creole culture. Written literature meanwhile had more currency with

---

FACT BOX

AREA: 964 sq km (São Tomé 854 sq km)
POPULATION: 120 000
CAPITAL: São Tomé
LANGUAGES: Portuguese
FORMER COLONIAL POWER: Portugal
INDEPENDENCE: 1975

---

the indigenous intellectual élite, many of whom had been educated in Portugal, and who therefore tended to write in Portuguese.

Caetano da Costa Alegre was one such writer. Born into a relatively wealthy black family in 1864, he was packed off to Portugal for his education, and there wrote *Verses*, a collection of 96 love poems. It was not until long after Alegre's death in 1890 that there emerged another writer of note. Franciso José Tenreiro, a Creole, born in 1928 to a black mother and a white father, also spent most of his life in Portugal. His collection of poetry *Ilha de Nome Santo* is now recognized as the first Lusaphone expression of the spirit and sentiments of *Négritude*.

It was not until more recently, with the appearance of poet Alda do Espírito Santo ◊, that there emerged a genuinely local written literature. Unlike her predecessors she has spent most of her life in São Tomé, and a little of her work has been translated and occasionally appears in anthologies (Extract 1). While there is what might be safely described as a minimal audience for Santomean and Principense literature outside the country itself, another inhibition to its development is a limited local market. Sadly, despite increasing literacy and the efforts of Santo and her contemporaries, there are still limited local possibilities for publication in either newspaper or book form.

Libraries and Bookshops
Fang: Municipal Library. **Songe**: Municipal Library.

BOOKLIST

Hodges and Newitt, *São Tomé and Príncipe: From Plantation Colony to Microstate*, Westview, Boulder, Co, 1988.

Santo, Aldo do Espírito, 'Where are the Men Seized in this Wind of Madness?', in *The Penguin Book of Modern African Poetry*, Gerald Moore and Ulli Beier, eds, Penguin, London, 1984. **Extract 1**.

Extract

(1) São Tomé and Príncipe: Independence

Aldo do Espírito Santo,
Where are the Men Seized in this Wind of Madness?

The poet recalls the struggles and the neglected cries of her countrymen in the fight for nationality and independence. This poem is included in The Penguin Book of Modern African Poetry – see Booklist.

And the blood of lives fallen
in the forests of death,
innocent blood
drenching the earth
in a silence of terrors
shall make the earth fruitful,
crying for justice.
It is the flame of humanity
singing of hope
in a world without bonds
where liberty
is the fatherland of men . . .

Biographies and important works

KINGSLEY, Mary (see under Gabon).

SANTO, Aldo do Espírito (1926–). Despite a brief spell in Lisbon, Santo has spent most of her life teaching in her native **São Tomé**. Her pre-independence poems with titles such as 'The Sacred Soil of the Land is Ours' describe several unsavoury suppressions that took place on the islands in the 1950s. She taught in schools in São Tomé until independence in 1975, when she was appointed the country's Minister of Education and Culture. She has since produced little poetry, though she remains an inspiration for local writers.

ZAIRE

'It had become a place of darkness. But there was in it one river especially, a mighty big river, that you could see on the map, resembling an immense snake uncoiled, with its head in the sea, its body at rest curving afar over a vast country, and its tail lost in the depths of the land. And as I looked at the map of it in a shopwindow, it fascinated me as a snake would a bird – a silly little bird.'
Joseph Conrad,
Heart of Darkness

When Joseph Conrad ◊ was a child in Poland he pointed his finger at the uncharted centre of a map of Africa and said, 'When I grow up I shall go there.' This was the undiscovered heart of the last unexplored continent, and as such the centre of Africa had long held a fascination for the European romantic imagination.

As a result of the Berlin Conference in 1855, this central territory, today occupied by Zaire, was given to the Belgian King as his personal possession. At that Conference the European powers divided up Africa among themselves – regardless of whether the territories in question had ever been explored by Europeans. It was not until over 20 years later that Sir Henry Morton Stanley (◊ Tanzania) became the first European to map the **Congo River** thus providing an overall picture of this region which had previously remained blank on the maps.

Such was the European 'scramble for Africa' that by the time Joseph Conrad eventually fulfilled his childhood dream and arrived here, he was appalled by the havoc created by unscrupulous colonial exploration. *Heart of Darkness* is based on his experiences as captain of a steamship on the Congo River in 1890 (Extract 5). The title expresses how, in the collective European imagination, the romantic heart of Africa became a symbol for evil.

This was not to deter the British writer Graham Greene (◊ Sierra Leone) who had already marched through Liberia and lived awhile in

FACT BOX

AREA: 2 345 410 sq km
POPULATION: 38 473 000
CAPITAL: Kinshasa
LANGUAGES: French, Swahili, Tshiluba, Lingala, Kikongo
FORMER COLONIAL POWER: Belgium
INDEPENDENCE: 1960

Sierra Leone. On the contrary, it was the writings of Conrad and the fascination of this 'heart of darkness' that drew him here. A *Burnt-Out Case* (Extract 2), written in 1961 and one of Greene's most profound later novels, is the result of his visit to a leper colony at **Yonda** up a tributary of the **Congo River**. The protagonist of the novel is the incongruous and spiritually exhausted Catholic architect Querry, whose situation was in many ways similar to Greene's own at the time.

The Belgians were to continue with their ramshackle exploitative colonial administration until the territory was awarded independence in 1960. This took place with practically no prior instruction in government, and the country quickly fell apart in a bloody civil war, encouraged by Europeans who wished to see the rich mining area of **Katanga** (today called **Shaba**) province secede. Bands of foreign mercenaries and local armies employed by the warring factions roamed the countryside, virtually at will. Massacres and atrocities were rife, and eventually the United Nations sent in troops to try to bring about some form of stability. During this period, two great leaders lost their lives. In 1961 Lumumba, the head of the government was murdered and the President of the United Nations, Hammarskjold, on a vain mission to sort out the chaos, was killed when his plane was shot down. The civil war finally came to an end when Mobuto took power in 1965, and in 1970 the Congo changed its name to Zaire – a local African name for a large river. Today Zaire is the third largest African country (after Sudan and Algeria) and its capital **Kinshasa** the largest city in black Africa.

The people of this region were the first in sub-Saharan Africa to write in a European language. About 500 years ago, the kings of the Kongo sent written messages, by way of the early Portuguese explorers, to their fellow monarchs in Portugal (see under Congo). At the end of the nineteenth century the Belgian missionaries began translating sections of the Bible and religious tracts into the local Kikongo language. But it was not until the 1940s that the first novelists appeared, in the form of Emile Disengomka and Jacques N. Bahele who began publishing works in Kikongo.

After the second world war, the magazine *La Voix du Congolais* was launched under the editorship of Antoine-Roger Bolamba ♭. This became a useful platform for a generation of new Zairean writers, despite the fact that it had to remain under paternalistic (and tight) colonial control. In 1955, Bolamba's book of poems *Esanzo: Chants pour mon Pays* became the first Zairean work to be published in Paris. This rhythmic and sensitive expression of the tenets of *Négritude* has since been translated into English (*Esanzo: Songs for My Country*), which is a considerable achievement for a Zairean writer for several reasons (Extract 3).

While Francophone writers in French (or former French) colonies could look to the cultural centre of Paris for appreciation and distribution throughout the Francophone world, the Zaireans had only Brussels, which is hardly a great cultural capital. (Even Belgian writers find it difficult to get their work appreciated, so what chance a member of their former African colony?) The effect of this handicap has been double-edged. Because of the difficulties of publication in Belgium, Zaire has established an unusually large number of indigenous publishing houses. This guarantees a lively local cultural scene – but a scene which is isolated from the global centres of culture. Consequently, though there are a good many Zairean writers of genuine talent, hardly any have been translated into English.

Besides Bolamba, the only other author to have crossed the cultural divide into English in any significant sense is V.Y. Mudimbe ♭, whose stylistic abilities have shown him to be the finest writer of his generation in Zaire. His novels *Before the Birth of the Moon* (Extract 1), and *Between the Tides* are both available in English. The latter is about a priest who becomes a Communist guerrilla, only to realize that he has merely exchanged one restrictive dogma for another.

Of the untranslated writers, several are worthy of note. Even before independence, Paul Lomani-Tshibamba, who was born in 1914, won a literary prize in Belgium for his novel *Ngando* ('The Crocodile'). Since independence Clementine Nzuzihas achieved renown for her researches into local folklore and Philip Masegabio has established himself as a poet of considerable national stature. Elebe Lisembe has produced prose works of interest, including the essayistic novel *Giambattista Viko*, which admirably attempts to relate the form of the novel to earlier Zairean oral traditions (see Extract 4 for a typically colourful and expressive example of oral literature).

LITERARY LANDMARKS

(See also under Congo – Literary Landmarks, Congo River)

Kinshasa. Formerly known as Leopoldville, after the King of the

Graham Greene in 1982

Belgians who 'owned' the Congo but never set foot in it. The controversial Irish 'traitor' Sir Roger Casement wrote the first assessment of the Congo for the British government, drawing attention to widespread corruption and malpractice while consul here in 1901–04. Joseph Conrad passed up river from Kinshasa as captain of one of the many riverboats.

Kisangani. Formerly known as Stanleyville, after the explorer Sir Henry Morton Stanley (◊ Tanzania). The nearby **Boyoma Falls** were also once named after him.

Yonda. The leper colony on a tributary of the **Congo River** (now called the **Zaire River**) which Graham Greene visited and described in his novel A *Burnt-Out Case*.

Libraries and Bookshops

Kinshasa. Éditions Edimaf, BP 16367, Kinshasa 1; Éditions de la Grue

Coinnée, BP 3986, Kinshasa-Gombe; Éditions Lokole, Département de L'Information Culture et Arts, Kinshasa-Gombe; Presses Universitaires du Zaire, BP 1682, Kinshasa 1.

Lubumbashi. Centre d'Études des Littératures Romanes d'Inspiration Africaine (CELRIA), Campus de Lubumbashi.

BOOKLIST

The following selection includes the extracted titles in this chapter as well as those mentioned in the introduction which are available in English and other titles for further reading. In general, paperback editions are given when possible. The editions cited are not necessarily the only ones available. For most of the extracted works, the original publisher in English can be found in 'Acknowledgments and Citations' at the end of the volume, as can the exact location of the extracts and the editions from which they are taken. Extract numbers are highlighted in bold for ease of reference.

Bolamba, Antoine-Roger, *Esanzo: Songs of My Country*, Sherbrook, Canada, 1977.

Bolamba, Antoine-Roger, 'A Fistful of News', in *The Penguin Book of Modern African Poetry*, Gerald Moore and Ulli Beier, eds, Penguin, London, 1984. **Extract 3.**

Conrad, Joseph, *Heart of Darkness*, Penguin, London, 1987. **Extract 5.**

Gide, André, *Travels in the Congo*, University of California Press, Los Angeles, CA, 1962.

Greene, Graham, *A Burnt-Out Case*, Penguin, London, 1991. **Extract 2.**

Greene, Graham, *Congo Journal*, Penguin, London, 1987.

Mudimbe, V.Y., *Before the Birth of the Moon*, Simon and Schuster, New York, 1989. **Extract 1.**

Mudimbe, V.Y., *Between the Tides*, Simon and Schuster, New York, 1991.

Myths and Legends of the Congo, collected by Jan Knappert, Heinemann, London, 1971.

Naipaul, V.S., *A Bend in the River*, Penguin, London, 1979.

Stanley, H.M., *Life and Finding of Dr Livingstone*, Dean and Sons, London, 1874.

Voices from Twentieth-Century Africa, Chinweizu, ed, Faber and Faber, London, 1988. **Extract 4.**

Extracts

(1) KINSHASA

V.Y. Mudimbe, *Before the Birth of the Moon*

In this story of the shifting relationship between a prostitute and a minister of state, Mudimbe is concerned with their innermost thoughts which reveal their true identity. Here the prostitute meets her girlfriend and they walk through the streets of Kinshasa.

She smiled at her as soon as she recognized her. The other responded in kind. Both of them had dark circles under their eyes, tired faces. She offered her a cigarette. It was refused.

'Things not going well?'

'No, I'm just exhausted, that's all.'

'Shall we take a cab?'

'No, please. Let's walk. I feel like walking. I think that'll do me good.'

Ten o'clock in the morning. The city was full of people. She takes her hand. They begin to walk: two good little girls walking quietly along the avenues. The shop windows don't appeal to them at all. They go down the Boulevard du 30 Juin; then, around Bata, they begin their climb up to the Great Market.

'What happened?'

'Nothing. Not really anything. Well, nothing special.'

'Is he pestering you, this politician of yours?'

'As always. He wears me out, but . . .'

'Don't tell me you're in love!'

'No, that isn't it.'

A faint smile appears. The pressing of her hand? As they reach the Memling Hotel, taxi drivers first whistle at them, then accost them verbally with blunt and obvious vulgarities. They're an easy target. They laugh it off and continue to push through the middle of a crowd that grows more and more dense. The poor were climbing up with the sun to attack the rich, European section of town. Multicolored waves, all cries, noise, song, and laughter. So as not to lose each other in this flow, they hold each other by the waist.

'So what about your politician? You were saying . . .'

'I don't feel like seeing him anymore.'

'That's not very hard. Send him on his way.'

(2) YONDA

Graham Greene, *A Burnt-Out Case*

*Querry, the protagonist and 'burnt-out case' of the novel has
'retired' to a leper colony at Yonda, up a tributary on the far
reaches of the Congo. Life was peaceful until the arrival of
Parkinson, a persistent American journalist who has come to
write a sensational story about the new life of this famous
Catholic architect.*

'You'd need to be a kind of a saint, wouldn't you, to bury yourself here.'

'No. Not a saint.'

'Then what are you? What are your motives? I know a lot about you
already. I've briefed myself,' Parkinson said. He sat his great weight
down on the bed and said confidingly, 'You aren't exactly a man who
loves his fellows, are you? Leaving out women, of course.' There is a
strong allurement in corruption and there was no doubt of Parkinson's;
he carried it on the surface of his skin like phosphorus, impossible to
mistake. Virtue had died long ago within that mountain of flesh for
lack of air. A priest might not be shocked by human failings, but he
could be hurt or disappointed; Parkinson would welcome any kind of
failing. Nothing would hurt Parkinson or disappoint him but the size of
a cheque.

'You heard what the doctor called me just now – one of the burnt-out
cases. They are the lepers who lose everything that can be eaten away
before they are cured.'

'You are a whole man as far as one can see,' said Parkinson, looking
at the fingers resting on the drawing-board.

'I've come to an end. This place, you might say, is the end. Neither
the road nor the river go any further.'

(3) ZAIRE: NÉGRITUDE

Antoine-Roger Bolamba, *A Fistful of News*

*In these lines from the poem, Bolamba expresses, in the name
and voice of Négritude, the anguish of identity and existence in
Zaire. 'A Fistful of News' is included in The Penguin Book of
Modern African Poetry – see Booklist.*

> The hills hunch their backs
> and leap above the marshes
> that wash about the calabash
> of the Great Soul

Rumours of treason spread
like burning swords
the veins of the earth
swell with nourishing blood
the earth bears
towns villages hamlets
forests and woods
peopled with monsters horned and tentacled
their long manes are the mirror of the Sun

they are those who when night has come
direct the regiments of bats
and who sharpen their arms
upon the stone of horror

(4) Zaire: Oral Tradition

Bakongo address for the Feast of the Dead

*This traditional address of the Bakongo tribe concerns behaviour
to be adopted at the Feast of the Dead.*

You have come to the festival,
Men and women.
Of quarrelsome people, let there be none among you.
The husband who has brought his wife
Must spend with her the night in the same place.
He who has no wife
Shall not take one belonging to someone else.
My whole village, I have pacified.
He who has the mastery over fetishes
Let him leave them in his own village.
If anyone wants to prowl at night like a witch,
Let him beware, our fetishes will make him jump.
It will be said: he has eaten bad food at the festival,
In truth, he will have devoured his own self.

Joseph Conrad

(5) ZAIRE RIVER

Joseph Conrad, *Heart of Darkness*

Conrad's classic story describes the sailor Marlow's journey up the Congo River, and his meeting with the infamous and evil Kurtz.

Going up that river was like travelling back to the earliest beginnings of the world, when vegetation rioted on the earth, and the big trees were kings. An empty stream, a great silence, an impenetrable forest. The air was warm, thick, heavy, sluggish. There was no joy in the brilliance of sunshine. The long stretches of the waterway ran on, deserted, into the gloom of overshadowed distances. On silvery mudbanks hippos and alligators sunned themselves side by side. The broadening waters flowed through a mob of wooded islands; you lost your way on that river as you would in a desert and butted all day long against shoals, trying to find the channel, till you thought yourself bewitched and cut off for ever from everything you had known once – somewhere – far away – in another existence perhaps. There were moments when one's past came back to one, as it will sometimes when you have not a moment to spare to yourself; but it came in the shape of an unrestful and noisy dream, remembered with wonder amongst the overwhelming realities of this strange world of plants, and water and silence. And this stillness of life did not in the least resemble a peace. It was the stillness of an implacable force brooding over an inscrutable intention. It looked at you with a vengeful aspect. I got used to it afterwards.

Biographies and important works

BOLAMBA, Antoine-Roger (1913–). Bolamba was born in Leopoldville (now **Kinshasa**). He became Editor of the prestigious literary magazine *La Voix du Congolais*. He published many articles and much poetry in this magazine, and later achieved fame when his book of poems *Esanzo: Chants pour mon Pays* (Songs for My Country) was the first Zairean work to be published in Paris. This was later translated into English with a preface by Léopold Senghor (◊ Senegal).

CONRAD, Joseph (1857–1924). Conrad was born in Poland. He worked for many years as a sailor in the merchant marine, eventually rising to the rank of captain. In the course of his work he travelled widely throughout the Far East. He abandoned the sea to become a writer of novels and short stories when he was 36 years old. *Heart of Darkness* (Extract 5) is considered by many to be one of the finest stories in the English language. It is based on Conrad's experiences while he was captain of a Congo River steamer in 1890. The 'Heart of Darkness' of the title is not only the heart of the dark continent of Africa, but also stands for the heart of evil, personified in this story by the infamous Kurtz, who is eventually encountered at the end of the narrator Marlow's journey up the river. The story formed the basis for Francis Ford Coppola's acclaimed 1979 film about the Vietnam war, *Apocalypse Now*.

GREENE, Graham (see under Sierra Leone).

MUDIMBE, V.Y. (1941–). Considered by many to be the outstanding novelist of his generation in Zaire, Mudimbe's works have deep psychological penetration and yet at the same time manage to reflect the social difficulties of developing Zairean society. His varying style is attuned to the latest developments in French-language writing, but manages to retain a distinctly African flavour. He is widely educated in economics, linguistics and sociology, and received a PhD at the University of Louvain, Belgium. In 1977 he received the Senghor Grand Prize, and he is at present Professor of Comparative Literature at Duke University in North Carolina. His novels *Before the Birth of the Moon* (Extract 1), and more recently *Between the Tides* have been translated into English.

ANGOLA

> 'Nowhere else in the world had I seen such a city, and I may never see anything like it again. It existed for months, and then it suddenly began disappearing. Or rather, quarter after quarter, it was taken on trucks to the port.'
> Ryszard Kapuściński,
> Another Day of Life

Agostinho Neto ◊, Angola's poet–President who warned his countrymen against cultural chauvinism and static socialism was remembered in the *Guardian* as 'a great man who not only wrote history and poetry, but made it'. He was the leader of the Popular Movement for the Liberation of Angola (MPLA) and became the country's first President in 1975. He was described by fellow-writer Oscar Ribas as 'an ideal representative of our country. He is black, his wife is white, and his children are *mestizo.*' In literary terms Neto's poetry is highly respected, coming clearly out of the *Négritude* tradition (Extract 5).

In the golden days of independence, even when his attentions were turned to politics, Neto still played a key part in the activities of the newly formed Angolan Writers Union. There was an unprecedented flurry of literary activity, with competitions, prizes and new publishing opportunities. Up to then, the rumblings of a new intellectual and literary movement (which challenged the colonial establishment) had limited vent. During the 1950s activity and protest centred around two sporadically produced magazines, *Mensagem* and *Cultura*, which came out of the Association of Angola's Native Sons. The members were militant poets and writers of mixed race, most of whom joined the MPLA.

Antonio Jacinto ◊, a poet of European descent, was a devoted contributor though his work is not so much from the guns-and-marching school of writing. More the purveyor of love and reflection on the role of the poet, he often adds a cherished touch of humour to his work (Extract 1). Sometimes clumsy, his work is nevertheless touching amid a sea of suffering. In 'Letter from a Contract Worker' the

---

FACT BOX

AREA: 1 246 000 sq km
POPULATION: 10 301 000
CAPITAL: Luanda
LANGUAGES: Portuguese, Kikongo, Kimbundu, Umbundu,
    Kioko, Fiote, Ganguela
FORMER COLONIAL POWER: Portugal
INDEPENDENCE: 1975

---

long-suffering poet writes 'I wanted to write you a letter/But my love, I don't know why it is,/why, why, why it is, my love,/but you can't read/and I – oh the hopelessness – I can't write.'

Castro Soromenho, who died in 1968, was another author of Portuguese origin, remembered as the 'first Portuguese writer to do justice to Africans'. His father was a mining contract labourer who came here when Castro was a child. He trained as a journalist and travelled widely, and his writing was in the 'realist' mode. Ironically his collection of stories about life in **Luanda Province** as suffered under Portuguese pacification policies won him the Prize for Colonial Literature. Pepetela (the guerrilla pseudonym of Artur Pestana) was born to a white colonial family and wrote several patriotic novels while posted on the front with the MPLA. Political and ironical, his work strives to weave together complicated plots with different levels of allegory and strands of African tradition with elements of a surreal European novel form. In his latest (as yet untranslated) book *O Cão e os Caluandas* (*The Dog and the People of Luanda*), a scruffy stray dog is the sometimes real and sometimes imagined symbol of the people's experience.

The élite of the white Angolan literary faction were Jacinto, the poet and short story writer Costa Andrade, and Luandino Vieira ◊. Despite his Portuguese origins Vieira, a novelist and short story writer, feels himself to be very much an African writer. As well as a forceful member of the MPLA, Vieira has also been credited with creating a literary revolution with his unconventional use of language. *Luuanda* (Extract 4), comprising his early short stories, uses a combination of the indigenous Kimbundu and Portuguese tongues, which are woven freely together. This 'anti-colonial' collection became a *cause célèbre* when it won a Portuguese literary prize in 1965. It has since been translated into English.

Another poet roaming among the ranks of the MPLA is Ngudia Wendel. Influenced by Vieira, his contemporary, he produced a collection called *We Shall Return, Luanda* in 1970.

Behind all the self-searching of the contemporary poets caught up in rhymes and reasons of revolution, lies a lively and lyrical oral literature (Extract 2). An early push to encourage Angolans to preserve the fruits of their oral traditions and to dedicate their 'leisure time to the founding of our literature' came from a Kimbundu, Joaquim Dias Cordeiro da Matta in the nineteenth century. Lost but not forgotten in the rush for cultural revolution, today's discoveries of old traditions are justly rewarding. Sings the proud Aandonga bridegroom, 'Namujezi, your eyes – how fresh-new they are!/And your teeth – as if you had gotten them only yesterday!/And your eyes – like those of hornless cow!'. The 'Song of a Bridegroom in Praise of His Bride' from Chinweizu's anthology *Voices from Twentieth-Century Africa* puts an unfamiliar perspective on *Little Red Riding Hood* and the coy conventions of the Western marriage ceremony. Also found in Chinweizu's anthology is a rare translation of a work by Oscar Ribas. Born in Luanda in 1909, Ribas is a locally famous short story writer, ethnologist and folklorist. His early 'romantic' writing was influenced by the works of the late nineteenth-century Portuguese writers and his later works by the Kimbundu traditional tales. Blind since the age of 21, he has nevertheless continued his writing, researches and his support for the MPLA, though he has relied on private publishing to disseminate many of his works in Angola. The reason, to quote one critic, is that 'he is regarded as intellectually isolated in a country where contemporary writers see literature primarily as a tool to build socialism'.

One of the truly modern generation of writers is Sousa Jamba ◊, an ex-member of the defeated Western-backed UNITA. *Patriots* (Extract 3) is the young author's first novel, which he claims is between 20% and 30% autobiographical. The hero flees Angola after his UNITA-supporting parents are killed. After ten years in exile in Zambia, Hosi Mbueti returns to fight against (and is captured by) the Soviet-supported MPLA of which his brother is a member. In one scene an MPLA soldier realizes there is no real difference between the men on either side: 'The politicians decide; we die.' Jamba's novel *A Lonely Devil*, published in 1993, is set on an imaginary island, not at all unlike Angola, and deals with the cruelty and wickedness engendered by unbending ideology.

While most civilians were trying desperately to escape this mire of mortar and rhetoric in the long war of independence which had started in 1961, there were some who actively sought it out. 'This is your last chance to get to Angola. How about it?' tempted Ryszard Kapuściński's ◊ boss at the Polish Press Agency in the summer of 1975. The civil war was well underway but, keen and determined as ever, Kapuściński managed to beg a lift from one of the last Portuguese military planes flying out of Lisbon. As one of a skeleton cast of foreign journalists there at the time, he spent the next three months travelling with the MPLA and watching the demise and desertion of **Luanda** (Extract 6). The capital was deserted first by the Portuguese, then the Police, the garbagemen, the doctors and finally the pedigree dogs abandoned by their owners. 'Later when all the barbers, repairmen, mail carriers and concierges had left, the stone city lost its reason for existing, its sense. It was like a dry skeleton polished by the wind, a dead bone sticking up out of the ground toward the sun . . . After the exodus of the dogs, the city fell into rigor mortis. So I decided to go to the front.'

In between several blood-curdling forays with the MPLA 'roving thus from checkpoint to checkpoint in an alternating rhythm of dread and joy', Kapuściński was back in the city consoling his solitude by spending time in an obsolete bookshop ('because I like to spend time in the company of books'). In mid-November the enemy were withdrawing from their positions around Luanda, and Kapuściński went to say goodbye to the new MPLA President, Agostinho Neto. They talked about poetry and, gesturing towards a map of the enemy positions, Neto complained about the lack of time he had had recently to compose poetry. As he left for Europe, Kapuściński recalled the words of a poem from Neto's most recent collection: 'Our lands/red as coffee berries/white as cotton/green as fields of grain/we will return.'

LITERARY LANDMARKS

Luanda. On 11 November 1975, while the town was still surrounded by enemy troops, Agostinho Neto proclaimed the People's Republic of Angola. Writer Ryszard Kapuściński spent three months in the frequently waterless and foodless **Tivoli Hotel**, frantically and sometimes furtively telexing his eye-witness reports back to the Polish Press Agency.

Libraries and Bookshops

Luanda. Angolan Institute of Education; Instituto Nacional do Livro e do Disco, CP 1281; Lello SARL, CP 1300; National Library of Angola; University of Angola.

BOOKLIST

The following selection includes the extracted titles in this chapter as well as those mentioned in the introduction which are available in English and other titles for further reading. In general, paperback editions are given when possible. The editions cited are not necessarily the only ones available. For most of the extracted works, the original publisher in English can be found in 'Acknowledgments and Citations' at the end of the volume, as can the exact location of the extracts and the editions from which they are taken. Extract numbers are highlighted in bold for ease of reference.

Harding, Jeremy, *Small Wars, Small Mercies: Journeys in Africa's Disputed Nations*, Viking, London, 1993.

Jacinto, Antonio, 'Poem of Alienation', in *The Penguin Book of Modern African Poetry*, Gerald Moore and Ulli Beier, eds, Penguin, London, 1984. **Extract 1**.

Jamba, Sousa, *A Lonely Devil*, Fourth Estate, London, 1993.

Jamba, Sousa, *Patriots*, Penguin, London, 1992. **Extract 3**.

Kapuściński, Ryszard, *Another Day of Life*, Pan, London, 1987. **Extract 6**.

Neto, Agostinho, 'Kinaxixi', in *The Penguin Book of Modern African Poetry*, Gerald Moore and Ulli Beier, eds, Penguin, London, 1984. **Extract 5**.

Neto, Agostinho, in *Poems of Black Africa*, Wole Soyinka, ed, Heinemann, London, 1987.

Neto, Agostinho, *Sacred Hope*, M. Holnes, trans, Journeyman Press, London, 1988.

Pepetela, *The Adventures of Ngunga*, Writers and Readers Publishing Cooperative, London, 1980.

Pepetela, *Mayombe*, Zimbabwe Publishing House, Harare, 1983.

Vieira, José, *Luuanda*, Heinemann, London, 1980. **Extract 4**.

Vieira, José, *The Real Life of Domingos Xavier*, Heinemann, London, 1978.

Voices from Twentieth-Century Africa, Chinweizu, ed, Faber and Faber, London, 1988. **Extract 2**.

Extracts

(1) ANGOLA: POETS

Antonio Jacinto, *Poem of Alienation*

The angst of an alienated poet in his search for 'the poem of my soul and of my blood', and his inspiration and purpose, is combined with surreal black humour and irony in these lines from Jacinto's 'Poem of Alienation'. The poem is included in the anthology The Penguin Book of Modern African Poetry – see Booklist.

My poem steps outside
wrapped in showy cloths
selling itself
selling
    'lemons, buy me le-e-e-emons'

My poem runs through the streets
with a putrid cloth pad on its head
offering itself
offering
    'mackerel, sardine, sprats
    fine fish, fine fi-i-i-sh . . .'

. . .

My poem comes from the township
on Saturdays bring the washing
on Mondays take the washing
on Saturdays surrender the washing and surrender self
on Mondays surrender self and take the washing

(2) ANGOLA: RAIN-MAN

Aandonga, *The Rain-Man's Praise-Song of Himself*

*These lines are from one of the Aandonga people's traditional
praise-songs which gives a characteristically lyrical and ironical
perspective on the vagaries of life and nature by which their lives
are ruled. Claims the rain-man . . .*

No house is ever too thick built
To keep me, the rain from getting in.
I am well known to huts and roofs,
A Grandson of Never-Been-There.

. . .

When I pour in the morning, people say:
'He has cut off our lips and stopped our mouths,
He is giving us juicy fruits.
He has rained and brought mushrooms,
White as Ivory.'

(3) ANGOLA: REVOLUTION

Sousa Jamba, *Patriots*

*Junior, a powerful member of the MPLA, takes the young
Osvaldo Mbueti for a walk, promises him great things and tells
him he must choose between his 'wretched' and 'reactionary'
father and the party 'who will always be on your side'. Later that
night Osvaldo confesses his decision to his brother.*

Osvaldo said: 'I understand everything you've been telling me, Comrade. But I need to know whether I am really going to Cuba to be
trained as a pilot?'

'An astronaut! You'll be the first African to step on the moon.
Imagine that. Your father and step-mother will be jealous; the
progressive people of the world will be very proud of you.'

Osvaldo smiled and nodded.

'So we are agreed?' said Junior. 'You are now an MPLA party
militant, right?'

'Right!' Osvaldo answered . . .

After dinner Nataniel Mbueti subjected Osvaldo to yet another
tirade for fraternizing with Junior and Xavier Ramos. In a fit of rage, he
said: 'If you continue seeing that man I will kill you. I really mean it.'

Hosi and Osvaldo were then sent to bed. Unable to sleep, Osvaldo
said to Hosi almost in a whisper: 'Can I tell you a secret?'

'Yes.'

'Promise not to tell anyone.'

'I promise.'

'Swear!'

'OK. I swear.'

'Upon what?'

'Upon God.'

'No. There is no God. Swear upon the people of Angola.'

'What will happen if I tell the secret to somebody?'

'You'll be a reactionary, a traitor, a worthless person.'

'I promise not to tell. Please tell me the secret.'

'I am going to Cuba. I will be leaving tomorrow. I will be a pilot. I might even go to the moon.'

Hosi's heart was beating fast. He did not believe what Osvaldo had just told him. He said: 'Never play with me like this again. You are not going anywhere. Papa is not going to let you go.'

Osvaldo said: 'Believe it or not, I am leaving. Don't tell anyone or you'll be shot. This is a revolution and, as Comrade Junior says, reactionaries are fit only for one place – the grave.'

Hosi felt then that even though Osvaldo was less intelligent than he was, he would become an important man.

(4) Coqueiros

Luandino Vieira, *Luuanda*

> *The rough musseque or shanty town of Coqueiros is an African ghetto where life is bleak and where Grandma Xixi has just eaten dahlia roots for lunch in the belief and hope that they were manioc.*

Over Coqueiros the breeze of the day's end spreads the colours of the sun fleeing into the sea; it is a great red sun that swells and burns the colours of the houses, the green of the trees, the blue of the sky . . .

. . . Seated on the wet floor in the doorway of the shanty, *nga* Xixi Hengele – as they call her in the *musseque* because she talks in a way that makes some people laugh and confuses all the rest – mutters as a narrow ray of sunlight escapes the clouds to fall on her old thin face. Grandma blinks her eyes, her body feels limp, her mouth bitter, head heavy. Then she remembers, she was day-dreaming; a sad smile twists the lines on her face, '*Nga* Xixi . . . Madame Cecília! . . . Why remember now?' She laughs a dull spent laugh, hoarse from the tobacco of the little cigars smoked lit end in. '*Auá!* Maybe it's the maniocs I ate.'

True her belly is aching. Only watery coffee for days and then all of a sudden she cooked those potatoes and ate every one, maybe that's what's made her sick. Their taste wasn't exactly manioc or even sweet potato, those tastes Grandma knows well, but she refuses to remember the words of her grandson when he left angry at lunch time. 'No!' she sighs. 'It's not my time to die and I'm not hungry now anyway.'

But still those images which came to her in her dream do not want to let go, they cling to her in memories unwilling to leave – nothing was lacking at home, plenty of food and clothes and no need to talk about money. It continues to eat at her even now, no longer being Madame Cecília Bastos Ferreira, and Grandma doesn't resist, doesn't struggle, what for? She lets those tattered bits of times passed play in her head, bringing regret, sorrow, and just goes on repeating very softly as if to excuse herself, 'So, it's life. The Lord has his own reasons . . . only He knows . . .'

(5) KINAXIXI

Agostinho Neto, *Kinaxixi*

Amid the gentle rhythm and warmth of ordinary everyday life in Angola, these lines from Neto's poem convey the weariness, responsibility and the resignation of the poet and first President of independent Angola. 'Kinaxixi' is included in The Penguin Book of Modern African Poetry – see Booklist.

> I was glad to sit down
> on a bench in Kinaxixi
> at six o'clock of a hot evening
> and just sit there . . .
>
> Someone would come
> maybe
> to sit beside me
>
> . . .
>
> After the sun had set
> lights would be turned on and I
> would wander off
> thinking that our life after all is simple
> too simple
> for anyone who is tired and still has to walk

(6) LUANDA

Ryszard Kapuściński, *Another Day of Life*

Barely two months before independence and in a flurry of activity, the Portuguese packed up 'the stone city' (their homes) into 'the wooden city' (crates) and the whole boxed-up city set sail for Portugal. As observed by Kapuściński, it was an eerie end to a city once known as the 'jewel of Africa'.

Nowhere else in the world had I seen such a city, and I may never see anything like it again. It existed for months, and then it suddenly began disappearing. Or rather, quarter after quarter, it was taken on trucks to the port. Now it was spread out at the very edge of the sea, illuminated at night by harbor lanterns and the glare of lights on anchored ships. By day, people wound through its chaotic streets, painting their names and addresses on little plates, just as anyone does anywhere in the world when he builds himself a house. You could convince yourself, therefore, that this is a normal wooden town, except that it's been closed up by its residents who, for unknown reasons, have had to leave it in haste.

But afterward, when things had already turned very bad in the stone city and we, its handful of inhabitants, were waiting like desperadoes for the day of its destruction, the wooden city sailed away on the ocean. It was carried off by a great flotilla with which, after several hours, it disappeared below the horizon. This happened suddenly, as if a pirate fleet had sailed into the port, seized a priceless treasure, and escaped to sea with it.

Biographies and important works

JACINTO, Antonio (1924–). Jacinto was born in **Luanda**. He was a pioneer of the cultural nationalist movement which was followed by armed struggle. A militant member of the MPLA, he was subsequently sentenced to fourteen years in prison in Portugal on political charges. He managed to escape in 1973, rejoined the MPLA, and worked for the new government after independence in 1975.

JAMBA, Sousa (1966–). Jamba was born in Angola and was forced to leave the country during the civil war. After a period of exile in neighbouring Zambia he returned to join UNITA in the struggle against the MPLA government. The plot of his first novel *Patriots* (Extract 3) closely resembles his life experiences. From the grotesque to the chaotic and the comical, Jamba involves us in every part of the difficult process of growing up as an exile and a freedom fighter. A second novel, *A Lonely Devil*, appeared in 1993. Jamba currently lives in London and writes columns for several magazines. He has won *The Spectator* travel writing prize.

KAPUŚCIŃSKI, Ryszard (1932–). Born in Eastern Poland, Kapuściński studied at the University of Warsaw. His first journalistic job was as a domestic reporter, and then he worked as a (or rather *the*) foreign correspondent for the Polish Press Agency (PPA) until 1981. During his time with the PPA he covered wars and revolutions in Africa, the Middle East and South America. Kapuściński had, at the last count, witnessed a mere 27 revolutions in the Third World. *Another Day of Life* (Extract 6) covers his adventures in Angola on the brink of independence. *The Emperor* is his evocative and as ever engaged account of the decline of the court of Ethiopia's Haile Selassie.

NETO, Agostinho (1922–1979). Neto was born in **Icolo e Bengo**. His parents were Methodist schoolteachers. Between 1944 and 1947 Neto worked for the colonial health services before going to Portugal where he graduated from Lisbon University with a degree in medicine. While in Portugal he was arrested twice for his activities with a democratic youth movement. In 1959 he returned to Angola to practise medicine and became involved with the movement for the 'rediscovery' of Angola's indigenous culture. In 1960

he became the President of the MPLA, but was arrested the same year and imprisoned in Cape Verde and Lisbon. With the help of the democratic resistance movement, he managed to escape in 1962. When independence was declared, he became the country's President, a post he held until his death by cancer in 1979. His poetry, written in Portuguese between 1945 and 1960, is wholly concerned with Angola's predicament. He was awarded the Lenin Peace Prize.

VIEIRA, Luandino (1935–). Vieira was born in Portugal. His parents emigrated to Angola when he was three. He was brought up in the *musseques*, or poor suburbs, inhabited by blacks, mulattos, and other whites. After leaving school at the age of fifteen, he joined an automobile firm. A member of the MPLA, at the age of 26 he was sentenced to 14 years imprisonment for disclosing information about secret lists of army deserters during an interview with the BBC. Part of his sentence was spent in a camp on Cape Verde with fellow poet Jacinto ◊. He was released in 1972, but was confined to Portugal until 1974. Vieira wrote much of his work while in prison. *Luuanda* (Extract 4), written in the African storytelling tradition, takes its name from the ancient spelling of the capital. Also translated into English is *The Real Life of Domingos Xavier*, about a truck driver who becomes a martyr to the MPLA cause. Vieira was last spotted living in Luanda, where he was working with the Union of Angolan Writers.

BOTSWANA

'Good-Bye . . . I am going to the great grey-green, greasy Limpopo to find out what the Crocodile has for dinner . . . and before he knew what he was doing he schlooped up a schloop of mud from the banks of the great grey-green, greasy Limpopo, and slapped it on his head, where it made a cool schloopy-sloshy mud-cap all trickly behind his ears.'
Rudyard Kipling, Just So Stories

Great, green and greasy no longer, the legendary **Limpopo River** is today dry and dusty. Racked by drought, this landlocked country, like many of its southern African neighbours, is said to be suffering a long slow death by desertification. The first people to feel the effects were the Bushmen, the original nomadic inhabitants of Botswana, properly known as San. Laurens van der Post ◊ in *The Lost World of the Kalahari* (Extract 1) wrote of them: 'He appeared to belong to my native land as no other human being has ever belonged. Wherever we went he contained, and was contained, deeply within the symmetry of the land. His spirit was naturally symmetrical because moving in the stream of the instinctive certainty of belonging he remained within his fateful proportions.'

The San once lived and hunted across the whole of Africa – today there are maybe only 30 000 left in Botswana, and the remainder in Namibia and Angola. Many of the San, forced out of their traditional hunting-and-gathering method of survival in Botswana, now live a sedentary life in the town of **Xade**. South African writer van der Post has travelled widely throughout the country, carefully and conscientiously recording the vestiges of this traditional way of life.

Neither San, nor English (the colonists' language), nor the main indigenous tongue, Tswana, has produced a national written literature to speak of. There was a vague rumbling of written literary activity in the 1940s and 1950s, but this was severely handicapped by lack of publishing opportunities and resulted in a few pedantic poems, novels

---

FACT BOX

AREA: 600 000 sq km
POPULATION: 1 285 000
CAPITAL: Gaborone
LANGUAGES: English, Ikalanga, San, Setswana (Tswana)
FORMER COLONIAL POWER: Great Britain
INDEPENDENCE: 1966

---

and some translations of Shakespeare into Tswana. However, traditional Tswana tales abound, and the praise-poems of the Tswana chiefs are legendary (Extract 2). It has been said of the latter, 'these compositions are regarded by the Bantu themselves as the highest products of their literary art'. Where once tribes and nature were applauded, today the poems have been adapted to the modern world and sing in praise of bicycles, trains and schools. Traditional Tswana tales are more rooted in proverbs and lessons from the animal and spirit world, and start not with our 'once upon a time', but more realistically with 'it is said that . . . there was once a man on whose head a tree grew'.

Over the years Botswana has been a harbour for people fleeing from tyranny, war and persecution in neighbouring lands. Writer Bessie Head ◊ who came here from South Africa was one of thousands of exiles the country has adopted. At the age of 27 she settled in a village called **Serowe** which was to be both a shock and an inspiration to her. 'Botswana was a traumatic experience to me and I found the people, initially, extremely brutal and harsh, only in the sense that I had never encountered human ambition and greed before in a black form.' Her initial impressions formed much of her first novel *When Rain Clouds Gather*, which follows the life of a black South African nationalist who flees to a small village in Botswana. *Maru* reveals the conflicts and chaos that take place when a new teacher arrives in a Botswana village.

If the events of Head's books look familiar, she would have been the last to deny that her works are autobiographical. She often made the main character male, because, as she once explained, 'Unfortunately, I think like a man and have a strong masculine style.' From 1968 until her nervous breakdown in 1970, she was haunted by nightmares and voices which taunted and tortured her. Unable to leave the country, she tried to identify and exorcise these demons in a moving book, *A Question of Power* (Extract 3). It is her most difficult and disturbing work, in that it obviously reveals her hardest times. Elizabeth, a coloured South African, works in a garden in a cooperative in

Botswana. The peace of mind she finds there is threatened by haunting images of her past and an imminent nervous breakdown. As Head explained in a letter to a correspondent and fan, Charles Sarvan, 'One day at the end of 1970 I collapsed. I did what I wrote in A *Question of Power*. I rushed out of my house and shouted at an old white volunteer, Mrs Jones. I put a paper up at the post office to the effect that so-and-so was a filthy pervert.' She was arrested and spent time in a mental hospital. 'My breakdown was the Botswana national joke.'

She sometimes wondered whether she should have written the book, but apart from the obvious apologies she wanted to make, it had a clearly cathartic effect. Later when she had recovered and was researching a non-fiction history of the village, *Serowe: The Village of the Rainwind*, she learnt a lot about local witchcraft that helped to vindicate and explain her experiences. Her longings for a restful life in Botswana were summed up by Makhaya in *When Rain Clouds Gather*. Arriving at one of life's busy crossroads he says, 'I shall choose the road of peace of mind. I shall choose a quiet backwater and work together with the people.'

Head's honesty and openness extend to her opinions on fellow African writers, which are worth noting for an insight into her own preferences and approach. Again in the candid letters to Sarvan, she says Chinua Achebe (◊ Nigeria) is 'grim and humourless in some way. Most of his writing bores me.' While she admitted she admired the clarity of Doris Lessing's (◊ Zimbabwe) political writing (something

Bessie Head

Head herself avoided), of Lessing's novels she said, 'I could never get past a few pages. I disliked the image of a woman continually in bed with men she despises.' In particular Nobel Prize winner Nadine Gordimer (◊ South Africa) raised her ire – 'The lady lacks human warmth and love and that chill, cold humourless world of hers repelled me so I never investigated her thought.' (Letter to Mr Charles Sarvan, *Wasafiri*, Autumn, 1990.)

Head is undeniably the dominant figure in Botswana's literary world, and the strength and poignancy of her writing make it something of a role model for writers dealing with today's conflicts and changes. Echoing Head's themes is one of the few successful contemporary popular novelists, Andrew Sesinyi. *Love on the Rocks* is about a man who tries to start a new life in the city after he is driven out of his village by family struggles. Forgetting the past is of course, as Head's work so eloquently shows us, much harder than he ever imagined.

The prolific British writer Naomi Mitchison (1897–) has lived and worked in Botswana. From 1963 to 1973 she was Tribal Adviser and Mmarona (mother) to the Bakgatla. Mitchison has written fiction, non-fiction and children's books about Africa.

LITERARY LANDMARKS

Kalahari Desert. 'After the rains there is a great invasion of life from the outside world into a desert which produces such sweetness out of its winter travail of heat and thirst. Every bird, beast and indigenous being waits expectantly in its stony upland for the summer to come round. Then as the first lightning begins to flare up and down below the horizon in the west as if a god walked there swinging a storm lantern to light his great strides in the dark, they eagerly test the winds with their noses.' (Laurens van der Post, *The Lost World of the Kalahari*.)

Limpopo River. The Elephant Child in Rudyard Kipling's *Just So Stories* '. . . went from Graham's Town to Kimberley, and from Kimberley to Khama's Country, and from Khama's Country he went east by north, eating melons all the time, till at last he came to the banks of the great grey-green, greasy Limpopo River, all set out with fever trees, precisely as Kolokolo Bird had said.'

Serowe. Bessie Head came to this village in eastern Botswana after leaving South Africa and wrote many books about her tragic and tortured life here. Known as the largest village in the country, Head described it as 'a very stimulating part of Botswana'.

Libraries and Bookshops

Gaborone. American Library; Botswana Book Centre, The Mall, PO Box 91; British Council Library; Gaborone Public Library.

BOOKLIST

The following selection includes the extracted titles in this chapter as well as those mentioned in the introduction which are available in English and other titles for further reading. In general, paperback editions are given when possible. The editions cited are not necessarily the only ones available. For most of the extracted works, the original publisher in English can be found in 'Acknowledgments and Citations' at the end of the volume, as can the exact location of the extracts and the editions from which they are taken. Extract numbers are highlighted in bold for ease of reference.

African Women's Writing, Charlotte Bruner, ed, Heinemann, London, 1993.

Head, Bessie, *The Collector of Treasures*, Heinemann, London, 1977.

Head, Bessie, *Maru*, Gollancz, London, 1971.

Head, Bessie, *A Question of Power*, Heinemann, London, 1974. **Extract 3**.

Head, Bessie, *Serowe: The Village of the Rainwind*, Heinemann, Oxford, 1990.

Head, Bessie, *When Rain Clouds Gather*, Penguin Books, London, 1971.

Head, Bessie, *A Woman Alone*, Heinemann, London, 1990.

Kipling, Rudyard, 'The Elephant's Child', in *Just So Stories*, Pavilion, London, 1989.

Mainane, Susheela Curtis, ed, Botswana Book Centre, PO Box 91, Gaberone. (Tswana tales.)

Mitchison, Naomi, *The Africans: A History*, Blond, London, 1970.

Mitchison, Naomi, *Images of Africa*, Canongate, Edinburgh, 1980.

Mitchison, Naomi, *A Life for Africa: The Story of Bram Fisher*, Merlin, London, 1973.

Praise Poems of Tswana Chiefs, Oxford University Press, Oxford, 1965. **Extract 2**.

Sarvan, Charles, 'Bessie Head: Two Letters', *Wasafiri*, Autumn 1990.

Sesinyi, Andrew, *Love on the Rocks*, Macmillan, London, 1981.

van der Post, Laurens, *The Lost World of the Kalahari*, Penguin, London, 1964. **Extract 1**.

van der Post, Laurens, *Testament to the Bushmen*, (with Jane Taylor), Viking, New York, 1984.

van der Post, Laurens, *The Voice of Thunder*, Chatto and Windus, London, 1993.

Extracts

(1) BOTSWANA: KALAHARI BUSHMEN

Laurens van der Post,
The Lost World of the Kalahari

Here van der Post describes his favourite of all the Bushman stories, which he heard from an old 'Chuana cattle-herder who had been raised in giraffe country'.

The Bushman, this old father told me, knew only too well that all giraffe were women at heart, utterly inquisitive and completely incapable of resisting a pretty thing. Moreover, the Bushman knew from long experience what hard and thankless work it could be stalking one who looked down on life from so great a height and out of such far-seeing eyes. So he thought up a wonderful plan. He took out a glittering magic stone he always carried on him and crawled into a bush which was just in sight of a troop of giraffe. He held the stone in his hand in the sun at the side of the bush, constantly turning it in the bright light so that the giraffe could not fail to see it. At first they thought nothing of it, dismissing it as a sparkle of sun on dew, or an effect of the mirage of the heat-mounting distortion and hallucination in the quicksilver light of day. But as the sun climbed higher and this sparkle followed them, so prettily, wherever they moved, they began to get curious. 'And there little master,' the old father would always exclaim, 'the fat was in the fire!' I could see the giraffe, vivid in the mirror of the old man's words, their timid hearts, despite all their other instincts and whatever they had of reason in their shapely Victorian heads, drawn slowly towards the concealed hunter. They would come so near that the Scheherazade pattern in the silk of their clothes would be distinct and visible and their wide slanted eyes, perhaps the loveliest of all animal eyes in the world, would shine behind their long dark lashes like wild honey deep within the comb. For a moment they would stand there in the hypnotic sparkle of so unusual and pretty a thing – and then the Bushman would send his arrows trembling like tuning forks into the tender place below the shoulder because, much as he loved the lard of 'fat little old aunt sea-cow', he loved more the marrow in the long giraffe-bone.

(2) Botswana: Tswana Praise-Poem

Gagomokgwa Kebotseng, *Tshekedi Khama*

This praise, written in about 1926 by Kebotseng, tells of an elephant hunting expedition led by Tshekedi to the Nata River area near Serowe. As is the privilege of such rulers, there is no doubt in the commissioned song as to whom is glorified.

The lion roared in wonder at Tshekedi,
for it saw the chief challenge it,
Ma Mphakere's and Bonyerile's brother challenge it.
The wind pierced the young' men's bones,
it pierced the young men's joints;
those born in Serowe were overcome,
there remained those born in Palapye;
Tshekedi alone did not shiver,
he, the Leletamotse, did not shiver.

. . .

The elephant of the acacia grove screamed,
the elephant trumpeted and broke our nerve;
the cowards were really frightened,
they fled, running frantically,
and not even looking behind them;
I say this because they came back from afar,
they came back from Bokalaka,
back from Domboshaba in Ririmaland.
    How blessed are you people with good sight,
for you have seen that fine person Tshekedi.

(3) Motabeng

Bessie Head, *A Question of Power*

A few months after arriving in Motabeng ('place of sand') at the edge of the Kalahari Desert, Elizabeth starts to see ghosts and spirits. One day when the kindly local white volunteer, Mrs Jones, comes to see how she is and to pray for her, Elizabeth slams the door. Later on when the hallucinations take over she exacts her revenge.

She swayed to the bed and collapsed. The whole room, her whole head was full of shifting ghostly shapes and images. It was Dan's seventy-one nice-time girls. They crawled over her in a slow death-dance. Hands moved, grabbing for the last treasures in the debris of her shattered life.

Sello was there with a boy-friend. His swollen, lopsided, greenish-hued face grinned at her evilly. His little girl still lay with her face upturned in death. The cackling Mrs Jones egged her offspring on to take everything while the going was good. Dan might have been the only presence there. A terrible weight was exterminating her. In her ears was a low, wild, panting hysteria:

'Die, die, die, you dog! I hate you! I hate you!'

Her mind struggled with the question: 'Why, why, why? What have I done?'

She struck an abyss of utter darkness, where all appeals for mercy, relief, help were simply a mockery. At what point did she come to the terrible decision – 'I'll die, but I'll take one of them along with me!' Because it was already pitch-dark when she stood up in her nightdress and ran out of the house. Sello and Dan lived at the extreme end of Motabeng village, twenty miles away, but the home of Mrs Jones was just a few yards from her own house. She ran up the brown road and turned in at the school gates. Old Mrs Jones had been out visiting a friend. She had a torch in her hand, and as she approached the gate of her house the light of the torch struck against the form of Elizabeth.

'Elizabeth!' she cried out.

An angry roar greeted her. Elizabeth rushed towards her.

'Don't you know?' she shouted, 'oh, don't you know? You make your children prostitutes!'

She raised one hand and struck the old woman a blow on the side of the head. Mrs Jones cringed. The torch dropped to the ground. They stood a moment, silent, breathless in the dark; then Elizabeth turned her face up to the stars and screamed.

Biographies and important works

HEAD, Bessie (1937–86). Head was born in Pietermaritzburg, South Africa. The consequence of an 'illicit' liaison between a white woman and a black man, she was fostered and then sent to a mission school until she was 18. She trained as a teacher, taught for a while and then worked as a journalist for *Drum* magazine. Following a failed marriage and the trial of a friend, she applied for a job in Bots-wana. Posted on an exit visa, she came to **Serowe** as a primary school teacher, and was to spend all of her literary life here. *The Collector of Treasures* is a collection of short stories which, in her distinctive simple and direct style, refashions the ancient myths and places them in a contemporary context. Her novels clearly reveal her disturbed and unsettled existence in Botswana. This was partly due to the fact that she came from a country 'with a broken sense of history' and was unable to return, and also to the unexpected prejudices and problems she suffered as a coloured exile/refugee. After two years at Serowe she lost her job and moved north, but returned later as different projects got underway there. In 1979, after 15 years of living with refugee status, she was finally granted citizenship of Botswana. When she did at the age of 49 in Botswana she was writing her 'real' autobiography. *A Woman Alone* is a posthumously published book of collected sketches, personal notes and autobiographical writings.

VAN DER POST, Sir Laurens (see under South Africa).

INDIAN OCEAN ISLANDS

'God saw Mauritius and designed heaven in its image.'
Mark Twain

While the smallest of the Indian Ocean Islands disappears regularly under the waves, the largest, **Madagascar**, is the size of France. Anchored off the east coast of Africa, this disparate scattering of dozens of islands has over the centuries been vulnerable to invasion, pillage and plunder from every side. While the Portuguese largely ignored the islands (in search of bigger bounty) they did, like many sailors and adventurers, use them as refuelling and resting stations. As the euphemism on **Rodrigues** goes, the visitors left 'one or two portraits behind'.

The South-east Asians, the Portuguese, the British, the mainland Africans and the Arabs all left their mark, but culturally it was the influence of the French colonists which presided in the majority of the islands. The French occupied **Madagascar** in the nineteenth century, a time when the island had more contact and influence from Europe than the nearby African continent. Compounding this was the early introduction of printing presses (the first in 1827) which promptly began to translate religious tomes and French fables into Malagasy. Nevertheless the presses were soon put to other uses by a lively group of Malagasy journalists, dramatists and writers who emerged before the turn of the century. But from the point at which Madagascar officially became a French colony in 1905, all teaching was in French. The effect on the vernacular writing was not as devastating as it could have been, thanks in part to the versatility of the creative corps, and a vital Malagasy oral tradition spiced with folktales, proverbs, *hain-teny* (prose poems), music and dance (Extract 4).

Jean-Joseph Rabéarivelo ◊ and Flavien Ranaivo ◊, the pride of the country's twentieth-century poetic production, both write in French and were influenced by the French poets. Nevertheless, both their best works proudly incorporate the distinct forms and rhythms of the

FACT BOX

Comoros
AREA: Grande Comore, 1148 sq km; Anjouan, 424 sq km;
  Mohéli 290 sq km
POPULATION: 518 000
CAPITAL: Moroni (on Njazida)
LANGUAGES: French, Arabic, Comoran
FORMER COLONIAL POWER: France
INDEPENDENCE: 1974

Madagascar
AREA: 586 486 sq km
POPULATION: 11 979 000
CAPITAL: Antananarivo
LANGUAGES: French, Malagasy
FORMER COLONIAL POWER: France
INDEPENDENCE: 1960

Mauritius
AREA: Mauritius, 1865 sq km; Rodrigues, 110 sq km
POPULATION: 1 103 000
CAPITAL: Port Louis
LANGUAGES: English, French, Creole, Bhojpuri
FORMER COLONIAL POWER: France and Great Britain
INDEPENDENCE: 1968

Réunion
AREA: 2512 sq km
POPULATION: 594 000
CAPITAL: St Denis
LANGUAGES: French, Creole
FORMER COLONIAL POWER: France
INDEPENDENCE: Officially a colony to 1964, today a French
  overseas département

Seychelles
AREA: 445 sq km
POPULATION: 70 000
CAPITAL: Victoria (on Mahé)
LANGUAGES: English, French, Creole
FORMER COLONIAL POWER: Great Britain
INDEPENDENCE: 1976

traditional *hain-teny*. Rabéarivelo, revered as 'a poet of genius' and 'a poet of cosmic visions', founded a literary review *Capricorne* and fronted a literary revival which swept through Madagascar in the 1920s and 1930s. A melancholic figure, he was so devoted to French literature and in particular to the work of Baudelaire that when he was refused permission to visit the land of his heroes, he killed himself. His most celebrated collection is *Translations from the Night* (Extract 2), which found its own form, free of French fashion and left a distinct impression on Malagasy and African literature: 'What invisible rat/ comes from the walls of night/gnaws at the milky cake of the moon?/Tomorrow morning,/when it has gone,/there will be the bleeding marks of teeth . . .'.

After Rabéarivelo's tragic death, it was Flavien Ranaivo who was to hold the literary mantle. Ranaivo's first love and education lay not so much with melancholic and romantic French poets, but his own country's rhythms and ballads and *hain-teny*. 'The slangy insolent tone of his verse reveals an authentic inspiration from the popular vernacular songs of the island', wrote anthologists Gerald Moore and Ulli Beier, ' "Song of a Young Girl" combines very successfully this lounging gait with a delightful impudence of language.' (Extract 3)

While Ranaivo's work has translated well into English, the work of his contemporary Jacques Rabémananjara has proved more difficult. Nevertheless he is an important figure. *Antidote* was inspired by the 1947 anti-colonial violence, and Rabémananjara spent many years in prison for his part in the struggle. Ironically, while independence was won in 1960, both he and Ranaivo have been living in exile in France since the military coup of 1972.

Meanwhile, scattered 2000 km off the coast of Africa, lie **Mauritius, Rodrigues** and a sprinkling of small islands and reefs that make up this independent island group. Colonized both by the French (who named Mauritius the Île de France) and by the British, they were populated by some 300 000 Indian labourers in the 1860s. Today, over one million of the population are descended from these Indian immigrants and each year a third of them take part in a traditional Hindu pilgrimage. Nevertheless, as a member of the Organization of African Unity, Mauritius counts itself very much as part of the African continent.

The crises and questions of identity arising out of such an ethnic melting pot were summed up by the country's foremost twentieth century poet Edouard Maunick ◊. He is, he says simply, 'not black enough to be a Black Man, not white enough to be a White Man and not Hindu enough to be a Hindi'. Nevertheless, he is 'a negro by preference'. One of Maunick's first memories of the effects of this 'racial limbo' is when, at the age of five, he learnt of the suicide of Madagascar's poet Rabéarivelo. Maunick was more fortunate in that he was allowed to travel abroad, leaving the island for the first time when he was 29. He recalls that when he first travelled he used to say to people who did not know Mauritius, 'This is the island where the stepfather of Baudelaire sent him.' He did not say 'that we were proud to belong to Africa. I was told by my mother, by my teachers, not to take heed of this side of myself.' Not surprisingly, he uses much maritime imagery, and in the mould of the *Négritude* poets seeks to highlight the African elements in his life and work (Extract 5).

Although English and French are both official languages here in Mauritius, the majority of people are French-literate and consequently there are few notable works in English. One English-language work which caused a storm of publicity was Azize Asgarally's play *The Hell-Hot Bungalow*, which was banned from being performed when it was first published. It depicts a devilish family quarrel in which the cast members change dramatically in the course of events. When the ban was eventually lifted, it enjoyed enormous success. Following the publication of several political works, Asgarally has taken to writing in Creole. The widely spoken and increasingly important Creole language is a French–Bantu–Malagasy fusion whose songs and tales play an important (though as yet untranslated) part in Mauritanian literature.

Geographically, historically and culturally close to Mauritius is the volcanic island of **Réunion**. Claimed by French settlers and traders in the seventeenth century, the island is still a *de facto* colony (technically an overseas *département*) of France, and French has long been the dominant tongue. The literature of this tiny country first came to European attention when two of its poets enjoyed minor celebrity status in Paris in the nineteenth century. It was about this time that Baudelaire's stepfather sent the young French poet to sea. The ports of call included Mauritius and Réunion, but as the captain reported, 'Nothing in a land and society that were quite new to him attracted his attention or aroused his aptitude for observation.' However, Baudelaire could not, as his step father had hoped and as the captain to his despair discovered, be distracted from his books (Extract 6). After a long period of strong influence from the French writers, Réunion's authors of today are moving towards the use of Creole and the local oral literature. When and if the poetry in particular wings its way into translation, look out for Alain Lorraine, Jean Albany and Jean Henri Azéma.

Paradise is a word that trips lightly off the tongue of visitors to the tropical Indian Ocean Islands. While each island lays its own claim to fame and beauty, it was **Praslin**, in the Seychelles group, that was officially declared to be the original 'Garden of Eden' by General Gordon, one-time British Governor of Sudan. **Farquhar Island** meanwhile was *the* home of Venus according to the Portuguese poet Camoëns. Today's measurement of paradise might be that no buildings are permitted to be taller than the palm trees. There are nearly 100 islands in all, whose origins are locally attributed to the 'crumb theory' of creation. According to this, the islands were the little bits left over after Africa was formed, a theory which echoes the lore of their Atlantic African Island counterparts, the Cape Verde Islands. Given the lack of available literature, one can only guess that in a choice between looking at 'paradise' and writing about it (in English), the former is the preferred option.

LITERARY LANDMARKS

Madagascar. The largest bird that ever lived, the extinct Aepyornis, lived here, and was the likely inspiration for the 'roc' in *Sinbad the Sailor*. 'I had heard in my youth from pilgrims and adventurers: how in a far island dwelt a bird of monstrous size called the roc, which fed its young on elephants.' Off the north coast lies the island of **Nosi Be** with the alluring capital of **Hell-Ville**. Irish writer Dervla Murphy ◊ made one of her tortured treks across the island in 1983 (Extract 1).

Mauritius. The French poet Baudelaire, who later inspired many of the island's writers, sailed here in 1841. Mauritius was once home of the now extinct Dodo bird.

Seychelles. When writer Stephen Grey cruised round the islands in 1990 he discovered 'the best-read paperback library in the world' in a clubhouse on **Aldabra** (population 8) – 'Mostly Hammond Innes and, of all things, a fat biography of Saint Augustine of Hippo.'

Libraries and Bookshops

Madagascar. La Librairie de Madagascar, 38 Avenue de l'Indépendance, Antananarivo; Librairie Mixte, 37 bis Avenue de 26 Juin, Antananarivo.

Mauritius. Nalanda & Co, 30 Bourbon Street, PO Box 202, Port Louis.

BOOKLIST

The following selection includes the extracted titles in this chapter as well as those mentioned in the introduction which are available in English and other titles for further reading. In general, paperback editions are given when possible. The editions cited are not necessarily the only ones available. For most of the extracted works, the original publisher in English can be found in 'Acknowledgments and Citations' at the end of the volume, as can the exact location of the extracts and the editions from which they are taken. Extract numbers are highlighted in bold for ease of reference.

Asgarally, Azize, *The Hell-Hot Bungalow*, Dawn Printing Co, Port-Louis, 1967.

Maunick, Edouard, *Les Manèges de la Mer*, extracted in *The Penguin Book of Modern African Poetry*, Gerald Moore and Ulli Beier, eds, Penguin, London, 1984. **Extract 5**.

Murphy, Dervla, *Muddling Through in Madagascar*, Century, London, 1986. **Extract 1**.

The Penguin Book of Modern African Poetry, Gerald Moore and Ulli Beier, eds, Penguin, London, 1984.

Pichois, Claude, *Baudelaire*, Hamish Hamilton, London, 1989. **Extract 6**.

Rabéarivelo, Jean-Joseph, *Translations from the Night*, John Reed and Clive Wake, trans, Heinemann, London, 1975. **Extract 2**.

Rabéarivelo, Jean-Joseph, *24 Songs*, Ulli Beier and Gerald Moore, trans, Mbari, Ibadan, 1963.

Ranaivo, Flavien, 'Song of a Young Girl', in *The Penguin Book of Modern African Poetry*, Gerald Moore and Ulli Beier, eds, Penguin, London, 1984. **Extract 3**.

Sinbad the Sailor, retold by N.J. Dawood, Puffin, London, 1989.

Voices from Twentieth-Century Africa, Chinweizu, ed, Faber and Faber, London, 1988. **Extract 4**.

Extracts

(1) MADAGASCAR: BARA

Dervla Murphy, *Muddling Through in Madagascar*

Murphy and her daughter Rachel are the only two vazaha (foreigners) leaving Ranohira early one morning on an epic truck ride that takes them through Bara country along Route Nationale No 7 towards Tulear in the south-west of Madagascar. With an average speed of around 15 miles per hour there was plenty of time for observation.

Suddenly we were overlooking an inhabited green oasis where dense foliage marked the course of a narrow river. The truck splashed and lurched through the foot-deep water – bridges are an unknown luxury hereabouts – then stopped to refresh its engine. A tall leafless tree, laden with russet bobbles, overhung a group of huts crudely assembled from wooden stakes, sheets of iron and strips of raffia matting; they had neither doors nor windows. 'Nobody here is afraid of bandits,' I remarked to Rachel. 'They probably *are* the bandits!' she retorted. Three women sat outside one shack, wrapped to the ears in gaily coloured blankets; for them this was a chilly morning. Black pigs, white geese and scrawny brown hens swarmed happily amidst the glossy riverside growth. An ibis and several cattle egrets flew past. A long-haired chocolate-coloured cat dozed on the edge of a table beside manioc-flour buns; there was no coffee. An old blanketed man squatted on the beige earth slowly stirring a large black pot on a small charcoal fire. A toddler in a short pink skirt cuddled a tiny white puppy; both had bloated bellies. 'They've given each other worms,' noted Rachel gloomily. Nobody took any notice of the *vazaha*: we were just another manifestation of the road-building team. When the driver had washed down a plate of mashed manioc with a swig of cane-spirits we rattled on, allowing the mantle of silence to fall again on that microscopic community.

(2) MADAGASCAR: DAWN

Jean-Joseph Rabéarivelo, *Daybreak*

Rabéarivelo's characteristic melancholy tints the colours of the sunrise over the ocean in Madagascar. For him it was a symbol of freedom and led to a place he was never allowed to visit. 'Daybreak' is included in Translations from the Night.

Have you seen the dawn go poaching
in night's orchard?
See, she is coming back
down eastern pathways
overgrown with lily-blooms.
From head to foot she is splashed with milk
like those children the heifers suckled long ago.
She holds a torch in hands
stained black and blue like the lips of a girl
munching mulberries.

Escaping one by one there fly before her
the birds she has taken in her traps.

(3) MADAGASCAR: HAIN-TENY

Flavien Ranaivo, *Song of a Young Girl*

A girl sings boldly of the man, the 'oaf', who is her lover who won't marry her because he has another mistress. The girl's sassy style and patter takes its form from the local songs and prose-poems or hain-teny. The poem from which these lines are taken is in The Penguin Book of Modern African Poetry.

Jealous
his mistress I saw two days since at the wash house
coming down the path against the wind.
She was proud;
was it because she wore a lamba thick
and studded with coral
or because they are newly bedded?
However it isn't the storm
that will flatten the delicate reed,
nor the great sudden shower
at the passage of a cloud
that will startle out of his wits
the blue bull.

(4) MADAGASCAR: PLAGUE

The Locust

'What is a locust?' begins this Malagasy traditional elegy which describes the farmer's blight with great detail. The parts of the insect are broken down with Kafkaesque precision, and it becomes an object of both beauty and destruction. This extract is taken from the anthology Voices from Twentieth-Century Africa – see Booklist. An editor's note explains that 'clothing for the dead' refers to the fact that 'some national mourning garments are particoloured'.

Its head, a grain of corn; its neck, the hinge of a knife;
Its horns, a bit of thread; its chest is smooth and burnished;
Its body is like a knife handle;
Its hock, a saw; its spittle, ink;
Its underwings, clothing for the dead.

(5) MAURITIUS: IDENTITY

Edouard Maunick, *Les Manèges de la Mer*

As a result of an upbringing that taught Maunik to emphasize the French part of his background and deny his African and Indian roots, his poetry displays a struggle to re-discover his identity. Two poems from Les Manèges de la Mer are included in The Penguin Book of Modern African Poetry – see Booklist.

Further off is the measured force the word of the sea
Further without leeway for the blueing shoulders of the horizon

harm is born of the light
when it capsizes under the voyages' assault
when it watches oblivion like a beast
and seeks the shipwreck of ten-year old villages
conclusive shifts of time in exile

. . .

I did not leave in order to forget
I am mulatto
the Indian ocean will never give way to the city of today

(6) Réunion: Saint-Denis
Claude Pichois, *Baudelaire*

Long after leaving Bordeaux, the boat on which Baudelaire was
bound arrived at Saint-Denis, Réunion, on 1 September 1841.
This amusing incident at the quay-side was later recalled in the
Chronique de Paris as an insight into the poet's idiosyncrasies.

At Saint-Denis de Bourbon, as everyone knows, due to the usual roughness of the sea and the difficulties experienced at the only point at which one can land, the disembarkation was effected in the past by means of a rope ladder hung, at the tip of a jetty constructed on piles, from a sort of gigantic scaffold. This ladder was maintained in a vertical position, taut and pulled down into the sea, by two enormous blocks of stone fastened to its lower end. In order to disembark, one had to grab hold of the rungs at the instant the rising wave had reached its highest point.

Though informed of this necessary precaution, Baudelaire stubbornly insisted on climbing the ladder with books under his arm – an original method right enough, but also a little awkward. He scaled the ladder slowly and solemnly, pursued by the mounting wave. In a few moments, the wave had reached him. He was submerged and covered in twelve to fifteen feet of water. With great difficulty, they fished him out; but, incredibly, he still had the books under his arm. Only then did he consent to leave them in the boat which was holding steady at the foot of the ladder. Yet as he climbed back up, once again he allowed the wave to reach him, but this time held on, and reached the shore, setting off towards the town, calm and collected, seeming not to notice the excitement of the onlookers. His hat alone had fallen prey to the sharks.

Biographies and important works

MAUNICK, Edouard (1931–). Maunick was born of African, Indian and French ancestry in **Port Louis**, Mauritius. 'My little island is not on most maps', he says sadly of Mauritius. Following the success of his first collection of poetry *Ces Oiseaux de Sang*, Maunick, who was director of **Port Louis Library**, moved to Paris in 1961. In France he worked for several years with *Présence Africaine*, which published his major collection *Les Manèges de la Mer* in 1964. His main theme is the sea and the insularity of living on the island. Rather than fighting against his inherited French tongue, Maunick saw it as a weapon to turn back on the French through

Dervla Murphy

his writing. He has worked as a journalist, a promoter of Francophone African writers, and a TV and radio producer.

MURPHY, Dervla (1931–). Murphy was born and convent-educated in Ireland. Her first forays out of her homeland were cycle trips in Europe. Since then, she has travelled widely in Africa and India by foot, donkey and bike (and reluctantly by bus) in notoriously difficult places, under (self-imposed) very strenuous conditions. In 1966 she journeyed alone through Ethiopia on a mule, later she was *Muddling Through in Madagascar* (Extract 1) with her equally remarkable and resilient fourteen-year-old daughter.

RABÉARIVELO, Jean-Joseph (1901– 1937). Born of an impoverished noble family in **Antananarivo**, Madagascar, Rabéarivelo's formal education ended when he was thirteen. He began to teach himself, reading the French Symbolists and Romantics whose work influenced his poetry. He married young, had three children and supported his family through his work as a printing press proofreader. A melancholic and restless character, he became increasingly frustrated at the refusal of the French to allow him to travel to France (his life's ambition). He became addicted to drugs, and finally killed himself in 1937 at the age of 36. He wrote seven volumes of poetry, six of which were published while he was alive. Two collections, *24 Songs* and *Translations from the Night* (Extract 2), are available in English.

RANAIVO, Flavien (1914–). Ranaivo was born in **Imerina**, near **Antananarivo**, Madagascar, where his father was a local Governor. Ranaivo started school at the age of eight, and could read music well before he could read the alphabet. Much of his childhood was spent wandering about the countryside, listening to the popular songs and ballads. His poetry shows these influences and his work bridged the gap between the new Francophone poetry and more traditional forms of oral literature.

MALAWI

'They call me a dictator! If I am then I am a dictator for the people . . .' enthuses President Osbong in Paul Theroux's ◊ *Jungle Lovers* (Extract 1). Open the cover of this excellent novel about guerrilla war in Malawi and you will notice two things: first, the absence of the usual disclaimer 'any resemblance to persons etc . . .', and second the striking resemblance of Theroux's Osbong to the country's real-life President Dr Hastings Kamuzu Banda. Under his despotic and seemingly eternal rule, the country is quietly referred to as a one-man Banda. Everything is named after him, from classrooms to highways, and his face beams from every 'respectable' bar room and bottom – even material for the kangas that women wear wrapped around them is stamped with his portrait.

> 'It was half-past six, the spectacle of the sun rehearsing its disappearance as usual in Malawi: the sun did not drop whole and round behind the earth, but rather broke like an egg low in the sky, making a fiery bloody omelette at the sharp rim of the sky's base. It was this wide thing, not the sun, that set scrap by scrap.'
> *Paul Theroux, Jungle Lovers*

Not to display his image is considered deviant, and the mildest criticism of the nonagenarian despot leads to jail. In the 1970s he jailed almost the whole of the free press corps, and the country's struggling writers and poets live in constant fear of this fate. Malawi's foremost poet Jack Mapanje ◊ was recently released from prison after four years in detention with only a Bible for company. There was no charge brought against him, and the reason for his detention remains a mystery, though rumour has it that it was something he said over a beer in a university bar. His collection of poems *Of Chameleons and Gods* has been deemed 'unsuitable for schools and colleges' by the Ministry of Education because of the said 'bitterness against the system'. As Mapanje said in his poem 'Messages', 'Did you think it was a hunting party/Where after a fall from chasing a hare/You laughed together an

---

FACT BOX

AREA: 94 080 sq km (20% of which is lake)
POPULATION: 8 800 000
CAPITAL: Lilongwe
LANGUAGES: English, Chichewa, Nyanja, Tonga, Yao, Timbuka
FORMER COLONIAL POWER: Great Britain
INDEPENDENCE: 1964

---

enemy shaking/Dust off your bottom . . ./Mother it's a war here, a lonely war/Where you hack your own way single handed . . .'. In June 1993, a referendum was held in Malawi on the introduction of a multi-party democracy. The vote was almost two-to-one in favour. Nevertheless, at the time of writing (August 1993), Banda is refusing all calls for his resignation.

Poetry is the dominant literary medium in Malawi. Helpful impetus has come from an active workshop at the university and *Odi*, a literary magazine. Among Mapanje's most successful protégés are Frank Chipasula ◊, Lupenga Mphande, Felix Mnthali, and Steve Chimombo ◊, whose work can be found in several anthologies of African poetry (see Extracts 3, 4 and 7 for Chimombo, Chipasula and Mapanje). As a result of his work, Chipasula has been forced into exile and currently lives in the USA. In 'A Love Poem for my Country' he writes, 'My country, remember I neither blinked nor went to sleep/My country, I never let your life slide downhill/And passively watched you, like a recklessly-driven car,/Hurrying to your crash while the driver leapt out.'

Yet another writer who has had to take the leap to safety in exile, is poet, novelist and critic David Rubadiri ◊, who is characteristically as critical, if sometimes appearing more covertly so (Extract 5). With his novel *No Bride Price* he joins Legson Kayira ◊ and James Ng'ombe as one of the country's few well known novelists. Ng'ombe's début novel *Sugarcane with Salt* is concerned with the struggle of a doctor who returns from England after eight years to discover unexpected changes within his country, himself and his family – his mother now living with a white man and his younger brother caught up in a drug racket.

The country's most successful novelist is still Legson Kayira. His great success and determination started with his extraordinary pilgrimage to America via Sudan, which is described in *I Will Try*. His powerful and convincing novel *The Detainee* (Extract 2) addresses tyranny and dictatorship from the eyes of a mystified and vulnerable man: 'The only remarkable thing about Napolo was his simplicity – the naive and trusting simplicity of a villager whose greatest worry in the

world is the failure of rain . . .' Kayira was regretful that he was not able
to write his second semi-autobiographical novel, *The Looming Shadow*,
in his native Timbuka language. Some 25 years later, there is still little
work published or translated into Malawi's indigenous languages.

LITERARY LANDMARKS

Kasungu. The area which is today the **Kasungu National Park** was
explored by David Livingstone (◊ Zambia) in 1863, shortly before his
death. The National Parks pamphlet for the area boasts, 'One of the
things which impressed Livingstone most . . . was the extent and
quality of the local iron-working industry.' A preserved furnace can be
seen near **Dwangwa** crossing.

   Lake Malawi. Standing at **Cape Maclear**, a rocky point poking into
Lake Malawi, Livingstone reputedly vowed to convert all Africans
around the lake to Christianity. In 1875 the Free Church of Scotland
founded the **Livingstonia Mission** here. It was here that Malawi's
foremost novelist Legson Kayira received his early education. The **Rest
House** was once a watering hole for the khaki and mosquito-net set
who stopped over in the flying boats on their way from London to Cape
Town. Today's transportation on the lake is via the power steamer *Ilala
II* which replaced *Ilala I*, named after the village tribe in Zambia (where
Livingstone died).

   Nyika National Park. The **Nyika Plateau**, celebrated for its beauty
and wildlife, is one of the places Sir Laurens van der Post (◊ South
Africa) explored (Extract 6).

   Zomba Plateau. Site of the renowned **Chingwe's Hole** in which is
said to lie many a man and mystery, and inspiration for one of Jack
Mapanje's poems (Extract 7).

Libraries and Bookshops

Blantyre. American Library; French Cultural Centre.

   Lilongwe. British Council Library; Malawi National Library; University of Malawi Library.

BOOKLIST

The following selection includes the extracted titles in this chapter as well as those mentioned in the introduction which are available in English and other titles for further reading. In general, paperback editions are given when possible. The editions cited are not necessarily the only ones available. For most of the extracted works, the original publisher in English can be found in 'Acknowledgments and Citations' at the end of the volume, as can the exact location of the extracts and the editions from which they are taken. Extract numbers are highlighted in bold for ease of reference.

Chimombo, Steve, 'Derailment: A Delirium', in *The Heinemann Book of African Poetry in English*, selected by Adewale Maja-Pearce, Heinemann, Oxford, 1990. **Extract 3**.

Chimombo, Steve, *Napolo Poems*, Manchichi, Zomba, 1987.

Chimombo, Steve, *The Rainmaker*, Popular Publishers, Limbe, 1978.

Chipasula, Frank, 'Manifesto on Ars Poetica', in *The Heinemann Book of African Poetry in English*, selected by Adewale Maja-Pearce, Heinemann, London, 1990. **Extract 4**.

Chipasula, Frank, *Nightwatcher, Nightsong*, Paul Green, Peterborough, 1986.

Chipasula, Frank, *O Earth Wait for Me*, Raven Press, Johannesburg, 1984.

Chipasula, Frank, *Whispers in the Wings*, Heinemann, London, 1991.

Kayira, Legson, *The Detainee*, Heinemann, London, 1974. **Extract 2**.

Kayira, Legson, *The Looming Shadow*, Macmillan, New York, 1970.

Kayira, Legson, *No Easy Task*, Heinemann, London, 1966.

Mapanje, Jack, *Of Chameleons and Gods*, Heinemann, London, 1981.

Mapanje, Jack, *The Chattering Wagtails of Mikuyu Prison*, Heinemann, Oxford, 1993.

Ng'ombe, James, *Sugarcane with Salt*, Longman, Harlow, 1989.

Poetry from East Africa, D. Rubadiri and D. Cook, eds, Heinemann, London, 1971.

Rubadiri, David, 'An African Thunderstorm', in *The Penguin Book of Modern African Poetry*, Gerald Moore and Ulli Beier, eds, Penguin, London, 1984. **Extract 5**.

Rubadiri, David, *No Bride Price*, East African Publishing House, Nairobi, 1967.

Shepperson, George, ed, *David Livingstone and the Rovuma*, Edinburgh University Press, Edinburgh, 1965.

Theroux, Paul, *Jungle Lovers*, Penguin, London, 1974. **Extract 1**.

van der Post, Laurens, in Eric Newby, ed, *A Book of Travellers' Tales*, Pan, London, 1986. **Extract 6**.

van der Post, Laurens, *Venture to the Interior*, Penguin, London, 1957.

Extracts

(1) BLANTYRE

Paul Theroux, *Jungle Lovers*

Calvin Mullet, an ill-fated insurance salesman, and his wife have just arrived from Hudson, Massachusetts. His posting here to the 'Switzerland of Africa' is, he believes, a 'promotion' and a last chance to save their marriage.

They arrived in Malawi in late afternoon, in time for tea at their hotel. Buttering scones at a veranda table they noticed a beggar walk out from a hedge and stand near, like a terrible angel. He wore rubber clogs cut from automobile tyres, and wings of rags, and a filthy skullcap.

'Tell him to go home,' Calvin's wife said.

The beggar stared: he made no gesture. His gaze penetrated to Calvin's innards. Calvin felt very white. The beggar looked fierce, strong even, a muscular man, capable of savagery. He could kill with his hands. Calvin knew the man hated him; he wanted to help him or at least tell the man that he was there to help. Calvin raised his hand, a timid salute. But a waiter took this as an annoyed signal and shooed the beggar away.

In the room they argued about the official photograph of Dr Osbong. It was hung over the bed, but Calvin's wife said, 'Even if it was in the john I'd take it down.'

'The President,' said Calvin. 'A nice way to talk.'

'Uncle Ben's Rice,' said his wife, and giggled mirthlessly.

'You insensitive bitch,' Calvin said. He took down the picture of Dr Osbong and banged it into a bureau drawer.

His wife locked herself into the bathroom and washed noisily. Calvin went to the window and threw back the curtains. It was still light, and it was cool. He peered down two storeys to the street, which was a side street, bordered by Hudson-like foliage: bushy-boughed trees, high hedges and even several tepees of pinetops showing. A man in a wide felt hat pushed a bicycle out of sight. There were no more people. But Calvin knew there was a beggar in the hedge, and there were odours, of fresh grass, of flowering trees, of sweet decay; there was a high whine of locusts building to tea-kettle pitch, and a sky so blue he could have cried.

(2) MALAWI: DICTATORSHIP

Legson Kayira, *The Detainee*

Napolo has ventured out from his remote native village to seek out the white doctor in Banya who will cure his hernia. On his journey he encounters gangs of thugs, the so-called Youth Brigade, who are terrorizing the land in the name of the President. Here Napolo has innocently asked about the President's tour of the country.

'Now, why do you want to know the movements of His Eminence, the Father of the Nation?'

'I'm going to Banya and . . .'

'What's the matter?' another Young Brigade asked.

'The old dog here is being disrespectful to Africa's greatest son, Sir Zaddock Mlingo, Doctor of Laws.'

'Is that true?' The rest of them had now gathered around Napolo.

'You've misunderstood me,' Napolo said nervously and he felt a prickling sensation on his forehead.

'He doesn't even have a current card.'

'He deserves to have his skull cracked.'

'Let's see if he knows his lesson,' the bandy-legged youth said. 'Answer me,' he added, addressing Napolo. 'Who is Sir Zaddock?'

'He's my one and only redeemer,' Napolo said, repeating a phrase which he had memorized.

'And?'

'He is the owner and ruler of this country. Everything in this country, including my life, belongs to him.'

'What about your wife and your children?'

'My wife and my children also belong to him.'

'Never forget that,' another warned.

'We'll spare your empty skull today,' the bandy-legged one said, 'but your rudeness will cost you ten shillings.'

'And five shillings for the new card.'

Napolo, relieved at being spared, paid the fifteen shillings with a profusion of thanks.

'You're lucky today. Next time it'll cost you ten pounds.'

'And three months in jail,' added another.

As they walked away in the direction of Patel's shop, laughing merrily, Napolo too got up. He felt old and tired and had vague pains in his stomach. He went back to his room in the rest house near the deserted bus depot.

(3) MALAWI: MALAISE

Steve Chimombo, *Derailment: A Delirium*

In this six-part poem Chimombo uses many analogies for the country's ills and ailments. Here the enemy, hepatitis, is what he calls 'an administrator' which lurks in the life-giving waters of the rivers. The poem is included in the anthology The Heinemann Book of African Poetry in English – see Booklist.

> Napolo spoke to me
> in the waters regenerating my car:
> 'What kind of hepatitis, son?'
> 'Premium, please,' I said trembling.
> And I saw hordes of them:
> layer upon layer,
> amoebas and viruses
> debating what to do
> with your liver.
> Premium or Regular?
> Amoebic or Viral?

(4) MALAWI: POETS

Frank Chipasula, *Manifesto on Ars Poetica*

Chipasula, a Malawian who lives in America, is able to voice his intentions as a poet. He speaks for his colleagues and compatriots who have either stayed behind, or been imprisoned for their beliefs and writings. This poem is included in the anthology The Heinemann Book of African Poetry in English – see Booklist.

I will undress our raped land and expose her wounds.
I will pierce the silence around our land with sharp metaphors
. . .

I will thread the voice from the broken lips
through my volatile verbs that burn the lies.
I will ask only that the poem watch the world closely;
I will ask only that image put a lamp on the dark
ceiling in the dark sky of my land and light the dirt.
Today, my poetry has exacted a confession from me.

(5) MALAWI: THUNDERSTORM

David Rubadiri, *An African Thunderstorm*

Rubadiri's imagery, using the ferocity of nature, can be read as a symbol for many of the changes that the country has weathered – from colonialism blowing in 'from the west' to the recent rumblings of revolution. 'An African Thunderstorm' is included in The Penguin Book of Modern African Poetry – see Booklist.

From the west
Clouds come hurrying with the wind
Turning
Sharply
Here and there
Like a plague of locusts
Whirling
Tossing up things on its tail
Like a madman chasing nothing.

. . .

The Wind whistles by
Whilst trees bend to let it pass.
Clothes wave like tattered flags
Flying off
To expose dangling breasts
As jaggered blinding flashes
Rumble, tremble, and crack
Amidst the smell of fired smoke
And the pelting march of the storm.

(6) NYIKA PLATEAU

Laurens van der Post, *Venture to the Interior*

On one of his expeditions into little known parts of southern Africa, Sir Laurens van der Post watches the wildlife 2000 m up on the Nyika Plateau in the Nyika National Park.

There was no wind any more. There was no cloud or mist in the sky. I have never known such stillness. The only sound was the sound of one's blood murmuring like a far sea in one's ears: and that serene land and its beauty, and the level golden sunlight seemed to have established such a close, delicate, tender communion with us that the murmur in my ears seemed also like a sound from without; it was like a breathing of the grasses, a rustle of the last shower of daylight, or the swish of the silk of evening across the purple slopes.

Suddenly Karramba touched my arm. We could hardly believe our eyes. A very big male leopard, bronze, his back charged with sunset gold, was walking along the slope above the pool on the far side about fifty yards away. He was walking as if he did not have a fear or care in the world, like an old gentleman with his hands behind his back, taking the evening air in his own private garden. When he was about twelve yards from the pool, he started walking around in circles examining the ground with great attention. Then he settled slowly into the grass, like a destroyer sinking into the sea, bow first, and suddenly disappeared from our view. It was rather uncanny. One minute he was magnificently there on the bare slope and the next he was gone from our view . . .

(7) Zomba Plateau

Jack Mapanje, *Glory Be to Chingwe's Hole*

Up on the 2000 m high Zomba Plateau is the legendary and mysterious Chingwe's Hole – reputedly so deep that no one has been able to measure its depth. This poem is included in the anthology The Heinemann Book of African Poetry in English *– see Booklist.*

Chingwe's Hole, you devoured the Chief's prisoners
Once, easy villagers decked in leopard colours
Pounding down their energies and the sight.
You choked minstrel lovers with wild granadilla
Once, rolling under burning flamboyant trees.

. . .

Chingwe's Hole, how dare I praise you knowing whose
Marrow still flows in murky Namitembo River below you?
You strangled our details boasting your plush dishes,
Dare I glorify your rope and depth epitomizing horror?

Biographies and important works

CHIMOMBO, Steve (1945–). As well as his poetry, which has been widely published in anthologies, Chimombo has published *The Rainmaker*, the dramatization of a Malawi myth that has its origins in a separatist religious cult of the seventeenth century. The dialogue, which follows the failure of a rainmaker, is punctuated by chants. Chimombo's collection *Napolo Poems* was published in Malawi and was commended in the 1988 NOMA Award for Publishing in Africa. He is currently employed as Assistant Professor of English at **Chancellor College, University of Malawi.**

CHIPASULA, Frank (1949–). The intention of Chipasula's work and the difficulty of being a poet in Malawi is described in 'Manifesto on Ars Poetica' (Extract 4), which outlines his philosophies and aims. He is above all an outspoken writer, and in order to protect his work and sanity he now lives in the USA, where he is Associate Professor in the Black Studies Department of the University of Nebraska. Most of his work has been published outside Malawi and *Nightwatcher, Nightsong* was even printed in a so-called 'Dangerous Writers series' in England.

KAYIRA, Legson (1940–). Educated initially in a Presbyterian mission, Kayira decided at an early age that he wanted to continue his education in the USA. In order to achieve this, he set out on foot with Bible and *Pilgrim's Progress* to Khartoum. Four thousand kilometres later he was befriended by the US Consul there who arranged for his wish to come true. In Washington he attended Skagit Valley Junior School and later the University. His first book, an autobiographical account of the trek, was entitled *I Will Try* after his school motto. Kayira followed up a degree in political science with a two-year scholarship to Cambridge. *The Looming Shadow* completes his early history with its description of his native village life. *Jingala* takes on the conflict between old and new, with the story of a feud between a retired tax-collector and his son who wants to be a priest. His fifth book, *The Detainee* (Extract 2) is a compelling novel concerned with dictatorship and the abuse of power.

MAPANJE, Jack (1945–). Mapanje was born at **Kadango** in southern Malawi. He studied at the **University of Malawi**, then at the University of London and went on to lecture at **Chancellor College, Zomba**. His first published collection of poetry, *Of Chameleons and Gods*, is a compilation of ten years' work. It was, he says, 'a way of hanging onto some sanity. Obviously where voices are too easily muffled, this is a difficult task to set oneself.' Until his imprisonment in 1987 without charge or trial he was Head of the English Department at the **University of Malawi**. Mapanje was also the founder and editor of *Odi*, the Malawian literary magazine, and a mentor for many of the country's poets. He is currently a research fellow at the University of York.

Paul Theroux

RUBADIRI, David (1930–). Rubadiri is a poet, novelist and critic. Though he has spent much of his life away from his homeland, Malawi is a strong theme in his work. He studied at Makerere College, Uganda, and was arrested during the crisis in Malawi in 1959. Following his release he went to England where he read English at Cambridge. He has taught at the University of Nairobi and the **University of Malawi**. His first novel, *No Bride Price*, is the story of the downfall of a civil servant against a familiar and confusing background of corruption and deception. It also considers conflicts between the Asian community and the indigenous population.

THEROUX, Paul (1941–). Theroux was born in Medford, Massachusetts. His first novel was published in 1967. Since then, he has published many travel books and novels, with settings as diverse as Africa, South-east Asia, and Central America. He spent five years in Africa and his experiences there provided the basis for several novels and stories. His poignant comedy *Jungle Lovers* (Extract 1) tells of the woeful fortunes of 'Cal' Mullet, an insurance salesman who sets out to sell policies in remote dusty dorps – 'But you still die isn't it', remarks one of his potential customers. The novel is a cool and observant evocation of a white man in Africa who, even when taken prisoner by a revolutionary, stubbornly still attempts to sell him a policy. *Fong and the Indians* is a novel about a Chinese immigrant in an East African country. *Girls at Play* focuses on a group of single white women in Kenya.

VAN DER POST, Sir Laurens (see under South Africa).

MOZAMBIQUE

'The coelacanth, oldest of fish, still lurks in the Gulf of Mozambique. Some wags say that Mozambique is a coelacanth trying to change itself suddenly into a salmon.'
Richard West,
The White Tribes of Africa

A roll call of the country's leading poets and prose writers looks not unlike the list of its main freedom fighters and government employees. When resistance to Portuguese rule culminated in the formation of Frelimo (the Mozambique Liberation Front) in 1962, many intellectuals and writers pledged their support to the leader Eduardo Mondlane. Exiled poet Marcelino dos Santos returned home as soon as Frelimo was formed and pledged his support: 'This is the land/where we were born/its sorrow/is our grief/and today's bitter cloud/is a moment's pain/which the rain must dry . . .' ('Here We were Born').

While some supporters took to the pen, others put down their pens and took up arms. Many took up both. It was not considered unusual, for example, that Armando Guebuza, the appointed Frelimo inspector of schools, and Jorge Rebelo, the Director of Information, dabbled in revolutionary verse. By 1967 poetic support from its members was such that Frelimo published a collection called *Breve Antologia Literatura Mozambicana.*

Following independence, one could well imagine the revolutionary poets queuing up for the post of Mozambique Poet Laureate. But without the place, purpose or money for such indulgences Frelimo gave them government posts. Some, like Noémia de Sousa ◊, one of Africa's first female writers, had given up the struggle early and gone into exile in Europe. The fate of the two leading literary lights of Frelimo, poet José Craveirinha ◊ and prose writer Luís Bernardo Honwana ◊, was revealed by a curious Swedish journalist, Per Wästberg ◊. In 1975, the year of independence, Wästberg found Craveirinha appropriately sandwiched between piles of dusty books, though less appropriately installed as the librarian in the Department of Trade (Extract 1). It was

```
┌─────────────────────────────────────────────────────────────┐
│                                                               │
│   FACT BOX                                                    │
│                                                               │
│   AREA: 783 000 sq km                                         │
│   POPULATION: 16 100 000                                      │
│   CAPITAL: Maputo                                             │
│   LANGUAGES: Portuguese, Makua-Lomwe, Ronga, Swahili         │
│   FORMER COLONIAL POWER: Portugal                             │
│   INDEPENDENCE: 1975                                          │
│                                                               │
└─────────────────────────────────────────────────────────────┘
```

a position that belied his power and militancy as a poet (Extract 4): 'All feel/uneasiness/at the undoubted whiteness of my bones . . . that the mingling in my veins should be/blood from the blood of every blood . . . ('The Seed is in Me'). His images often include railways which were built by forced labour, and along which workers were then shipped off to toil in the mines of South Africa, 'Belching steam the miners' train pulled out/and in the pistons a voice sang/Joao Tavesse went to the mines . . .' ('Mamana Saquina').

Wästberg was equally surprised to find the country's foremost prose writer, Luís Honwana, installed as the Prime Minister's secretary. He explained to Wästberg that the reason that practically no-one (other than himself) wrote prose, was, quite logically, because it took too long and was seen as a distraction (Extract 3). At the time it also apparently owed something to the fact that inflation had made paper scarce, and in the resulting competition for space in newspapers, poetry and prose were first to be sacrificed. At the time, Honwana was gathering literary material for teaching in schools from the country's oral tradition. He was looking to the rhymes, themes and tales of the type that built up the feelings of solidarity during the fighting. He hoped they would recall a peaceful rhythm of daily life – as opposed to early Frelimo material, which focused on blood, guts and struggle.

Education, or the widespread lack of it, was one of the prime reasons for the slow development of the literature here. Neglect under Portuguese rule had left 90% illiterate at independence. There was also disruption of schooling during the struggle for independence, and independence itself did not precipitate a burst of patriotic literary activity. The exceptions include the works of a white Mozambican poet, Orlando Mendes, who in 1975 published two collections of patriotic prose. Since 1975 a seemingly endless civil war has done much to disrupt the country's education and literary programmes.

Today Mia Couto ◊ is hailed as one of the few short story writers worthy of comparison to Honwana (Extract 2), and poet Luís Patraquim to Craveirinha's. Still, most of the work available in English lies buried in anthologies gathered by a dedicated few. These include some quite unexpected pieces such as the writing of Valente Malangatana who was born at **Marracuene** in 1936. His mother went mad and his father was often away in the mines of South Africa and he appears to have been brought up by his grandmother. As well as writing poetry, which appeared in *Black Orpheus* in the 1960s, he developed his skills as a painter. A strange family history resulted in similarly strange poetry – 'Women's hair shall be the blanket/over my coffin when another Artist/calls me to Heaven to paint me . . .' ('Woman'). Like every 'respectable' Frelimo poet, Patraquim did a spell in jail for his political activities.

LITERARY LANDMARKS

Maputo. Richard West described the capital in *The White Tribes of Africa* as he saw it in the 1960s (it was then known as Lourenço Marques): 'the only town I have been to in Africa that really seems like Europe. The South Africans on holiday look as the English on holiday in Spain: the men in blazers and flannels, the women in head-scarves and sun-red necks; the jokes about garlic and "Mozambique belly"; the prevailing sense of naughtiness . . . The Southern Rhodesians go rather to Beira up the coast, which they have turned into a kind of hot Blackpool.' The **Museum of the Revolution** is said to be worth a visit.

Mozambique Island. This was the country's capital for 400 years following the arrival of the Portuguese explorer Vasco da Gama in 1498, who declared all visible land as the property of the King of Portugal. At **San Sebastian Fortress** the statue of Vasco da Gama looking towards the mainland was engraved with the inscription 'discoverer of Mozambique'.

Tete Province. When Frelimo entered the area in 1974, it effectively marked the end of some 500 years of Portuguese rule. At **Cabora Bassa** the **Zambezi River** was navigable to the coast; 'the place where the hard work stops' said a travel-weary Livingstone (◊ Zambia) who had stopped here to recuperate.

Libraries and Bookshops

Maputo. Centre for African Studies; Eduardo Mondlane University Library; Municipal Library; National Documentation Centre; National Library.

BOOKLIST

The following selection includes the extracted titles in this chapter as well as those mentioned in the introduction which are available in English and other titles for further reading. In general, paperback editions are given when possible. The editions cited are not necessarily the only ones available. For most of the extracted works, the original publisher in English can be found in 'Acknowledgments and Citations' at the end of the volume, as can the exact location of the extracts and the editions from which they are taken. Extract numbers are highlighted in bold for ease of reference.

Couto, Mia, 'The Tale of the Two Who Returned from the Dead', David Brookshaw, trans, *Wasafiri*, No 10, Summer 1989. **Extract 2**.

Couto, Mia, *Voices Made Night*, Heinemann, Oxford, 1990.

Craveirinha, José, 'Poem of the Future Citizen', in *African Writing Today*, Ezekiel Mphahlele, ed, Penguin, London, 1967. **Extract 5**.

de Sousa, Noémia, 'If You Want to Know Me', Art Brakel, trans, in

The Penguin Book of Modern African Poetry, Gerald Moore and Ulli Beier, eds, Penguin, London, 1984. **Extract 4**.

Harding, Jeremy, *Small Wars, Small Mercies: Journeys in Africa's Disputed Nations*, Viking, London, 1993.

Honwana, Luís Bernardo, 'Dina', in *African Writing Today*, Ezekiel Mphahlele, ed, Penguin, London, 1967. **Extract 3**.

Honwana, Luís Bernardo, *We Killed Mangy-Dog and Other Mozambique Stories*, Heinemann, London, 1969.

Malangatana, Valente, in *The Penguin Book of Modern African Poetry*, Gerald Moore and Ulli Beier, eds, Penguin, London, 1984.

Rebelo, Jorge, 'Poem', Art Brakel, trans, in *The Penguin Book of Modern African Poetry*, Gerald Moore and Ulli Beier, eds, Penguin, London, 1984. **Extract 6**.

Wästberg, Per, *Assignments in Africa*, The Olive Press, London, 1986. **Extract 1**.

West, Richard, *The White Tribes of Africa*, Jonathan Cape, London, 1965.

Extracts

(1) Maputo

Per Wästberg, *Assignments in Africa*

In Mozambique's year of independence, Swedish writer and journalist Wästberg tracks down the country's leading poet to the Department of Trade in the capital. Craveirinha told Wästberg that during his four years of imprisonment he resorted to writing with a pin on toilet paper. Maputo was formerly known as Lourenço Marques.

Dawn in Lourenço Marques in 1975. Outside the large office block in the town centre, nightwatchmen are making tea and preparing to leave. The sun rises before six, high summer south of the Equator. Indian families living near the ocean are bathing, going down to the water with towels over their shoulders, then returning at dusk, when they park their cars in long lines and sit and talk to each other as they watch the sun setting.

Dockers are on their way to the harbour. Occasional policemen are on patrol. Some people are waiting for the first bus of the day. The market is not yet open in Chipamanine. At a quarter past six, the town is suddenly awake, the shops on the outskirts selling food, tea brewing, and at half past six everyone seems to be up and about, servants, street-sweepers, workers and cyclists.

At half past seven in the morning, I go to see José Craveirinha, fifty-four, a mulatto, librarian in the Department of Trade. The country's leading poet is sitting in the dim light between old-fashioned bookcases and shelves full of enormous reference books and dictionaries of trade terms and international statesmen of the 1950s.

He is a gentle, melancholy man.

'Why take a photograph of me when we're so near to the zoo? You must be disappointed to see me. Maybe you'd thought you'd see a poet?'

(2) Mozambique: Bureaucracy

Mia Couto,
The Tale of the Two Who Returned from the Dead

Missing and presumed dead in a flood, two men return to find that far from being pleased to find them alive, the local officials are thrown into a bureaucratic spin. This is a cautionary tale about the dangers of cumbersome hierarchies and burgeoning bureaucratic powers in a newly independent country. The story was published in Wasafiri – see Booklist.

The official arrived on the scene. He was a tubby man, his belly inquisitive, peeping out of his tunic. They were complimented with the respect due to the dead. The official explained the difficulties and the extra burden they represented, as two dead people who had returned without warning.

– Look: they've sent us supplies. Clothes, blankets, sheets of zinc, a lot of things. But you two weren't included in the estimate.

Aníbal became agitated when he heard they had been excluded:

– What do you mean not included? Do you strike people off just like that?

– But you have died. I don't even know how you came to be here.

– What do you mean died? Don't you believe we are alive?

– Maybe, I'm not sure any more. But this business of being alive and not alive had best be discussed with the other comrades.

So they went to the village hall. They explained their story but failed to prove their truth. A man dragged along like a fish only seeks air, he's not interested in anything else.

After some consultation the official concluded rapidly:

– It doesn't matter whether you are completely dead or not. If you're alive, it's worse still. It would have been better to take advantage of the water to die.

The other, the one with the tunic that played tug-of-war with its own buttons, added:

– We can't go along to the administrative cadres of the district and tell them a couple of ghosts have turned up. They'll tell us we've got ourselves mixed up in obscurantism. We could even be punished.

– That's true – agreed the other. We did a political orientation course. You are souls, you're not the material reality that I and all the others with us in the new village are.

The fat one added emphatically:

– To feed you, we'd have to ask for an increase in our quota. How would we justify that? By telling them we'd got two souls to feed?

(3) Mozambique: Forced Labour

Luís Bernardo Honwana, *Dina*

*Out in the 'Molungo's' (white man's) cornfields in the midday
sun, the labourers are performing backbreaking work under the
intensive watch of the Portuguese Overseer. When 'Dina'
(dinner, pronounced 'deena' by returning migrant labourers) is
finally called, those who still are able move quickly through the
fields to the 'chicafo' (from 'scoff'). 'Dina' is included in the
anthology African Writing Today – see Booklist.*

Gradually Tandane, Djimo and Muthambi emerged from the field,
with their eyes fixed on the Overseer.

Djimo's body was covered with sweat, but even so Madala observed
the nervous dance of his jittery muscles under his skin of the colour of
river sand.

'Let's get going to the *chicafo*,' commanded the Overseer, shutting
the book he had in his hand. 'That will be the day when a fellow
manages to write a book without these whores . . .' he added, looking
at the picture on the cover of the book.

The Overseer started the march, and the others followed in silence.

Madala gazed around him, feeling a certain·pleasure in hurting his
eyes on the fragments of sun that sprang from the smooth corn leaves.
'Cornfields are like the sea.'

The others were far ahead, half submerged in the thick greenness of
the field, walking slowly as if they were really pushing through a liquid.

Madala remained motionless: 'Molungo's cornfields are like the sea . . .'
he insisted, as his eyes followed the gentle waving of the even surface of
the fields. Madala's gaze travelled along a wave which broke far away in
the distance, assailed by a thousand silver sparks – small suns turned
into comets by the wind. When he could no longer bear the burning in
his eyes, he turned them away.

Suddenly Madala tired of comparing the cornfields to the sea,
because he realized that this idea always occurred to him when he raised
himself at the stroke of Dina and cast his eyes on the vastness that
encircled him: 'The sea is different . . .,' he murmured, frowning.

(4) MOZAMBIQUE: IDENTITY

Noémia de Sousa, *If You Want to Know Me*

*One of the rare female Mozambican poets, de Sousa encompasses
here the sweep of Mozambique's ailments. She is also 'Africa
from head to toe', feeling the pains and the burden of her
continent's troubles. 'If You Want to Know Me' is included in
The Penguin Book of Modern African Poetry – see Booklist.*

If you want to understand me
come and bend over my African Soul,
in the groans of the Negroes on the docks
in the frenzied dances of the Chopes
in the rebelliousness of the Shanganas
in the strange melancholy evaporating
from a native song, into the night . . .

And ask me nothing more
if you really wish to know me . . .
for I am no more than the shell of flesh
in which the revolt of Africa congealed
its cry swollen with hope

(5) MOZAMBIQUE: INDEPENDENCE

José Craveirinha, *Poem of the Future Citizen*

*Craveirinha, a Frelimo fighter, calls for independence for
Mozambique, for a country he can call his own. 'Poem of the
Future Citizen' is included in the anthology African Writing
Today – see Booklist.*

. . .

I have a heart
and cries which are not mine alone
I come from a country which does not yet exist.

Ah! I have love in plenty to give
of what I am
I!
A man among many
citizen of a nation which has yet to exist.

(6) MOZAMBIQUE: REVOLUTION

Jorge Rebelo, *Poem*

The poet, looking for fuel to fire his revolutionary poems, calls on his fellow countrymen to show him 'the marks of revolt', their wounds, defeats and dreams. It is a call to arms that could also be seen as a way to embarrass those who have not sacrificed something for the cause. Rebelo's 'Poem' is included in The Penguin Book of Modern African Poetry – see Booklist.

Come brother and tell me your life,
come relate me the dreams of revolt
which you and your fathers and forefathers
dreamed
in silence
through shadowless nights made for love

. . .

And later I will forge simple words
which even children can understand
words which will enter every house
like the wind
and fall like red hot embers
on our people's souls.

Biographies and important works

COUTO, Mia (1955–). Couto was born in **Beira**. From a journalistic background, his stories deal with the country's post-independence problems. Described as a young Honwana ◊, his work is similarly laconic, and often set in a rural landscape. His 1986 published collection *Vozes anoitecidas* (Extract 2), translated as *Voices Made Night*, is a mixture of symbol, fantasy and reality, where faith in the supernatural and traditional myths play an important part in the characterization.

CRAVEIRINHA, José (1922–). Born in **Maputo**, Craveirinha worked as a journalist in the capital for many years before joining Frelimo. In 1966 he was arrested and tried with 12 other Mozambican intellectuals for criticizing the colonial regime. He was imprisoned from 1965 to 1969, after which time he composed a collection that came out of his moods and dreams of that period. His poetry is the voice of protest. All his poems are written in Portuguese, but selected ones have been translated for several anthologies (Extract 5). His poetry has won prizes in Mozambique, Italy, and Portugal. Fellow writer Luís Honwana ⧫ dedicated his book of short stories to him. In 1991 Craveirinha was reported by a passing author to have given up writing and declined to talk about poetry.

DE SOUSA, Noémia (1922–   ). de Sousa was born in **Maputo**. Her poetry was at its best while she was active in the early liberation struggle of the 1950s. She now lives quietly in exile in Paris. Her poetry in Portuguese appears in several anthologies.

HONWANA, Luís Bernardo (1942–). Honwana grew up in **Moamba**, a suburb of the capital, with seven siblings. His father worked as an interpreter for the Portuguese. Honwana's education was interrupted due to lack of funds, and he took up a post as a cartographer. His interest in writing grew when he contributed to the literary page of a local newspaper and he eventually became a reporter and then an editor in **Beira**. His work for Frelimo involved a spell in Lisbon in 1970, where, under the pretext of studying law, he was on assignment to rally communists and socialists together for the cause. He spent three years in prison, was released in 1967 and by 1975 was the Prime Minister's secretary. He was written several short stories, published as *We Killed Mangy-Dog and Other Mozambique Stories.* Among Honwana's other talents are documentary film-making and photography.

REBELO, Jorge (1940–   ). Born in **Maputo** and educated at Coimbra University in Portugal, Rebelo worked as Frelimo's Director of Information during the war of liberation and Editor of the magazine *Mozambique Revolution.* When the liberation group published *Breve Antologia Literatura Mozambicana* in 1967, several of his poems were included in the collection.

WÄSTBERG, Per (see under Tanzania).

NAMIBIA

'On my first evening, when a port official had led me to the edge of the desert, and asked me to look at it, I asked him what lay above, below and out beyond us. "Nothing!" he said, with a note of hysteria in his voice. "It's just miles, and miles, and miles – and MILES! – of Sweet Fanny Adams!" '
Negley Farson,
Behind God's Back

With one of the most inhospitable coastlines and deserts in Africa, if not the world, it is a wonder that Namibia's independence was won only a few years ago. The first colonists, the Germans, appeared on the barren shores in 1878, and waged a merciless campaign of genocide a few years later against the indigenous Herero and Nama peoples, who had protested against the invasion. Although the Germans were eventually usurped by South Africa in 1915, they maintain a strong presence numerically and culturally. Pictures of the Kaiser can be found lurking in shops and houses, and in **Swakopmund** a flag with a swastika mysteriously appears on Hitler's birthday.

For the South Africans, Namibia was an economically and politically strategic country and they occupied it illegally (without formal ratification), using it as an extension of their homeland with the same system of apartheid and suppression of the blacks. Negley Farson, on his travels here in the 1930s, remarked often on the 'South-Africanism' whose fragrance he described as 'something like the combination of "the odour of sanctity" and a dead buffalo'. Despite worldwide protest and the efforts of the South West Africa People's Organization (SWAPO) they held on to it until 1990.

The local literature reflects quite clearly the years of oppression and brutality. The Anthology *Voices from Twentieth-Century Africa* includes a dour local chant of the Bergdama people called 'Desperation', in which they sing, 'May the days kill me, that I perish!/May the years kill me that I perish!/I call out 'Woe!'/I call the days!/Years – I do not

455

FACT BOX

AREA: 824 292 sq km
POPULATION: 1 834 000
CAPITAL: Windhoek
LANGUAGES: Afrikaans, Damara, English, German, Herero,
  Kavango, Ovambo
FORMER COLONIAL POWERS: Germany (1892–1915),
  South Africa
INDEPENDENCE: 1990

---

believe that I shall live them./Days – I do not believe that I shall live them./Any measure of time – I do not believe that I shall live it.' The deep despair felt by the people before independence was reflected in a poetic prayer entitled 'Why, O Why, Lord?' by Zephania Kameeta. As well as declaring a strong affinity with the plight of the blacks in South Africa, Kameeta begs for 'release, righteousness, redemption' and an end to the relentless suffering in Namibia: 'We call to you, save us in our deadly fear!/We are trembling and feeble. Take our destiny in your strong right hand; through us let the world see your wonders!' (*Voices from Twentieth-Century Africa*).

One of the first modern Namibian works to appear in English was *Battlefront Namibia*, the autobiography of John Ya-Otto, a key member of SWAPO, who describes the terror and hopes of life as a freedom fighter in the 1970s. *Born of the Sun* (Extract 1) by Joseph Diescho ◊ is a more entertaining and poignant novel. It follows the story of how life changes in a village, first following the arrival of pious German missionaries and later when South Africa sends a 'Commissioner for Native Affairs' to collect taxes. As a young boy, Muronga, the hero, is frequently bemused and amused by the rituals and symbols of the church. Peering at a picture of a bleeding Christ carrying a heavy wooden cross over his shoulder, Muronga 'cannot help wondering how these white people came to be so cruel . . . Is it any wonder that not many of us want to become Christians.' Later forced to go to work in a gold mine in order to pay the taxes, he chants 'our only sin is the colour of our skin'.

While the prayer for independence has been answered for Namibia, in this fledgling state there are still many things to be done and much confidence to be restored before a true body of national literature can and will emerge.

LITERARY LANDMARKS

Swakopmund. In the 1930s, when Negley Farson came here and feasted on Bismark Herring, Frankfurters and beer served by a German Fräulein, it was said to be 120% Nazi.

Windhoek. Windhoek means 'windy corner'. 'This hilly capital is God's gift to the picture postcard industry . . . even the grave-yard, which is one of the showplaces of the town, is laid out with vistas of cypress and classic urns . . .' (Negley Farson, *Behind God's Back*). The **Lutheran Evangelical church** here was consecrated in 1910 to mark the end of the German genocide of the indigenous peoples.

Libraries and Bookshops

Windhoek. Estorff Reference Library; Old Mutual Library; Windhoek College of Education; Windhoek Public Library.

BOOKLIST

The following selection includes the extracted title in this chapter as well as those mentioned in the introduction which are available in English and other titles for further reading. In general, paperback editions are given when possible. The editions cited are not necessarily the only ones available.

Diescho, Joseph, *Born of the Sun*, Friendship Press, New York, 1988. **Extract 1.**

Farson, Negley, *Behind God's Back*, Gollancz, London, 1940.

Harding, Jeremy, *Small Wars, Small Mercies: Journeys in Africa's Disputed Nations*, Viking, 1993.

It is No More a Cry: Namibian Poetry in Exile, Henning Melber, ed, Basler Afrika Bibliographien, Basel, 1982.

Philander, Frederick, *The Curse: A Four Act Play on the Namibian Struggle*, Skotaville Publishers, Braamfontein.

Pickford, Peter, and Jacobsohn, M., *Himba: Nomads of Namibia*, New Holland Publishers, London, 1990.

Voices from Twentieth-Century Africa, Chinweizu, ed, Faber and Faber, London, 1988.

Ya-Otto, John, *Battlefront Namibia*, Heinemann, London, 1982.

Extract

(1) NAMIBIA: MISSIONARIES

Joseph Diescho, *Born of the Sun*

Muronga is in the German church trying to make head and tail of the Ten Commandments, the five laws of the Catholic church, and the rest of the catechism that he is being taught. When asked by the priest, he cannot remember who is God's representative on earth.

'I will tell you again. This is very important,' he goes on. 'God's representative on earth is the Pope, who is sitting in Rome, the holy capital. I told you this before, remember?' They nod their heads. Now they remember. How could they forget? They have been told many times about the pope. He is the man who wears dresses day and night! Muronga smiles quietly at the thought of this man who looks like a woman, but he says nothing . . .

Muronga and Makena nod in bewildered agreement as the priest lists the powers of the Holy Father. They haven't the faintest idea about what the Pope is and where Rome is. They cannot even figure out if this 'Pope' is male or female. The pictures Pater Dickmann has, show him wearing dresses all the time, as women would, but the priest and *Katekete* speak of him as a man. Maybe the Pope is a she-man, like Shamwaka, the man in the next village, who wears women's clothes and cannot get married, Muronga speculates. But Shamwaka is not the chief. I don't understand how a she-man can be a chief. A she-man could never be a chief, Muronga says to himself. He is tempted to ask the priest or *Kakekete* more about the Pope. But he remembers that it is this priest who chased one catechist away from the mission when he asked whether Mary, the mother of Jesus Christ, broke the marriage law by sleeping with the Holy Ghost. That would have explained how Mary got pregnant without sleeping with her man, Joseph. The catechist's question made perfect sense to Muronga, but kept the priest in a bad temper all week long . . .

From that day on they all learned that it was best just to believe what the priest said. They have been taught that believing, or faith, does not necessarily bring understanding. They do not even ask whether the Pope is a white or a black person.

Biography and important works

DIESCHO, Joseph. Diescho was born in the north of Namibia to uneducated peasant parents. He was educated in a Roman Catholic school by missionaries. Later he went on to study law and political science at Fort Hare University in South Africa. As a student, he was active in the anti-apartheid movement and helped found a workers' union while working in a diamond mine. Diescho later studied at Columbia University, New York. *Born of the Sun* (Extract 1), while not declared specifically as autobiographical, contains many ironical and sharp observations of the workings of the missionaries in Africa, and life in the gold mines.

SOUTH AFRICA

'Bees were the most sad . . . They took a long time to die, too. Sometimes two to three days of an agonizing wait for death. A day is a long time in a South African prison . . . As soon as I certified them dead, I . . . would take them to the rubble in the corner to perform the death ceremony, remembering the many funerals I had attended in Soweto.'
Molefe Pheto, And Night Fell

When Nadine Gordimer ◊ was awarded the Nobel Prize for Literature in 1991 she was, naturally, congratulated by her country's president F.W. De Klerk. 'A noteworthy achievement from any point of view', he said. His words brought attention to the fact that it is indeed her *particular* point of view for which she, and many of her fellow writers, are internationally recognized and for which their books were banned in South Africa. *Burger's Daughter* was originally marked down by the censors as nothing less than 'a full-scale attack on the republic', though today all Gordimer's books are available throughout the country. Since her first book was published in 1952, Gordimer's work has focused on the liberation movement in South Africa. She is an outspoken opponent of apartheid and a member of the African National Congress (ANC). In her recent collection of short stories *Jump*, she attempts to see and smell and feel the world from inside a black skin. Her *forte* in characterization, however, remains her portrayal of white South Africans (Extract 3).

A reviewer in *The Sunday Times* remarked that 'If one were never to read any other literature about South Africa, Gordimer's work would be enough.' This is something Gordimer herself would, I hope, strongly disagree with. There is an enormous body of work in many forms, styles and languages. The predominant themes are the unequal relations between the races and the long struggle for the liberation of 'Azania' since the first European settlement was established in the seventeenth century. As necessary expressions of identity and dissent, the historical

---

FACT BOX

AREA: 1 221 042 sq km (including Lesotho)
POPULATION: 36 762 000
CAPITAL: Pretoria
LANGUAGES: English, Afrikaans, Pedi, Sotho, Tsonga, Tswana,
   Venda, Xhosa, Zulu
FORMER COLONIAL POWER: Great Britain
INDEPENDENCE: 1910

---

importance of poetry, song, theatre and novels and short stories cannot be underestimated in a country like South Africa.

The most extreme cases of literature as a lifeline are those works by political prisoners. One of the modern classics is *Bandiet: Seven Years in a South African Prison* by Hugh Lewin, who served his sentence for sabotage. His memoirs spare no details as he takes us through his arrest, interrogation, torture (physical and emotional), and eventual release. Molefe Pheto, Steve Biko ◊ and Nelson Mandela (imprisoned 1962–90) have also written powerful political documentary-style books of their horrific experiences leading up to and/or during their imprisonment (see Extract 10 for Biko). Often found in these books, movingly recalling the roots of the prisoners and the old oral traditions, is the sound of song. Hugh Lewin, for example, writes 'Up behind the huge sign in the hall saying *Stilte/Silence*, the Condemned sing, chant, sing through the day and, before an execution, through the night. At times the chant is quiet, a distant murmur of quiet humming, softly. Then it swells; you can hear a more strident, urgent note in the swell, sounding through the prison . . .'.

Dennis Brutus ◊, one of South Africa's most highly regarded poets, spent 18 months in the notorious **Robben Island Prison**. Not only were writing and reading materials banned during imprisonment, but Brutus, an outspoken intellectual, was also banned from writing poetry following his release (Extract 9). His collection *Letters to Martha* was cleverly concealed in the form of letters to his sister-in-law. While his writing was distinguished by protest without malice – 'state the bare fact and let it sing' – it spoke precisely of the nightmares, loneliness and conditions he and his fellow prisoners suffered: 'and the resort of the weak/is to invoke divine revenge/against a rampaging injustice;/but in the grey silence of the empty afternoons/it is not uncommon/to find oneself talking to God.'

The resonant voice of exile, Brutus had a great effect on both his countrymen and his students. One of his students and friends, poet

Arthur Nortje ◊, wrote most of *Dead Roots* while in exile in England, shortly before he committed suicide at the age of just 28. One poem, written before his departure for England, summed up his reasons for leaving and was strangely prophetic about his own fate: 'All one attempts is talk in the absence/of others who spoke and vanished without so much as an echo./I have seen men with haunting voices/ turned into ghosts by a piece of white paper/as if their eloquence had been black magic'.

Despite the banning of his writings, short story writer Richard Rive ◊ was determined to live in his homeland. He was, he explains, 'part of a small élite of South African writers not allowed to read their own works in case they became influenced by them'. Rive's pithy short story 'The Bench' (Extract 12), is a classic and sensitive piece which was written in response to the South African Defiance of Unjust Laws Campaign 1952–53.

Rive was one of a group of writer–journalists along with Can Themba and Lewis Nkosi ◊ who got their first break on *Drum* magazine in the 1950s and 60s (see Extract 11 for Nkosi). They were the harbingers of the short sharp literary punch at apartheid. Themba's banned journalistic short stories in *The Will to Die* display the rich roughness of the life and jargon in **Sophiatown**: 'The near-animal, amorphous, quick shifting lingo that alarms farm-boys and drives cops to all branches of suspicion'. It is, believes Nkosi, this 'very absorbing, violent and immediate nature of experience which impinges on individual life' and which inhibits black writers from producing 'long and complex works of literary genius'.

While short fiction, be it oral fable or urban prose, has undoubtedly played a central role, plays and novels have not been overlooked. The first novel in English by a black South African was written in 1917. Published 13 years later, *Mhundi* by S.T. Plaatje describes the early skirmishes and struggle for land. Regarded as political, poetical and 'wonderfully old-fashioned', it is considered *the* epic of native life a century ago. The landmark (liberal) white novel around this time was *The Story of an African Farm* (Extract 4) by Olive Schreiner ◊, published in 1883. It follows the life of two cousins brought up by a large lazy Boer woman in the **Great Karroo** farming area. It was quickly courted for its powerful descriptions of the arid landscape, controversial for the rejection of conventional marriage by one of the main protagonists, and later hailed as prophetic on the question of race conflicts. Schreiner wrote of her countrymen (and the subjects of her fiction) in 1890, 'Fancy, a whole nation of lower middle class Philistines, without an aristocracy of blood or intellect or muscular labourers to save them.'

It was during the 1930s that the maverick English-language poet Roy

Campbell enjoyed a measure of popularity in his homeland. Following
the publication in 1924 of *The Flaming Terrapin*, a long derivative poem
in the manner of Eliot and Pound, he entered a fertile period of
inspiration. A great fan of Nietzsche and the Portuguese poet,
Camoëns, he had a reputation as an incurable teller of tall stories (the
autobiography *Light on a Dark Horse* is notoriously unreliable), as a
'talking bronco', a fascist and an anti-semite. His poems are often
colloquial, coarse, and epigrammatic, but as Marcia Leveson claims in
the introduction to *Roy Campbell: Selected Poems*, 'he remains certainly
our most prolific and possibly still our greatest poet'. The epigram for
which he is best remembered and oft quoted is the sharp 'On Some
South African Novelists' – 'You praise the firm restraint with which
they write – / I'm with you there, of course:/They use the snaffle and
the curb all right,/But where's the bloody horse?'

With the 1930s came the first 'African-coming-to-town' stories
which took the bit by the teeth. Provocative novels such as *In a
Province* (Extract 6) by Laurens van der Post ◊, published in 1934, is
the story of Johan, a white, who is taught by a charismatic and liberal
tutor who openly confesses his controversial views and desires for black
women – 'You must be very careful of this silly superstition that white
people in this country have about the black. In your own case, the
superstition has already got such a hold that it has deadened your sense
of what is beautiful . . . I want you to remember, in case you should
one day meet people who feel about black women as I have felt about
Johanna, that every white man who *does* sleep with a black woman
commits a social act of the greatest value.' The tutor is sacked and
Johan travels to a town called Port Benjamin where he strikes up a
friendship with a young black boy.

When Peter Abrahams' ◊ classic tale of transition, industrialization
and exploitation, *Mine Boy* (Extract 5), appeared in 1946 it was the
first novel by a black South African to have appeared in over fifteen
years. Two years later, Alan Paton's ◊ *Cry the Beloved Country* (Extract
8) was the white man's attempt to deal with this increasingly familiar
theme: 'The tragedy is not that things are broken', says one black
priest, 'The tragedy is that they are not mended again. The white man
has broken the tribe. And it is my belief . . . that it cannot be mended
again.' The book, set in **Johannesburg** and the **Umzimkulu valley**,
marked what one critic referred to as 'the apex of liberal humanism' in
South African literature.

A wave of Boer nationalism, heralded by the victory in 1948 of the
Afrikaner National Party, rapidly cast a grave silence over the literary
landscape of the 1950s and 1960s. As the voices of protest against the
growing restrictions and apartheid laws increased in volume, so did the
work of the censors. Peter Abrahams, returning briefly on a journalistic

assignment in 1952, cried 'it seemed to me that one did not have to die to go to hell. This was hell.' Abrahams and Ezekiel Mphahlele were two of the strongest novelists to come out of the *Drum* scene (*Drum* was the outspoken magazine founded by young African journalists – see under 'Literary Landmarks'). Mphahlele went on to establish himself as an important critic, essayist and anthologist. Banned from teaching in South Africa, he turned to writing and shortly afterwards left for Nigeria. In his autobiography *Down Second Avenue*, he describes his dilemma and the problems of living as an exile: 'Thirty seven years of age in a country of tensions is too long for one suddenly to develop a sense of guilt over escape. Yet it is too long for one to forget, to be lost in the new-found freedom. One develops a habit of thinking about oppression, and I was still wiping off the sweat in which I woke up when I jumped physically out of the *apartheid* nightmare.'

Beneath the deepening and darkening shadows of the 1950s and 1960s in South Africa, writing and a political career became inseparable for novelist and short story writer Alex La Guma ◊. As a result of his outspoken opposition to the regime he suffered years of house arrest, solitary imprisonment, and eventually found sanctuary in exile. Using a racy Coloured tongue, his first novel, *A Walk in the Night* (Extract 2), is about the breakdown of humanity in the slums of **Cape Town**. One of the distinguishing and welcome features that imbue his books is a spirited freshness and ironic humour of observation – a rare literary commodity amid such circumstances and when dealing with such themes.

A lightness of touch is also applied to this period in expatriate novelist Christopher Hope's retrospective *The Love Songs of Nathan J. Swirsky*, published in 1993. Set in a new suburb of **Johannesburg** in

---

Notes to map: [a]*Home of the progressive Market Theatre. Home town of **Nadine Gordimer**. Birthplace of **Miriam Thali**, known for her portrayals of life in Soweto. Setting for **Alan Paton's** Cry the Beloved Country. In Sophiatown, outside Johannesburg, the weekly magazine Drum was founded, whose contributors included **Richard Rive**, **Lewis Nkosi** and **Can Themba**. Peter Abrahams and Ezekiel Mphahlele were among the leading novelists to come out of the Drum literary scene;* [b]*Birthplace of **André Brink**;* [c]***Laurens van der Post** was born near Philippolis;* [d]*This farming region provided the setting for **Olive Schreiner's** The Story of an African Farm (Extract 4);* [e]*Birthplace of **Arthur Nortje**;* [f]*Birthplace of **J.M. Coetzee**, **Richard Rive**, and **Alex La Guma**, whose A Walk in the Night is set in the slums of the city (Extract 2). In Table Bay, off Cape Town, lies Robben Island, site of the notorious prison;* [g]***Olive Schreiner's** grave is near here;* [h]***Steve Biko** was brought up here;* [i]***Athol Fugard** was brought up here. He achieved international recognition in the 1960s with the so-called 'Port Elizabeth plays'. **Arthur Nortje** grew up in Port Elizabeth;* [j]*Birthplace of the Zulu poet **Mazisi Kunene**.*

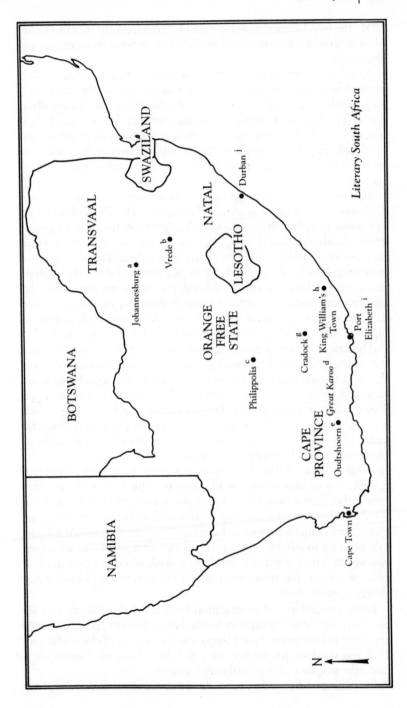

Literary South Africa

NAMIBIA

BOTSWANA

CAPE PROVINCE

TRANSVAAL

SWAZILAND

ORANGE
FREE
STATE

NATAL

LESOTHO

Johannesburg [a]

Vrede [b]

Durban [j]

Philippolis [c]

Cradock [g]

King William's [h]
Town

Port
Elizabeth [i]

Great Karoo [d]

Oudtshoorn [e]

Cape Town [f]

N

1951, the novel comprises a sequence of scenes from the small-town life of an apartheid community and uses humour to point up its ironies and absurdities.

Another rare appearance on the bookshelves, though perhaps for less explicable reasons, are works by black woman writers. Miriam Thali ◊ had problems getting her first novel, Muriel at the Metropolitan, published. Because it simply relates the everyday life of a black shop office clerk, the book has been described as 'circumcised in action' and 'negligible in plot'. Ironically it was the ordinariness of this viewpoint and Thali's experiences that gained her recognition and eventual success.

The most, and possibly the only really influential English-language dramatist to emerge was Athol Fugard ◊. The Blood Knot, first performed in 1961, has been described as 'probably the most important event South African theatre ever had'. The 'knot' is what holds together two half-brothers, one of whom is lighter than the other, as they struggle to hold on to their dream of a farm and their relationship. In a country where years of abuse numb the senses and wear down the capacity for compassion, it takes Fugard's daring in improvisation and experimentation combined with his raw energy and stark realism to make an audience sit up and take notice. Better seen than read.

The first real movements away from realism in English fiction came during the 1970s and 1980s with the work of J.M. Coetzee ◊ who sets the violence and oppression around him into a wider moral, psychological and historical context (Extract 1). From frontier men and **Cape Town** ladies, to megalomaniac Boers, Coetzee's books are infused with a macabre sense of death and the smell of decaying humanity. Says the callous Boer explorer in Dusklands, returning from wiping out a tribe of Hottentots in 1762, 'My essence is to open what is closed, to bring light to what is dark. If the Hottentots comprise an immense world of delight, it is an impenetrable world, impenetrable to men like me who must either skirt it, which is to evade our mission, or clear it out of the way.' Coetzee's character, in this his first work of fiction, symbolizes an eternal and ubiquitous terror – 'I can be seen as superfluous. At present I do not care to inhabit such a point of view; but when the day comes you will find that whether I am alive or dead, whether I ever lived or never was born, has never been of real concern to me. I have other things to think about.'

Exile, censorship and intimidation have affected publication of all contemporary 'liberal' writers in South Africa. Even the popular 'beach and bath' fiction writer Tom Sharpe was thrown out of the country in 1970 and was back for the first time in 1991. His satirical writing is a flashlight snapshot of the Afrikaners' society.

Censorship and prejudice have also inhibited the means and will for

J.M. Coetzee

translation from languages other than English. Zulu, Xhosa, Pedi, South Sotho and Tsongo are the main traditional languages. The earliest works in these languages kept close to the oral traditions; many then became influenced by the missionaries; and later writers developed more urban and political themes. Chinweizu, in his excellent anthology *Voices from Twentieth-Century Africa*, includes work from all over Azania. Born out of the lively Zulu oral literary tradition, for example, is the poet and historian Mazisi Kunene ◊. *Zulu Poems* (Extract 14), like most of his work, was written first in Zulu and then translated by the author into English. Kunene has also (somewhat poetically) translated *Chaka* (Extract 13) written in Sesotho in 1910 by Thomas Mofolo ◊. A much recounted legend, Mofolo's version of the Emperor's life focuses on his destruction and repudiation. Preparing for kingship, Chaka goes to a 'doctor' who tells him, 'the medicine with which I have vaccinated you is a medicine of blood; if you do not spill much blood, it will turn against you and kill you instead. Your sole purpose should be to kill without mercy, and thus clear the path that leads to the glory of your kingship.'

The movement to establish Afrikaans as a national language at the turn of the century resulted in several waves of writing. Notable were the early pastoral poets Eugène Marais and Jakob D. du Toit, whose work was a refuge from the horrors of the Anglo–Boer war of 1899–1902. Looking at later Afrikaans literature, you could work on the principle that if it was banned it must be good. If it was banned *and* translated, then it must be even better. The first popular politically committed (ie banned) Afrikaner writer to be translated (by himself) was André Brink ◊. *An Instant in the Wind*, *Rumours of Rain* and *A Dry White Season* (Extract 15) are among his best known novels. *An Act of Terror*, described as a 'polyphonic novel', takes the country's history and ethos in one sweep, dipping into the animal and crustacean kingdom for cruel but effective metaphors. The crayfish in one scene are seen to represent black Africa. As the fisherman twists off their tails and they scuttle away dismembered and disorientated, the fisherman (black) remarks, 'The crayfish get used to it.'

Brink's 1993 novel *The First Life of Adamastor* reflects some of the trends and concerns of the fiction emerging in the 'end-of-apartheid' era. Writers are adopting more experimental and personal approaches and formats, and the re-examination of South African history is a key concern. *The First Life of Adamastor* deals entertainingly with the racial, cultural and religious conflicts that have divided South African society and with the undeniable forces of sexual attraction that have so often defied those artificial barriers. *On the Contrary*, also 1993, appropriates the real-life eighteenth century figure of Estienne Barbier to anatomize the South African crisis. Barbier, originally sent out by the Dutch government, became involved in tribal wars and was eventually imprisoned and executed.

Another example of the new approach to fiction is the third novel of a younger Afrikaner writer, Karel Schoeman. In *Take Leave and Go*, Schoeman looks into the near future, portraying a society in civil war, in the grips of great change, its previous reference points swept away.

Since the release of ANC leader Nelson Mandela from prison, the government's strangle-hold of apartheid on the literature appears to be loosening and restrictions (which once banned the likes of *Black Beauty*) are being lifted. After so many decades of getting used to a siege mentality, authors, old and new, have greeted the changes with a natural cautious relief and sense of bewilderment. As Steve Biko said, 'We are looking forward to a nonracial, just and egalitarian society in which colour, creed and race shall form no point of reference.'

LITERARY LANDMARKS

Alice. The **University of Fort Hare** is South Africa's oldest university for blacks, and the Alma Mater of its black leaders. It is described as the 'Oxford' for the intelligentsia.

Johannesburg. The **Market Theatre** is a leading showcase for mixed-race drama and actors. Its most celebrated play is the witty *Woza Albert*, by director Barney Simon about what would happen if a black Jesus Christ arrived in South Africa today. Johannesburg is the home town of Nadine Gordimer.

Robben Island. Writers and political prisoners, including Dennis Brutus and Nelson Mandela, were held for many years under horrific circumstances.

Sophiatown. Here, outside Johannesburg, a group of young African journalists founded the racy and outspoken weekly magazine *Drum*. A book about the life and times of the magazine by Mike Nicholson entitled *A Good-Looking Corpse* takes its name from the local catch-all: 'live fast, die young and have a good-looking corpse'.

Libraries and Bookshops

Alice. University of Fort Hare Library.

Cape Town. South African Library.

Durban. Arcade Book Exchange, 14 Ajmeri Arcade, Grey Street; Municipal Library.

Johannesburg. Public Library.

Lesotho. National Library, Maseru.

Pretoria. State Library.

Swaziland. National Library, Mbabane.

Zululand. University of Zululand Library.

BOOKLIST

The following selection includes the extracted titles in this chapter as well as those mentioned in the introduction which are available in English and other titles for further reading. In general, paperback editions are given when possible. The editions cited are not necessarily the only ones available. For most of the extracted works, the original publisher in English can be found in 'Acknowledgments and Citations' at the end of the volume, as can the exact location of the extracts and the editions from which they are taken. Extract numbers are highlighted in bold for ease of reference.

Abrahams, Peter, *Mine Boy*, Heinemann, London, 1963. **Extract 5**.

Abrahams, Peter, *A Night of Their Own*, Faber and Faber, London, 1965.

Abrahams, Peter, *Tell Freedom*, Allen and Unwin, London, 1978.

Biko, Steve, *Black Consciousness in South Africa*, Vintage, New York, 1979.

Biko, Steve, *I Write What I like: A Selection of Writings*, Penguin, London, 1988. **Extract 10**.

Brink, André, *An Act of Terror*, Secker and Warburg, London, 1991.

Brink, André, *A Chain of Voices*, Faber and Faber, London, 1982.

Brink, André, *A Dry White Season*, Flamingo, London, 1984. **Extract 15**.

Brink, André, *The First Life of Adamastor*, Secker and Warburg, London, 1993.

Brink, André, *An Instant in the Wind*, Flamingo, London, 1983.

Brink, André, *Looking on Darkness*, Minerva, London, 1993.

Brink, André, *Mapmakers: Writing in a State of Siege*, Faber and Faber, London, 1983.

Brink, André, *On the Contrary*, Secker and Warburg, London, 1993.

Brink, André, *Rumours of Rain*, W.H. Allen, London, 1978.

Brutus, Dennis, *Letters to Martha and Other Poems from a South African Prison*, Heinemann, London, 1969.

Brutus, Dennis, 'Prey', in *Voices from Twentieth-Century Africa*, Chinweizu, ed, Faber and Faber, London, 1988. **Extract 9**.

Brutus, Dennis, *A Simple Lust*, Heinemann, London, 1973.

Campbell, Roy, *Light on a Dark Horse*, The Bodley Head, London, 1951.

Campbell, Roy, *Selected Poems*, A.D. Donker, Johannesburg and London, 1981.

Coetzee, J.M., *Age of Iron*, Penguin, London, 1991. **Extract 1**.

Coetzee, J.M., *Dusklands*, Penguin, London, 1983.

Coetzee, J.M., *In the Heart of the Country*, Secker and Warburg, London, 1977.

Coetzee, J.M., *Life & Times of Michael K*, Penguin, London, 1985.

Coetzee, J.M., *The Master of Petersburg*, Viking Penguin, New York, 1993.

Coetzee, J.M., *Waiting for the Barbarians*, Penguin, London, 1988.

Colours of a New Day: Writing for South Africa, Sarah Lefanu and Stephen Hayward, eds, Penguin, London, 1991.

du Toit, Jakob, D., in *Afrikaans Poems with English Translations*, Grove and Harvey, eds, Oxford University Press, London, 1969.

Fugard, Athol, *Boesman and Lena*

and Other Plays, Oxford University Press, London, 1980.

Gordimer, Nadine, Burger's Daughter, Jonathan Cape, London, 1979.

Gordimer, Nadine, My Son's Story, David Philip, Cape Town, 1990.

Gordimer, Nadine, July's People, Penguin, London, 1982.

Gordimer, Nadine, Jump and Other Stories, Bloomsbury, London, 1991.

Gordimer, Nadine, No Place Like: Selected Stories, Penguin, London, 1978. Extract 3.

Gordimer, Nadine, Something Out There, Jonathan Cape, London, 1984.

Harding, Jeremy, Small Wars, Small Mercies: Journeys in Africa's Disputed Nations, Viking, London, 1993.

The Heinemann Book of African Poetry in English, selected by Adewale Maja-Pearce, Heinemann, Oxford, 1990. Extract 7.

Hope, Christopher, The Love Songs of Nathan J. Swirsky, Macmillan, London, 1993.

Kunene, Mazisi, Anthem of the Decades, Heinemann, London, 1981.

Kunene, Mazisi, Emperor Shaka the Zulu, Heinemann, London, 1979.

Kunene, Mazisi, Zulu Poems, André Deutsch, London, 1970. Extract 14.

La Guma, Alex, In the Fog of the Season's End, Heinemann, London, 1972.

La Guma, Alex, The Stone Country, Seven Seas Books, Berlin, 1967.

La Guma, Alex, Time of the Butcherbird, Heinemann, London, 1979.

La Guma, Alex, A Walk in the Night, Heinemann, London, 1967. Extract 2.

Lewin, Hugh, Bandiet: Seven Years in a South African Prison, Heinemann, London, 1983.

Mandela, Nelson, No Easy Walk to Freedom, Heinemann, London, 1965.

Marais, Eugène, in Afrikaans Poems with English Translations, Grove and Harvey, eds, Oxford University Press, London, 1969.

Mofolo, Thomas, Chaka, Mazisi Kunene, trans, Heinemann, London, 1981. Extract 13.

Mphahlele, Ezekiel, Chirundu, Nelson, Walton-on-Thames, 1980.

Mphahlele, Ezekiel, Down Second Avenue, Faber and Faber, London, 1959.

Mphahlele, Ezekiel, The Unbroken Song, Raven, Johannesburg, 1981.

Nicholson, Mike, A Good-Looking Corpse, Secker and Warburg, London, 1991.

Nkosi, Lewis, 'The Prisoner', in African Writing Today, Ezekiel Mphalele, ed, Penguin, London, 1967. Extract 11.

Nortje, Arthur, Dead Roots, Heinemann, London, 1973.

Paton, Alan, Cry the Beloved Country, Jonathan Cape, London, 1977. Extract 8.

Paton, Alan, Too Late the Phalarope, Penguin, London, 1971.

Pheto, Molefe, And Night Fell: Memoirs of a Political Prisoner in South Africa, Heinemann, London, 1983.

Plaatje, Solomon Thekiso, Mhundi, Heinemann, London, 1978.

Rive, Richard, 'The Bench', in The Penguin Book of Southern African Stories, Penguin, London, 1985. Extract 12.

Rive, Richard, Emergency, Faber and Faber, London, 1964.

Rive, Richard, Selected Writings, A.D. Donker (Pty) Ltd, Johannesburg, 1975.

Rive, Richard, Writing Black, David Philip, Cape Town, 1981.

Schoeman, Karel, Take Leave and Go, Sinclair-Stevenson, London, 1993.

Schreiner, Olive, The Story of an

African Farm, Penguin, London, 1971. **Extract 4.**

Sharpe, Tom, *Indecent Exposure*, Pan, London, 1974.

Sharpe, Tom, *Riotous Assembly*, Pan, London, 1973.

Simon, Barney, *Woza Albert*, Methuen, London, 1983.

Soho Square V, S. Kromberg and J. Ogude, eds, Bloomsbury, London, 1992.

Thali, Miriam, *Muriel at the Metropo-litan*, Longman Group, London, 1979.

Vita Anthology of New South African Writing, The, Marcia Leveson, ed, Justifed Press, Pretoria, 1988.

Themba, Can, *The Will to Die*, Heinemann, London, 1972.

van der Post, Laurens, *In a Province*, Penguin, 1988. **Extract 6.**

Voices from Twentieth-Century Africa, Chinweizu, ed, Faber and Faber, London, 1988.

Extracts

(1) CAPE TOWN

J.M. Coetzee, *Age of Iron*

Elizabeth Curren's life changes when she finds out she has cancer, and Vercueil, a down-and-out alcoholic (her angel of death) takes up residence by her house. One night when trouble breaks out in a township she drives her domestic there to look for her son. Here they get caught up in a modern-day version of Dante's Inferno.

It was from the people gathered on the rim of this amphitheatre in the dunes that the sighing came. Like mourners at a funeral they stood in the downpour, men, women and children, sodden, hardly bothering to protect themselves, watching the destruction.

A man in a black overcoat swung an axe. With a crash a window burst. He attacked the door, which caved in at the third blow. As if released from a cage, a woman with a baby in her arms flew out of the house, followed by three barefoot children. He let them pass. Then he began to hack at the door-frame. The whole structure creaked.

One of his fellows stepped inside carrying a jerry-can. The woman dashed in after him, emerged with her arms full of bedclothes. But when she tried to make a second foray she was hurled out bodily.

A new sigh rose from the crowd. Wisps of smoke began to blow from inside the shack. The woman got to her feet, dashed indoors, was again hurled out.

A stone came sailing out of the crowd and fell with a clatter on the roof of the burning shack. Another hit the wall, another landed at the feet of the man with the axe. He gave a menacing shout. He and half a dozen of his fellows stopped what they were doing and, brandishing sticks and bars, advanced on the crowd. Screaming, people turned to flee, I among them. But in the clinging sand I could barely lift my feet. My heart pounded, pains shot through my chest. I stopped, bent over, gasping. *Can this really be happening to me?* I thought. *What am I doing here?*

(2) CAPE TOWN

Alex La Guma, *A Walk in the Night*

Willieboy, a petty criminal living in the coloured slums of Cape Town, goes for a walk in the night thinking about the dead body of a white man he accidently stumbled on earlier.

In the dark a scrap of cloud struggled along the edge of Table Mountain, clawed at the rocks for a foothold, was torn away by the breeze that came in from the southeast, and disappeared. In the hot tenements the people felt the breeze through the chinks and cracks of loose boarding and broken windows and stirred in their sweaty sleep. Those who could not sleep sat by the windows or in doorways and looked out towards the mountain beyond the rooftops and searched for the sign of wind. The breeze carried the stale smells from passageway to passageway, from room to room, along lanes and back alleys, through the realms of the poor, until the massed smells of stagnant water, cooking, rotting vegetables, oil, fish, damp plaster and timber, un-washed curtains, bodies and stairways, cheap perfume and incense, spices and half-washed kitchenware, urine, animals, and dusty corners became one vast, anonymous odour, so widespread and all-embracing as to become unidentifiable, hardly noticeable by the initiated nostrils of the teeming, cramped world of poverty which it enveloped.

Willieboy strolled up the narrow back street in District Six, keeping instinctively to the shadows which were part of his own anonymity, and thought with sudden anger: Well, I had *mos* nothing to do with it. They can't say it's me. I found him *mos* like that. But years of treacherous experience and victimization through suspicion had rusted the armour of confidence, reduced him to the nondescript entity which made him easy prey to a life which specialised in finding scapegoats for anything that steered it from its dreary course. So that now he longed for the stimulants which would weld the seams of the broken armour and bring about the bravado that seemed necessary in the struggle to get back into the battle that was for hardened warriors only.

(3) Durban

Nadine Gordimer, *The Catch*

On a beach near Durban an Afrikaner couple make 'friends' with a local Indian who is also spending his holiday there. The couple congratulate themselves on 'The fact that he was an Indian hardly troubled them at all. They almost forgot he was an Indian.' Gordimer carefully reveals the ingrained attitudes and awkwardness in the Afrikaners' conduct. 'The Catch' is included in No Place Like – *see Booklist.*

He was 'their Indian'. When they went home they might remember the holiday by him as you might remember a particular holiday as the one when you used to play with a spaniel on the beach every day. It would be, of course, a nameless spaniel, an ownerless spaniel, an entertaining creature existing nowhere in your life outside that holiday, yet bound with absolute intimacy within that holiday itself. And, as an animal becomes more human every day, so every day the quality of their talk with the Indian had to change; the simple question-and-answer relation that goes with the celluloid pop of a ping-pong ball and does so well for all inferiors, foreigners and children became sudddenly a toy (the Indian was grown-up and might smile at it). They did not know his name, and now, although they might have asked the first day and got away with it, it was suddenly impossible, because he didn't ask them theirs. So their you's and he's and I's took on the positiveness of names, and yet seemed to deepen their sense of communication by the fact that they introduced none of the objectivity that names must always bring. He spoke to them quite a lot about Johannesburg, to which he assumed they must belong, as that was his generalization of city life, and he knew, sympathetically, that they were city people. And although they didn't live there, but somewhere near on a smaller pattern, they answered as if they did. They also talked a little of his life; or rather of the processes of the sugar refinery from which his life depended. They found it fascinating.

'If I were working, I'd try and arrange for you to come and see it,' he said, pausing, with his familiar taking his own time, and then looking directly smiling at them, his head tilted a little, the proud, almost rueful way one looks at two attractive children. They responded to his mature pleasure in them with a diffusion of warm youth that exuded from their skin as sweat is released at the touch of fear. 'What a fascinating person he is!' they would say to one another, curious.

(4) GREAT KARROO

Olive Schreiner, *The Story of an African Farm*

Out in the Great Karroo lies the isolated farm where live Tant' Sannie the big Boer and her young charges Lyndall and Em. It is 1862, the year of the great drought, and this peaceful moonlit picture belies the trouble that is to come.

The full African moon poured down its light from the blue sky into the wide, lonely plain. The dry, sandy earth, with its coating of stunted 'karroo' bushes a few inches high, the low hills that skirted the plain, the milk-bushes with their long, finger-like leaves, all were touched by a weird and an almost oppressive beauty as they lay in the white light.

In one spot only was the solemn monotony of the plain broken. Near the centre a small, solitary 'kopje' rose. Alone it lay there, a heap of round iron-stones piled one upon another, as over some giant's grave. Here and there a few tufts of grass or small succulent plants had sprung up among its stones, and on the very summit a clump of prickly-pears lifted their thorny arms, and reflected, as from mirrors, the moonlight on their broad, fleshy leaves. At the foot of the 'kopje' lay the homestead. First, the stone-walled 'sheep-kraals' and Kaffir huts; beyond them the dwelling-house – a square red-brick building with thatched roof. Even on its bare red walls, and the wooden ladder that led up to the loft, the moonlight cast a kind of dreamy beauty, and quite etherealized the low brick wall that ran before the house, and which enclosed a bare patch of sand and two straggling sunflowers . . .

In the farm-house, on her great wooden bedstead, Tant' Sannie, the Boer-woman, rolled heavily in her sleep.

She had gone to bed, as she always did, in her clothes; and the night was warm and the room close, and she dreamed bad dreams. Not of the ghosts and devils that so haunted her waking thoughts; nor of her second husband, the consumptive English man, whose grave lay away beyond the ostrich-camps; nor of her first, the young Boer; but only of the sheep's trotters she had eaten for supper that night. She dreamed that one stuck fast in her throat, and she rolled her huge form from side to side, and snorted horribly.

(5) JOHANNESBURG

Peter Abrahams, *Mine Boy*

Xuma, a young boy from the north, has just arrived at Malay Camp, Johannesburg to work in the mines. Alone and naive, he is befriended by a family who offer him food, shelter, and advice.

'Tell him about the custom and the city,' she repeated patiently, helping him into a chair.

'The custom and the city,' he murmured, then his eyes lighted up and he smiled. 'The custom and the city, ah. Oh yes, funny about the custom and city, Xuma. Very funny. Just you listen . . .'

He got up and walked up and down the room. He rubbed his hands, smiled knowingly and smacked his lips. He lifted first one shoulder then the other.

'Very funny,' he said. 'One day the city came to visit the custom, Xuma. And the custom was kind. It gave the city food and it gave the city beer and it gave the city beautiful young women . . .'

'No, Daddy,' Leah interrupted.

'Quiet, woman!' Daddy said very firmly.

Leah smiled.

'. . . As I was saying, it gave the city beautiful young women. And then what do you think? Unbelievable. The city didn't say a word. It didn't say "No thank you" and it didn't say "thank you." And the people said, "Ah, everything will be all right now, the custom and the city are friends." Hmmmm. . . . They did say that and they went out into the fields to look after their crops. And when the sun was going down they came back and looked for their beer but their beer was gone. And then they looked for the custom but he had gone too. And the city was there laughing at them. And now they go to jail if they drink beer. That's why I like beer . . . Very funny, heh, Xuma? Well, that is it and I want to go to sleep . . .'

(6) SOUTH AFRICA: A BOARDING HOUSE
Laurens van der Post, *In a Province*

Johan and Kenon, an Afrikaner and a black, both find themselves as homesick new arrivants in a bleak boarding house. Johan soon makes friends with Kenon, who is working there, much to the disapproval and suspicion of the other lodgers. One evening at supper Major Mustard asks Johan if he knows a particular poem of Kipling's.

' "Oh! East is East, and West is West, and
       never the twain shall meet." '
'You mean Kipling?'

'One can easily substitute for that, with as much justification,' said the Major, ignoring his remark, ' "Oh! White is White, and Black is Black, and never the twain shall meet." And if they do meet, by God, there shall be trouble.'

'I don't think I know what you're driving at,' van Bredepoel answered.

'I think you'll know presently,' the Major said mysteriously, and went on eating.

Van Bredepoel knew after dinner, for as he came out of the dining-room Mrs Harris beckoned him nervously to her room.

'I don't like talking to you, Mr van Bredepoel,' she said, trembling with nervousness, 'and I'm sure, of course, there's nothing in it, but several of my guests have been talking to me and complaining, not that I attach the slightest importance to it, but you know what these complaints are, one must attend to them if only to be tactful . . . Oh, where was I? Yes! Some people have been complaining that they often see that new boy Joseph going into your room.'

'It is perfectly true, Mrs Harris,' he replied, and then sought the most plausible explanation, not because he had anything to conceal but because he knew it was quite hopeless to try to make Mrs Harris and her lodgers realise that he was interested in Kenon as a human being. They would not have understood. 'You see, I'm very interested in native folklore, and as this boy is still fresh from his country it occurred to me that he might have a great deal of useful information to give me. It's so rare that one gets the chance of talking to a raw native in Port Benjamin, isn't it?'

'Oh! I'm so glad it's that!' she replied. 'I'll tell them that immediately, and I do hope you don't mind my talking to you like this, but of course no one would dream of interfering with your private studies. But you know, Mr van Bredepoel, you students are sometimes a little unconventional!'

The following night, at dinner, Major Mustard looking at him over his plate of soup and said: 'So you are interested in anthropology?' And before van Bredepoel could reply, added: 'It must be an interesting subject, that – ahem! – anthropology.'

(7) South Africa: Exile

Arthur Nortje, *Waiting*

Written in exile shortly before Nortje committed suicide at the age of 28, 'Waiting' describes what he calls the 'radiation burns of silence'. The agony of feeling helpless and lonely that is present in much of Nortje's work speaks also for many of his fellow exiles. The poem is included in The Heinemann Book of African Poetry in English – see Booklist.

The isolation of exile is a gutted
warehouse at the back of pleasure streets:
the waterfront of limbo stretches panoramically –
night the beautifier lets the lights
dance across the wharf.
I peer through the skull's black windows
wondering what can credibly save me.

(8) South Africa: Fear

Alan Paton, *Cry the Beloved Country*

In the course of this story of a priest looking for his son in Johannesburg, many of Paton's passages are sermon-like in their expression of hopes and fears for the future of his country. The book was first published in 1948.

Yes, there are a hundred, and a thousand voices crying. But what does one do, when one cries this thing, and one cries another? Who knows how we shall fashion a land of peace where black outnumbers white so greatly? Some say that the earth has bounty enough for all, and that more for one does not mean less for another, that the advance of one does not mean the decline of another. They say that poor-paid labour means a poor nation, and that better-paid labour means greater markets and greater scope for industry and manufacture. And others say that this is a danger, for better-paid labour will not only buy more but will also read more, think more, ask more, and will not be content to be for ever voiceless and inferior.

Who knows how we shall fashion such a land? For we fear not only the loss of our possessions, but the loss of our superiority and the loss of our whiteness. Some say it is true that crime is bad, but would this not be worse? It is not better to hold what we have, and to pay the price of it with fear? And others say, can such fear be endured? For is it not this fear that drives men to ponder these things at all? . . .

Cry, the beloved country, for the unborn child that is the inheritor of our fear. Let him not love the earth too deeply. Let him not laugh too gladly when the water runs through his fingers, nor stand too silent when the setting sun makes red the veld with fire. Let him not be too moved when the birds of his land are singing, nor give too much of his heart to a mountain or valley. For fear will rob him of all if he gives too much.

(9) SOUTH AFRICA: HOPE

Dennis Brutus, *Pray*

Ex-political prisoner and current exile, poet Dennis Brutus'
prose conveys the reality of life in his homeland with images from
its harsh natural environment. The images recall Robben Island
Prison where he was held for 18 months. 'Pray' is included in
Voices from Twentieth-Century Africa – see Booklist.

we have soared among cloudpeaks
and splintered our hearts on their marble whiteness
we were sodden in the drizzling harmattan of tears
now we sear, sere, in the sirocco of lost hopes

we have known the rocks and the shoals
the diapson breakers and talismanic spray
we have stood transfigured and effulgent
we have known the jagged edges and the taloned reefs

Pray,
if you believe in prayer,
for those shipwrecked by love;
or pity us:
for still it will not rain.

(10) South Africa: Interrogation

Steve Biko, *I Write What I Like*

*These thoughts on death, pride and interrogation were taken
from an interview given to an American businessman some
months before Biko's final detention and death.*

You are either alive and proud or you are dead, and when you are dead,
you can't care anyway. And your method of death can itself be a
politicizing thing. So you die in the riots. For a hell of a lot of them, in
fact, there's really nothing to lose – almost literally, given the kind of
situations that they come from. So if you can overcome the personal
fear of death, which is a highly irrational thing, you know, then you're
on the way.

And in interrogation the same sort of thing applies. I was talking to
this policeman, and I told him, 'If you want us to make any progress,
the best thing is for us to talk. Don't try any form of rough stuff, because
it just won't work.' And this is absolutely true also. For I just couldn't
see what they could do to me which would make me all of a sudden
soften to them. If they talk to me, well I'm bound to be affected by
them as human beings. But the moment they adopt rough stuff, they
are imprinting in my mind that they are police. And I only understand
one form of dealing with police, and that's to be as unhelpful as
possible. So I button up. And I told them this: 'It's up to you.' We had
a boxing match the first day I was arrested. Some guy tried to clout me
with a club. I went into him like a bull. I think he was under
instructions to take it so far and no further, and using open hands so
that he doesn't leave any marks on the face. And of course he said
exactly what you were saying just now: 'I will kill you.' He meant to
intimidate. And my answer was 'How long is it going to take you?'

(11) South Africa: Prisoner

Lewis Nkosi, *The Prisoner*

*The story of George and his former servant Mulela, this is black
humour at its driest and most sardonic. George, a white South
African bigwig, succumbs to his (illegal) weakness for a 'dark
stormy body' in the form of his maid and finds himself
blackmailed, then held prisoner by his own 'prisoner'. This short
story is included in the anthology African Writing Today – see
Booklist.*

I know, you must be impatient to see him at close range. You want to
examine his physical condition with a thoroughness which is his proper

due. That I appreciate. Also the Social Welfare Department, as you say, is anxious about his condition, what with all the ugly rumours about torture and other unmentionable brutalities, though I must say, I'm surprised that people in your Department (people of your background and training) can be so completely misled by false and unjustified reports in the newspapers. We all know what newspapers are like – garbage cans of rumour and scandal, that have an insatiable love of tragedy and of the slightly unsavoury. . .

At any rate, I think I can reveal to you quite frankly that apart from an occasional whipping with a leather thong which is permitted by the Prison Code, George has never been tortured. It is true that once or twice I have been compelled to put his thumb in a screw when he failed to address me properly as 'master'. Nothing very serious, as I say; besides, in the modern world we have learned to live with such unpleasantness as a kind of necessity. George emitted a few horrible screams, but then George has always been something of a physical coward. While he was boss and jailer, protected by a white skin, you wouldn't know it. I also feel it is necessary to mention the fact that while George was master here it was foolhardy in the extreme to forget to address him as 'bwana', 'baas', or some such tedious nomenclature. Where titles were concerned, whatever sense of humour George possessed deserted him altogether. He took these social conventions most seriously. So we wouldn't let him get away with anything, we had to insist that he observe the same social obligations. There were times when I felt it necessary to apply electric shocks in order to revive him from what seemed a fatal lapse of memory.

(12) SOUTH AFRICA: SEGREGATION

Richard Rive, *The Bench*

Emboldened and enlightened following a conversation about challenging the system, Karlie decides to visit a friend. He heads purposefully into the train station where suddenly everything looks and feels different: 'He saw the station through the eyes of a fresh convert.' 'The Bench' is included in The Penguin Book of Southern African Short Stories – see Booklist.

Then it dawned on him. Here was his chance. The bench. The railway bench with the legend WHITES ONLY neatly painted on it in white.

For a moment it symbolized all the misery of South African society. Here was his challenge to his rights as a man. Here it stood. A perfectly ordinary wooden bench like the hundreds of thousands of others all over South Africa. Benches on dusty stations in the Karoo; under ferns

and subtropical foliage in Natal; benches all over the country each with
its legend. His challenge. That bench now had concentrated in it all
the evils of a system he could not understand. It was the obstacle
between himself and his manhood. If he sat on it, he was a man. If he
was afraid, he denied himself membership as a human in human
society. He almost had visions of righting the system if only he sat on
that bench. Here was his chance. He, Karlie, would challenge.

He seemed perfectly calm as he sat down, but his heart was thumping
wildly. Two conflicting ideas now seeped through him. The one said,
'You have no right to sit on the bench.' The other questioned, 'Why
have you no right to sit on the bench? The first spoke of the past, of the
life on the farm, of the servile figure of his father and Ou Klaas, his
father's father who had said, 'God in his wisdom made the white man
white and black man black.' The other voice had promise of the future
in it and said, 'Karlie, you are a man. You have dared what your father
would not have dared. And his father. You will die like a man.'

Karlie took out a Cavalla from the crumpled packet and smoked. But
nobody seemed to notice him sitting there. This was also a let-down.
The world still pursued its natural way. People still lived, breathed and
laughed. No voice shouted triumphantly, 'Karlie, you have conquered!'
He was a perfectly ordinary human being sitting on a bench on a
crowded station, smoking a cigarette. Or was this his victory? Being an
ordinary human being sitting on a bench?

(13) SOUTH AFRICA: ZULU KING

Thomas Mofolo, Chaka

*Even as a young boy Chaka stood out from his peer group. He
was a skilled fighter and as the villagers began to question
whether or not he was human, he became linked with all things
evil and was treated accordingly.*

In those days, long ago, wild beasts used to terrorize the people a great
deal. On many evenings, while the people were sitting around or as
they were about to turn in, a hyena, if it had found no goats to eat,
would come into the village and grab a person and run off with him,
with no one brave enough to go in pursuit and force it to abandon its
prey. That poor person would scream continuously in the middle of the
darkness, saying: 'It's picking me up! It's putting me down! It's picking
me up again! It's putting me down! Now it's eating me!' He would
shout these words in an attempt to raise the alarm so that the people
would know where he was and come to his rescue. But in spite of all
that, it would eventually eat him with no one coming to help him.

Since there were no strong doors, very often children such as Chaka were placed near the door in the young people's hut, so that the hyena should take them and the others should escape. Chaka himself was made to sleep by the door there in the young men's hut, so that such hazards of the night, including those involving witchcraft, should begin with him. He had been turned into a barricade used to protect the others. But, in spite of all that, such dangers kept passing him by: a hyena would simply sniff at him and pass to the far end of the hut and grab someone there. Indeed, it appears that a hyena always avoids taking a person sleeping right by the door, just as if it knew that the ones who sleep near the door are the hated ones.

Twice or three times, Chaka had his hands tied right there in the young people's hut, and was made to sleep outside near the door tied up like that, so that the hyena should see him as soon as it came. This would be done on a day when a hyena had been seen near the village, and it was expected that it would catch some people after dark; but on those occasions the hyena would feast on goats and leave the people alone. Chaka's growing up was truly painful.

(14) SOUTH AFRICA: ZULU TRADITION

Mazisi Kunene, *Cycle*

Here during traditional festival celebrations the Zulu are conscious of the presence of their ancestors. Speaking of his own translation of Zulu Poems, Kunene reminds us that 'these are not English poems, but poems directly evolved from a Zulu literary tradition'.

So many are asleep under the ground,
When we dance at the festival
Embracing the earth with our feet.
Maybe the place on which we stand
Is where they also stood with their dreams.
They dreamed until they were tired
And handed us the tail with which we shall dance.

(15) SOWETO

André Brink, *A Dry White Season*

It is 1976, just after the Soweto riots, and Ben Du Toit is on a mission to uncover the truth about the death of his black friend Gordon at the hands of the security police. Here his investigations take him into the Johannesburg township.

In the dark it was a different city. The sun was down when they reached Uncle Charlie's Roadhouse; by the time they left the main road near the bulky chimneys of the power station, the red glow was already darkening through smoke and dust, smudged like paint. A premonition of winter in the air. The network of narrow eroded paths and roads across the bare veld; then the railway-crossing and a sharp right turn into the streets running between the countless rows of low, squat houses. At last it was there, all around them, as overwhelming as the previous time, but in a different way. The dark seemed to soften the violence of the confrontation, hiding the details that had assaulted and insulted the eyes, denying the squalor. Everything was still there, stunning in its mere presence, alien, even threatening; and yet the night was reassuring too. There were no eyes conspicuously staring. And the light coming from the small square windows of the innumerable houses – the deadly pallor of gas, the warmer yellow of candles or paraffin lamps – had all the nostalgic intimacy of a train passing in the night. The place was still abundantly alive, but with a life reduced to sound: not the sort of sound one heard with one's ears, but something subterranean and dark, appealing directly to bones and blood. The hundreds of thousands of separate lives one had been conscious of the first time – the children playing soccer, the barbers, the women on street corners, the young ones with clenched fists – had now blurred into a single omnipresent organism, murmuring and moving, devouring one like an enormous gullet that forced one further down, with peristaltic motions, to be digested and absorbed or excreted in the dark.

Biographies and important works

ABRAHAMS, Peter (1919–). Abrahams was born in **Vrededorp Johannesburg** to a 'Cape Coloured' mother and an Ethiopian father. As a child, he 'lived in two worlds' – that of the slums and that of his books (Shakespeare and Keats were his favourites). He worked his passage to Europe on a boat at the age of nineteen and eventually made his way to

Jamaica. Abrahams has written many short stories, novels and essays. *Mine Boy* (Extract 5) was significant as one of the first books to bring to light the condition of blacks lured into the industrialized cities and exploited by the machinations of the apartheid system. The autobiographical *Tell Freedom* relates the struggle of a bright educated boy to escape his country. *A Night of Their Own* portrays the plight of the oft-overlooked Indian community. Abrahams now works as a journalist and a broadcaster in Jamaica.

BIKO, Steve (1946–1977). The nationalist leader was brought up in **King William's Town** where he was born to a clerk and a domestic for white families. In 1966 he joined the non-European section of the medical school of the **University of Natal, Durban**. In 1968 he helped found the South African Student's Organization and later the Black People's Convention. Expelled from university in 1972, he joined the Black Community Programmes. *I Write What I Like* (Extract 10), a collection of his political writings, cries out against the tyranny in South Africa. Banned and therefore silenced in 1973, Biko made his last public statement when he was called to testify at the trial of nine blacks charged with terrorism. *Black Consciousness in South Africa*, the transcript of this legendary explanation, is a testimony to his courage and commitment and to the principles and objectives of the Black Consciousness movement of which he was 'father'. Biko was brutally murdered while he was in police detention in 1977.

BRINK, André (1935–). Brink was born in **Vrede**, Orange Free State. He studied English, Afrikaans and Dutch at a university in **Transvaal**. A prolific writer, his early work was unashamedly influenced by Albert Camus (◊ Algeria) and the existentialists. He spent a year in Paris in 1968. An Afrikaner, although he finds apartheid morally insupportable, he chooses to remain in South Africa. *Mapmakers: Writing in a State of Siege* is a collection of his essays published almost a decade ago on the responsibilities of his fellow authors. Since 1980 Brink has been Head of the Department of Afrikaans and Dutch literature at **Rhodes University, Grahamstown**. His work first came to notice when he was the first Afrikaner writer to be banned under the 1963 censorship laws. His first novel was *A Dry White Season* (Extract 15) which, along with *Rumours of Rain*, is generally regarded as the best, and least sentimental and sensationalist of his works.

BRUTUS, Dennis (1924–). Brutus was born in Harare, Zimbabwe, but graduated from **Fort Hare University** and taught English and Afrikaans for many years in South Africa. Of mixed parentage, he was classified there as 'Coloured' and as such subjected to the vagaries of apartheid. He was a leading political activist and, as a keen sportsman, campaigned against racism in sport. Shot in **Johannesburg** by the South African police, Brutus was sentenced to one-and-a-half years' hard labour on **Robben Island**, during which *Sirens, Knuckles, Boots*, his first volume of poetry, was awarded the Mbari Prize. After his release in 1966, he was defined as a banned person and went into exile in London and later the USA. He is currently a professor at North-Western University in Chicago. *A Simple Lust* is a selection of his work including reflections on exile, and reveals how, in order to dodge cen-

André Brink

sorship in his homeland, Brutus cleverly circulated work under a pseudonym. Among several awards he received for his writing during the 1970s was the 1979 Award for Humanism from Kenneth Kaunda of Zambia.

COETZEE, J.M. (1940–). Coetzee was born in **Cape Town** and is a graduate of the **University of Cape Town** and the University of Texas. He has worked as a computer programmer and lectured widely. His work is often described as modern political fable. It is marked by a persistent concern with the theme of exploitation. In the two novellas of *Dusk-lands*, Coetzee bluntly juxtaposes life in southern Africa in the 1760s with the dealings of the US State Department during the Vietnam war. *Waiting for the Barbarians* was followed by *In the Heart of the Country*. Prize-winning *Age of Iron* (Extract 1), set against Coetzee's usual measure of blood and violence, is a stark but beautiful portrait of a lonely widow dying of cancer. His 1993 novel *The Master of Petersburg* concerns Dostoevsky's search for his stepson who turns out to have been killed by the secret service because of his involvement in political activities. Coetzee has been awarded several literary prizes, including the Booker Prize in 1980.

FUGARD, Athol (1932–). Brought up by mixed English and Afrikaner parents in **Port Elizabeth**, Fugard's first involvement with theatre was in **Cape Town**, with an experimental group. His first works were inspired by his job in a Native Commissioner's court where he met numerous Africans who had fallen foul of the 'pass laws'. Among his first books was a novel, *Tsotsi*, written in 1959 but unpublished until 1979. In the early 1960s, the so-called 'Port Elizabeth plays', *The Blood Knot, Hello and Goodbye* and *Boesman and Lena* brought him into the international literary limelight. The last two were two- or three-handed plays written especially for a drama group in Port Elizabeth in 1963. In the late 1960s Fugard and his actors discovered and devised improvisational theatre. Drawing on the actors' real experiences with the pass laws and **Robben Island Prison**, they produced several powerful pieces.

GORDIMER, Nadine (1923–). Gordimer is the *grande* (white) *dame* of South African literature, and, as *Time* put it, 'South Africa's restless white conscience'. She began writing at the age of nine, was first published when 15, and made her literary début in 1952 with *Lying Days*. During the 1950s her house became something of a meeting place for *Drum* writers. *Burger's Daughter*, published in 1979, tells the story of the daughter of an Afrikaner Communist whose father dies in prison. The book showed a move in her writing in the 1970s towards white heroes who are wholly committed to black liberation. Gordimer helped found the Congress of South African Writers in the 1980s. Of her reputation a critic once said, 'In South Africa her stature as a major writer goes largely unacclaimed. Abroad . . . she is the country's most celebrated writer.' Gordimer was awarded the Nobel Prize for Literature in 1991. She is married to a South African art dealer and currently lives in **Johannesburg**.

KUNENE, Mazisi (1930–). The Zulu poet Kunene was born in **Durban** where he later studied history and Zulu at the **University of Natal**. *Emperor Shaka the Zulu* is his 17 book-long praise-song. *Anthem of the Decades* ('The Age of the Gods', The Age of Fantasy' and 'The Age of the Ancestors') is concerned with the philosophy and origin of life as perceived by Zulu tradition, and was inspired by the author's great-grandmother. Kunene has taught and lectured widely on African literature. A founder member of the anti-apartheid movement, he has worked for the ANC.

LA GUMA, Alex (1925–). La Guma was born and educated in **Cape Town**, where he joined the local Communist party. He went on to become a leading figure in the liberation movement, for which activity he was frequently arrested and imprisoned. For years nothing he wrote was permitted to be published or quoted, and he was charged for possessing banned literature. *A Walk in the Night* (Extract 2), his first novel was published abroad. His prison experiences resulted in *The Stone Country* which is dedicated to 'the daily 70351 prisoners in South African jails in 1964.' About *In the Fog of the Season's End*, a poetic novel written whilst in exile, it is often remarked that he has since lost touch intellectually with events in his homeland. He currently lives in exile in England.

MOFOLO, Thomas (1876–1948). Born in **Lesotho**, Mofolo was prolific

Nadine Gordimer

at the beginning of the century when he wrote two books which were published in Sesotho by the Morija Mission. Around 1909, he left his job as proofreader, reviewer and reporter for the Mission's publications, and wrote his best known work, *Chaka* (Extract 13). Although he finished this work about Chaka, the ambitious and legendary Zulu leader, in 1910, it was not published until 1925. It has since been translated by the poet Mazisi Kunene ◊.

NKOSI, Lewis (1936–). Nkosi is an essayist, a critic, and a playwright. Driven by early ambition and literary interest, he had at the age of nineteen already embarked on a career in journalism on the *Natal Sun*. He soon joined *Drum*, where he became Chief Reporter living in notorious **Sophiatown**. When he left to study in the USA, he became an exile and his works were banned in South Africa. He has since written for numerous British and American magazines, including *The New Yorker*, *The Spectator*, and *Africa Today*. When his play *The Rhythm of Violence* was published in England in 1965 it was, somewhat remarkably, celebrated as the first English-language play to be written by a black South African since 1936. Returning to Africa, Nkosi became senior lecturer in literature at the University of Zambia.

NORTJE, Arthur (1942–1970). Nortje was born in **Oudtshoorn** and educated in **Port Elizabeth**. He attended the segregated **University of Western Cape** where he studied English and Psychology. Following a nervous breakdown he went to live abroad, where the pain and suffering of both his country and his feelings as an exile were revealed in his poetry and were to lead eventually to his suicide in his room at Oxford University. He was just 28 years old when he took a fatal overdose of barbiturates. His posthumously published collection *Dead Roots* includes several dedications to the poet Sylvia Plath and was written while working for a doctorate at Jesus College. Nortje's work has been widely anthologized.

PATON, Alan (1903–1988). Brought up by deeply religious English parents, Paton was a founding member of the anti-apartheid Liberal Association in the 1950s. Almost all his works display his belief in the power of love and brotherhood and his suspicion of institutional power, and are characterized by a simple and rhythmic use of pseudo-biblical language. The book which established his reputation as a novelist was *Cry, the Beloved Country*. Subtitled *A Story of Comfort in Desolation*, the novel is set in **Johannesburg** and tells the touching story of a Zulu minister who has come to the city to search for his son.

RIVE, Richard (1931–). Rive was born in the infamous **District Six** slum of **Cape Town**. He was educated at local schools, and the Universities of Cape Town, Columbia and Oxford, where his doctoral studies were on the life and work of Olive Schreiner ◊. His *forte* as a short story writer became evident while he was still a student of English. His subjects are, he says, simply 'tsotsis, life in the slums, the consequences of overt protest and the ironies of racial prejudice and color snobbery'. (A 'tsotsi' is a violent, typically young criminal living on his wits in a township.) Rive's novel *Emergency*, about three days in the life of a Coloured schoolteacher in **Cape Town** (like himself), took its title from the state of emergency declared following the **Sharpville** massacre in 1960. Associated with the *Drum* school of writers, Rive is also an editor and anthologizer. *Writing Black* is his autobiography.

SCHREINER, Olive (1855–1920). Born in **Wittebergen** to missionary parents, Schreiner was educated informally on mission stations. She became a governess. After a liberating spell in Europe, she returned to South Africa and took up political journalism and women's rights. Despite this, her best known work, *The Story of an African Farm* (Extract 4), was first published under a male pseudonym. She married a liberal South African farmer, spent the last few years of her life in England, and returned to South

Africa to die. Her grave is near **Cradock** in Cape Province.

THALI, Miriam (1930–). Thali was born in **Doornfontein, Johannesburg**. Her further education was interrupted – first when the **University of Witwatersrand** was closed to blacks, and again when lack of funds forced her to give up her studies at **Roma University** in **Lesotho**. Her first job as a clerk was to provide the basis for her first novel. *Muriel at the Metropolitan* was completed in 1968 and published in 1975. Following its success and a writers' workshop in America, Thali decided to write full-time. She is known for her vignettes of the lives of working men and women in **Soweto** published in *Staffrider*, a radical arts journal.

VAN DER POST, Sir Laurens Jan (1906–). A writer, farmer, soldier and journalist, van der Post was born near **Philippolis** and went to school in **Bloemfontein**. During his youth he worked aboard the Durban whalers and in 1925–26 was a journalist in **Durban**. He has divided his time between England and South Africa. In 1939 van der Post enlisted and served under the British in Africa and the Far East. The lines in his work can be drawn back to many of his childhood fascinations, such as the time spent as a child on the family farm learning about the rhythms, legends and instincts of the Bushmen and other tribes. *In a Province* (Extract 6), his first novel and generally regarded as his best, is narrated by a young white South African whose black friend falls foul of the law. *The Lost World of the Kalahari* and *The Heart of the Hunter* are the result of expeditions to visit the few remaining Bushmen in Botswana. He relates their symbolism, rituals, and other remnants of a disappearing lifestyle.

ZAMBIA

> 'Kaunda came to believe he was the embodiment of his nation. He had wrested it from the colonial power, led it to independence, moulded its policies. His picture was in every public building, his face on the money. He *was* Zambia.'
> *Richard Dowden on Kenneth Kaunda, in The Independent*

Before the country's first democratic elections in 1991, the then President Kenneth Kaunda banned publication of the independent press. Months later, he was swept peacefully from power and Frederick Chiluba of the Movement for Multiparty Democracy was brought into office amid euphoric cries of 'The hour has come!' – the hour of Kaunda's accountability, that is. During his long Presidency (1964–1991), Kaunda's favourite slogan was 'One Zambia, One Nation'. This was a necessary strategy in a country whose borders – thanks as ever to the absurd colonial carve-up of Africa – do not correspond to any one complete tribe. In 1962 he set out his ideas in *Zambia Shall Be Free*, less a literary work than a pronouncement of political intent. As one of the most widely available books in English, it was therefore hailed as one of the most widely read books in Zambia.

The first genuinely popular books were short novels which flourished in the 1950s. Published in the indigenous languages they are reminiscent in style of the Onitsha Market Literature of Nigeria (see under Nigeria), and boast extraordinary titles such as *How Not to Treat Animals, Every Day Brings Something New* and *You Have Survived by Luck*. But when English was made the teaching language for schools in 1965, many writers turned from their native languages. Writer Fwanyanga Mulikita switched from Lozi to English with the poignantly entitled *A Point of No Return*, a collection of short stories published in 1968. Mulikita also wrote a poetic epic, *Shaka Zulu*, about the founder of the Zulu nation.

The first English-language novel proper did not appear until 1971.

FACT BOX

AREA: 724 614 sq km
POPULATION: 8 300 000
CAPITAL: Lusaka
LANGUAGES: English, Bemba, Lozi, Lunda, Tomga, Nyanja
FORMER COLONIAL POWER: Great Britain
INDEPENDENCE: 1964

The Tongue of the Dumb by Dominic Mulaisho ◊ was followed eight years later by *The Smoke That Thunders* (Extract 2). From the one-time economic adviser to Kaunda, this novel about the internal and external struggles of the rising nationalist party has particular insight and resonance.

Apart from Mulaisho, who has managed to combine an estimable political career with novel writing, and without imprisonment, very few authors have reached international ears or eyes. Yet what Zambia lacks in printed literature, it makes up for with a lively performing arts scene. The University sponsors a pioneering theatre group, Chikwak-wa, which, instead of playing in gloomy indoor theatres, takes plays to the people – travelling to remote villages the group performs in the open air. With a combination of music, dance and plays that use traditional themes, the group is bringing back the spirit of traditional celebration and communication to the local literature.

LITERARY LANDMARKS

Kasanka National Park. In a village of the Ilala people is the **Livingstone Memorial**. When Livingstone ◊ died here in 1873, his faithful bearers Susi and Chuma buried his heart under a tree and then dried his body and carried it to Zanzibar.

Victoria Falls. 'No one can imagine the beauty from anything seen in England' said Livingstone, the first white man to see the Falls (Extract 1). Today there is a **statue** of him looking over them. It is rumoured that he carved his name on a tree on an island in the river above the Falls. Dominic Mulaisho uses the local name for the Falls, *The Smoke That Thunders*, as the title for his second novel.

Libraries and Bookshops

Livingstone. Livingstone Municipal Library; Livingstone Museum Research Library.

Lusaka. British Council Library; Central Reference Library; Helen Kaunda Memorial Library; Lusaka City Library; University Library.

BOOKLIST

The following selection includes the extracted titles in this chapter as well as those mentioned in the introduction which are available in English and other titles for further reading. In general, paperback editions are given when possible. The editions cited are not necessarily the only ones available.

Kaunda, Kenneth, *Zambia Shall Be Free*, Heinemann, London, 1980.

Livingstone, David, *Livingstone's Travels*, James McNair, ed, Dent, London, 1954. **Extract 1.**

Mulaisho, Dominic, *The Smoke That Thunders*, Heinemann, London, 1979. **Extract 2.**

Mulaisho, Dominic, *The Tongue of the Dumb*, Heinemann, London, 1971.

Mulikita, Fwanyanga, *A Point of No Return*, Macmillan, London, 1968.

Mulikita, Fwanyanga, *Shaka Zulu*, Longman, London, 1967.

Extracts

(1) VICTORIA FALLS

David Livingstone, *Livingstone's Travels*

In November 1855 Livingstone and his entourage visited the 'falls of Victoria' on the Zambezi River. The local name for them, he noted was, Mosi-oa-tunya which means 'the smoke that thunders'.

After twenty minutes' sail from Kalai, we came in sight, for the first time, of the columns of vapour appropriately called 'smoke,' rising at a distance of five miles, exactly as when large tracts of grass are burned in Africa. Five columns now rose, and bending in the direction of the wind, they seemed placed against a low ridge covered with trees. The tops of the columns at this distance appeared to mingle with the clouds. They were white below, and higher up they became dark so as to simulate smoke very closely. . .

When about half a mile from the falls, I left the canoe by which we had come down thus far, and embarked in a lighter one with men well acquainted with the rapids, who, by passing down the centre of the stream in the eddies and still places caused by many jutting rocks, brought me to an island situated in the middle of the river, and on the edge of the lip over which the water rolls. In coming hither there was danger of being swept down by the streams which rushed along each side of the island, but the river was now low, and we sailed where it is totally impossible to go when the water is high. But though we were within a few yards of the spot, a view from which would have solved the whole problem, I believe that no one could perceive where the vast body of the water went. It seemed to lose itself in the earth, the opposite lip of the fissure into which it disappeared being only eighty feet distant.

(2) Zambia: Revolution

Dominic Mulaisho, *The Smoke That Thunders*

Kawala, the driving force of the People's Army of Liberation Party (PALP), is approached by Katenga, just released from prison, and eager to join the revolutionaries. But the arms of the the PALP are not as welcoming as he might have hoped.

A few days later as Kawala walked out of a shoe store, Katenga ran to him and said:

'I don't think you know me. But you have done something good for us. My name is Katenga.'

Kawala offered his hand to Katenga. The eyes of the two men met: one pair narrow and sunken, but piercing, the other bulgy and criss-crossed with reddened veins. Kawala's face was smooth and clean shaven: the other's was rough and wore a fuzzy goatee which fluttered ominously in the small breeze.

'I have lots of time. I'm unemployed. Can I join the party?'

'We don't allow loafers.'

'No, I mean, I'm tired of my life. Drink, women, from one job to another. I'm tired of living for myself. I know I can get a job any time, but . . .'

Kawala looked into his face. He felt a mysterious togetherness with the man standing before him. What was it? Katenga did not batter his eyes. He too was looking into Kawala's face steadily.

'Show you can keep a job first. Then I'll know you can stick the rough life of party workers.'

Katenga tore off his hand from Kawala's. Grunting with disgust he said:

'I'll make it my own way,' and walked away.

They're all the same, these politicians of Africa, Katenga was thinking. They come in with a bang and die with a whimper.

Biographies and important works

LIVINGSTONE, David (1813–1873). The greatest of all the nineteenth-century African explorers, Livingstone was born in Blantyre, Scotland, the son of poor but pious and hard-working parents. One of seven children, he was brought up as a strict Christian. He studied medicine and theology while working part-time in a cotton mill, and set out for South Africa as a missionary in 1841. In 1853 he undertook a major expedition into the interior, where he 'discovered' the **Victoria Falls** (Extract 1) on the **Zambezi River**. When he returned to England he found that his exploits had turned him into a celebrity. In 1866 he mounted an expedition to discover the source of the Nile – a project which gripped the imagination of the Victorian public. Some time after he had set out, conflicting reports began to filter back to the coast that Livingstone had died or was ill. The journalist H.M. Stanley (◊ Tanzania) was dispatched by the *New York Herald* to try to find Livingstone. Stanley finally met up with him at Ujiji in Tanzania. After months of joint exploration, he returned to England. By now Africa was beginning to take its toll on Livingstone. His wife, who had come out to join him, died of fever within a few months, and he himself was a sick man. Despite this he pressed on, turning south into what is now Zambia. On 1 May 1873, his African servant discovered him dead, kneeling at his bedside as if in prayer. Livingstone's body (minus his heart, which was appropriately buried in Africa) was transported to England, where, amid an orgy of Victorian pomp, the great missionary explorer was buried in Westminster Abbey.

MULAISHO, Dominic (1933–). Mulaisho was born at **Mkando**. His first educational experiences in a mission school were to provide the theme for *The Tongue of the Dumb*. In this, his first novel, Mulaisho takes the year 1949 and the dissatisfaction of the Kaunga people, who are understandably reluctant to be schooled by the white man and to pay hut tax. While noted for its realism, the novel is not predominantly autobiographical. Mulaisho completed his education at the then University College of Rhodesia and Nyasaland (Malawi), where he studied English, economics and history. Following a successful career as a teacher he joined the government and held several prestigious posts, including that of Economic Adviser to Kenneth Kaunda. Politics and the wrangling of business and politicians are the main themes of his second novel, *The Smoke That Thunders* (Extract 2). Although it does not claim to retell directly the story of the country's struggle for independence, the character Kawala does, you might venture, bear a remarkable resemblance to Kaunda.

ZIMBABWE

'Hundreds of people who heard singing and the sound of Kudu horns, drums and other instruments, left their homes and joined the pilgrimage to Zimbabwe, till the procession was like the mighty Zambezi river, stretching and meandering along valleys, and vales, through forests and hills and across the plains.'
Stanlake Samkange,
The Year of the Uprising

'Today in Zimbabwe, *before* remains a loaded word', say the authors of *Squandering Eden.* 'If many blacks have forgiven, few have forgotten.' This is very much the opinion demonstrated by the country's writers. The literary references today still hark back to the arrival of the original white settlers, brought at the turn of the century to this temperate plateau by mining mogul Cecil Rhodes. He was, as Evelyn Waugh (◊ Ethiopia) puts it in *A Tourist in Africa,* 'not a politician; or rather he was a minor one. He was a visionary and almost all he saw was hallucination.' Waugh also recalls how at the funeral of Rhodes the Bishop of Mashonaland read a poem which Rudyard Kipling had, in rather pompous style, composed for the event: 'There till the vision he foresaw/Splendid and whole arise/And unimagined Empires draw/To council neath his skies/The immense and brooding Spirit still,/Shall quicken and control.'

Nevertheless, it is still hard to imagine that independence came only 15 years ago to Zimbabwe. By the time Ian Smith declared his renegade Unilateral Declaration of Independence (UDI) in 1965, there were some 250 000 white residents behind him. Contemporary poet Musaemura Zimunya wrote in his poem 'Arrivants', 'Came to Hope-dawns and democracy with strings attached/and so we were reconciled to white faces/whose pride and heads had watered UDI and racism . . .'. Tensions with the dominant Shona and Nbedele tribes grew quickly, for while the rest of the British colonies were gaining 'real' independence, Rhodesia, as it was known, was still clearly under white rule. 'Genuine independence can only come out of the barrel of a gun,'

FACT BOX

AREA: 390 580 sq km
POPULATION: 10 100 000
CAPITAL: Harare
LANGUAGES: English, Shona, Ndebele
FORMER COLONIAL POWER: Great Britain
INDEPENDENCE: 1980

---

said first President-to-be Robert Mugabe. The bloody liberation war that followed claimed nearly 30 000 lives.

In retaliation, gunfire of words burst forth, divided into the three main languages – English, Shona and Ndebele. Early Shona and Ndebele literature stayed closely rooted to traditional myth – with most of the translations available taken from oral legend. Imaginative works in the indigenous languages were supported by The Southern Rhodesian African Literature Bureau, who published Solomon Mutswairo's Shona epic *Feso*. In his Shona poem 'NeHanda Nyakasikana' he writes; 'We are weary of drinking our tears./How long shall we have forbearance?/Even trees have a rest,/When their leaves are shed . . .' (from *Voices from Twentieth-Century Africa*). The first Ndebele novel, by Ndabangingi Sithole and published in 1956, was less discreet about its political intent, and, like many vernacular works in the 1960s, was banned by the Smith regime.

English-language literature was also forced to develop cautiously but for one character, Dambudzo Marechera ◊. The literary rebel of Zimbabwe, Marechera was a self-consciously Rimbaudesque figure who died of Aids in 1987 at the age of 35. His short life has been described as a 'wild work of art' and his writing as egotistical, derivative, obsessed *and* iconoclastic. Doris Lessing ◊, on reading his first book, *The House of Hunger* (Extract 2), said frankly 'It is no good pretending this book is an easy or pleasant read.' It won the writer *The Guardian* Fiction Award in 1979. His later works are no less nebulous or imaginative. Violence, apartheid, tyranny and incest all colour all his fantastical montages of life from *Black Sunlight* to *The Black Insider*. In a tribute to the 'scandalously gifted' Marechera, David Caute in *The Independent* described his singular style of fiction as black-hole autobiography: 'His ego was ungovernable, likewise his intake of alcohol . . . In a short sentence he could take in Chaka Khan, Hieronymous Bosch and, well, Dylan Thomas. His wit matched his solemnity: "If . . . we all have something to hide then my whole life has been an attempt to make myself the skeleton in my own cupboard."'

Against this colourful and prodigious writer it is not surprising that

Dambudzo Marechera

the rest of the talents of the country are somewhat shaded. Marechera himself often charged his fellow authors as weak collaborators, who were just part of the masses from whom he was clearly distinguished. Nevertheless, there are some worthy of note and by whom Marechera was almost certainly influenced.

One of the first sepulchral voices about the effect of white settlerdom came from historian and novelist Stanlake Samkange ◊ whose distinctive work combines both talents (Extract 1). For the early part of *On Trial for My Country*, he used many real memoirs from the settlers. *The Mourned One* is, claims Samkange, the story of 'Ocky', a condemned man in Salisbury (now **Harare**) jail, who narrates the ironical twists in his life from his prison cell. Life started when he was rescued from drowning in a river by a missionary, and ended with accusations of rape of a white colleague at a missionary school.

As it became increasingly clear that the Smith regime could not last, there entered a mood of 'sombre realism' into the fighters and the writers. This literary shift was characterized by the writings of Charles

Mungoshi ◊ (Extract 5), and more consummately by Marechera. Mungoshi's prize-winning *Waiting for the Rain* is a powerful story of family tensions unleashed as the son prepares for his departure to England.

Another popular writer is Samuel Chimsoro, whose book *Nothing is Impossible* is a lesson in perseverance against the odds of apartheid. The ambitious and talented hero Simbai believes, 'the state of affairs of the country went out of alignment with the ambitions of the people. This raised the need for the people to scrutinise and understand their environment, just as the people at the farm learnt to repair punctures even though they did not have bicycles.'

Poetry in English is also a quietly maturing medium in Zimbabwe, encouraged locally by poetry magazines and the Mambo Press in Gweru, which published *And Now the Poets Speak* and *Zimbabwean Poetry in English*. Musaemura Zimunya, Chenjerai Hove ◊ and the illustriously named Wonder Banda are but a few to watch out for in anthologies (see Extract 4 for Hove). Hove's poetic novel *Bones*, about the struggles of a labourer on a white farm, is rich in Shona idiom and imagery: 'Arise all the bones of the land. Arise all the bones of the dying cattle. Arise all the bones of the locusts. Wield the power of the many bones scattered across the land and fight so that the land of the ancestors is not defiled by strange feet and strange hands.'

White society in Zimbabwe has been copiously written about by the settlers themselves – the most celebrated and worthwhile of whom is Doris Lessing ◊. A prolific writer, she sets many of her most successful novels against the time she grew up here in the 1930s and 1940s (Extract 3). While she succeeded in shocking her (mainly European) audience with her depiction of the arrogance and ignorance of the archetypal boorish white settler, she has been criticized for the conspicuous absence of parts played by Africans in her books. Nevertheless, she is normally seen as an Zimbabwean writer. Her dichotomy was that she was never, like all white settlers, really at home in any one place. Lessing wrote in *Going Home* 'Africa belongs to the Africans; the sooner they take it back the better. But – a country also belongs to those who feel at home in it.'

LITERARY LANDMARKS

Harare. According to writer David Lamb, 'It feels very British, reminding me of what York would look like if it were stuck in the middle of the Montana Plains.' The impressively wide boulevards were apparently designed by Cecil Rhodes to allow an eight-team ox cart to do a U-turn. Maverick writer Dambudzo Marechera apparently slept rough in **Cecil Rhodes Square** after yet another rejection of his work, 'while keeping a close eye on a parade of white liberal ladies who paid his rent or his price' (David Caute in *The Independent*). Every year up to 1980, descendants of the first white pioneers who came to live here (as organized by Cecil Rhodes) at the turn of the century, held a Pioneers' Day celebration in the Square.

Masvingo. About 28 km south-east of the city lies the **Great Zimbabwe National Monument** which is one of the most important archaeological sites in Africa. The enormous stone structures, that date back to 1200 AD, are the remains of a large empire that was partially destroyed by the arrival of the Portuguese in the sixteenth century.

Libraries and Bookshops

Bulawayo. Municipal Library; National Free Library of Zimbabwe; Public Library.

Harare. Booklovers' Paradise Book Exchange, 48 Angwa Street; British Council Library; City Library; University of Zimbabwe Library.

BOOKLIST

The following selection includes the extracted titles in this chapter as well as those mentioned in the introduction which are available in English and other titles for further reading. In general, paperback editions are given when possible. The editions cited are not necessarily the only ones available. For most of the extracted works, the original publisher in English can be found in 'Acknowledgments and Citations' at the end of the volume, as can the exact location of the extracts and the editions from which they are taken. Extract numbers are highlighted in bold.

And Now the Poets Speak, Mambo Press, Gweru.

Chimsoro, Samuel, *Nothing is Impossible*, Longman, Harlow, 1983.

Dangarembga, Tsitsi, *Nervous Condition*, The Women's Press, London, 1988.

The Heinemann Book of African Poetry in English, selected by Adewale Maja-Pearce, Heinemann, Oxford, 1990.

Hove, Chenjerai, *Bones*, Heinemann, Oxford, 1990.

Hove, Chenjerai, *Red Hills of Home*, Mambo Press, Gweru, 1985. **Extract 4**.

Hove, Chenjerai, *Up in Arms*, Zimbabwe Publishing House, Harare, 1982.

Lessing, Doris, *African Laughter: Four Visits to Zimbabwe*, Flamingo, London, 1993.

Lessing, Doris, *Martha Quest*, Paladin, London, 1990.

Lessing, Doris, *Collected African Stories, Volume 1: This was the Old Chief's Country*, Paladin, London, 1992.

Lessing, Doris, *Collected African Stories, Volume 2: Sun Between Their Feet*, Panther, New York, 1979.

Lessing, Doris, *Going Home*, Panther, New York, 1968.

Lessing, Doris, *The Grass is Singing*, Paladin, London, 1989. **Extract 3**.

Lessing, Doris, *Landlocked*, Paladin, London, 1990.

Lessing, Doris, *A Proper Marriage*, Paladin, London, 1990.

Lessing, Doris, *A Ripple from the Storm*, Paladin, London, 1990.

Lord, Graham, *Ghosts of King Solomon's Mines*, Sinclair-Stevenson, London, 1991.

Marechera, Dambudzo, *The Black Insider*, Lawrence and Wishart, London, 1992.

Marechera, Dambudzo, *Black Sunlight*, Heinemann, London, 1980.

Marechera, Dambudzo, *The House of Hunger*, Heinemann, London, 1978. **Extract 2**.

Marechera, Dambudzo, *Mindblast*, College Press, Harare, 1984.

Mungoshi, Charles, *Coming of the Dry Season*, Zimbabwe Publishing House, Harare, 1982.

Mungoshi, Charles, *The Milkman Doesn't Only Deliver Milk: Selected Poems*, Poetry Society of Zimbabwe, Harare, 1981.

Mungoshi, Charles, 'The Mountain', *The Setting Sun and the Rolling World*, Heinemann, Oxford, 1989. **Extract 5**.

Mungoshi, Charles, *One Day Long Ago: More Stories from a Shona Childhood*, Baobab Books, Harare, 1991.

Mungoshi, Charles, *Waiting for the Rain*, Heinemann, London, 1975.

Mutswairo, Solomon, *Chaminuka: Prophet of Zimbabwe*, Three Continents Press, Washington, DC, 1978.

Mutswairo, Solomon, *Mapondera: Soldier of Zimbabwe*, Three Continents Press, Washington, DC, 1978.

Rosenblum, Mort, and Williamson, Doug, *Squandering Eden*, Paladin, London, 1990.

Samkange, Stanlake, *The Mourned One*, Heinemann, London, 1975.

Samkange, Stanlake, *On Trial for My Country*, Heinemann, London, 1969.

Samkange, Stanlake, *The Origins of Rhodesia*, Heinemann, London, 1968.

Samkange, Stanlake, *The Year of the Uprising*, Heinemann, London, 1978. **Extract 1**.

Sithole, Ndabaningi, *The Polygamist*, Hodder and Stoughton, London, 1972.

Sithole, Ndabaningi, *Roots of a Revolution*, Oxford University Press, Oxford, 1977.

Voices from Twentieth-Century Africa, Chinweizu, ed, Faber and Faber, London, 1988.

Waugh, Evelyn, *A Tourist in Africa*, Methuen, London, 1985.

Zimbabwean Poetry in English, Mambo Press, Gweru.

Zimunya, Musaemura, 'Arrivants', in *The Heinemann Book of African Poetry in English*, selected by Adewale Maja-Pearce, Heinemann, Oxford, 1990.

Extracts

(1) MASVINGO

Stanlake Samkange, *Year of the Uprising*

In the search for a leader to conquer the colonists, the different peoples join forces and march to Great Zimbabwe where a huge ceremony takes place. A key site in Zimbabwe's ancestral history and mythology, the stone structures at Masvingo date back to 1200 AD.

When the sun was highest in the heavens and, standing erect, a man stood on all his shadow, the priests of Mwari and Munyati's kraal at Matojeni that day blew their kudu horns, long and loud, a hundred thousand times, till the mountains, hills, kopjes, rocks, boulders and stones of the Matopo shook and trembled, as the blast reverberated and echoed in their caves and caverns. Chizungu, Munyati's father and High Priest of Mwari, was dressed in *madumbu*, monkey and buck skins worn round the waist, complete with hooves trailing on the ground, and *nabgamaringa*, black limbo, about five yards in length, draped over one of his shoulders; he had special black beads round the wrists, up to the elbow, and a necklace of similar beads round the neck, and he held an exceptionally beautiful *mudonzvo*, carved stick, as he led the long procession to the premier shrine of the land. Hundreds of people who heard singing and the sound of kudu horns, drums and other instruments, left their homes and joined the pilgrimage to Zimbabwe, till the procession was like the mighty Zambezi river, stretching and meandering along valleys and vales, through forests and hills and across the plains.

(2) ZIMBABWE: ALCOHOL

Dambudzo Marechera, *The House of Hunger*

Dambudzo and his friend Harry are sitting in a bar talking about writing and life. 'You literary chaps are our only hope,' says Harry as they knock back a few more drinks.

I looked up. As I did so the old cloth of my former self seemed to stretch and tear once more. The pain flashed through my head and like a cold hand squeezed my bloody lungs. (What shall I see when the cloth rips completely, laying everything bare? It is as if a crack should appear in the shell of the sky. The human face in close-up is quite incredible –

Swift was right. And what of the house inside it? And the thing inside the house? And the thing inside the thing inside the thing inside the thing? I was drunk, I suppose, orbiting around myself shamelessly. I found a seed, a little seed, the smallest in the world. And its name was Hate. I buried it in my mind and watered it with tears. No seed ever had a better gardener. As it swelled and cracked into green life I felt my nation tremble, tremble in the throes of birth – and burst out bloom and branch.) . . .

Harry's glass clinked my glass and we drank each other's health.

I suppose I was beyond worrying about health; dead souls have no such worries. An extreme case of the left hand not caring a piss about what the right hand was doing. I was, I knew, a dead tree, dry of branch and decayed in the roots. A tree however that was still upright in the sullen spleen of wind. And caught among the gnarled branches were a page from Shakespeare's *Othello* and page one of the *Rhodesia Herald* with a picture of me glaring angrily at the camera lens.

But Harry was saying something.

'. . . in the evening edition,' he said. 'I couldn't believe it, but you've always been rather a closed fist.'

'No. It's just that I've no friends.'

Harry stared; wounded.

'I've always liked you, you know,' he said.

'Don't let's get personal,' I said, feeling sick. 'It might be painful.'

He cleared his throat.

'Let's get drunk instead.' He swallowed phlegm.

I laughed and said:

'That's more lethal.'

I looked up. The barman's eyes bored into mine. The laughter was hurting my gums; something was twitching uncontrollably above the barman's left eye. I got up hastily and, escaping into the toilet, just made it to the bowl where I was violently sick. As I came out, wiping my mouth with the back of my hand, I collided with two massive breasts that were straining angrily against a thin T-shirt upon which was written the legend ZIMBABWE.

'You better watch where you're going, deary,' she said.

(3) ZIMBABWE: SETTLERS

Doris Lessing, *The Grass is Singing*

Mary Turner, wife of an Afrikaner farmer, is ill at ease with the land, the people and the lifestyle in the Zimbabwe countryside. Her unease is manifested in her tragic relations with her latest servant Moses.

'I told you I only wanted tea,' she said sharply.

He answered quietly: 'Madame ate no breakfast, she must eat.' On the tray there was even a handleless cup with flowers in it: crude yellows and pinks and reds, bush flowers, thrust together clumsily, but making a strong burst of colour on the old stained cloth.

As she sat there, her eyes bent down, and he straightened himself after setting down the tray, what troubled her most was this evidence of his desire to please her, the propitiation of the flowers. He was waiting for a word of approval and pleasure from her. She could not give it; but the rebuke that sprang to her lips remained unspoken, and she pulled the tray to her and began to eat, without a word.

There was now a new relation between them. For she felt helplessly in his power. Yet there was no reason why she should. Never ceasing for one moment to be conscious of his presence about the house, or standing silently at the back against the wall in the sun, her feeling was one of a strong and irrational fear, a deep uneasiness, and even – though this she did not know, would have died rather than acknow-ledge – of some dark attraction. It was as though the act of weeping before him had been an act of resignation – resignation of her authority; and he had refused to hand it back.

(4) ZIMBABWE: SHONA FOLKLORE

Chenjerai Hove, *Lost Bird*

In Shona lore, the migratory bird is the harbinger of the rainy season while the sighting of a secretary bird roaming the sky is said to foretell death. Here the migratory bird has been swallowed up by the smoke-laden city. 'Ngauzani Ngauzani' is a song children sing when they see the migratory birds. 'Lost Bird' is included in Red Hills of Home – see Booklist.

And the children still stare
at the empty sky
with no season's song on their lips.
That year the rains failed.
Then the sky had its share
of empty prayers, tasty meat for dogs.

Later, the bird's nest was empty:
so the secretary bird roamed
the sky in uproarious song,
And women complained to their husbands,
Some nocturnal visitor
has castrated the women too,
So nobody would sing:
Ngauzani Ngauzani.
Ngauzani Ngauzani.

(5) ZIMBABWE: SPIRITS

Charles Mungoshi, *The Mountain*

Two young boys set off at first cock-crow to the bus station 8 km away. Taking a short cut across the mountain in the eerie half-light, Chemai tells his companion about the spirits which scared away the Europeans looking for gold. 'The Mountain' is included in The Setting Sun and the Rolling World *– see Booklist.*

Suddenly through the dark trees a warm wind hit us in the face as if someone had breathed on us. My belly tightened but I did not stop. I heard Chemai hold his breath and gasp, 'We have just passed a witch.' I wanted to scream at him to stop it but I had not the voice. Then we came out of the trees and were in the bush and short grass, climbing again. I released breath slowly. It was much lighter here, and cooler.

Much later, I said, 'That was a bad place.'

Chemai said, 'That's where my father met witches eating human bones, riding on their husbands.'

'Oh, you and your . . .' He had suddenly grabbed me by the arm. He said nothing. Instinctively I looked behind us.

There was a black goat following us.

I don't know why I laughed. Then after I had laughed I felt sick. I expected the sky to come shattering itself round my ears but nothing happened, except Chemai's fear-agitated hand on my shoulder.

'Why shouldn't I laugh?' I asked. 'I'm not afraid of a goat.' . . .

'You have insulted her,' Chemai said accusingly.

I said nothing. It was no use pretending I didn't know what I was doing. I knew these goats. Lost spirits. Because I had laughed at it it would follow me wherever I went. It would eat with me, bathe with me, sleep with me. It would behave in every way as if I were its friend or, better still, its husband. It was a goat in body but a human being in spirit.

Biographies and important works

HOVE, Chenjerai (1956–). A novelist, poet and former teacher, Hove was born in **Mazvihwa**. He has published several collections of poetry. His novel *Bones* won the 1988 Zimbabwean Publishers/Writers Literary Award and the 1989 Noma Award. He has also received literary acclaim for his volumes of poetry *Up in Arms* and *Red Hills of Home* (Extract 4). He currently works as a cultural journalist in **Harare**.

LESSING, Doris (1919–). Lessing was born in Persia to British parents. They moved to Zimbabwe in 1925, where they bought a 300-acre farm. Lessing was educated at a Catholic convent and then a state school until the age of fourteen. At fourteen, she read Olive Schreiner's (◊ South Africa) *The Story of An African Farm* which was a great inspiration to her. During the second world war she joined a small local Marxist group. Following a career as a legal secretary, and two failed marriages, Lessing left for England in 1949 at the age of 30 with a son, £20, and the manuscript of *The Grass is Singing* (Extract 3). For 25 years she was a 'prohibited immigrant' in Zimbabwe. Many of her most successful books take up African themes. *The Grass is Singing* was followed by a five-part, distinctly autobiographical series called *Children of Violence*, which spans the life of Martha, born of first-generation settlers (comprising *Martha Quest, A Proper Marriage, A Ripple from the Storm, Landlocked,* and *The Four-Gated City*). It is the deep conflict between European and African culture which characterizes Lessing's

African Stories. Since independence, she has been able to return and explore her childhood homeland. *African Laughter* is an account of four such journeys made during the past ten years. Lessing is particularly fascinated with the people's post-independence energy and ingenuity (or less euphemistically, corruption). The book includes sketches of a feminist nun who refuses to wear a habit, and her brother, an archetypal hard-line white settler. Doris Lessing now lives in West Hampstead, London.

MARECHERA, Dambudzo (1952–1987). Marechera was born in **Rusape** to a lorry driver and a nanny. He was educated at a mission boarding school and later at the University of Rhodesia, where he edited a student magazine, and the University of Oxford. Marechera was expelled from both universities – the former pending imprisonment, and exit from the latter was apparently the alternative to voluntary psychiatric treatment. As well as 'enjoying' imprisonment in both Zimbabwe and Cardiff, Marechera was an exile in Britain. *The House of Hunger* (Extract 2), his first novel, describes the cyclical violence of life in a Zimbabwean township. *Black Sunlight* also embraces the themes of social chaos and urban guerrillas amid what one reviewer described as 'streams – or rather torrents – of consciousness, and verbal extravagance'. Marechera was unashamedly extravagant in his use of literary references – an aspect of his style which did not always endear him to publishers. *Mindblast*, a ruth-

Doris Lessing

less and brutal exposé of the Special Branch which plagued him, has not yet been published in England. *The Black Insider*, published in 1991, was the first of his unpublished works to be released since he died from Aids at the age of 35.

MUNGOSHI, Charles (1947–). *The Coming of the Dry Season*, Mun-

goshi's first collection of short stories, was followed by *Waiting for the Rain* – 'Rarely has an African writer composed such a powerful story about family turmoil and the generation gap', was the acclaim from *Books Abroad*. The *Sunday Times*, meanwhile, reported more soberly, 'That impartial eye, balanced against the passionate involvement . . . gives this remarkable book its almost

Charles Mungoshi

SAMKANGE, Stanlake (1922–1988).
A historian and a novelist, Samkange
was the son of a Methodist minister.
He was educated in Zimbabwe, South
Africa and the USA. After graduating with a history degree from Fort
Hare University College, he returned
to Zimbabwe where he became a
teacher, and General Secretary of the
ANC. He also worked as a journalist
and for an advertising firm. He wrote
several historical tomes, including the
prize-winning *The Origins of Rhodesia*.
Sometimes it would seem that Samkange was more historian than novelist, but an effective combined use of
documentation, memoirs and imagination enabled him to produce
several popular novels. *On Trial for
My Country* envisages the meeting
between Cecil Rhodes and Lobengula
the Ndebele King. *The Mourned One*
sees colonial society through the eyes
of a condemned man. *The Year of the
Uprising* (Extract 1) is the story of the

visionary double dimension.' Mungoshi has also written an intriguingly
entitled book of poems, *The Milkman
Doesn't Only Deliver Milk*. Other collections of his short stories are *The
Setting Sun and The Rolling World* (Extract 5) and *One Day Long Ago: More
Stories from a Shona Childhood*.

suppression and subsequent uprising
of the Matabele and Mashona people
in 1896. Drawing richly on the customs and spiritualism of his people,
some portions of the book have been
likened to the Old Testament for
their mesmeric quality.

Acknowledgments and Citations

The author and publisher are very grateful to the many literary agents, publishers, translators, authors, and other individuals who have given their permission for the use of extracts and photographs, supplied photographs, or helped in the location of copyright holders. Every effort has been made to identify and contact the appropriate copyright owners or their representatives. The publisher would welcome any further information.

EXTRACTS

BENIN: (1) Paul Hazoumé, *Doguicimi*, Richard Bjornson, trans, Three Continents Press, Washington, DC, 1990, pp 92–93. By permission of Three Continents Press. (2) Bruce Chatwin, *The Viceroy of Ouidah*, Pan, London, 1982, pp 96–97. By permission of Random House UK Ltd. (3) Olympe Bhêly-Quénum, *Snares Without End*, Longman, Harlow, 1981, pp 15–16. Originally published in French as *Un Piège Sans Fin*, Présence Africaine, Paris, 1985. By permission of La Société Nouvelle Présence Africaine. (4) Emile Ologoudou, 'Liberty', Gerald Moore, trans, in *The Penguin Book of Modern African Poetry*, Gerald Moore and Ulli Beier, eds, Penguin, London, 1984, p 46. Originally published in French as 'Liberté in *Nouvelle Somme de Poésie du Monde Noir*, Présence Africaine No 57, Paris, 1966. By permission of La Société Nouvelle Présence Africaine. (5) Bruce Chatwin. 'A coup', in *The Best of Granta Travel*, Granta, London, 1991, pp 72–73. By permission of Aitken, Stone and Wylie Ltd. (6) Sir Richard Burton, *A Mission to Gelele, King of Dahome*, Routledge and Kegan Paul, London, 1966. **CAPE VERDE ISLANDS:** (1) Onésima Silveira, 'A Different Poem', Margaret Dickinson, trans, in *The Penguin Book of Modern African Poetry*, Gerald Moore and Ulli Beier, eds, Penguin, London, 1984, p 59. Originally published in *When Bullets Begin to Flower*, Margaret Dickinson, ed, East African Publishing House, Nairobi, 1972. (2) Kaoberdiano Dambara, 'Judgement of the Black Man', Margaret Dickinson, trans, in *Poems of Black Africa*, Wole Soyinka, ed, Heinemann, Oxford, London, 1987, p 196. **CÔTE D'IVOIRE:** (1) Ahmadou Kourouma, *The Suns of Independence*, Adrian Adams, trans, Heinemann, London, 1981, p 5. By permission of Adrian Adams. (2) Bernard Dadié, *Climbié*, Heinemann, London, 1971, p 21. (3) Charles Nokan, 'My Head is Immense', Gerald Moore, trans, in *The Penguin Book of Modern African Poetry*, Gerald Moore and Ulli Beier, eds, Penguin, London, 1984, p 116. Originally published in French as 'Ma tête est immense' in *Nouvelle Somme de Poésie du Monde Noir*, Présence Africaine, No 57, Paris, 1966. By permission of La Société Nouvelle Présence Africaine. (4) V.S. Naipaul, 'The Crocodiles of Yamoussoukro', in *Finding the Center*, A.A. Knopf, New York, 1984, pp 77–78. By permission of Aitken, Stone and Wylie Ltd. **THE GAMBIA:** (1) Ebou Dibba, *Chaff on the Wind*, Macmillan, Basingstoke, 1986, p 51. By permission of Macmillan London Ltd. (2) Tijan Sallah, 'Shadows of Banjul', in Samuel Baity Garren, 'Exile and Return: The Poetry and Fiction of Tijan Sallah', *Wasafiri*, Spring 1992, pp 15–16. By permission of *Wasafiri*. (3) Lenrie Peters, 'Home Coming', in *Satellites*, Heinemann, London, 1967, p 39. By permission of Lenrie Peters. (4) Alex Haley, *Roots*, Doubleday, New York, 1976, pp 2–3. By permission of Bantam, Doubleday, Dell Publishing Group, Inc. **GHANA:** (1) Ayi Kwei Armah, *The Beautyful Ones Are Not Yet Born*, Heinemann, Oxford, 1988, p 3. By permission of Heinemann Educational, Oxford. (2) Kofi Awoonor, *This Earth, My Brother . . .*, Heinemann, London, 1971, pp 16–17. By permission of David Higham Associates Ltd. (3) Amu Djoleto, *Hurricane of Dust*, Longman, Harlow, 1987, p 71. By permission of Longman Group UK Ltd. (4) B. Kojo Laing. *Search Sweet Country*, Picador, London, 1987, pp 14–15. Originally published by William Heinemann Ltd. By permission of Reed International Books. (5) J.E. Casely Hayford, *Ethiopia Unbound: Studies in Race Emancipation*, Frank Cass, London, 1969. By permission of Frank Cass and Co Ltd. (6) Kwesi Brew, 'The Woods Decay', in *The Shadows of Laughter*, Longman, London, 1969. By permission of Longman Group UK Ltd. **GUINEA:** (1) Tierno Monénembo, *The Bush Toads*, Longman, Harlow, 1983, pp 7–8. (2) Alioum Fantouré, *Tropical Circle*, Longman Drumbeat, Harlow, 1981, p 123. Originally published in French as *Le Cercle des Tropiques*, Présence Africaine, Paris, 1972. By permission of La Société Nouvelle Présence Africaine. (3) Graham Greene, *Journey Without Maps*, Penguin, London, 1976, p 145. © 1936 Verdant SA. By permission of David Higham Associates Ltd. (4) Camara Laye, *The African Child*, Fontana, London, 1977, pp 101–102. By permission of HarperCollins Publishers Ltd. **GUINEA-BISSAU:** (1) David Lamb, *The Africans*, Vintage Books, New York, 1987, p 3. **LIBERIA:** (1) Bai T. Moore, 'Murder in the Cassava Patch', in *Liberian Writing*, Horst Erdmann Verlag, Tübingen, 1970, pp 91–92. (2) Roland Tombekai Dempster, *A Song Out of Midnight*, privately published, 1959, p 11. (3) Graham Greene, *Journey Without Maps*, Penguin, London, 1976, pp 132–133. © 1936 Verdant SA. By permission of David Higham Associates Ltd. (4) Barbara Greene, *Too Late to Turn Back*, Settle Press, London, 1981, pp 173–174. Published in hardback by Settle Press, with an introduction by Paul Theroux (£9.95, Settle Press, 10 Boyne Terrace Mews, London W11 3LR). First published by Penguin in 1990. By permission of Settle Press. **MALI:** (1) Amadou Hampâté Bâ, *Kaidara*, Three Continents Press, Washington, DC, 1988, p 83. By permission of Three Continents Press. (2) D.T. Niane, *Sundiata: An Epic of Old Mali*, London, Harlow, 1974, p 41. Originally published in French as *Soundjata ou L'Epopée Mandigue*, Présence Africaine, Paris, 1960. By permission of La Société Nouvelle Présence Africaine. (3) Yambo Ouologuem, 'When Negro Teeth Speak', in *The Penguin Book of Modern African Poetry*, Gerald Moore and Ulli Beier, eds, Penguin, London, 1984, p 147. (4) Leland Hall, *Timbuctoo*, Harper and Brothers, London, 1927, pp 172–173. (5) Mungo Park, *Travels in the Interior Districts of Africa*, London, 1799. (6) William Seabrook, *The White Monk of Timbuctoo*, Harrap, London, 1934, pp 83–84. **MAURITANIA:** (1) A.G. Gerteiny, *Mauritania*, Pall Mall Press, London, 1968, p 86. (2) Geoffrey Moorhouse, *The Fearful Void*, Penguin, London, 1986, pp 78–79. By permission of Aitken, Stone and Wylie Ltd. (3) Odette du Puigaudeau, *Barefoot Through Mauritania*, Routledge, London, 1937, pp 74–76. (4) Bruce Chatwin, *The Songlines*, Jonathan Cape, London, 1987, p 129. By permission of Random House UK Ltd. **NIGER:** Paul Stoller and Cheryl Olkes, *In Sorcery's Shadow*, University of Chicago Press, Chicago and London, 1987, pp 64–65. © 1987 by The University of Chicago. By permission of the University of Chicago Press. **NIGERIA:** (1) Adewale Maja-Pearce, *In My Father's Country: A Nigerian Journey*, Heinemann, London, 1987, pp 25–26. By permission of Adewale Maja-Pearce. (2) *The Life of Olaudah Equiano*, Paul Edwards, ed, Longman, Harlow, 1988, pp 10–11. (3) Gabriel Okara, *The Voice*, Heinemann, London, 1970, pp 38–39. By permission of André Deutsch Ltd. (4) J.P. Clark-Bekederemo, *Ozidi*, in *Collected Plays 1958–1988*, Howard University Press, Washington, DC, 1991, pp 117–119. Copyright © 1991 by J.P. Clark. Introduction Copyright © 1991 by Howard University Press. By permission of Howard University Press. (5) Cyprian Ekwensi, *Jagua Nana*, Heinemann, London, 1988, pp 12–13. (6) Buchi Emecheta, *The Joys of Motherhood*, Fontana, London, 1988, pp 102–103. By permission of HarperCollins Publishers Ltd. (7) Ben Okri, *The Famished Road*, Vintage, London, 1992, pp 7–8. (8) Odia Ofeimun, 'The Poet Lied', in *The Heinemann Book of African Poetry in English*, selected by Adewale Maja-Pearce, Heinemann, Oxford, 1990, pp 188–189. (9) Christopher Okigbo, 'Hurrah for Thunder', in *The Heinemann Book of African Poetry in English*, selected by Adewale Maja-Pearce, Heinemann, Oxford, 1990, p 26. (10) Chinua Achebe, *Things Fall Apart*, in *The African Trilogy*, Pan, London, 1988, pp 123–124. First published in England by William Heinemann Ltd. By permission of Reed International Books. (11) Biyi Bandele-Thomas, *The Man Who Came in from the Back of Beyond*, Bellew, London, 1991, pp 14–15. By permission of Bellew Publishing Company. (12) Amos Tutuola, *The Palm-Wine Drinkard*, Faber and Faber, London, 1977, pp 20–21. By permission of Faber and Faber Ltd. (13) Wole Soyinka, *Death and the King's Horseman*, in *Soyinka: Six Plays*, Methuen, London, 1984, pp 185–186. By permission of Reed International Books. **SENEGAL:** Birago Diop, quoted in *The Gambia and Senegal*, Insight Guides, APA Publications, London, 1990, p 101. (2) Ousmane Socé, 'Karim', in *African Writing Today*, Ezekiel Mphahlele, ed, Penguin, London, 1967, p 162. By permission of Nouvelles Éditions Latines, Paris. (3) Malick Fall, *The*

Wound, Heinemann, London, 1973, pp 14–15. (4) Aminata Sow-Fall, *The Beggar's Strike*, Longman, Harlow, 1986, pp 72–73. By permission of Longman Group UK Ltd. (5) David Diop, 'Sell-out', in *Poems of Black Africa*, Wole Soyinka, ed, Heinemann, Oxford, 1987, pp 85–86. (6) Léopold Sédar Senghor, 'Congo', in *Lépold Sédar Senghor: Prose and Poetry*, selected and translated by John Reed and Clive Wake, Heinemann, London, 1976, pp 139–140. (7) Sembène Ousmane, Heinemann, London, 1970, p 266. (8) Mariama Bâ, *So Long a Letter*, Virago, London, 1982, pp 5–6. First published in England by Heinemann Educational. By permission of Heinemann Educational, Oxford. **SIERRA LEONE**: (1) Yulisa Amadu Maddy, *No Past, No Present, No Future*, Heinemann, London, 1973, p 45. (2) Graham Greene, *The Heart of the Matter*, Penguin, London, 1971, pp 14–15. © 1948 Verdant SA. By permission of David Higham Associates Ltd. (3) Graham Greene, *Journey Without Maps*, Penguin, London, 1976, pp 37–38. © 1936 Verdant SA. By permission of David Higham Associates Ltd. (4) Sarif Easmon, 'Bindeh's Gift', in *African Writing Today*, Ezekiel Mphahlele, ed, Penguin, London, 1967, pp 70–71. (5) Abioseh Nicol, 'The Devil at Yolahun Bridge', in *The Truly Married Woman and Other Stories*, Cambridge University Press, Cambridge, 1965, pp 24–25. By permission of Cambridge University Press. (6) Syl Cheney-Coker, 'The Philosopher', in *The Blood in the Desert's Eyes*, Heinemann, Oxford, 1990. By permission of Heinemann Educational, Oxford. (7) Syl Cheney-Coker, *The Last Harmattan of Alusine Dunbar*, Heinemann, Oxford, 1990. By permission of Heinemann Educational, Oxford. **TOGO**: (1) George Packer, *The Village of Waiting*, Vintage, New York, 1988, pp 142–143. (2) Tété-Michel Kpomassie, *An African in Greenland*, James Kirkup, trans, Secker and Warburg, London, 1983, pp 45–46. By permission of Reed International Books. **ALGERIA**: (1) Fadhma Amrouche, *My Life Story*, Dorothy S. Blair, trans, The Women's Press, London, 1988, pp 62–63. First published in Great Britain by The Women's Press Ltd, 34 Great Sutton Street, London EC1V 0DX, UK. By permission of The Women's Press Ltd. (2) Fettouma Touati, *Desperate Spring*, Ros Schwartz, trans, The Women's Press, London, 1987, pp 17–18. First published in English by The Women's Press Ltd, 34 Great Sutton Street, London EC1V 0DX, UK. By permission of The Women's Press Ltd. (3) Albert Camus, 'Summer in Algiers', in *Albert Camus: Selected Essays and Notebooks*, Philip Thody, trans, Penguin, London, 1979, pp 83–84. Copyright © Éditions Gallimard, 1950, 1951, 1954, 1956, 1958, 1959, 1963;

translation copyright © Hamish Hamilton Ltd and Alfred A. Knopf Ltd, 1967. By permission of Penguin Books Ltd. (4) Nicholas Nicholay, 'Navigations at Peregrinations Orientales', in *Purchas his Pilgrimes*, 1625. (5) Isabel Eberhardt, *The Passionate Nomad: The Diary of Isabel Eberhardt*, Beacon/Virago, London, 1988, pp 28–29. **EGYPT**: (1) C.P. Cavafy, *The Complete Poems of C.P. Cavafy*, Chatto and Windus, London, 1961. Extract translated by Paul Strathern. (2) Lawrence Durrell, *The Alexandria Quartet*, Faber and Faber, London, 1960, pp 667–668. By permission of Faber and Faber Ltd. (3) Waguib Ghali, *Beer at the Snooker Club*, Serpent's Tail, London, 1987, pp 14–15. By permission of Serpent's Tail Ltd. (4) Gamal Al-Ghitani, *Zayni Barakat*, Farouk Abdel Wahab, trans, Penguin, London, 1990, pp 52–53. (5) Naguib Mahfouz, *Palace Walk*, Doubleday, New York, 1990, pp 45 and 47–48. By permission of Bantam, Doubleday, Dell Publishing Group, Inc. (6) William Shakespeare, *Antony and Cleopatra*, Act IV, Scene XII. (7) Nawal El Saadawi, 'Thirst', in *She Has No Place in Paradise*, Shirley Eber, trans, Minerva, London, 1989, p 27. First published in English by Methuen. By permission of Reed International Books. (8) *The Book of Exodus*, I vv 8–14. (9) Yusuf Idris, 'Faharat's Republic', in *Modern Arabic Short Stories*, selected and translated by Denys Johnson-Davies, Oxford University Press, Oxford, 1967, p 14. By permission of Oxford University Press. (10) Tewfik Al-Hakim, 'Miracles for sale', in *Modern Arabic Short Stories*, selected and translated by Denys Johnson-Davies, Oxford University Press, Oxford, 1967, p 114. By permission of Oxford University Press. (11) and (12) Herodotus, *Histories*, Book II, H.H. Huxley, ed, Bradda, Oxford, 1979. Extracts translated by Paul Strathern. (13) Gustave Flaubert, *Flaubert in Egypt*, Francis Steegmuller, ed and trans, The Bodley Head, London, 1972, pp 49–50. (14) Ferdinand de Lesseps, *The History of the Suez Canal: A Personal Narrative*, Blackwood, London, 1876. (15) Howard Carter, *The Tomb of Tutankhamen*, Casell, London, 1923, pp 88–89. **LIBYA**: Antoine de Saint-Exupéry, *Wind, Sand and Stars & Flight to Arras*, Lewis Galentière, trans, Picador, London, 1987, pp 103–104. First published in this translation by William Heinemann Ltd. By permission of Reed International Books. **MOROCCO**: (1) Paul Bowles, *The Sheltering Sky*, Paladin, London, 1990, pp 149–151. First published in England by Peter Owen Ltd. By permission of Peter Owen Ltd. (2) Driss Chraïbi, *Heirs to the Past*, Len Ortzen, trans, Heinemann, London, 1971, pp 45–46. By permission of Heinemann Educational, Oxford. (3)

Wyndham Lewis, *Journey into Barbary*, C.J. Fox, ed, Penguin, London, 1987, p 74. © Wyndham Lewis and the Estate of the late Mrs G.A. Wyndham Lewis. By kind permission of the Wyndham Lewis Memorial Trust (a registered Charity), and Penguin Books Ltd. (4) Tahar Ben Jelloun, *The Sacred Night*, Alan Sheridan, trans, Quartet, London, 1989, pp 13–14. By permission of Quartet Books Ltd. (5) Peter Mayne, *A Year in Marrakesh*, Eland, London, 1984, pp 38–39. Published in the UK, Commonwealth and USA by Eland. By permission of Eland Books. (6) Extract taken from Eric Newby, *A Book of Travellers' Tales*, Picador, London, 1986, pp 86–87. Originally from Colette, *Places*, David Le Vay, trans, Peter Owen, London, 1970. By permission of Peter Owen Ltd, (7) Mohammed Mrabet, *Love with a Few Hairs*, Paul Bowles, trans, Arena, London, 1986, pp 29–30. First published in England by Peter Owen Ltd. By permission of Peter Owen Ltd. (8) Mohammed Choukri, *For Bread Alone*, Paul Bowles, trans, Grafton, London, 1987, pp 83–84. First published in England by Peter Owen Ltd. By permission of Peter Owen Ltd. **TUNISIA:** (1) Virgil, *Aeneid*, in John Dryden, *Works of Virgil*, Oxford University Press, Oxford, 1961, p 236. (2) Rainer Maria Rilke, extract translated by Paul Strathern from *Rilke: Briefe 1907–1914*, Insel Verlag, Leipzig, 1933. (3) Albert Memmi, *The Pillar of Salt*, Elek Books, London, 1956, pp 96–98. (4) Gisèle Halimi, *Milk for the Orange Tree*, Dorothy S. Blair, trans, Quartet, London, 1990, pp 63–64. By permission of Quartet Books Ltd. **DJIBOUTI:** (1) Wilfred Thesiger, *The Life of My Choice*, Fontana, London, 1987, pp 122–123. First published by Collins. By permission of HarperCollins Publishers Ltd. (2) *Contes de Djibouti*, Conseil International de la Langue Française, Paris, 1980, pp 59 and 63. Adapted from the French by Paul Strathern. (3) Evelyn Waugh, in *A Book of Travellers' Tales*, Eric Newby, ed, Picador, London, 1986, p 89. Originally from *When the Going was Good*. By permission of Peters Fraser and Dunlop Ltd. (4) Arthur Rimbaud, letter of 3 December 1885, translated by John Edmondson from *Illuminations, Suivi de Correspondance 1873–1891*, Flammarion, Paris, 1989. **ETHIOPIA AND ERITREA:** (1) Fikré Tolossa, *The Coffin-Dealer and the Grave-Digger*, Übersee-museum, Bremen, 1982, Act 1, Scene 1. (2) Evelyn Waugh, *Waugh in Abyssinia*, Longman, London, 1936, p 47. By permission of Peters Fraser and Dunlop Ltd. (3) Daniel Worku, *The Thirteenth Sun*, London, 1973, p 2. By permission of Daniel Worku. (4) Paul Strathern, *A Season in Abyssinia: An Impersonation of Arthur Rimbaud*, Macmillan, London, 1972,

pp 10–11. By permission of Paul Strathern. (5) Sahle Sellassie, *Warrior King*, Heinemann, London, 1974, pp 93–94. (6) Sir Richard Burton, *First Footsteps in East Africa*, Longman, London, 1856, pp 290–292. (7) Arthur Rimbaud, letter of 15 February 1881, translated by John Edmondson from *Illuminations, Suivi de Correspondance 1873–1891*, Flammarion, Paris, 1989. (8) James Bruce, *Travels to Discover the Source of the Nile, Volume III*, Robinson, London, 1790. **KENYA:** (1) Jared Angira, 'No Coffin, No Grave', in *Poems of Black Africa*, Wole Soyinka, ed, Heinemann, Oxford, 1987, p 111. (2) Ngugi wa Thiong'o, *Devil on the Cross*, Heinemann, Oxford, 1987, pp 58–59. By permission of Heinemann Educational, Oxford. (3) David Mulwa, *Master and Servant*, Longman, Harlow, 1979, pp 36–37. (4) 'The Call' by the Mau Mau, in *Voices from Twentieth Century Africa*, Chinweizu, ed, Faber and Faber, London, 1988, p 59. Originally published in *Thunder from the Mountains*, Maina wa Kinyatti, ed, Zed Books, London. By permission of Zed Books Ltd. (5) Swahili traditional verse, in *Poems of Black Africa*, Wole Soyinka, ed, Heinemann, Oxford, 1987, p 175. Originally published in *Swahili Poetry*, Lyndon Harries, ed, Oxford University Press, Oxford, 1962. By permission of Oxford University Press. (6) Grace Ogot, *The Promised Land*, East African Publishing House, Nairobi, 1966, pp 44–45. (7) C.J. Jung, *Memories, Dreams, Reflections*, Collins, London, 1983, also quoted in Elspeth Huxley, *Nine Faces of Kenya*, Collins Harvill, London, 1990, pp 356–357. By permission of HarperCollins Publishers Ltd. (8) Meja Mwangi, *Going Down River Road*, Heinemann, London, 1984, pp 18–19. By permission of Heinemann Educational, Oxford. (9) V.S. Naipaul, *North of South*, André Deutsch, London, 1978, also quoted in Elspeth Huxley, *Nine Faces of Kenya*, Collins Harvill, London, 1990, pp 209–211. By permission of Aitken, Stone and Wylie Ltd. (10) Karen Blixen (Isak Dinesen), *Out of Africa*, Penguin, London, 1984, pp 15–16. By permission of Florence Feiler, Literary Agent, and Random House UK Ltd. (11) Charles Mangua, *A Tail in the Mouth*, East African Publishing House, Nairobi, 1972, p 135. (12) Elspeth Huxley, *The Flame Trees of Thika*, Penguin, London, 1977, pp 118–119. First published in England by Chatto and Windus. By permission of Random House UK Ltd. **SOMALIA:** (1) Nuruddin Farah, *A Crooked Rib*, Heinemann, London, 1970, p 23. (2) Sir Richard Burton, *First Footsteps in East Africa*, Tylston and Edwards, London, 1894, pp 9–11. (3) Omar Eby, 'A Long Ride', in *The Sons of Adam*, Herald Press, Scotsdale, PA, 1970, pp 91–92. By permission of Omar Eby. (4)

Hassan Sheik Mumin, *Leopard Among the Women*, B.W. Andrzejewski, trans, Oxford University Press, London, 1974, pp 107–109. (5) Faarax M.J. Cawl, *Ignorance is the Enemy of Love*, Zed Books, London, 1982, p 16. By permission of Zed Books Ltd. (6) Anonymous poem quoted by John Darnton in 'A barren Ethiopian desert is Promised Land to Somalis', *New York Times*, 14 September 1978, pp 1, 7. Also published in David D. Laitin and Said S. Samatar, *Somalia: Nation in Search of a State*, Westview Press, Boulder, CO, p 34. SUDAN: (1) Tayeb Salih, *Season of Migration to the North*, Denys Johnson-Davies, trans, Heinemann, London, 1976. By permission of Heinemann Educational, Oxford. (2) Bruce Chatwin, *The Songlines*, Jonathan Cape, London 1987, p 129. By permission of Random House UK Ltd. (3) Anai Kelueljang, 'My Cousin Mohamed', in *The Myth of Freedom*, New Beacon Books, London, 1985. By permission of New Beacon Books Ltd. (4) Jamal Mahjoub, *Navigation of a Rainmaker*, Heinemann, Oxford, 1989, pp 176–177. By permission of Heinemann Educational, Oxford. (5) Edward Hoagland, *African Calliope: A Journey to the Sudan*, Penguin, London, 1981, pp 139–140. Copyright © Edward Hoagland, 1978, 1979. By permission of Penguin Books Ltd. (6) Charlie Pye-Smith, *The Other Nile*, Penguin, London, 1987, p 147. Copyright © Charlie Pye-Smith, 1986. By permission of Richard Scott Simon Ltd. TANZANIA: (1) M.G. Vassanji, *The Gunny Sack*, Heinemann, Oxford, 1989, pp 87–88. By permission of Heinemann Educational, Oxford. (2) Peter Palangyo, *Dying in the Sun*, Heinemann, London, 1969, pp 92–93. By permission of Ngalo & Company Advocates on behalf of Mrs Emeline Palangyo. (3) William Boyd, *An Ice Cream War*, Penguin, London, 1983, p 34. First published by Hamish Hamilton. Copyright © William Boyd, 1982, 1983. By permission of Penguin Books Ltd. (4) Ernest Hemingway, 'The Snows of Kilimanjaro', in *The Snows of Kilimanjaro and Other Stories*, TriadGrafton, London, 1977, pp 28–29. (5) Per Wästberg, *Assignments in Africa*, The Olive Press, London, 1986, pp 87–88. By permission of Impact Books/Olive Press. (6) Yusuf O. Kassam, 'Maji Maji', in *Poems of Black Africa*, Wole Soyinka, ed, Heinemann, Oxford, 1987, p 203. (7) Shabaan Roberts, 'Laugh with Happiness', in *Anthology of Swahili Poetry*, Ali A. Jahadhmy, ed, Heinemann, London, 1977, p 22. (8) Evelyn Waugh, *A Tourist in Africa*, Methuen, London, 1985, pp 96–97. By permission of Peters Fraser and Dunlop Ltd. (9) H.M. Stanley, *Life and Finding of Dr Livingstone*, Dean and Sons, London, 1874, pp 189–190. UGANDA: (1) Barbara Kimenye, 'The

Village', in *Kalasanda*, Oxford University Press, Oxford, 1965, pp 1–2. (2) Patrick Marnham, 'You Still Exist', in *Fantastic Invasion: Dispatches from Contemporary Africa*, Jonathan Cape, London, 1980, p 257. By permission of Random House UK Ltd. (3) John Hanning Speke, *Journal of the Discovery of the Source of the Nile*, W.M. Blackwood, London, 1863, pp 446–467. (4) Omunjakko Nakibimbiri, *The Sobbing Sounds*, Longman, London, 1975, pp 32–35. By permission of Longman Group UK Ltd. (5) Peter Nazareth, *In a Brown Mantle*, East African Literature Bureau, Kampala, 1972, pp 135–136. (6) Enriko Seruma, *The Heart Seller*, East African Publishing House, Kampala, 1971, pp 58–59. (7) Okot p'Bitek, 'The Song of the Prisoner', in *Two Songs*, East African Publishing House, Nairobi, 1971, p 42. (8) Taban lo Liyong, 'He and Him', in *Fixions*, Heinemann, London, 1969, pp 32–33. By permission of Taban lo Liyong. CAMEROON: (1) Ferdinand Oyono, *The Old Man and the Medal*, Heinemann, London, 1967, pp 46–47. (2) Mongo Beti, *Perpetua and the Habit of Unhappiness*, Heinemann, London, 1978, p 191. © Éditions Buchet/Castel. By permission of Rosica Colin Ltd. (3) Mbella Sonne Dipoko, 'Autobiography', in *African Writing Today*, Ezekiel Mphahlele, ed, Penguin, London, 1967, p 201. (4) Nigel Barley, *The Innocent Anthropologist*, British Museum Publications, London, 1983. By permission of the British Museum Press on behalf of Nigel Barley. (5) André Gide, *Travels in the Congo*, University of California Press, Los Angeles, CA, 1962, pp 324–325. (6) Francis Bebey, *Agatha Moudio's Son*, Heinemann, London, 1971, p 10. CENTRAL AFRICAN REPUBLIC: (1) André Gide, *Travels in the Congo*, University of California Press, Los Angeles, CA, 1962, pp 324–325. CONGO: (1) Sylvain Bemba, 'The Dark Room', in *African Writing Today*, Ezekiel Mphahlele, ed, Penguin, London, 1967, p 125. (2) Tchicaya U Tam'si, 'The Scorner', in *Selected Poems*, Gerald Moore, trans, Heinemann, London, 1970, p 68. By permission of L'Harmattan, Paris. (3) *Myths and Legends of the Congo*, collected and translated by Jan Knappert, Heinemann, London, 1971, 69–70. By permission of Dr Jan Knappert. (4) Henri Lopes, *The Laughing Cry*, Readers International, London, 1982, pp 156–157. By permission of Readers International. (5) William Boyd, *Brazzaville Beach*, Penguin, London, 1990, p 287. First published by Sinclair Stevenson Ltd. By permission of Reed International Books. (6) King Dom Affonso, in *The African Past*, Basil Davidson, ed, Penguin, London, 1966, pp 194–195. (7) André Gide, *Travels in the Congo*, University of California Press, Los Angeles,

CA, 1962, pp 32–37. **EQUATORIAL GUINEA**: (1) Mary Kingsley, *Travels in West Africa*, Virago, London, 1986, pp 47–48. (2) Robert Klitgaard, *Tropical Gangsters*, I.B. Tauris, London, 1991, p 47. By permission of I.B. Tauris & Co Ltd. **GABON**: (1) Mary Kingsley, *Travels in West Africa*, Virago, London, 1986, pp 329–332. (2) 'Song of the Will-o'-the-Wisp', in *Voices from Twentieth-Century Africa*, Chinweizu, ed, Faber and Faber, London, 1988, pp 350–351. Originally published in *The Unwritten Song*, Vol 1, Willard R. Trask, ed and trans, Macmillan, New York, 1966. Copyright © 1966 by Willard R. Trask. By permission of Macmillan Publishing Company. (3) 'Pygmy Song', in *The Unwritten Song*, Willard R. Trask, ed and trans, Jonathan Cape, London, 1969, p 65. First published by Macmillan, New York, 1966. Copyright © 1966 by Willard R. Trask. By permission of Macmillan Publishing Company. (4) Albert Schweitzer, *From My African Notebook*, George Allen and Unwin, London, 1938, pp 101–102. By permission of Rhena Schweitzer Miller. **RWANDA AND BURUNDI**: (1) Ryszard Kapuściński, Granta Books, London, 1990, pp 80–81. Published by Penguin Books in 1991. Copyright © 1969, 1990, Ryszard Kapuściński. By permission of Penguin Books Ltd. (2) Dian Fossey, *Gorillas in the Mist*, Penguin, London, 1988, pp 141–142. Copyright © 1984. By permission of Hodder and Stoughton Ltd/New English Library Ltd. (3) Jean-Baptiste Mutabaruka, 'Song of the Drum', in *African Writing Today*, Ezekiel Mphahlele, ed, Penguin, London, 1967, p 148. **SÃO TOMÉ AND PRÍNCIPE**: (1) Aldo do Espírito Santo, 'Where are the Men Seized in this Wind of Madness?', Gerald Moore, trans, in *The Penguin Book of Modern African Poetry*, Gerald Moore and Ulli Beier, eds, Penguin, London, 1984, p 226. Originally published in *Antologia de la poesia negra de espressão portuguesa*, Mario de Andrade, ed, Lisbon, 1953. **ZAIRE**: (1) V.Y. Mudimbe, *Before the Birth of the Moon*, Simon and Schuster, New York, 1989, pp 39–40. Originally published in French as *Le Bel Immonde*, Présence Africaine, Paris, 1976. By permission of La Société Nouvelle Présence Africaine. (2) Graham Greene, *A Burnt-Out Case*, Heinemann and The Bodley Head, London, 1974, pp 124–125. © 1960 Verdant SA. By permission of David Higham Associates Ltd. (3) Antoine-Roger Bolamba, 'A Fistful of News', Gerald Moore, trans, in *The Penguin Book of Modern African Poetry*, Gerald Moore and Ulli Beier, eds, Penguin, London, 1984, p 290. Originally published in French in *Esanzo*, Présence Africaine, Paris, 1956. By permission of La Société Nouvelle Présence Africaine. (4)

Bakongo address for the Feast of the Dead, in *Voices from Twentieth-Century Africa*, Chinweizu, ed, Faber and Faber, London, 1988, p 307. From J. Van Wing, 'Bakongo incantations and prayers', *Journal of the Royal Anthropological Institute*, Vol 60. By permission of the Royal Anthropological Institute of Great Britain and Ireland. (5) Joseph Conrad, *Heart of Darkness*, Penguin, London, 1987. **ANGOLA**: (1) Antonio Jacinto, 'Poem of Alienation', Michael Wolfers, trans, in *The Penguin Book of Modern African Poetry*, Gerald Moore and Ulli Beier, eds, Penguin, London, 1984, pp 32–33. Originally published in *Poems from Angola*, Michael Wolfers, ed, Heinemann, London, 1979. (2) 'The Rain-Man's Praise-Song of Himself', in *Voices from Twentieth-Century Africa*, Chinweizu, ed, Faber and Faber, London, 1988, p 215. Originally published in *The Unwritten Song*, Vol 1, Willard R. Trask, ed and trans, Macmillan, New York, 1966. Copyright © 1966 by Willard R. Trask. By permission of Macmillan Publishing Company. (3) Sousa Jamba, *Patriots*, Penguin, London, 1992, pp 68–69. Copyright © Sousa Jamba, 1990. By permission of Penguin Books Ltd. (4) Luandino Vieira, *Luuanda*, Heinemann, London, 1980, p 11. By permission of Heinemann Educational, Oxford. (5) Agostinho Neto, 'Kinaxixi', W.S. Merwin, trans, in *The Penguin Book of Modern African Poetry*, Gerald Moore and Ulli Beier, eds, Penguin, London, 1984, p 29. Originally published in *Black Orpheus*, 15, 1964. (6) Ryszard Kapuściński, *Another Day of Life*, Picador, London, 1987, p 17. By permission of Pan Macmillan Ltd. **BOTSWANA**: (1) Laurens van der Post, *The Lost World of the Kalahari*, Penguin, London, 1987, pp 20–21. First published in England by Chatto and Windus. By permission of Random House UK Ltd. (2) Gagomokgwa Kebotseng, 'Tshekedi Khama', in *Praise Poems of Tswana Chiefs*, I. Schapera, ed, Oxford University Press, London, 1965, pp 226–227. By permission of Oxford University Press. (3) Bessie Head, *A Question of Power*, Pantheon, New York, 1973, p 173. **INDIAN OCEAN ISLANDS**: (1) Dervla Murphy, *Muddling Through in Madagascar*, Century, London, 1986, pp 150–151. First published in England by John Murray. By permission of John Murray Publishers Ltd. (2) Jean-Joseph Rabéarivelo, in *Translations from the Night*, John Reed and Clive Wake, trans, Heinemann, London, 1975, p 17. By permission of Clive Wake. (3) Flavien Ranaivo, 'Song of a Young Girl', Gerald Moore, trans, in *The Penguin Book of Modern African Poetry*, Gerald Moore and Ulli Beier, eds, Penguin, London, 1984, p 133. Originally published in French by Presses Universitaires de France. By permission of Presses Universitaires de France. (4) 'The Locust', in *Voices from Twentieth-Century Africa*, Chinweizu, ed, Faber and Faber, London, 1988, p 352. Originally published in *The Unwritten Song*, Vol 1, Willard R. Trask, ed and trans, Macmillan, New York, 1966. Copyright © 1966 by Willard R. Trask. By permission of Macmillan Publishing Company. (5) Edouard Maunick, 'Les Manèges de la Mer', Gerald Moore, trans, in *The Penguin Book of Modern African Poetry*, Gerald Moore and Ulli Beier, eds, Penguin, London 1984, p 155. Originally published in French by Présence Africaine, Paris, 1964. By permission of La Société Nouvelle Présence Africaine. (6) Claude Pichois, *Baudelaire*, Hamish Hamilton, London, 1989, p 76. **MALAWI:** (1) Paul Theroux, *Jungle Lovers*, Penguin, London, 1971, pp 45–46. By permission of Aitken, Stone and Wylie Ltd. (2) Legson Kayira, *The Detainee*, Heinemann, London, 1974, pp 9–10. By permission of the Peters Fraser and Dunlop Group Ltd. (3) Steve Chimombo, 'Derailment: A Delirium', in *The Heinemann Book of African Poetry in English*, selected by Adewale Maja-Pearce, Heinemann, Oxford, 1990, p 95. By permission of Steve Chimombo. (4) Frank Chipasula, 'Manifesto on Ars Poetica', in *The Heinemann Book of African Poetry in English*, selected by Adewale Maja-Pearce, Heinemann, Oxford, 1990, p 182. By permission of Heinemann Educational, Oxford. (5) David Rubadiri, 'An African Thunderstorm', in *The Penguin Book of Modern African Poetry*, Gerald Moore and Ulli Beier, eds, Penguin, London, 1984, p 137. By permission of David Rubadiri. (6) Laurens van der Post, *A Book of Travellers' Tales*, Eric Newby, ed, Pan, London, 1986. Originally from *Venture to the Interior*, published by Chatto and Windus, London. By permission of Random House UK Ltd. **MOZAMBIQUE:** (1) Per Wästberg, *Assignments in Africa*, The Olive Press, London, 1986, pp 122–123. By permission of Impact Books/Olive Press. (2) 'The Tale of the Two who Returned from the Dead', David Bookshaw, trans, *Wasafiri*, No 10, Summer 1989, pp 10–11. By permission of *Wasafiri*. (3) Luís Bernardo Honwana, 'Dina', in *African Writing Today*, Ezekiel Mphahlele, ed, Penguin, London, 1967, p 321. (4) Noémia de Sousa, 'If You Want to Know Me', Art Brakel, trans, in *The Penguin Book of Modern African Poetry*, Gerald Moore and Ulli Beier, eds, Penguin, London, 1984, p 163. Originally published in *Ba Shiru*, Spring 1970. (5) José Craveirinha, 'Poem of the Future Citizen', in *African Writing Today*, Ezekiel Mphahlele, ed, Penguin, London, 1967, p 315. (6) Jorge Rebelo, 'Poem', Margaret Dickinson, trans, in *The Penguin Book of Modern African*

Poetry, Gerald Moore and Ulli Beier, eds, Penguin, London, 1984, pp 166–167. Originally published in *When Bullets Begin to Flower*, Margaret Dickinson, ed, East African Publishing House, Nairobi, 1972. **NAMIBIA:** (1) Joseph Diescho, *Born of the Sun*, Friendship Press, New York, 1988, pp 36–37. **SOUTH AFRICA:** (1) J.M. Coetzee, *Age of Iron*, Penguin, London, 1991, p 88. First published in England by Secker and Warburg. By permission of Reed International Books. (2) Alex La Guma, *A Walk in the Night*, Mbari Publications, Ibadan, pp 47–48. (3) Nadine Gordimer, 'The Catch', in *No Place Like: Selected Stories*, Penguin, London, 1978, p 39. By permission of Random House UK Ltd. (4) Olive Schreiner, *The Story of an African Farm*, Penguin, London, 1971, pp 35–36. (5) Peter Abrahams, *Mine Boy*, Penguin, London, 1972, pp 24–25. Also published by Faber and Faber. By permission of Faber and Faber Ltd. (6) Laurens van der Post, *In a Province*, Penguin, London, 1988, pp 67–68. First published in England by Chatto and Windus. By permission of Random House UK Ltd. (7) Arthur Nortje, 'Waiting', in *The Heinemann Book of African Poetry in English*, selected by Adewale Maja-Pearce, Heinemann, Oxford, 1990, p 75. (8) Alan Paton, *Cry the Beloved Country*, Jonathan Cape, London, 1977, pp 76–79. By permission of Random House UK Ltd. (9) Dennis Brutus, 'Pray', in *Voices from Twentieth-Century Africa*, Chinweizu, ed, Faber and Faber, London, 1988, p 409. From *Rhythms of Creation: A Decade of Okike Poetry*, D.I. Nwoga, ed, Fourth Dimension, Enugu, Nigeria. By permission of Fourth Dimension Publishing Co Ltd. (10) Steve Biko, *I Write What I Like*, Penguin, London, 1978, pp 172–173. By permission of the Bowerdean Press. (11) Lewis Nkosi, 'The Prisoner', in *African Writing Today*, Ezekiel Mphahlele, ed, Penguin, London, 1967, pp 296–297. (12) Richard Rive, 'The Bench', in *The Penguin Book of Southern African Stories*, Stephen Gray, ed, Penguin, London, 1985, p 190. From Richard Rive, *Advance, Retreat: Selected Short Stories*, David Philip, Cape Town. By permission of the Richard Rive Estate and David Philip Publishers (Pty) Ltd. (13) Thomas Mofolo, *Chaka*, Heinemann, London, 1981, p 27. By permission of Heinemann Educational, Oxford. (14) Mazisi Kunene, 'Cycle', in *Zulu Poems*, André Deutsch, London, 1970. By permission of André Deutsch Ltd. (15) André Brink, *A Dry White Season*, W.H. Allen, London, 1979, p 167. By permission of André Brink and Reed International Books. **ZAMBIA:** (1) David Livingstone, *Livingstone's Travels*, James MacNair, ed, Dent, London, 1954, p 151. (2) Dominic Mulaisho, *The Smoke that Thunders*,

Heinemann, London, 1979, pp 34–35. **ZIM-BABWE**: (1) Stanlake Samkange, *The Year of the Uprising*, Heinemann, London, 1978, p 36. By permission of Mrs T.M. Samkange. (2) Dambudzo Marechera, *The House of Hunger*, Heinemann, London, 1978, pp 17–19. By permission of Heinemann Educational, Oxford. (3) Doris Lessing, *The Grass is Singing*, Heinemann, London, 1973, p 190. First published by Michael Joseph, 1950. Copyright © Doris Lessing, 1950. By permission of Penguin Books Ltd. (4) Chenjerai Hove, 'Lost Bird', in *The Heinemann Book of African Poetry in English*, selected by Adewale Maja-Pearce, Heinemann, Oxford, 1990, p 207. From *Red Hills of Home*, Mambo Press, Gweru, 1985. (5) Charles Mungoshi, 'The Mountain', in *The Setting Sun and the Rolling World*, Heinemann, Oxford, 1989, p 41.

PICTURES

Front cover and spine – photograph taken in Rora Habab, north-east Eritrea by Bill Robinson, © Bill Robinson; Back cover – Rimbaud House in Harar by Oona Strathern; p 13 – Bruce Chatwin, courtesy of Pan; p 29 – V.S. Naipaul, courtesy of Penguin; p 30 – Bernard Dadié, courtesy of Heinemann, p 45 – B. Kojo Laing, courtesy of Heinemann; p 53 Ayi Kwei Armah, courtesy of Heinemann, © Camera Press; p 96 – Geoffrey Moorhouse, courtesy of Penguin, © Tara Heineman; p 106 – Chinua Achebe, courtesy of Heinemann; p 108 – Wole Soyinka, courtesy of Reed Publishing Group; p 129 – Cyprian Ekwenski, courtesy of Heinemann; p 130 – Buchi Emecheta, courtesy of Harper-Collins; p 131 – Adewale Maja-Pearce, courtesy

of himself; p 133 – Ben Okri, courtesy of Random House; p 137 Mariama Bâ, © George Hallett, courtesy of Virago; p 146– Sembène Ousmane, courtesy of Heinemann; p 152 – Graham Greene by William Karel; p 177 – Albert Camus, courtesy of Penguin; p 203 – Lawrence Durrell, © Caroline Forbes, courtesy of Faber and Faber; p 225 – Paul Bowles by Roy Round, courtesy of Peter Owen Ltd; p 226 – Tahar Ben Jelloun, courtesy of Quartet; p 236 – Gisèle Halimi, courtesy of Quartet; p 248 – Amharic script, from Edward Ullendorf, *An Amharic Chrestomathy*, Oxford University Press, Oxford, 1965, p 47; pp 250 and 251 – photographs by Oona Strathern; p 268 – Elspeth Huxley, courtesy of Penguin, © Tara Heineman; p 284 – Karen Blixen, courtesy of Penguin; p 285 – Ngugi wa Thiong'o, courtesy of Heinemann, © Carrie Craig; p 290 – Nuruddin Farah, courtesy of Heinemann; p 298 – Omar Eby, courtesy of himself; p 313 Moyez Vassanji, courtesy of Heinemann, by Milne Photography, Toronto, Canada; p 323 – Ernest Hemingway, courtesy of HarperCollins; p 324 – Peter Palangyo, courtesy of Mrs Emeline Palangyo; p 337 Taban lo Liyong, courtesy of himself; p 350 – Mongo Beti, courtesy of Heinemann, © Tessa Colvin; p 384 – Dian Fossey, courtesy of Hodder and Stoughton; p 400 – Joseph Conrad, courtesy of Raffles Hotel, Singapore; p 416 – Bessie Head, courtesy of Heinemann; p 433 – Dervla Murphy, by Michael Brophy, courtesy of John Murray; p 467 – J.M. Coetzee, courtesy of Penguin; p 486 – André Brink, courtesy of Reed Publishing Group; p 488 – Nadine Gordimer, courtesy of Random House; p 498 – Dambudzo Marachera, courtesy of Heinemann, © The Guardian; p 507 – Doris Lessing, courtesy of HarperCollins; p 508 – Charles Mungoshi, courtesy of Heinemann.

INDEX

This is an index to authors. (E) = extract. Bold type = biographical entry.